ROUTLEDGE LIBRARY
MILITARY AND NAVAL

Volume 8

THE FORTRESS IN THE AGE OF VAUBAN AND
FREDERICK THE GREAT 1660–1789

THE FORTRESS IN THE AGE OF VAUBAN AND FREDERICK THE GREAT 1660–1789

CHRISTOPHER DUFFY

Routledge
Taylor & Francis Group
LONDON AND NEW YORK

First published in 1985

This edition first published in 2016
by Routledge
2 Park Square, Milton Park, Abingdon, Oxon OX14 4RN

and by Routledge
711 Third Avenue, New York, NY 10017

Routledge is an imprint of the Taylor & Francis Group, an informa business

© 1985 Christopher Duffy

All rights reserved. No part of this book may be reprinted or reproduced or utilised in any form or by any electronic, mechanical, or other means, now known or hereafter invented, including photocopying and recording, or in any information storage or retrieval system, without permission in writing from the publishers.

Trademark notice: Product or corporate names may be trademarks or registered trademarks, and are used only for identification and explanation without intent to infringe.

British Library Cataloguing in Publication Data
A catalogue record for this book is available from the British Library

ISBN: 978-1-138-90784-3 (Set)
ISBN: 978-1-315-67905-1 (Set) (ebk)
ISBN: 978-1-138-92458-1 (Volume 8) (hbk)
ISBN: 978-1-138-92464-2 (Volume 8) (pbk)
ISBN: 978-1-315-68424-6 (Volume 8) (ebk)

Publisher's Note
The publisher has gone to great lengths to ensure the quality of this reprint but points out that some imperfections in the original copies may be apparent.

Disclaimer
The publisher has made every effort to trace copyright holders and would welcome correspondence from those they have been unable to trace.

Christopher Duffy

The Fortress in the Age of Vauban and Frederick the Great 1660–1789

Siege Warfare Volume II

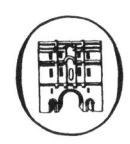

Routledge & Kegan Paul
London, Boston, Melbourne and Henley

*First published in 1985
by Routledge & Kegan Paul plc*

14 Leicester Square, London WC2H 7PH, England

9 Park Street, Boston, Mass. 02108, USA

*464 St Kilda Road, Melbourne,
Victoria 3004, Australia and*

*Broadway House, Newtown Road,
Henley on Thames, Oxon RG9 1EN, England*

*Set in Monophoto Ehrhardt
and printed in Great Britain by
BAS Printers Limited, Over Wallop, Hampshire*

© *Christopher Duffy 1985*

*No part of this book may be reproduced in
any form without permission from the publisher,
except for the quotation of brief passages
in criticism*

Library of Congress Cataloguing in Publication Data

Duffy, Christopher, 1936–

*The fortress in the age of Vauban and Frederick the
Great, 1660–1789.
(Siege warfare; v. 2)
Bibliography: p.
Includes index
1. Fortification—Europe—History—17th century.
2. Fortification—Europe—History—18th century.
I. Title.   II. Series: Duffy, Christopher, 1936–
Siege warfare; v. 2.
UG401.D83   1985 vol. 2   355.4'4s [355.7'094]   83-24685 [UG428]*

British Library CIP data available

ISBN 0-7100-9648-8

Contents

	Preface	xiii
One	Louis XIV and the Apogee of the Old Fortress Warfare 1660–1715	1
Two	The Masters: Coehoorn and Vauban	63
Three	The Resolution of the Conflict: the Last Struggles of Habsburg and Bourbon	98
Four	The Age of Frederick the Great 1740–86	112
Five	A Time of Doubt: the Standing of Permanent Fortification in the Eighteenth Century	149
Six	The Subjugation of Ireland and Scotland	168
Seven	The Battle for Sweden's Trans-Baltic Bridgeheads	176
Eight	The Last Crusade – the Repulse of Ottoman Turkey	218
Nine	The Collision of the Colonial Empires	253
Ten	Conclusions	291
	Glossary	296
	Bibliography	300
	General Index	311
	Subject Index	317

Illustrations

Essentials of the bastion system
1. Profile of fortification — 2
2. Trace (ground plan) of a simple bastioned front — 3
3. Intersecting lines of cannon fire and musketry — 3
4. Gun battery (Fort George, Inverness) — 4
5. Ravelin (Montmédy Citadel) — 4
6. View down a covered way to a snow-topped traverse (Mont-Louis) — 5
7. Covered way with multiple traverses (Montmédy Citadel) — 5
8. The new fortifications at Lille — 7
9. Louis XIV at the sieges — 10
10. Vauban's trench attack, with zigzag approaches and three parallels — 11
11. Sturm's reconstruction of the Rimpler trace — 15
12. L. C. Sturm, the foremost interpreter of German manners of fortification — 16
13. Gründler von Aachen's manner 1683 — 17
14. The Marienberg Citadel at Würzburg, seen from the Main bridge — 17
15. The Wülzburg Fortress — 18
16. The Rothenberg Fortress — 19
17. Newmann's Machicolation Tower, Marienberg Citadel — 19

The Schönborn style
18. The Rosenberg Fortress — 21
19. The Nürnbergertor, Forchheim 1698 — 21
20. Bastion cartouche, Forchheim 1664 — 22
21. Sentry box, Würzburg town — 22
22. Spandau Citadel — 24
23. Frontispiece, Matthias Dögen — 24
24. Siege of Luxembourg 1684 — 28
25. Attack on Bastions II and III of Lille town 1708 — 39
26. Attack on Lille Citadel 1708 — 40
27. Siege of Ath 1697 — 42
28. The sieges of Le Quesnoy 1712 — 43
29. Landau — 46
30. Verrua — 50
31. The front of attack, Turin Citadel 1706 — 53
32. Turin Citadel — 56
33. Sack of a fortress-town — 59
34. Acropolis of Aragon – the cathedral and fortress of Lerida — 61
35. Menno van Coehoorn — 65
36. Plan of Naarden — 66
37. Bastion at Naarden — 67
38. Double retired bastion flank at Naarden, showing guns emplaced in lower storey — 67
39. Coehoorn's 'first manner' — 68
40. Coehoorn's 'second manner' — 69
41. Coehoorn's 'third manner' — 70
42. Sébastien Le Prestre de Vauban — 71
43. The Maintenon Aqueduct — 73
44. Bastion at Fort Nieulay, Calais — 74
45. Countermine gallery, ravelin at Le Quesnoy — 75

Vauban's France I
46. Entrevaux — 76

47	Colmars	76	77	The Prussian siege of Schweidnitz 1758	123
48	Redoubt outside Colmars	77	78	Frederick's siege of Olmütz 1758	124
49	Sisteron	77	79	Sieges of Dresden 1759 and 1760	126
50	Street plan of Neuf-Brisach	79	80	Prussian siege of Schweidnitz in 1762	127
51	Redoubt in a place of arms at Mont-Dauphin	80	81	The attack on the Jauernicker-Fort at Schweidnitz 1762	129
52	Villefranche-de-Conflent, Bastion du Dauphin	82	82	Königgrätz	130
53	Bastion at Villefranche-de-Conflent	83	83	Theresienstadt	131
54	Bastion tower, on the bend of the River Doubs at Besançon	84	84	The south-eastern front at Josephstadt	132
55	Bastion tower at Belfort	85	85	One of the surviving bastions at Josephstadt, on the western front	133
56	The 'third system' at Neuf-Brisach	86	86	Plan of Schweidnitz, showing the detached forts and the Austrian retrenchment	140
57	Rampart at Neuf-Brisach, showing the recessed curtain, bastion flank and face, and the bastion tower	86	87	Plan and profile of a star fort at Schweidnitz	141
			88	The old castle at Glatz	143
			89	Neisse, with Fort Preussen	145

Vauban's France II

58	Bastion salient, Montreuil	88
59	Fortified harbour, Saint-Martin de Rhé	88
60	Brouage	89
61	Montmédy Citadel	90
62	Plan of Belfort, showing the enceinte with bastion towers and the citadel	91
63	Belfort Citadel, with shell damage from the famous Prussian siege of 1871	91
64	Mont-Louis	92
65	Ravelin of the hornwork at Mont-Louis	92
66	View along one of the branches of the hornwork at Mont-Louis	93
67	Hornwork gate, Mont-Louis	93
68	Treadwheel, for raising water from the well in Mont-Louis Citadel	93
69	Plan of Blaye	95
70	Powerful double bastion at Blaye	95
71	Ravelin Dauphine at Blaye	96
72	Cuneo, the barrier of the Stura valley	103
73	Fort d'Exilles	105

The Elvas position

90	View of the Elvas fortifications as they existed in the later seventeenth century	146
91	Forte de Graça, seen from the town	146
92	View from the Forte de Graça over the town towards Forte de Santa Luzia	147
93	The Durance gorge at Briançon, with the Pont d'Asfeld	151
94	The Roc de Briançon, Briançon town	151
95	The fantastic elaboration of one of Virgin's traces	155
96	La Joumarière's squirt system 1785	156
97	Fort St Elisabeth, showing the caponnière and part of the ground plan	158
98	Details of the caponnière at Fort St Elisabeth	159
99	Montalembert's coastal tower	160
100	Bastion and polygonal flanking compared	160
101	Montalembert's caponnière	161
102	The polygonal manner, as illustrated by Montalembert in an imaginary scheme for the defence of Cherbourg	162
103	The floating batteries at Gibraltar 1781	165
104	Siege of Athlone 1691	170
105	Fort George, Inverness	174

The siege of Bergen-op-Zoom 1747

74	First French trenches and batteries	108
75	The mine war for the covered way and the powerful redoubts	109
76	The final French breaching batteries in the covered way	109

106	Gateway of Rüsensteen's *Kastell* at Copenhagen	178
107	Guardians of the Sound	179
108	Kongsten Fort, Fredrikstad	180
109	The Dahlberg Monument, Karlskrona	183

Dahlberg's Sweden

110	Vadstena Castle, Lake Vättern	185
111	Kalmar Castle	185
112	The Eda Fort	186
113	The Eda Fort today	186
114	The Aurora Bastion, Karlskrona	187
115	The Västerport, Kalmar town	187
116	The central keep, Nya Älvsborg Fort, Göteborg	187
117	The Fars Hatt Tower, Bohus Castle	188
118	The tower at Carlsten Fort, Marstrand	188
119	Water gate, Kalmar town	189
120	The Landskrona Bastion, Landskrona Citadel	189
121	The castle, Landskrona Citadel	190
122	Wismar, the new fortifications by Dahlberg	191
123	Dahlberg's fortifications at Göteborg	192
124	Trace and profile of the Göta Lejon Fort	193
125	Göta Lejon Fort	194
126	Kronan Fort	195
127	Siege of Stralsund 1715	203
128	Fredriksten, the main fortress	204
129	Fredriksten, with Stortårnet and Overberget forts	205
130	Fort Gyldenløve, the southern face	206
131	Siege of Fredriksten 1718	207
132	Augustin Ehrensvärd	209
133	The Gustavsvärd Fort, Sveaborg	211
134	Virgin's mortar casemates	212
135	Virgin-style mortar casemates at Fort Concepçion, Spain	213
136	The bastioned fortifications at Moscow, built 1707–8	215
137	Opening of the siege of Candia 1649	219
138	The Panigra and Sant'Andrea Bastions, Candia	220
139	The Athens Acropolis as a Turkish fortress	225
140	Raab, with reminders of the barbarities of the Turkish wars	229
141	Siege of Vienna 1683	230
142	Explosion of the Turkish magazine at Ofen 1686	234
143	Another view of the same	235
144	Munkacz, in the Carpathians	237
145	The northern front at Karlsburg	238
146	Kamenets	241
147	Peterwardein	243
148	Louisbourg	265
149	Fort Duquesne	269
150	Fort Chambly, Richelieu River, Canada	273
151	The Long Island and Manhattan fortifications	279
152	Siege of Savannah 1779	285
153	Siege of Yorktown 1781	288
154	Modern French engineer troops clearing vegetation at Blaye	293

Maps

The Netherlands in the seventeenth and eighteenth centuries	9
The Rhine and south Germany in the seventeenth and eighteenth centuries	23
The Netherlands in the War of the Spanish Succession	34
Piedmont and neighbouring states in the War of the Spanish Succession	51
Spain and Portugal	58
Central and eastern Pyrenees and Catalonia	94
Piedmont and neighbouring states in the War of the Austrian Succession	102
West Germany in the Seven Years War	115
Central Europe in the time of Frederick the Great	121
Europe against Frederick in the Seven Years War	122
Scotland and the Borders	173
The Baltic lands	177
Denmark, with south Norway and south Sweden	181
Gulf of Finland	199
Poland and western Russia	201
The Turkish empire 1683	222
Southern Greece and Crete	224
Austro-Hungarian borderlands	227
India	255
West Indies and Central America	259
North America in the colonial period	263
The theatres of war on the St Lawrence, Hudson and Ohio	267
The Southern States in the War of Independence	283

Preface

This book has two aims:

(a) to seek to explain how, in what is rightly accepted as the classic age of artillery fortification, military engineering came to be of less relative importance at the end of the period than at the beginning

(b) to integrate the study of fortress warfare with the military and general history of the time

Here I must set out my order of priorities. I assign little importance to the manifold paper 'systems' of fortification which were compiled in the seventeenth and eighteenth centuries by drawing-masters, clerical tutors, and chatty old retired engineers. If these schemes bulk so large in the compendia of Max Jähns and others, it is only because they are the kind of evidence which bookish people most readily understand.

I attach far more significance to works of fortification that have been actually carried out on the ground. The student of military engineering cannot rest until he has toured as many strongholds as it is physically possible for him to reach, and even then he must be aware of how much more has been done – and remains to be done – by those enthusiasts who are nowadays recording and preserving the fabric of artillery fortifications, and those newly minted historians who are working through the relevant archives.

I know from experience that it is more difficult to persuade people of the relevance of certain other perspectives. The problem relates directly to the present crisis of serious historical studies, which derives partly from an uncertainty as to what history ought to be about, and partly from the close-range defensive strength of modern scholarship which has encouraged a deplorable narrowing of interests and sympathies. Among fortress specialists themselves it is rare to find an individual who will be equally interested in the design of a stronghold, the symbolism of its architecture, the costs of construction, the character of the engineer who drew up the plans, the sieges which the place might have undergone, or the strategy which determined its location.

Lest it should be thought that I am pronouncing from a standpoint of superior wisdom, I must confess that it was only upon the last re-writing of the present work that I came to appreciate how rewarding it is to bring together the 'old-fashioned' history of events and ideas with what is termed with all too much accuracy 'immobile history' – the study of conditions and structures over a long period of time. It now seems clear to me that, for example, the difference in expertise between French and German engineers, or the success of Vauban and Coehoorn at their sieges, was directly related to the strength and continuity of support which these experts enjoyed from their masters. Hence the importance of the political dimension.

Again, the concept of military professionalism, as explored recently in the United States, proves most revealing when applied to engineers of the seventeenth and eighteenth centuries, who were evolving an institutional equivalent of those brotherhoods of Italian masters who had transformed military architecture at the time of the Renaissance.

The theme of professionalism pulls together the stories of military engineering throughout Europe and the wider world. In the narrower European context it is as important – and as difficult – to avoid Francocentricity in studies of the time of Vauban as it is to eschew excessive Italocentricity when we look at the Renaissance. I have therefore responded to the call of Scandinavia, and Central and eastern Europe, defying all the talk of trolls, vampires or superstitious peasantry. My linguistic ambitions terminated some time ago, when I discovered that I was forgetting 'old' languages at the same rate as I was trying to acquire new ones. For voyages still further afield I have therefore not hesitated to rely on the tales of other travellers. It is no great crime to depend on third- or fourth-hand accounts when you are seeking not to compile a history which will be complete or authoritative, but merely one that will perhaps bring together things which have not been brought together before.

Two further comments are in order. In military engineering, questions of originality and attribution are very difficult to resolve without hard documentary proof from the archives. We shall never know with certainty where Vauban obtained the inspiration for his siege parallels. Again I suspect – though I cannot prove – that Montalembert copied the form of his famous caponnières directly from the Austrian Fort St Elisabeth on the Danube, but I am reluctant to lend any credence to authorities who are driven by national pride to claim precedence for caponnière-like devices which appear in medieval castles in Germany, Italy or Scotland. It is one thing to run a gallery from one work to the next, and knock some gun-ports in it, but quite another to set out, like Montalembert, to re-shape fortification on first principles. Intention and continuity must be our touchstones in such matters.

Finally, the demands of publishing economy dictate that most of the military operations and sieges in this volume can be treated only in summary fashion, to illustrate points of outstanding technical or strategic interest. The siege of Vienna in 1683, which is deliberately discussed at greater length, will have to stand in for all the other sieges on the eastern theatre. By the same token the struggle for Turin in 1706 will represent western baroque siegework at its most elaborate. The sacrifice of detail in the other episodes is all the more painful, since for a number of reasons the record of sieges is of far greater reliability than the evidence for combats in the open field: the process of siege and defence extended on occasion over a period of several months, and was not confined to a few hectic hours or minutes; the location of the contest may be determined with nearly absolute precision, and is often marked by fortifications which survive to the present day; lastly the direction of the operations lay largely in the hands of formally trained engineers and gunners who, if they survived, left meticulous journals of what had passed.

Directly and indirectly I owe a great deal to my associates in the Fortress Study Group, and in particular to Anthony Kemp, who has an unrivalled network of international correspondents, and who introduced me to the fascinating and little-known fortresses of central Germany. I am left with a debt which I cannot possibly repay to the scores of folk who gave freely of their time and expertise to assist me in my travels. Only a matter of weeks ago I was forced to revise my notions of French and Austrian engineering in the later eighteenth century, in the light of what I was told of Bohemian fortresses by Pavel Mertlík, of the Local Museum at Jaroměř in Czechoslovakia. It is merely from convention, and the lack of space, that the names of people like these do not appear on the title page. Now, more than ever, military history bears a collective character.

Secretariats of useful organisations:

Great Britain:
Fortress Study Group (journal *Fort*), 24 Walters Road, Rochester ME3 9JR.

The Netherlands:
Stichting Menno van Coehoorn (journal *Jaarboek*), Postbus 110, 5060 Oisterwijk, The Netherlands.

United States:
Council on America's Military Past, PO Box 1151, Fort Myer, Virginia 22211.

West Germany:

Deutsches Gesellschaft für Festungsforschung (journal *Zeitschrift für Festungsforschung*), Pelikanweg 38, 4230 Wesel, West Germany.

Supra-national:

Internationales Burgen-Institut (journal *Bulletin*), Chateau de Rosendael, 6891 Da Rozendaal (Gld.), The Netherlands.

There are two companion volumes to the present work:

Fire and Stone. The Science of Fortress Warfare 1660–1860, Newton Abbot, 1975. This book deals with the techniques of siting, designing, building, garrisoning, defending and attacking artillery fortifications in the classic age (out of print).

Siege Warfare. The Fortress in the Early Modern World 1494–1660, London, 1979. Similar in style to the present work, but contains additional sections on oriental engineering, and on urbanism and the architectural and literary symbolism of artillery fortification.

For the best general history of fortification please consult Quentin Hughes, *Military Architecture*, London, 1974.

One Louis XIV and the Apogee of the Old Fortress Warfare 1660–1715

Allegro marziale 1660–78

The personal rule of Louis XIV
The classic age of artillery fortification takes its origins from late fifteenth-century Italy, the theatre of war which first experienced the full effect of two important advances in gunpowder artillery – the advent of truly mobile siege guns, and the employment of the dense and compact shot of iron, which slowly began to supplant the missiles of stone. Neither of these revolutions was as sudden or as complete as used to be thought by military historians. Over the following decades, however, gunners and engineers were impelled to re-shape fortification and siege warfare in ways that influenced the thinking of military technologists until the middle of the nineteenth century.

On the side of the attack, the Spanish were the first to evolve the 24-pounder cannon, the king of siegework, which represented the ideal combination of hitting-power, economy and mobility. In the matter of the defence, the Italian engineers presented Europe with the 'bastion system', which re-worked fortification in three important respects:
(a) Fortress walls crouched lower and lower until they became massive banks of earth, lined on their outer side by masonry retaining walls or (in the case of Dutch fortresses) by slopes of turf that were planted with stakes. The new ramparts gave enhanced protection against view and cannon shot, while providing the defenders with a wide and solid platform for their own artillery.
(b) Novel outworks endowed the bastioned fortress with the very desirable attribute of defence in depth. The most important of these defences were the 'ravelin' (a free-standing diamond-shaped fortification), and the 'covered way' (an infantry position running around the outer rim of the ditch).
(c) The overall plan assumed a characteristic star shape, and the lines of all the works were geometrically interrelated so as to bring a lethal cross-fire to bear along the ditches or over the ground outside the fortress.

There remained the very considerable problems of how best to employ these brilliant and various inspirations in the gross physical world. It was in fact an immensely time-consuming process to achieve a mastery of fortress warfare. You had to think in terms of decades or generations if you wished to form your construction engineers and gunners, assemble powerful siege trains, and win and consolidate coherent state frontiers. The thing was fundamentally a matter of politics rather than technology.

Only a recurring political instability held back France from claiming what we would now call 'superpower status' in the European context. That nation owned large physical resources, a united population which by the middle of the seventeenth century reached more than eighteen million, and a geographical position which enabled her to intervene with force in the Low Countries, in Germany and in the Mediterranean world. From about 1599 Henry II, the last of the Valois kings, showed what could be achieved in the way of sieges and fortress-building by gifted men who enjoyed the support of royal authority. Henry was assassinated in 1610, and his legacy was lost in the period of religious strife and weak rule which supervened before the rise of another great Frenchman, Cardinal Richelieu, who rationalised the fortress system, and waged a series of lively if ultimately ruinous wars on the territory of his neighbours. Richelieu died in 1642, and within a few years the government became the prize of noble factions in the semi-comic Wars of the *Fronde*. However, Richelieu had begun the process of bureaucratisation in the armed services, and an element of continuity was provided by the nearly fifty-year rule (1643–91) of two successive *Sécretaires d'Etat de la Guerre* – Michel Le Tellier and his son the Marquis de Louvois.

The advent of Louvois in 1661 followed closely upon the coming to full power of the young King Louis XIV, who terminated the era of civil unrest and, more importantly, proceeded to break the feudal world which had made such an aristocratic indulgence possible. Within three decades some of the other leading states of Europe had to re-shape their affairs to survive in competition with the novel phenomenon of this absolutist monarchical state, controlling a 'de-feudalised' army of unprecedented size and efficiency.

Some of the transformations in the French army were obvious to the eye – the bearing and address of the soldiers, which came from the loving attentions of the drillmasters, or the building of the stark and regular barrack blocks where the garrisons of the fortresses lived out their existence in peacetime. More far-reaching, however, were the decrees and practices which brought home to officers that they were servants of the state, and no longer semi-independent leaders of mercenary bands. The power of promotion was taken from their grasp by the *Ordre de Tableau* of 1675, which established the principle of advancement by seniority, except in cases of extraordinary merit. In operational matters

Essentials of the bastion system

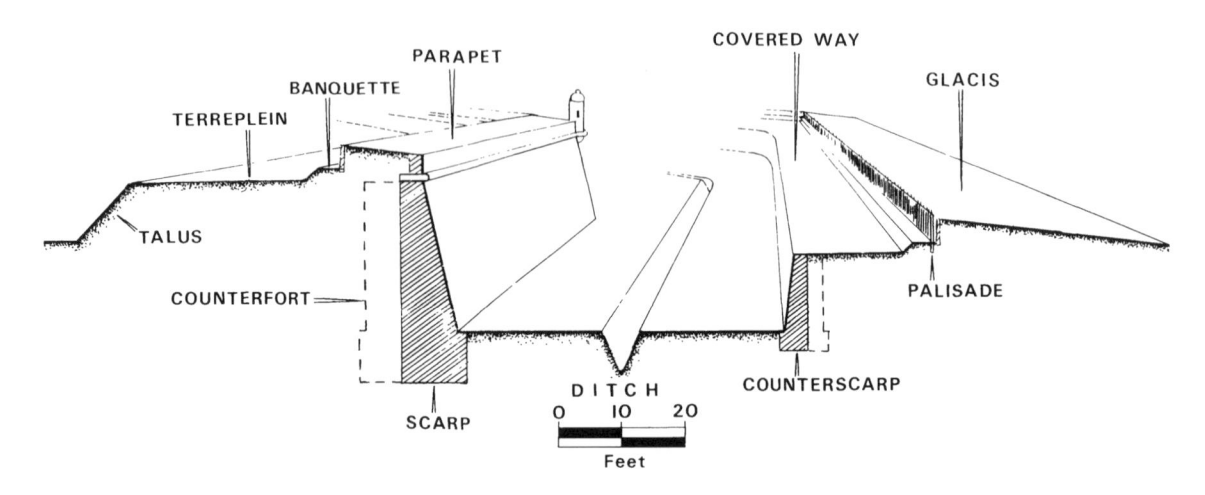

1 Profile of fortification. On the left is the great mass of the rampart. From the interior of the fortress an earthen slope (*talus*) rises to the wide *terreplein*, or fighting platform. An infantry firing step (*banquette*) lies immediately behind the cannon-proof *parapet*. The earthen mass of the rampart is retained on the outer side by a masonry *scarp* of brick or stone; this in turn is supported by *counterforts*, or interior buttresses, buried in the rampart. The far side of the wide ditch is marked by a corresponding *counterscarp*, or retaining wall. Beyond the counterscarp stretches the infantry position called the *covered way*, which has a banquette of its own, and a palisade set back a little way from the lip of the *glacis*, the clear, fire-swept zone which descends gradually to the open country

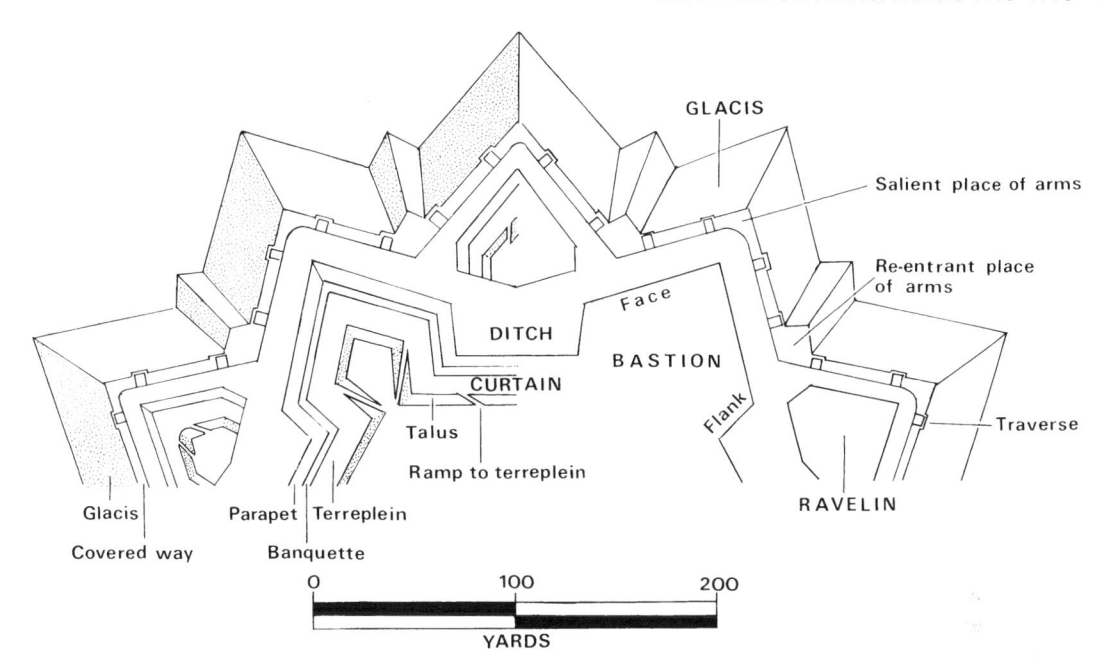

2 *Trace* (ground plan) of a simple bastioned front. Showing how the *enceinte*, or main perimeter, is indented to form the long straight walls of the *curtain*, and the angular projections called *bastions*. The diamond-shaped *ravelins* provide additional defence, and the zigzag line of the covered way is interrupted by breastworks (*traverses*), which intercept enemy cannon shot, and enable the infantry to dispute the covered way sector by sector. Infantry could concentrate in strength in the *places of arms* of the covered way, whether to repel attack, or to prepare for a sortie

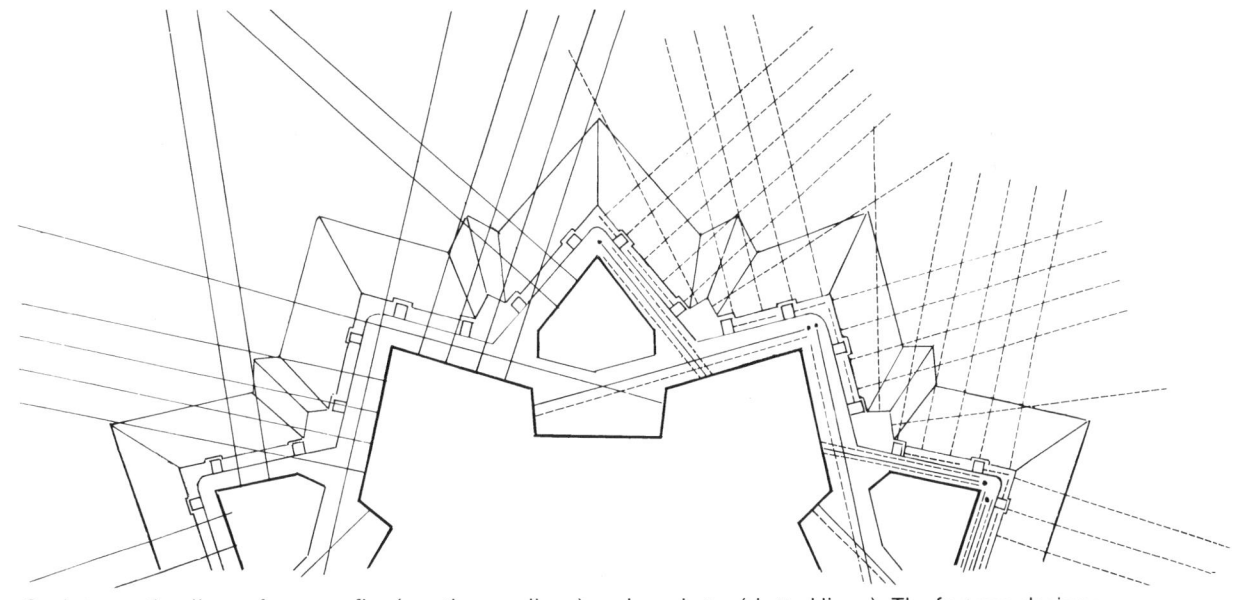

3 Intersecting lines of cannon fire (continuous lines) and musketry (dotted lines). The fortress-designer worked on the reasonable assumption that the gunners and musketeers fired more or less blindly to their front, and he aligned the works accordingly. The zone in front of the bastion was the least well covered by fire, which was why it was normally chosen as the point of attack

4 Gun battery (Fort George, Inverness). The banquette was cut away at intervals, to enable fortress cannon to be wheeled forward all the way to the parapet, and the barrels were pointed through outward-splaying slots called *embrasures*, cut through the thickness of the parapet

5 Ravelin (Montmédy Citadel)

Louis XIV and Old Fortress Warfare 1660–1715 5

6 View down a covered way to a snow-topped traverse (Mont-Louis). The covered way is commanded by a ravelin (right), and by the embrasures of the bastion face beyond

7 Covered way with multiple traverses (Montmédy Citadel). A small re-entrant place of arms is at the left centre

the establishment of march routes and chains of supply magazines made it possible to direct forces to where they were most needed, and not simply where the army commanders fancied they ought to go. In 1673 the two great men Turenne and Condé protested in vain against the *stratèges de chambre* of Louvois, who took on himself the higher management of the war against the Dutch.

The supporting services, the navy and the technical arms of gunnery and engineering began to realise their potential during this long period of stable and purposeful government, Ministers of proven loyalty and efficiency came to the fore, imbued with something of the confidence and ambition of *Le Grand Monarque* himself. Louis's right-hand man in military affairs remained the Marquis de Louvois, whose presence at sieges counted for almost as much as that of the king. Almost as significant was the work of Colbert, the minister of finances and of the navy, who by a strange dispensation saw to colonial and coastal fortresses, as well as works within the historic borders of France.

In their turn Louvois and Colbert gave full support to the most able military engineer of the time, Sébastien Le Prestre de Vauban. In 1675 Colbert wrote a typically blistering rebuke to an engineer who had ventured to criticise some of Vauban's designs:

Get it into your head that it is not for the likes of you to tamper with Vauban's arrangements without express order. Before showing such presumption again, you should work and study another ten years under his direction. (To Niquet, 11 December 1675, Rochas d'Aiglun, 1910, II, 134)

King Louis put military engineering near the centre of his own interests. In 1650, as a young monarch, he had learnt the principles of the art from a fort that was built for him in the gardens of the Palais Royal. Now, as absolute ruler, he devoted many hours a week to reviewing projects of fortifications, and he kept himself up to date with all the developments of siegework. He was present at nineteen of the sieges directed by Vauban, and he liked in particular to be remembered for his activity at the attack on Maastricht in 1673:

He seemed perfectly tireless in this operation. He issued excellent orders, and saw that every need was provided for. He was on horseback from dawn to dusk. He visited the trenches, regulated the attacks, and was present at all the assaults. Inspired by his example, the soldiers became heroes who were always ready to sacrifice themselves for his service. (Quincy, 1726, I, 353)

Out of all the operations of war, a grand siege was in fact Louis's favourite. Not only did it follow a predictably successful course (thanks to Vauban), but it provided a magnificent spectacle in the baroque style, at once vigorous and theatrical.

All of this bore significant implications for French military engineering. Vauban and his companions sharpened the edge of siegework through their technical advances. Moreover an 'absolute power, strongly centralised, became for them the driving force for a prodigious undertaking which transformed the physical aspect of their country' (Truttmann, 1976, 73). The new or newly rebuilt fortresses were usually capacious affairs, designed to accommodate the troops of the new standing army, as well as magazines and arsenals which sustained offensive operations, and Louis, Louvois and Vauban were careful to site these strongholds where they would serve coherent strategic ends. Here the central direction of state policy was of direct relevance.

The technical oeuvre is still impressive, even in these days of mechanised engineering. Work was going on at 160 or more places, embracing nine or so completely new fortress towns and a dozen new citadels. The enterprise at Longwy alone involved shifting 640,000 cubic metres of rock and earth, and raising 120,000 cubic metres of masonry, and this was far from the largest of the undertakings. Louis seemed almost indifferent to the cost, providing his engineers could run up a *belle place*, and Colbert caught the mood of the time perfectly when he wrote a letter concerning a fortress gate:

We do not live in a reign which is content with little things. With due regard to proportion, it is impossible to imagine anything which can be too great. (*ibid.*, 38)

The war with Spain 1667–8

Surprisingly enough, France's first territorial gains in the new age were bought with gold, not blood. Duke Charles of Lorraine began the process by practically renting his duchy to the French forces. In 1662 his equally hard-up namesake, Charles II of Britain, was glad to sell the Cromwellian conquest of Dunkirk back to France. These accessions gave France some first-class military bases within easy reach of the Spanish territories of Franche-Comté and the Netherlands.

Spanish pride was not a commodity that was up for sale, but Louis calculated that the King of Spain (yet another Charles II) was such a mental and physical weakling that he would not put up much of a fight if France stole some territory in the Spanish Netherlands. Everything considered, it was difficult to think of two opponents less well matched than resurgent France and the ramshackle empire of the Spanish Habsburgs.

In the summer of 1667 the French swept over the border. While de Créqui kept the fortress of Luxembourg contained in the east, his colleague d'Aumont overran the coastlands, and the main army of 35,000 troops pressed into the heart of the country and took Charleroi, Ath, Douai and Oudenarde in rapid succession. The triple advance compelled the Spanish to divide their forces, and they were powerless to prevent the French from investing Lille, the capital of Spanish Flanders, on 28 August.

The direction of this important new siege was entrusted to Vauban, who had won Louis's confidence by his activity in the trenches before Douai. The Spanish rule was popular in Lille, and armed townspeople did everything they could to assist the garrison of 2,600 troops. However, the French guns

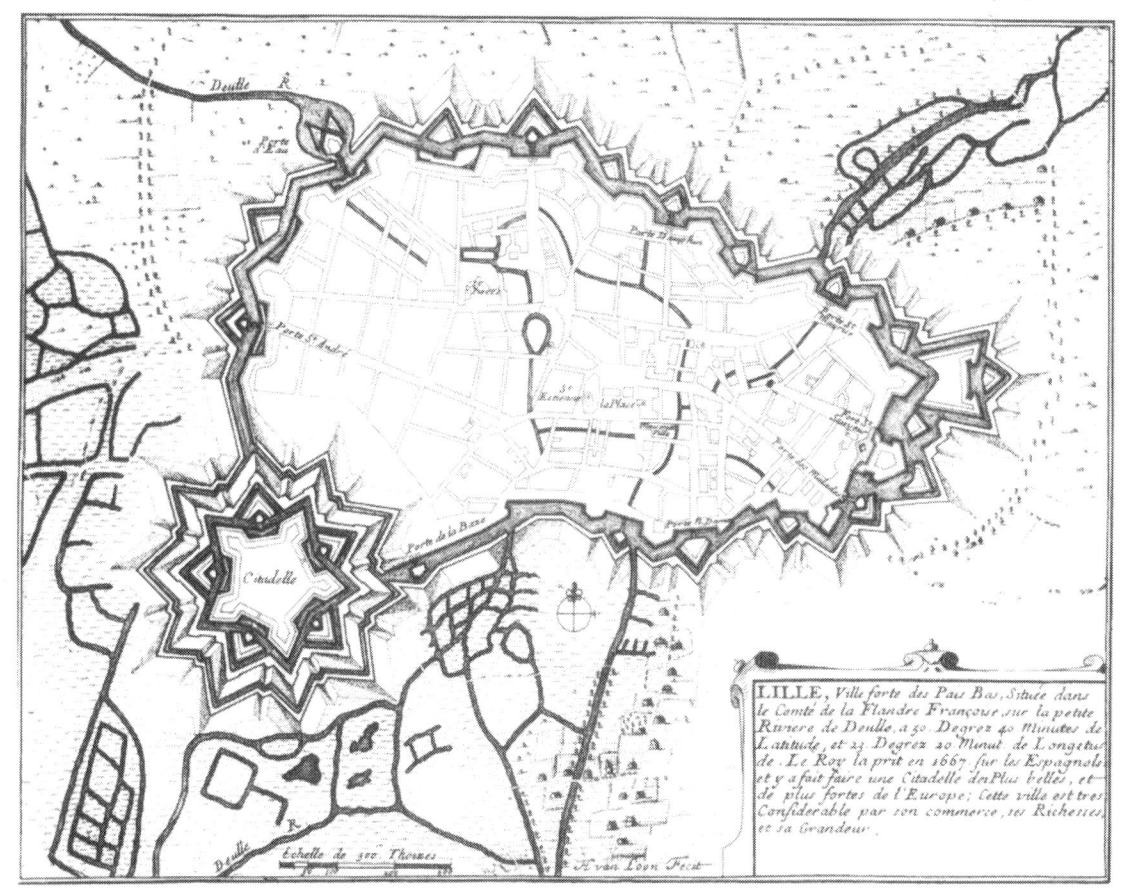

8 The new fortifications at Lille

opened up to devastating effect on 21 September, and within a week the besiegers had razed the parapets of the rampart and established their lodgments in the ravelins. On the 27th the Spanish capitulated for an evacuation.

Vauban thereby staked his claim to be the best person to re-fortify the great prize. He proposed to build a handsome citadel on the classic pentagonal plan, which would give ample space for all kinds of military establishments, and he carried the day against his nominal superior, the Chevalier de Clerville, who wanted a miserable affair of four bastions. Clerville pottered around planting surveying sticks at random, then departed the scene for good. By 1670 Vauban's fine new citadel was complete, and over the next two decades his work on the city walls extended the area of Lille by one-third.

As Spain still refused to come to terms, Louis turned his armies south-eastwards into Franche-Comté. The unprepared fortresses fell in the single month of February 1668 to the same combination of meticulous preparation and lightning movement which had delivered a great part of Flanders to the French in 1667. The English and Dutch began to make their displeasure known to Louis, and on 2 May 1668 the French deputies came to terms with the Spanish at Aix-la-Chapelle. Franche-Comté was restored to Spain, but the French retained their conquests in the Netherlands.

The worth of the newly captured fortresses (Lille, Courtrai, Oudenarde, Tournai, Douai, Ath and Charleroi) consisted in giving the French firm bases of aggression on the water avenues of the Lys, the Yser, the Scheldt, the Dender and the Sambre, and in affording Vauban the space to begin to build the *frontière de fer* – his famous double barrier for the northern borderlands. At the heart of the new territory was Lille, which had an importance of its own as the earliest, and perhaps the greatest of Louis's conquests, and as the fortress which Vauban came to regard as his *fille aînée dans la fortification*.

The Dutch campaign of 1672
As the next step in extending his dominion to the north, Louis decided to leave the Spanish Netherlands to one side and strike a blow at the Dutch, who deserved to be punished for their lack of respect in the peace talks in 1668. He laid the diplomatic groundwork carefully, so as to leave the Dutch isolated, and he hoped that his offensive would be so rapid and so brilliant as to browbeat these people into allowing him a free hand in the Spanish Netherlands in the following years.

The examination of the consequent campaign of 1672 partakes less of the nature of a military analysis than of a pathological investigation of all the ills that are capable of infecting a fortress system. The Dutch were eventually saved by their water barriers, but the months that preceded this providential deliverance were marked by a collapse of defensive arrangements which finds no parallel until the Prussian débâcle of 1806.

Decay was most evident in the bricks-and-mortar (or rather sand-and-slime) aspect of the Dutch fortresses. As early as 1652 the Council of State, or central cabinet, had drawn attention to the 'urgent need of repairing the national fortifications' (Ten Raa *et al.*, 1911, etc., V, 517). As usual the province blithely ignored the warnings from The Hague, and in 1672 a French intelligence report on Doesburg could make a scornful reference to 'those old and ruinous earthen ramparts which, as you know, surround all the wretched little towns of this country, and which offers useful cover to any besieger who wishes to "attach" his miners to the foot of the defences' (Chamilly to Louvois, 1 April, Luxembourg, 1759, 41). Three years before the war the rich but parsimonious province of Holland actually suspended work on Naarden and all its other fortresses.

Everything to do with physical preparations for defence was in a bad state. Flood damage was left unrepaired, the Ijssel river barrier was allowed to silt up, and the magazines held horrors like the dried fish at Rees, which were found to be thirty years old and, as an official unnecessarily added, 'completely ruined and unfit for consumption' (Ten Raa *et al.*, 1911, etc., V, 517). There were few trained gunners to be had, and the guns themselves had been bought by the individual provinces from all over northern Europe.

Worst of all was the state of moral unpreparedness. A review of the garrisons of Dutch Brabant states that the recruits were 'drawn from every

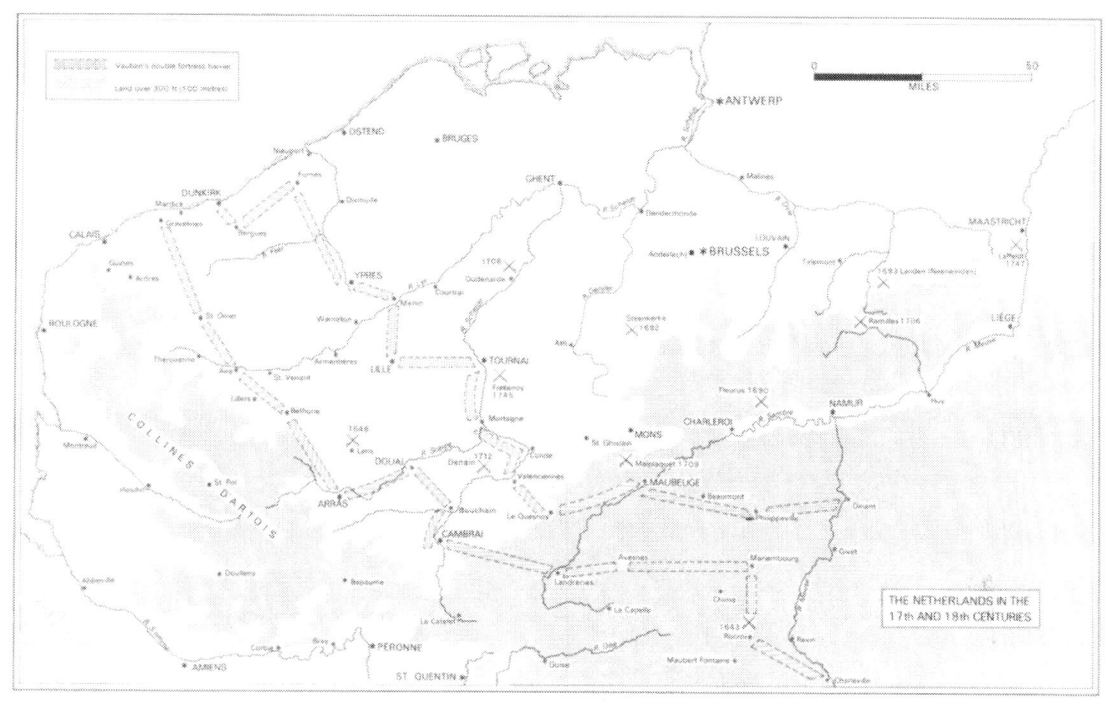

The Netherlands in the seventeenth and eighteenth centuries

nation, and indisciplined and licentious. The French are the worst of the lot, for there are so many of them, and this number surely includes a good contingent of spies' (*ibid.*, V, 300). The townspeople disliked and despised their garrisons, and the morale of the Dutch forces as a whole had scarcely recovered from the reverses inflicted upon them by the army of the Bishop of Münster in 1665. Since then many of the troops had been on watch winter and summer against a new irruption from Münster, 'a labour which is by no means agreeable to the Dutch national character' (Chamilly to Louvois, 2 February 1672, Luxembourg, 1759, 15).

In so far as the Dutch had a plan of defence, it turned on holding Maastricht, the fortress which seemed to be the most endangered by the new French foothold on the Sambre at Charleroi. Instead, Louis and Louvois decided to leave the place isolated harmlessly to the west, and bring the army of 110,000 men on a right-flanking circuit along the Rhine and the lower Meuse to the interesting area of Gelderland where the Rhine divided into the Waal, the Neder-Rijn and the Ijssel.

In June 1672 the strategy was put into effect, and the first results were spectacular. The strongholds of Arnhem, the Schenckenschans and Zutphen succumbed most abjectly, and only Nijmegen offered a creditable defence. As a last resort the Dutch summoned the elements to their aid. They had just enough time to open the sluices at Muiden, which permitted the waters of the Zuider Zee to fill the inundation of the *Oude Hollandse Waterlinie*, which ran southwards from Muiden behind the unoccupied towns of Naarden, Woerden and Oudewater to the Neder-Rijn (Lek). The heartland province of Holland was now sealed off by a glittering barrier, and ingloriously but unarguably the Dutch had brought Louis's runaway progress to an end.

The continuation of the war in the Netherlands 1673–8

Like his father in 1635, Louis XIV was drawn by the prospect of a rapid and decisive local victory into a prolonged war of European dimensions. The Dutch refused to be brought to terms, and their appeals for support met with a response from Spain and the Emperor of Germany. King Louis was not at first particularly worried, and in 1673 he decided to address himself to some unfinished business from the last campaign, and eliminate the Dutch garrison in Maastricht. Once in French hands, Maastricht could be easily supported from friendly territory, and its position on the middle Meuse would facilitate communications with the French armies now operating in Germany.

Thirty-five thousand troops converged on Maastricht on 6 June 1673 and laid the place under close investment. Everything seemed to indicate a long resistance, for the town was held by a garrison of 6,000 men under Major-General Jacques de Fariaux, 'a brave man with a good record' (Saint-Hilaire, 1903–4, I, 118). Twenty thousand peasant labourers duly opened the trenches against the Tongres Gate on the night of 17–18 June. This, however, was no ordinary siege, for Vauban was in charge of the operation, and in an access of inspiration he brought about the greatest advance in the siege attack since mobile siege artillery was introduced in the 1490s. Louis wrote that:

the way in which we conducted the trenches prevented the defenders from doing anything against us, for we advanced towards the fortress in broad and spacious trench lines, almost as if we were drawn up for a field battle. The lines were furnished with firing steps, so that we were able to meet the enemy on a very wide frontage. Neither the governor nor his officers had ever seen anything comparable, even though Fariaux was a veteran of five or six sieges – he was used to dealing with narrow approach trenches which were untenable against the smallest sortie. (Louis XIV, 1806, III, 549)

The progress of these novel trenches was greatly facilitated by the fact that they were directed by 'a single commander [Vauban], who received his orders directly from the king and reported to His Majesty alone' (quoted in Lazard, 1934, 156–7).

Parallel gave way to zigzag saps, zigzags to a further parallel, and so on until the French were close enough to take the hornwork and ravelin of the Tongres Gate by battering and assault. Fariaux capitulated on 1 July, in return for an evacuation

9 Louis XIV at the sieges

for the 3,000 survivors of his garrison.

The siege parallel was the culmination of a striving which had been expressed in devices such as Montluc's *arrière coins* of 1558 (see *Siege Warfare*, 1979, p. 54), the siege redoubts of the Netherlands wars (*ibid.*, p. 93), and the transverse trenches of some unsung French engineers of the earlier part of the seventeenth century.

The siege parallels had the simplicity of genius, and they fulfilled a variety of functions with extraordinary ease. The first of the parallels was dug just out of effective cannon shot. It replaced the old countervallation entirely or in part, and acted as the foundation for the whole of the rest of the siege. As further parallels were dug closer to the fortress, so they offered the besiegers secure sites for their batteries, a defence against sorties, and start lines and supports for assaults. In other words, Vauban assailed the fortress with a marching fortress of his own, and stole for the siege attack the tactical advantages which had hitherto been the preserve of the defence.

Not just the siege tactics of the French, but their entire way of making war seemed machine-like and

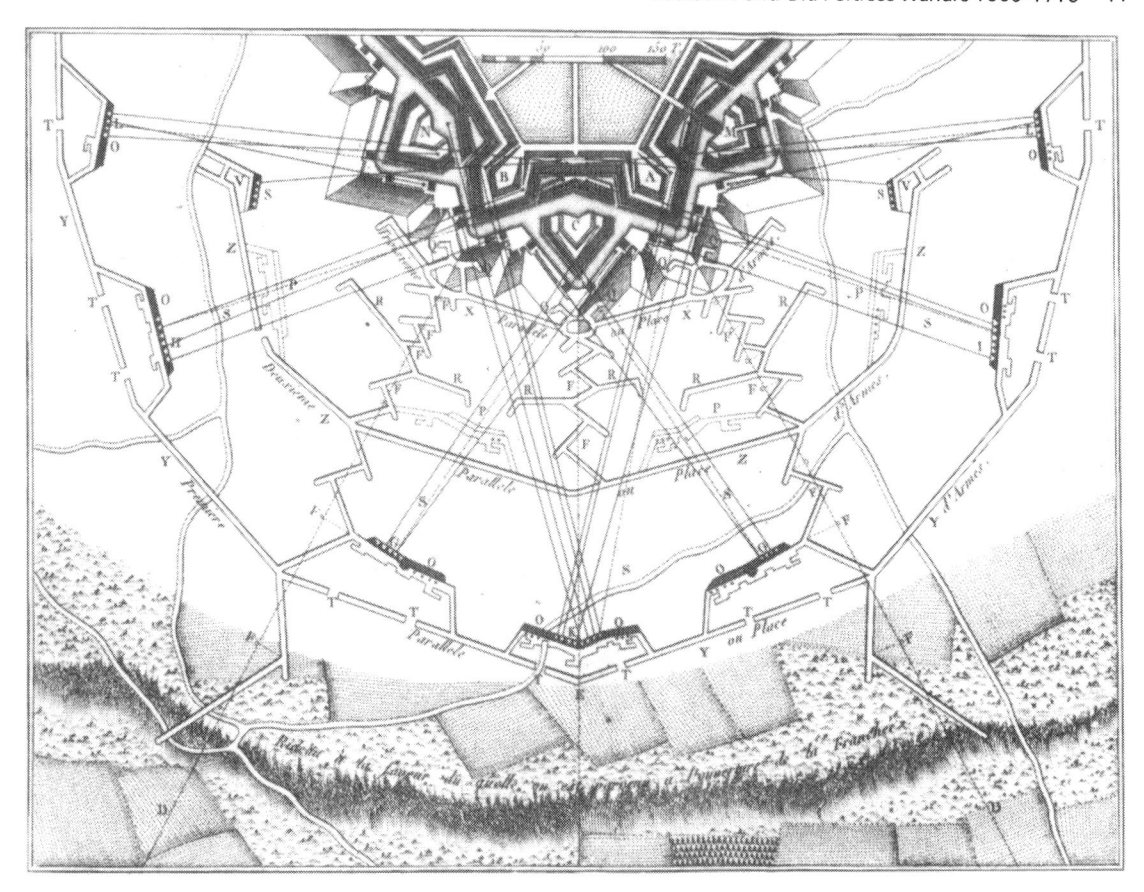

10 Vauban's trench attack, with zigzag approaches and three parallels

irresistible. While the Prince of Orange spent the early spring of each year in extracting money from the Dutch provinces, and prodding the decaying Spanish forces into a semblance of life, Louis was able to proceed without hindrance to attain whatever objectives he had set himself for that campaign. The Dutch Council of State observed that:

the French habitually made considerable progress in the Spanish Netherlands in the winter and early spring, before we could subsist in the open field. This advantage is not just a question of superior forces, but proceeds from the practice of making magazines on the borders, from which they may support their troops at a time of year which would otherwise be unsuitable for military operations. On our side, in that season, the forces are scattered in garrisons, and we lack the fodder to enable them to be concentrated. (Ten Raa *et al.*, 1911, etc., VII, 41)

After a couple of successful sieges, the French liked to maintain a restful equilibrium in the Netherlands for the rest of the year. This they did by holding the army in strong positions, and juggling with the useful intermediate corps which they held in the region of the Moselle and the upper Meuse. As the Earl of Orrery explained:

the French with great prudence attack places in the beginning of the spring, when there is no army to relieve them; and in the summer, when the whole confederacy is in the field, they are on the defensive, and cover what they have took; and in my weak judgment, they do at least as much by their always providing well to eat, and by their entrenched encampings, as by their good fighting. (Orrery, 1677, 139)

The French rarely had to take to the open field in these final months of the campaigning season, for the allies were gratifyingly incompetent at the business of fortress warfare, as was proved when they laid siege to Oudenarde and Grave (1674), Maastricht (1676) and Charleroi (1677).

These conditions made it possible for Vauban to shape campaigns in accordance with ultimate strategic objectives. The sieges of 1675 (Dinant, Huy and Limburg) gave the French a continuous line of Meuse fortresses as far down as Maastricht, except for a single enemy foothold at Namur. All the same, the sight of the jagged French border was still displeasing to Vauban, and in particular he was dissatisfied at the fashion with which the provisions of the last peace had given the French a wedge of fortresses (Lille, Armentières, Courtrai, Oudenarde, Ath and Tournai) which jutted into the midst of Spanish territory as an awkward salient, with enemy fortresses poised dangerously on the flank and rear. On 21 September 1675 he accordingly wrote to Louvois that the king should think seriously about creating a *pré carré* – an untranslatable expression which carries the general meaning of 'defensible frontier zone'. On 4 October he went on to suggest that the French ought to begin to even out their frontier by eliminating the Spanish fortresses to the right (east) of the Lille salient, for he saw that the places of Condé, Bouchain, Valenciennes and Cambrai had excellent intercommunication along the Scheldt, and that once they were in French hands they would form a bastion from which Louis could not be evicted in a score of years.

In 1676 the French began to put Vauban's programme into effect, reducing Condé, Bouchain and Aire. The States General rightly attributed the misfortunes of the last two years to the fact that on their side 'affairs were not regulated as speedily as was called for by the needy state of the alliance and the might of the enemy' (Ten Raa *et al.*, 1911, etc., VI, 61). However, the performance of the allies was not a whit better in the next year, when the French were allowed to expand their conquests to the east of Lille. As if to demonstrate his versatility in all branches of fortress warfare, Vauban took Valenciennes by a decidedly unconventional daylight assault on 17 March, then reduced Cambrai for formal siege in the following month.

Away on the coastal flank Saint-Omer fell to a French detachment on 19 April. This was a clear sign that Louis intended to build up his *pré carré* to the west, as well as to the east of the Lille salient. Indeed, Saint-Omer by itself was such a useful prize that the French could afford to suspend all work on their rearward fortresses in Picardy.

The campaign of 1678 followed the clearly established routine. The Prince of Orange could not begin to move to help the threatened fortresses, and he had to look on impotently while Louis wrested Ghent from the Spanish on 11 March, and went on to reduce the marsh-fortress of Ypres on the 25th. The French then assumed their usual smug and unassailable defensive posture in the Netherlands for the rest of the campaigning season.

Rather than go through the whole painful process yet another time, the allies came to terms with the French at Nijmegen in August and September 1678. The Dutch regained Maastricht, but the Spaniards had to sacrifice the patently untenable Franche-Comté, and give the French a solid and continuous *pré carré* in the Netherlands by yielding a wide constellation of fortresses which stretched from Maubeuge on the Sambre to within sound of the Channel waves at Furnes (Valenciennes, Cambrai, Bouchain, Condé, Menin, Ypres and Saint-Omer). The return of Charleroi was the one concession they were able to wring from the French. Altogether, Louis had gained almost everything he wanted on his northern frontiers. His ambitions were now to be channeled towards the east.

For the Dutch, the first priority was to mend or replace the fortresses which had let them down so badly in 1672. Bergen-op-Zoom, s'Hertogenbosch and Kampen were considerably strengthened, and Naarden, Grave, Breda and Sas van Gent were completely rebuilt. The old Dutch school of fortification was dead and discredited, and Menno van Coehoorn, the creator of a 'new' Dutch school, was still known only as an officer of infantry who had a strong interest in engineering and gunnery. In the absence of native masters the Raad van Staate and the Stadhouder William III therefore turned to French models, as brought to them by Paul Storff de Belleville. Unusually far-travelled, even by the standards of military adventurers, Belleville had served Swedish, Venetian, Spanish and Palatine masters before joining the French in the late war (on a commission from Charles II of England) and acting, as he claimed, as chief engineer under Vauban in the Low Country sieges. Belleville came to Holland in 1678, and he designed and directed the early stages of the construction of the works at Grave (1680–9), and probably also at Naarden (1678–85), Breda and Sas van Gent. He bade a hasty farewell to the Dutch at the end of 1683 or early in 1684, following the subsidence of the new bastions at Grave, and he returned to the service of Venice, commending himself as the creator of those last four places, 'which are reckoned at present to be the strongest fortresses in Europe' (Wieringen, 1980–1, 73).

German military engineering

The war with the Dutch rapidly brought Louis into collision with Austria, Bavaria, Brandenburg and the lesser powers of the Empire. What was the calibre of these German enemies?

If prolixity in military literature had the power to win wars, then the Germans would have reached Paris in the first campaign. A host of authors carried a mass of international motifs forward into the seventeenth and eighteenth centuries. In the earlier years we discover writers like Grotte (*Neue Manier mit Wenigen Kosten Festungen zu Bauen*, Munich, 1618), J. H. Sattler (*Fortificatio*, Bale, 1619, 1620 and 1627), and the Wilhelm Dilich (*Peribologia*, Frankfurt, 1640), who sensibly eschewed complicated geometrical calculations and referred the reader instead to his beautiful engravings of various fortress types.

Over the next three-quarters of a century the Germans more than made up for their previous reticence on the subject of fortification. The mere list of some of the lesser writers is lengthy enough:

Matthias Dögen, the Brandenburger (see p. 23)

Christoph Heidemann, the Bavarian (see p. 24)

Johann Bernhard Scheither (see p. 14) *Novissima Praxis Militaris*, Brunswick, 1672)

Hans Zader, a Swedish officer of German birth (*Manuale Fortificatorie*, Alt-Stettin, 1679; *Der Verstärckten Vestung*, 1691)

C. Neubauer (*Discursus et Verae Architecturae Militaris Praxis*, Stargard, 1679)

Ernst Friedrich Borgsdorf, the Austrian (*Die Unüberwindliche Festung*, Ulm, 1682; *Die Befestigte Stütze eines Fürstenthums*, Nuremberg, 1686; *Academia Fortificatoria*, Vienna, 1694; *Neu-Triumphirende Fortification*, Vienna 1703)

Werdmüller, the Swiss colonel (*Der Probierstein der Ingenieure*, Frankfurt, 1685; *Schauplatz der Alten und Neuen Fortifikations-Maximen*, Frankfurt, 1689)

Johann Heinrich Behr (*Der aufs Neu-verschantzte Turenne*, c. 1677, and Frankfurt, 1690)

Voigt (*Nouvelle Manière de Fortifier*, Jena, 1713)

Harsch (*Dissertatio de Architectura Militari*, Freiburg, 1719)

Leonhard Christoph Sturm (*Architectura Militaris Hypothetico-Eclectica*, Vienna and Nuremberg, 1729, 1736, 1739, 1755)

Landsberg, a Dutchman who entered the Saxon service (*Neue Grund-Risse und Entwürffe der Kriegs-Bau-Kunst*, Dresden and Leipzig, 1737, a translation of his French original of, 1712)

An impressively large number of the German authors were practical engineers and gunners, and several of them appear to have been spurred on to commit their thoughts to paper by shared experiences like the defence of Candia in aid of the Venetians, or the humiliations at the hands of the French, who were ravaging much of western Germany. On this matter Behr wrote in about 1677:

nowadays everybody is talking about the destruction and exactions being visited upon our lands, the burning-down of towns, and the besieging, storming and capture of fortified cities and castles which used to be considered, if not absolutely impregnable, at least very well secured. Field battles are in comparison scarcely a topic of conversation. . . . Indeed at the present time the whole art of war seems to come down to shrewd attacks and artful fortifications. Strongholds are being assailed and taken one after the other. We do not know whether to attribute their fall to the effective techniques, superior forces and skill of the enemy, or to considerations like the inexperience and corruptibility of the governors, the weakness of the garrisons, the terror and rebelliousness of the townsmen, or slowness in mounting expeditions of relief. (*Der aufs Neu-verschanzte Turenne*, Introduction)

From Italy the Germans inherited the bastion, with the general proportions given to it by Speckle, and the retired flanks which reached their extreme in the six-fold monstrosity advocated by Neubauer. The Netherlandish fausse-braye was held in high regard by many authors, even after it had gone out of fashion in its homeland, and it was applied on a large scale when Dresden was re-fortified in the 1680s. There was, however, no German equivalent of Pagan, to transform the most useful of the old inventions into a harmonious whole.

Of all the German authors of the time, Georg Rimpler certainly caused the most stir. His career exemplified the exciting and varied life which was open to the contemporary engineer. Rimpler was born in 1634 or 1635, the son of a butcher in Leisnig in Upper Saxony, hard by the Castle of Colditz. At about the age of twenty he entered the Swedish service as a simple musketeer, which accorded with the affinity between the Swedish and German nations, and the mood of the time:

Rimpler would not have embraced military service by chance. He was a man of lively, vaulting spirit, and a soldier through and through, as was to be shown later. The whole century was military in its character. The endless wars offered a rapid succession of honourable tasks and employments to every man of boldness and enterprise. (Kittler, 1951, 144)

After taking part in the defence of Riga against the Russians in 1654, Rimpler found time to acquire a liberal education in Nuremberg under the direction of the painter and mathematician Georg Gork. In 1669 he accompanied the Swedish general Count Königsmarck to the Venetian fortress of Candia, then under siege by the Turks, and he shared in the bitter defence which so influenced his thinking and that of all his comrades. In marked contrast, a period in the French employ enabled Rimpler to join in the Dutch campaign of 1672 and witness the defence of fortresses at its feeblest. Thereafter his doings are obscure until he emerges in 1683 as chief engineer in the Imperial service, and Rüdiger Starhemberg's right-hand man in the defence of Vienna against the Turks. On 25 July, while leading a sortie, he received a shot which shattered his arm. He died of the effects on 2 August.

The heroic Rimpler's fame was reinforced by a number of writings in which he expressed his views in peculiar and forceful language. His first book was *Ein Dreyfacher Tractat von den Festungen*, Nuremberg, 1673. His friend Christian Neubauer claimed that the designs were complicated and expensive (*Wohlmeynende Gedancken*, Kölln-am-Spree, 1673). Rimpler replied in *Die Befestigte Festung*, Frankfurt, 1674, and he went on to defend himself against another critic (and veteran of Candia) in his *Herrn Joh. Bernh Scheithers Ingenieurs, Furiöser Sturm auf die Befestigte Festung totaliter abgeschlagen*, Frankfurt, 1678.

In general terms Rimpler deplored the abandonment of the hollow, casemated wall in favour of the earth-filled rampart of the last century. In Rimpler's opinion the only use of the open ramparts was to

remind the soldier of his mortality, calling out to him: 'Comrade! Thou art dust, and through the action of bombs and mines to dust thou shalt return. Therefore prepare thyself to meet thy God and die in a Christian manner!' (Kittler, 1951, 216)

He admitted that there was a good deal of prejudice against casemated works, but pointed out that their great resistance at Candia showed powerful advantages.

Thus far Rimpler's case was clear and well-argued, but when he came to put forward a design of his own he was overcome by the Gothic obscurity that was the affliction of fortification writers of Teutonic blood. The body of his work is a mass of jargon, contradictions and bewildering detail, and lacks any plans which might have made any sense of the tangle – one story has it that he ordered all his drawings to be burnt before his eyes, while he lay on his death-bed at Vienna. There is no indica-

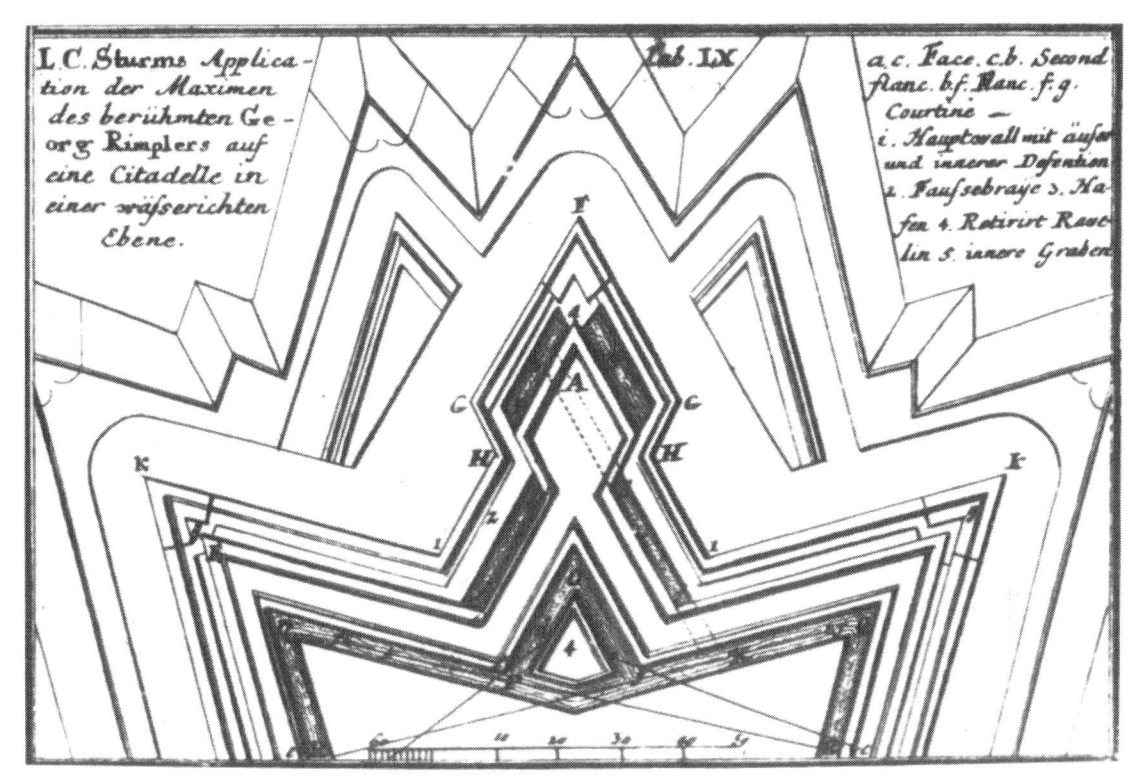

11 Sturm's reconstruction of the Rimpler trace

tion of where, if anywhere, he intended to site his famous casemates. All that is certain is that any fortress built according to his notions would have been very complicated and very expensive.

What became known as the 'Rimpler trace' was the product of later writers and editors who possibly found more sense in Rimpler's ramblings than they actually held. These were L. C. Sturm (*Freundliche Wettstreit der Französischen, Holländischen und Deutschen Kriegsbaukunst*, Augsburg, 1718, 1740) and L. A. Herlin (*Herrn Georg Rimplers ... samtliche Schriften der Fortifikation*, Dresden and Leipzig, 1724).

However, there were probably good reasons why Rimpler (and indeed Vauban and Coehoorn) left such disappointing printed memoranda on the subject of fortification.

His master [the Emperor] afforded him pay and bread over a period of time, and it was quite justifiable for Rimpler to have reserved his principles for the eyes of the Emperor alone, to have explained them to him in detail, and to have applied them to the defence of his lands. An engineer who hangs out his art for public display at every crossroads is the equivalent of a counsellor of state ... who gives the enemies of his fatherland written notification of all the policies and principles which tend to the maintenance and improvement of his sovereign's interests. (Behr, 1690, Introduction)

Vanity was also at stake. Sturm compared the great engineers with 'those fencing-masters who hold back a particular thrust, which they never teach to their pupils, and which for this reason they call the "master stroke"' (Sturm, 1710, Introduction).

How far is it possible to detect 'national' tendencies in German fortification of the time? In the nineteenth century, when such things were considered important, Rudolf Eickmayer (*Die Kriegskunst nach Grundsätzen*, Leipzig, 1821) made some very far-fetched connections between the casemated gunports to be found in the designs of Dürer and Rimpler and those advocated in the later eighteenth century by the maverick French innovator Montalembert (see p. 159), whom all authorities correctly accepted as the immediate inspiration for the new principles then gaining acceptance in northern Europe. This dubious pedigree was given credence through General Heinrich von Zastrow's widely-read *Geschichte der Beständigen Befestigung* (Leipzig, 1828, and later editions and translations), but it was convincingly destroyed in the 1880s by General G. Schröder ('Rimpler, Berichtigung einer Berumtheit', in *Beihefte zum Militär-Wochenblatt*, Berlin, 1884). Schröder's lead was followed by Max Jähns, the famous military bibliographer, who showed the absurdity of trying to claim that any school of fortification could possibly have traced its paternity to the muddled writings of Rimpler.

We are on slightly firmer ground when we turn to the 'tenaille' plan of fortification. The motif originated in sixteenth-century Italy, but it was taken up more enthusiastically in Germany than in most other places, and inspired some of the manners of Grotte, Borgsdorf, Werdmüller, Voigt, Harsch and the ex-Dutchman Landsberg. The tenaille was the simplest of all possible traces, being made up entirely of straight faces which were joined together as zigzags. 'The whole fortification takes on the shape of a star', wrote its enthusiastic advocate Leibniz in 1670. 'If the besieger plants himself between the salients, he comes under fire from the branches on either side: if he attacks one of the salients directly, he can be shot up by the adjacent salients' (Jähns, 1889-91, I, 347). Another advantage of the tenaille trace lay in the fact that it could enclose a given area more economically than any other shape except the circle. Unfortunately, tenaille fortification was the kind which was the most vulnerable of all to enfilade fire. The prolongation of the two faces reached out into the country in an acute angle, and it was all too easy for the besieger to plant his batteries on those lines, and make the long unbroken ramparts untenable in a single day's cannonade.

Probably these considerations were in the minds of the engineers who carried out very large-scale works in a modified tenaille style at Würzburg and Mainz from 1653. The first impetus came from Johann Philipp von Schönborn, a man of intelli-

12 L. C. Sturm, the foremost interpreter of German manners of fortification

gence and taste, who was elected Bishop of Würzburg in 1642 (while still serving as a cavalry officer), and Archbishop and Electoral Prince of Mainz five years later. For the defence of the Mainviertel quarter of Würzburg, and of the city of Mainz itself, he fell in with a novel scheme which seems to have been devised by the Salzburg master mason Johann Baptist Driesch, and carried out by Colonel Baron Alexander von Claris. The resulting ramparts were undeniably of tenaille inspiration in general character, being formed of saw-tooth projections and retired flanks, with very short connecting walls.

All the same geometry counted for little in the wider fields of strategy and frontiers. If some impressive advances were made by France, as a unified nation of nineteen million people, 'Germany' at that time was in the midst of those centuries of division and comparative helplessness – when the only semblance of unity was provided by some antiquated constitutional forms and the moral authority of the Emperor, when the word 'Dachau' called to mind a hunting-lodge of the Elector of Bavaria, and

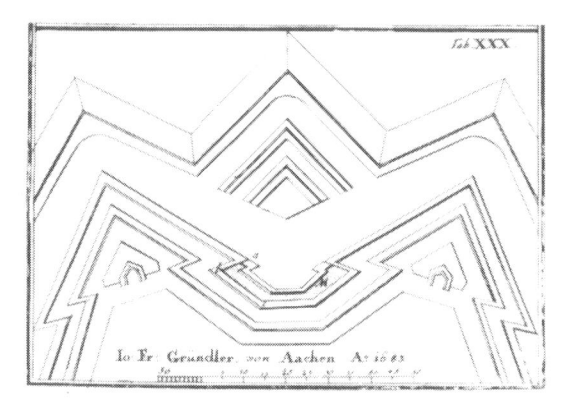

13 Gründler von Aachen's manner 1683. It closely resembles the traces of Driesch and Claris at Mainz and Würzburg

Goethe's favourite tree already graced the forest of Buchenwald.

On the defensive, the German Empire displayed merely the dispersed vitality of a low organism. Kehl and Philippsburg counted as the only 'Imperial' fortresses, all the rest being maintained directly from the revenues of citizens or princes. The bishopric of Mainz had an unusually heavy responsibility, for it guarded the access to the Main valley and thus to central Germany. For some time the enceinte of Mainz city was left in a neglected condition, after it was recaptured from the French in 1689, but in 1713 the Elector Lothar Franz von Schönborn began work on an ambitious system of outer defence, comprising a ring of interconnected forts – Karl, Elisabeth, Philipp, Joseph and Hauptstein. The complex was finished in 1736. It was in recognition of the importance of this state that in 1749 the Austrians, who had just set up their own engineering corps, lent the bishopric the artillery colonel Ferdinand Christoph Reichel von Reichelsheim to perform the same office for Mainz.

Meanwhile the internal tensions between the German princes continued unabated. Deeper into Germany the bishops of Würzburg were much concerned with the security of the vital crossing of the middle Rhine at Würzburg town. Here the Marienberg citadel (the 'stout heart of Franconia') was in a defensible state by 1653, as was the Mainviertel by the late 1670s. It was obviously to the advantage of the empire as a whole to have this vital point in secure hands. However, the Würzburgers gave at least as much attention to their eastern borders fronting on to Bavaria and the Protestant states and cities of central Germany. They had a strong Italianate fortress-town at Forchheim, on the right bank of the Pegnitz, twenty miles due

14 The Marienberg Citadel at Würzburg, seen from the Main bridge

15 The Wülzburg Fortress

north of the heretical city of Nuremberg. To the north-north-east again the medieval castle of Rosenberg (above Kronach) was expanded into a sprawling pentagonal citadel, serving as an ultimate refuge in the case of attack from the west, and as an outpost towards Thuringia, in which context it withstood an attack by the Prussians in the Seven Years War. Amongst their other competitors in the region we come across the Ansbachers, who built the somberly functional fortress of Wülzburg near Weissenburg, and the Bavarians, who owned the fortified town of Amberg, and who employed Pierre de Coquille and a team of Frenchmen to run up the show fortress of Rothenberg from 1730.

Coldly rational calculation was not always evident in the way the little princes went about building their fortresses. The Electors Palatine, for instance, were fond of sending for plans from foreign engineers, and building the works in text-book style regardless of the nature of the site. Even at Würzburg the bishop, Peter von Dembach (1675–83), reverted to a bad old practice, and commissioned projects from several engineers at a time, each of whom was kept in ignorance of the existence of his rivals until the bishop put a botched-up compromise into effect.

Appearances counted for a great deal among the Germans, as Vauban appreciated. The bishops of Würzburg were prepared to spend heavily on ramparts of beautifully dressed stone, rusticated gateways, baroque cartouches, and an architectural folly like Balthasar Neumann's mock-medieval 'Machicolation Tower' at the Marienberg. On its hill in the Bavarian enclave of Schnaittach, the

Louis XIV and Old Fortress Warfare 1660–1715 19

16 The Rothenberg Fortress

Rothenberg with its tall white walls was a military insanity, but it probably served its purpose of imposing on the lower ground about, and particularly the city of Nuremberg on the south-western horizon.

Meanwhile the French were threatening the western frontiers. The tamed and polluted Rhine of the present day gives little indication as to the strategic importance of that river in the seventeenth century, when it coursed swiftly through myriad channels, and every now and again burst over the surrounding landscape in devastating floods. The permanent crossings of this barrier were consequently very important.

On the upper (southern) Rhine the Empire was linked with Alsace by just two bridges, one leading from Breisach, and another from the fort of Kehl to the independent city of Strasbourg. For most of the century these strategic bridgeheads made it fairly easy for German commanders to wage war on the west bank in Alsace. It was a different story from the 1680s onwards, for by then the French had made themselves masters of Strasbourg, and won their way to the river bank along a broad frontage.

The contest was rather more equal on the Middle Rhine, for the Germans managed to wrest Philippsburg from the French in 1676, and made the place into their main depot on the Rhine. The area of Philippsburg and Mannheim now became the central point of assembly for the Imperial armies, possessing as it did these two fortified *points d'appui*,

17 Neumann's Machicolation Tower, Marienberg Citadel

and good rearward communications with central Germany by way of the Neckar.

The French responded by a sustained frenzy of fortress-building which even Vauban considered excessive. On the right, or southern flank, they strengthened Huningue (from 1680), and built mighty new fortresses at Belfort (1687) and Neuf-Brisach (1698) to cover the upper Rhine and Franche-Comté.

In the centre no effort was considered too great to safeguard Lower Alsace and the new acquisition of Strasbourg. Not content with the powerful new citadel at Strasbourg, and the little fortresses which were scattered over Alsace and Lorraine, the king built Fort Louis du Rhin on an island in the direction of Philippsburg. As a further check on Philippsburg, Vauban threw up extensive and powerful fortifications at Landau, well inside the borders of modern Germany. Significantly enough the last two undertakings, Fort Louis and Landau, were begun in the late 1680s, when Louis saw that the German princes were ganging up against him. Landau was so exposed that it actually fell to the Imperialists twice over in the War of the Spanish Succession. By then, however, the French had learnt to cover territory by lines and positions, and they effectively sealed off the incursions by holding the Moselle and Saar crossings to the north-west and west, and by guarding the gate to Alsace in the south at the successive lines of the Lauter and the Modder.

We end our journey down the Rhine at the lower, or northern end, where the Germans had some powerful fortifications along the 'Bishops' Alley' at Mainz, Coblenz, Bonn and Cologne. Here the French usually chose to open their way through political means, by agreement with one or more of the bishops. On the French side of the frontier Vauban attended to Luxembourg, after he took it from the Spanish in 1684, and he planted the fortress of Mont-Royal (1687) as an advanced post in a loop of the Moselle in the direction of Trier. French raiding parties sallied out frequently from Mont-Royal, and they brought back 'contributions' that were the equivalent of the revenues of an entire French province.

Once the French were across the Rhine in force, it was difficult for the Germans to offer a coherent defence, for the right-bank tributaries of the Rhine (the Kinzig, the Neckar, the Main, and much further downstream the Lippe) flowed in a general east–west direction, which offered the French natural paths of invasion into the heart of the empire, but obstructed the German lateral communications. Everything, therefore, came to rest upon the fortresses which guarded the individual valley routes to the heart of Germany.

The first of these tutelary fortresses, in succession from the south, was Freiburg, the capital of the Austrian enclave of Vorder-Österreich, which occupied the southern of the two main routes across the Black Forest. Somewhat more tempting, from the French point of view, was the northern route up the Kinzig valley, which could be unbottled by taking the fort of Kehl, lying within cannon-shot of the great French depot of Strasbourg. This road by-passed Freiburg by a wide margin, and was obstructed only by the medieval walled town of Villingen. A branch of this second route led off westwards towards Stuttgart by way of the Württemberg fortress of Freudenstadt, which was rebuilt in 1667.

The area of the old 'Bavarian block' of Mercy's time (See *Siege Warfare: the Fortress in the Early Modern World*, 1979, 130) was losing much of its former strength, because its many small strongholds were vulnerable to the new methods of siege attack. Also the French could avoid the Black Forest altogether if they chose to skirt the northern flank by way of the Neckar route. The access to that valley was inadequately defended by a cluster of Palatine fortresses – the old stronghold of Heidelberg and the newer but badly-sited fortresses of Mannheim and Frankenthal. Once they had broken through these defences, the French needed only to take the imperial city of Heilbronn in order to have the freedom of a network of roads spreading through south Germany.

By the 1690s the imperial and German commanders were able to offer the French a good fight in the open field, for they had profited greatly by their experience in the Turkish wars. However, their conduct of sieges rarely occasioned Louis much anxiety. The reason, as always, lay in the political weakness and disunion of the empire.

Months of paper-work and wrangling were

The Schönborn style

18 The Rosenberg Fortress

19 The Nürnbergertor, Forchheim 1698. Bearing the arms of Prince Bishop Lothar Franz von Schönborn

20 Bastion cartouche, Forchheim 1664

21 Sentry box, Würzburg town

required to mobilise the resources of the individual princes and cities for a projected siege. In 1702, for instance, the Emperor had to supplement the Austrian siege train through an 'Association', by which the Imperial cities and the Elector of Trier promised to add their guns to the number. The train still fell short of what was needed, and in 1703 the Emperor had to ask the *Reichsrath* at Regensburg for thirty-six mortars, forty demi-cannon and thirty-five 12-pounders, together with all their equipment, 25,000 27-pounder shot, 16,000 12-pounder shot, four lifting machines and 896,000 pounds of gunpowder. Small wonder that as the wars dragged on, many of the princes were content to become spectators, interested only in hiring out their troops on the best terms they could get. Narrow, isolated trench attacks were the hallmarks of German sieges, reflecting the division of the armies into princely contingents, and a general backwardness in fortress warfare.

The Germans subjected their allies to a variety of irritations. Already by 1703 Marlborough had learnt that 'whatever promises may be made by the princes of Germany, they are by no means to be relied upon' (Marlborough, ed. Murray, 1845, I, 92). In the following year the chaplain Samuel Noyes explained that the Allies had to give generous terms to the little fortress of Rain because

ammunition is not so plentiful with us as in Holland or Flanders, the Germans were very slow in providing it, and therefore we were content not to be obliged to spend any more. Besides, the German gunners are good for nothing. The time they did fire on the wall they made no work of it, and after all, I believe that we were glad to have the place at any rate that we might go forward (Noyes, *J.S.A.H.R.*, 1959, 145).

The three major states of the Empire were rarely in a condition to give a lead in engineering matters. Brandenburg-Prussia was already one of the prominent powers of north Germany, yet its engineers displayed little skill or originality until the middle of the eighteenth century. Bastion fortification first came to Brandenburg in 1537, when Margrave Johann commissioned an unknown Italian to fortify

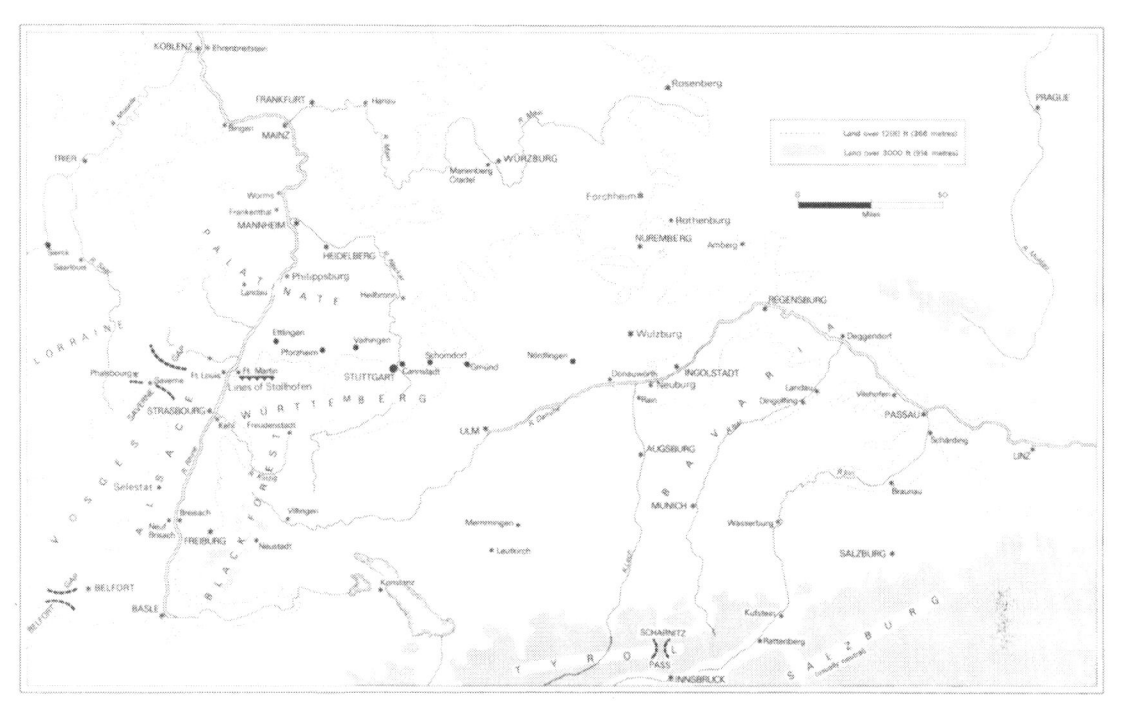

The Rhine and south Germany in the seventeenth and eighteenth centuries

Küstrin on the Oder. The citadel of Spandau, another essay in the same style, was designed in 1559 by the Italian Giromela and the native master Christoph Römer. In 1602 we hear for the first time of a Dutch engineer, in the person of one Nicolas de Kemp. The Netherlandish fortification rapidly supplanted the Italian, and the new works that were carried out in the duchy of East Prussia, which was acquired in 1618, were all executed in the new style. The foremost examples were the earthen enceintes of Königsberg and Pillau, which were begun in 1626. The leading native exponent of Netherlandish fortification was Matthias Dögen, who learnt the manner while he was serving as the Brandenburg resident in The Hague. His massive treatise *Heutiges Tages Übliche Kriegs Baukunst* was published in German and Latin in 1646 and 1647, and in French in 1648.

That most formidable ruler the Great Elector Frederick William (1640–88) called on the services of Dögen to help him to carry out a comprehensive scheme of national defence. Berlin, which had been girdled with an enceinte as recently as 1624, was re-fortified from 1658 according to the designs of Dögen, with contributions thrown in by Field-Marshal Sparr and the Great Elector himself. Fortification work was in progress at the same time at Lippstadt, Kolberg, Magdeburg, and at Königsberg, where the Great Elector had crushed civil liberties and was in the process of building the citadel of Friedrichsburg to overawe the townspeople.

Prussian officers went forth to help Peter the Great of Russia and his immediate successors in their sieges and fortress-building, which is one of the few instances in which we find that German experts were numerous and well-qualified enough to be in a position to help foreigners. The Prussians got on much less well with the Dutch, when they were allies in the War of the Spanish Succession. The Prussian officers were inclined to be patronising and boastful, and their gunners were such careless shots that the cannon-balls used to fly right over the besieged fortresses and land in the Dutch trenches on the far side.

Passing to south Germany, we discover that in Bavaria, the largest state of the region, military engineering could not even lay claim to the crude vigour that was one of the redeeming features of the

22 Spandau Citadel (Merian, 1637)

Prussian variety. Elector Maximilian I completed the new bastioned fortifications of Munich in 1645, which was a wise precaution in view of the freedom with which the Swedes tramped back and forth across his land. The names of three engineers alone survive from the reign of his successor, Elector Ferdinand Maria (1651–79). Among these the single one of note was the *Kriegsbaumeister* and *Oberingenieur* Christoph Heidemann, who worked on almost every stronghold of the electorate, and converted Ingolstadt into a powerful modern fortress. His literary monument was the *Nue-Herfürgegebene Kriegs-Architectur* (Munich, 1673), which was essentially a commentary on a number of beautifully engraved plates of fortress designs in the Italian style. Heidemann died in 1684, and with him the brief line of native engineers became extinct. The electorate was almost entirely dependent on foreign engineers from then onwards until 1744, the date of the foundation of the Bavarian engineering corps. Worse still, from the point of view of the Empire, Bavaria fought as an ally of the French in the wars of the Spanish and Austrian Successions, and offered the hereditary enemy a wide base in the heart of Germany.

The thing was a grave embarrassment to the Austrians, for their defences all faced to the north and east, against old enemies like the Swedes and Turks, and they had nothing to put in the way of an attack down the Danube valley. At Vienna there was no single body of engineering officers and bureaucrats who could direct sieges or attend to state defence. The *Hofkriegsrath* (Court War Council) gave the initial orders for military construction, but left the execution entirely to the *Fortifications Bau-Zahlamt*, which sent the appropriate instructions to

23 Frontispiece, Matthias Dögen

the fortress commandant concerned, or dispatched engineers of its own from Vienna. Nearly all of these experts were foreigners, and especially Huguenots, who were given formal contracts and military rank.

However, specialists of any kind remained very rare birds in the Austrian service. In the 1660s and 1670s the Imperialists were lucky to have as their leading military man the celebrated Raimondo Montecuccoli, who maintained an old tradition according to which great captains were expected to have a working acquaintance with fortification, siegework and gunnery. In the Austrian arsenals he discovered a

chaotic accumulation of artillery, heaped together without regard for order, category or proportion. They used to ransack the dictionary to find sufficient names to distinguish all the types of pieces, so that there was hardly a snake, an animal or a bird which had not lent its name to some gun or other. (Montecuccoli, 1735, bk I, ch. 2)

Montecuccoli did what he could to remedy this state of affairs, reorganising the Vienna Arsenal in 1677, and casting new designs of guns from the evidence of statistical experiments.

Montecuccoli's common-sense remarks on fortification stand in marked contrast to the faddish rantings of much of the literature of the time. He was not particularly concerned with the geometrical properties of traces, provided they conformed, within wide limits, to the accepted dimensions:

To sum up, every fortress is good ... when it is spacious enough to allow a large number of troops to come into action together, to mount a good quantity of artillery, and to allow the defenders to throw up several flanks and retrenchments. (*ibid.*, bk I, ch. 5)

Prince Eugene of Savoy represented a new generation, which largely resigned the management of technical affairs to the so-called experts. He might have been speaking for all the Austrian commanders of his time when he wrote to the Emperor in 1710

I do not have a single engineer who knows how to build a proper fortress. The engineers have either been broken by misery and hardship, or they have deserted in order to avoid their imminent ruin. That is why we have been unable to fulfil our project of setting up an engineering corps and school of military architecture of the sort on which all the other princes lavish so much money. (Kriegsarchiv, 1876-91, XII, Appx 290)

The war with the Empire, 1672-8

At the beginning of the new conflict the French were content to remain on the defensive on the Rhenish theatre, which encouraged the Earl of Orrery to believe that he could detect an essential difference between the campaigns in Germany and those in the Netherlands:

As the French king manages his wars on the German side by his captains, and makes it oftener defensive there than invasive; so on the Flanders side, he makes it generally offensive, and leads his armies himself.... On the side of Alsace, the French keep but very few garrisons, and those excellently furnished, and the country generally wasted; so that if the forces of the Circles of the Empire besiege and reduce one of them the ensuing summer, that will probably be the most they can aim at, and possibly all things considered, more than they can effect. (Orrery, 1677, 132, 139)

By manoeuvre and counter-attack, and by resolutely holding on to the little fortresses of Haguenau and Saverne in 1675, the French were able to preserve Alsace against the German offensives, and limit their losses to some places on the Rhine. The events along that river were certainly alarming enough. Late in 1673 45,000 Germans, Austrians, Dutch and Spanish wrested Bonn from the Elector of Cologne and his French friends. Three years later another powerful siege army took Philippsburg after two and a half months of attack. The fall of this place was particularly painful, as the French had held Philippsburg in full sovereignty, and they lost with it their one bridgehead on the 'German' bank of the middle Rhine.

It was some consolation that the French were able to take the offensive towards the end of the war, reducing Freiburg in 1677 and the fort of Kehl in 1678. The peace treaty of 5 February 1679 confirmed the military *status quo*. Louis had to cede all his rights on Philippsburg, but he retained his recent conquest of Freiburg, and thereby consolidated a French grip on both banks of the upper Rhine.

The French aggrandisements of the 1680s

The decade of the 1680s marks in many ways the end of the period of almost unresisted successes which Louis had enjoyed since he first assumed power. He certainly kept up an aggressive front, as we shall see, but in the process he awakened wide fears of a universal monarchy and a universal Gallican–Catholic religion. In response the purposeful Prince William of Orange began to spin a network of alliances, and the states of north Italy found unsuspected virtues in Habsburg Spain. More dangerously still, the armies of Habsburg Austria returned from the Turkish wars full of fight and trailing clouds of *gloire*.

None of this would have been of much consequence if France had been able to preserve its relative military superiority. However, the monarchy as a whole was weakened by an agrarian recession and the gradual ossification of the bureaucratic machine. The army was under-strength, and the hard work of fortress-building served to reduce the remaining troops to a state of exhaustion. The French generals began to fall behind the times, at least in warfare in the open field, and Vauban himself was about to be faced with an enemy worthy of his talents in the great Dutch engineer Menno van Coehoorn.

Strasbourg 1681
Turenne died in action on 27 July 1675, leaving the memory of one of the foremost captains of Louis's reign, and the commission to France to capture Strasbourg. In April 1674 he had pointed out that as long as the Germans had the use of that city, they would always be able to spend the winter on the 'French' side of the Rhine, and concentrate their forces in safety for a move into the heart of France by way of Lorraine and Champagne. The Strasbourgers lent force to Turenne's argument in September of the same year, when they threw over all pretence of neutrality and admitted a German garrison. In 1676 they made so bold as to provide the artillery, ammunition and barges which enabled Prince Frederick of Baden-Durlach to reduce Philippsburg.

The Strasbourgers were immensely confident in their 260 cannon, their 800 mercenary troops, their 4,600 militia, and above all in their fine sandstone ramparts. The important Roseneck Bastion had been built in the last century by Strasbourg's native son Speckle. The other defences were reconstructed on the plans of the Swedish engineer Mershäuser, who had been hired in 1633. By 1680 the entire enceinte of sixteen bastions was complete.

The citizens did not know that they were as good as building for the King of France. Exploiting the ambiguities of the Peace of Münster (1648), the French had already secured a number of territorial adjudications which enabled them to grope towards the Rhine on a number of sectors. The whole of Alsace was pronounced to be theirs, as were the duchy of Zweibrücken and parts of the Palatinate. Finally Louis made underhand approaches to some of the leading burghers of Strasbourg, giving assurances that the privileges of the city would be respected. Now that the ground was fully prepared, a French force of occupation entered by the open gates on 30 September 1681. Vauban accompanied the first troops into the city, and as early as 16 November he was able to send Louvois his plans for improving the enceinte and building a very strong new citadel of five bastions at the southeastern corner.

Thus 'the course of a river became a political frontier, and the concept of a Rhine frontier entered the sphere of international diplomacy' (Livet, in Hatton, 1976, 65).

Casale 1681
At the same time as Strasbourg was being swallowed up in the north, the French appeared to give a clue to their sinister intentions elsewhere in Europe when they occupied Casale, a fortress in the Montferrat forty miles east of Turin. The Duke of Mantua was one of those hard-up petty potentates who abounded at the time, and after being sounded by the French he willingly parted with his enclave at Casale in return for a bribe.

It was bad enough that Louis got Casale at all,

for it supplemented Pinerolo as a base for French operations on the Italian side of the Alps. The way in which the enterprise was carried out was more significant still, because the occupying force and the subsequent reliefs marched straight across Piedmontese territory without the formality of gaining the Duke of Savoy's leave.

In a similarly cavalier fashion the French made a naval bombardment of Genoa in 1684, simply because the republic appeared to be too friendly with Spain. This drastic measure confirmed the impression that Louis regarded north Italy as part of his own domains.

The Netherlands and Luxembourg 1683–4
Not content with snatching slices of territory, Louis wished to force the Emperor and the King of Spain into signing a formal recognition of his recent aggrandisements. Without any proper declaration of war, Marshal d'Humières and Vauban made a short incursion into the Spanish Netherlands at the beginning of November 1683, and captured Courtrai in a two-day siege.

In the next year Louis addressed himself to the siege of the mighty Spanish fortress of Luxembourg. In normal circumstances this would have been a risky enterprise, both militarily and politically, for Luxembourg was a rocky fortress which was accessible only on its northern side, and the duchy was situated on the narrow and sensitive junction of the Empire and the Spanish Netherlands. Louis, however, trusted that the meticulous preparations of Louvois and Vauban's skill would bring the place rapidly into his power.

An army of 27,000 men was devoted to the siege, and trenches were opened on the night of 8–9 May 1684. The further progress of the siegeworks was greatly aided when Vauban built some 'trench cavaliers', which he describes as

breastworks of gabions which are situated half-way up the glacis around the main salient angles of the counterscarp. By this means we have been able to capture the covered way without recourse to a general storm, which has saved us many casualties. (Rochas d'Aiglun, 1910, II, 229–30)

As always in Vauban's sieges, the advance of the saps was covered by a well-directed artillery fire, and in this case the mortars worked to particularly devastating effect. On 28 May a large crownwork in front of the Barlemont Bastion was wrecked by mines and taken by storm. The bastion itself was now threatened with the same treatment, which induced the surviving 1,800 defenders of Luxembourg to conclude a capitulation on 3 June. Vauban reported to Louvois

This is the finest and most glorious conquest the king has made in his life, and the one which best guarantees the prosperity of all his affairs. I beg you as a personal favour to come and see the trenches before we raze them. I am so eager to see you here that if you disappoint me I shall forswear the trade of sieges and fortifications for ever. (*ibid.*, II, 237)

This well-calculated aggression brought a further, if temporary, reward in the shape of the Truce of Regensburg of 15 August 1684, by which Emperor Leopold acquiesced in Louis's occupation of Strasbourg and Luxembourg. No concession could have been more grudging. As soon as the immediate Turkish danger to Austria's eastern borders had passed, Leopold hastened to form the hostile League of Augsburg in 1686. Once again Louis was faced with war on a European scale.

The War of the League of Augsburg 1688–97

The Netherlands, the lower Rhine and the struggle for Namur
The first years of the new conflict brought home to Louis the unpleasing fact that the Dutch, for the first time since the days of Frederick Henry of Nassau, were displaying some efficiency in siege warfare.

Everywhere there were signs of a willingness to learn and improve. The Dutch artillery was given a military organisation in 1677, and over the next two decades the gunners learnt to make effective use of such devices as the day and night sighting mechanisms of Willem Meesters, and the arrangements (probably attached cartridge and shot) which the Danish captain Jan Zeger introduced to enhance the rate of fire. Experiments were made into grenade-throwers, and from 1693 the imported

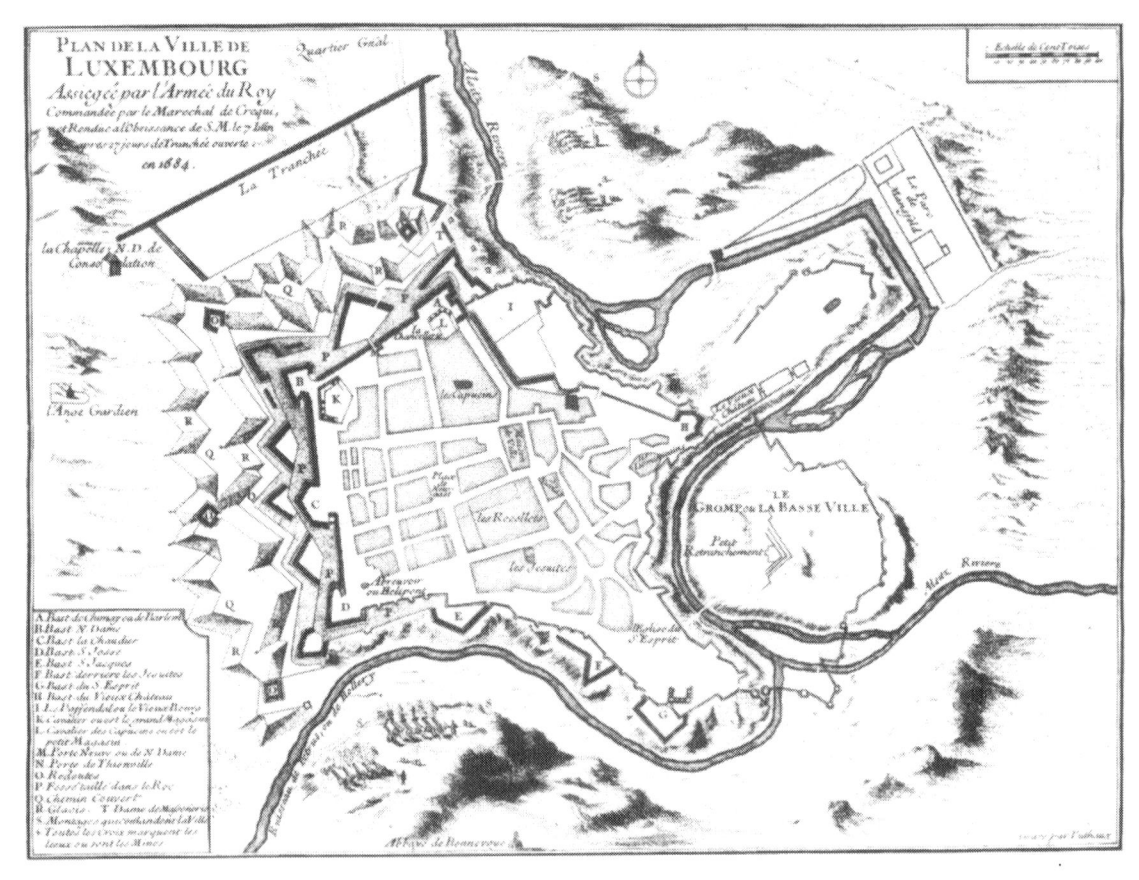

24 Siege of Luxembourg 1684. The Barlemont Bastion is indicated by 'A'

howitzers were replaced by the products of the native gun-founder Hermanus Nieupoort.

In the realm of strategy the Dutch had absorbed the lesson of 1672, and they made it their first concern to secure the lower Rhine and the Meuse, the river avenues which curved into the United Provinces from the south-east. Dutch contingents were therefore sent to join the German armies which were bent on evicting the French from the electorate of Cologne at the beginning of the war. The most gifted of the Dutch engineers, Menno van Coehoorn, assisted at the siege of Kaiserswörth, which capitulated on 26 June 1689, after two days of attack. From there he went to join the Brandenburgers and Austrians who sat before Bonn with an enormous train of siege artillery. However the siege of this place proved

long and difficult, for to begin with the attacks were not very well directed. One day Coehoorn made bold to speak his mind on the subject. His arguments reached the ears of the Elector of Brandenburg, then present at the siege, who changed the method of attack accordingly. This brought about the rapid capitulation of the fortress. (G. Coehoorn, 1860, 8)

The main change wrought by Coehoorn was to concentrate the fire on the fortifications, instead of dissipating the effect in a general bombardment of the town. He had given the same advice at Kaiserswörth.

After a lull in the Netherlands theatre in 1690, the following year opened in the old style 'with an exceedingly bold and well-concerted enterprise on the part of the French' (Quincy, 1726, II, 342). This was when they attacked Mons, the capital of Hainault, before the allies were in a condition to take the field. The details were revealing.

The preparation was left to Louvois, a person who 'could be relied upon to attend to every detail necessary to form a powerful army, and forward ample supplies and convoys of provisions and ammunition' (Villars, 1884-9, I, 127). For many months now the contractors had 900,000 rations of hay in constant readiness near the Scarpe and the Scheldt, and in January 1691 Louvois ordered the fodder to be bound in fifteen-pound bales ready for transport. The canals and roads were surveyed and improved, and Mesgrigny, the governor of the citadel of Tournai, was summoned to Paris, sworn to secrecy, and told to prepare boats and bridges to convey the provisions and ammunition along the Scarpe, the Scheldt and the Haine. Great quantities of foodstuffs, including 220,000 red-skinned Dutch cheeses, were heaped up in his citadel.

All the time the Lieutenant-General of Artillery, de Vigny, was engaged in assembling a siege train of forty-five 36- and 24-pounders, twenty 16- and 12-pounders, and thirty-one mortars and pierriers. A battalion of bombardiers was assigned to serve the mortars, and Vauban collected no less than sixty engineers to help him to direct the trenches.

On 17 March 1691 the circumvallation around Mons was begun by 20,000 labourers, a gigantic force which is a further indication of the impressive scale of the siege. By early April the French cannonade was so furious that it sounded like a continuous roll of musketry, and the Spanish fire was so subdued that it was safe for the French soldiers to stand on the parapets of the trenches and watch the spectacle. The garrison of 4,800 men yielded on 8 April. The fat and overworked Louvois died unexpectedly nine weeks later, but not before he had given his master this one last proof of his ability and devotion.

The Allies were thrown into such confusion by the fall of Mons that they were good for nothing for the rest of the year. In 1692 the French were ready to mount another offensive, which was directed this time against the major Spanish fortress of Namur, which stood astride the junction of the Sambre and the Meuse. The stronghold stood in the first line of frontier fortresses, now that the Treaty of Nijmegen had delivered Givet to the French. 'The loss of this place would be a mortal blow to the Spanish cause', wrote the governor of the Spanish Netherlands (Pro Civitate, 1965, 315). He scarcely overstated his case, for the fall of Namur threatened to open up the south-eastern flank of the Netherlands, and place the French in a good position for future campaigning down the Meuse against the Dutch.

The resulting siege was of unusual technical interest, for it pitted directly against each other the two great engineers of the age, Coehoorn and Vauban (for detailed descriptions of the sieges of Namur in 1692 and 1695 see the author's *Fire and Stone. The Science of Fortress Warfare 1660-1860*, 1975, pp. 163-74).

On 25 and 26 May 1692 King Louis descended on Namur with a host of 60,000 men, accompanied by a siege train of 151 pieces. Vauban drove the trenches forward with vigour and skill, and after reducing the town he cut off and captured Coehoorn in the strongpoint of Fort William, where the Dutchman had hoped to stage a last-ditch defence. The final resistance was beaten down on 28 June.

In 1693 the French exploited their success by expanding their hold on the Meuse-Sambre line. In July they took the Meuse fortress of Huy and beat the allies in the open field at Neerwinden (almost their last victory of the kind), and Vauban urged that the next objective must be Charleroi on the Sambre. The offending place was

> responsible for the ruin of a tract of land which is equivalent to a good province in area. Moreover Charleroi denies us the navigation of the Sambre, makes it difficult to support Namur, and compels the king to maintain 15,000 or 16,000 additional men in his fortresses. (To Le Peletier, 29 June, Rochas d'Aiglun, 1910, II, 390)

Vauban's opinion in strategic matters weighed just as heavily as it did in the 1670s, and the king accordingly sent Villeroi with a large detachment to undertake the siege of Charleroi in September. As if revelling in his power, Vauban refused to be hurried out of the systematic march of his attack, and he turned to some impatient officers with the famous remark: '*Brûlons de la poudre, et versons moins de sang!*' ('Burn your powder and spare your blood!')

Charleroi capitulated on 11 October, as a mass

of rubble and half-buried corpses. 'The capture of this place', wrote Vauban, 'is one of the most needful conquests which the king has made in his entire reign. This success presents him with the finest frontier which France has enjoyed for a thousand years' (to Le Peletier 19 Oct., *ibid.*, II, 398). By this he meant that France now commanded the line of the Sambre from Maubeuge eastwards to the confluence with the Meuse at Namur.

The Allies screwed themselves up to a major offensive in 1694, but by the end of the year they had nothing to show for their efforts except the capture of the little stronghold of Huy. In 1695, however, a renewed Allied move offered Coehoorn a target more worthy of his talents – namely Namur itself.

Namur was actually a good deal stronger than it had been three years earlier, for the French had a garrison of 13,000 in the place, and they had surrounded the fortifications with an outer zone of arrow-shaped works called 'lunettes'. The Allied army of Dutch, English, Spanish and Germans got off to a bad start, for at first the siege was entrusted to the uninspired direction of King William III's Grand Master of Artillery, Julius von Tettau, and the Director General of Fortifications, the Huguenot du Puy de l'Espinasse. Coehoorn spoke out boldly in a council of war:

He argued that it was essential to avoid a long and very difficult siege, which would cost many officers and soldiers their lives. He knew the fortress well and had made some works there himself, and he was confident that he could wipe out the powerful garrison by a continuous fire of cannon and mortars. (G. Coehoorn, 1860, 12)

The Elector of Bavaria (the new governor of the Spanish Netherlands) was mightily impressed, and he made the protesting von Tettau fall in with every one of Coehoorn's directions.

Coehoorn's technique of well-timed bombardment and assault was aimed as much at shattering the morale of the garrison as at gaining ground, and on 1 September he was rewarded when the French unexpectedly asked to capitulate. This very important re-conquest cemented Coehoorn's reputation. King William now promoted him lieutenant-general and made him Director General of Fortifications in place of du Puy de L'Espinasse, who had been mortally wounded in the siege. On his side Charles II of Spain showed his appreciation by bestowing on Coehoorn the title of baron – an indication of how far the Spanish and Dutch had progressed in interdependence since the end of the Eighty Years War.

In 1696 both sides drew breath after the high drama of the previous year, but in 1697 the French went to war in something like their time-honoured fashion, taking the field before the Allies, and advancing into Hainault to besiege Ath. Ironically enough, Vauban had been responsible for rebuilding the place after the French first gained it in 1667, and he now planned a model siege to bring his lost child back again. Perhaps also he was on his mettle, after Coehoorn's performance at Namur.

The first parallel was opened on the night of 22–23 May at a distance of 650–700 paces from the covered way on the eastern side of Ath. This was followed on the night of the 24–25th by the digging of the second parallel, three hundred paces nearer the fortress. Vauban spent the next days bringing forward his guns, and on 27 May he opened fire with thirty-six cannon, which were disposed in five batteries along the prolongation of the faces of the fortress works. These batteries were arranged in a completely novel manner, for they embraced all the front under attack, delivering an enfilading and cross-fire into the bastions, ravelins and covered ways. For this purpose Vauban ordered the cannon to be fired with reduced charges, so that the round-shot, instead of following a flat trajectory, dropped over the parapets and bounced along the length of the ramparts. The gunners were disappointed of their crashes and bangs, but this 'ricochet fire' cleared the ramparts in less than six hours. The mortars added their voices on 28 May, and on the night of 28–29 May Vauban planted his breaching batteries on the covered way opposite the bastions of Limburg, Brabançon and Namur. The inevitable capitulation was signed on 5 June. At a cost of 53 dead and 106 wounded the French had reduced an eight-bastioned modern fortress which was held by 3,850 men.

The conquest of Ath was more than one of those

typically sure and economical sieges which Europe had come to expect from Vauban. By his devastating employment of the 'ricochet batteries' he had made a significant addition to the vocabulary of fortress warfare, and provided the natural complement, in the artillery attack, to the parallels with which he had already revolutionised the trench attack. Nearly a century later Montalembert went so far as to say:

This is a siege which makes the highest state of perfection to which the art of attacking fortresses has ever been brought. As soon as the batteries had been cunningly planted along the prolongations of the faces and flanks of the fortifications, it became quite impossible for the defenders to preserve their artillery. Once the fire of the guns of a besieged fortress is silenced, no garrison, even the most active, is capable of postponing the capitulation for more than a few days. (Montalembert, 1776-96, I, 8)

The reduction of Ath provided a useful bargaining counter for Louis to employ in the negotiations which were bringing this increasingly costly and burdensome war to an end. At the Treaty of Rijswijk in September 1697 Louis restored to Spain the fortresses of Charleroi, Ath, Courtrai and Luxembourg. Vauban found it particularly hard to reconcile himself to losing Luxembourg, which again placed the enemy within dangerously close reach of the upper Meuse. With these reservations, he and his master could be fairly content with the peace provisions, for they had won a breathing space, and retained intact the northern *pré carré* which they had carved out for themselves in the 1670s.

The war on the middle and upper Rhine
In contrast to the long drawn-out campaigning on the Netherlands frontier of France, the struggle on the Rhine was decided in a spectacular way in the first year of hostilities.

In early October 1688 the Dauphin with a siege army of twenty-nine battalions and forty-five squadrons descended upon Philippsburg without the formality of declaring war. Vauban accompanied the expedition, but for once his habitual confidence and address appeared to have deserted him. The rain, the wind and the cold made life in the trenches a misery; the newly delivered cannon from the Keller brothers' foundry were bursting like pottery; worst of all, the Germans were using their own 127 guns 'wonderfully well' (to Louvois, 17 October, Catinat, 1819, I, 306-7). At last on 23 October the French artillery began to gain the upper hand. The outworks were taken by assault, and Governor Richard Starhemberg surrendered his fortress at the end of the month rather than risk a general storm.

The tenth of November found Vauban before the Palatine fortress of Mannheim, and with his confidence fully restored. He had just opened the trenches, he was again speaking in a tone that befitted a general officer of King Louis:

These Germans are very good-natured people. Last night, while we were quietly cutting their throats by digging towards the citadel, they responded with fanfares and music on their trumpets, drums and woodwind. They gave splendid renderings of all our favourite minuets and tunes from the operas, and kept up the performance for as long as they kept up their drinking – in other words all night. (To Louvois, 10 November, Rochas d'Aiglun, 1910, II, 299-300)

The next day twenty mutinous German soldiers presented their musket barrels to the governor's stomach and forced him to surrender.

A thirty-six hour siege brought about the capitulation of the neighbouring fortress of Frankenthal on 18 November, and Vauban gave Louvois a scornful professional verdict on the fortresses of the Elector Palatine:

I cannot understand what goes on in these people's minds. They fortified Mannheim in the way you would draw a fortress plan on a blank sheet of paper, without deriving any advantage from the presence of the Neckar or the Rhine – if they had lodged themselves in the fork between these two rivers, they could have used them in the office of main ditch or outer ditch. . . . Again, what are we to make of Frankenthal, which has been set down in a plain two leagues from Mannheim? It seems a ridiculous mistake for a sovereign as badly off as the Prince Palatine to wish to keep up such a useless and expensive fortress. (18 November, *ibid.*, II, 304)

The Dauphin's army had more than achieved Louis's objectives in Germany. The winning-back of Philippsburg had not only relieved the king of his almost paranoid anxiety for Alsace, but given him a strong east-bank bridgehead on the middle Rhine which complemented the hold he had on the upper Rhine by means of Freiburg, Breisach and Kehl. Thereafter the French were content to maintain these fortresses as the strategic equivalent of outworks, the Rhine as a ditch, and the whole region as a bare uninviting glacis after they had devastated the German towns and villages in 1689. The one failure was a diplomatic one. The Spanish and the Emperor still refused to come to terms, and German public opinion as a whole was outraged by the barbarities of 1689. Thus Louis's lightning 'preemptive strike' on the Rhine led him, against every calculation, into a general continental war. When the French handed back Philippsburg, Kehl, Breisach and Freiburg by the peace treaty of 1697, it was out of Louis's desire to put an end to European hostilities, rather than a reflection of the way the war had been going on the Rhine.

The war in Italy
Just as in their contest with the empire, the French took the initiative at the beginning of hostilities in Italy, and won an advantage which they preserved, with a couple of small exceptions, for the rest of the war. The chief victim was the state of Piedmont-Savoy, and the men who dealt these damaging blows were Marshal Catinat and his engineer Lapara des Fieux.

An official Piedmontese memorandum explained that:

When the French attacked our lands they found the country unprepared for war and the fortresses in a bad state. Since we were enjoying a restful peace, it was easy for the enemy to take Nice, Villefranche (1691), Susa (1690) and Montmélian (1691). By this act of aggression the French sealed off the entry to Provence from Dauphiné and the Lyonnais, and erected a frontier which placed them in complete safety. The enemy were now free to choose between two courses, to carry the war into the Piedmontese lowlands by way of Susa and Pinerolo, or simply to stay on the defensive by holding the ground on either side of these fortresses and the rearward slopes of the Alps. (Enclosed by Victor Amadeus to the Marquis del Borgo, 3 March 1704, R. Deputazione, 1907-10, II, 347)

The trouble was that the Duke of Savoy's dominions were scattered very awkwardly over both sides of the Alps. Two of his territories were actually situated on the 'French' side of the mountain barrier – these were the Duchy of Savoy (fortresses Annecy, Montmélian) and the County of Nice (fortresses Nice, Vintimille and Villefranche). The mountain chains did not even compensate the Piedmontese by offering a barrier against French advance into the northern plain, for Louis held Turin neatly bracketed by his garrisons at Pinerolo and Casale (see pp. 27-8).

Duke Victor Amadeus found no effective means of striking back, apart from a solitary raid into the valley of the upper Durance in 1692, which caused Louis a disproportionate amount of worry for his southern borders. Victor Amadeus did not entirely welcome the presence of the Austrians, who came to his aid, and the only fruit of the alliance was a joint siege of Pinerolo in 1693. The enterprise merely laid him open to retaliation from Catinat, who slipped around his rear by way of Susa. Victor Amadeus called off the siege, and marched to a heavy defeat at Marsaglia on 4 October.

The hostilities between the French and Piedmontese petered out in a prolonged blockade of Casale in 1694 and 1695. Playing the ancient political balancing-trick of the dukes of Savoy, Victor Amadeus now checked the expanding power of his over-mighty Austrian friends by striking a bargain with the French. The French garrison yielded Casale in July 1695, as soon as the Piedmontese lodged on the glacis. Victor Amadeus thereupon razed the works, as his part of the deal, and returned the emasculated town to its original Mantuan owners. The Austrians were furious, but the French and Piedmontese laid a joint siege to Valenza and persuaded the Imperialists to accept a general settlement of north Italy's affairs in October 1696.

Casale went to the Duke of Mantua, as had already been arranged, and the French ceded Pinerolo to the Piedmontese. When he abandoned these invaluable outposts on the Italian plain, Louis showed just how much he was now willing to pay for a peace.

The war in Catalonia
Every war between France and Spain brought about a state of hostilities in the Pyrenees. For half a century now the rival forces had been content to make no more than brief forays into each other's territory, for Catalonia was quiescent under the rule of Madrid, and there seemed to be no cause for France to renew the adventures of the 1640s. In the first campaigns of the present war the French got the better of what small encounters took place, and they were able to edge a short way down from the Pyrenean passes, taking Rosas in 1693, and the virgin fortress of Gerona in 1694.

There was nothing in these last few Pyrenean campaigns, or indeed in the last three wars, which could give an inkling of the scale of ferocity of the siege of Barcelona, the event which closed the War of the League of Augsburg. Louis believed that the capture of this great fortress-port, the capital of Catalonia, would be such a mighty blow that Spain might come to terms. He accordingly put Marshal Vendôme in command of 30,000 men, and ordered Vice-Admiral d'Estrées to supply the expedition from the sea and transport the siege train of sixty cannon and twenty-four mortars.

The Spaniards, for their part, suspected that something was afoot, and they piled 9,500 troops (including about 4,000 Germans) into the fortress to assist the 4,000 citizen militia.

Vendôme invested Barcelona on 12 June 1697. His engineer Lapara des Fieux, the 'Vauban' of France's southern campaigns, made a wise choice and directed his attack against the New and San Pedro bastions on the northern sector of the enceinte. On the 26th, however, this ingenious engineer had his wig removed by a cannon ball, and he did not recover from the experience for eighteen days. The accident could not have happened at a worse time, for the Spaniards were resisting in a style which seemed quite alien to observers who had witnessed their feeble performance in the Netherlands in recent decades.

In the absence of any informed direction the generals bludgeoned themselves forward by means of bloody assaults, and tore great chunks out of the ramparts by the uncouth but very effective technique of firing mortar bombs from heavy cannon. Governor Corsana declared a truce on 5 August, once the French had lodged some mines in the old enceinte, and Barcelona finally yielded by capitulation on the 10th.

By their own calculations the French had spent fifty-two days of trenches and lost 8,000 men in taking Barcelona. It is a matter of debate whether the place could have been bought more cheaply, for the siege fitted nowhere into the strategic or technical pattern of recent wars. Vauban declared that the operation had succeeded only by a miracle, and already we can detect some of that tension between 'scientific' engineering and the vigorous ways of the French field commanders, which was going to have such important consequences in the next war. The veteran de Guignard, in reviewing the wars of Louis's reign, flatly states that 'it is quite certain that you have seen the very best of fortress warfare when you have witnessed Vendôme in his siege of Barcelona, and Boufflers in his defence of Lille [1708]' (Guignard, 1725, II, 439). Both of these gentlemen were known to have flouted the prescriptions of Vauban.

One thing was certain, namely that the Catalans, however strong their dislike of being ruled from Madrid, no longer wished to place themselves under the patronage of France. Vendôme's troops marched out at the end of the year, after the peace settlement, and 'the aversion of the inhabitants was so strong that they poured scalding water on us as we marched through the streets' (Drake, 1960, 15).

The War of the Spanish Succession 1701–14

The war in the Netherlands
The new strategic balance. In 1700 Louis decided to abide by the will of Charles II, the last of the Spanish Habsburgs, and annex Spain and its dominions to the House of Bourbon, in the person

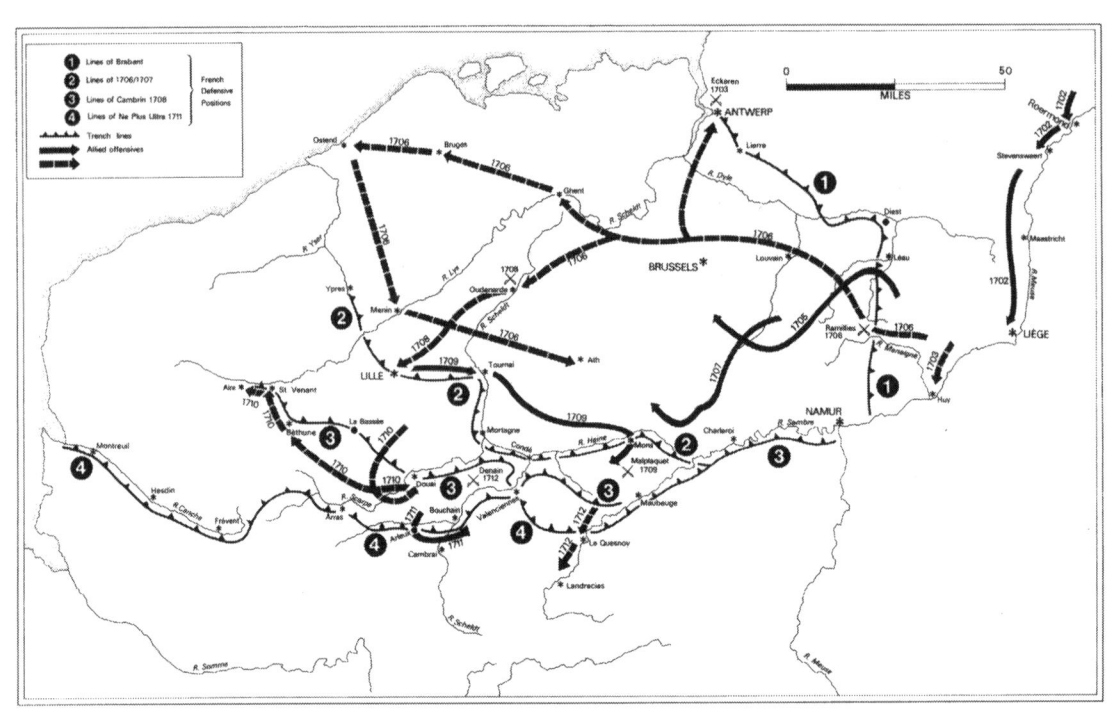

The Netherlands in the War of the Spanish Succession

of his grandson Philip. Most of the other rulers of Europe responded violently to the prospect of a new Franco-Spanish superpower arising in their midst, and they unleashed a war that lasted for more than a dozen years.

The fighting put in question the survival not just of small states like Bavaria and Piedmont, but of the great French and Austrian monarchies. The Dutch may therefore be forgiven for supposing that when King Louis occupied the Spanish Netherlands in 1701, along with the bishoprics of Liège and Cologne, he placed the Republic in as much danger as in the terrible crises of 1573 and 1672, when the existence of Holland came to depend on a single water line.

The outbreak of the new hostilities certainly caught the United Provinces at an embarrassing moment. At the end of the last war Coehoorn and the field deputies of the States General had carried out inspection of the frontier fortresses, and William's Council concluded that urgent attention must be paid to 'some of the strongholds along the Ijssel, as also to Coevorden, Groningen and Bergen-op-Zoom, which all stand where the frontiers are at their weakest and most exposed to the first enemy onslaught' (Ten Raa *et al.*, 1911, etc., VII, 395).

Four million florins were voted for the new programme of defence, of which 800,000 came as a windfall from the East India Company as the fee for the renewal of its licence. Such, however, was the multiplicity of the frontier fortresses that the money was swallowed up without producing any obvious results, and in August 1702 the Council informed the States General that 'work on the fortifications has come to a halt, at the very time when it ought to be continued with the greatest energy' (*ibid.*, VII, 399). As one example of the nation's state of defence we may take the case of Bergen-op-Zoom, the guardian fortress of Dutch Brabant, where Coehoorn had razed the southern fronts but was not given the time or the money to build the new works he intended to throw up in their place. Dutch confidence was dealt a further blow in 1702 through the death of William III, 'whose courage, whose wisdom, whose care, whose very name afforded the state more security than the best frontiers' (quoted in *ibid.*, VII, 399).

In these circumstances it was not surprising that

the Dutch were 'not inclined to venture any action, the event of which is doubtful; knowing, that battles decide the fate of states, and may, in an instant, ruin them' (Berwick, 1779, I, 180-1). They intended to take only such measures as would, with the minimum of risk, enable them to bar the Meuse and Rhine invasion routes, and win a strategic barrier in the Spanish Netherlands.

Even before the Bourbonisation of the Netherlands, the Dutch were aware that it was no use relying on the Spaniards to provide them with a shield to the south, and in 1697, by one of the provisions of the Peace of Rijswijk, they gained the right to station troops at Nieupoort, Oudenarde, Mons, Charleroi, Namur and Luxembourg. These garrisons were taken prisoner when the French swept over the Netherlands in 1701, but the Dutch ensured that the Grand Alliance of September the same year committed itself, albeit in vague terms, to the policy of establishing a 'Barrier' in the Netherlands. This institution was to become one of the most enduring and significant features of eighteenth-century international politics.

The Dutch thinking was probably most clearly revealed in 1706, through some words of the Grand Pensionary Heinsius:

We know that Spain will not be in a condition to render us secure by herself, and we have learnt by disastrous experience that the troops of that country, together with the Dutch troops we kept in the Netherlands before this war, did not guarantee us from the seizure of that country and our Barrier. The reason is obviously because we were not masters there either of the troops or of the fortresses in which they were stationed. It is clear, therefore, that the mere country cannot serve us as a Barrier, and that, for the security which is our right, it is not just that we should repose on others like the Spaniards. We should keep troops in the country for its defence, and place them where they are required for this purpose. (Geikie and Montgomery, 1930, 54)

The Dutch and their allies would have been very surprised to learn that the French commanders regarded the annexation of the Netherlands with something less than enthusiasm. Marshal Boufflers toured the Flemish towns in April 1701, and reported:

you will scarcely credit the state of decay of all these fortresses. It defies description. All the works are of earth, without storm-poles or palisades, and the exterior slopes have subsided and are easy to climb. But for their wet ditches, every single one of these places would be open to insult along its entire perimeter. (To Louis XIV, 27 April, Vault, 1835-62, I, 62)

From this state of affairs arose the paradox that the French actually fought at a severe disadvantage in the Netherlands until they were pressed back into the *pré carré* of the old French frontier. Thus in 1704 they were restrained from taking the offensive by the fear of leaving open the province of Brabant 'which', according to Marshal Villeroi, 'does not possess a single fortress which could withstand an enemy army for twelve hours without the support of a French army' (To Louis XIV, 13 April, *ibid.*, IV, 12). In the next year Marshall Villars explained that it was the same reprehensible weakness of the northern fortresses which prevented him from carrying out the time-honoured strategy of relying on the Netherlands frontier to hold off the enemy, while the field forces were switched to the Rhine (To Chamillart, 30 September, *ibid.*, V, 92).

The French began to strengthen the ragged frontier by means of continuous trench lines. The 'Lines of Clare', a first essay in this kind of fortification, had been constructed between the sea and the middle Scheldt in 1694. The idea was taken up on a much more ambitious scale in 1701, in the form of an entrenchment which extended eastwards from Cantelmo, near Sluis, as far as Antwerp, and thence under the names of the 'Lines of Brabant' to the Meuse at Huy. The whole was almost 130 miles long, and consisted of a curtain, furnished with bastions and redans, and preceded by a ditch twenty-four feet wide and twelve feet deep. Save for a few unavoidable overland stretches, the entire length was protected by the Flemish canals and the successive river lines of the Demer, the Gette and the Mehaigne.

The usefulness of lines was the subject of much debate. The immediate purpose was to protect friendly territory from the enemy cavalry who would otherwise penetrate between the fortresses and carry off fodder and contributions of cash. Coehoorn was a strong advocate of *razzias* of this kind, for as governor of Dutch Flanders he was entitled to one-tenth of all the contributions. Boufflers explained in 1701

The whole of the people of the countryside, as well as the local officials, look upon these lines as their salvation. All the generals, whether French or Spanish, believe that the lines are essential and that they can be held against attacks. They demand fewer troops than are needed for the defence of fortresses, canals or rivers. (To Louis XIV, 27 April, *ibid.*, I, 66)

Where the performance of the lines was questionable was in their capacity to resist a determined assault by a regular army, as Louis was careful to point out. Vauban, however, inclined to the side of Boufflers, and argued that a system of lines could serve very well as long as the defenders were vigilant and quick on their feet.

The later campaigns of the War of the Spanish Succession brought about an essential change in the object of the Netherlands lines. 'Old' France was threatened with invasion, and the lines, from being a mere shield against 'contributions', were converted into prepared fields of battle for entire armies. Now that the main French forces were directly engaged in the defence, the quantity of troops relative to the extent of the front became much greater than at the beginning of the war. It is not too extravagant to claim that the Lines of *Ne Plus Ultra* were a presage of the trench systems that were dug over the same territory in the Great War.

The struggle for the eastern river avenues. Coehoorn proposed to begin the war in a most un-Dutch style, by advancing to give battle in the heart of 'Belgium'. His masters, however, decided they must cling to historical precedent and turn the French from the fortresses along the lower Rhine and Meuse, just as they did in the last war.

As luck would have it, Coehoorn was absent in Flanders when, in mid-April 1702, the Dutch and their Brandenburger allies reached Kaiserswörth, on the Rhine, and set about the first siege of the war, The operation was bloody and mismanaged, and the assaulting troops were cut down on the glacis 'like grass before the mower's scythe' (Marquis de Blainville to Boufflers, *ibid.*, II, 688). When the garrison finally capitulated, on 15 June, it had defied the Allies for fifty-nine days. Altogether the army paid very dearly in labour and blood for 'a hole like that' (Vauban to Chamillart, *ibid.*, III, 571).

After Coehoorn rejoined the army the Allies made easier weather of their sieges. To please the Dutch, the new commander-in-chief, John Churchill, Earl of Marlborough, swung westwards to the Meuse and made the capture of Venlo the next objective, 'The situation of this place being between Roermond and Maastricht makes it very necessary that we have it' (Marlborough to Godolphin, 14 September, *Marlborough-Godolphin*, 1975, I, 111). Louis wrote urgently to Boufflers:

If you let the enemy get possession of Venlo, you must give up Gelders as lost, as with it the Rhine fortresses, the town of Liège and the alliance with the Elector of Cologne. . . . Without Gelders I am powerless. Only through the channel of Gelders and the Rhine fortresses can I carry my armies to the heart of Holland. (23 August, Vault, 1835–62, II, 92)

Marlborough was impatient with the slowness of the preliminaries, but Coehoorn took care to build up great stocks of every category of ammunition, for he had no wish to see the siege languish for lack of powder and shot, as had happened at Kaiserswörth. Once he was satisfied that everything was ready, he pushed ahead with spirit. A well-prepared storm gave the Allies the possession of Fort St Michael, on the western bank of the Meuse, which enabled Coehoorn to build trenches and batteries beside the river with the vast quantity of 40,000 fascines and 2,000 gabions which he had kept in readiness for the purpose. On 21 September the morale of the people and garrison of Venlo was cracked by a violent cannonade which the besiegers set up to celebrate the fall of Landau in Germany to another Allied army (see p. 45). Negotiations began almost at once, and the French and Spanish governors yielded Venlo on the 24th. This efficiently managed siege consituted one of the most important defensive victories of the Grand Alliance.

The Dutch were now content to consolidate their success, and for the next couple of years the Allies merely exploited a short distance up the Meuse (Roermond and Liège in October 1702, Huy in August 1703), and eastwards to the Rhine (Rijnberk in February 1703 and Bonn in May). On their side the French sat securely behind the Lines of Brabant.

In 1704 the attention of Europe was focused on the drama of the Blenheim campaign in the heart of Germany. The war in the Netherlands languished, and the only important news that came from that part of the world was that Coehoorn had died from natural causes on 17 March. On the Amsterdam stock exchange the prices immediately plummeted, for the Allies had lost a talisman of victory. 'The name of Coehoorn frightens all the ladies of Bonn', Marlborough had reported in 1703, 'which has given me an occasion of obliging them, for I have refused no one a pass to go to Cologne, amongst which are all the nuns of a monastery' (to Godolphin, 27 April, *Marlborough-Godolphin*, 1975, I, 169). However, the full extent of the loss was appreciated only in later years, when the Allies invaded France and were faced with the problem of attacking Vauban's double line of fortresses. As William Horneck observed, 'his death prolonged the war, and those towns which cost us almost a campaign, would have come much cheaper to us, had he been there to attack them' (Horneck, 1738, xv–xviii).

This judgment is reinforced by Prince Eugene's complaint in 1710 that the siege of Douai progressed so slowly

because of the mistaken ambition of the engineers, who try to invest themselves with the same authority that was enjoyed by the late General Coehoorn. I never met Coehoorn, but I know that there can be no comparison between his ability and that of the horrible little men we have with us now. (To Count Sinzendorff, 20 June, Kriegsarchiv, 1876–91, XII, Appx 140)

The French never seriously threatened to deprive the Allies of Coehoorn's last legacy, the conquest of the fortresses of the lower Meuse and Rhine. Marshal Villeroi certainly sallied forth from the Lines of Brabant and recaptured Huy, on 11 June 1705. Marlborough, however, returned to the Netherlands in force from Germany, and under his direction the Allies retook Huy in July, and went on to penetrate and raze the southern end of the Lines of Brabant near Leeuw. He had unmistakably settled the struggle for the eastern river approaches in favour of the Grand Alliance.

The Allied conquest of the Spanish Netherlands 1706–7. At the Battle of Ramillies, on 23 May 1706, the Duke of Marlborough broke the French field army upon which the decaying fortresses of the Spanish Netherlands entirely depended for their safety. Oudenarde, Malines, Brussels and Bruges opened their gates with hardly a show of a fight, and it was 'almost unprecedented for so many fortresses and their associated territories to have surrendered in such a short time' (Marlborough, 4 June, Murray, 1845, II, 560).

The sieges of the fortresses that still remained were more noisy than demanding. As for their objectives, the Allies settled on Ostend and Menin 'so as to open a path by which we may enter the southern Netherlands and Old France' (General Dopf, in Ten Raa *et al.*, 1911, etc., VIII, ii, 72). Ostend held out for just twelve days, after which Marlborough moved inland against Menin, the 'key to France', or rather the doorway to coastal Flanders. By 10 August the governor, de Bully, had to confess that he could do nothing to stay the progress of the siegeworks – 'the fire of their artillery is so frightful that you cannot discharge a cannon or a musket without being immediately crushed by a hundred cannon shot and as many bombs' (journal of the siege of Menin, Vault, 1835–62, VI, 543–4). The Allies were now using Vauban's system of parallels as a matter of course, and the place capitulated on the 22nd, as soon as the direct breaching batteries opened fire from the counterscarp.

For the rest of the year the French were granted an unexpected reprieve. The autumn rains fell with great violence, and the Allies abandoned all thoughts of invading Old France. Marlborough had to be content with trudging eastwards through the mud and laying siege to Ath. The fortress fell on 1 October, and Brussels was now reasonably secure from the attentions of French raiding parties.

Marshal Vendôme was meanwhile looking to the safety of his own territory. Because the Lines of

Brabant had been lost in the general catastrophe of May, he was forced to construct a new barrier – a gentle concave line of trenches which ran for more than one hundred miles from Ypres through Lille, Tournai, Mons and Charleroi to the eastern anchor on the Meuse at Namur. Vendôme gradually built up the numbers and confidence of his army behind the shelter of this new military frontier, and in 1707 he was able to put 100,000 men into the field. The Allies were inferior by about 20,000, and, because Vendôme refused to be lured from his lair, Marlborough achieved still less than in the barren campaign two years earlier in 1705, when Villeroi was lurking behind the Lines of Brabant.

The advance into the Vauban pré-carré *1708–July 1712.* In 1708, after having kept up an advantageous defensive for nearly two years, the French were ill-advised enough to sally from their lines and try their luck in the open field. On 11 July they were repaid by a sharp defeat just outside the little fortress of Oudenarde, which guarded the Allies' one remaining passage over the Scheldt.

Marlborough would have liked to have followed up the success by launching an all-out invasion of France, but the Imperial commander, Prince Eugene, wanted to go about things systematically and reduce the city of Lille. Nobody stopped to consider that this place was the first and probably the strongest of the fortresses which Vauban had built to defend the French border proper. Moreover, Lille was held by 15,000 men commanded by the dwarfish Marshal Boufflers, who was a paragon of the military virtues. At his side stood the engineer du Puy Vauban, who was clutching the memorandum on defence which had been written by his late uncle Sébastien Le Prestre.

Into French Flanders the Allies brought 95,000 men – a characteristically motley mass of English, Dutch, Austrians, Prussians, Hessians and Palatines, of whom 55,000 were detached under Marlborough to hold Vendôme at a respectful distance.

The siege army proper stood under the orders of Prince Eugene, who relied for technical advice on the incompetent Huguenot engineers du Muy and Le Vasseur des Rocques. An unco-ordinated trench and artillery attack was opened against Bastions II and III on the northern sector of the city enceinte, which left the capture of the works to the infantry, who had to assault across open ground. The Dutchman Landsberg sourly commented that the engineers were reckless with other peoples' lives, 'but I have always noticed that the officers who propose such assaults are careful never to take part in them in person' (Ten Raa *et al.*, 1911, etc., VIII, ii, 391). On the evening of 7 September it took nearly 3,000 dead and wounded for the Allies to establish just four isolated lodgments on the covered way, and when the sun rose on the next morning the French saw that the grass of the glacis was entirely covered with bodies.

The Allies were saved by a change in the character of the siege. Even Huguenot engineers were capable of learning from their mistakes, and, according to the Saxon general Schulenburg:

six weeks after the opening of trenches the engineers appreciated that they had opened the attack on too broad a front, and tried to breach the fortifications at too many points, namely twelve. It would have been better to confine the breaching fire to the two main bastions and the intervening curtain. (Kriegsarchiv, 1876–91, X, 456)

By mining, sapping, concentrated artillery fire and well-planned assaults, the Allies finally managed to conquer the ravelin between Bastions II and III as well as the covered way on either side. At last, at ten in the morning of 21 October, they opened fire against the main enceinte with fifty-six cannon, sixteen howitzers and nineteen mortars. This caused the French to beat *chamade* on the next day, and on the 23rd the 4,500 survivors agreed to relinquish the town and retire to the citadel. Thus far the siege had cost the Allies almost 12,000 casualties.

The engineers now proceeded to attack the citadel from the town side with an almost extravagant regard for the formalities of siegework. They proceeded by sap from the very first, and by these cautious methods they were able to reach the covered way with few casualties, and plant their breaching batteries on the counterscarp. On 9 December the gallant Boufflers capitulated for an evacuation with the honours of war. The Allied butcher's bill for the capture of this very powerful

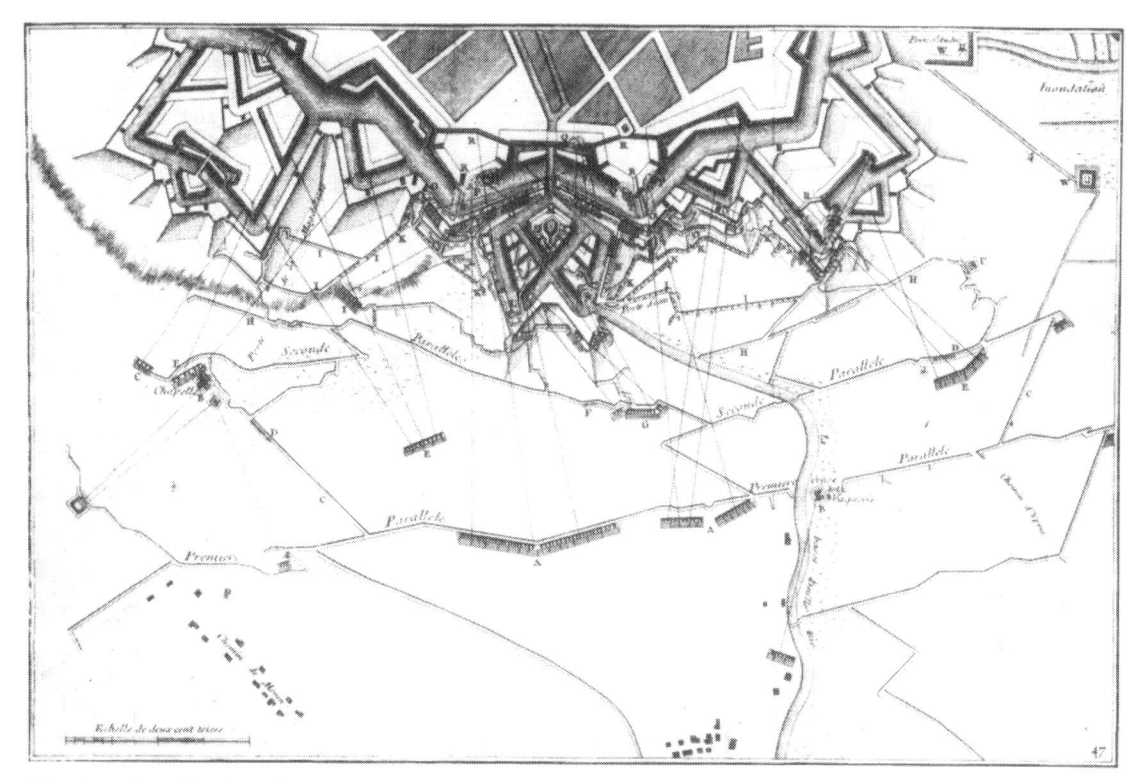

25 Attack on Bastions II and III of Lille town 1708

citadel was 1,252 dead and wounded, which was clear evidence that Vauban-style trench attacks were economical.

In strategic terms all that the Allies had done by taking Lille was to effect a single breach in the first of the two lines of Vauban fortresses which guarded the northern frontier of Old France. The French were now fighting on their own ground, and the depth, the number and the strength of the fortresses prohibited any direct Allied advance on Paris. The two years following the capture of Lille were therefore spent by the Allies in sliding up and down the frontier, seeking to broaden the first penetration they had made at Lille. The determining factor in the selection of a stronghold for attack was often the winning of water communications, for it was much easier to convey siege ordnance and supplies by barge, than to haul the whole mass overland. Marlborough had written earlier in 1708:

This country lies all open to us, but for want of cannon we are not able to do anything considerable.... That which hinders us from acting with vigour is, that as long as the French are masters of Ghent, we can't make use of neither the Scheldt nor the Lys... which are the only two rivers that can be of use to us in this country. We have ordered twenty battering pieces to be brought from Maastricht, and we have taken measures for sixty more to be brought from Holland. The calculation of the number of draught horses to draw this artillery amounts to 16,000 horses, by which you will see the difficulties we meet with, but we hope to overcome them. (Marlborough to Godolphin, 19 and 23 July, *Marlborough-Godolphin*, 1975, II, 1030, 1033–4)

The reduction of the individual fortresses showed every sign of being a costly business. The Austrian official history praises Eugene's conduct at Lille in the following terms:

The endurance and tenacity he displayed in this operation are all the more... worthy of the admiration of posterity, when we bear in mind that the whole inclination of his talent was towards dealing rapid and heavy blows. Fortress warfare was foreign to his nature. (Kriegsarchiv, 1876–91, X, 495)

The last sentence was intended as a compliment, but it gives a clue to a significant change in the aspect of siege warfare since the days of Condé, Turenne and Montecuccoli, when a versatile captain was quite capable of taking over the direction of sieges in an authoritative way. Since then, however, the perfection of such mysterious-sounding devices as parallels, trench cavaliers and ricochets had elevated siegework into something of a black art, which became less and less accessible to busy field commanders. France owned a whole generation of engineers who had been bred up by Vauban to put the new techniques at the service of Louis's marshals. The Allies, on the other hand, had to rely on a dwindling, overworked and demoralised band of cosmopolitan experts. Marlborough and Eugene had precious little confidence in their ageing Huguenot engineers, but they could not trust themselves to take over in their place. It was as if a patient had handed himself over to the mercies of some

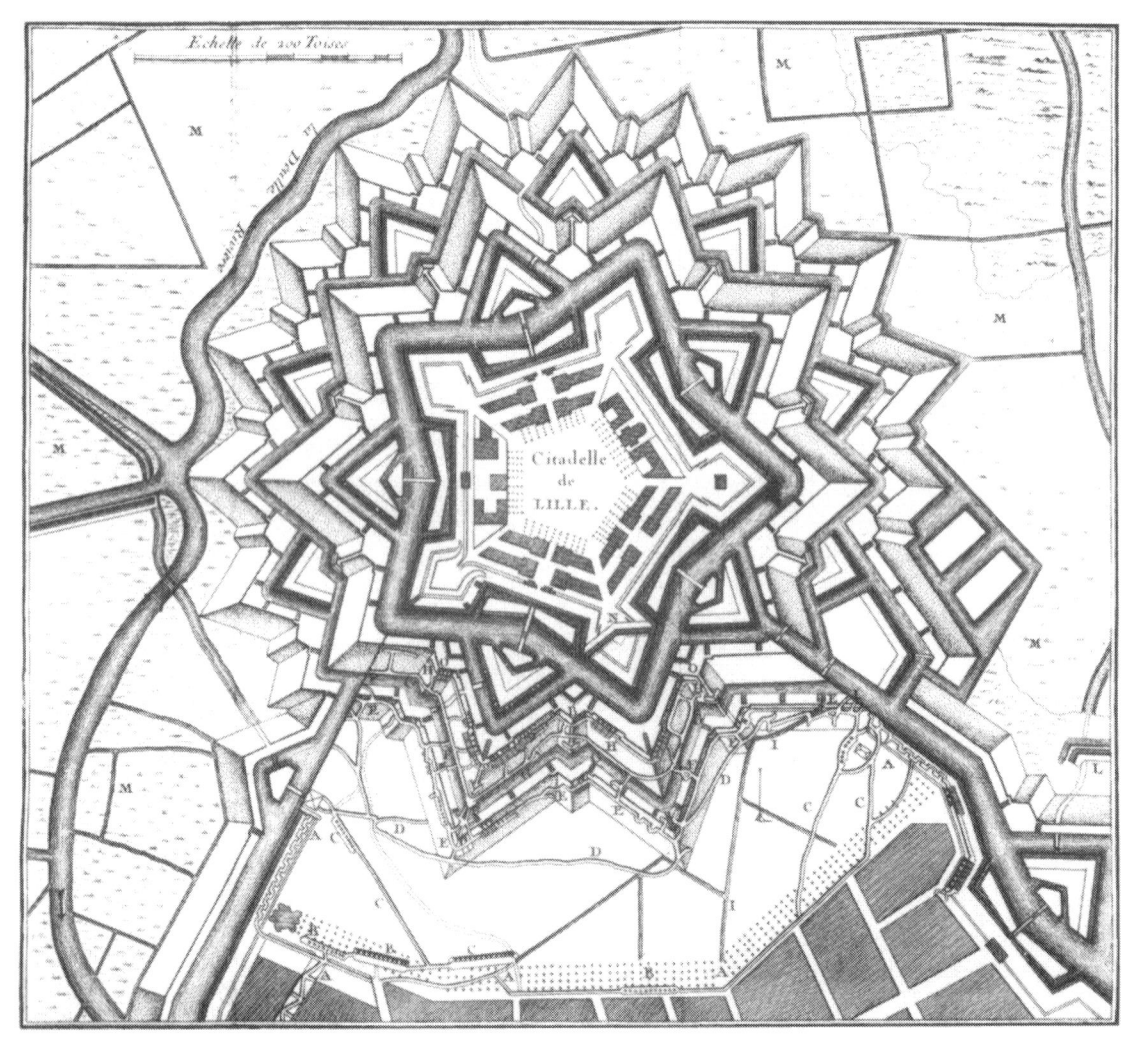

26 Attack on Lille Citadel 1708

shabby surgeon, and was forced to look on while the old man scanned through the yellowing pages of his textbooks, and fumbled indecisively with his rusty instruments.

The western sector of the Vendôme lines was rendered untenable by the fall of Lille, but Marshal Villars, the energetic new French commander, more than made up for the loss by taking up a 'switch line' about fifteen miles further to the rear. Lille was sealed off by a semi-circle of entrenchments which looped from the marshy ground near La Bassée along the Lens canal to the fortress of Douai and the line of the Scarpe. From the Scarpe the lines described a curve to the south by way of Condé and Valenciennes, before they resumed the original easterly direction to the Sambre and the Meuse. The advent of these 'Lines of Cambrin', guarded as they were by a vigilant field army, forced the Allies to renounce any thought of prosecuting an advance south from Lille in 1709. They resolved instead to march to the east and attack the front-line fortresses which had been stranded outside the Lines. Tournai was the first on their list, for it was the nearest place to Lille, and it held a commanding position on the water avenue of the Scheldt which was comparable with that of Menin on the Lys. The decision was a disappointment to Marlborough's political ally in London, the Lord Treasurer Godolphin, who had just written:

I know, as well as certainly as I can know anything, that nothing can please the enemy better than to see your army engaged in a siege. Nor do I see that the taking of any one place, gives you more liberty and opportunity of pressing France itself than you have now. (6 June, *Marlborough-Godolphin*, 1975, III, 1277)

The main technical problem at Tournai turned out to be the strength of the modern pentagonal citadel, with its double ramparts and its peculiarly elaborate system of permanent masonry-revetted countermines. The whole complex had been built by the former governor, Mesgrigny, to the designs of Vauban's colleague Deshoulières. The French had fifty miners to direct their underground defence, and before the end of this obstinately contested siege they had forced the Allied miners to dig in thirty places. The lack of provisions compelled Governor Surville to capitulate on 3 September. By then the Allies had suffered 3,100 casualties in the siege of the town, and between 1,800 and 1,900 more in the attack on the citadel.

Mons fell in October, at the cost of one month in time and about 1,450 casualties. This comparative economy was, however, more than offset by the 20,000 dead and wounded that were the price of evicting the French field army from its position at Malplaquet on 11 September. By one means or another, the Allies paid very heavily for effecting what was still only a shallow erosion of the French frontier.

King Louis was now a convinced partisan of frontier defence by means of lines, and on 20 April 1710 he wrote to Marshal Montesquiou d'Artagnan: 'The Lines of Cambrin are strong enough to permit fifty-eight battalions and seventy squadrons to halt an entire army. I give your decision to defend the Lines my enthusiastic approval' (Vault, 1835–62, X, 18). However, before the marshal received the letter Marlborough and Eugene had entered the field unexpectedly early and pierced the Lines at two points. After this brisk start, the Allies nevertheless gave themselves up to the weary old process of shuffling along the frontier, and away from the direct line of advance on Paris. The French field army was as watchful as ever, and the Allies could devise no better response than a succession of sieges which were intended to widen the Lille-Tournai breach in a westerly direction.

To reduce the vast works of Douai the Allies expended 8,000 men and fifty-two days. The conquest of Béthune, Saint-Venant and Aire added a further 10,800 men to the Allied losses for 1710, mainly because the commanders laboured 'under a great misfortune of being obliged to carry on the war ... by sieges almost without engineers' (Marlborough to Stanhope, 18 August, Murray, 1845, V, 105).

In 1711 the Allies gathered their forces and resolution for their first direct push southwards in the direction of the valley of the Oise, the ancient path of invasion from the Netherlands to the Ile de France. The campaigns of the last two years had taken the form of an exploitation in breadth, rather

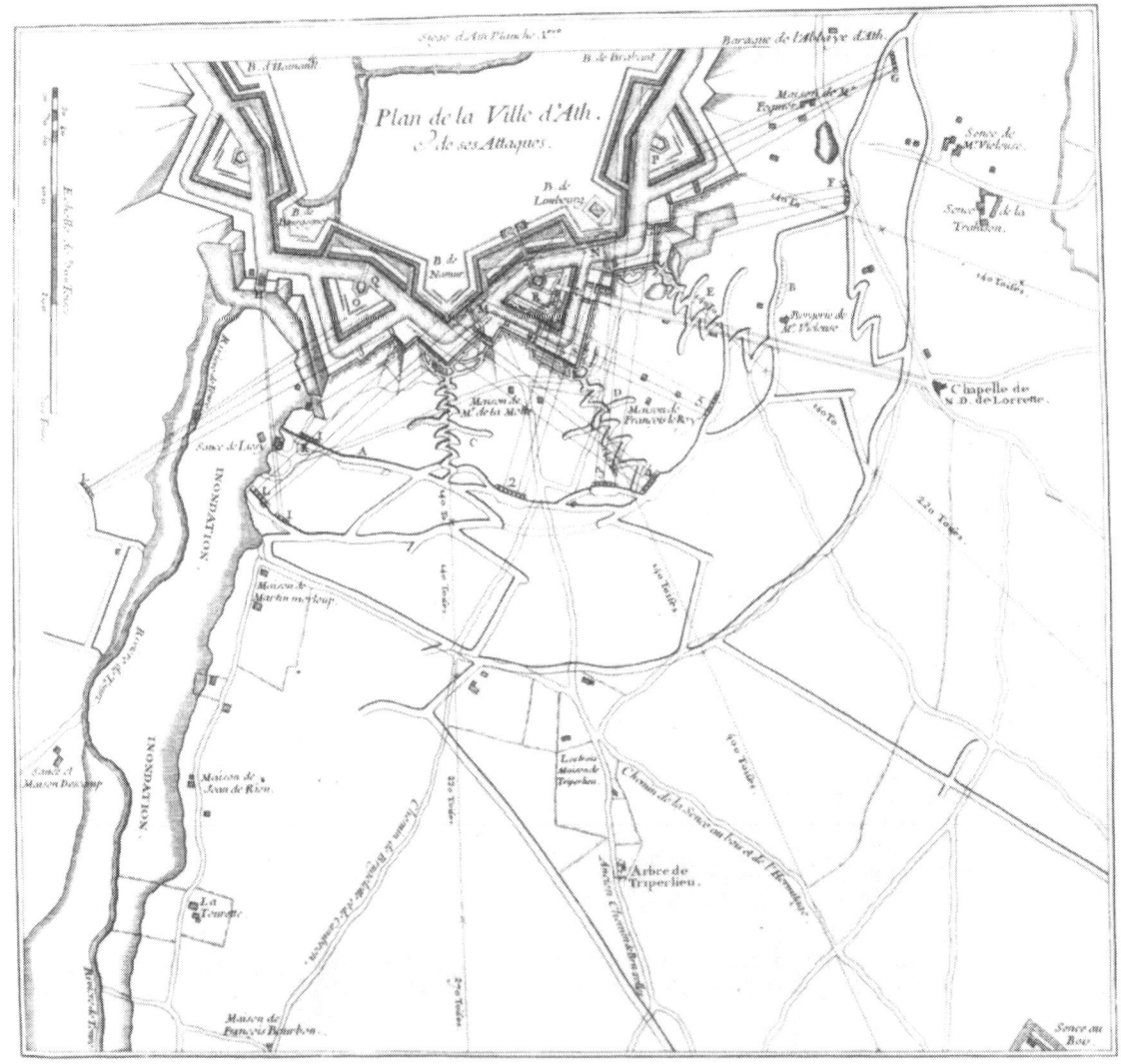

27 Siege of Ath 1697. Showing the arrangement of the ricochet batteries (Goulon, 1730). The ideal of sieges throughout the eighteenth century

than depth, and up to now the French had been left in undisputed possession of the second-line fortresses of Arras, Cambrai, Bouchain, Denain, Valenciennes, Le Quesnoy and Maubeuge.

In immediate support of these strongpoints Villars was casting up the last, and at about 160 miles the longest of all his fortified postitions – these were the famous Lines of *Ne Plus Ultra* (No Further!), which began on the Channel coast at Etaples, followed stretches of the Canche, the Scarpe, the Sensée and the Scheldt to the Sambre near Maubeuge, then clung to the south bank of that river as far as the Meuse at Namur.

Despite every effort Marlborough could not collect enough troops to justify the risk of a field action – or so at least his supporters claim. The campaign passed in waiting and manoeuvring until early August, when Marlborough took the initiative by bursting over the Lines near Arleux, then clapping a siege on Bouchain. The attack on Bouchain was the last of Marlborough's sieges, and ironically enough it was one of the best conducted. The casualties were fairly light, at 3,600, but the siege lasted five weeks, and the end of the campaigning season was so near that the Allies could not undertake another such operation. In these last years, time was as precious a commodity for the Allies as human blood, for opinion in Britain was rebelling against the war, and the Tory party was working to extricate the army from the struggle.

The French continued to work on the Lines of *Ne Plus Ultra* in the same spirit as those housemartins that wall up intruding birds with mud. In 1712 Villars concentrated his army behind the marshy Sensée in the centre of his lines – Arras served as a firm *point d'appui* for his left, while the right flank was anchored on the Scheldt and the fortress-depôt of Cambrai. For once, however, the Allies had a clear superiority in force (122,000 as against 100,000), and Prince Eugene boldly executed a march around the Cambrai flank of Villars' position and assailed the last fortresses which stood between the Allies and the Oise. Marlborough had been recalled to England, but Eugene must have blessed the name of his former colleague for having heaped up great quantities of artillery, ammunition and provisions for the coming campaign in depôts along the Scheldt and the Scarpe.

The London Ministry dealt a serious, if not fatal blow at the enterprise by placing the new English commander, the Duke of Ormonde, under 'restraining orders' which permitted his 12,000 troops to act as a corps of observation, but not to take part in a siege or battle. Eugene was not deterred from invest-

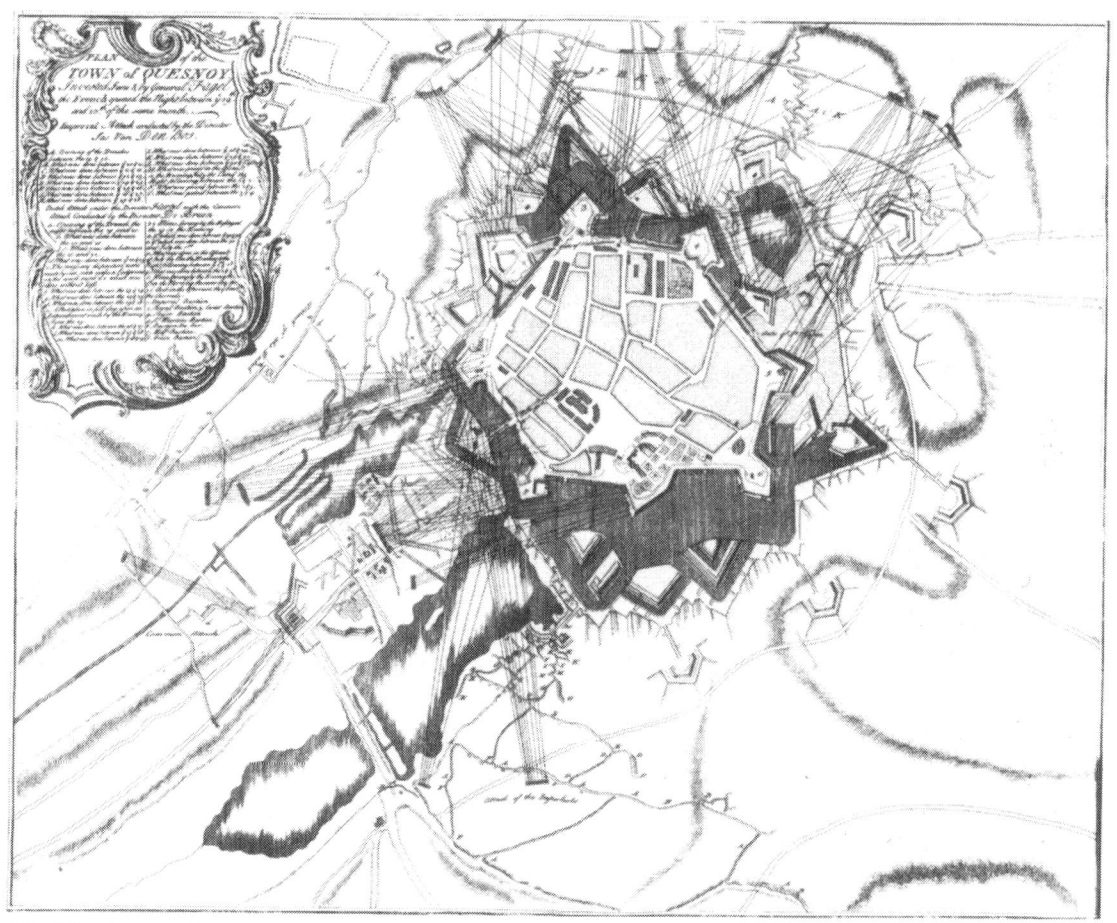

28 The sieges of Le Quesnoy 1712. The Allied siegeworks of June and July are worming up from the left; characteristically, they have divided their attacks into three isolated corridors. The French siege attack of September–October is approaching on a wide front from the top right-hand corner

ing Le Quesnoy on 8 June 1712, for he still had his Gothic hordes of troops from Holland, Austria, Hanover, the Palatinate, Wolfenbüttel, Saxony, Hesse, Holstein and Münster. The ensuing operation bore unmistakable signs of the bad old sieges of earlier years. The governor, however, unaccountably lost his nerve, and at midnight on 4–5 July he surrendered his garrison as prisoners of war.

Villars's counter-offensive July–October 1712. Perhaps a check at Le Quesnoy would have deterred Eugene from advancing what Clausewitz would have termed the 'culminating point' of the decades of Allied campaigning in the Netherlands. As it was, the fall of this place led the Allies naturally on to attack Landrecies, a small fortress just fifteen miles short of the Oise. This one further push exposed Eugene to a French counter-offensive which turned the balance of the war decisively against the Alliance. The march on Landrecies had left thirty miles of communication dangerously open to a thrust from Villars's redoubt behind Cambrai. At the king's call the French army therefore emerged from the Lines, and on 24 July it routed the 8,000 troops guarding Denain, which was a key point on Eugene's communications.

Villars exploited his victory by reducing the fortified depôts along the Scarpe. The most important of them, Marchiennes, fell on 30 July, and the Allies abandoned the siege of Landrecies three days later. De la Colonie writes that:

all of these magazines were of the greatest use in the sieges undertaken by us later on. One hundred and twenty-five beautiful pieces of cannon, quite new, were found therein, over and above the munitions of war and food. (Colonie, 1904, 366–7)

In earlier times Eugene would have welcomed the opportunity to bring the French to a decisive battle, but now Ormonde's 12,000 British were withdrawn from the war altogether.

Villars at once began to reclaim the lost ground by prosecuting a series of exceptionally energetic sieges. He drove his engineers hard, and (in retaliation for the happening at Le Quesnoy) he usually demanded that the enemy must surrender 'at discretion', that is as prisoners of war at the mercy of the besiegers. His advance guard was kept in constant movement, sweeping down to invest the next fortress before the main army was quit of the last. By these means Douai, Le Quesnoy and Bouchain were brought down in the third week of October.

Through his offensive Villars restored the integrity of the French frontier, and helped the king's plenipotentiaries at the peace congress at Utrecht to gain terms in 1713 that were more generous than would have seemed possible a year or two before. Out of the fortresses still in French possession, Louis had to demolish Dunkirk, and yield up Ypres, Furnes, Tournai, Charleroi, Namur and Luxembourg. In return he received back Aire, Béthune, Saint-Venant and the great fortress-city of Lille. A sizeable dent had been made in Vauban's *pré carré*, but along the central sector of the Netherlands frontier the French retained a double line of fortresses – the base from which Louis XV was to conquer the Austrian Netherlands in the 1740s, and the bulwark against which monarchical Europe was to break fifty years later.

Nothing, however, could equal the service which had already been performed by Vauban's *frontière de fer*, which was remembered as one of the most considerable rendered by a defensive system in modern history. It cost the Allies 47,000 troops in the direct attack on the fortresses alone, and it saved Louis XIV from the just consequences of years of ambition and miscalculation.

The war in Germany
The struggle for Bavaria 1702–4. The Marquis de Chamlay summed up the prospects for campaigning in Germany as they seemed to stand for the French at the outset of the new war:

We must begin by saying that the system of waging war in Germany has completely changed. In earlier times the king used to have several fortresses along the Rhine [Philippsburg, Fort of Kehl, Breisach], not to mention a considerable stronghold well advanced on the far side [Freiburg] which enabled his armies to cross to the other bank and subsist in German territory. Since the Peace of Rijswijk the state of affairs is different, for the same fortresses are now in the hands of the Emperor and the Germans, which bars the passage of the Rhine to

French armies, and compels us to retain our forces in Alsace so as to cover that province.
(Memorandum of February 1702, Vault, 1835–62, III, 756)

It was some consolation that Elector Max Emanuel of Bavaria decided to defy the rest of the Empire and throw in his lot with the French. In order to exploit this exciting opportunity which opened in the heart of Germany, the French had to ward off the Allied offensives over the middle Rhine, while breaking through the Black Forest to join their new Bavarian friends.

As the French had feared, the war on the middle Rhine opened with an attack by the combined forces of the empire on Landau, the guardian-fortress of Lorraine and Lower Alsace. The Margrave Ludwig of Baden-Durlach duly surrounded the place with no less than 36,000 men in the midsummer of 1702. However, Vauban's new fortifications were exceptionally strong, and the tough and ingenious governor, Lieutenant-General Mélac, built two earthen lunettes at the foot of the glacis, which compelled the Germans to dig no less than five parallels, and helped to spin out the siege to the inordinate length of 140 days of investment and eighty-five of siege attacks. By the time Mélac capitulated, on 10 September, the Army of the Empire was incapable of further effort.

Mélac's lunettes, or flèches, were an improved version of similar works which Vauban had constructed around Namur in the 1690s. The lunettes constituted an economical application of the principle of defence in depth, and were imitated later in the war at the defences of Turin in 1706, Le Quesnoy and Bouchain in 1712, and Freiburg in 1713. Taken together with the system of 'lines' in the Netherlands, they indicate that the belligerents were turning more and more to improvised expedients to supplement the effort of their fortresses.

The loss of Landau by no means deterred the French and Bavarians from working to effect their union in southern Germany. By bluff, impudence, and where absolutely necessary, clapping on a little siege, Max Emanuel eliminated a scattering of hostile garrisons (the independent cities of Ulm, Regensburg, Memmingen, and the isolated Palatine fortress of Neuburg on the Danube), and in the summer of 1703 he felt inspired to stage a brief but spectacular invasion of the Tyrol. De la Colonie and other French engineers came to help him with technical advice, for Max Emanuel

had not felt the want of engineers in the previous war when allied with the Emperor, for both the Dutch and the king of England had a sufficient number present with them. Besides, his ministers were so ignorant of the science of engineering that they did not foresee the necessity of making provision on this point. (Colonie, 1904, 366–7)

On their side the French won a wide base on the upper Rhine for future operations in Germany. Villars began the process in February 1703, when he crossed the Rhine near Strasbourg and laid siege to the Fort of Kehl. He pushed the works ahead with all the enthusiasm he was to display in the Netherlands sieges, and disregarded a memorandum which Vauban sent him on the subject, outlining a formal siege of thirty-nine days. On 9 March Villars was rewarded by the sight of the enemy coming out to parley.

Side-stepping Ludwig of Baden's celebrated 'Lines of Stollhofen', Villars marched south-east from Kehl with a little army to join the Elector of Bavaria. The united force beat the Imperialists under Styrum at Höchstädt on 20 September, and further reinforcements brought the Franco-Bavarian army to a strength of 23,000 men, and enabled it to besiege and capture the independent city of Augsburg. The French army could now spend the winter in security and relative comfort in the Danube valley.

Meanwhile the rearward forces were usefully expanding their hold along the Rhine. On the southern flank Vauban in person brought down Breisach in September, and in the following month his gouty confidant Lapara reduced Freiburg, the sentinel of the southern route over the Black Forest. To the north another of Vauban's engineers, Pierre Filley, managed to win back Landau after thirty days of siege attack, which was little more than one-third of the time the Army of the Empire had taken over the same operation in 1702.

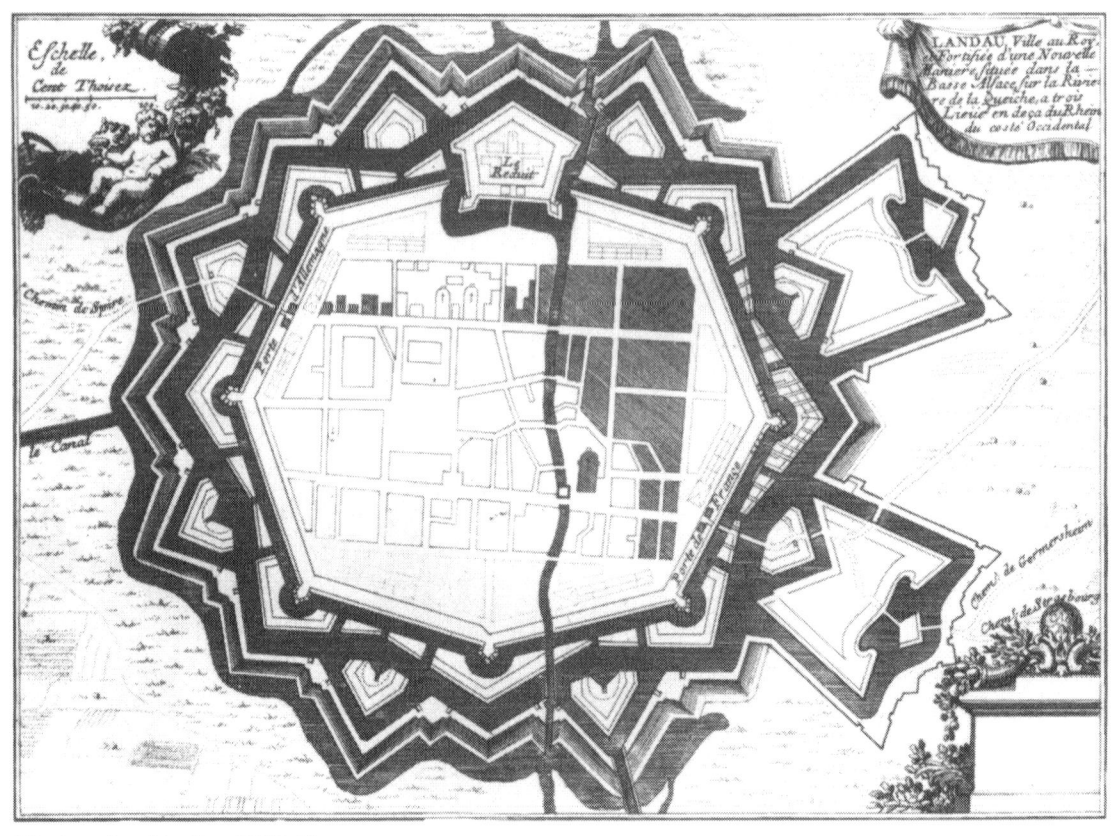

29 Landau (De Fer, 1690–5)

Thanks to Vauban and his comrades, France had never been so favourably placed for carrying on war in Germany than at the outset of 1704. The alliance with Bavaria and the reduction of the free cities gave the French a base in the heart of the Empire, while the conquests along the Rhine won a secure communication over the Black Forest by way of the Kinzig and Freiburg routes.

Such was the situation which led Marlborough to prosecute his famous march from the Netherlands to the Danube with an army of British and Allied troops in 1704. Marlborough irrupted into Bavaria in fine style, but found that the Bavarian troops slipped out of his reach into their fortresses, following the very sound custom of their ancestors in their old wars against the Swedes and French. This proved highly embarrassing for Marlborough, who had left his siege artillery behind in the Netherlands for the sake of speed on the march, and he was left with no alternative but to devastate the open country of Bavaria, like his former master Turenne in 1647.

The Bavarians finally left their refuges when a fresh batch of French reinforcements arrived in the theatre of war under the command of Marshall Tallard. The combined force thereupon marched to a catastrophic defeat at Blenheim (13 August), which undid most of the good work of the last couple of years. Marlborough saw that his task was accomplished, and he returned to the Rhine to see how best to exploit his success by making some progress in that part of the world. A detachment of empire troops was left behind to besiege Ulm, which capitulated on 10 September, and two months later the Electress of Bavaria agreed to surrender all the fortresses which still held out in her husband's name.

Landau now exercised its old lure. It was isolated from the other French fortresses, and lay within easy reach of the great Imperial depôt at Philippsburg. The Allies also bore in mind that once they were masters of the place, they would have a good *point d'appui* for an advance into Alsace, or against the Saar and the Moselle. Landau was accordingly laid under siege. The garrison put up an exemplary defence, and finally capitulated on 25 November, having inflicted 9,322 casualties on the Allies, and detained them for an inordinate seventy-two days of siege. Marlborough had already written in October: 'If it shall please God that we take this place, I shall be careful never more willingly to engage with the Germans for the taking of a town that is of any strength' (To Duchess Sarah, 20 October, *Marlborough-Godolphin*, 1975, I, 384).

The stalemate on the Rhine 1705–12. The last impetus deriving from the victory of Blenheim was dissipated in 1705, when Marlborough spent weeks on the Moselle, checked by Villars's blocking position on the right bank at Sierck.

Thereafter the war in Germany reverted to its time-honoured pattern of marching and raiding on either side of the Rhine. Neither party had the numbers of the ambition to upset the rough equilibrium. The forces of the empire held Germany east of the Rhine, together with Landau and a large bulge of territory on the west bank as far south as Lauterbourg. The French, for their part, were content to hold the Line of the Lauter, as protection for Alsace, and to maintain their bridgeheads on the German bank of the Rhine at Kehl, Breisach, Neuingen and Huningue.

The French counter-attack of 1713. The general return of French aggressiveness towards the end of the war was manifested in Germany by a siege of the much-battered fortress of Landau. By this time most of the sovereigns of the Empire were showing little more than a pretence of taking part in the war, and Landau was put in a passable state of defence only through the efforts of the energetic Prince Carl Alexander of Württemberg. He completed Mélac's ring of lunettes, and planted a new work of his own, which compelled the infuriated Marshal Villars to open his attack more than two miles from the main rampart. Prince Carl contrived to hold out fifty-six days, until 20 August, which was long by German standards, and represented one of the earliest and most striking examples of the kind of resistance which could be put up by works disposed in depth.

As a final, spectacular blow against the Emperor, the French determined to cross the Rhine and capture the town and double rock castle of Freiburg. Villars passed the river at Fort Louis, Kehl and Breisach, and opened his trenches towards the end of September 1713. He conducted the operation in his characteristically brutal style. On 14 October he lost 2,000 men in taking the covered way of the town in an assault which was described in Paris as being 'the most obstinately-fought of its kind in the entire war' (Austrian agent, Kreigsarchiv 1876–91, XV, 292). Two weeks later, when a storm on the town was imminent, the governor withdrew his men to the castle rock. There was no prospect of relief, and on the night of 16–17 November the Austrians capitulated in return for a free evacuation.

Villars had achieved the *succès d'estime* that his royal master desired. In any other circumstances he might have found it difficult to justify such an un-French and costly method of reducing the stronghold.

The war in Italy
Piedmontese military engineering. King Louis began the new war as an ally of Piedmont and the virtual owner of Spanish Lombardy. The Austrians, his enemies, seemed likely to be shut out of Italy for ever more. This impression was confirmed by the first campaigns in the theatre.

In the summer of 1701 Prince Eugene led an Austrian army south 'over steep and barren mountain passes into a country where no towns or fortresses were holding out in the Emperor's name' (Saint-Hilaire, 1903–4, III, 90). His one chance to win a foothold in Italy was to take the lake-fortress of Mantua, the capital of the duchy of the same name. Mantua was sited a full fifty miles from the débouché of the Brenner pass (in other words about a week's march from the safety of the Tyrol), but in compensation it stood far enough into the plain to permit the garrison to influence events in Lombardy. Unfortunately the French had already grasped the value of the place. As General Tessé wrote to Louis, after expounding the possible avenues of Austrian advance into Italy: 'Your Majesty sees, from the position of Mantua, that it is vital to gain this place at any cost, if the Emperor continues with his design of carrying the war into Italy' (17 February 1701, Vault, 1835–62, I, 217).

The French got to Mantua first, and they held out there in 1701 and 1702 in the face of Austrian blockades. In 1703 Marshal Vendôme was emboldened to invade the South Tyrol, with a view to linking up with the Bavarians, but he had still failed to take Trent before a dangerous development in Italy recalled him to the lowlands.

Alarmed at the growing power and arrogance of the French and Spanish, Duke Victor Amadeus II of Savoy and Piedmont drew back from his alliance with the Bourbons and went over to the Emperor. The aspect of the war in Italy altered at once, for by their change of sides the Piedmontese had interposed a block of hostile territory between France and the Bourbon armies in Italy. A Piedmontese memorandum explained that, unlike the situation in the last war, the French no longer owned

any fortresses in Piedmont which furnish them with a free entry for their armies or provide magazines for their subsistence. The strongholds in Nice and Montmélian have been so well fortified and equipped through the foresight of His Royal Highness that they are capable of offering a long resistance, and retaining a Piedmontese foothold beyond the Alps even in the event of the loss of Savoy. (Enclosed by Victor Amadeus to the Marquis de Borgo, 3 March 1704, R. Deputazione, 1907–10, II, 347)

Once the French were thrown on to the defensive, the conformation of the Alps would force them to array their troops on the wide arc of the circle from Lake Geneva to the Riviera, whereas the Piedmontese could hold a central position in the midst of the semi-circle of heights. This is what the Irish-French general Dillon had in mind when he wrote that:

there is one important thing to remember about this frontier – namely that it is much easier for an army to penetrate from Piedmont into France than from France into Piedmont. ('Mémoire . . . sur la Guerre dans les Alpes', Vault, 1835–62, XI, 563)

The most urgent problem was to do something to support the stranded French armies in Lombardy. There was just one good route at hand, if the French steeled themselves for a direct attack over the mountains against the Piedmontese obstruction. This lay by the Mont-Genèvre Pass on the northern flank of the Cottian Alps, which had been the chosen path for the invasions of Italy by Charles VIII, Francis I and Richelieu. The new fortress-depôt of Briançon was stationed conveniently close to the entrance to the pass to the west, and once the French were over the Col they were faced with little more than fifty miles of straight road between there and Turin. The box-like fort of Exilles was already in their power, and they knew that they would have to reckon on determined opposition only at Susa. The branch of the Mont-Gènevre route which ran south of the Colle dell'Assiette ridge by way of Fenestrelle had lost much of its importance to the French since they had demolished Pinerolo, at the entrance to the plain.

The next three campaigns in Italy represented a war of attrition in its purest form. Probably no other power in contemporary Europe relied quite so heavily as Piedmont upon fortresses for national defence. The Italian Official History comments:

The quantity of fortified towns and positions, which was one of the characteristics of Piedmont, offered the state its best guarantee of integrity, given the slow and methodical strategy of the time. These strongholds guaranteed the means of prolonging resistance, even after a rout in the open field, until the arrival of the help which Piedmontese diplomats had summoned up from one or other of the neighbouring powers. From this state of affairs proceeded the policy – which would nowadays seem incomprehensible – of preserving every single fortress from demolition, and of keeping the strongholds in a condition to offer at least a short resistance. (R. Deputazione, 1907–10, X, 327)

Recognising that his 20,000 regulars and his six new militia regiments were incapable of withstanding the French in the open field, Duke (Later king) Victor Amadeus committed almost his entire forces to defending strongholds. He trusted that he could hold out long enough to enable Prince Eugene and the Austrians to fight their way through Lombardy to his help. The prince's genius in field warfare was therefore to be matched against the skill of the French engineers in a race which had the survival of Piedmont as its stake.

Victor Amadeus had some reason to be so confident in passive defence. His predecessor Charles Emmanuel II (1638–75) had shown a marked interest in fortification, though not always with happy results. His chief memorial in this branch of architecture was the curious fortress of Vercelli, where Ancanio Vitozzi had tried to combine Italian and Netherlandish styles, and allowed himself too little space in his Italianate ditch for his Dutch fausse-braye. The work therefore possessed a walk-way no more than nine or ten inches wide, from which wounded soldiers rolled off screaming to their deaths – a neat but doubtless unintentional solution to the problem of tending casualties. Charles Emmanuel's most useful legacy was, paradoxically enough, his reconstruction of the town buildings of Turin in baroque style by the architects Castellamonte, Lanfranchi and Guarini. His *Azienda General delle Fabbriche e delle Fortificazioni* was responsible for fortifications and artillery, as well as public buildings of all kinds, and he therefore bequeathed to Victor Amadeus a flourishing and versatile generation of technicians who, in sterner times, could devote their talents to the problems of state defence.

In 1677, two years after Victor Amadeus's succession, the loyal Jesuit C. F. Milliet Dechales reminded the young duke that his family had always excelled in fortress warfare. At the moment Piedmont was not at war,

but it is precisely in peacetime that you should consider the defence of your territories, following the example of His Royal Highness, your late, august father, who carefully fortified all his main strongholds in a time of undisturbed calm, exploiting all the advantages of nature and the resources of the engineering art. (Milliet Dechales, 1677, dedication)

Victor Amadeus was caught rather badly off his guard when the French attacked in 1690, but otherwise he heeded Dechales's advice. He became an expert on fortress warfare on his own acount, and sent out a constant stream of instructions on how the works were to be built and defended.

In 1699, which was otherwise in a period of retrenchment and economy, Victor Amadeus spent a great deal of money on strengthening his fortresses. During the War of the Spanish Succession the expenditure rose more steeply still, and the monies were chiefly devoted to planting palisades and storm-poles, and building the fascine-revetted earthworks that were a Piedmontese speciality. In 1704 237,265 lire were spent on Vercelli alone, which is some indication of the cost of the far more ambitious works which were being undertaken at Turin.

The struggle for the approaches to Turin. From the outset of hostilities with Piedmont, Marshal Vendôme had impressed on Louis that there was 'no worthwhile objective in Piedmont except the siege of Turin' (12 October 1703, Vault, 1835–62, III, 288). The king, however, was sure that it was best to approach the capital in a roundabout way, by first undertaking a few, apparently easy sieges of the lesser fortresses.

A detached corps came from France under the command of the Duc de la Feuillade, and opened the Mont-Genèvre route by taking Susa on 12 June 1704. Marching from the side of Lombardy, Vendôme simultaneously began his operations against the fortresses around Turin. Against every expectation, the work of opening up these approaches lasted until July 1705. The sieges were expensive in every regard. Verrua, for instance, fell on 8 April 1705, and gave the French the facility of shipping their siege train from Lombardy a few extra miles up the Po, but for this one gain they had expended 166 days, fired away 200,000 cannon shot and 50,000 bombs, and lost no less than six generals, 547 senior officers and 12,000 men.

The engineers suffered particularly hard in the process. Twelve of their band were lost at Verrua alone, and the surviving officers were worn out by the endless succession of sieges. The chief engineer, Lozières d'Astier, groaned during the attack on Ivrea in 1704

The heat is terrible, and although we are in the mountains the air we are breathing seems to issue from a furnace . . . The commanders would lose many fewer engineers if they employed them as

30 Verrua. The barrier of the Po below Turin

engineers, and not like grenadiers. (To Le Peletier, 27 August and 2 September, *ibid.*, II, 556, 565)

The contemptuous feelings of the generals towards their engineers are best illustrated with regard to the events on the Mediterranean flank, where de la Feuillade captured the town of Nice in the spring of 1705. The duke wrote in condescending praise of his chief engineer,

I have every reason to be pleased with Filley. He is able and willing. He also has a certain amenability of character which leads him to be somewhat less dogmatic than are most engineers. (To Chamillart, *ibid.*, V, 122)

This concept of the good engineer, as a humble technician who was aware of his place, goes far to explain the disaster which overtook the French in Italy in the next year (see also p. 33).

The great siege of Turin 1706. The French devoted two great armies to the intended climax of the campaigns in Italy, the reduction of Turin in 1706. While Vendôme and 48,000 men held off Eugene and the Austrians, the Duc de la Feuillade was to undertake the siege proper with another 40,000. Some 110 heavy cannon and forty-nine mortars were assigned to the siege, and were assembled partly at Susa, which was the depot for the guns from Dauphiné, and partly at Chivasso, the park for the artillery that was being shipped up the Po.

For all their gigantic preparations, the French commanders took a number of decisions which doomed their enterprise before it was under way. Vauban had hoped to crown his life's work by undertaking the siege of Turin in person. This was not to be, for he was too old for distant campaigning, and his presence was urgently needed on the Netherlands frontier. Vauban therefore wrote to de la Feuillade on 13 September 1705, giving him the benefit of his years of meditation on the subject of an attack on Turin. As the first step he proposed that the besiegers should close off the place from outside help by digging an effective line of circum-

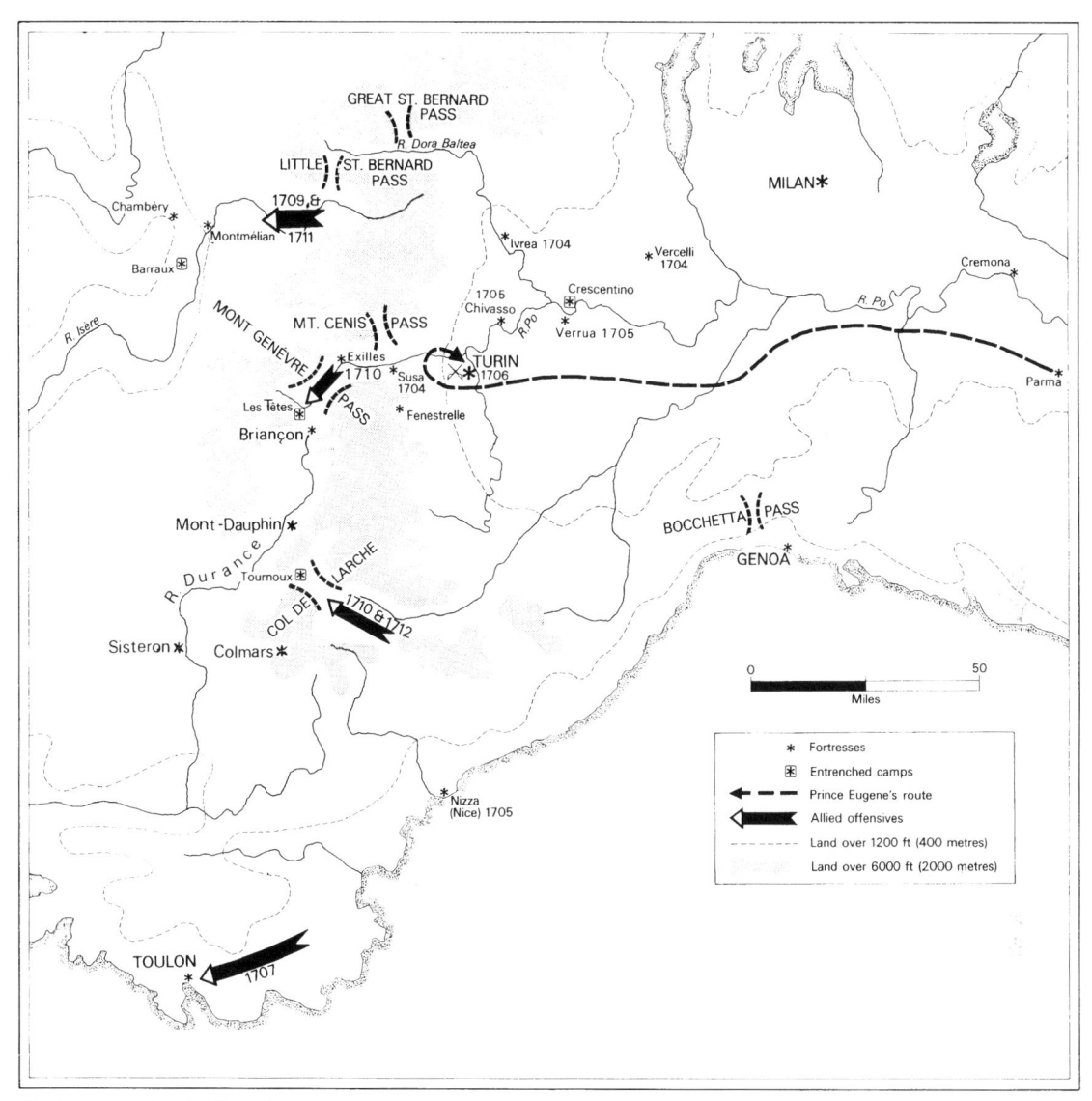

Piedmont and neighbouring states in the War of the Spanish Succession

vallation. Then the French should concentrate all their efforts on reducing the town, and leave the powerful citadel strictly alone at the beginning of the siege:

I am absolutely against any idea of attacking *à la Coehoorn*. This method is effective only against miserable and feeble places like Venlo, Roermond, the citadel of Liège and Bonn... none of which would have held out for eight days against a formal attack. The citadel of Turin is in a different class,

for its works are solid, tested and well-flanked, and they would withstand any cannonade that was delivered from Coehoorn's favourite range of six hundred paces.... The only way to open up a revetment and effect a breach is to plant your batteries on the covered way and batter away at the foot of the bastions. (*ibid.*, V, 654)

Once the town had fallen, claimed Vauban, the citadel would be isolated and fall into the hands of the French easily enough.

Vauban's advice was received in Italy with something less than enthusiasm. Vendôme wrote to Louis on 1 October:

To begin with, I have the honour of saying to Your Majesty that, whatever Vauban alleges, the siege of Turin is a perfectly ordinary operation. Contrary to Vauban's claims, I believe that it is quite unimportant whether a fortress is well or badly invested, if the magazines are already full to capacity and the enemy are unable to throw in any further help . . . I am convinced that if Your Majesty had consulted Vauban we should never have taken Verrua or Chivasso. These two sieges were conducted against the rules, but the fortresses fell anyway, and I guarantee that Turin will follow in their train. (*ibid.*, V, 664)

De la Feuillade was still less amenable. As a raffish, restless 33-year-old, who had risen to high rank by marrying the ugly daughter of Louis's secretary Chamillart, he found the notion of accepting the guidance of an aged technician entirely alien to his character and ambitions. On 1 September 1705 he wrote to his influential father-in-law:

Just have confidence in me, and I shall repay you and the king for your trust more handsomely than all the engineers in the world. There are certain men who are born to command: by the same token there are other men, like the engineers, who exist merely to carry out the orders which are issued to them by their superiors. (Augoyat, 1860–4, I, 303)

The siege that was shaped by these deliberations may be fairly accounted the most striking episode of the great age of fortress warfare, even when we bring into the reckoning the sieges of Namur in the 1690s, and the attack on Lille in 1708. The scale of the struggle for Turin, and the determination with which it was waged, reflect the magnitude of the issue which hung upon its outcome, namely the survival of Piedmont. The progress of the operation is documented with a thoroughness which is probably not to be seen again in any siege until the attack of Sevastopol, and the emotions of the defenders are preserved in the journal of the Piedmontese chief gunner Solar de la Marguerite, a narrative enlivened with much descriptive colour. As for the besiegers,

de la Feuillade and Vendôme not only rejected the notions of regular attack as laid down by Vauban, but defied the principle of centralised direction of warfare which had replaced the gay campaigning of the young days of Condé and Turenne. If the French commanders had succeeded in taking Turin, they would have destroyed everything that had made French military engineering what it was.

How well prepared was Turin to meet the French? Many of the permanent works dated from the last two centuries, and consisted of a town enceinte of nineteen bastions, and of Paciotto's famous pentagonal citadel, which was founded in 1564, and occupied a side on the western side of the town ramparts. The works had been strengthened in the 1670s, ironically enough with Vauban's advice, and the last few years had seen much urgent activity (see p. 49). More recently still, enough publicity had been given to de la Feuillade's plan of attack to warn the Piedmontese that they ought to concentrate their efforts on the three exterior bastions of the citadel: these works were furnished with fascine-revetted counterguards (detached bastions), which lurked behind flèches with palisaded gorges.

The system of masonry-revetted permanent countermines took the form of two storeys of 'capital galleries' which ran along the imaginary prolongations of the centre lines of the bastions. The upper level began at the counterscarp gallery, but the lower one extended all the way from the interior of the citadel, a fact which was to be of some importance towards the end of the siege. The two storeys united under the inner glacis, then dived beneath the dry ditch and extended for twenty-five paces under the outer glacis. These underground defences were now hung with oil lamps, and the galleries and branches were prolonged in new ramifications so as to give adequate protection to the flèches. The whole complex formed what was 'almost a second, invisible fortress, vaster still than the one on the surface' (Amoretti, 1978, 35).

The defenders were led by the Austrian Lieutenant-General Wirich Daun, a firm, active but accessible kind of man, very well suited to command a fortress-city. He disposed of a regular garrison of 14,700 Austrians and Piedmontese. Half of these

Louis XIV and Old Fortress Warfare 1660–1715 53

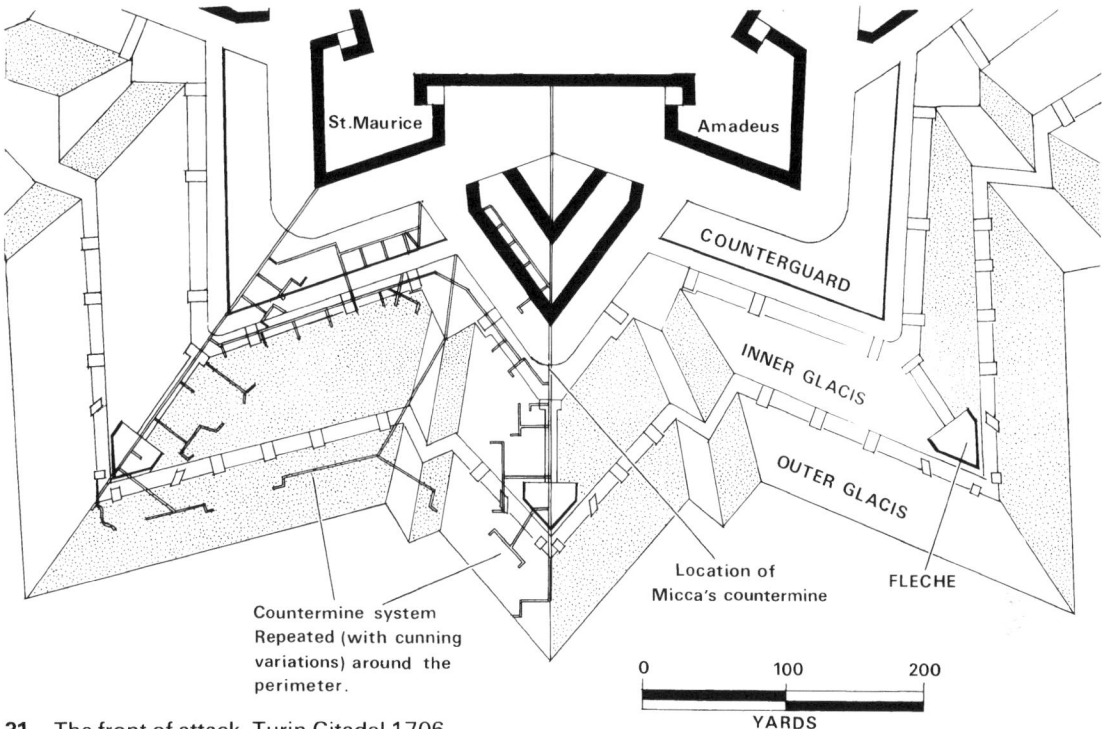

31 The front of attack, Turin Citadel 1706

men were recruits, and Daun would have been hard put to it to defend Turin if the townspeople had not given him their whole-hearted support. Over the last three years a good deal of work had been put into reviving the urban militia, and during the siege the 8,000 armed citizens gave an extremely good account of themselves on the ramparts. Hundreds of women toiled on the defences under fire, while

the orphans of the Spedale della Carità, who had no other guide than their innocence, marched in small squads to lend a hand in the mine workings. Some of the boys were crushed to death beneath the débris, from where their little bodies were retrieved with some difficulty, and carried shoulder-high to burial within the same precincts they had left such a short time before. (Diary, in R. Deputazione, 1907–10, VII, 244)

So much for the lie which talks about a divorce between governments and subjects in the eighteenth century.

The French assembled around Turin in the middle of May, 1706. They had no intention of forming an investment, and for some time the Piedmontese roved with some freedom over both banks of the Po. Victory Amadeus remained in the city until 17 June, and convoys of supplies contrived to reach Turin for several weeks more.

Early on the morning of 3 June a fluttering of flags revealed that the French had opened a first parallel at five hundred paces from the outer covered way of the citadel bastions of St Maurice (facing north-west), Amadeus (facing west) and the Royal Bastion (where the citadel met the town). The defenders greeted the French with fire from the new flèches, and on 5 June

having learnt from deserters that several enemy generals had arranged to dine in some farm houses within artillery range of the citadel, so as to have a better view, we opened fire at noon with all the artillery of the citadel, aiming at all the farm houses in the neighbourhood. This unpleasant surprise caused a horrid upset to the Frenchmen's lunch, and afforded great amusement to the people who knew the circumstances. (Marguerite, 1838, 15)

The French threw up their second parallel on the night of 8–9 June, and on the next day they opened fire with a battery of fifteen mortars. Some of the bombs were

of an enormous weight which enabled them to break through joists and arches, wrecking houses from top to bottom, and scattering the bones of the dead in the tombs of the principal churches. (*ibid.*, 20)

By the middle of the month twenty 24-pounders were firing from two batteries in the second parallel, and under the cover of this fire the French began to drive forward their saps on the night of 19–20 June. The artillery barrage grew to a crescendo on 24 June, when the French opened up with sixty-six cannon and thirty-four mortars, and the garrison replied by 'unmasking' a large number of hidden embrasures. Since the successive fortifications climbed to the rear in gradations of scarcely two feet each, the greater part of the French shot flew straight into the town, bounding down the streets and sometimes reaching the far side of the Po. On the 25th,

the day had scarcely dawned when the French artillery thundered out again, though the effect was to cause more disorder inside the town than actual damage to the ramparts. Near the Arsenal six Austrian soldiers and a woman were carried away by a single shot, and the ball would have continued on its way if, by a happy chance, it had not been stopped by a large ox who received it in his belly. (*ibid.*, 37)

The French chose this stage of the siege to open their third parallel at the foot of the outer glacis, on the night of 25–26 June. The ground had to be won by the laborious means of covered saps, and the Piedmontese fed cobblestones into six newly cast pierriers in order to pelt the supporting troops who were standing in the open trenches behind. Chamillart wrote unhelpfully to his son-in-law, de la Feuillade: 'Vauban announces to his friends and to the world at large that he is quite willing to have his throat cut, if you ever succeed in taking Turin by keeping up the attack on the point you have chosen (6 July, Vault, 1835–62, VI, 193).

Below ground the French made scarcely better progress. The mine attacks against Bastion Amadeus and the adjacent ravelin were begun in the last week of June. It was a nerve-wracking business from the start, for the exploding bombs on the surface caused earth to sift through the wooden frames of the galleries, and the dread noise of countermining frightened the French into exploding the first of their camouflets on 5 July.

News of the underground war reached Vauban at Dunkirk, and he was moved to write to Chamillart:

Do me the honour of believing me when I say, once and for all, that they will never take Turin by the sector they have chosen for the attack . . . all this clever business about the mines will go on for ever, and serve only to entomb the best men in your army. This is because the enemy are the sitting tenants, and they just have to wait for you to come at them . . . (Mengin, 1832, 45)

The attack on the ravelin was brought to a temporary halt when, on 15 July, a Piedmontese countermine blew in two galleries and produced a crater of twenty paces diameter on the surface. The Piedmontese took steps to dominate the reeking area by employing criminals from the city prisons to drag away the corpses, and blowing fresh air into the galleries by bellows attached to metal pipes. The French were less well prepared. Their miners

used every kind of device to expel the stale air and draw in the fresh, but the miners suffered so terribly underground that a fair number of them died. In addition some of the labourers suffocated in galleries which were infected by the stench of corpses which nobody wished to remove. (Saint-Hilaire, 1903–4, IV, 286)

The siege took an unexpected step forward on the night of 21–22 July, when four French grenadier companies seized the three flèches, lost them again to a determined counter-attack, but finally stormed in once more and made their lodgments. Three nights later the French made their fourth parallel on the inner glacis, and from now onwards the contest for Turin was fought out on the few yards which separated the lip of the glacis from the bastions.

From the evening of 5 August the French sought to win a lodgment for their breaching batteries on the covered way – 'their musketry rang out with great violence, and the bombs were discharged from their mortars twenty-six at a time, like a volley of rockets darting suddenly into the air' (Marguerite, 1838, 82). The defenders in their turn burnt some of the gabions of the lodgments, and dragged others into the ditch by means of grapnels.

The French opened fire from the covered way with the first of the breaching batteries on 14 August. More and more guns were brought into action, despite the fulminating counter-batteries and countermines, and a number of dangerous breaches were opened in the ravelin and the counterguards. On the night of 26–27 August the French blew long sections of the counterscarp into the ditch, and the waiting grenadiers swarmed across and gained the crumbling fortifications on the far side. The defenders held out in the inner bastions and the redoubt of the ravelin, and launched a counter-attack on the 27th which evicted the enemy from the counterguards. The French, however, held firm in the main body of the ravelin, where they began to throw up a battery. The resistance had been prolonged well beyond the point where the conventions of the time allowed an honourable capitulation, but the Piedmontese and Austrians were still full of defiance. They piled fascines and timber into the ditch, flung torches on top of the piles, and jeered and swore at the French across the flames.

On 29 August the floor of the ditch was still glowing with the embers, and a lucky bomb landed on the magazine of the French battery in the ravelin:

The grenades and bombs which were stored there blew up with a noise that sounded like a mass assault – muskets, coats, hats, everything that was in the battery was flung to a great height. The cannon cartridges and their voluminous paper wrappings flew into the air, broke apart and scattered in little tatters which swirled about in a dense cloud of smoke like some miraculous blizzard in high summer. (*ibid.*, 109–10)

The delighted General Daun distributed money among the bombardiers, and read out a letter which caused the soldiers to crowd around him – Prince Eugene had written to say that he had out-manoeuvred Marshal Marsin, Vendôme's successor, and that an army of relief would shortly reach Turin.

That eventful day closed with the most memorable event of the siege. At the bottom of the counterscarp the French had found a way into the upper storey of countermines, and they were now bent on forcing the door which gave onto the flight of steps which led to the lower gallery, and thus to the interior of the citadel. The Piedmontese miner Pietro Micca was stationed beneath the steps, waiting to demolish the entrance with a charge of powder:

Hearing that the enemy were breaking down the door with axe-blows, he urged his comrade to apply the match to the fuze. Consumed with impatience he shouted 'Get out of the way!' Seizing him by the hand he said 'For heaven's sake, how much longer are you going to take? Make yourself scarce and let me get on with it!' He touched the end of the fuze with the match. The charge exploded, killing the poor man and flinging him forty paces from the stairway. (*ibid.*, 112)

All the same, Micca had done his work, and the French had no means of penetrating through the smoky rubble to the lower gallery.

Between the night of 30 August and the afternoon of the 31st the French made their last desperate assaults. The wretched troops were scourged by a flanking fire from twenty-four cannon (probably including four breech-loaders purchased from the German inventor Embser), and the morale of the besiegers was finally broken by a last, dreadful countermine which scattered the breaching cannon like straw.

On 2 September Prince Eugene and Victor Amadeus mounted to the cupola of the new basilica of Superga, and took in a view which extended from the Ligurian Apennines across the Piedmontese plain to the Alps. From what they saw, they decided to bring the Austro-Piedmontese army of relief around to the west of Turin, and attack the French positions between the Dora and the Po.

Their opponents were already half beaten. On 30 August Marshal Marsin reported that the French infantry were being burnt out, and that the technical services were no better off:

Poor Tardif is the chief engineer and the director

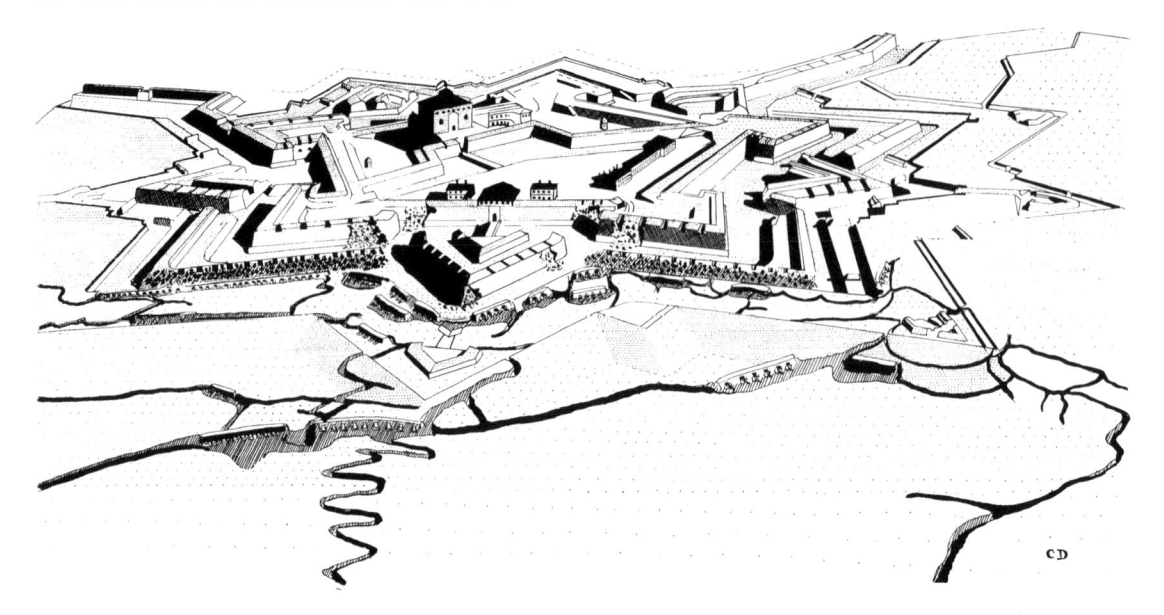

32 Turin Citadel. The state of affairs on about 20 August, after the French had lodged on the flèches and inner covered way, and begun to breach the counterguards, the ravelin and the main enceinte

of the siege. He is an old acquaintance of mine, for he once served under me. I know that he is a good and brave man, but I am also aware that he is not up to the conduct of an operation like this – he is crushed by his responsibilities, and he is at loggerheads with the subordinate engineers. . . . It is much the same story with the artillery officers. The Sieur d'Houville, the chief gunner, earned the displeasure of the Duc de la Feuillade. Anyway he was killed a few days ago. The Sieur de Chantelou, who followed him, seemed to have won the duke's high regard, but he was found yesterday morning dead in his bed of apoplexy. The present incumbent, the Chevalier de Saint-Perrier, is a very capable officer and at the same time the only one we have left. If he too is removed from the scene, which could easily happen, I have no idea who will be able to take over the artillery. (To Chamillart, Vault, 1835–62, VI, 267–8)

The Allied army attacked and defeated the French outside Turin on 7 September, and Daun contributed to the victory by making a sortie against the enemy camp. The French retreated towards the Alps and home, leaving behind 5,000 prisoners, 10,000 dead and wounded, fifty-six mortars and over one hundred cannon.

The Allied exploitation 1706–8. The French veteran de Guignard conceded that:

The powers with which we were fighting . . . excelled us in the art of bringing help to besieged fortresses, most notably in the way they relieved the vitally important strongholds of Barcelona and Turin in 1706. These two blows would have been enough to overturn any other state than the French. As it was, we received such a violent shock that we had to summon up all our forces to prevent ourselves from going under. (Guignard, 1725, II, 422)

The defeat of the French at Turin not only brought the loss of all the scattered garrisons in Italy, but enabled the Allies to pierce the long and apparently indefensible arc of France's Alpine frontier. In the summer of 1707, while Marshal Tessé and 38,550 men were guarding the Mont-Genèvre route into Dauphiné, the Austrians and Piedmontese invaded Provence with the support of British warships. The French would probably have lost Toulon, their premier port on the Mediterranean, if the engineer Lozières d'Astier had not made some hasty repairs to the 'garden wall' that surrounded the town, and made arrangements to defend the nearby heights.

Tessé was granted the time to march down the 'French' side of the Alpine barrier and occupy the entrenched camp of Sainte-Anne, which was situated on the hills to the north and north-west of Toulon. This was quite enough to deter Prince Eugene, who decamped from Toulon on the night of 21–22 August. Here we have a convincing enough testimonial to the efficacy of entrenched camps, a kind of fortification which Vauban had tried to persuade the French to adopt as early as the 1690s.

It was much the same story in 1708. Louis expected a new invasion of Provence, but the Allies instead took the initiative in the north and cleared the approaches to the Mont-Genèvre by reducing Exilles and Fenestrelle. Villars found that their covering positions were everywhere too strong to be attached – this went to show, said the expert topographer Jean François de la Blottière, that 'the first tenants of mountain-tops are very difficult to dislodge' (Augoyat, 1860–4, I, 340).

The Allies wasted their opportunity, for the Emperor succumbed to the age-old temptation of the conquerors of north Italy, and diverted a large part of his forces to attack Naples. A network of sympathisers had prepared the way for the Austrian invasion of 1708, with the result that only the fortresses of Pescara and Gaeta put Wirich Daun to the trouble of having to make a formal siege.

The defence of the French Alpine barrier 1709–12.
It was left to Jacobite exiles from Britain to teach the French how to defend their two-hundred-mile concave Alpine frontier. In November 1708 the Irishman Dillon, who commanded at Briançon, suggested that the surest means of blocking the exit from the Mont-Genèvre Pass would be to build an entrenched camp on the heights of Les Têtes, which towered above his fortress. The project was put into execution, and the new camp at Briançon became the pivot of a highly effective strategy that was evolved by the Duke of Berwick, the illegitimate son of James II:

I chose Briançon for the fixed position, or centre, where I intended to place the main body of my troops, and whence they were to file off to the right or left, according to the motions of the enemy. . . .
It is to be observed, that in a war carried on among mountains, when one is master of the heights, the enemy is necessarily stopped; and this is what I had made my principal object in the line I had laid down for myself. (Berwick, 1779, II, 61–2, 67)

The Briançon position was supplemented by a number of entrenched camps which blocked the lesser-used lateral passes. The Allies accordingly spent the last four years of the war making fruitless marches up one valley or another, without daring to force the positions. In each case Berwick had time to match the enemy moves by executing parallel marches on the French side of the frontier. Thanks to his mastery of military topography, France was able to maintain the integrity of the 'natural border' that ran along the Alpine summits from Savoy to the County of Nice.

The dividing line was consecrated by the peace settlement of 1713, though the French had to buy off the Piedmontese by renouncing the long-lost strongholds of Exilles and Fenestrelle. Piedmont likewise gained Sicily, as her price for recognising the Bourbon dynasty in Spain – 'never had Piedmont found herself in such happy circumstances' (Saluces, 1817–18, V, 267).

The Emperor made peace with the Bourbons in 1714. His designs on the Spanish homeland were frustrated, but he was awarded the Spanish Netherlands, the Milanese, Naples, Mantua and Sardinia. The Austrians not only possessed a wide and deep strategic bridgehead in Italy, but they became a power in Italy in their own right.

The war in the Iberian peninsula

The Portuguese theatre. The succession (or, as some said, the imposition) of the Bourbon king, Philip V, at Madrid had the effect of reviving all the old quarrels which had wracked the Peninsula over the last two centuries. The bitter Spanish struggle with Portugal was revived in 1703, when the Portuguese threw in their lot with the Grand Alliance. Two years later the Catalans rose in revolt, and welcomed an Austrian archduke as 'King Charles III' of Spain.

A dangerous interval of three and a half decades had intervened between the 1660s, which was a period of busy military reform in Portugal, and Portugal's entry into the War of the Spanish Succession.

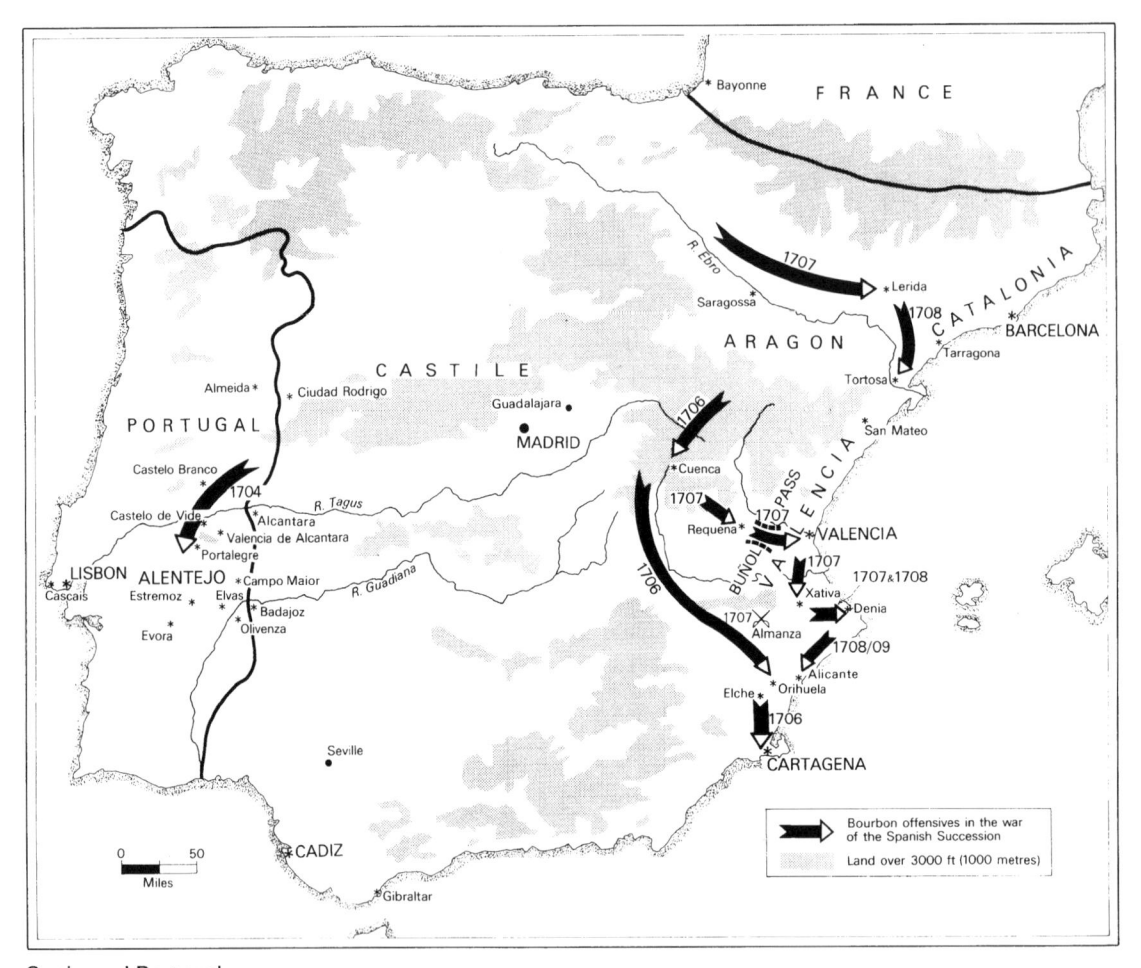

Spain and Portugal

The Portuguese troops were ill-disciplined, the fortresses were ruinous and badly stocked, and the Portuguese commanders were observed to be expansive in their promises of ammunition and artillery, but slow to produce the actual objects.

In an attempt to improve at least the technical arms, Marlborough looked up one of his several acquaintances among the Irishmen who were then wandering Europe. This was Colonel John Richards, a Williamite engineer who had taken service with Saxony-Poland and Venice against the Turks. By 1703 he had probably accumulated as much practical experience of fortress warfare as all except a handful of Continental engineers.

Not all the expertise of Richards could forge the Portuguese into a particularly useful instrument of the Grand Alliance. They had a bad fright in 1704, when the Duke of Berwick (as Bourbon commander) turned the northern flank of the Alentejo fortresses, and they accordingly demanded that their British and Dutch allies must bend their efforts to reducing the fortified enemy bases just inside the Spanish border. Badajoz, the southern depot, was attacked in vain in 1705, but in the spring of the following year the combined army marched northwards parallel with the border and captured the corresponding northern base of Ciudad Rodrigo.

It took the news of the French defeat at Ramillies and their failure at Barcelona to give the Portuguese enough confidence to leave their borderlands and advance on Madrid. The allied host entered the city on 26 June 1706. The Portuguese now developed

33 Sack of a fortress-town. Engraving by Rigaud, inspired by episodes of the war in Spain

a taste for parading in the capital of their enemies, which was of purely symbolic importance, and it was a long time before the Allies reached out to join the troops from the Mediterranean coast at Guadalajara. Away in Portugal, the guard of the frontier could be safely entrusted to small parties of Portuguese and Allied troops.

The Catalan theatre. The Catalans were hardly less promiscuous than the Portuguese when it was a question of embracing a foreign friend. In the 1640s and early 1650s these people had given the Castilians a good run for their money with the help of the French. Now, in the War of the Spanish Succession, the Grand Alliance was surprised and delighted by the ardour with which the Catalans turned their affections towards Archduke Charles of Austria, as the Habsburg candidate for the Spanish throne. The liaison was presided over by the Catholic and *simpatico* Austrian general Prince George of Hesse-Darmstadt, who was already known to the Catalans for his defence of Fort Montjuich at Barcelona in 1687, and who had increased his standing with the Allies by leading the land forces to the capture of Gibraltar in 1704.

In 1705 Spain's Mediterranean provinces were ripe for revolt, and an Allied fleet set sail from Gibraltar to back up the dissidents by armed force. The Allies chose Barcelona as their objective, for it was the focal point of Catalan sentiments, and owned one of the finest ports on the entire coastline.

The little expedition of 12,000 British, Dutch and Catalans landed near Barcelona on 23 August. Once on shore the Allies were aghast at theit own temerity, and the Earl of Peterborough had already decided to decamp when the rock citadel of Montjuich, the key to Barcelona, fell into their hands in an almost casual assault. The beloved Prince George was killed during the operation, but Peterborough pressed on with the siege and the city of Barcelona capitulated on 5 August. The revolt in favour of Archduke Charles now flared down the Mediterranean coastlands 'like a blaze in the dry fields at harvest time' (San Felipe, 1957, bk III), running south from Gerona by way of Lerida and Tarragona to the city of Valencia, the capital of the province of the same name.

The French and Bourbon Spanish tried to win back Barcelona in 1706. Montjuich was actually reduced in a bitterly fought operation, which cost the life of the gifted French engineer Lapara des Fieux, but the besiegers were still stuck fast before the southern ramparts of the city when their supporting ships fled before an Allied fleet. After a few days of anxious deliberation the Bourbon forces marched away on 12 May, leaving behind 2,000 sick and wounded, together with 140 cannon and twenty-seven mortars. This débâcle, like the simultaneous failure before Turin, revealed how sorely the French missed the presence of Vauban at their sieges. The reverse also made a deep impression on the Bourbon Spanish, and provoked the Marquis of Santa Cruz into discoursing at some length, in the eighth book of his *Reflexiones Militares*, on the difficulties which so often made a siege inadvisable.

Archduke Charles, now to be known as Charles III, King of Spain, had brought into his power a great tract of land which he could not possibly retain with his motley and thinly spread army of militia, Catalan miquelets, British, Dutch, Portuguese and Germans. Over the following years the Bourbons attacked this Habsburg Spain from two directions – coming from the Pyrenees, the French armies battered at the northern perimeter of Catalonia in a series of major sieges (Lerida 1707, Tortosa 1708, Gerona 1711); at the same time forces of Spanish and French advanced eastwards from the heart of Spain and chopped up and digested the southern corridor (Cartagena 1706, occupation of Valencia 1707, Denia 1708, Alicante 1709). It was essentially the same strategy which the Union was to employ to bring down the Southern Confederacy in the American Civil War.

The Catalans and their allies never effectively broke through the tightening cordon. The Earl of Galway very optimistically struck for Madrid in 1707, but was crushed when he ran into the Duke of Berwick's concentration of 30,000 men at Almanza on 25 April. Using powerful Austrian reinforcements, Field-Marshal Guido Starhemberg broke out of the Catalan strategic box in 1710 and actually endangered the communication between the French armies and their homeland. However, the Catalans and Portuguese were interested only in lording it over the Castilians in Madrid, and after

34 Acropolis of Aragon – the cathedral and fortress of Lerida. Captured by the French in 1707, it was fortified with a bastion perimeter in 1708, and became an important base of Bourbon power in north-eastern Spain

a short occupation (21 September–11 November) the army made back for the Mediterranean coast. In the process the British contingent of 2,500 troops was cut off and captured at Brihuega.

Otherwise the war resolved itself into the remorseless succession of sieges. On the one side the 'Habsburg' Spanish and their foreign friends showed an almost fanatical determination to hold out to the last. Already in December 1705 a Bourbon detachment had been repulsed by the militia and population of San Matheo, a little fortified town which occupied a position on the inland route between Catalonia and Valencia. The magistracy recalled with pride:

It is impossible to express the readiness of the clergy in taking arms, doing duty at their posts, and going the rounds. Nor is the unparalleled valour and bravery of the religious women to be omitted, who like so many brave Bellonas, stood sentinel on the curtain of the monastery wall, armed with firelocks, and boldly firing upon the enemies' troops. (Anon., 1707, 23)

A particularly horrible happening occurred at Alicante on 3 March 1709, when John Richards and a party of troops stood on guard on the parade ground of the castle rock, in the full knowledge that the French engineer d'Asfeld had packed a gigantic charge of 117,000 pounds of gunpowder into a mine chamber below. At six in the morning a wisp of smoke was seen to emerge from the entrance of the mine tunnel, and shortly afterwards the parade ground opened in a great mouth which swallowed up Richards, eight officers and forty-five soldiers, and closed over them as if they had never been.

At the same time there was a good deal to admire in the ingenuity of the French, when they seemed to be able to conjure up siege trains from the air. It was

> always very difficult to assemble heavy artillery and munitions, and most of all in Spain, where you are unable to dip into any reserve arsenals. The materials from France had to come a great distance over bad roads and mountain passes, and they reached their destination only after we had expended much money, effort and time. (Saint-Hilaire, 1903–4, V, 81)

The British and Dutch withdrew their fleets from the Mediterranean in December 1712, which forced King Charles III (or rather the Emperor Charles VI, as he should now be called) to retrieve his troops from Spain. Charles was in one of those weepy moods that sometimes overtook the Habsburgs when they bowed to the demands of statecraft, and he wrote that the extraordinary loyalty of the Catalans made it 'all the more painful to me ... to have to abandon such faithful subjects ... but I must accept this heavy though well-deserved punishment from God with resignation' (Kriegsarchiv, 1876–91, XV, 365).

Starhemberg and the Austrians embarked at Barcelona in December 1713, and advised the Catalans to make what terms they could with the Bourbons. The Catalans appreciated Starhemberg's good intentions, but they made up their minds to hold Barcelona against the united power of France and Spain.

Sixteen thousand French and Spanish gradually assembled around the defiant city, and came under the command of the Duke of Berwick in July 1714. The Gallispans directed their attacks along the coastal plain from the north, well away from the Montjuich hill of bloody history, but the city enceinte put up an unexpectedly heavy resistance, and the garrison repulsed no less than three storms. Far less vindictive than his Castilian allies, Berwick persuaded the Catalans to admit the besiegers on 13 September. Berwick kept his word to hold his troops in check, but over the following years the Spanish reimposed the rule of Madrid in a most ruthless way, and extinguished the Catalan customs and privileges which had survived the earlier catastrophe of the 1650s.

It was not wholly out of character that this great war closed on an episode that showed, almost eighty years before the French Revolution, the kind of effort which could be put forth by a people fighting for its nationhood and liberties.

Two   The Masters: Coehoorn and Vauban

Menno van Coehoorn 1641–1704

Career and character
During six decades of the most crowded and intensive fortress warfare in history we have so far caught only unrelated glimpses of Coehoorn and Vauban, the two military engineers who are generally reckoned to be the greatest masters of their art.

Vauban's great rival in war and fame was born at Lettinga, near Leeuwarden, in March 1641, to a family which had emigrated from Frankfurt-am-Main to the United Provinces at the time of William the Silent. Together with several brothers Menno pursued his studies under a private tutor until, at the age of sixteen, he was admitted to his father's infantry regiment with the rank of captain, and sent to the garrison of Maastricht:

He showed a particular liking for mathematics and military drawing, as well as mastering all that had to do with the service in general. He distinguished himself so well in both the scientific and mundane branches of his profession that the old Rhinegrave, who was the governor of this town, conceived a liking for him and honoured him with his generosity. He made Coehoorn his aide-de-camp, and introduced him to the young count, his son. The two youths travelled together to France, so as to see all the finest sights of that great and vast kingdom. (Coehoorn, 1860, 6)

Coehoorn was wounded while he commanded a company of grenadiers at the defence of Maastricht in 1673, and it was also as an infantry officer that he fought at the field actions at Senneff in 1674, Mont Cassel in 1677, Saint-Denis in 1678, and at Fleurus in 1690, where he was nearly taken prisoner.

These were years of frustration and disappointment for Coehoorn. He was unpopular among his brother infantry officers, and even as a budding engineer he was overlooked in favour of the Huguenot engineers who flooded over Protestant Europe in the years following the revocation of the Edict of Nantes in 1685.

It took years of the most varied effort for Coehoorn to get himself established as the natural successor to the foreign experts. He had established his name as a controversialist and theoretician in his *Nieuwe Vestingbouw* of 1685, and four years later he began his career as a taker of fortresses by assuming the direction of the siege of Bonn, in which he mightily impressed the Great Elector of Brandenburg. Coehoorn declined the offer of a major-generalship in the Brandenburg service, and his talents and loyalty were finally rewarded by his own masters towards the end of 1691, when William III entrusted him with 27,000 florins and told him to reinforce the citadel complex at Namur. Coehoorn won the attention of Europe by his spirited defence of the same works in 1692. Three years after, with the roles reversed, he came to the rescue of the floundering Allied siege army and brought about the capture of Namur on 1 September 1695.

Honours and positions were belatedly heaped upon Coehoorn. Before the end of 1695 he was major-general of infantry, and as *Ingenieur Generall*, the effective successor of the Huguenot Charles du Puy de l'Espinasse. In November 1697 he became *Meester Generall van de Artillerie*, and his career was crowned with the award of the potentially lucrative governorship of West Flanders in June 1701.

William III had meanwhile charged Coehoorn with taking up the work of national re-fortification, which had been interrupted by the War of the League of Augsburg (see p. 34). Coehoorn toured the frontiers, and in May 1698 he was able to lay before the king at Windsor his projects for new works at Bergen-op-Zoom, Breda, Grave, Zutphen, Doesburg, Zwolle, Coevorden and Groningen. Coehoorn then returned to the United Provinces, and used his authority as overlord of the technical arms to put his plans into effect.

Bergen-op-Zoom was to be a new, first-class fortress. Elsewhere, however, Coehoorn had to be content with reinforcing the existing works. Speed and economy were vital, and in a vain attempt to anticipate the outbreak of war he made extensive use of tenaille lines, and of the outworks he had affected to scorn in his treatise of 1685.

The prospect of power and fortune suddenly receded for Coehoorn when his royal patron, William III, died in 1702. Coehoorn made an unfortunate essay in field command in his Flemish campaign of 1703, which did nothing to commend him to his new masters, and the tale of misfortune was complete when his secretary stole away to France with his precious portfolios of plans and memoranda. Casting around for a new start in life, Coehoorn approached the Piedmontese envoy with a view to entering the service of Duke Victor Amadeus. Before he could take the matter any further he died, on 17 March 1704, leaving his family with scarcely enough money for their daily bread.

We shall always do an injustice to Coehoorn's achievement unless we bear in mind that he aspired for a mere seven years to a position of authority which Vauban enjoyed for five decades.

Disappointingly little of Coehoorn's character and ambitions is revealed by the scanty documentary evidence which survives. What remains is a distinct impression of a spiky, difficult temperament, which constantly placed Coehoorn at odds with his peers and immediate superiors. The field deputies of the States General were the targets of his special scorn. One of these gentlemen, Geldermalsum, was incautious enough to order an artillery officer to open fire at the siege of the citadel of Liège in 1702:

At this, Coehoorn gave the gunner some new and strict orders to cease fire, and he went without delay to Geldermalsum's quarters and asked him unceremoniously whether he was the person who had had the effrontery to instruct Colonel Ijssel to open up. The deputy replied that he was, and asked Coehoorn whether he was aware of who he was speaking to. Without blinking an eyelid Coehoorn said that he knew very well whom he was addressing, namely Geldermalsum, field deputy of the States General. He went on to challenge the deputy to say the same. 'Yes', he answered, 'I know it's the commanding general of the artillery.' 'You are wrong', retorted Coehoorn, 'it is me, Coehoorn in person. I can become what you are in a single day, whereas you could spend a whole lifetime and still not become what I am!' He promptly returned to his quarters, wishing to take no further part in the siege. (*ibid.*, 36–7)

Fortunately for the Allies, Coehoorn's old and close friend Ginkel was at hand to patch up the quarrel, and the indignant engineer was persuaded to return to his work.

The siege attack

Coehoorn was something more than the mad bombardier of the legend which was so assiduously cultivated by Vauban and the French, although it is certainly true that the time-table of his sieges rarely approximated to Vauban's well-established routine. There were some important reasons for the difference.

Whereas Vauban frequently sketched out a whole plan of campaign, the Dutchman was usually excluded from strategy-making, and he was sometimes forced to attack a fortress which he would much rather have left alone, as happened at Kaiserswörth in 1702. Such freedom as Coehoorn possessed in conducting a siege was usually won by dint of making a direct appeal to the commanding prince, over the heads of his immediate seniors.

Since he had no Dutch 'Louvois' to prepare the material resources for the siege, Coehoorn's next task was to lash the commissaries and field deputies into some belated activity, and supply what was still lacking by asking for help from nearby princes or cities. After that he had to slot perhaps as many as a dozen separate contingents into a combined plan of attack. Above all, Coehoorn had to bring some order into the plentiful if ill-assorted artillery which the Allied contingents usually carried to their sieges. Spectacular bombardments were deeply rooted in North European usage, and the gunners would have been content to blast away at everything which came into their view if Coehoorn (like Vauban) had not set himself firmly against the cannonade of towns, and compelled the artillery to concentrate its fire on the fortifications.

Two new weapons made high-trajectory fire with explosive bombs especially formidable. The first was the howitzer, which the Dutch began to manufacture for themselves in the 1690s, and which they employed in batteries to supplement the fire of the heavier and less mobile mortar. Both howitzer and mortar were nevertheless fairly clumsy weapons, and unsuitable for giving close support to infantry when it attacked covered ways or small detached works. In May 1701 Coehoorn therefore brought an invention of his own to the notice of William's Council. This was a miniature iron mortar of about five-inch calibre, which could throw a 16- or 18-pound bomb up to an extreme range of seven hundred paces. It was small and light enough to be pulled by one man, or carried bodily by two, and it could be planted anywhere in the trenches. This 'cohorn mortar' was probably first employed, to the number of seventy-four, at the siege of Kaiserswörth in 1702. Later in the same year 125 were in action against Venlo, and no less than 250 against the citadel of Liège. This number climbed to about 300 in the siege of Bonn in 1703.

Coehoorn could never forget that the bulk of the troops at his disposal were Germans, who were then sunk in a state of apparent feeble-mindedness concerning all that had to do with fortress warfare. Rather than attempt a lengthy sap attack, which would have been well beyond the capacity of these people, Coehoorn chose to launch the best troops

35 Menno van Coehoorn (Netscher). This portrait is reckoned to be the best likeness of the choleric engineer

of the army into mass assaults, once he had satisfied himself that the overwhelming Allied fire had breached the walls and cracked the morale of the defenders. Timing and *coup d'œil* were all important, for Coehoorn had to stake everything upon the outcome of a couple of hours of combat.

These energetic methods corresponded more closely to the instincts of French commanders like Boufflers, Vendôme and Villars than did the apparently slow march of Vauban's attack. Where the essential difference between the methods of Coehoorn and Vauban resided was not so much in the ability of the two engineers, or even in the resources at their command, as in the almost unlimited authority which the Frenchman possessed to shape the progress of the attack according to his wishes.

The Dutch engineering corps
Coehoorn gave the Dutch engineering service a stability and a cohesion which it had not known since the days of Frederick Henry of Nassau. Up to Coe-

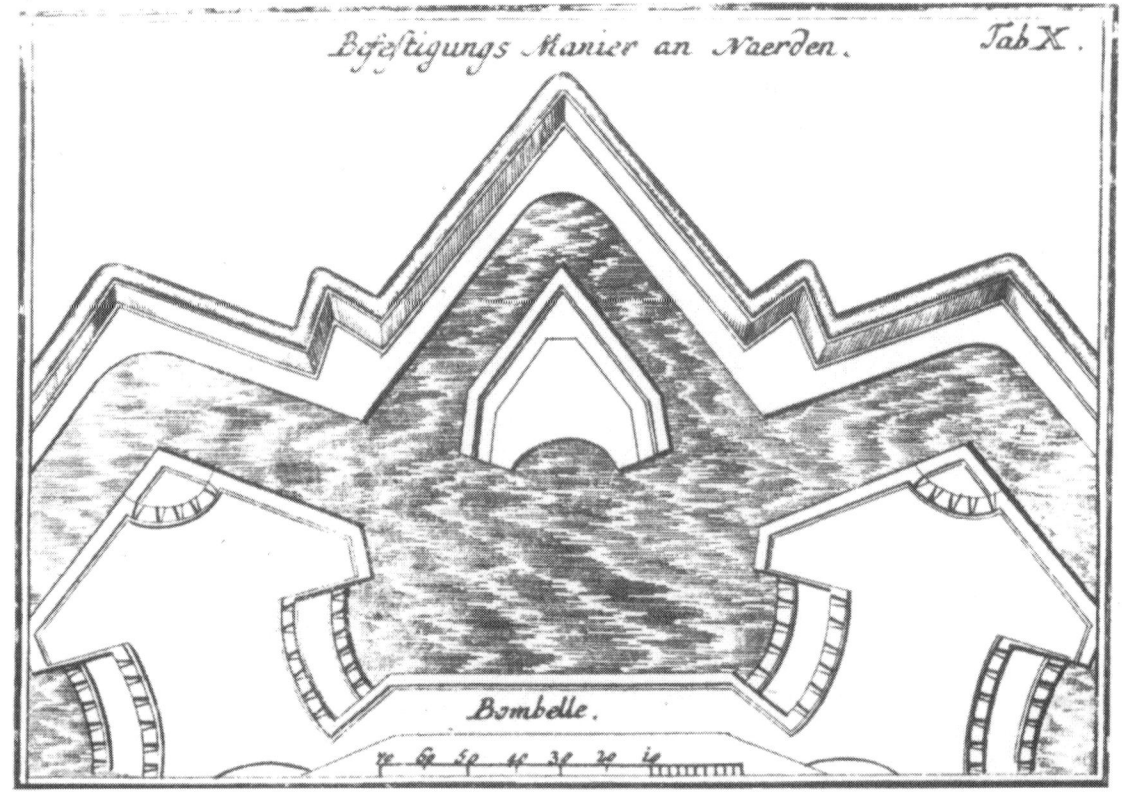

36 Plan of Naarden (Sturm)

hoorn's time it had been the practice to hire a large number of engineers at the beginning of every war, and dismiss all the survivors with the return of peace. A change was apparent soon after Coehoorn became head of military engineering. In 1697, at the end of the War of the League of Augsburg, he had about seventy engineer officers under his command – the largest number in Dutch history until then. Two-thirds of these people were Huguenots, an exceptionally footloose kind of person, but Coehoorn was able to retain most of the Frenchmen in the service of the United Provinces through the unheard-of expedient of retaining all his engineers on the peacetime establishment.

Coehoorn's concern for his engineers sprang from the conviction that fortress warfare was much more than the pitting of material against material. On the contrary, it was about the application of an informed intelligence, 'which explains why some petty fortress with useless works is able to offer a stiff resistance, whereas some strongly-fortified places are lost in no time at all (*Nieuwe Vestingbouw*, 1741, preface).

Coehoorn's fortifications
In contrast to the magnificence and fluency of Vauban's writings, all that Coehoorn has to offer us is a singularly dry, arid and obscure little book, the *Nieuwe Vestingbouw* of 1685 (Full title *Nieuwe Vestingbouw op een Natte of Lage Horisont*, Leeuwarden. German trans. *Des Freiheern von Coehoorn neuer Festungsbau*, Wesel, 1709. French trans. *Nouvelle Fortification*, The Hague, 1706 and 1741).

Written before the period of Coehoorn's greatest achievements, the *Nieuwe Vestingbouw* betrays no sign of personal experience, or of the lessons of the recent war with the French. As we might have expected from Coehoorn's character, however, the argument is clear and forceful when it voices the Dutchman's dislikes. He had little time for the bloated French hornworks, and he launched a concerted attack on the French main rampart, claiming that the revetment was costly and vulnerable –

37 Bastion at Naarden

costly, because it was prolonged all the way down to the bottom of the ditch, and vulnerable because it rose almost to the summit of the rampart and could be seen easily from the open country.

As far as Coehoorn's own principles can be disentangled from the verbiage, they may be summed up as follows:

(i) Powerful close-range defence: like many of his contemporaries, Coehoorn was impressed by the work of the hidden Venetian batteries in delaying the fall of Candia. He sought to reproduce these conditions, in the terrain of the Netherlands, by subjecting the attacker to successive zones of flanking fire, variously delivered from loopholed redoubts in the re-entrant places of arms, from earthen faussebrayes, and from long, concave double bastioned flanks. These works were screened from view by their low profiles, and, in the case of the flanks, by narrow, tower-like orillons of solid masonry.

(ii) Active infantry and cavalry defence: the defend-

38 Double retired bastion flank at Naarden, showing guns emplaced in lower storey

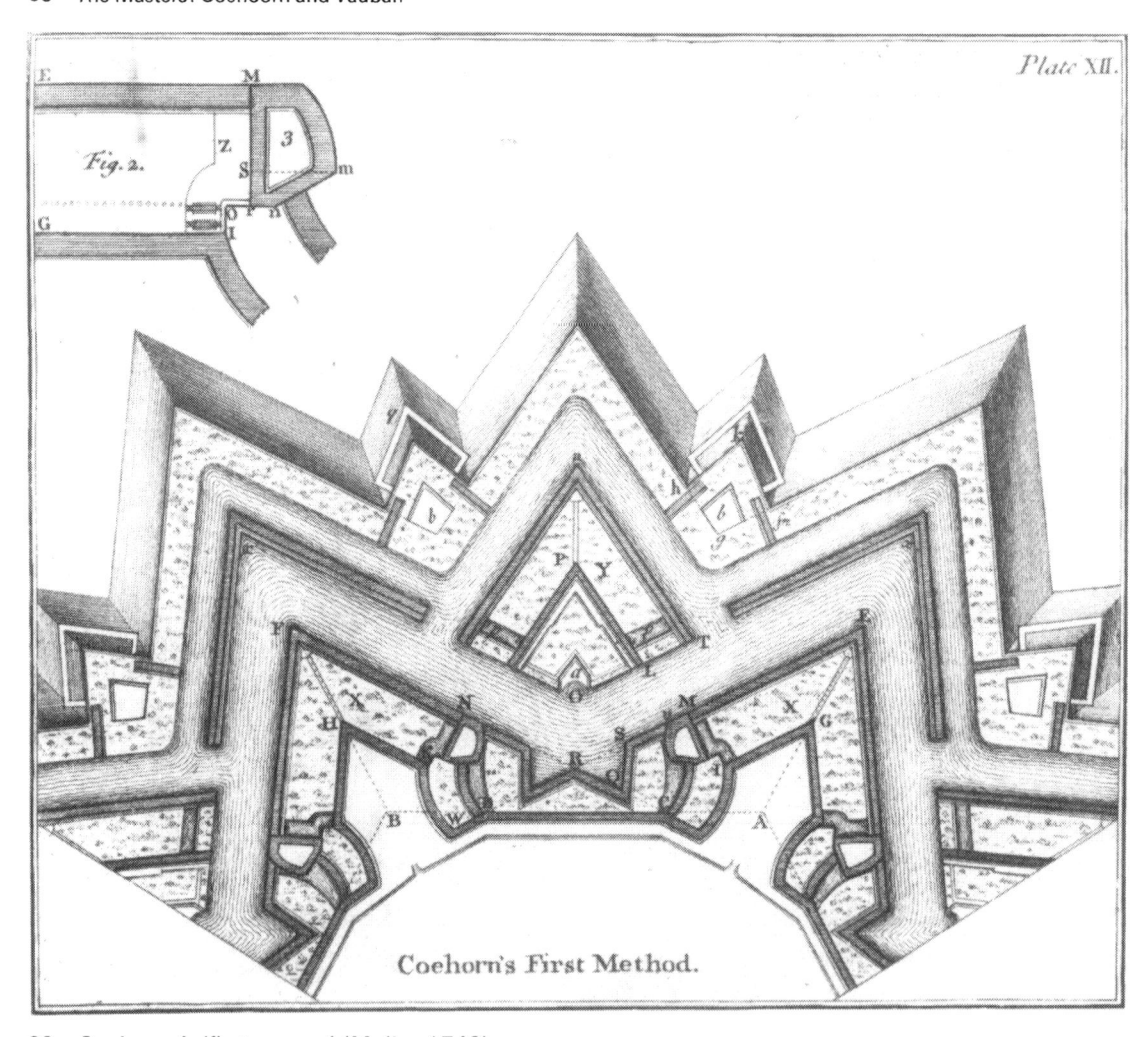

39 Coehoorn's 'first manner' (Muller, 1746)

ing troops were afforded ample space to assemble and move on the wide covered ways and the spacious places of arms.

(iii) *Denial of earth*: Coehoorn protected his works by digging alternate ranks of wet and dry ditches. The dry ditches and covered ways were cunningly cut down to within a few inches of the water table, which gave the defenders freedom of communication, but compelled the besiegers to make their 'passage of the ditch' by the laborious expedient of transporting earth from some distance away. If they dug into the floor of the ditch in the normal way, they would be soon flooded out.

(iv) *Economy of construction*: Coehoorn claimed that his fortress demanded only two-thirds of the quantity of masonry which was needed for the French constructions: 'This great economy results from our practice of beginning our walls on ground

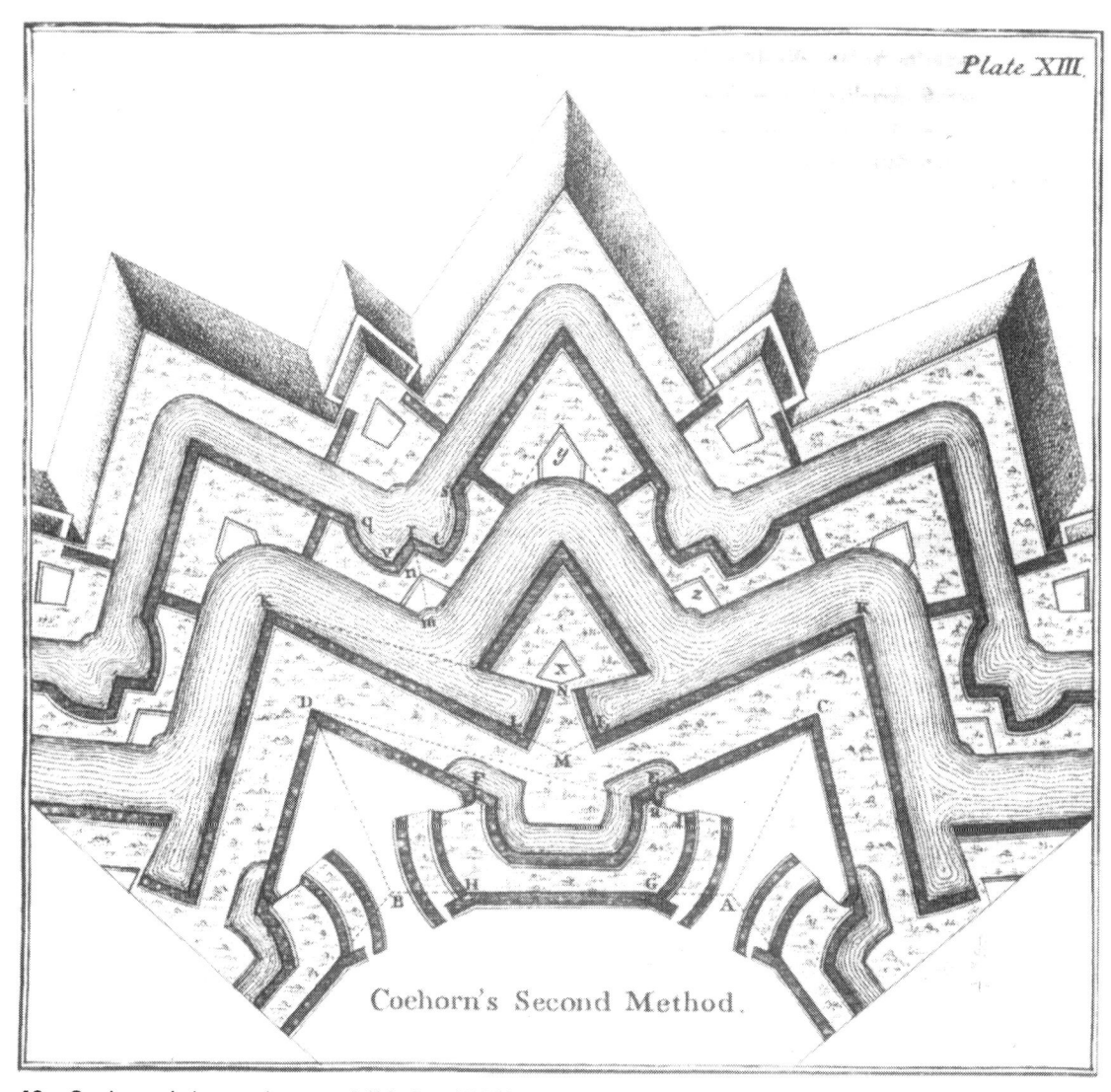

40 Coehoorn's 'second manner' (Muller, 1746)

level, and not from the bottom of the ditch, which is the only means by which "modern systems" may guarantee themselves against surprise' (ibid., 127). This was disingenuous, for Coehoorn relied on the presence of a high water table to avert the danger of mining. He is suspiciously reticent as to how he proposed to construct his own revetments, 'for I wish to keep something secret concerning this method of fortifying' (ibid., 35). Leonhard Christoph Sturm went to Breda and Naarden to see if he could uncover the great mystery, 'but I must say that at neither of these two places could I detect anything of this peculiar economy in masonry, even though I examined the works most attentively both inside and out' (Sturm, 1736, 261). Sturm's voyage to Naarden was bound to end in frustration, since the spectacular fortifications there were not the handiwork of Coehoorn at all, but were probably

70 The Masters: Coehoorn and Vauban

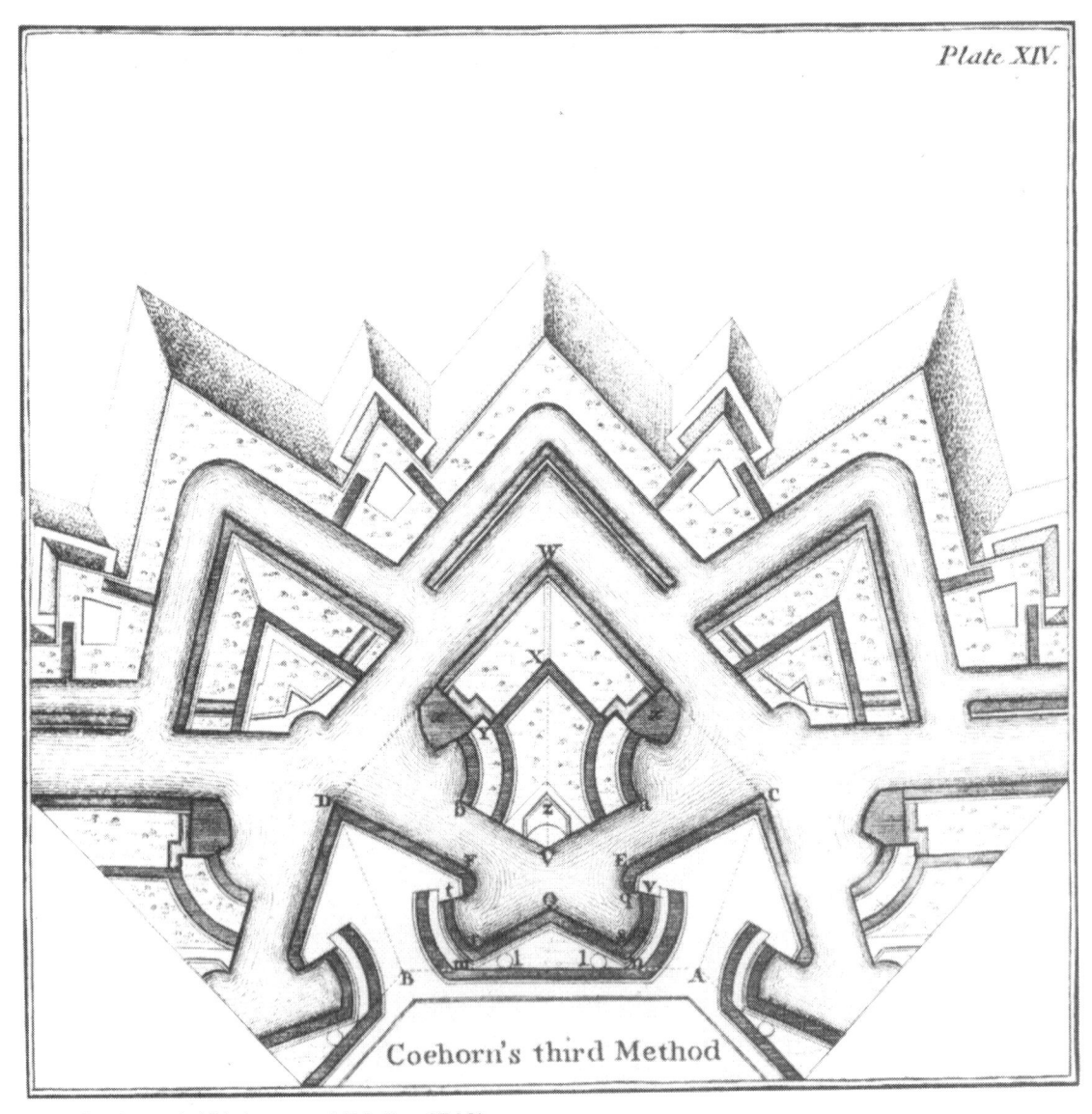

Plate XIV.

Coehorn's third Method

41 Coehoorn's 'third manner' (Muller, 1746)

conceived by Paul Storff de Belleville (see p. 13), and represented French principles as applied to a flat and wet site. Coehoorn, in fact, condemned Naarden ('a certain fortress built in recent years') and Belleville's other fortress at Grave, and he disliked in particular the wide ditches, which opened the scarps to view and fire, and left the covered way without effective support from the main rampart.

Coehoorn gives three traces to illustrate the application of his own principles. In the first of these designs, the weight of the defence rests heavily on the complex which is formed by a combined bastion and fausse-braye. The second trace transfers the emphasis to a continuous envelope, while in the third plan the bastions shrink and the envelope disappears, and their function is largely taken over by enormous ravelins and lunettes.

When it came to actually building on the ground, Coehoorn interpreted his notions on a more modest scale. Elements of his traces may be detected at Bergen-op-Zoom, Nijmegen, Fort William at Namur, Coevorden, Groningen, and at Mannheim, which was re-fortified according to his prescriptions in the early eighteenth century. He by no means considered that he was bound by the recommendations of his own textbook. Outside Groningen, for instance, he built a very Germanic-looking fort which fronted onto the country with a tenaille trace. At Bergen-op-Zoom he subordinated everything to the demands of the site. Here the enceinte took the shape of an hour-glass laid upon its side. The western bulge had a dozen salients, while the eastern side had nine readily recognisable bastions, each with double concave flanks and small orillons. The chief strength of the place resided, however, in the spacious covered way, and in particular in those casemated redoubts that were to give the French such a lot of trouble in 1747.

Sébastien Le Prestre de Vauban 1633–1707

Career and character

Sébastien Le Prestre was born to a poor family of Burgundian gentry on 15 May 1633. He first left his native province in 1651, when he entered as a volunteer in the regiment of the rebel leader the Prince of Condé. Taken prisoner two years later, he was won over to the royalists by Cardinal Mazarin, and sent back to the wars to serve his engineering apprenticeship under the Chevalier de Clerville.

By the late 1660s Vauban's fame had already eclipsed that of his master, but he had to wait until Clerville's death before he was formally recognised as *Commissaire Général des Fortifications* in Louvois's department in 1678. Even then his power derived less from formal rank than from his moral authority and his standing with King Louis. In 1688 he was promoted lieutenant-general, and in January 1703 he became a Marshal of France. He was the first engineer to have ever reached such exalted field

42 Sébastien Le Prestre de Vauban

ranks. He died on 30 March 1707, having sustained eight wounds, directed some forty-eight sieges, and drawn up projects for about 160 fortresses.

Everywhere we find evidence of the strength and breadth of mind which forced from the cynical Saint-Simon the comment:

Vauban concealed outstanding qualities of valour, goodness and probity beneath a rough, coarse and brutal exterior. He was by far the greatest man of his century in the art of fortifications and sieges, and the art of sparing the blood of his men. With all that he was the very soul of simplicity. (Lazard, 1934, 83)

In appearance and manner Vauban was certainly fearsome enough. His great, scarred, leonine head was set on a powerful frame which endured over half a century of hardship and unrelenting activity. His tongue was quick to speak his pronounced likes and dislikes, and ran to Burgundian dialect or words of Vauban's own invention when polite French was incapable of expressing what he intended. He served Louis with a loyalty which stopped very far short of servility, and more than any other soldier of the time he had a concern for the mass of unimportant human beings who sometimes served the royal ambitions, and sometimes stood in the way of them. In February 1669, in the course of an inspection of Pinerolo, he took the trouble to ask Louvois to do something on behalf of

a poor man with eight children, whose only property consists of a few plots of land on the road between Mont Sainte-Brigitte and the citadel. The citadel esplanade has eaten up some of them, and the rest have been stripped of their earth. (22 February, Rochas d'Aiglun, 1910, II, 24–5)

Vauban also entered the lists against the kind of economy which saved money at the expense of the men under his command. In 1675 he declared to Louvois that he

feared for the state of the monarchy when I see garrisons which are made up of companies of children or other poor little wretches who have been snatched from their homes and subjected to all kinds of ill-treatment, and who are commanded by officers who for the most part are as badly off as they are.... How can we rely on the troops, when in most of the fortresses they are lodged like pigs, half naked and half dead of hunger? (11 January, *ibid*., II, 121)

Behind Vauban's correspondence on even the most routine matters we can observe the compassion, the bad temper, the acute observation and the years of experience of the man himself. In such an arid literary form as a topographical report he can describe Château-Queyras as an isolated rock 'surrounded by four great mountains which seem intent on crushing it by their towering mass' (to Le Peletier, 27 September 1700, *ibid*., II, 487) – an almost Wordsworthian image. In 1704 he gives his nephew du Puy Vauban a detailed instruction on his responsibilities as governor of Béthune, and can end with the reminder that

you have a pretty wife... you should do nothing in your household affairs without consulting her. But you must rigidly exclude her from anything which has to do with the king's service or your command. Nothing makes a man more ridiculous than to be ruled by his wife's opinion concerning the execution of his duties.... Well-born little women who know that they are pretty are liable to get above themselves and become difficult to live with. (2 October, *ibid*., II, 550–1)

Vauban attracted and held a wide circle of friends, ranging from Louvois himself, with whom he corresponded on the easiest of terms, to the learned ex-diplomat Baron Woerden, who supplied him with historical arguments, and with Latin inscriptions to set above his gateways.

The scope of the present work provides no opportunity for discussing Vauban's activities as civil engineer, naval strategist, infantry tactician or political economist. Here again the last word must be with Saint-Simon:

You could imagine no finer man or finer patriot. He was always concerned with the promotion of the glory of the state, and the well-being of all its component parts. (Lazard, 1934, 95)

Methods of work
Vauban had to work very hard indeed to give his sieges and fortresses their aspect of almost mechanical perfection. In the course of the attack on Luxembourg in 1684 he let slip the rare admission that 'these labours, together with the effort of the two journeys I have to make to the trenches every day, leave me so exhausted that when I return to my quarters I am incapable of moving hand or foot (to Louvois, 4 June, Rochas d'Aiglun, 1910, II, 245).

Vauban spent almost every winter in Paris, poring over sheets of plans. For the rest of the year (when he was not actually on campaign) he spent most of the time touring the frontiers in his coach, or, when the going was especially bad, in a litter suspended between two mules. He once complained half-seriously to Louvois about the labour of inspecting a fortress. When you were reviewing troops, they at least marchd to the mustering place on their own feet, but

there is not a single watch-tower in all the king's fortresses which will move so much as an inch at my command.... Just think of all the tramping

43 The Maintenon Aqueduct. Built from 1685, at the insistence of Louvois, to carry the waters of the Eure to the new palace of Versailles. One of Vauban's most famous essays in civil engineering

back and forth which is involved in making a thorough inspection of those huge masses of inert material which make up a fortress. (10 May 1696, *ibid*., II, 203)

Fortunately Vauban possessed such a sharp eye for ground that he could draw up his projects with great speed, even though on every occasion he had to compose a large portfolio which was made up of the *lettre d'envoi* (a covering letter), the main *mémoire* (giving details of the site, of the projected works, of the methods of construction, and of the properties of the works when complete), and several sheets of plans which he usually drew up in his own hand. The local engineers usually saw to the details, though Vauban was always in touch with what was going on. He never forgot the consequences of a brief moment of inattention in 1667, when he had almost brought his career to an abrupt end by unwittingly signing his name to false accounts for the fortifications at Breisach.

The defensive works proper formed only one element of the complex which made up a seventeenth-century stronghold. The gates were supposed to look good, as well as guard the entries securely, and in 1681 Vauban was quick to defend himself against Louvois's accusation that the two portals of the Strasbourg citadel were too splendid and costly:

I must beg to differ . . . for Strasbourg is the

44 Bastion at Fort Nieulay, Calais. Showing the salient of dressed stone, the outer skin of bricks, laid end-on into the scarp, and the interior of courses of bricks and unshaped stones. A rare example of the collapse of one of Vauban's structures, probably caused by the heavy shelling of 1940

gateway to France for the whole of Germany, and because the Germans (who are possessed of an insatiable curiosity and who are usually good connoisseurs) are liable to form their estimation of the magnificence of the king and the strength of the fortress from the beauty of its gates. (10 December, *ibid.*, II, 203)

Barracks were formed around the inner rim of the enceinte, to accommodate the garrisons of the powerful new standing army, and for this purpose Vauban evolved a rather gloomy-looking standard block, built up of staircase modules housing 144 men each. More successfully, perhaps, Vauban designed a powder magazine which remained the official type in France until 1874. The building reconciled security with ventilation, and consisted of a thick roof, resting on a massive single-span arch which sprang from below ground level. Artillery, tools and muskets by the thousand were likewise stored in purpose-built arsenals.

To help him in his calculations, Vauban worked out sets of tables, which related the garrison, armament and interior space to various numbers of bastions. Except in the smallest works, the stronghold invariably embraced a civilian community, which forced Vauban and his engineers to become urbanists. Where he had freedom of action, Vauban liked to arrange the streets in a gridiron fashion, formed around a central square where you found such imposing establishments as the garrison church and the governor's *hôtel*. Uniformity of architectural taste was imposed throughout the town by *cahiers de charge*, which went into some detail on matters like ornaments, building lines and heights of elevations.

The French engineering corps

We have already touched on the rise of Vauban to supreme power in engineering matters. Already in 1668 he had replaced Clerville as adviser to Louvois, the Minister of War, and ten years later, after Clerville's death, he was formally made *Commissaire Général*. Two further deaths promoted the centralisation of control. The Marquis de Seignelay, who was the son of Jean-Baptiste Colbert, and his successor as Minister of Marine, died in 1690. Louvois himself died in July 1691, and now at last it was possible to think about uniting the two branches of engineering administration – that of the War Ministry, which saw to fortifications in the newly conquered territories, and had a predominance of semi-military attack engineers (*ingénieurs de Tranchée*), and that of the Ministry of Marine, which was responsible for coastal and interior fortresses, and was staffed by civilian construction engineers (*ingénieurs de places*). On 22 July 1691 the whole of engineering administration was united under a *Directeur Général*, Michel Le Peletier de Souzy, as chief of a new *Département des Fortifications des Places de Terre et de Mer*. Le Peletier's expertise was of an administrative kind, and for advice on technical matters he looked in the first place to the immensely experienced engineer Louis Lapara des Fieux. However, Le Peletier was an old associate of Vauban's, and the new *Département* promoted rather than detracted from Vauban's control of engineering affairs.

45 Countermine gallery, ravelin at Le Quesnoy. Revealed by tree-damage at this sadly neglected fortress

Vauban's France I

46 Entrevaux. Part of the town wall, as re-fortified to the designs of Vauban after his visit in 1700. Sited at the end of a descending knife-edge of rock, this closely packed medieval town barred the upper valley of the Var. It was again put in a state of defence during the Austro-Piedmontese invasion of the Mediterranean coastlands in 1746–7

47 Colmars. A small town in the foothills of the Alpes Maritimes, re-fortified by Vauban with casemated towers and a free-standing loopholed wall (shown here) in the shape of a ravelin

The Masters: Coehoorn and Vauban 77

48 Redoubt outside Colmars. Now called 'Fort Soult', this little work occupies a hillock which could not be incorporated in the main position

49 Sisteron. The plug-like limestone rock of Sisteron is sited at a point where the valley of the Durance narrows between tall hills. It therefore commanded an important avenue between Provence and Dauphiné. The rock was originally fortified in 1597 by Jean Errard de Bar-le-Duc, and drastic measures were taken to protect the interior from fire from the outlying heights – most notable is the tall arcaded screen wall to the right of the photograph. Vauban re-made some of the works after the Piedmontese incursion down the Durance in 1692

What Vauban thought about the demands of his profession is best shown in a celebrated letter to Le Peletier of 17 February 1693:

Engineering is a trade which is beyond our capacity, for it embraces so many things that no individual is able to master all the elements with real proficiency. I am vain enough to believe that I am as good an engineer as any ... but when I look at myself I see that I am still only half an engineer, after forty years of furious application and an unrivalled experience. (*ibid.*, II, 380)

Vauban's own activity went far towards increasing the number and proficiency of the king's engineers. By 1696 France possessed 280 of these officers, and all of them had felt the influence of Vauban through his personal example, his correspondence, and the circulation of his memoranda in manuscript form.

Vauban was able to exercise his authority in a more direct form after 1697, when Le Peletier ruled that in future the king would admit as engineers only those officers who had undergone examination by Vauban, or, in his absence, the mathematician Sauveur. From the evidence of *Le Directeur Général des Fortifications* (a memorandum written by Vauban in 1676 or 1677) it is likely that he first subjected the candidates to tests in geometry, surveying, mechanics, arithmetic, geography, civil architecture and drawing, then sent them away for a one- or two-year practical noviciate before recalling them for a final examination. He appointed some of the most proficient engineers as regional *ingénieurs directeurs*, responsible for groups of fortresses, a principle which was incorporated in the bureaucratic structure of the eighteenth century.

If anything, the new stringency concerning standards seems to have enhanced the attractiveness of the profession of military engineer. Nobles and commoners were represented in roughly equal proportions (where you might have expected the bourgeois element to predominate), and in 1706 Jean-Anténor de Caligny noted that 'this trade has become so fashionable that numbers of officers of good family are making haste to secure admission' (Blanchard, 1979, 120).

This was, in fact, the formative period of the French engineers, and Vauban endowed the corps with an unrivalled prestige and professionalism. In the nineteenth century the Prussian general von Zastrow paid a striking compliment:

Any soldier must be filled with the deepest respect for the French engineering corps, looking back on the past or the more recent episodes of fortress warfare in which French engineer officers have played a part, whether as defenders or assailants of strongholds. These officers fight not only with intelligence but with the most selfless courage, and they are as adept with the sword as the pen. (Zastrow, 1854, 463)

In some ways, indeed, Vauban's ambitions were so far ahead of his time that they were impossible to realise. In 1672 and again in 1675 Vauban asked Louvois to allow him to create 'Brigades' of trained sappers, gunners, miners and artificers. These would help the engineers proper to direct siegeworks and field fortifications, and in general spread the doctrine of true engineering in the army. He returned to the theme in 1684, complaining that 'at the moment I have to use a collection of men who have been scavenged from various sources. I don't know them – and they don't know or understand me' (6 June, Rochas d'Aiglun, 1910, II, 249).

Louvois could not grasp what Vauban meant when he applied the word 'sapper' to these strange mixed bodies of engineer officers and expert private soldiers. This was a kind of organisation which became firmly established in Europe only in the nineteenth century. Vauban had to be satisfied with being able to found the first permanent company of French miners in 1679.

The siege attack
Vauban established the routine of the siege attack as it was to remain almost unaltered for the best part of two centuries.

At Maastricht in 1673 he showed how the trenches could march forward by successive parallels and zigzags, taking a major fortress in just ten days and at a fraction of the cost in lives that might have been expected. The principles were summed up in the manual *Military Engineering (Part II) Attack and Defence of Fortresses*, 1910, which the British Army took to France in 1914:

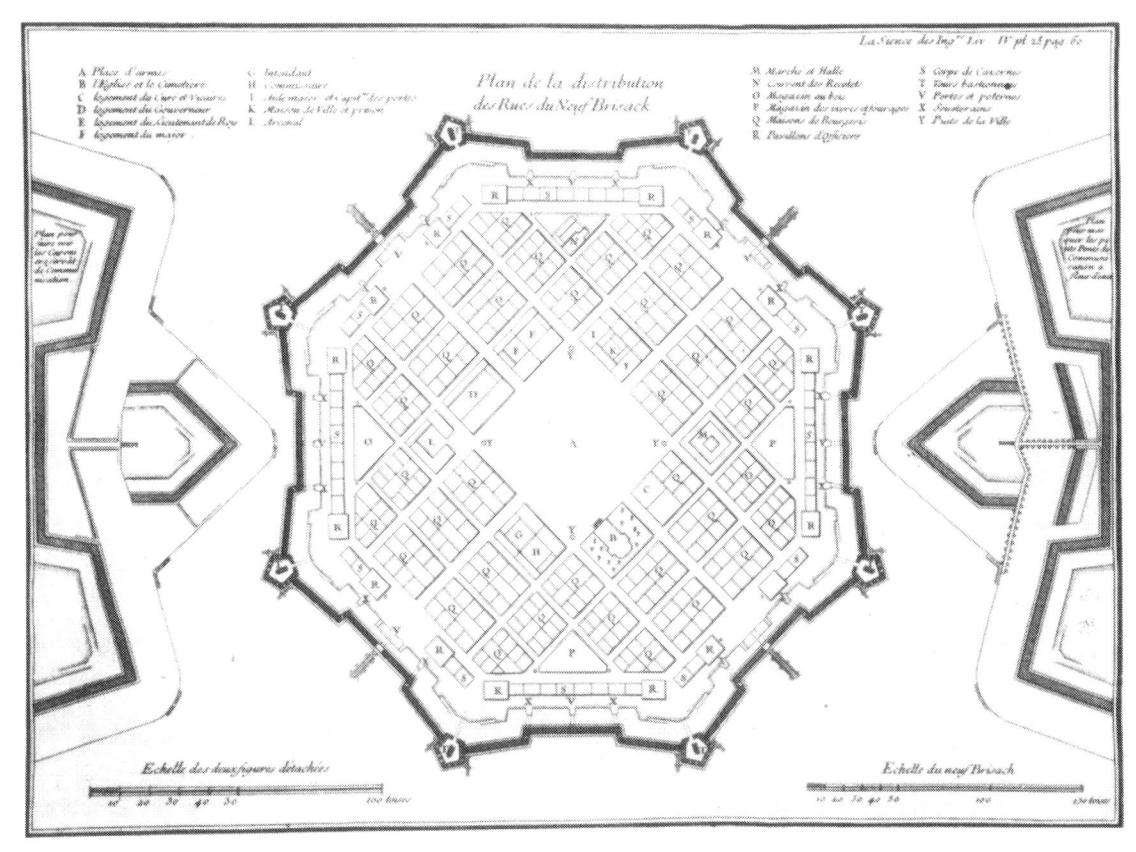

50 Street plan of Neuf-Brisach

It is necessary that approaches be so laid out that they cannot be enfiladed from any part of the enemy's position. For a considerable portion of the advance to the fortress this object can be attained by making each approach in zigzags. . . . Since an approach is practically end on to the fortress, it can as a rule furnish little effective fire towards its own defence, and must be protected by other works. Therefore, after the approaches have been pushed forward for some distance, or concurrently with the work on them, a position must be prepared . . . to protect them, roughly parallel to the line of the enemy's works. Such a position is called a parallel. (p. 22)

Under Vauban's direction, the corresponding artillery attack finally attained the degree of specialisation towards which it had been tending since the beginning of the seventeenth century. From their position in the second parallel the ricochet batteries cleared the fortress parapets of men and guns, and permitted the saps to reach the covered way, from where the breaching batteries could open up the bastions and ravelins at close range. The siege of Luxembourg in 1684 had shown the mortars to be a powerful adjunct of the attack. These too were assigned a specialised task – that of raining down their bombs on the interior of the fortifications. Vauban, however, believed that the generalised cannonade of a town was as useless as it was brutal, and he opposed the idea of bombarding Brussels when it was first mooted in 1691,

for it seems to me that the cannonades of Oudenarde, Luxembourg and even that of Liège not only failed to win an inch of ground for the king, but used up great quantities of ammunition to no purpose, and tired and weakened the troops. (17 July, Rochas d'Aiglun, 1910, II, 327)

51 Redoubt in a place of arms at Mont-Dauphin, showing 'mouse steps' leading from the ditch

Like Coehoorn, Vauban devised a special weapon to help him to clear the enemy infantry from the outworks of a fortress. The first experiments were staged in 1672, when he showed that whole wheelbarrows' worth of stones could be fired from a mortar with devastating effect. The example was followed all over Europe, and for this purpose the standard mortar was eventually replaced by a light but large-calibre version called the 'pierrier'.

Vauban lacked direct authority over the artillery corps, and it was not until 1697, at the siege of Ath, that he could bring the artillery attack to its perfection. He had complained four years earlier that the artillerymen were

ignorant of the principles of fortification, and never knew how to aim and fire their pieces.... I do not find this altogether surprising, since most of them are soldiers who are assigned from the infantry, and recognise the authority of the professional gunners [*commissaires*] only when it pleases them. (To Le Peletier, 19 October, *ibid.*, II, 399–400)

The mine attack was the subject of important experiments in 1685 and 1686. Vauban was particularly pleased at the work of Lamotte at Valenciennes, who devised tables of charges and the resulting craters. Unfortunately, Vauban drew the false conclusion that no charge, however heavy, was capable of producing a crater the diameter of which would exceed the 'line of the least resistance' (the depth of the charge beneath the surface) multiplied twofold. The development of mine warfare was therefore retarded until Belidor invented the 'globe of compression', or supercharged mine, in the middle of the eighteenth century.

By the time Vauban had completed his work it took an exceptionally obstinate defence to compel the besieger to go to the trouble of digging mines at all. As Vauban observed,

You should not be surprised ... that fortresses give up more quickly than in earlier times. Nowadays the garrisons are severely weakened by having to guard the additional outworks, the defence of which exhausts and consumes a great many troops, and by the advantages of the attack, which are more pronounced than in former days.... There is not a single garrison (and I mean that literally) which will be rash enough to commit itself to a last-ditch defence, and incur the almost certain fate of being overpowered and cut to pieces. (*Traité des Siéges*, 1704, 1829, 201)

Later engineers were in no doubt as to the extent of the debt they owed to Vauban:

Before he came on the scene, the siege attack was an indiscriminate and senseless chaos, a labyrinthine accumulation of dangerous and numberless works. This was because the only resource of the besiegers was an inexhaustible courage, which was often more fatal than beneficial in its results. If we have made a few discoveries since Vauban's time, the glory still belongs to him, because he was the man who set us on the right path. (Lefèbvre, 1778, I, vii–viii)

The defence

Compared with the revolution which Vauban effected in the art of taking fortresses, his views on how to defend them are of no great significance. His *Traité de la Défense des Places* was composed in a hurry, directly after the manifold French disasters of 1706, and it is an extraordinary fact that Vauban, the great master of fortress warfare, was never once discovered in a fortress under siege. His draftsman Thomassin unhelpfully records:

Like many other people I often heard him say that his one remaining wish was to find himself under siege, for he had worked out an infallible method of defending a fortress. His friends often questioned him on this head, but he died without giving a word of his secret away. (Augoyat, 1860–4, I, 300)

More than most authorities of the time Vauban placed the main burden of the defence on the artillery, and especially on the 18- and 12-pounders and guns of even smaller calibre. He maintained that the government could afford to equip the fortresses with a great quantity of cannon, if the barrels were of iron instead of the exceedingly costly bronze. However, he was never able to persuade the *Grand-Maître de l'Artillerie*, the Duc de Maine, to experiment in the manufacture of iron pieces. As for the carriages, he argued that the best model was the naval type which he had devised in the early 1690s for Dunkirk, Ypres and Mons: 'Without using carriages of this kind there are all sorts of places where you will be unable to lodge your cannon – namely lower flanks, round towers and bastion towers (to an unknown correspondent, 15 January 1693, Rochas d'Aiglun, 1910, II, 369). Here again Vauban proved to be too far in advance of his time. King Louis ruled that all fortress cannon must be mounted on the ordinary field carriages, for otherwise the armies would not be able to borrow them for use on campaign.

Vauban's other chief concern was to husband the human resources of the defence: 'Do not waste the courage and strength of your troops in useless enterprises ... do not commit them unless you are sure that they will be able to retreat, and that they will remain close enough to be supported by your fire' (to the Marquis de Blainville, 14 March 1702, *ibid.*, II, 505). Vauban actually believed that it was wrong to hold out for too long in the covered way, a doctrine which Boufflers deliberately ignored in his defence of Lille in 1708.

Vauban's fortifications

The neo-Pagan trace. It must also come as a surprise to consider that Vauban never got down to writing a treatise on fortification. For most of his plans he simply worked on the basis of the straightforward, well-proportioned trace which he inherited from Pagan. This was Vauban's so-called 'first system', which he actually used in all normal cases throughout his life. The conformation of the bastions was one which the eye readily accepts as natural – neither so obtuse and bulky as the Italian, nor so acute or spiky as the Netherlandish. The flanks were sometimes straight, and sometimes retired and concave and furnished with orillons. In the more important fortresses, such as Ypres and Lille, hornworks were employed with profusion, 'and placed ... often so near each other, as would incline one to believe that

52 Villefranche-de-Conflent, Bastion du Dauphin. This little fortress in the eastern Pyrenees shows how Vauban solved the problems presented by a narrow site overlooked by mountains. Here we see a loopholed and casemated bastion which offered good protection against Spanish miquelet snipers

he rather intended more to terrify an enemy by their numbers, than to strengthen the place' (Muller, 1746, 83).

Vauban's one contribution to the Pagan trace was to take up a suggestion of Floriani (*Difesa et Offesa della Piaze*, Venice, 1630, 1654) and apply a stretch of the Netherlandish fausse-braye to protect the curtain. This tenaille also served to screen the assembly of sorties, and to command the bottom of the ditch by fire.

Vauban applied the motifs of the neo-Pagan trace with great freedom and flexibility. Very often he had to reckon with existing fortifications and town buildings. At Tournai, for instance, he decided to keep the medieval town wall as a continuous curtain, and reinforce it by four hornworks and ten detached bastions. Mountainous sites were the most challenging of all:

Vauban was the first engineer who consistently arranged the trace and regulated the profile of his fortresses according to the surrounding terrain. He managed to keep his works low-lying, and thus screened from external view – an effect which earlier engineers had been able to produce only by dint of heaping up traverses and cavaliers. (Bousmard, 1797–9, I, 22–3)

Vauban also had to consider the element of time, as well as the more obvious demands of ground. At some vital sites the first priority was to plant a powerful citadel outside the old enceinte, to serve as an independent and rapidly-available focus of defence (e.g. Lille, Arras). Once the work was complete, he ran long straight ramparts (*branches de jonction*) from the citadel to the enceinte. When these in turn were ready, he considered it safe to demolish

53 Bastion at Villefranche-de-Conflent. Here the rampart is protected by a heavy timber gallery

the now-superfluous town fronts which faced the citadel.

Vauban's freshness of outlook retained a strong appeal for soldiers who were repelled by the spirit of academic formalism which pervaded French military engineering in later times. One century afterwards Michaud d'Arçon pointed out that 'Monsieur Vauban was so skilful at adapting himself to the various irregularities of terrain, that you frequently find no sign of uniformity or even of a systematic layout' (1786, 11). Even the Prussian Zastrow conceded that Vauban surpassed all engineers before or since in his masterly application of fortification to ground, 'and the possession of this art is the hallmark of a truly great engineer' (1854, 167).

Vauban's 'bastion tower' system. Vauban's search for compact, fully-covered works, which would be tenable even when the fortress was dominated by neighbouring heights, led him in 1687 to devise the hollow, loopholed masonry bastions which are called 'bastion towers' (Vauban's 'second system'). In April of that year he designed bastion towers for two fronts at Besançon. Going on to Belfort, he devised a double enceinte which consisted of an inner rampart set with bastion towers, and an outer circuit of detached bastions and tenailles. Vauban was so pleased with his invention that in October he adopted it in his design for Landau, a fortress which was set in a marshy plain. All three schemes were carried out. In other words the bastion tower arrangement had become a system which could be applied on almost any site, providing that very considerable funds were available. Vauban explains that:

In essentials the bastion tower is a very strong retrenchment, which is capable of putting up a powerful resistance after the detached bastion in front has fallen. In an ordinary fortress, when the bastions are breached the whole enceinte is breached, and you cannot hold out unless you run the risk of seeing the garrison overwhelmed at the same time as the bastions. This cannot occur in the new system, where the only troops at risk are the ones in the individual work actually under attack. (Augoyat, 1860–4, I, 144–5)

In 1697 France suffered such heavy losses at the Peace of Rijswijk that the king sent Vauban once more to the Rhine plain, this time to build a fortress

54 Bastion tower, on the bend of the River Doubs at Besançon

that had the heavy responsibility of holding Freiburg and Breisach in awe. 'Neuf-Brisach', as the place was called, was fortified according to a project which Vauban put forward in June 1698. Significantly enough he turned to the bastion tower trace, and added a few modifications – giving the ravelin a casemated redoubt, and recessing the central portion of the curtain so as to provide casemated shoulders or flanks on either side of the bastion tower (the 'third system'). This design probably represents the culmination of bastion fortification, combining as it did the advantages of a well-proportioned enceinte on the conventional plan, with those of hidden, casemated works which remained intact for the last, decisive stage of the defence.

The system was magnificent, but nobody was prepared to take it up after Vauban died. In the first place the numerous corridors and casemates made the undertaking far more costly than 'solid' fortresses of the same dimensions. Neuf-Brisach alone is known to have consumed 2,916,565 livres by the end of 1705. The deciding factor against the adoption of the system was, however, the increasing dogmatism of the eighteenth-century French engineering corps, which dismissed most casemates as smoky and Germanic.

Entrenched camps

Vauban and his royal master had done their work almost too well. Decades of French aggrandisement ultimately provoked a European reaction which became all the more formidable when the enemy alliances borrowed some of Vauban's siege techniques. The evolution of the bastion tower represented just one of the efforts to bottle up the genie which the French had so unwisely released.

Vauban saw that static, permanent fortresses alone were incapable of staying the Allied counter-offensive, and with increasing urgency he tried to convince the French that they must follow the example of their German enemies, and ensconce their armies in fortified camps and lines. On 28 May 1693 he asked his correspondent Baron Woerden to supply him with historical examples of entrenched camps from the time of Ziska the Hussite to that of Ludwig of Baden, who was the greatest modern practitioner of the art of fieldworks:

I am very well aware of the value of entrenched camps, but I need the authority of great men to help me to convert our misguided nation, which believes that you must be ready to do battle wherever you happen to be, and that as long as you strike hard you need not bother about anything else. (Rochas d'Aiglun, 1910, II, 388)

The French certainly learnt to be mighty diggers in the War of the Spanish Succession, and before he died Vauban had the satisfaction of seeing the marshals try their hand at every branch of field fortification – there was Villars's blocking position at Sierck on the Moselle in 1705, there were the Lines of Brabant, and finally there was Vauban's own entrenched camp outside Dunkirk, which helped to deter the Allies from penetrating French Flanders after the battle of Ramillies.

The national frontiers
Whether Vauban was building a fortress of his own, or snatching one from the enemy, his consistent aim was to create a coherent, defensible frontier, which was arranged, if possible, 'in two lines of fortresses . . . like an army drawn up for battle' (*Mémoire sur les Places Frontières de Flandres*, November 1678, *ibid.*, I, 189).

In the north he created the *frontière de fer*, the

55 Bastion tower at Belfort

86 The Masters: Coehoorn and Vauban

56 The 'third system' at Neuf-Brisach. The dotted lines indicate the angle of Illustration 57

57 Rampart at Neuf-Brisach, showing (left to right) the recessed curtain, bastion flank and face, and the bastion tower (with blocked-up embrasures)

double line of fortresses which was never completely broken through even in the blackest days of the War of the Spanish Succession (first line: Dunkirk, Bergues, Furnes, Knocke, Ypres, Menin, Lille, Tournai, Fort de Mortagne, Condé, Valenciennes, Le Quesnoy, Maubeuge, Philippeville, Dinant. Second line: Gravelines, Saint-Omer, Aire, Béthune, Arras, Douai, Bouchain, Cambrai, Landrecies, Avesnes, Mariembourg, Rocroi, Charleville. All according to the above memorandum.)

The frontier was prolonged to the south-east by another double row of fortresses which interposed a corridor between the debatable lands of Luxembourg and Lorraine (first line: Sedan, Montmédy, Longwy, Thionville. Second line: Verdun, Metz). The possession of Metz by itself, said Vauban, was as good as having a corps of troops in the centre of Lorraine. On the Rhenish frontier the fortresses of Landau, Philippsburg, Breisach and Freiburg came and went, but Vauban built rearward supports at Belfort and Besançon, and France never lost the advantage she derived from the bloodless occupation of Strasbourg in 1681, a place that was 'worth more by itself than the whole of the rest of Alsace' (Vauban to Racine, 13 September 1696, Rochas d'Aiglun, 1910, II, 446). Considering the northern and eastern frontiers as a whole, Vauban was entranced by the reflection that (except for a couple of gaps) you would be within earshot of French fortress guns all the way from the Swiss border to the Channel.

On the other hand Vauban was utterly weary of the Italian wars, which resulted from Louis's desire to gain territorial equivalents which he might exchange for tracts of land elsewhere. Vauban believed that it was mad extravagance to allow a fortress like Casale, which was isolated in the Italian plain, to take more than six million livres out of the kingdom between 1691 and 1695. In his view it was better to put the mountain frontier in good order than to pursue 'vain ambitions beyond the Alps' (to Le Peletier, 17 February 1693, *ibid.*, II, 376). He was sure that his works at Briançon would prove to be a fine investment,

for the two most practicable roads from Dauphiné to Piedmont branch off from here. This fortress should therefore support Exilles and Fenestrelle by its magazines, and in the event of one or the other being lost, it should supply the deficiency, halting the progress of the enemy and covering the country. (To Le Peletier, 27 September 1700, *ibid.*, II, 491)

The course of the War of the Spanish Succession bore out Vauban's reasoning – Italy proved untenable, and Briançon became the pivot of the manoeuvres by which Berwick defended the 'natural frontier' of the Alps.

The next avenue to the south was the valley of the middle Durance, down which the Piedmontese ranged so destructively in 1692. It was therefore under some pressure from Louis and the interests in Haut-Dauphiné that Vauban built the new fortress of Mont-Dauphin, occupying the plateau of Mille-Aures on a site that commanded the Durance valley and the exit of the Queyras valley.

Southwards again, towards the Mediterranean, Vauban strengthened the little castles and towns on the French side of the mountains (Colmars, Entrevaux, etc.), for 'it seems to me illogical to bolster up all our other frontiers with two lines of fortresses, and not have a single line of strongholds in Upper Provence' (to Le Peletier, 19 November 1700, *ibid.*, II, 491). The seaward flank was closed up by the new fortifications at Antibes and the conquered strongholds of the County of Nice, 'a fortified region which will prove impenetrable to enemy attack by land or sea' (to Le Peletier, 15 February 1693, Lazard, 1934, 239. Vauban's use of the term 'fortified region' seemed strikingly modern to Frenchmen in the 1930s). Well inside this frontier, the authorities sought to subjugate the Huguenots of Languedoc by building roads across the stony Cevennes, and building or strengthening citadels or enceintes like those at Carcassonne, Narbonne, Pont-Saint-Esprit, Nîmes, Sommières, Alès and Saint-Hyppolyte-du-Fort.

On the Pyrenean frontier the citadel and fortress town of Perpignan continued to fulfil their well-established role as depot and support for campaigning in Catalonia. Further inland a potentially dangerous avenue from the Cerdagne was sealed off by the fortified village of Villefranche, and the powerful

Vauban's France II

58 Bastion salient, Montreuil. Bastions were added to the walls of this medieval fortress in the reign of Henry IV. Its position above the Canche made it of some value even in the later seventeenth century, by when the advance of the frontier had left it stranded well to the rear of the main lines of northern fortresses

59 Fortified harbour, Saint-Martin de Rhé

60 Brouage. This old Huguenot stronghold on the Bay of Biscay was one of the most important commercial ports of the Atlantic coast. The decision to re-fortify the place was taken by the royal government in 1628, and work was completed in 1640 to the designs of d'Argencourt. However, the gradual silting of the harbour defied all the efforts of the engineers, including Vauban in 1685, and Brouage became the sleepy place it is today, where the loudest noise is often the clicking and purring of the frogs in the boggy levels outside

90 The Masters: Coehoorn and Vauban

61 Montmédy Citadel. An old fortress adapted by Vauban – one of his new ravelins is on the right. This was once a Spanish outpost on the north-eastern borders of France, in an area heavily disputed since the old wars of Habsburg and Valois. Captured by the French with the aid of Vauban in 1657, in one of the most hard-fought sieges of his early career. Recently restored, and well repays a visit

new citadel and massive hornwork of Mont-Louis (1679–c. 91) – a high and remote posting which was regarded with horror by French officers. On the corresponding western flank of the Pyrenees the town of Bayonne was encased in new fortifications and put under the guard of a citadel on the north bank of the Adour. Northwards up the Biscay coast the access up the Gironde to Bordeaux was barred by an island fort, and by the immensely strong right-bank citadel of Blaye (built 1685–9), a work which caused Vauban immense satisfaction. In the most distant north-west, the Tour de Camaret and other works around Brest helped to preserve France's opening to the north Atlantic.

Vauban knew that his fortresses comprised just one element in the scheme of national defence, and he was very well aware that every one of his larger strongholds represented an average loss of two or three thousand men to the field armies, and a heavy annual drain on the treasury. He wrote prophetically to Catinat on 7 April 1687:

You are quite correct to say that the excessive number of fortresses in France is an inconvenience which it is easy to overlook, as long as we are on the attack rather than the defensive. I could not agree with you more. If we are faced with a great war I fear very much that the danger will be all too evident with the first campaign. (Catinat, 1819, I, 35)

When Vauban demolished many superfluous places he was therefore making a substantial contribution to France's defence (among the slighted fortresses were Ham, Corbie, Le Castelet, La Capelle and La Fère in Picardy; Château-Porcien, Damvillers, and Stenay in the Meuse-Argonne region; Bellegarde in Burgundy). He even proposed three of his own creations for destruction, namely Mont-Louis, Mont-Royal and Huningue.

In all of this we must not forget that Vauban's role was primarily a consultative and executive one. The choice of priorities and the ultimate decisions

The Masters: Coehoorn and Vauban 91

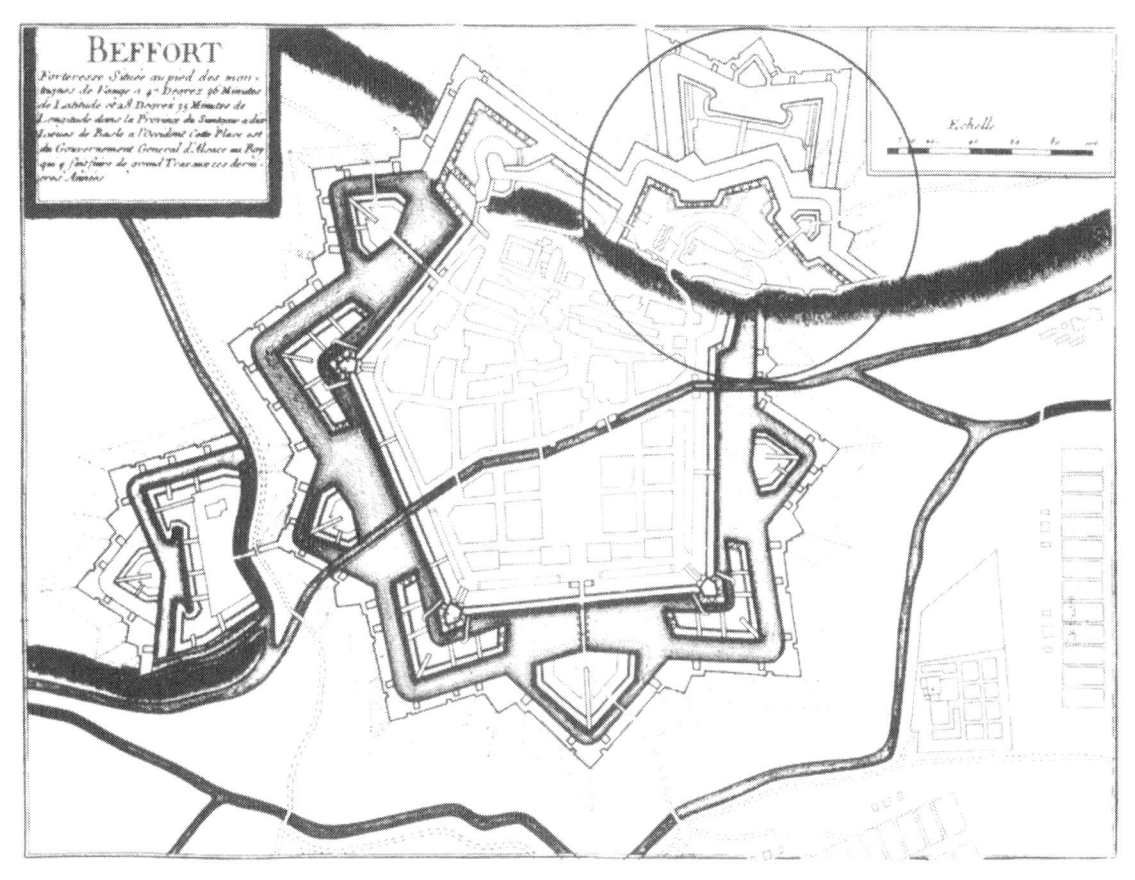

62 Plan of Belfort, showing the enceinte with bastion towers and the citadel (circled) at the top right (De Fer, 1690–5)

63 Belfort Citadel, with shell damage from the famous Prussian siege of 1871

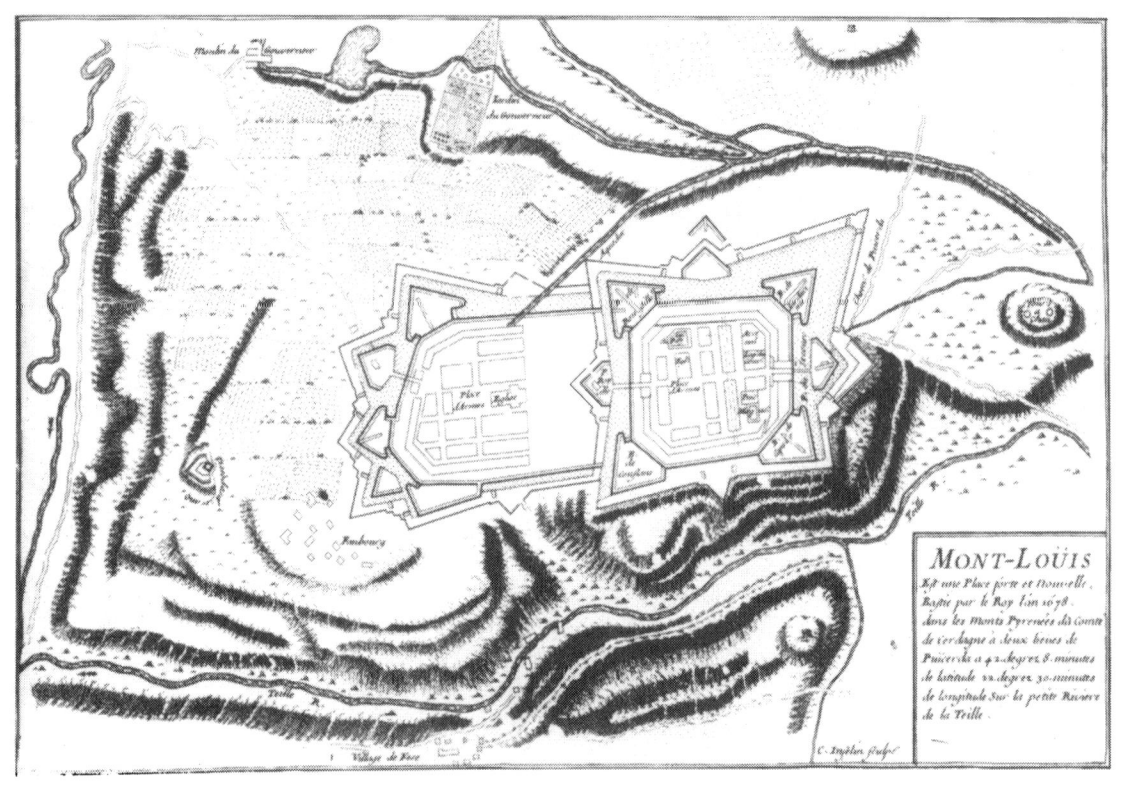

64 Mont-Louis. Plan of the citadel, and the town inside the massive hornwork (De Fer, 1690–5)

65 Ravelin of the hornwork at Mont-Louis

The Masters: Coehoorn and Vauban 93

66 View along one of the branches of the hornwork at Mont-Louis

68 Treadwheel, for raising water from the well in Mont-Louis Citadel

67 Hornwork gate, Mont-Louis

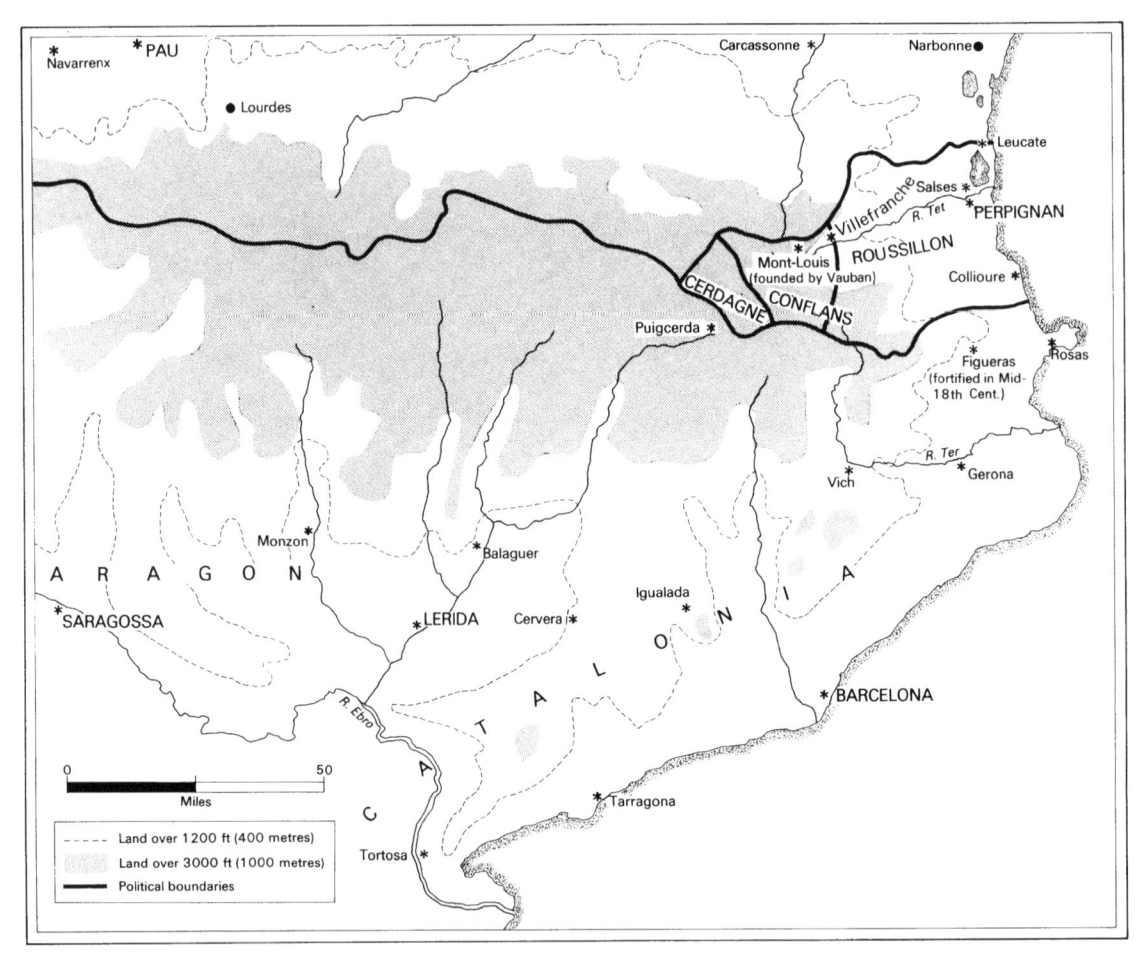

Central and eastern Pyrenees and Catalonia

were taken elsewhere: 'We must also do justice to Louis XIV, and the man who acted as the intermediary between the king and the technician, namely the Minister of War [Louvois]' (Corvisier, 1983, 373).

Vauban's influence and legacy
Vauban established his immortality in more concrete form than any other human being since the time of the building of the Pyramids. In the 1770s Montalembert projected a new system of fortification, supposing that Vauban's fortifications would soon crumble away. Two centuries later we are still waiting for them to fall down.

Vauban's frontier shielded the young Republic in the 1790s from a well-merited retribution at the hands of monarchical Europe – and the Jacobins repaid their benefactor by breaking into his tomb, ripping up the coffin and melting the lead into bullets to fire against the enemies of France. The old marshal would have disapproved of the politics of the thing, while applauding the spirit. In the early 1800s Napoleon was very well aware of how much he owed to Louis XIV's enormous capital investment in Vauban's fortress walls. When, finally, Napoleon was beaten down, and the victorious Duke of Wellington began to arrange the defence of the new kingdom of the United Netherlands, he found that in almost every case he had been anticipated on the best sites by Vauban a century and a quarter before. Vauban's fortifications could still give a good account of themselves in the Franco-Prussian War,

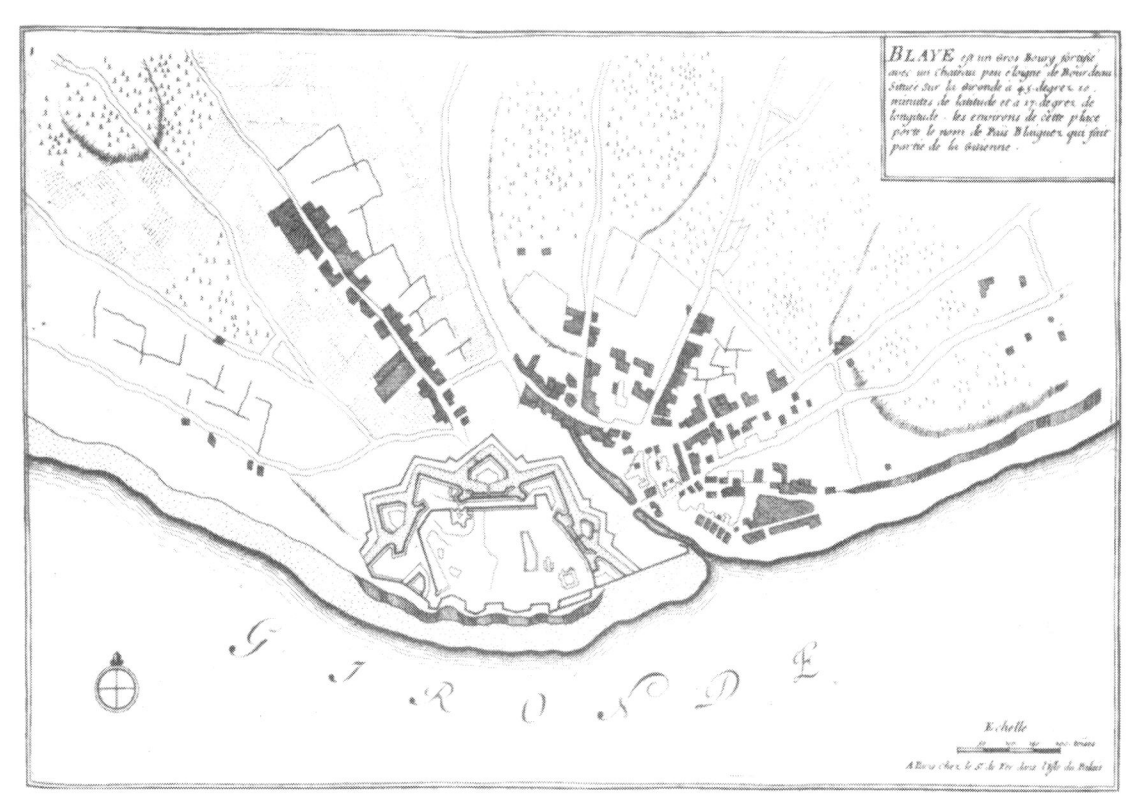

69 Plan of Blaye

70 Powerful double bastion at Blaye

71 Ravelin Dauphine at Blaye. This is the one shown on the far right of the enceinte on the plan

and amongst other services they helped to preserve Belfort for France in the otherwise humiliating peace of 1871.

Vauban's impressive contribution to the defence is eclipsed by his still greater achievement as a taker of fortresses. The later engineers were allured, exercised and finally frustrated by the quest to undo his work by restoring the defence to an equilibrium with the Vauban-style attack. They were still hard at work when rifled artillery arrived in the middle of the nineteenth century and made their task almost impossible.

Why did the attack owe so much to Vauban, and so little, in the long run, to his energetic rival Coehoorn? One reason was that Coehoorn's siege methods were inimitable, in the strictest sense of that word. Few soldiers could ever equal the furious energy with which Coehoorn marshalled the resources for a siege, or aspire to the intuition and the *coup d'oeil* which told him when to commit everything to an all-out assault. Vauban, on the other hand, established a nearly-infallible routine which was accessible to ordinary mortals who were willing to take the trouble to become versed in it.

Writing close to Vauban's own time, de Guignard claimed that the new prestige of French military engineering had produced a revolution in the nobility's view of fortress warfare which was comparable with the change of heart which overcame the Renaissance aristocracy:

It was . . . to follow the example of such a celebrated leader as Vauban that the French nobility embraced the art of engineering, and freed itself of the old prejudice to the effect that it was disgraceful to engage in warfare except as an officer of the field arms. . . . Just as the nobility had once abandoned the lance for the pike, so now they readily laid aside the pike to take up the measuring-rod. (1725, II, 234)

Vauban's *oeuvre* is so vast that it offers little resistance to men who search in it for vindication rather than instruction. Thus Carnot was able to commend Vauban to his contemporaries as a kind of Republican before his time. Thus the French authorities in the 1930s could find a gratifying comparison between Vauban's fortress barriers and the new Maginot Line, 'the various governments remaining faithful to the doctrine of national security which had already been conceived by Vauban' (Ricolfi, 1935, 23). Thus in 1967 President de Gaulle conjured up the shade of Vauban to support his policy of breaking away from entangling alliances in favour of a *défense à tous azimuths*:

He fortified all our frontiers – the Pyrenees, the Alps, our ports and even Belgium. We went everywhere, we made war everywhere. There is no reason why this strategy, which has always protected us against everything, should not be perpetuated.

What remains beyond dispute is that Vauban survives as one of the most complete mortals whom history has to show. Hard-headed but warm-hearted, he was able to reconcile success in warfare, an inherently bloody trade, with the demands of common humanity.

Three   The Resolution of the Conflict: the Last Struggles of Habsburg and Bourbon

The War of the Spanish Succession was followed by a period of exhaustion, readjustment and consolidation. Such quarrels as arose were provoked by old grievances, waged in familiar theatres of war, and fought out by veterans who employed the same techniques that had stood them in good stead in the old wars. The general impression of antiquity was reinforced by that most unlikely of events, a revival of the military power of Spain.

Hispania rediviva 1717–27

The Spanish military renaissance
The French had battled for more than a decade to place a Bourbon dynasty on the throne of Spain, but harsh *Realpolitik* asserted itself as soon as they had made Philip V undisputed master of that kingdom. As early as 1712 Louis XIV had declared his intention to demolish Gerona, and so deprive Spain of a frontier fortress against France: the scheme was not carried out, owing to the silent opposition of the Duke of Berwick. The Spanish, for their part, were encouraged by Queen Elizabeth Farnese and the mighty minister, Cardinal Alberoni, to behave as if Charles V still ruled southern Europe from Toledo. They laid claim to Sicily, which was now in the possession of Piedmont, and to the succession to Tuscany, Parma and Piacenza, on the southern and eastern flanks of the Milanese territory which Austria had gained at the peace.

For a time it seemed as if Spain actually had the means of putting these aggressive schemes into effect. The army became leaner and more efficient, and the rebuilt dockyards turned out a large number of excellent warships. This general renewal of the military spirit was provoked, in part, by sheer frustration at the way the French boasted about their leadership in the arts of war. The engineer officer Juan Martin Cermeño insisted that the first announcement of Vauban's 'first system' for fortification was its orillons and curved flanks (in a pirated edition at Amsterdam in 1689) had been anticipated by two years by Sebastián Fernández de Medrano, the director of the Royal Military Academy of the Spanish Netherlands (*El Ingeniero Práctico*, Brussels, 1687). According to Cermeño, Vauban had improved upon an original suggestion of Marchi:

Don Sebastián de Medrano did no less, and his trace (apart from being a little laborious to carry out) owned all the advantages you could desire. But this general had the misfortune to be a Spaniard, and to work in an unfortunate century, when the military art in our monarchy did not attain the same height as in other times. (Quoted in La Mina, 1898, I, 14)

A sense of inferiority, or rather, as the Marqués de la Mina said, an all-pervading laziness, prevented all but a few Spanish authors from following Medrano's footsteps. The sole Spanish military writer of the period to gain a European reputation was Don Alvaro de Navia Ossorio, Marqués de Santa Cruz, the author of *Reflexiones Militares* (twenty books in nine vols, Turin, 1724). Even this work was old-fashioned in tone, enumerating every possible eventuality in war, and delighting in ruses, spies, signals and secret messages.

A useful, if modest contribution was made to Spanish engineering by the Jesuit Joseph Cassini, who was mathematics master at the Imperial College of Madrid, and taught a number of the abler officers who were to serve in the Italian campaigns of the 1730s and 1740s. His literary monument was the *Escuela Militar de Fortificación Ofensiva y Defensiva*, which was published at Madrid in 1705. One of Cassini's pupils was the Marqués de la Mina, who felt strongly that Spanish military men must redeem their reputation as much with the intellect as with the sword, and drew up a practical dictionary to help young officers to find their way about the terminology of fortification. Eighteenth-century Spain being the place that it was, de la Mina's dictionary never appeared in print.

It was some consolation that Spanish military engineering was at last given a solid institutional basis. The founder of the engineer corps was the Fleming Jórge Prospero Verboom (1665–1744), 'the outstanding member of his profession, the Euclid of his age, the best-read among our officers, and a man who was respected by foreigners' (*ibid.*, I, 377). Verboom was made Engineer-General on 13 January 1710, but was wounded and captured in the bloody defeat of the Bourbon forces at Almenara on 27 July. While still a prisoner at Barcelona he conceived a plan to organise the engineer officers into a unified corps, which would attract high prestige, high pay and well-qualified recruits. He sent the programme to Philip V, who received it with enthusiasm and founded a proper hierarchy of engineering ranks on 11 April 1712. Verboom was released in the same year, and at once set about transforming the new corps into a passable imitation of the French model.

Such were the difficulties of transporting and maintaining forces in the remoter Mediterranean theatres that in the new war of 1717–20 it was almost unknown for two well-found armies to confront each other at the same time. The first-comer therefore had a great advantage, and was free to devote all his attention to taking the enemy fortresses.

In the late summer of 1717 an expeditionary force of 8,000 Spanish descended on the Austrian island of Sardinia and cracked open the strong points of Cagliari, Alghero and Aragonese before the Vienna government could send any help.

The Spaniards came out of Barcelona in 1718, this time in a strength of 30,000, and landed in Sicily to reclaim it from the Piedmontese, who had entered into possession five years before. The expedition was accompanied by Verboom, who contrived to produce sixty engineers and fifty miners for the occasion. Undeterred by the cutting of his sea communications by the British, through the naval battle of Passaro on 11 August, the diminutive Spanish commander de Lede bottled up the Piedmontese and 2,234 Austrians in the citadel of Messina, an impressive-looking work which the Spaniards had built in 1685. The Piedmontese governor capitulated on 29 September, after a bloody siege which cost the Spanish the lives of nineteen of their engineers. Verboom was furious with de Lede, and a few months later the commander told him to leave the army and go back to Sardinia. Seventeen thousand Austrians spent sixty-four days to get the place back again in the following year.

Western Europe was quick to show its indignation at Alberoni's adventures. The French joined with the British, Dutch and Austrians in a highly unnatural league called the Quadruple Alliance, and the Duke of Berwick was sent with 40,000 men to the western Pyrenees to invade the Biscayan provinces of Spain. The coastal gateway of Fuenterrabia fell on 17 June 1719, and Berwick went on to attack the peninsula-fortress of San Sebastian. He planted some heavy guns on the far bank of the Urumea, so as to open up the river fronts of the place, and then drove his trenches along the beach on the near bank. The fortress capitulated on 19 August. Wellington adopted exactly the same procedure when he besieged San Sebastian ninety-four years later. Perhaps he had read his history.

These manifold disasters brought about the fall of Alberoni, and in February 1720 King Philip V made peace. By a reshuffling of the terms of the Peace of Utrecht the Spanish evacuated Sicily in favour of the Austrians, and the dispossessed Piedmontese received Sardinia in return. Philip had not given up his ambitions in Italy, but he appreciated how dangerous it was to try to put them into effect without foreign friends.

Gibraltar seemed to be the one objective which could be attained without the help of allies, and early in 1727 the Conde de las Torres and an army of 20,000 men began the siege of the offending garrison of one thousand British. Verboom was in charge of the technical side of the operation, and suggested that Gibraltar should be attacked from the sea. The commander-in-chief disagreed, and Verboom argued so violently that for the second time in his career he was dismissed from a campaign and sent home. The affair was symptomatic of the growing discord between field commanders and their technicians, of which the century furnished so many examples.

After long and useless artillery duels the Spanish concluded a truce on 23 June, 'and thus ended a siege of five months, in which we had about two thousand men killed or wounded, and in which all we gained was the knowledge that the place was impregnable by land' (Keith, 1843, 75).

The War of the Polish Succession 1733-5

The array of rival powers took on a more familiar appearance in the 1730s, when the Bourbon powers of France and Spain stood once more shoulder-to-shoulder against Habsburg Austria. The cause of the quarrel was the support which the French gave to the candidacy of Stanislaus Leszczynski for the throne of Poland. The Russians had a candidate of their own, in the bulky person of Augustus III of Saxony, and with Austrian encouragement they occupied Warsaw on 10 October 1733. The French party among the Polish nobles might still have put up an effective opposition, if most of them had not taken refuge in the Baltic fortress of Danzig. With their enemies thus conveniently isolated and concentrated, the Russians began a long and muddled siege. Their Field-Marshal Münnich declared that 'since the Russians have never besieged any fortress which may compare with Danzig, I am unaware of any engineer officer who has the experience to direct a successful siege of this strong and modern fortress'

(Vischer, 1938, 347). Münnich arrived to take charge of the operation in person, but he was unable to move affairs along with any greater speed. Danzig finally capitulated on 30 June 1734, after 135 days of resistance, and the French party in Poland was as good as lost. Near to home, however, the Bourbon cause fared much better.

The Rhine

The events of the Rhenish campaigns of the 1730s could have been taken from any one of the wars of the last three-quarters of a century. As always, the Empire had a garrison in the fort of Kehl, which was separated by a narrow channel of sliding brown river water from the French bank and, a little further away, the great fortress-depot of Strasbourg. As always, the fortresses of the Empire were in little state to offer resistance, and Kehl fell on 29 October 1733 after a two-week siege.

The archaic flavour was still more pronounced in the campaigning of 1734, when the 62-year-old Berwick came out of retirement and led the French army to the siege of the middle Rhine fortress of Philippsburg, which had been so often attacked in the days of the old king. One of the motives of the present siege was to

reaccustom the troops to fire, after an interval of twenty years of peace. The army is willing enough, but physically not up to fighting a war. Sieges are particularly useful for getting soldiers used to the rigours of warfare. (Noailles, 1850, 285)

The Austrian army was kept at a distance by the last great circumvallation ever built in Western fortress warfare – a complex of lines and earthen bastions which extended for more than six miles.

Early on 16 June Berwick visited the trenches and climbed a parapet to gain a better view. This sort of thing was very dangerous, as Charles XII of Sweden had shown a few years before, and Berwick was promptly beheaded by a cannon shot. France lost with him a living link with the age of Vauban. Berwick had sometimes disagreed with the great engineer, but he was at one with him in his concern for the 'grand principle of humanity' (Berwick (continuation), 1779, II, 359), and the belief that systematic siegework was a good way of saving lives.

Seventy thousand Germans and Austrians advanced to the relief under the command of Prince Eugene, who was now merely 'an honourable relic of olden times' (Seckendorff, quoted in Kriegsarchiv, 1876-91, XIX, 238). Eugene refused to attack the circumvallation, much to the chagrin of the ambitious young Crown Prince Frederick of Prussia, who was attending the campaign. Philippsburg capitulated within sight of the army on 18 July 1734, and the Imperialists made no attempt to disturb the French hold on the Rhine for the rest of the war.

Italy
The rheumaticky Marshal Villars, another survivor of the old war, had meanwhile led an army of 38,000 French against Austrian Lombardy in 1733. They came at the invitation of King Victor Amadeus II of Piedmont-Sardinia, 'the gate-keeper of the Alps' (Foissac—Latour, 1789, 30), who was anxious to have the help of the Bourbons in pushing forward his eastern border. In return he promised to provide the French with siege artillery and ammunition – which was not quite so generous as it seemed, for the French would henceforth be unable to attack a fortress without his consent.

The allies flooded over the plain of Lombardy, and brought the Austrians face-to-face with their age-old strategic problem of how to emerge from the Alps into northern Italy. Mantua was their only sizeable fortress, but it offered no satisfactory base for the army, being marooned in a malarial swamp dangerously remote from the exits of the Alpine passes (see p. 47). The Austrian commanders could see no alternative to launching blind offensives through the 'strong' north Italian countryside of ditches, dykes, small fields and massive *cassines* (farmhouses). So it was that the French were able to smash successive Austrian armies in 1734 at Parma, on 29 June, and at Guastalla on 19 September.

In 1735 the Austrian field army abandoned the garrison of Mantua to its fate and retired into the Tyrolean valleys. The French duly advanced to Mantua, but they were content to lay the place under passive blockade until a truce brought an end to hostilities in November. In the meantime Don Carlos, son of Philip V of Spain, had carved out a kingdom for himself in Naples and Sicily. the Austrians were direly short of troops and money, and their last stronghold fell in July 1735.

The affairs of Europe were settled in a complicated manner by the Preliminaries of Vienna, in October 1735. Don Carlos clung onto his Kingdom of the Two Sicilies. As some compensation the Emperor received Parma and Piacenza in northern Italy, and gained the reversion of Tuscany to his son-in-law, Prince Francis Stephen, who was to yield to France his native Lorraine, the untenable western bulwark of the empire. Victor Amadeus of Piedmont-Sardinia carried away from the war the prize for which he had entered it – a slice of the Austrian duchy of Milan, which included the fortresses of Tortona and Novara.

The Emperor Charles VI could never reconcile himself to the thought that he would have to be more polite to the Piedmontese than ever before, complaining that Milan

a completely open city, is now on the borders, and is a prey to whatever army chooses to cross the Ticino. Thanks to the territory he has gained, the King of Sardinia can pass the river at any time, and in future he will be able to make himself master of Milan whenever he likes. (Kriegsarchiv, 1876-91, XX, 247).

The War of the Austrian Succession (western and central Europe) 1740-8

The Habsburg political entity had stood in less danger during the great Turkish siege of Vienna in 1683 than in the years which immediately followed the death of Emperor Charles VI in 1739. His daughter Maria Theresa, an untrained girl of twenty-three, found that the powers of Europe considered her to be just one of the many claimants to the succession of the Austrian domains. Frederick II ('the Great') of Prussia invaded the northern province of Silesia in 1740, and his action gave the signal for the older enemies of the dynasty, the French, the Spanish and the Bavarians, to go over to the offensive on both sides of the Alps.

Piedmont and neighbouring states in the War of the Austrian Succession

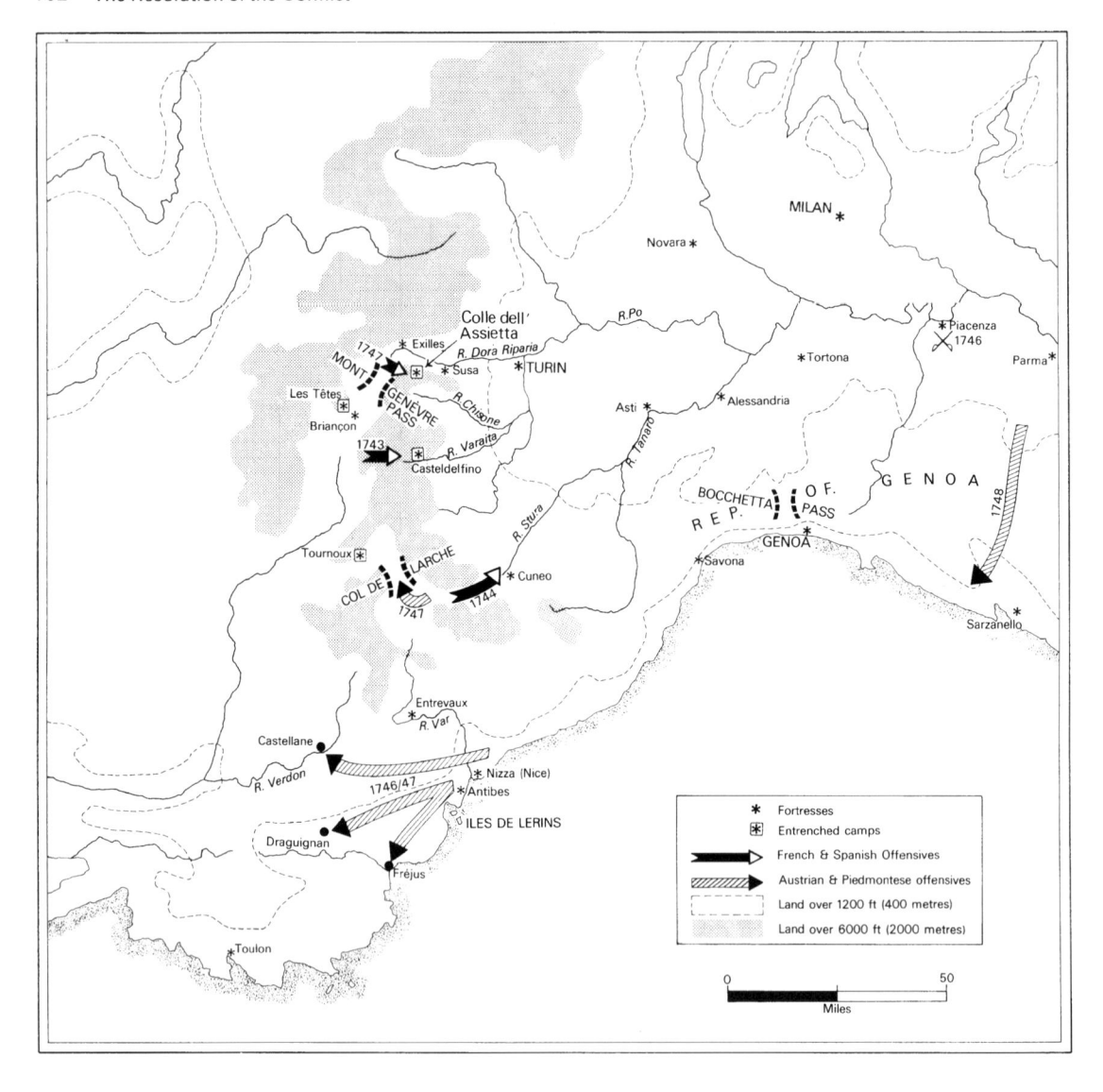

Italy

The most important event of the new war in Italy was the unexpected success of the British and Austrian diplomats in detaching Piedmont-Sardinia from the Bourbon alliance. Charles VI had regarded the recent advance of Piedmont with unadulterated dread. Fortunately for the Habsburg cause there were enough Austrians, like General Maximilian Browne, who saw the King of Piedmont-Sardinia as a person who was to be cultivated, and his realm as 'the outer wall of the State of Milan' (Duffy, 1964, 165). By now Piedmont certainly deserved that title. The border with France ran along the watershed of the Alps (since 1713), while the immensely strong new citadel of Alessandria and the recent acquisitions of Tortona and Novara were a useful check on the Spaniards if they attempted to invade Lombardy from Genoa or central Italy. Lastly, the already high professionalism of the Piedmontese engineering corps was given a solid foundation through the establishment in 1739 of the *Regie Scuola Teoriche e Pratiche di Artigliera e Fortificazioni*. The formative years of the new academy were presided over by successive director generals of high ability – Ignazio Roveda (Conde di Exilles), and Alessandro Papacino, 'the most gifted gunner of Europe'.

Piedmont proved to be an impenetrable barrier to every advance from the French side of the Alps. The first attempt, by way of the little-used Varaita valley, was checked by the entrenched position of the Piedmontese near Casteldelfino in October 1743.

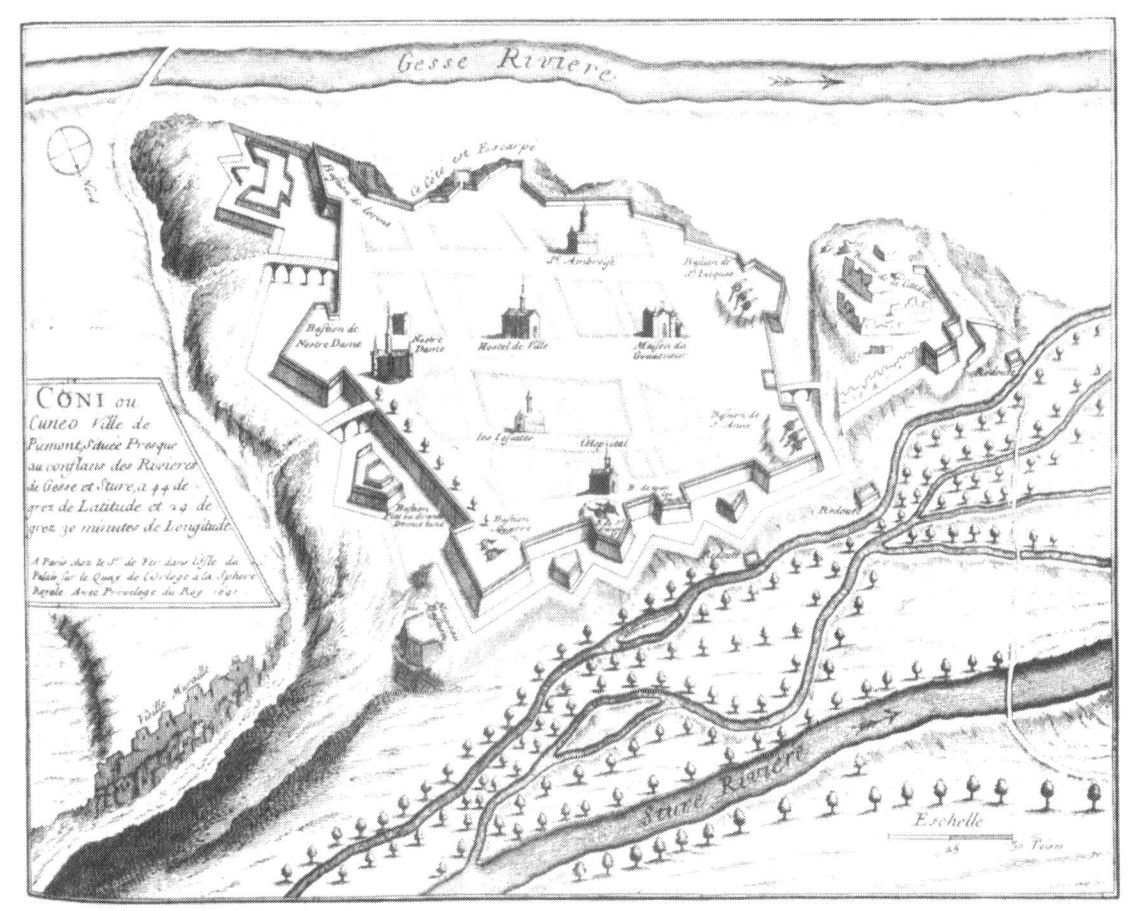

72 Cuneo, the barrier of the Stura valley. The side (furthest away from us) facing the River Gesso was reckoned to be weak and badly flanked. However, in 1744 the Franco-Spanish army saw fit to attack (from our left) the strong front between the Gesso and the Stura (De Fer, 1690–5)

In the following year the French staff officer Pierre Bourcet (who was brought up in the Alps) accomplished a clever concentration of 33,700 French and Spanish troops in the Stura valley further to the south. This venture too came to an end in front of a Piedmontese strongpoint, in this case the pentagonal fortress of Cuneo. The place was held by 3,000 men under the command of a fine old Saxon soldier of fortune, Major-General Leutrum, and few sieges have ever undergone such varied and comprehensive misfortunes – disagreements in command, floods, and guerrillas roving around on the lines of communication. The French and Spanish raised the siege on the night of 21–22 October and marched back over the Alps, having fired away 43,000 rounds of shot and bombs, and having lost 15,000 men through enemy action, sickness and desertion.

One final attempt to pierce the Alps, by way of the Mont-Genèvre route, was shattered on the ridge of the Colle dell' Assietta on 19 July 1747.

Meanwhile the Republic of Genoa had come over to the Bourbons in 1745, and given the French the means of by-passing the Alpine barrier simply by taking ship to the port of Genoa. In the summer of that year a new Franco-Spanish army marched north from Genoa over the Ligurian Alps and undertook a galloping offensive in Lombardy which must have reminded veterans of the events of 1733. However the allies were unbalanced by the very speed of their success. First of all they failed to clear their communications by reducing the citadel of Alessandria, which lay hard by the vital road back to Genoa. The Piedmontese managed to relieve the place on 11 March 1746, by which time the defenders had held out well beyond the point which could have been expected of brave, or even decent men:

> The garrison, having consumed the horses, the cats and the dogs, was left with three days' supply of bread, of which even the officers received only a ration of five ounces. The wretched soldiers were seen to eat the flesh of their dead comrades, such was their terrible state, but nobody talked of surrender. (Saluces, 1817–18, V, 487–8)

Here we have another refutation of the legend concerning the feeble spirit of eighteenth-century warfare (see p. 53).

Worse still the French and Spanish were caught completely off their guard by a new Austrian army which pounded over the Brenner pass in the depth of winter and poured into the plain of Lombardy from the east. Taken between two jaws of a pincer, the Gallispans were defeated at Piacenza on 16 June 1746. By late August they had given up the fight in Italy and were in full retreat along the Genoese Riviera towards France.

The enemy were now tempted to renew Prince Eugene's experiment of forty years before, and carry the war into Mediterranean France. In November 1746 an Austro-Piedmontese army irrupted into Provence in fine style, but the small French garrison of Antibes was enough to wreck the whole campaign. This place represented the only sheltered roadstead on the coast, and it was firmly held by the Marquis de Sade (distant relation of his notorious namesake). Finally the tenuous Austrian supply system collapsed altogether when the population of Genoa, the rearward base, rose in rebellion. Fifty thousand French counterattacked in the New Year of 1747, and drove the hungry and enfeebled allies over the Var.

Taken together, the Franco-Spanish campaign of 1745–6 and the Austro-Piedmontese campaign of 1746–7 were salutary object lessons in what could happen to eighteenth-century armies which over-extended themselves and left too many unreduced fortresses along the communications.

Peace was concluded in 1748, and the confines of Austrian Lombardy shrank still further than in the settlement of 1735. Piedmont-Sardinia gained the western part of the Duchy of Milan as far as the river lines of the Ticino and the Nure. This was a reasonable price for Piedmont's help in the war. What was far more galling to Maria Theresa was that, having beaten the Bourbons soundly in Italy, she was forced by de Saxe's victories in the Netherlands to yield up the duchies of Parma, Piacenza and Guastalla to the Infant Don Philip, second son of Philip V of Spain.

Germany and Bohemia
French statesmen were delighted to see the German Empire tear itself to pieces in the argument over the

73 Fort d'Exilles. Typical box-like Piedmontese *maison forte*. By obstructing the valley of the Dora Riparia in 1747, it tempted the French to make the bloody assault of the ridge of the Colle dell'Assietta

Austrian succession. As might have been expected from his father's record in the 1700s, Elector Charles Albert of Bavaria was quick to take the field against Austria with French help, and propose himself for election as the Emperor Charles VII, no less. Rather more disgraceful was the decision of Saxony and Prussia to join in the hostile league, for these two powers had been old helpmates of the Habsburgs.

Astonishingly enough, the Austrians still had no fortress which was capable of checking any enemy who desired to walk down the Danube valley to Vienna. However, the members of the disreputable enemy coalition were anxious to stake their respective claims to the north-western Habsburg province of Bohemia, and so the Bavarians and French unexpectedly 'turned left' and assembled with the Saxons outside Prague. There was general agreement that a formal siege would be *überaus ruinös* for their unequipped armies. Instead the allies carried out a daring escalade – a model of its kind – which brought Prague into their power in the dismal early hours of 26 November 1741.

Charles Albert entered Prague in triumph and had himself crowned emperor. This news only served to strengthen the wonderful pigheadedness of Maria Theresa, who resolved to carry on the war at any cost. Her armies went over to the offensive early in 1742, and by June they had bottled up more than 30,000 French in Prague. Now the Austrians discovered to their embarrassment that they had not a single engineer who was qualified to attack a fortress. Major-General Harsch had a knowledge of engineering from his youth, but he stepped into the affair with nearly disastrous results – he set almost the whole army to work to trim brushwood for the 400,000 fascines which he needed for his enormous siegeworks; he wove heavy gabions which scarcely anyone could carry; he appealed for volunteer sappers, with the usual consequence that the regiments sent their most stupid men to the trenches; finally he opened a breaching fire at the extravagant range of six hundred paces, and was shot up in retaliation by the French artillery.

The active siege came to an end in September, and Prague was laid under blockade. However, the bulk of the garrison contrived to break out on the night of 16–17 December, leaving a sickly four thousand men to capitulate three days later.

The French were evicted from Bohemia, and they now encountered the greatest difficulty in maintaining themselves even in Germany. The client state of Bavaria was repeatedly overrun by the Austrians, and Maria Theresa's diplomats were able to conjure up a 'Pragmatic Army' of sympathetic German princes and British to sustain her cause.

The French plucked up the courage to emerge from their hiding holes only when war broke out anew between Austria and Prussia in 1744. King Louis XV in person made so bold as to accompany the army across the Rhine in September and lay siege to Freiburg, which was stranded beyond the Rhine at the foot of the Black Forest. After putting up a fine defence the Austrian garrison capitulated at the end of November. It was now the French policy to destroy their neighbours' fortresses while they had the chance, and so they packed 800,000 pounds of gunpowder into Vauban's fine sandstone ramparts and blew them into the sky.

By the summer of 1745 the Habsburgs could marshal an overwhelming majority of the German Electors in their interest, and on 13 September Maria Theresa's husband, Francis Stephen of Lorraine, was chosen Holy Roman Emperor at Frankfurt. Early in 1746 the rival armies drew back from the Rhine, and nearly a century was to pass before the river was again disputed between France and the empire.

The Netherlands

Louis XV and his counsellors contemplated the approach of active hostilities in the Netherlands with unmitigated dread. The theatre stood very near the centres of strength of the king's wealthy enemies, the Maritime Powers. Moreover, the Dutch seemed to have converted 'Belgium' into a military colony. According to the Third Barrier Treaty of November 1715 the southern Netherlands had been delivered to Austria under a number of stringent conditions. Not only did the Austrians have to accept Dutch garrisons in eight fortresses (Namur, Tournai, Menin, Warneton, Ypres, Furnes, Fort Knocke and Dendermonde) but they had to contribute to their upkeep. All this was very galling, especially as the Dutch put heavy restrictions on commerce, and did not even live up to their part of the bargain by keeping effective garrisons in the fortresses.

The French remained unaware of the weakness of the Dutch and Austrian military establishment in the Netherlands. All that Louis XV knew was that the Peace of Utrecht of 1713 had reduced the defences of France's northern frontier on some sectors to one line of fortresses – the coastline had been laid bare by the enforced demolition of the fortifications of Dunkirk, and there was a dangerous inland gap between Maubeuge and Philippeville. Marshal Noailles wrote in February 1743 that the Flemish border was at once

the most important, the most exposed, and yet for a long time the most neglected of the entire kingdom ... the situation was different in the days when Dunkirk was fortified, and before the late king was compelled to cede Furnes, Ypres, Knocke and Menin. In those times it was possible to regard Gravelines, Calais, Ardres and Saint-Omer as places which were buried in the interior of the kingdom. (Colin, 1901–6, II, 25)

When the French took the initiative in opening hostilities in 1744 it was not with the ambition of conquering the Netherlands, but with the aim of forestalling an attack by the Austrians, Dutch and British on Dunkirk. The French were, if anything, still more surprised than the enemy at the brilliant success which attended this first tentative move. It took no more than two months of sieges in the early summer of 1744 to wrest Menin, Ypres, Fort Knocke and Furnes from the nerveless grip of the Dutch. The Duchess of Châteauroux lent comfort and support to King Louis during this campaign, and after it had finished she wrote to a friend that 'there could be nothing quite so glorious or so flattering for me than to have Ypres taken in nine days. The king's grandfather [Louis XIV], great though he was, never achieved anything comparable' (*ibid.*, II, 333).

Almost by accident the French had fallen into a routine which seemed capable of resolving every strategic problem. The field army was liberated from all direct responsibility for siegework, and under the leadership of the Marshal de Saxe it roamed over the theatre of war, outmanoeuvring the allies, or beating them in open combat (Fontenoy 1745, Rocoux 1746, Laffeldt 1747). The actual sieges were taken over by a separate army, which dug its trenches in the confidence that no enemy relief force could disturb the proceedings, and so the generals rarely found it necessary to cast up lines of circumvallation. This division between 'army of observation' and 'siege army' was to become a commonplace of eighteenth-century strategy.

By these means the French reduced Tournai and the best part of the Austrian Netherlands in 1745. They took Namur in 1746, and in the following year Marshal Löwendahl carried the war into Dutch Flanders, where the engineers showed notable skill in directing their siege approaches over flooded ground. This happy progress met a temporary check after Löwendahl moved into Dutch Brabant and was brought up short by the defiance of Bergen-op-Zoom.

Three considerations conspired to help the allies to restore the honour of their arms at Bergen-op-Zoom. The first was the unyielding nature of the governor, the 86-year-old Cronstrum, who declared that he was but one man

but if I can find fifty bold fellows to stick by me, I will keep the town or be buried in the ruins ... for Bergen-o-Zoom is a virgin, and she shall die like the daughter of the brave old Roman, Virginius, before she shall be polluted and ravished from us by the faithless Gaul. (Anon., 1747, 5–6)

Here was the perfect opponent to set against Löwendahl, the ruthless international adventurer who had sworn to sacrifice half his army, if needs be, to capture the fortress.

Secondly, the works of Bergen-op-Zoom were very well adapted to the terrain, and the fortress as a whole was regarded as the best that Coehoorn had ever designed. The arrangements for close-range defence were particularly formidable (see p. 71).

Most importantly of all, the allies had a fleet in the nearby Scheldt, and they were able to funnel men and supplies into the fortress under the protection of a line of earthworks which extended to Bergen-op-Zoom from Steenbergen in the north.

Löwendahl opened trenches before the southern fronts on the night of 14–15 July 1747, but he very soon realised that he had bitten off rather more than he could chew: 'I am engaged in attacking a stronghold which is a masterpiece of fortification, and which I am unable to invest. The garrison is numerous, and it has an army behind to back it up' (Augoyat, 1860–4, II, 414).

By the middle of August the French miners and sappers had won a number of lodgments on the covered way. However, the retired bastion flanks were still largely intact, and the covered way was enfiladed from end to end by the redoubts which Coehoorn had craftily sited in the re-entrant places of arms nearly half a century before. Every now and then the French lodgments erupted skywards in a cloud of flame, earth, rubble and bodies – the work of the Dutch counter-miners.

The bloody work was furthered by sorties of the British Highlanders, and by members of a 'brigade' of English engineers, the first ever formed in the British Army. They arrived in small groups in the last weeks of the siege, and were accompanied by the noted ballistician Benjamin Robin, whom Admiral Anson recommended as 'a perfect master of all the theory of that science.... He has an excellent understanding and great firmness of temper, and therefore I think he will do well' (Porter, 1889–1958, I, 163).

Mid-September found the French still stuck fast in the covered way, facing a few steep and narrow breaches in the Dedem Ravelin and the adjacent bastions. Löwendahl therefore nerved himself to carry out a desperate enterprise. At half past four in the morning of 16 September two salvoes of mortars gave the signal for three columns of volunteers to

The siege of Bergen-op-Zoom 1747

74 (*below*)   First French trenches and batteries

75 (*opposite, top*)   The mine war for the covered way, and (K and L) the powerful redoubts in the places of arms. The craters produced by the Dutch countermines are shaded

76 (*opposite, bottom*)   The final French breaching batteries (nos. 33–7) in the covered way

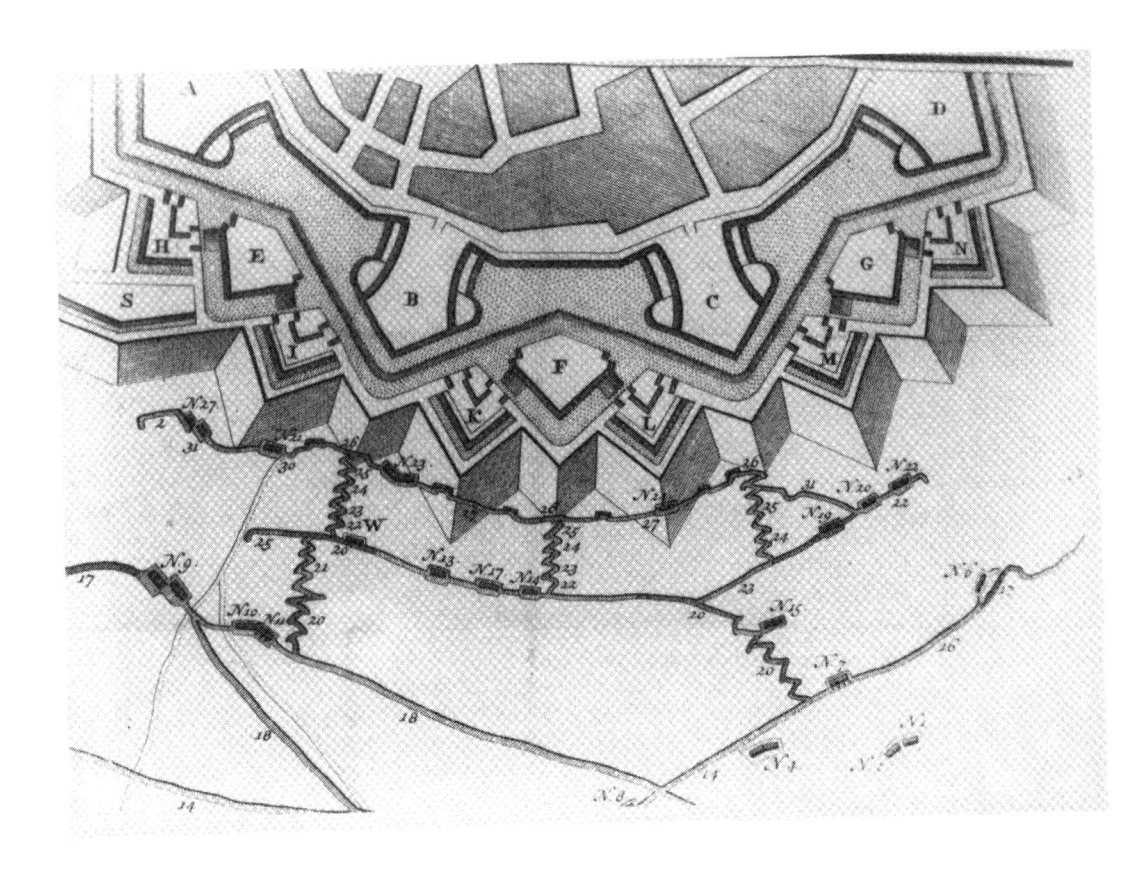

The Resolution of the Conflict 109

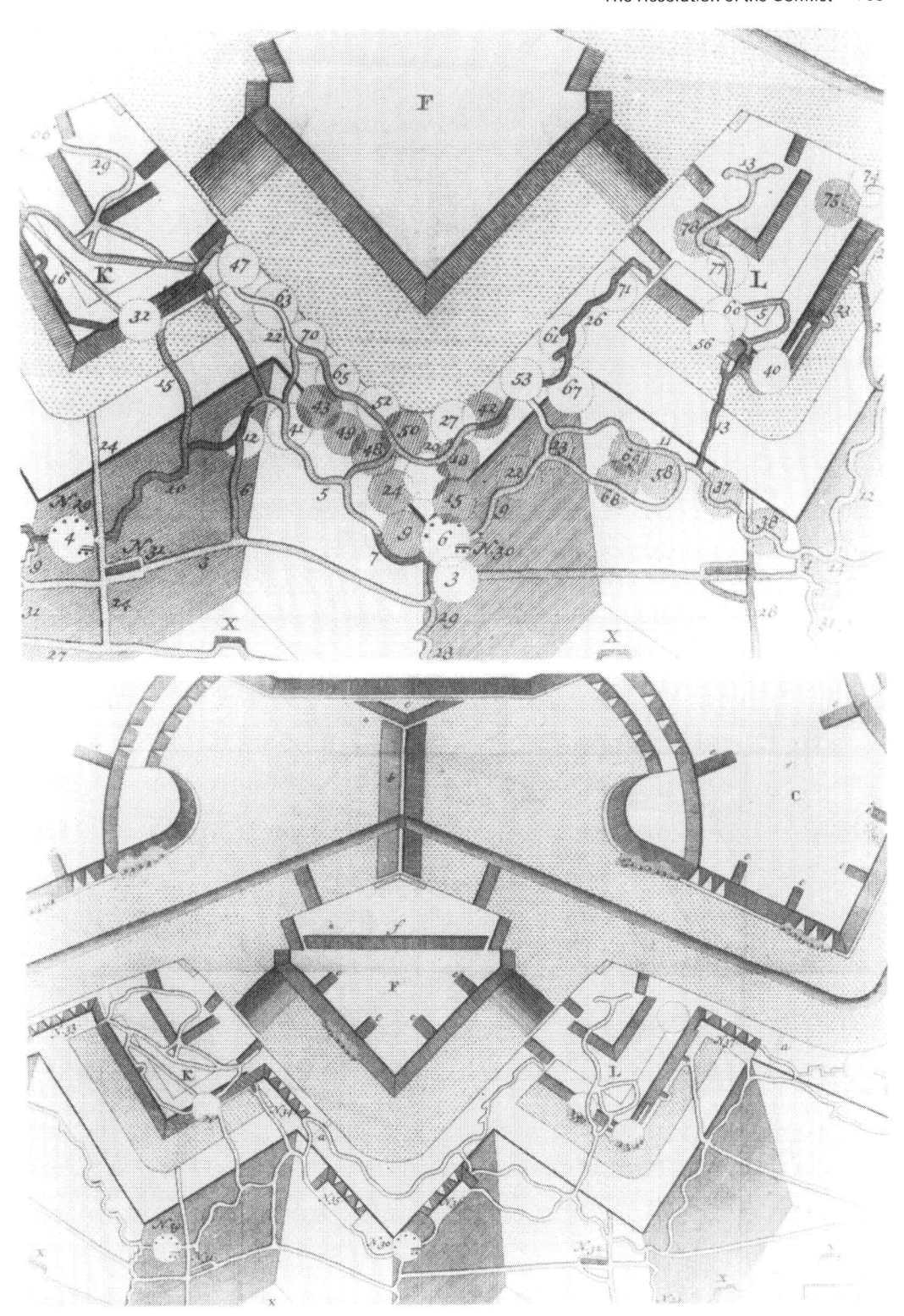

rush across the ditch and scramble up the breaches. The French pushed the feeble guard aside and made their way into the town, where they battled for nearly half an hour outside Cronstrum's headquarters before the deaf old general woke up, 'for Dutchmen will sleep unaccountably sometimes' (Anon., 1747, 67). It was too late to rally an effective defence, and the allies beat a retreat through the Steenbergen Gate, leaving Bergen-op-Zoom to the mercy of the French.

In the way Bergen-op-Zoom fell after a resistance of sixty-four days, Cronstrum's achievement was especially remarkable because it subjected the French to the one major frustration they encountered in their otherwise almost uniformly successful campaigning in the Netherlands. The episode was also of interest for British military affairs. It 'blooded' the new brigades of engineers, and forced the English to admire unsuspected qualities in their new comrades-in-arms, the Highland Scots. One of the English officers testifies that

the behaviour of the North Britons has removed a prejudice which I had conceived against them in the time of the Rebellion, which was, that I thought no virtue could reside in a vulgar untaught Scot, but I find, if they are not misled, they are both faithful and brave. (*ibid.*, 68)

In 1748 the war resumed its more accustomed train. Marshal de Saxe threatened the allied lines at Breda, as if to expand the breach that had been opened in the Dutch frontier in 1747. The enemy obligingly bunched together in the west, which gave the French the opportunity to cut back over the heaths of Limburg and capture Maastricht in the last siege of the war.

The significance of the Low Country Sieges. The Netherlands sieges of 1744–8 represented one of the most crucial turning points in eighteenth-century warfare and politics. In part they were the legacy of Vauban, for they proved that he had succeeded, where all other great engineers had failed, in institutionalising his art, and founding a corps which could apply and develop his teachings long after his death. It was of little consequence that no new 'Vauban' emerged among the French engineers, during these remarkable campaigns, for they conducted their sieges with a quiet professionalism that was the finest tribute to Vauban's work. Frederick of Prussia owned that

the great strength of the French armies resides in their siegework. They have the finest engineers in Europe, and they employ a powerful artillery which is a further guarantee of the success of all their enterprises. (*Histoire de Mon Temps*, in *Oeuvres Historiques*, 1846–7, II, 44–5)

No less importantly, the ordeal of the allies, as the celebrated fortresses fell one after the other, made the Austrians look again at their commitment to the Netherlands. Failing to gain assurance from the Maritime Powers, they began to turn to the French and initiated the complicated processes of the Diplomatic Revolution (see p. 114). The 1780s found the Austrians still in reluctant possession of that part of the world, and in his frustration Emperor Joseph II ordered the fortresses to be slighted, with significant consequences for the course of the campaigns against the French Republic (see the next volume in our series, *Siege Warfare III. The Fortress in the Age of Revolutions 1789–1871*).

The military experts were likewise in a state of agonised cogitation, for they were forced to revise their ideas as to the usefulness of existing fortresses. The Swedish engineer J. B. Virgin was one of those who concluded that the days of the open rampart were over:

I can prove my assertion from what I saw of the course of the eight sieges [in the Netherlands] which I attended in 1745 and 1746.... In the first days of the siege the fortress duly saluted the enemy with a great thunder of artillery, but as soon as the besieger replied to this civil greeting with some fire of his own the defending artillery fell silent. Thus the garrison could put up little or no opposition to the progress of the trenches. I have seen saps driven forward in full daylight, and the workmens' shovels were flashing above the gabions at the head of the sap without drawing a single musket shot from the fortress. This made the sappers so confident that they abandoned the usual precautions, and the sap advanced with no less speed. (Virgin, 1781, 7)

We may discern two trends of thought as the pundits explored means to restore the equilibrium between the attack and the defence:

(i) an attempt to secure better protection for the fortress artillery was clearly evident in vaulted works like the caponnières of Marc-René Montalembert, and the mortar casemates of Lazare Carnot and Virgin;

(ii) Montalembert and Carnot also re-examined the component parts of fortification, searching to identify and isolate their functions, and adapt them to serve their purposes more efficiently. Montalembert abandoned the bastion trace in favour of a new scheme of long straight ramparts, which commanded the open country, and low-lying projections – the caponnières – which had the specialised task of sweeping the ditch by short-range fire (see p. 159). At the beginning of the next century the proposals of Carnot retained the conventional ground plain, but took the rampart to pieces, positioning the masonry revetment as a free-standing 'Carnot wall' in the ditch, and converting the main body of the rampart behind into a sloping massif of earth.

The settlement of 1748

The Peace of Aix in 1748 confirmed the strategic verdict of the recent campaigns. The French had been unable to maintain themselves for any length of time in central Germany or north Italy. At the same time the Austrians had failed in their invasions over the Rhine and Var, and the Austro-Dutch Netherlands proved to be untenable against a French push from the south. The losses and gains were so evenly balanced that the terms of peace restored the borders of western and southern Europe, with some minor exceptions, to the lines which had existed in 1740. The Austrians regained their Netherlands, but found that the French had systematically wrecked the defences, just as they had done at Freiburg.

Everything considered, there was little incentive for Bourbon and Habsburg to resume their quarrels, but every reason why they should stay behind their own borders. By the autumn of 1756 the French (with a good deal of prompting from the Austrian chancellor Kaunitz) had become good friends with the Austrians, and the Empress Maria Theresa was free to bring all her armies to bear against a new and most dangerous enemy, Frederick the Great of Prussia.

Four   The Age of Frederick the Great 1740–86

First round: the Silesian Wars 1740–2 and 1744–5

The theatre
In 1740 Frederick of Prussia invaded the Austrian province of Silesia. This unprovoked aggression gave rise to a competition which extended over four decades of the eighteenth century and into the nineteenth, and which was settled in the bloodiest of fashions by the defeat of the Austrians at Königgrätz in 1866.

The scene of the conflict embraced the whole of the territory which stretched between Berlin and the approaches to Vienna – namely Brandenburg, Saxony, Silesia, Bohemia and Moravia. The theatre was divided horizontally by a three-hundred-mile range of forest-clad hills extending from the border with Bayreuth in the west to the edge of the Moravian Gate, the saddle which connected the ridge with the Carpathians. The hills helped to determine the outcome of the contest – which left the plain to the north of the range as a Prussian sphere of influence, while the provinces of Bohemia and Moravia to the south remained with the Austrians. This came about not because the heights interposed an absolute barrier, but because the passage of supplies and artillery over the passes proved to be laborious in summer, and almost impossible in winter.

On the whole, the character of the theatre favoured the Prussians. The land north of the hills formed part of the great north European plain which swept from Ypres to the Urals. In the German sector the lowlands were intersected by two respectable and navigable rivers, the Elbe on the west and the Oder to the east, which flowed roughly north-westwards on parallel courses about one hundred miles apart. These gave the Prussians the inestimable advantages of water transport. It was no coincidence that Frederick opened his two great wars by 'pre-emptive strikes' which brought the rivers into his power – the offensive of 1740 won him the rich Austrian province of Silesia and the regime of the Oder; the corresponding blow in 1756 conquered the neutral electorate of Saxony and a long stretch of the Elbe.

South of the hills the Austrians laboured under all sorts of disadvantages. They had no navigable waterways, apart from a very few miles of the upper Elbe, and so all their supplies and heavy ordnance had to be hauled overland. Worse still, the loss of Silesia and its many fortresses left the rearward Austrian provinces almost destitute of protection. The western territory of Bohemia was innocent of defences, save for the crumbling brick walls of Prague. Moravia, to the east, stood on the direct road between Silesia and Vienna, but was only slightly better protected, having fortresses at Olmütz and Brünn.

The First Silesian War 1740–2
In the eighteenth century the state of readiness of a nation's fortresses, engineers and gunners offered one of the most direct indications of the degree of power possessed by the central government. In the

Habsburg domains in 1740 the monarch and its officers represented hardly more than a single strand in the ragged network of municipal and noble interest which barely held the whole together. The defences suffered accordingly. Since 1717 professional engineers to the number of 317 had been turned out by the Engineering Academy in Vienna, but many of these men had lost their lives in the disastrous wars of the 1730s, or had been absorbed into the other arms – Vienna had no means of ascertaining the number or the whereabouts of the remainder.

In few places was the central authority more feebly felt than in the northern province of Silesia, which had been untrodden by enemies for almost a century, and where the fortresses, armaments and garrisons were in the last stages of decay. All priority had been given to the Turkish theatre (see p. 243). Frederick and 27,000 Prussian troops irrupted into this undefended province in the middle of December 1740, and on 3 January the king was welcomed into the capital fortress-city of Breslau by the Lutheran populace. Only at Neisse and Brieg did the Austrians offer any effective defence, and these two places were doomed after Frederick defeated the Austrian field army at Mollwitz on 10 April 1741.

The Prussians settled down to besiege Brieg at their leisure. Almost the only piece of ordnance available to the garrison was a curious gun of coiled leather which had been

abandoned here by the Swedes ninety-nine years ago. It was said to have been left loaded all this time. The garrison artillery captain did not want to fire, but an army gunner touched the gun off without his knowledge. It burst, wounding twelve people. (Kriegsarchiv, 1896–1914, II, 318)

On 9 October 1741 Maria Theresa's plenipotentiary struck a strange bargain with the Prussians at Klein-Schnellendorf. Frederick won Lower, or western, Silesia, and in return he allowed the Austrian field army to march away unmolested and deal with the French and Bavarians. For the sake of appearances the solitary fortress of Neisse was to be surrendered after a mock siege. The commandant was accordingly instructed to

put up a brave resistance for fourteen days from the date of the first enemy cannon shot. On the fifteenth day, however, you are to capitulate and deliver the fortress to the King of Prussia on terms (*ibid.*, II, 521)

Nobody thought to let the siege corps in on the secret, with the result that the Prussians rained down shot and shell so plentifully that the commandant had to capitulate on 31 October, after holding out only eleven days.

In the months following the Klein-Schnellendorf deal the Austrians made such good headway in Bohemia and on the Danube that Frederick took fright, and in the middle of February 1742 he invaded Moravia with a force of 32,000 Prussians, Saxons and French. The cavalry raided as far ahead as Korneuburg, a matter of seven miles from Vienna. However, the invaders' communications were dangerously exposed to sorties from Brünn, where the able and determined General Wilhelm Roth was holding out in the name of Maria Theresa. The Saxons failed to produce the siege artillery they had promised, and early in April Frederick had to order the retreat. Roth had effectively parried a thrust aimed at the heart of the monarchy. Frederick was never to come so near his goal again, and an important flaw had been revealed in his capacity for waging offensive warfare – namely the difficulties he experienced in tackling a properly defended fortress.

It was some consolation that the isolated stronghold of Glatz capitulated on 28 April after a three-and-a-half month blockade. On 17 May Frederick beat the Austrian army at Chotusitz, which lent further weight to his arguments, and Maria Theresa finally agreed to come to terms. On 13 June the Preliminaries and Breslau granted Frederick the possession of Lower Silesia, the county of Glatz and most of Upper Silesia.

The Second Silesian War 1744–5
Recent history ought to have convinced Maria Theresa that Frederick would be content to remain within his borders only so long as the Austrians were doing badly against the French and Bavarians. The spectacular Austrian successes in Germany (see p. 106) duly incited Old Fritz to invade Bohemia on

a broad front in the summer of 1744. The Austrians were taken unawares, and Prague fell on 16 September, after the feeblest of defences.

After the reduction of Prague, on Frederick's own admission, he committed an endless catalogue of mistakes. He spread his forces all over southern Bohemia, but in his excitement he neglected to bring up his rearward magazines or consolidate his position in the north. The veteran Austrian Field-Marshal Traun proceeded to clear the countryside of people and cattle, and his well-timed flanking movements (together with Saxony's declaration in favour of Austria), forced Frederick to begin a painful retreat from Bohemia.

The Prussians had to abandon all hope of making a stand at Prague, thanks to the eccentric behaviour of Frederick's chief engineer, General Walrave. During the Prussian occupation this aptly-nicknamed *Général Voleur* shamelessly plundered the Gallas Palace in order to fit out his own Schloss Liliput at Magdeburg, and he wrote to Frederick for permission to take some leave 'so that I can make arrangements to show off the beautiful furnishings from Prague to the best advantage in my own house' (*ibid.*, VII, 238). Having thus outraged the citizens, the least he could have done would have been to strengthen the fortifications. Instead, he 'devoted all his efforts to constructing some impossibly ambitious outworks which demand a garrison of 20,000 men. All the fortifications are consequently useless' (quoted in Grosser Generalstab, 1890–1914, *Zweite Schlesische Krieg*, I, 230). This episode began Frederick's disenchantment with the first of his long line of engineer chiefs. Prague was evacuated on 26 November 1744.

However, Frederick was still unbeatable in the open field, and in 1745, after two defeats in battle, Maria Theresa had to sign over the whole of Silesia in perpetuity. The balance of power in Central Europe was now heavily weighted in favour of the Prussians.

Second round: The Seven Years War 1756–63

The Diplomatic Revolution
The War of the Austrian Succession had shown that the Austrian obligations in the Netherlands were as dangerous as they were burdensome. The French had wrecked the fortresses, and now, after the peace, Vienna was unwilling to face up to the effort and responsibility which would have been involved in a full restoration of the Barrier. There were the damaged works to be repaired, the annual subsidy of 1,400,000 florins to the Dutch to be renewed, and all this while the Austrians had to build up their forces against Frederick of Prussia.

For some years the Austrians were content to press for some amelioration of the terms under which they held the Netherlands. As they pointed out to the Maritime Powers:

everything considered, the maintenance of this bulwark, which the Empress-Queen supports out of her spirit of magnanimity and her friendship for the allies ... serves much more to cover the frontiers of the Dutch Republic and Great Britain than the remnants of the Austrian monarchy.
(Khevenhüller-Metsch, 1907–72, III, 279)

Austria had lived up to its obligations religiously, but in return the Maritime Powers had formed the habit of regarding the Netherlands 'almost as a tributary province' (*ibid.*, III, 435).

No satisfaction was forthcoming, and so the Austrian chancellor Kaunitz turned aside from the Maritime Powers and set in train the series of events called 'The Diplomatic Revolution'. By the early summer of 1757 Maria Theresa was leagued in an anti-Prussian alliance with her old enemies the French, as well as with the Russians, Swedes and Saxons.

It is no disparagement of the diplomacy of Kaunitz to claim that Vauban was one of the prime movers of the Diplomatic Revolution. The ease with which the marshal had taken the Netherlands fortresses had frightened the Maritime Powers into setting up their Barrier, under unrealistic terms, in the 1700s. Then, four decades after Vauban's death, his pupils had so convincingly broken down the same barrier that the Austrians began to wonder what they were doing in that part of the world in the first place.

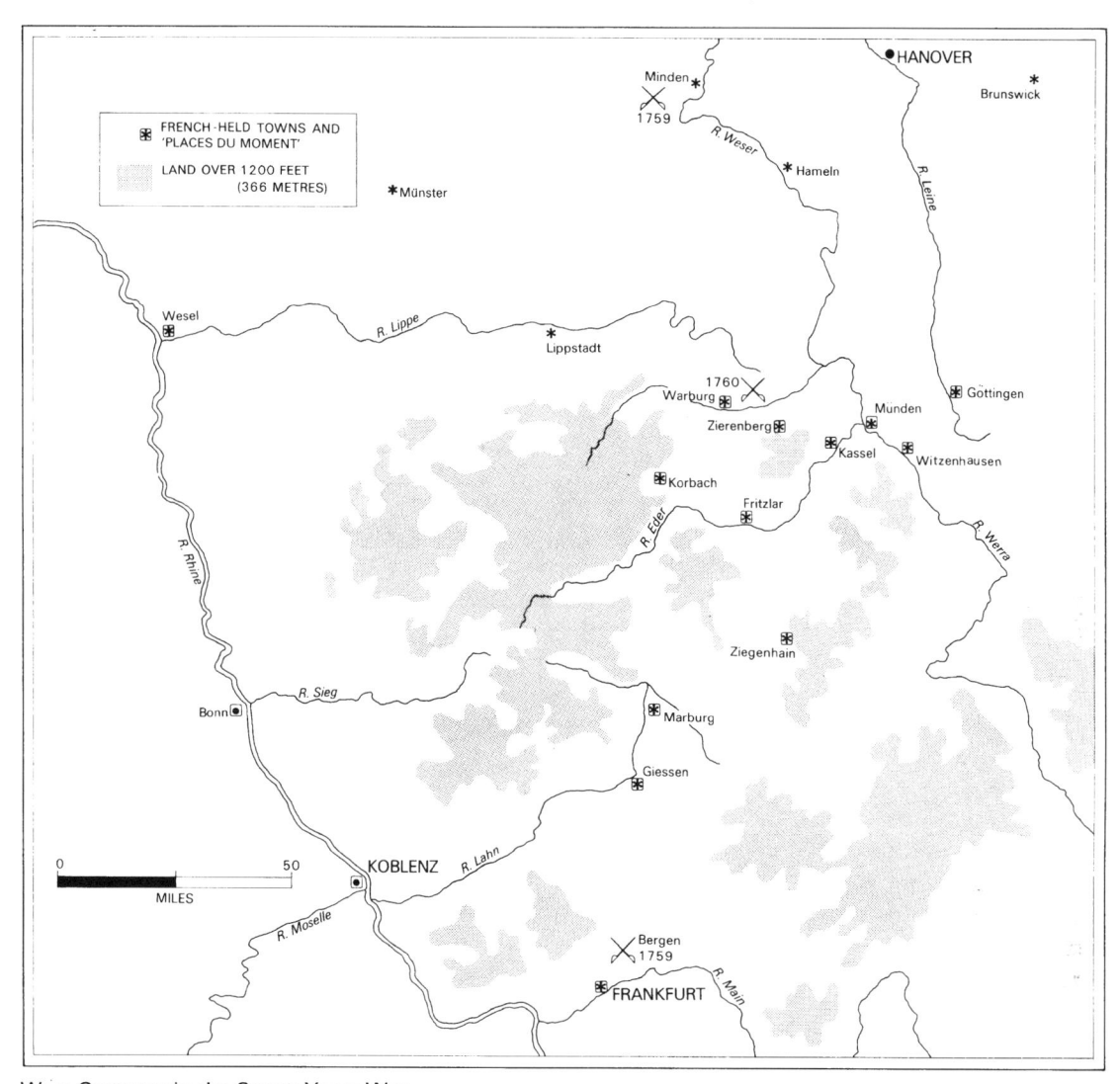

West Germany in the Seven Years War

Western Germany

The most important obligation taken on by France in the new alliance was to tackle Frederick by his western flank, while the Austrians, Russians and Swedes came at him from the other points of the compass.

The French army of the 1750s was far from fitted for this responsible task. The fighting qualities of the infantry and cavalry had undergone a sudden and almost catastrophic decline since the days of the Marshal de Saxe, and everybody complained about the unhappy marriage of 1755, which bound the engineers and gunners in a united corps (see p. 150). According to Count Clermont, the commander in Westphalia,

> When I ask for an engineer, they give me an artilleryman who does not know what he is up to. When I ask for a gunner, I am presented with an engineer who understands nothing of what I want him to do. (Augoyat, 1860-4, II, 459)

It is significant that the best achievements of the French engineers date from after 1758, when the divorce between the partners was arranged.

The French were fortunate that for the most part they had to fight mixed armies of Hanoverians, British, Hessians and Brunswickers. This colourful host had a decidedly modest capacity for fortress warfare. The Brunswick engineers, for instance, were decrepit old men who had begun work as footmen and valets, and slowly risen through the ranks of the army. Institutional support was lacking, and so was any systematic technical education. 'What could reasonably be expected of an engineer who had been brought up in this way? Effectively nothing at all ... so it was that in the army nobody except Count von der Lippe had any comprehension of what siege warfare was about' (Mauvillon, 1794, II, 293-4).

In purely geographical terms, the theatre of war had much in common with the scene of the Austro-Prussian arguments further to the east. The Rhine, the French base of operations, was the counterpart of the Elbe, while 120 miles further east the Weser provided a possible imitation of the Oder, and lent a degree of protection to Hanover and Brunswick. The wooded hills of Hesse were the continuation of the Bohemian heights, and they descended to the plains of northern Westphalia, which were the prolongation of the levels of Brandenburg and Saxony. Two essential differences between the theatres remain. North-western Germany had innumerable towns with weak old fortifications, but not a single stronghold which could compare with Olmütz, Brünn or the new Prussian fortresses in Silesia. Prussia had some isolated holdings in the region, but Frederick evacuated the garrisons of Wesel and Minden at the beginning of the war. Secondly, the rival parties faced respectively east and west, rather than north and south, and they found that the rivers were obstacles rather than aids to movement and supply.

One hundred thousand chattering Frenchmen crossed the Rhine in 1757. They were hugely confident, and made no attempt to establish secure depots along the line of advance, or to prepare the fortified towns to receive the débris in the event of a defeat. By the spring of 1758 their chastened remnants were back on the Rhine, having been badly mauled by the Prussians at Rossbach, and by Prince Ferdinand of Brunswick with his army of British and Germans.

The war entered a new phase when the French began to adopt a more effective strategy. They created a wide and firm rearward base by re-fortifying the abandoned Prussian fortress of Wesel, at the confluence of the Rhine and the Lippe, and by surprising the city of Frankfurt-am-Main on 1 January 1759. Advancing from these strongpoints, the French made their way systematically eastwards through the towns of the central hill-country of Hesse, creating a salient which eventually extended beyond the Weser. The better-sited of the towns were converted into improved fortresses of the kind which the French called *places du moment*:

In the last resort it was due to the support of these strongpoints that, despite defeats, blunders and setbacks of every kind, we managed to maintain ourselves in enemy country ... until the time we arranged a voluntary evacuation at the peace.... Their role was not just a passive one. At first they appeared to serve merely as refuges for the mobile troops, or as strongholds under whose shelter we could extend our winter quarters, but in the course of time they came to promote genuinely offensive purposes, for they seconded our repeated raids on the enemy quarters. (d'Arçon, l'An III, 61-2, and 1786, 48)

The allies for a time blunted the point of the French advance by the victory of Minden, on 1 August 1759. Some of the most advanced French strongpoints on or near the Weser were now patently untenable. Minden and Kassel were both packed with wounded and sick, and they capitulated as an immediate result of the battle. Over the following weeks, however, Prince Ferdinand had to detach more and more troops from his field army to reinforce the Hanoverian general Imhof, who was laying sluggish siege to Münster. The place finally capitulated on 20 November, having made a useful contribution to sapping the momentum of the allies after their victory.

Throughout 1760 the French expanded and consolidated their holdings. They were unshaken by their defeat at Warburg on 31 July, and on the same day they contrived to seize Kassel, the largest town of the Hessian theatre. Marshal Broglie did not hesitate to dispatch forces beyond the Weser to the

Werra, and in November he set Lieutenant-General de Vaux to work on fortifying Göttingen, as an outer bastion to the Hessian salient. The new lunettes and palisades seemed to rise out of the earth by magic, and the French made this strongpoint into a base for some very damaging raids.

Prince Ferdinand drew his forces together to the north of the Hessian salient. In his own words:

We have three firm bases from which we can operate against the enemy. These are Münster, Lippstadt and Hameln. All our efforts must be directed towards keeping them intact. The two first-named cover our communications with Holland and England, as well as the lower Weser, which is the source of our subsistence. The third, Hameln, covers the upper Weser, the Electorate of Hanover and the Duchy of Brunswick. (To Bute, 13 April 1761, Savory, 1966, 312)

In the late autumn of 1760, 400 yoke of oxen dragged Ferdinand's siege train from these three fortresses over flooded roads against Wesel, on the far left flank and rear of the French salient. There the Hereditary Prince of Brunswick found that the French were gathering so threateningly that he had to order the retreat, on 17 October. The guns were pulled all the way back without ever having come into action.

Early in 1761 Ferdinand essayed a direct approach into the Hessian salient, and saw his army melt away in a multitude of blockades and sieges. The most ambitious of these operations was undertaken against Kassel, by thirty-three battalions under the command of Count Wilhelm zu Schaumburg-Lippe. The investment was tenuous and incomplete, and the coming of the thaw softened the ground to a sponge-like consistency. Schaumburg-Lippe now had no hope of bringing his guns against the tenaille-like lunettes which the French had built around the fortress, and on 27 March he abandoned the siege.

The outcome of this campaign fully justified the odd distribution of the French forces: 45,000 troops occupied the Bergen position in front of Frankfurt, and 23,544 more were guarding Göttingen, Kassel, Ziegenhain, Giessen, Marburg, Dillenburg, Hanau and Frankfurt itself. Ferdinand's 77,000 men were dispersed and powerless, and in October a French detachment had the impudence to subject the city of Brunswick to a short investment.

In June 1762 Ferdinand bravely entered the Hessian maze once more, but this time he made sure that he swept Soubise and d'Estrées and their 80,000 men back to the Ohm before he set about reducing the strongholds. Kassel was laid under blockade from 16 August, and by 12 October 12,298 men were ready to see to the siege proper. Seventy guns of various calibres were brought up the Weser from Nienburg and Hameln, and upon their arrival on 15 October they were immediately planted in ready-made batteries – a time-saving expedient which had been attempted at the siege of Wesel in 1760. Kassel was subjected to repeated assaults and a very heavy cannonade, but it took an order from Soubise to induce Major-General Diesbach and his 5,300 men to capitulate on 1 November. Preparations were being made for the siege of Ziegenhain when hostilities came to an end on 14 November.

We admire the skill and the adaptability which enabled the French to hold the Hessian salient so long and so successfully. No other engineers could have performed nearly so well. In grand strategic terms, however, these years of intelligent effort contributed nothing towards the larger aim of eating away Frederician Prussia on its western flank. We shall now have to see whether France's partners fared any better.

The Swedish and Russian campaigns

Between 1721 and the opening of the Seven Years War, Swedish military prowess had fallen almost as far as that of France. 'They were brave once', said the Russian commander Saltykov, 'but now their time is past' (Montalembert, 1777, II, 62). Their military spirit inevitably suffered from the way Count Rosen maladministered the army, and from the bitter arguments among the politicians. Their engineers could still build imposing fortresses, and men like Major Röök and the generals Carlsberg and Virgin could still propose 'systems' of interest and originality, but the Swedish means of waging offensive fortress warfare had declined considerably since the days of Charles XII. Arms and equipment were antiquated, and the siege artillery was notably cumbersome by the standards of the second half of the eighteenth century.

Nowhere were the operations of the Seven Years War more repetitious and circumscribed than in Swedish and Prussian Pomerania. Campaigning was mostly confined to Swedish forays from the bridgehead fortress of Stralsund against the line of the Peene and its small strongholds at Demmin, Anklam and Peenemünde. These works were almost always lost again when the Strelasund froze over with the coming of winter, for the Swedes had to hasten back to Stralsund and the offshore island of Rügen to prevent the Prussians from getting there first by marching across the ice.

There was no chance whatsoever that the Swedes would fulfil their part in the strategy that was sketched out for them by the French staff officer Marc-René Montalembert, who urged that 'the Swedish and Russian armies will accomplish nothing useful for the common cause until they have taken the town of Stettin' (March 1759, *ibid.*, II, 11). This was a powerful Prussian fortress on the lower Oder, which effectively blocked the way from Swedish Pomerania to the Russians operating on the east side of the Oder. As for the Russians, they claimed that any siege of Stettin would require '200,000 men and more artillery than Russia and Sweden can possibly furnish' (31 August 1759, *ibid.*, II, 62). Perhaps also the Russians perceived that Montalembert deliberately wished them to waste their time and strength in this enormous operation, for by now the French lived in fear of the westward advance of Russia.

The Austrians, however, still looked to the Russians for positive help. Founded by Peter the Great (see p. 216), the Russian engineering corps had been reorganised by Field-Marshal Münnich in the 1730s, and by the time of the Seven Years War it comprised the very respectable total of 1,302 officers and men. Unfortunately, nearly all of these people were inextricably committed to civil engineering and topographical projects, leaving the Russians bereft of technical expertise when they came to attack fortresses.

The chief burden of Russian sieges therefore rested upon the gunners, not the engineers. The Saxon officer Tielke wrote from direct experience that:

the Russians differ from all other nations, in their method of carrying on sieges – instead of first opening trenches to cover themselves from the enemy's fire, and making batteries with strong parapets for the cannon and mortars, they advance as near as possible up to the town, bring up their artillery without covering it in the least, and after they have cannonaded and bombarded the town about forty-eight hours, they begin to break ground and make regular trenches and batteries. They think that this method inspires the assailants with courage, at the same time as it intimidates the defenders, and may possibly induce these latter to surrender. Both officers and soldiers are on these occasions equally exposed to fire. (Tielke, 1788, II, 133)

Since the Russians conducted their battles and sieges in a nearly identical fashion, the Master-General of the Ordnance, the brilliant and wayward Petr Shuvalov, embarked on a search for a universal general-purpose artillery piece. The result was a curious long-barrelled howitzer called the 'unicorn', which fired an explosive shell to a considerable distance but with no great accuracy. In 1758, after the futile cannonade of Küstrin, General Fermor complained that he would rather have more of the conventional siege artillery instead, but Shuvalov was adamant in defence of his 'unicorns', claiming that

although their bombs are not especially weighty, they travel with such speed, and along such a flat trajectory that, according to the experiments we have conducted here, they penetrate seven feet into an earthen rampart, and produce a large crater when they burst. (Maslovskii, 1888–93, I, 331–2)

The Russian operations in the Seven Years War fall into two clearly defined phases. The first objective was to reduce the Prussian enclave of East Prussia, which was isolated on the Baltic coast and surrounded by Polish territory on every landward side. The small defending army was beaten in the open field in 1757, and although the Russians fell back to winter quarters, they came on again in January 1758 and occupied the capital of Königsberg.

The Russians could now embark on the second stage of their war. By taking East Prussia they had opened the way to the River Vistula (Weichsel), which gave them a shield for the conquered lands and a start-line for the advance into Brandenburg. The Prussian heartland was ultimately saved by five strongholds. First of all the works at Kolberg offered the Prussians a base for partisan-type warfare in eastern Pomerania, and denied the Russians the use of the only sizeable harbour on the 150-mile stretch of sandy coast between Danzig and the mouth of the Oder. The lure of Kolberg repeatedly induced the Russians to weaken their army to form siege corps, and they finally reduced the place only in December 1761, after months of blockade and siege. The other four fortresses, the Oder strongholds of Stettin, Küstrin, Breslau and Glogau, managed to defy the Russians for the rest of the war. In 1759 and again in the summer of 1760 the Russians and a powerful corps of Austrians joined forces on the Oder, but the generals could not summon up the energy or the resources to attack the quartet of Prussian fortresses. This was why

they [the Russians] were never able to establish themselves in winter quarters. It never crossed their minds to secure themselves supplies or points d'appui on the Oder, and so they always had to march back to quarters behind the Vistula. These retreats deprived them of the fruits of the campaigns they had just fought, and of all the advantages they had gained. By the same token they experienced considerable delays in opening their next campaigns, and every time they had to re-do everything from the beginning. (Silva, 1778, 41)

Frederick's field army, the other prop of the Prussian monarchy, was, however, reduced to a parlous state, and without its support the fortress would certainly have fallen in a couple of campaigns. Old Fritz was saved in the nick of time by the death of Empress Elizabeth of Russia on 5 January 1762, which brought in its train the collapse of the anti-Prussian coalition.

The Austrian campaigns
The Austrian military renaissance. The performance of France, Sweden and Russia fell far short of Maria Theresa's expectations. The Empress-Queen was therefore forced to place all the more dependence on Austria's own military resources. By any reckoning these were now very formidable indeed.

The field forces were improved in every respect, and the artillery became probably the most powerful in Europe, thanks to the labours of the General Director Prince Liechtenstein. If the engineers lagged behind the other arms, it was only because they had so much more ground to make up. After the abysmal performance of her engineers in the last war, Maria Theresa commissioned Colonel Paul Bohn to set up a proper corps of professionals. Bohn worked fast and well, and on 20 July 1747 Maria Theresa sanctioned a *Regulament* which founded a corps of ninety-eight officers, and prescribed their activities in some detail. Another essential foundation was laid seven years later, when the teaching of engineer cadets was concentrated in a school at Gumpendorf, a suburb of Vienna.

The work of the 1740s and 1750s was going to produce gratifying results towards the end of the century. However, the Seven Years War found the Austrians still desperately short of native engineers, and Maria Theresa was deeply indebted to a number of French technicians who helped to fill the gap, and in particular to the brilliant gunner Jean-Baptiste de Gribeauval, who entered the Imperial service in 1759. It was on the advice of Gribeauval that Maria Theresa set up a corps of 255 sappers, who were to provide a skilled labour force for the engineers proper. The sappers performed brilliantly in Loudon's *coup de main* on Glatz in 1760, and again in the epic defence of Schweidnitz in 1762.

The Treasury could spare no money to build new fortresses, but there was enough cash to allow the Austrians to reconstruct Olmütz, the sentinel of Moravia, which gave a degree of protection to the dangerously open northern borders. The value of this investment was to be shown in 1758.

Frederick countered this sinister activity by casting a siege train of eighty cannon and twenty mortars. He also took the precaution of encrusting the Silesian fortresses with new works of a highly original design, but

since the Austrians had shown little capacity in the last war for the attack and defence of fortresses, I was content to build the works in a flimsy fashion.

This was a gross miscalculation, for strongholds should be constructed to do service for ever, and not just a period of time. And besides, I ignored the possibility that the Empress-Queen might attract to her service some able engineer who would teach the Austrians the skills they used to lack. (*Histoire de la Guerre de Sept Ans*, in Frederick, 1846–57, III, 6)

The French officer de Morainville went so far as to describe the Prussian fortresses as 'Badly-assembled trash. The fascines and palisades are worthless, and an unparalleled ignorance and negligence reigns among the commandants and engineers' (Arneth, 1863–79, VI, 467).

Offensive and counter-offensive 1756–8. Frederick boldly took the initiative in the first two campaigns of the new war. In the autumn of 1756 he surrounded and captured the Saxon army, and in the following spring he carried the war across the hills into Bohemia, smashing the main Austrian army just outside Prague on 1 May 1757.

Now the rival forces revealed the full extent of their ignorance of siege warfar. Prague held only the remnant of the defeated Austrian army, but Frederick wasted time and ammunition by laying the city under a generalised bombardment. The roundshot and shell splinters embedded themselves in the walls of the buildings like currants in a cake, and the Austrian commander reported that

the enemy are doing everything they can to annihilate the town ... so that from their manner of proceeding up to now they seem bent on waging war on the wretched townspeople rather than our troops, who have so far suffered virtually no casualties. (*ibid.*, V, 502)

Vienna was granted the time to assemble an army of relief under Field-Marshal Daun, who marched against Frederick and defeated him on the field of Kolin on 18 June 1757. The victorious Daun entered Prague in triumph, and the reunited Austrian army of 93,000 men chased the enemy from Bohemia. It was not easy for Frederick to extricate all his troops, and in late June the Austrians caught one of the stranded formations in the Lusatian textile town of Zittau. In true Central European style the Austrians subjected the place to indiscriminate bombardment. The conflagration took twenty-four hours to die down, and when the Austrians entered they found it 'dangerous to walk through the streets, on account of the stones which still crashed down from the buildings. It was terrible to enter the cellars and find whole families which had suffocated to death (Ligne, 1795–1811, XIV, 33).

The impetus of the victory at Kolin carried the Austrians over the border hills, and in October 1757 the Duke of Arenberg was sent off with 43,000 men to capture the brand-new fortress of Schweidnitz, and so establish a firm footing in Silesia. From 1748 onwards Frederick had been busy fortifying the place on an ingenious and novel plan, which placed the main weight of the defence on a ring of five detached forts and four intermediate flèches or redoubts, all of which seems to have thrown besiegers and besieged alike into a state of some uncertainty. After a tentative start to a formal siege, the Austrians lost patience and stormed three of the works on 12 November, at which the governor surrendered.

The Austrians now had the opportunity of viewing Frederick's new fortress at their leisure, but they were still at a loss to discover the guiding principles:

The works are very solidly built and possess some very fine casemates, but the engineers have clearly made a number of grave mistakes. The ditches are mostly narrow, and the glacis is too cramped and small (though the ground is planted with a live hedge). None of the works are connected by curtains or ditches, so that it ought to be possible for the besieger ... to dispense with the first parallel, and go straight on to take the town by storm at the cost of one hundred casualties at the very most. (Khevenhüller-Metsch, 1907–72, IV, 398)

The fortress-city of Breslau, the capital of Silesia, now changed hands with some rapidity, without putting either side to the trouble of making a formal siege. The place surrendered to the Austrians on 25 November, after a Prussian detachment was defeated outside. Frederick then hastened up with the main field army, and trounced the Austrians at Leuthen. Breslau was packed with no less than

The Age of Frederick the Great 1740–86   121

Central Europe in the time of Frederick the Great

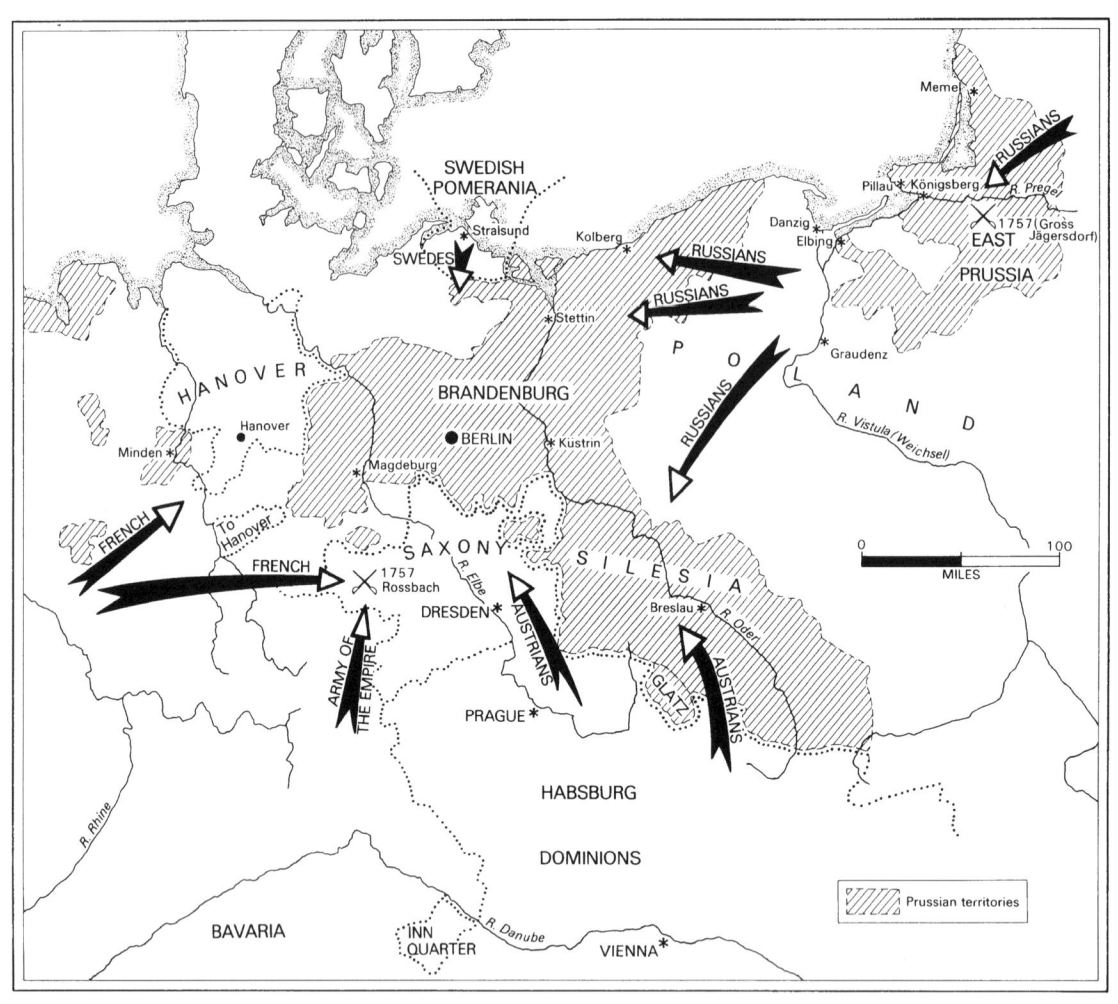

Europe against Frederick in the Seven Years War

17,000 demoralised Austrian troops, who gave themselves up as prisoners of war on 20 December.

Frederick held the initiative at the start of the campaigning season of 1758. The events of 1744 and the early summer of 1757 had disgusted him with campaigning in Bohemia, and he made up his mind to strike at the heart of the Austrian monarchy by way of the eastern province of Moravia. An essential preliminary was to recapture Schweidnitz, the one remaining enemy foothold on the northern plain.

On 22 March 1758 Lieutenant-General Tresckow arrived before Schweidnitz to undertake the siege with 10,000 men.

The enterprise was made far more difficult by the smallness of the corps. Generally speaking the strength of the Prussian army did not reside in sieges, since Frederick was not too fond of this kind of military operation. His disinclination was reinforced by his parsimonious spirit, and by the low esteem in which he held his engineer officers, the most able of whom had little hope of promotion, and had to give way in advancement and everything else to the most ignorant of the infantry officers. The numbers of the king's miners, guns and gunners were also insignificant.

So testifies the Prussian veteran Archenholtz (1911, 157–8).

The siege of Schweidnitz progressed with agonising slowness, and nothing seemed capable of subduing the Austrian fire. One day, while visiting the siege, Frederick had himself bled for the good of his health:

While the gash was still bleeding, a bomb from the fortress landed right next to Frederick, ploughing up the loose earth and covering the king and the barber-surgeon with dust... the surgeon uttered a shriek of terror, disappeared in panic and left the king sitting where he was, with the blood flowing from the vein. (Hildebrandt, 1829–35, II, 46)

Frederick was furious at the poor performance of his own gunners, and the deadlock was broken only when the Prussians escaladed the Galgen-Fort on 16 April. The whole fortress complex was immediately surrendered.

Using the amply-stocked fortress of Neisse as their base, the Prussians swept over the Moravian border hills at the end of April. The aim of the operation was to reduce Olmütz, the best-found of all the Austrian fortresses, and the principal obstacle on the road to Vienna. The masonry works had been rebuilt before the war, and the glacis was covered with some of those useful earthen lunettes which had come into general fashion in the War of the Spanish Succession.

Colonel Balbi was nominally entrusted with the direction of the siege, for he was the only one of the technical officers to have emerged with any credit from the attack on Schweidnitz. However, nothing could prevent Frederick from intervening in his usual unconstructive way. He ordered the artillery to fire with reduced charges, for the sake of economy, with the result that the first Prussian battery, on the Tafelberg, was incapable of reaching the

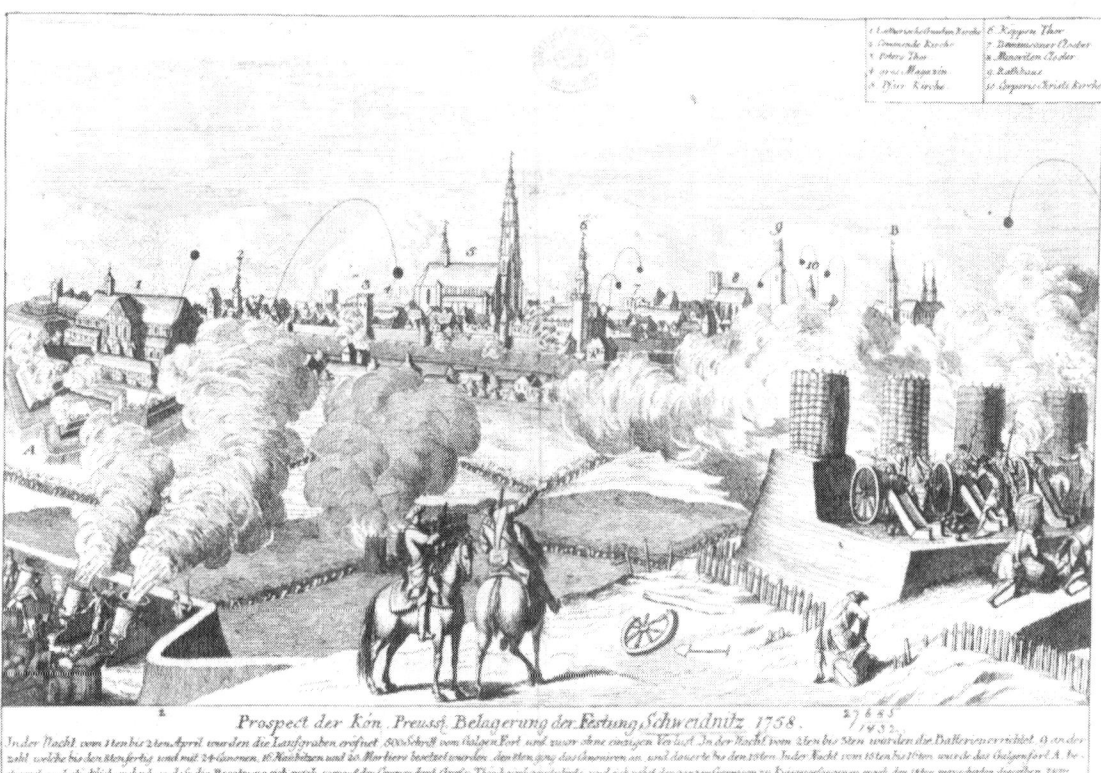

77 The Prussian siege of Schweidnitz 1758

124 The Age of Frederick the Great 1740-86

78 Frederick's siege of Olmütz 1758

fortress. The king therefore took the siege out of Balbi's hands altogether. He threw up a new parallel further down the Tafelberg, and established some batteries of his own. The guns proved to be further away from the target than the original battery on the Tafelberg, according to measurements taken by the Prince de Ligne after the siege.

Another grave mistake, which the French would never have committed, was to plant the batteries in front of the parallel, instead of to the rear. The Prussians thereby nullified the fire of the sector of the trench behind, exposed their own guns, and built a redoubt which the garrison could seize and hold when they launched a sortie. (Ligne, 1795–1811, XIV, 117–18)

None of this prevented Frederick from heaping all the blame on his engineers:

What! Is it not shameful to have failed to reach the glacis after fifteen days of open trenches? Just think! If Coehoorn and Vauban came to life again, they would surely present dunces' caps to the people who meddle in their trade nowadays, (11 June, Frederick, 1879–1934, XVII, 60)

The Prussians raised the siege on the night of 1–2 July, after the enemy had bushwacked a convoy of 4,000 waggons, carrying badly-needed ammunition and supplies. The Prussian officer Warnery gives the verdict of the army on the whole sorry affair:

As somebody had to take the blame for the failure to capture Olmütz, the lot fell on the engineer officer Balbi, the king's former favourite. He was disgraced, and he did not show his face again until the siege of Dresden [1760]. To be perfectly frank, nobody was in favour of the attack on Olmütz – an 'escapade' is just about the only way to describe it. (Warnery, 1788, 267)

The contest for the northern plain 1758–61. The siege of Olmütz represented the culmination of the third and last of Frederick's offensives over the border hills. He fared much better when he resumed campaigning in the territory to the north of the heights, where by ceaseless marching he was able to extract the last ounce of advantage from his central position, and survive reverses that were apparently more serious than the failure before Olmütz. The motions of the main Austrian army were confined for the most part to the area in southern Saxony around Dresden, while the combined German 'Army of the Empire' spent its time reducing the towns of western and central Saxony, and losing them again to the Prussians.

Frederick's one attempt at a major siege concerned Dresden, the capital of Saxony, which had fallen into the hands of the Austrians. In mid-July 1760 Frederick simply wheeled all his available artillery into position before the walls, and opened fire. Saxon cities burnt very easily (as witness the events at Magdeburg in 1631, Zittau in 1757 and Dresden again in 1945), and soon

the fire was raging ... terribly in the city and the suburbs. Many of the foremost streets were burning from end to end, and wherever you looked you could see houses crashing down. The Prussians noticed that Austrian officers were observing their movements through telescopes from the tower of the Kreuzkirche, and were reporting the information by signals. The Prussian guns fired at the tower. It flared up and collapsed, causing a wide conflagration. (Archenholtz, 1911, 327–8)

The heavy visage of General Johann Sigismund Macquire von Inniskillen, the Austrian commandant, remained quite unmoved. After a couple of days the Prussians therefore marched tamely away, having achieved nothing save the destruction of one of the foremost centres of Baroque civilisation. If Frederick hastened to put the blame for the débâcle on the technicians, one of his officers was willing to testify that

no one purposely failed in his duty. But we should not have been asked to perform the impossible, and what was demanded of us was really beyond human capacity. Moreover in this operation the high command departed from all the rules of the engineering art – instead of opening regular trenches and guarding them properly, we simply occupied the ditch of an old ruinous rampart and prolonged it a little. At the beginning of the siege we were completely devoid of siege artillery.... The history of sieges in general, and in particular that of Prague in 1757, ought to have proved to the king that it is impossible to force a sufficiently-garrisoned fortress to surrender just by a bombardment, especially when there are armies of relief in the offing. (Retzow, 1803, II, 273–4)

The one commander of the time who showed a genuine mastery of improvised siegework was the Austrian general Gideon Ernst Loudon, a taciturn, craggy-faced soldier of fortune whose exploits threatened to turn the balance of the war. On 26 July 1760 he cannonaded and successfully stormed the fortress of Glatz, which commanded a fertile enclave in the wall of border hills, and one of the avenues between the northern and southern theatres. It was a stroke of timing that would have done credit to Coehoorn himself. More dangerously still, Loudon dodged around Frederick's blocking position at Bunzelwitz at the end of September 1761, and stormed the vital Silesian fortress of Schweidnitz on the first of the next month. Some of Loudon's Austrian rivals affected to dismiss the capture of Schweidnitz as a simple *tour de Croate*, but elsewhere there was general agreement that 'this master-stroke demonstrated how Loudon excelled in the art of taking fortresses at the first onset, a technique he first employed at the capture of Glatz' (Silva, 1778, 208).

Frederick had to fall back to Breslau. Taken together with the loss of Kolberg to the Russians

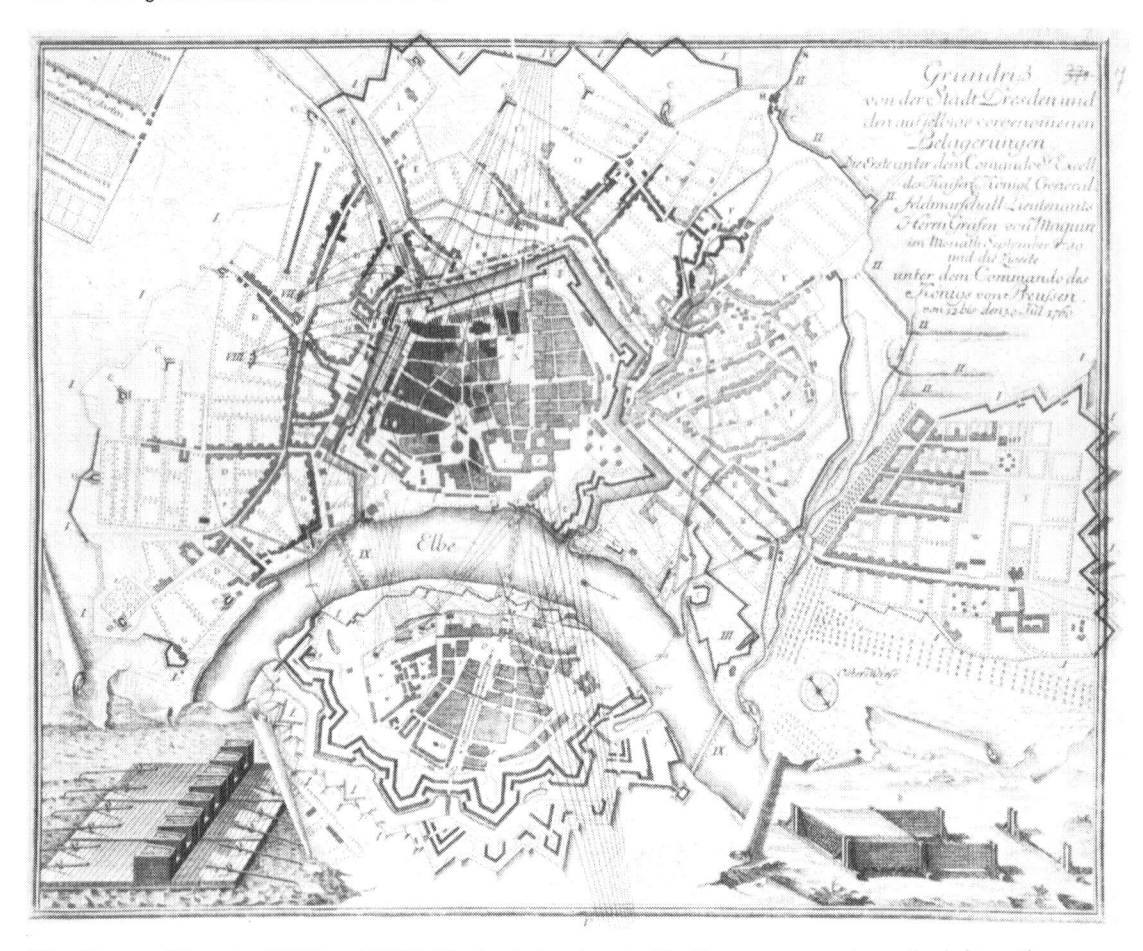

79 Sieges of Dresden 1759 and 1760. The batteries denoted by Roman numerals on the left are the Prussian bombardment batteries of 1760. The inset 'A' at the bottom left-hand corner shows a floating battery which was moored in the Elbe by the resourceful General Macquire in 1760

on 16 December, the reduction of Schweidnitz seemed to indicate that the Prussian body politic was in the process of dissolution.

The decision at Schweidnitz 1762. The Empress Elizabeth of Russia died on 5 January 1762, which brought about a convulsion in European politics no less far-reaching than the Diplomatic Revolution of the 1750s. Her crazy successor, Peter III, made peace with Frederick in May, and on 16 June he went so far as to conclude an armed alliance. Prussia's survival was assured, but Frederick still had to wrest his southern borders from the Austrians by force.

Now that the odds were weighing in his favour, Frederick manoeuvred the Austrian field army away from Schweidnitz, then addressed himself to the siege of that much-disputed place. The fortress was packed with a respectable garrison of 10,000 picked troops from all the regiments of the Austrian army, and entrusted to the command of Lieutenant-General Peter Guasco, an experienced engineer and topographer.

Because of its exceptional strategic and technical interest, the attack on Schweidnitz takes its place as the foremost siege of the middle of the eighteenth century. The operation represented the ultimate effort of the Prussians and Austrians for the possession of Silesia, and upon that issue hung the outcome of the struggle for the upper hand in Central Europe. The siege called forth commensurate efforts – the Austrians were making a determined defence of a stronghold with detached forts (the first in history), while the Prussians tried to break in by employing mines of unprecedented power. Indeed, 'this siege is truly notable, since both the attack and the defence were carried out according to all the rules of the art and prosecuted with the greatest energy' (H++++, 1774, 3-4).

Frederick chose as his chief technician a renegade Frenchman, Simon Deodat Lefèbvre, who had assisted at the siege of Bergen-op-Zoom. He later passed into the Prussian service, and was fortunate enough to spend 1758 in Austrian captivity, which exempted him from any part in the disastrous siege of Olmütz. This was probably why Frederick could still regard him as 'the most able engineer that I have' (to Tresckow, May 1759, Frederick, 1879-1939, XVIII, 269).

As chief engineer for the attack on Schweidnitz, Lefèbvre gloated at the prospect of being able to employ the 'globe of compression', the last word in military mining. In 1754 he had written to the distinguished French military technician Belidor, asking him for information about the 'globes' which he had exploded in the previous year on Marshal Belle-Isle's estate at Bissy in Normandy. Belidor was generous enough to reply in some detail.

The 'globe of compression', as it turned out, was simply a very large charge of gunpowder at the end of an ordinary mine gallery. Belidor found that Vauban had been mistaken to suppose that, beyond a certain weight of charge, the force of a mine explosion was dissipated in casting material higher into the air. On the contrary, not only did the diameter of the crater continue to increase proportionately with the charge, but the explosion threw out a crushing underground shock wave. Belidor arrived at the weight of his charge in pounds by multiplying the length in feet of the 'line of least resistance' (distance between charge and surface) by three hundred.

Lefèbvre lost no time in planting a charge of 3,300 pounds fifteen feet below ground in the park at Potsdam:

When everything was finished, His Majesty came to see the mine exploded. He himself gave the signal for the fuze to be ignited, and the result was a plume of earth and dust which rose high into the air. The crater was sixty-six feet wide and eighteen deep, with smoothly-scoured sides which showed no subsidence. (Lefèbvre, 1778, II, 92)

The weight of this charge was below Belidor's specifications (probably because the soil was light and sandy) but the compressive force staved in a demonstration mine gallery forty-two feet distant on the same plane, and destroyed another gallery sixteen feet below the seat of the explosion. Frederick was duly impressed, but the siege of Schweidnitz was to show that it was much easier to set off a 'globe of compression' in a royal park than in an actual operation of war.

On the night of 7-8 August 1762 the Prussians broke ground about nine hundred paces from the Jauernicker Fort on the north-western side of Schweidnitz. Their misfortunes began immediately, for the Austrians responded by erupting from the

80 Prussian siege of Schweidnitz in 1762

fortress in the first of a series of devastating sorties. The place seemed to be crammed with Hungarians, who were fighting mad, and with Irishmen who were even worse. In the trenches the youthful Prussian troops were literally reduced to tears by the ordeal.

Further deficiencies were revealed in the period following the night of 22–23 August, when the Prussians made their third parallel and the miners sank a sixteen-foot deep shaft on the left of the new trench. Now the lack of a true technical corps began to be severely felt. Lefèbvre observed that:

It is only in the French service that you can carry out such operations with real proficiency, for in that army the technical officer is treated with respect and given everything he needs. It is not the individual who carries the burden, but the corps as a whole. (*ibid.*, II, 69)

Here we have the measure of the difference between French and German military engineering in the eighteenth century.

The Prussian miners met their match in the Bohemian miners of the Austrians, who were guided by the Frenchman Gribeauval and their own Captain Pabliczek. Lefèbvre's 'globes of compression' therefore gained him disappointingly little ground, and in the second half of September he suffered a nervous collapse.

Guasco was managing his resources with much skill. As regards the static defences, he was aware that the low profile of the works offered little security against storm, and that his principal trust must be in the palisade, which was assiduously repaired every night. Gun carriages and ammunition had never been abundant, even at the beginning of the siege, but Guasco imposed a strict fire-discipline on his gunners, and he thereby secured for himself

the means of putting up a vigorous defence of the palisade and covered way by means of a lively fire of musketry, but more particularly the resources to rain down a continuous stream of bombs, pierrier stones and grenades into the mine craters, which inconvenienced the enemy extremely. (Guasco, 1846, 32)

Frederick now arrived on the scene to take charge in person. He was able to give the operation his undivided attention, which was probably why he directed it with much more success than his earlier sieges. By the last week in September a chain of craters extended right up to the palisade of the Jauernicker-Fort, and Guasco could not longer think of using countermines, for fear of wrecking his own defences. He turned once more to the infantry, and on the night of 26–27 September the elegant First Lieutenant Waldhütter and a party of thirty Hungarian grenadiers led a sortie:

They uprooted the palisade to open the way to the nearest crater, and Waldhütter and his men jumped into the hole without hesitation. The Prussians were on their guard – some of them opened fire, while others were kneeling and held their muskets high with bayonets planted on the end. Our people threw themselves recklessly on their opponents with drawn sabre. A number of the Hungarians were skewered on the bayonets, but the rest set about the enemy and hacked them down to the last man. (Guasco, 1846, 27)

The supporting forces occupied this crater and two more, and destroyed the mine galleries they found leading from the nearly parallel.

Early in October the Austrians at last began to show clear signs of exhaustion. The carriages of their heavy cannon were in splinters, while the roundshot for the lighter pieces were fast running out, and the reserves of musket cartridges could be counted in days. Almost every one of the engineers was dead or wounded.

The resistance was broken by two blows. On 8 October a Prussian bomb landed outside the magazine of the Jauernicker-Fort, and a mighty explosion blew down the rearward front of the work from one end to the other, burying three hundred grenadiers. The last stroke was dealt on the following night. The Prussians had driven a deep gallery for ninety-six feet from the bottom of the crater of their third globe of compression, and they now exploded a charge of 5,000 pounds beneath the covered way of the fort. A stretch of the covered way vanished, and a ramp of earth was thrown across the narrow ditch to the top of the rampart.

On 9 October Guasco and the 9,000 surviving members of his garrison surrendered as prisoners of

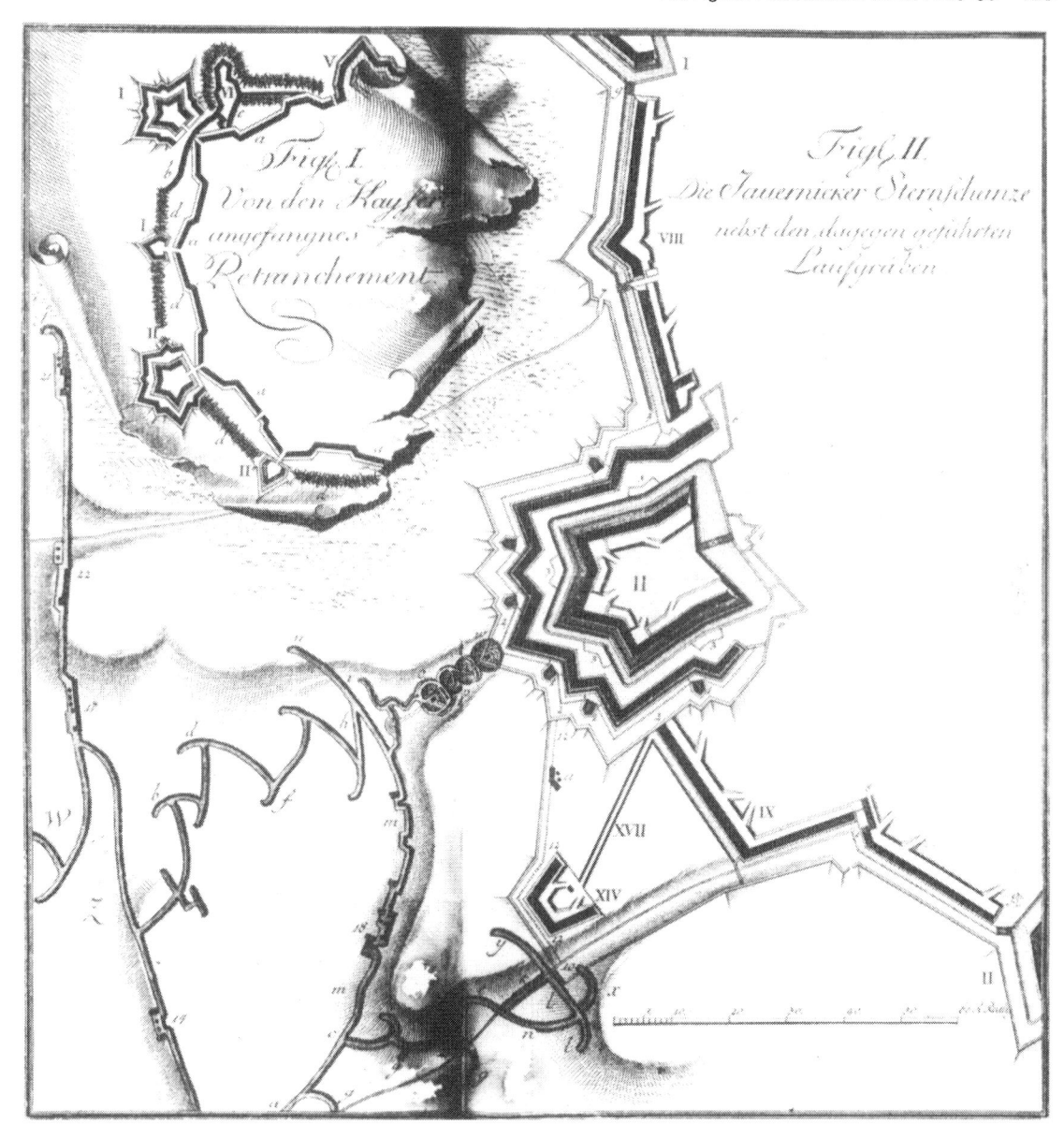

81 The attack on the Jauernicker-Fort at Schweidnitz 1762 (Tielke, 1778)

war, after a resistance which had lasted for sixty-three days of open trenches. By the admission of the besiegers, 'the Austrians defended themselves with bravery and coolness. Gribeauval ran through all the resources and tricks of his art, in order to frustrate the Prussian siegeworks' (Retzow, 1803, II, 515).

On 15 February 1763 Austria, Saxony and Prussia concluded a treaty of peace which restored their borders to the lines they had followed in 1756. In other words, Frederick retained Silesia.

The struggle for Schweidnitz had been rich in technical and human interest. The globes of compression had been efficient in moving great masses of earth, but the prolonged underground war emphasised that mining was still the most difficult branch of the besieger's art, and that no single invention could offer a substitute for the skill and nerve of the tunnellers.

Likewise, the bitter defence of the ring of detached forts owed more to the moral qualities of the garrison than to the novel lay-out. The Austrians rightly concentrated their resources to defend a single sector, just as if Schweidnitz had been a conventional fortress with a continuous permanent enceinte. A living garrison was not like some primitive creature which could be chopped into a multitude of viable parts.

Third round: The War of the Bavarian Succession 1778–9

The rivalry between Austria and Prussia for influence in the German empire led to a new outbreak of hostilities in July 1778. This time the Prussians owned a convincing superiority in numbers, thanks to the support of the Saxons, and Frederick accordingly planned to put 220,000 men into the field and carry out a giant pincer movement by way of Silesia and Saxony.

Old Fritz did not know that some essential changes had been wrought in military geography. In 1764 the Austrian general Franz Lacy had urged that more attention should be paid to the possibility of defending north Bohemia along the line of the upper Elbe, a hitherto little-regarded stretch of the river which curled eastwards and northwards to its sources in the border mountains with Silesia.

82 Königgrätz. (The model in the Krajské Muzeum, Hradec Králové)

The Austrians, as was their way, appointed a commission to look into the affair. They now had an engineering corps of their own, but French technicians stood very high in credit with them, after the stout resistance of the works of Olmütz (built 1742–57 by P. F. Bechade de Rochepine), and Gribeauval's prolonged underground defence of Schweidnitz in 1762. Now in 1764 the Austrians brought in for consultation the French brigadier-general d'Ajot and a team of four of his officers. This informed opinion concluded that the best way to bolster up Lacy's river line would be to place a new fortress at Pless, where there was a plateau of ideal height and dimensions, falling gently down to the confluence of the Elbe with the Mettau. In 1765, however, the *Genie-Director* Prince Charles of Lorraine and the obstinate General Harsch made a new reconnaissance, and perversely recommended the fortification of the existing town of Königgrätz, which occupied a narrow site a short distance down the Elbe at the confluence with the Adler. The Pless scheme was abandoned, and the foundation stone of the works at Königgrätz was laid in 1766.

Twelve years later, when the new war broke out, the Austrians made the fortress of Königgrätz their principal *point d'appui*, and arrayed their main army along the Mettau and the upper Elbe in the way which had been sketched out by Lacy in 1764. That is why the invaders found the Austrians entrenched in the very area which Frederick had chosen for the junction of the two jaws of his pincers. The king's army, coming from Silesia by way of Glatz, did not dare to attack the lines, while Prince Henry of Prussia and the Saxons at first made good progress into north-west Bohemia, but ran out of supplies and resolution a few miles short of Prague. Hostilities, such as they were, came to an end early in 1779 without a single siege or battle having taken place.

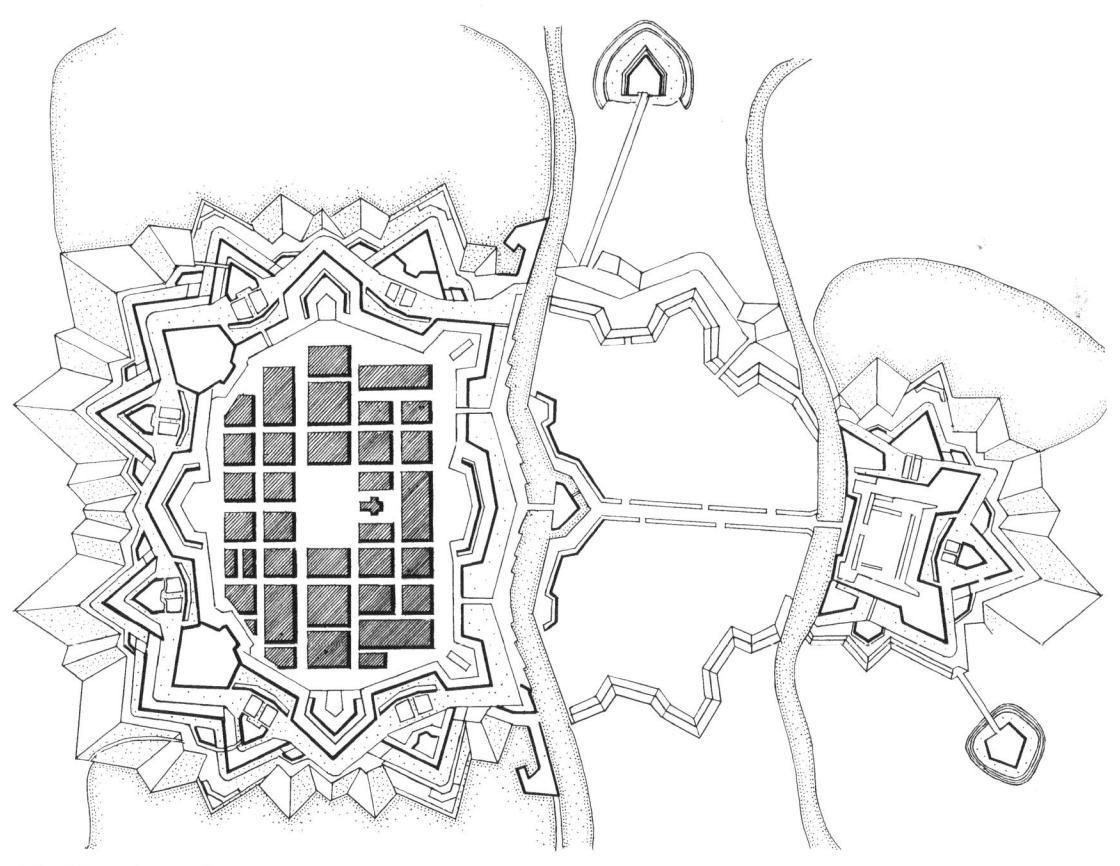

83 Theresienstadt

The quarrel was settled by the Treaty of Teschen on 13 May 1779. The Austrians failed in their larger aim of taking over the whole of Bavaria, but as some recognition of their local defensive victory they gained a small slice of eastern Bavaria along the Inn. The ceded territory included the little fortress of Braunau (the birth-place of Adolf Hitler), and afforded the Austrians better communications with the Tyrol.

After the war the Austrians hastened to review the defence of north Bohemia. Their field forces had been brought near to breaking-point in the late campaign, and the military men were now agreed as to the urgency of sealing off the avenues of invasion by additional permanent fortifications.

In order to guard the route up the lower Elbe from Saxony, the fortress of Theresienstadt was planted at Kopist in northern Bohemia, at the confluence of the Elbe and the Eger. Before that time, the unresisted passage of the Elbe had given the Prussians the facility of transporting provisions, ammunition and siege guns up to the effective head of navigation at Leitmeritz (which now lay under the guns of Theresienstadt). The new fortress stood too far back from the frontier to prevent the Prussians from entering Bohemia in the first place, but they would now be unable to penetrate into the heart of the kingdom 'without leaving an important fortress on the flanks or rear of their positions. This stronghold, with its powerful garrison, will stand in the way of the further enterprises of the enemy, and render the transport of their provisions very dangerous' (Romaňák, 1980, 714). The words are those of General Pellegrini, who designed the sprawling fortress complex, which comprised a main fortress on the left bank of the newly regulated Eger, and a *Kleine Festung* which was sited on the right bank to control the sluices. The main fortress was a massive affair of eight bastions and six ravelins, and it owned three effective zones of defence: the main rampart with its curtains, bastions, and four bastion cavaliers; the ravelins which, together with the connecting counterguards on some of the landward fronts, formed a nearly continuous wall of works; and lastly the elaborate covered way, which owned no less than ten masonry lunette-redoubts in the reentrant angles. The building work extended over the ten years from 1780, and the five brick kilns produced twenty million or more bricks per annum, many of which were used to line the eighteen miles of underground galleries.

A companion fortress was positioned far to the east on the upper Elbe on the Pless plateau site, and named 'Josephstadt' in honour of Austria's emperor

84 The south-eastern front at Josephstadt

and co-regent Joseph II. The work was begun in 1780 and completed in thirteen years, and so, adding Josephstadt to Königgrätz, the Austrians owned two modern fortresses on an eleven-mile stretch of the upper Elbe.

These 'Austrian' fortresses in north Bohemia are of great technical interest, for the French engineers of the later eighteenth century had run out of places to fortify in their homelands, and these virgin sites presented them and their imitators with their one opportunity to execute the elaborate designs they had been devising in their stuffy offices over the last decades. If Königgrätz and Theresienstadt are clearly products of the accepted school of Mézières, then Josephstadt was an eclectic *omnium gatherum* of motifs from that place, from Cormontaigne, and from the old master Vauban himself. The whole was brought together by Louis Querlonde du Hamel, who had come to Bohemia as a captain in d'Ajot's suite in 1764, and was now a major-general in the Austrian service. At Josephstadt he constructed a crownwork bridgehead beyond the river, and occupied the low plateau of Pless with a main fortress of eight bastions (some with counterguards), powerful ravelins (some with casemated redoubts and caponnière rearward communications), a loopholed counterscarp, and large double redoubts in the re-entrant places of arms. The ramparts were inter-

85 One of the surviving bastions at Josephstadt, on the western front. Such Franco-Austrian fortifications are of impressive scale and finish – contrast with p. 204

sected with casemated traverses *à la Mézières*, and the outworks and glacis were riddled with permanent countermine galleries amounting in total length to twenty miles or more. The dimensions of the scarps were drawn directly from Cormontaigne and Fourcroy, and the masonry was carried out in a hard reddish-brown brick of local manufacture.

Regarding Theresienstadt and Josephstadt, the Prince de Ligne commented:

In former times campaigning in Bohemia was like an English country dance in which the rival parties joined hands, then ran to the end of the room. Now that our two fortresses have been built, the fate of Bohemia can no longer be decided by battle – Frederick himself would have been incapable of invading the province as often as he did, on four or five occasions, if the fortresses had been constructed in his time. (Ligne, 1795–1811, XVII, 22)

Unfortunately the northern Bohemian fortress system was built too late to participate in the wars of Frederick the Great, it was too remote to influence the Napoleonic campaigns to any great extent, and it was technically unequal to meet the demands of the middle of the nineteenth century. Königgrätz and Josephstadt had inspired Joseph II to declare 'this is naturally the weakest stretch of the Elbe ... but it now seems to me impossible for an enemy to pass between these two fortresses' (Peters, 1902, 309). In their triumphal campaign of 1866 the Prussians swept past the two places almost as if they had not been there, which showed how much the art of war had changed in the meantime.

Frederician military engineering

Frederick and his engineers

Probably no other great captain of modern history has been cursed with such bad relations with his engineers as Frederick of Prussia. While the rest of Europe was trying, with unequal success, to institutionalise its military engineering, Frederick actually chose to reverse the progress which his father, Frederick William I, had made towards the same end.

The old king had commissioned the Dutch-born lieutenant-colonel Gerhardt Cornelius Walrave (1692–1773) to draw up a rank-list of engineers, and with the help of this information Frederick William was able to issue two comprehensive sets of engineering regulations in 1729.

In the 1730s, the formative years of the new corps, Walrave went on to build extensive fortifications at Stettin and Magdeburg which influenced the style of Prussian military architecture for more than a century to come. The ditches of the new works were deep and narrow, and they were in places flanked by caponnières – low-lying casemated galleries which jutted perpendicularly across the ditch. The scarps (rampart walls) seemed dangerously low by French standards, but they were shielded by high counterscarps and earthen envelopes. Both bastioned and tenaille motifs were used as the terrain suggested.

Among the other 'Prussian' traditions which were established by Walrave was the principle of maintaining the strictest secrecy concerning fortress designs. This stood in marked contrast to the habits of some of the French governors, who were only too delighted to guide foreign officers around their works.

Walrave's proficiency and standing were confirmed when, in 1733, the Empire commissioned him to restore the decayed fortifications at Kehl and Philippsburg at a cost of 300,000 florins. Walrave's designs had commended themselves on account of their efficacy and cheapness, and they were preferred to the projects of the Austrian captain Lüttich, and Colonel von Welsch from Mainz.

When he began to cast about for engineers, the young king Frederick naturally considered Holland to be the most likely source of able non-French officers. On 11 January 1741 he accordingly asked his military mentor, Field-Marshal Leopold of Anhalt-Dessau, to suggest the names of five or six good engineers in the Dutch service. The Old Dessauer replied that the Dutch had had no experience of active military operations since the War of the Spanish Succession, and that in any case he could recommend twenty-two engineers already standing in the Prussian service, headed by their own Dutchman Walrave. In addition to his fortress-building at Magdeburg and Stettin, this gentleman had assisted at eleven sieges and two *coups de main*, and this practical experience, together with the Old Dessauer's recommendation, gained him the promotion of major-general on 4 May 1741, and the effective leadership of a corps of forty-four officers. In 1742, after the end of the First Silesian War, Walrave was appointed chief of the new pioneer regiment which was set up at Neisse, and in 1747 Frederick gave his approval to Walrave's *Mémoire sur l'Attaque et la Défense des Places*, and made use of it in his instructions to fortress commandants.

Frederick liked an element of eccentricity in his companions, and he was certainly willing to tolerate a good deal in Walrave – the string of mistresses, the fitting out of his palace of Liliput with plundered goods, and a bizarre character which permitted Walrave to extort money from monasteries, while prompting him to send wax candles to the church at Czestochowa, and repair war-damaged religious pictures at his own expense. The king was finally forced to move when Walrave opened suspicious relations with foreign envoys.

On 10 February 1748 Frederick entertained Walrave and others to lunch, and chatted and joked with him over table:

When lunch was finished Walrave, like the other guests, asked leave to return home. In the royal anteroom, however, a general requested him to hand over his sword. Walrave took it for a prank, but when the general assured him in all seriousness that he was carrying out the royal intention, Walrave returned in haste to the king's chamber to discover from the monarch in person whether he had really ordered his arrest. Frederick's only reply was: 'The general must have received an order to this effect', whereupon he ducked into a side room without listening to a word that Walrave had to say. Count Haake then placed Walrave under arrest. (Hildebrandt, 1829–35, II, 126)

The investigations revealed that Walrave had embezzled more than 40,000 thaler in Silesia alone, but also showed that his foreign contacts had been unwise rather than treasonable. What probably told most heavily against Walrave, however, was the fact that he was a manifestly dangerous repository of the innermost secrets of Prussian fortresses. He was therefore sentenced to perpetual imprisonment in his own Sternschanze fort at Magdeburg. Walrave sent a copy of the 88th Psalm to plead for his release ('I am counted with them that go into the pit; I am as a man that has no strength: Free among the dead, like the slain that lie in the grave, whom thou rememberest no more', etc.). Frederick coolly sent back the 101st ('He that worketh deceit shall not dwell in my house: he that telleth lies shall not tarry in my sight', etc.). The wretched man was allowed some comforts, and the company of a menagerie of animals, but his liberation came only with his death on 16 January 1773, after nearly a quarter of a century of imprisonment.

The disgrace of Walrave effectively killed the corporate life of the Prussian engineers. If Major Balbi now became the engineer highest in favour with the king, it was not because he assumed any leadership of the corps, but because he offered some of the things he desired most in a friend – a gift for telling stories, a willingness to tolerate Frederick's social cruelties, and a touch of the outlandish. Balbi, who hailed from Genoa, was a man of extreme ugliness, and he used to say that before he enjoyed the royal grace his hideous countenance used to earn him some of the most unpleasant jobs in the Prussian service, like clearing the churchyard at Stettin. More domesticated than Walrave, Balbi once tried to smuggle a melon from the royal table to take home to his wife. Frederick pretended not to notice, but then affected to search in the fruit bowl for a good melon, and called out: 'Hey Balbi, give me the specimen you have hidden in your bag, it's the only eatable one here!' (Kalkreuth, 1840, IV, 136).

Balbi's term as favourite ended with the débâcle at Olmütz in 1758: 'Until then the king had always called him "dear little Balbi", but after the raising of the siege of Olmütz there was no more talk of our "dear little Balbi". He remained in disgrace until the end of his life' (Kalkreuth, 1840, IV, 136).

The most horrific fate of all awaited the third in succession of Frederick's engineering favourites, Simon Lefèbvre, who was one of the experts recruited by Balbi during his tour of the French sieges in the Netherlands in 1747 and 1748. Lefèbvre was admitted to the Prussian service as a captain, and in the period before the Seven Years War he recommended himself to Frederick's favour by compiling a survey of Brandenburg, and conducting the successful experiments with the 'globes of compression' at Potsdam. However, the king was sorely disappointed by Lefèbvre's check at the siege of Schweidnitz in 1762, and in the following year he withdrew a special pension from him, declaring 'you must bear in mind that the most important quality in any officer must be to possess and maintain a cool head, and not allow himself to lose it in any circumstances' (Bonin, 1877, I, 10).

Lefèbvre gradually regained a little of the king's grace, and in the summer of 1771, as a newly promoted lieutenant-colonel, he completed a casemate at Neisse. The work cost 200,000 thaler, but when the props were removed the roof fell in, killing between 120 and 130 men. Frederick came to Silesia to demand an account, but rather than face the interview Lefèbvre took up a kitchen knife and killed himself by repeated blows to the stomach and chest. Frederick was genuinely shocked, and exclaimed 'I would never have been so hard on him' (Zimmermann, 1790, II, 341).

After the Seven Years War foreign adventurers could scarcely complain that they were left in ignorance of the kind of treatment which awaited them in the Prussian service. The Piedmontese colonel Pinto fell out with the king over the designs for hilltop forts in Silesia, as did the French-born Count d'Heintz over the siting of the large new fortress to be built in West Prussia. D'Heintze repeatedly complained to Frederick about the lack of promotion, and in 1786 he finally elicited the reply that engineers were not to be ranked with the other officers of the army. He discovered like the rest that it was no help to be in the right in one's quarrels with the king.

Less excusable still was the neglect of reliable German engineers, like the senior engineer, Colonel Regler, who designed the fortress of Silberberg, or the valiant and long-serving Paul von Gontzenbach, who directed the works at Graudenz. The consequence was a shameful neglect of native talent:

Generally speaking the German is studious, hardworking, meticulous and a lover of order: when he takes up a profession, he strives to improve himself in it.... Now the French engineering corps enjoys a very high and well-deserved reputation, and Frederick concluded that it was simply because the French were born good engineers. As soon as a Frenchman came forward and said that he was an engineer, Frederick made him a captain in his own engineering corps. He did not stop to think that no officer capable of serving among the distinguished members of the French royal corps, where ability and honour are rewarded with a sure and well-regarded career, would ever contemplate entering such an abject body of engineer officers as the Prussian. (Mirabeau and Mauvillon, 1788, 173, 172)

Alone in his army the engineers were allowed to have no settled establishment, pay, or path of promotion – by the time of Frederick's death in 1786 some engineers who had served in the Seven Years War were still lieutenants, while their comrades in the other arms had risen to become colonels or generals.

Rather than permit his experts to enjoy any kind of corporate existence, Frederick sought to manage engineering affairs by wayward and sporadic personal interventions, corresponding directly with engineers and individual fortress commandants on even the most trivial matters. No kind of routine was established for fortress construction. As a general rule Frederick liked to build as cheaply as possible from state or local resources – labour raised by the local administration, carts from the large landowners, timber from the royal forests, and some at least of the bricks from state-owned kilns. Only when the local authorities fell down on the job did Frederick usually have resort to contractors. These people were inadequately supervised, and frequently defrauded the state in collusion with the engineer officers.

On the matter of theoretical education and scientific progress Frederick did not welcome initiatives from the body of the corps. In 1747 he thanked one Major Humbert for the present of a *Traité* on siegework, but characteristically added 'I cannot conceal from you that in this trade I prefer good practical skill, enlightened by experience, to the most profound theory' (Preuss, 1832–4, I, 52). The French

Professor Marson was allowed in 1775 to establish an engineering preparatory school of sorts in a single room in the Berlin Schloss. Marson certainly met Frederick's requirements for freakishness, standing just three feet high, and owning one eye, but his academy enjoyed so little royal support that it disappeared without trace before the end of the reign. Major Pullet observed:

with a few exceptions, the engineering corps consisted of what for lack of a better expression I will call 'guild tradesmen', who went about clutching ruler and set square, with which they drew the systems of Pagan, Vauban, Coehoorn and others, without understanding the ideas behind them, or who were capable of reciting the dead print of these masters forwards and backwards without a slip. . . . A body formed on these principles became . . . a corporation of craftsmen of limited expertise, or a dumping ground for individuals who could not be fitted in elsewhere. (Bonin, 1877, I, 141)

It is not easy to find a convincing explanation as to why the greatest soldier of his age so badly misused his experts. If the Prussian engineers were notoriously corrupt, the fault lay largely with the king himself, who always slashed bills for fortress construction by half; the engineers learnt to ask for double their real needs, and so lying and fraud became part of their routine.

This kind of behaviour reinforced the distaste which Frederick felt towards commoner officers. Middle-class men were allowed to become engineers with no restriction, as was only sensible, but Frederick did nothing to enhance the prestige or efficiency of the corps when he used it as a rubbish heap for officers who had offended the delicacy of their aristocratic comrades in the infantry and cavalry regiments.

Possibly Frederick was temperamentally incapable of allowing his engineers to develop as an organism. His royal interference, or more charitably 'personal interest', had been commonplace in fortress warfare a century or two earlier, when a king and his army might spend a whole campaigning season immured in trench lines before a single stronghold. Since then, however, the development of the 'science' of siege warfare rendered it almost impossible for an individual to supervise both a field army and a complicated siege operation. When Frederick had to drive his marching regiments into the ground to gain a single hour over the enemy, it seemed to him that the engineers at their sieges were grossly extravagant with time, which of all commodities was the most precious to him. Frederick, the foremost field commander of the middle of the eighteenth century, retained in some respects the habits of a Renaissance prince, who regarded his engineers as hired artists who were incapable of showing judgment or initiative unless it was to line their own pockets.

The engineers enjoyed precious little support from other quarters. Walrave's pioneer regiment was disbanded in the Seven Years War, while the great siege of Schweidnitz showed that the companies of miners (three by 1761) were not the match of Pabliczek's Bohemians. The permanent guard of fortresses was entrusted to second-rate *Land-Regimenter* and fortress gunners, which was useful economy in wartime, but it is difficult to understand why Frederick seemed to go out of his way to express his contempt for these units long after the Seven Years War was over. The townspeople, the other living element in the Prussian fortresses, were accorded an essential but subordinate role in the state's affairs, and the king told his officers to shun all social contact with such common folk.

All of this added up to a sorry inheritance for Frederick's successors. It is little wonder that the crisis of 1806 found the Prussian fortresses in the hands of aged commandants and demoralised garrisons, and peopled by citizens who were accustomed to believe that they had no stake in the defence of their country.

The attack and the defence
To judge from his writings alone Frederick might be accounted one of the most faithful disciples of classic siegecraft. According to his *Principes Généraux de la Guerre* (1748) 'the art of conducting sieges has become a trade like that of carpenter or clock-maker. Certain infallible rules have been established, and we follow an unvarying routine, applying the identical procedure in the same cases'.

He acknowledged his debt in these matters to Marshal Vauban, and to the Old Dessauer, who had drawn up a huge instruction for his benefit in 1738. 'They are our masters. They are responsible for reducing to precepts a science which was hitherto known to very few people' (*Oeuvres Militaires*, Frederick, 1846–57, I, 65, 66).

Frederick's theoretical knowledge was supplemented by his admittedly fleeting acquaintance with siegework in the two Silesian Wars, and by the mass of practical experience which Balbi, Lefèbvre and others brought from the French sieges in the Netherlands in the middle 1740s. He learnt from Balbi of the 'unparalleled utility' (Duvernoy, 1901, 72) of the howitzers at the siege of Bergen-op-Zoom. He likewise adopted the distinction between 'siege' and 'observation' armies which had served de Saxe so well, and he was well up with leading opinion when he declared that the days of the circumvallation were over:

I invariably prefer to have an observation army to cover the siege instead of an entrenched camp. This is because experience shows that you cannot put your trust in the old system of entrenchments. ('Principes Généraux', 1748, in *Oeuvres Militaires*, Frederick, 1846–57, I, 31)

In the last week of July 1752 Balbi, Lefèbvre and the gunner major Dieskau conducted a mock siege of a 'polygon' of two bastions and an intervening ravelin at Potsdam. This operation was intended to acquaint the officers of Potsdam, Berlin and the other garrisons in the business of a siege. An officer of the First Battalion of the Garde wrote that:

We attentively observed the work that went ahead, and the king explained everything with such clarity, and in such detail, that everybody acquired a very good grasp of what it was about. I cannot pay sufficient tribute to the extraordinary eloquence and inexhaustible energy which His Majesty employed to instruct the officers, who were looking on, in every conceivable procedure which might be employed in a siege. We could scarcely hear or see enough to satisfy our curiosity. (Duvernoy, 1901, 83)

The park at Potsdam thundered with a still bigger explosion on 28 April 1754, when Lefèbvre ignited his 'globe of compression' (see p. 127).

The actual performance of the Prussians in the sieges of the Seven Years War fell far short of what might have been expected. Such operations usually amounted to little more than blockades, bombardments or sketchy attempts at formal attack. The blame rests partly in Frederick's overdeveloped sense of economy – he did not lack for good engineers or gunners, 'but he always desired miracles to be accomplished, and always at the least possible cost. He invariably did away with half the resources which are customarily used and required for a siege' (Zimmermann, 1788, 202). Still more important was the unexpected duration and intensity of the field campaigns of the Seven Years War, which left Frederick with so little time to devote to his sieges, as has already been indicated. On 16 April 1758 he congratulated Lieutenant-General Tresckow on the risky but successful escalade of the Galgen-Fort, which brought the first siege of Schweidnitz to an unexpectedly early end: 'Time is something which is very precious to me at the present moment' (Frederick, 1879–1939, XVI, 386). Frederick assumed the immediate direction of a formal siege on only one occasion, at Schweidnitz in 1762, and that was after the Austrian field army had been pushed into the mountains by the action at Burkersdorf.

Old Fritz had some sensible things to say about the ways of defending a fortress: 'The two elements of fire and water, each employed in its appropriate place, are the defensive resources which occasion the greatest difficulties to the besieger, while making the least demands on the troops of the garrison' ('Testament Politique' of 1752, in *Politischen Testamente*, Frederick, 1920, 91). In suitable low-lying sites, as on some fronts at Neisse, Frederick made extensive use of inundations and wet ditches. When the terrain did not lend itself to an aquatic defence, he laid all the more stress on countermines:

Mines prolong the resistance further and defend the fortress better than surface works. They force the enemy to proceed with caution, and when they are made at water level it is quite impossible for the besieger to disarm them. A well-made arrangement of mines ought to be able to explode three times – firstly as a fougasse on the surface, secondly as a chamber resting ten feet below ground, and thirdly as a mine proper, which will often be as much as twenty-five feet deep and more. ('Testament Politique' of 1752, in *Politischen Testamente*, Frederick, 1920, 91)

Frederick was all for keeping up a lively artillery defence throughout the siege. In contrast he looked on sorties with a jaundiced eye, as a kind of operation which caused the defenders a disproportionate amount of casualties. Certainly the Austrians were his superiors in those risky enterprises.

Fortress design
Frederick wrote of the fundamental principles of defence with the clarity of a master tactician. Two things appeared to him to be of fundamental importance: that the layout of fortifications must derive the greatest possible benefit from the terrain; and that the attacker must be held at a distance by a system of detached works. Such outworks were to be secure against enfilade and *coup de main*, to have secure communications, and to be swept by the fire of the main fortress behind. Interestingly enough, Frederick tacitly rejected the accepted doctrine of the 'equilibrium of defence', by which a fortress was supposed to be equally strong on all sides. Instead, one of the functions of detached works was to assure 'that the enemy cannot approach any front with like advantage, but is able to attack only one side of the fortress, upon which the commandant may therefore concentrate all his attention ('Aphorismen des Königs über die Befestigungs-, Lager- und Gefechtskunst', June or July 1757, *Oeuvres Militaires*, Frederick, 1846–57, III, 226).

In general terms Frederick hailed the achievement of Vauban the fortress-builder. In the fourth 'song' of his poem *L'Art de la Guerre* (1751) he proclaimed:

Vous, célèbre Vauban, favori du Dieu Mars,
Vous le sublime auteur des modernes ramparts,
Que votre ombre aparaisse à nos guerriers novices;
Montrez-leur par quels sciences et par quels artifices
Vous avez assuré les places des Français
Contre les bras germains et les canons anglais

Frederick added, however, that the art of defence was by no means exhausted. Indeed, he had already demonstrated his independence of mind in 1743, when Walrave proposed to fortify an awkward height near Neisse by a number of small works. Instead Frederick pushed through his own design for a single star-fort, and showed a model to the French envoy, boasting that even his masters would be unable to take it. Walrave conceded that this new work, Fort Preussen, was designed on a *schönes System*, and in 1747 he modestly owned that Frederick had originated the schemes for all the Silesian fortresses, leaving him merely with the honour of executing his orders.

Frederick arrayed his fortifications, like his subjects, in a highly specialised order. The short-range defence rested on features like narrow and deep ditches, high counterscarps and multiple covered ways. Casemated works, which had been forgotten when Brandenburg engineers came under Dutch influence, were now revived for bastion flanks and counterscarp coffers. Walrave's caponnières were also given a new lease of life, and were attached to the counterscarp, or, in the case of the Schweidnitz enceinte, to the middle of the curtain.

For long-range defence Frederick looked to detached flèches and forts. In some places these works supplied obvious local needs, as when they were planted on commanding hills (Neisse, Glogau, Glatz, Silberberg), or sited to guard inundation sluices (Kosel, Glogau). Much more interesting was the 'pure' application of detached works as a means of producing a deeper and more economical defence than could be afforded by the hornworks of the Dutch and French schools. In this respect the ring of outworks around Schweidnitz constituted a truly revolutionary re-shaping of fortification. These were built on flat and open ground, with the deliberate intent of increasing the depth of defence, and not dictated by local needs, as was the case with Fort Preussen at Neisse or the many other detached forts we find in earlier periods of military history.

At the heart of the Schweidnitz complex lay the old town wall, rebuilt in places, and furnished with ditch caponnières and an irregular outer rampart of earth. Facing the little Weistritz, which ran past the eastern side of the town, the Wasser-Fort hornwork

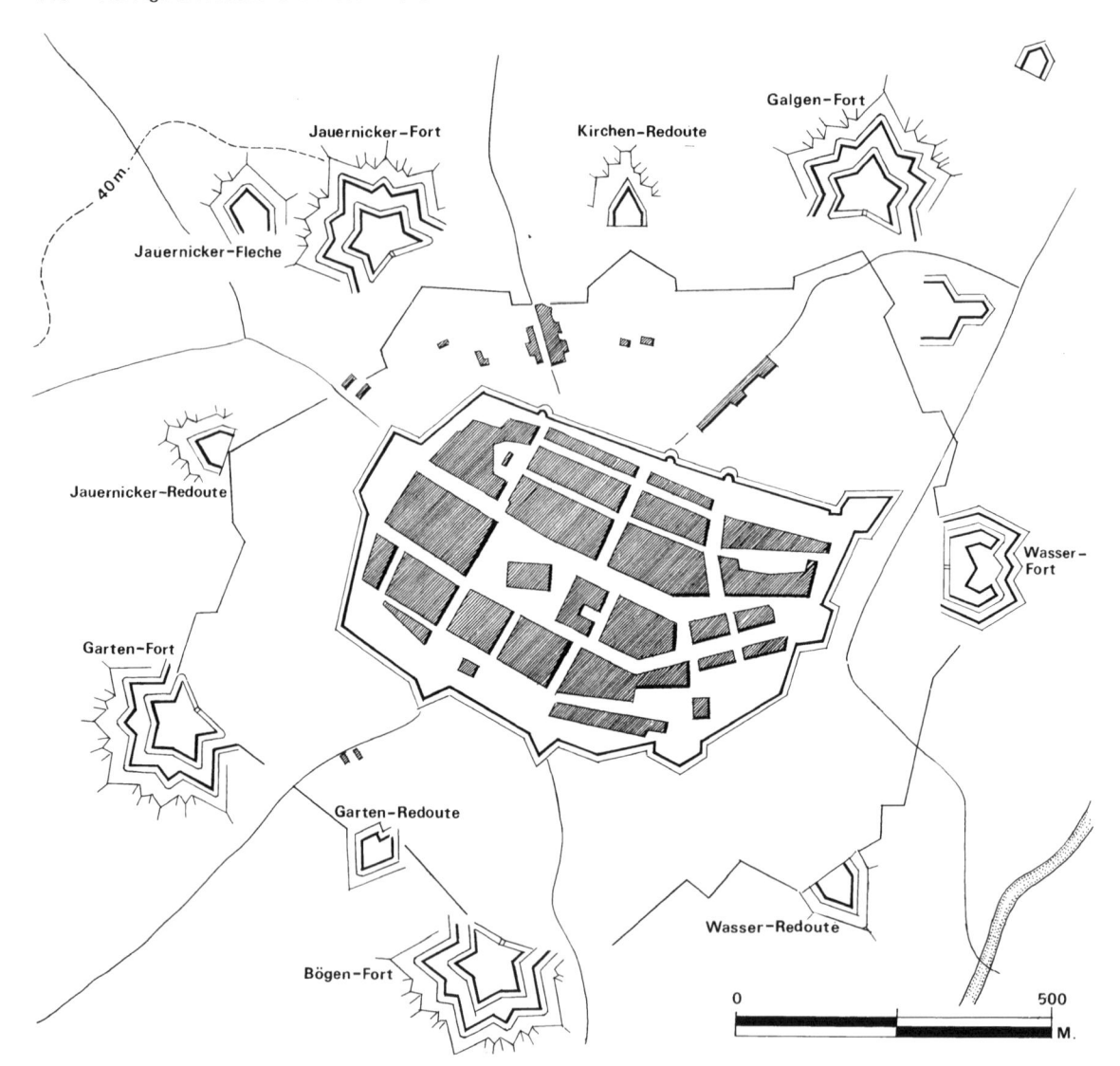

86 Plan of Schweidnitz, showing the detached forts and the Austrian retrenchment

and the nearby Wasser-Redoute owned sites that were strong by nature. To cover the other approaches, the Galgen-, Jauernicker-, Garten- and Bögen-Forts were built on the plateau which extended to the north, west and south; three intermediate redoubts (the Kirchen-, Jauernicker- and Garten-Flèches) were sited to cover some of the wide intervals between the forts. The ring of outworks stood up to more than five hundred paces into the country.

The forts proper were built on a typically Old Fritzian star plan, which was the natural outcome of applying the German tenaille trace to a small work. On their four outer sides the forts owned a double rampart of curious design. As you approached from the open country, a gentle 'countersloping' glacis led down to the dry ditch at the foot of the ten-foot high scarp of the envelope, or outer rampart. The earthen body of the envelope rose to the lip of an eighteen-foot high retaining wall, which simultaneously served as the counterscarp to the rearward rampart, and which offered the fort's

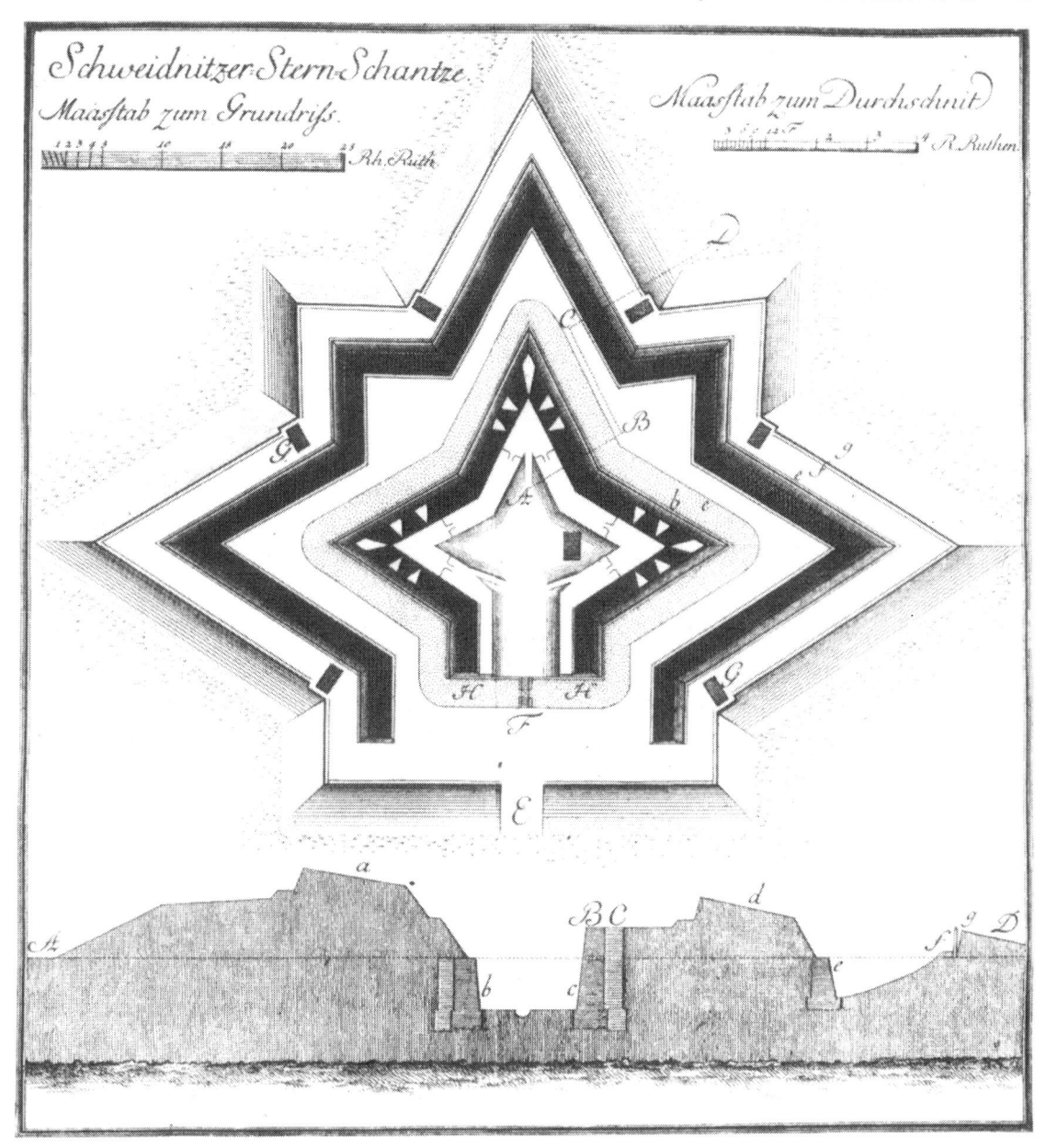

87 Plan and profile of a star fort at Schweidnitz (Tielke, 1778)

chief passive defence. The envelope and the main rampart were separated by a narrow dry ditch, which was commanded by fire from the re-entrant angles of the inner rampart, and (on the broad rearward side of the fort) from caponnières which were placed at the postern gates. The chief rampart owned another surprisingly low revetted scarp, and an earthen parapet which reached to twenty-four to thirty feet above ground level.

The fortification of Schweidnitz was carried out from 1747 under the direction of Colonel von Sehrs, and was completed just in time for the place to fall to the Austrians in November 1757. The new masters could make no sense of the gaps between the forts, and, assuming that the fortress complex was unfinished, they hastened to join the outworks by a continuous retrenchment.

To sum up, the Walravian-Frederician style of fortification was characterised by:

1. Detached forts as a means of affording defence in unprecedented depth, and imposing the defender's will on the shape of the attack
2. A preference for the tenaille, or star trace
3. Deep and narrow multiple ditches
4. Double ramparts, with low masonry scarps
5. A high inner counterscarp, and a gently sloping outer counterscarp on the 'Walrave Profile' to facilitate sorties
6. Active casemated defence from artfully-sited caponnières or counterscarp galleries
7. Passive casemated defence in the form of bomb-proof shelters for troops and stores. Where the water table was too high, or the profile of the works too low, to permit the construction of bombproofs underneath the ramparts, Frederick instead built free-standing single-storey *Hangard* shelters, as at Kosel and in some locations at Schweidnitz.

Frederick constantly revised his notions on fortification through his reign, and he was an avid reader of the earlier volumes of Montalembert, whose ideas accorded so much with his own. So enlightened on engineering matters in general, Frederick was, however, unable to confront his engineers on their own terms. Old Fritz was very bad at mathematics, and still worse at drawing, and, on occasion, when he encountered a defect in a work, the only response open to him was to chase the man responsible with raised stick.

Absolute precision of measurement was of less importance in field fortification, which was the branch of active military engineering which the Prussians practised with the most conspicuous success. In the Seven Years War Frederick's great army camps at Schmottseiffen and Bunzelwitz became celebrated among experts. Less well known were the little works which Frederick ordered to be built in 1758 at nearly all the towns, villages and features of the ground along the edges of the Silesian plain facing the border mountains with Bohemia. By 1763 no less than 288 such strongpoints were to be found in the Circle of Schweidnitz alone.

The Frederician fortress system

It is easy to overlook the benefit which Frederick derived from two powerful fortresses which were built by his father, Frederick William I, and which never came under direct attack in the wars. Stettin, the tutelary fortress-port of the lower Oder, relieved Frederick of much anxiety which he would otherwise have felt for the defence of Pomerania against the Swedes and Russians, as we have seen. Still more important were the many roles of Magdeburg, in Frederick's words 'the ultimate resource of the state' (Duvernoy, 1901, 56), the great depot on the middle Elbe which became the foundation of the war effort in Saxony and deep into Bohemia, and which received the royal court and its treasures in the crisis of the Seven Years War.

Frederick's immediate priority in his own fortress-building was to secure the newly conquered province of Silesia against the vengeful Austrians. As a first line of defence along the borders with Bohemia and Moravia, Frederick extended and rebuilt the works at Glatz and Neisse, and made what were virtually new fortresses at Schweidnitz and Kosel. These four places by themselves absorbed 1,500,000 thaler between 1745 and 1756, whereas only a quarter of a million was spent on all the other fortresses of the monarchy together. Less pressing works went ahead at Glogau, Breslau and Brieg, to secure the line of communication along the Oder.

The interest of the little town of Glatz came from its site in the centre of the county of the same name, a mountain-rimmed salient which was lodged in the border, and which provided the warring parties with one of their best entrances into north Bohemia or central Silesia. The strengthening of Glatz began in 1743, and was directed by Major von Wrede. The town was now furnished with an envelope and a covered way, and an earthen flèche, the 'Kranich', which projected to the north. The old castle continued to do service as a citadel, and from its highlying position it dominated the square and the two main streets of the town. Viewed from the country 'it appeared little more than a large house, built on the summit of a mountain, and devoid of any defence save the rock and its massive walls' (Stille, 1763, 68).

The importance of Glatz was underlined in the Seven Years War when it came under investment by the Austrians in 1757, and was captured by them in 1760. After the Seven Years War the Prussians therefore completed the '*Neue Festung*', a powerful pentagonal tenaille fort on the Schäferberg on the far bank of the Neisse; the ditch was swept by casemated galleries, and three redoubts sprawled over the slopes outside the fort. At the same time the old castle was rebuilt by Lieutenant-Colonel von Regler as a strong casemated donjon. On one of his visits to view the progress of the various works, Frederick was shown the statues of St Florian, who protected against fire, and St Nepomuk, the guardian of Silesia. '"I have no use for Florian", replied Frederick, "because I don't fear fire anyway, but you must put Nepomuk on the new observation tower facing Bohemia, and I hope that he will be on his guard to prevent them invading my country". This order was punctiliously obeyed, and the statue stands even now at its assigned station on the said tower' (Anon., 1788–9, IV, 21–2).

As early as 9 December 1741 Frederick wrote that the re-fortification of Neisse was something which had 'caught my fancy' (Preuss, 1832–4, I, 5). The town was sited on a principal border avenue, and its importance for the defence of Upper Silesia was matched by its utility as a depot for offensives into Moravia. The low-lying town on the right bank of the Neisse river was re-fortified by a double envelope, and a system of between eighteen and twenty sluices which was capable of laying two-thirds of the surrounding country under water. Frederick's main attention was, however, directed towards the hill on the left bank of the Neisse. This feature offered the only suitable dry ground for the emplacement of his stores, and he knew that he had to deny this dominating site to anybody who might be tempted to copy his own bombardment of Neisse in 1741. The foundation stone of Fort Preussen was laid on 30 March 1743, and the attention of foreign engineers was soon caught by the boldness of the

88 The old castle at Glatz, seen from the town

scale and conception of this novel star fort, and its deep ditches, its extensive countermine system, and its two-storey under-rampart casemates with space for one thousand men and huge magazines of stores and ammunition. So many labourers were set to work that the fort was essentially complete in 1744.

Neisse successfully withstood a siege in 1758, but its fame in the Seven Years War was far eclipsed by that of the new fortress complex of Schweidnitz, which lay in a fertile area between the Oder supply line and the main passes of the Bohemian mountains. Schweidnitz changed hands several times during the conflict, and it is scarcely possible to over-exaggerate the importance which the belligerents attached to its ownership in the final stages: its loss in 1761 helped to persuade Frederick that he had lost the war, and, after the death of the Empress Elizabeth gave him an unexpected reprieve, he made its recovery his chief objective in his last campaign.

Kosel, the fourth of the Silesian border strongholds, was in comparison an unimportant place, serving principally as an obstacle in the way of Hungarian raiding parties which might irrupt into the remote south-eastern corner of Upper Silesia. Walrave cast an extensive tenaille enceinte around the old perimeter in the 1740s, and a further scheme of reinforcement was undertaken from 1765.

With his strict sense of priorities, Frederick believed that it was enough to strengthen the existing works of the rearward Oder fortresses – little Brieg, the city of Breslau, and Glogau. However, Frederick's calculations led him astray in the matter of the defences on the far strategic flanks of the Prussian state, for in the 1740s and early 1750s he never conceived that he might come under attack from the French and Russians as well as from the Austrians. In the Seven Years War the fortresses of Wesel and Minden in Prussian Westphalia were therefore abandoned to the French without a fight, and it was only through prodigious efforts that Kolberg in eastern Pomerania was sustained so long against the Russians.

Two new fortresses of radically differing design were built after the Seven Years War, testifying to the open-mindedness and adaptability of Frederick and his engineers. On several occasions in the late war the Austrians had by-passed Glatz, and raced to the passes of the Eulengebirge, a long ridge which struck out from the border mountains and separated the County of Glatz from the Silesian plain. In 1763 Regler recommended the pass of Silberberg as the best blocking position in the Eulengebirge, and over the following years a most curious complex of detached forts sprawled crab-like over the surrounding hilltops. The ditches of the works were blasted out of the living rock, and in 1778 an officer describes the assemblage as a place

which puts Königstein [in Saxony] in the shade, thanks to the artistry with which it is sited, and the extraordinary difficulties which thereby had to be overcome. The more I get to know this fortress, however, the more thankful I am that I do not have to stay here forever, because it is dreadful to live in the casemates. The only people who have to reside here permanently are the commandant, the fortress major, and an official in charge of the wells. The garrison is accommodated in the little town of Silberberg, which lies at the foot of the mountain. (Krockow, 1884, 27)

Clausewitz describes Silberberg as 'a fool with his nose against the wall', but the siting made sense in the context of Frederick's earlier campaigning against the Austrians.

In 1772 the First Partition of Poland delivered to Frederick the greater part of West Prussia, though without Danzig or the fortress of Thorn. Old Fritz therefore considered it all the more vital to give himself a secure crossing of the Vistula (Weichsel). The first site of the intended fortress, on the low-lying Grabau island near Marienwerder, was abandoned in 1776 after drifting ice swept away the works and with them most of the reputation of the engineer in charge, Count d'Heintze. Frederick determined on a new site on the higher lying right bank below Graudenz, and he roughed out a plan for a tenaille enceinte and five detached bastions, which were intended to serve as supports for a future entrenched camp. It was the job of Captain Paul v. Gontzenbach to make sense of the scratchy pen sketch, and from 1776 until the king's death he had to contend with Frederick's suspicions and desire for economy, the practical problems of building the very extensive casemates and countermines, and the inability of the

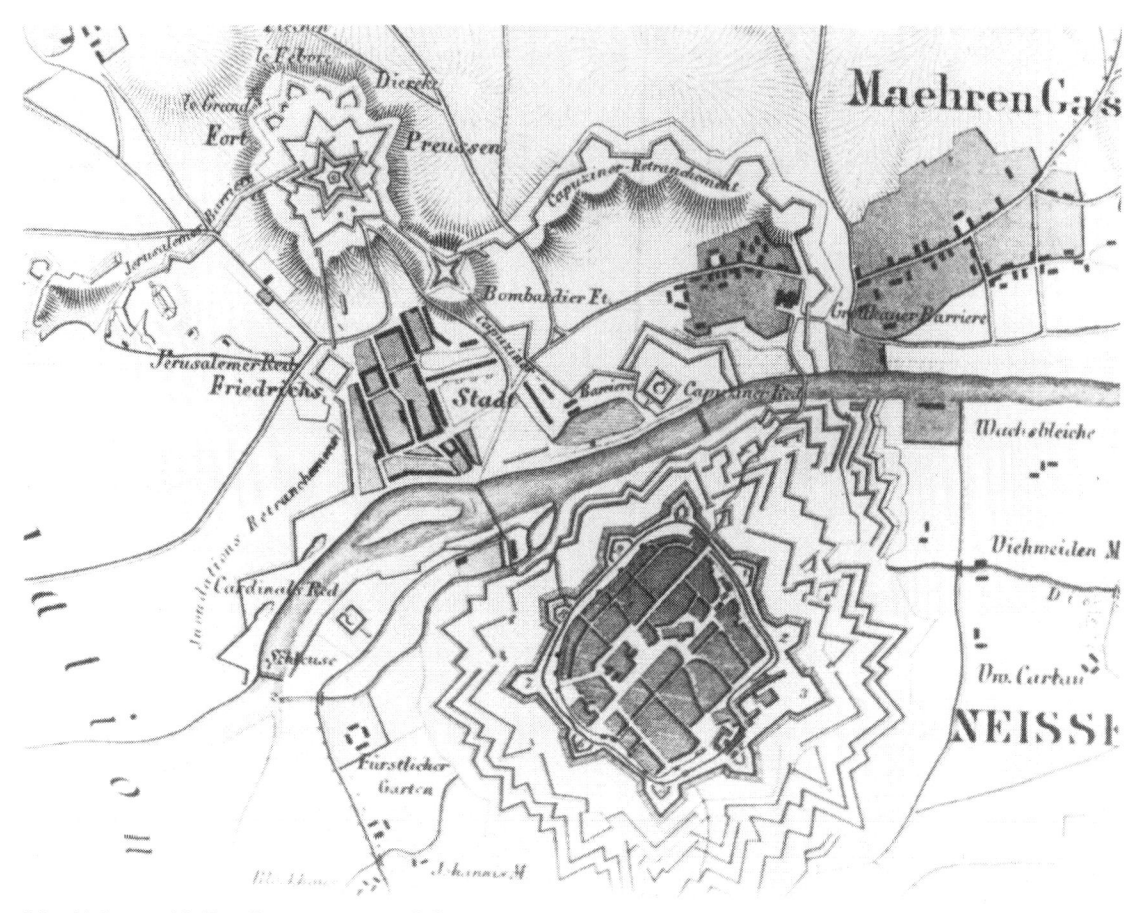

89 Neisse, with Fort Preussen at top left

Marienwerder *Kammer* to meet the demands for bricklayers, masons, labourers and transport.

The fortress in Frederick's strategy

Fortresses are mighty nails which hold and attach the provinces to the dominion of the sovereign. In wartime they serve as *points d'appui* to the army which happens to be in their proximity. They are the support of the troops – their massive ramparts afford a secure refuge to the army's magazines, sick, wounded and munitions. The fortresses which lie nearest the frontier become the guards of the cantonments where we may assemble large bodies of troops – whether we wish to rest in the area during the winter, carry the war into enemy country, or let the men encamp in safety while we are waiting for other troops to join them.
(*Politischen Testamente*, Frederick, 1920, 90)

This statement, from the Political Testament of 1752, is a striking indication of Frederick's conception of the fortress as a versatile instrument of war, not a mere slave of the defensive.

During the Silesian Wars provisions were shipped up the Oder to the main magazine at Breslau, from where Frederick filled the successive depots along his lines of advance. This method of proceeding anticipates the great offensives of Napoleon. Fortresses likewise gave Frederick powerful assistance during his famous marches across the northern plain in the Seven Years War, for they secured his river crossings, and spared him the trouble of having to carry all the heavy artillery with

The Elvas position

90 View of the Elvas fortifications as they existed in the later seventeenth century. The Amoreira Aqueduct comes in from the right, and the Forte de Santa Luzia is at the top left. The site of Forte de Graça is off the bottom of the map (Mallet, 1673)

91 Forte de Graça, seen from the town

92 View from the Forte de Graça over the town towards Forte de Santa Luzia

the field army. The big guns from Glogau, for example, helped him to smash the Austrians at Leuthen. Thus the fortresses fitted very well into the strategy which the king outlined to Frederick of Brunswick in 1758 – 'The model of our conduct may be perceived from what we have practised during the present year, namely, while conducting a fundamentally defensive war, we remain perpetually on the attack' (21 November, Frederick, 1879–1939, XVII, 396).

The Austrians were perfectly aware of what Old Fritz was up to, even if they could do little to frustrate it. Major-General Tillier told the Russians in 1759:

The King of Prussia has a river on either side (the Oder and the Elbe), fortresses and depots in his rear, and magazines scattered all over the place. Thus he has reliable support in flank and rear in case of misfortune, while the magazines enable him to turn speedily against one after another of his enemies in succession, and each time match them with superior or at least equal force. (16 January, Vorontsov, 1870–95, VI, 394)

This goes to the heart of Frederick's system of war.

Frederick certainly allowed some of his fortresses an important defensive role, but 'an excess of strong garrisons only serves to enfeeble an army and render it almost incapable of serving in the open field' (Political Testament of 1752, *Politischen Testamente*, Frederick, 1920, 91). He was clearly determined to hang on to Magdeburg, the Silesian fortresses, Stettin and Kolberg, but he did not hesitate to abandon the fortresses of Prussian Westphalia at the outset of the Seven Years War.

Few commanders have ever possessed a more acute awareness than Frederick of what fortresses could and could not do. No one, not even Napoleon, ever achieved such a finely judged interaction of field forces and static defences. Frederick might well have earned the title of the foremost practitioner of fortress warfare in modern history if he had not so sadly maltreated his essential helpmates, the engineers.

Peninsular postscripts

In the Seven Years War French expeditions twice took the offensive against British interests in southwestern Europe. If it was unrealistic to contemplate an attack on Gibraltar itself, France rapidly eliminated the second British naval base in that part of the world, namely Port Mahon on Minorca. In May 1756 the Duc de Richelieu and 15,000 troops got safely ashore on the island, and on the 9th they opened trenches against St Philip's Castle, the guardian citadel of Port Mahon. The siege was a scrappy one, compared with the recent episodes in the Low Countries, for the ground was a hard rock, and the French knew that a British fleet intended to return to the scene with troops recently arrived at Gibraltar. The outworks of the castle was taken by storm on the night of 27–28 June, and the next day the garrison capitulated.

Considerations of grand strategy lay behind the next enterprise, the attack on Portugal in 1762. The operation was just one of the schemes by which Choiseul, the French first minister, hoped to draw British attention away from the Channel, and so facilitate a direct assault on Britain. The allied Spanish forces were pushed into opening hostilities in May, and before long 42,000 Spanish troops and French auxiliaries were marching into Portugal on three sectors.

Portuguese defences and military institutions were in a state of extreme decay, but the Portuguese premier Pombal summoned up assistance from Britain just in time to avoid collapse. First on the scene was Count Wilhelm of Schaumburg-Lippe-Bückeburg, who was said to be an illegitimate grandson of George I, and who, more relevantly perhaps, had been serving with great credit in western Germany (see p. 116). Lippe was equally distinguished as a practical and intellectual soldier, and in his little empire in Germany he founded the excellent Wilhelmstein academy of artillery and engineering, where he conducted the mathematical classes in person. In the short time available to him Lippe embarked on the modernisation of the Portuguese army, and the advent of 7,000 British reinforcements put a total of about 15,000 troops at his disposal for the open field.

The Portuguese fortresses capitulated in rapid succession, without putting the enemy to the trouble of opening regular siegeworks, and even the well-found stronghold of Almeida, on the central northern route to Lisbon, gave up the fight on 26 August, when Lippe had ordered it to hold out until the middle of September at the least. However, displaying considerable resource, Lippe countered the Gallispans by falling back from one blocking position after another, while dealing out damaging local counter-attacks against enemy depots and communications. The advance of the main division down the Tagus was halted by a raid on 6 October, which overran the post of Villa Velha, and finally the advent of the winter rains compelled the French and Spanish to retire across the frontier. Peace came to this theatre on 3 February 1763.

At the urgent request of the Portuguese, Lippe stayed behind after the war to help them to put their defences in order. He had to leave Portugal in September 1764, but he returned for a brief visit in 1767, to see how the work was going on, and he maintained an assiduous correspondence with the Portuguese authorities until he died in 1777.

Bearing in mind the failure of the Portuguese fortresses in 1762, Lippe paid particular attention to the fixed defences. He toured the entire frontier, and he concluded that it was particularly important to bar the direct road to Lisbon by doing something to strengthen Elvas, which was impressively sited where the wooded hills of the frontier gave way to the plain in which sat the grimy Spanish fortress-town of Badajoz. Just north of Elvas, on a smooth-sided conical hill, Lippe planted the symmetrical bastioned Forte de Graça (1763–78), surely one of the most beautiful creations of the great age of artillery fortification. The glacis extended down the hill slopes in long, even pleats, and the work was crowned with an elegant pavilion which commanded views for more than one hundred miles into Spain. A line of earthworks connected the Forte de Graça to the enceinte of Elvas town, and this in turn was joined by a broad caponnière communication with the old Forte de Santa Luzia (1648) to the south. The water supply for the town came by the Amoreira Aqueduct, which dwarfs the famous aqueduct at Maintenon, Vauban's essay in the same form.

Five A Time of Doubt: the Standing of Permanent Fortification in the Eighteenth Century

The interpreters of Vauban

The first generation
The eighteenth century accepted the superiority of Vauban's teaching on the defence and the attack without having a very precise idea of what those teachings were. Vauban's definitive treatises of 1704 and 1706 existed only in defective pirated editions and closely guarded manuscripts, and access to their secrets restricted to a small circle of engineers until the first authentic editions were published in 1829 (*Traité des Siéges* (1704), ed. M. Augoyat; *Traité de la Défense* (1706), ed. de Valazé). As for the fortifications proper, Sturm noted that 'Vauban did not present his systems to public gaze in any printed book. Various professors of mathematics have set about reconstructing them, though not in entirely uniform ways' (Sturm, 1736, 95). Among the more accurate reconstructions Sturm himself recommended the *Véritable Manière de Fortifier de Mr. de Vauban*, which was published in Paris in 1693 with the permission of Vauban himself. The work was generally attributed to the Abbé du Fay, who in fact only wrote the introduction. The original was the deed of the Chevalier de Cambray, and its publication at Amsterdam in 1689 was presented as 'a kind of conquest which we have made from the French'.

Likewise, Belidor complained in 1729 that the details of Vauban's methods of constructing fortresses were retained only in the heads of his old colleagues:

They maintain a glorious silence. The king has entrusted them with the guard of the barriers of the realm, and, ceaselessly occupied with making new works or maintaining the old ones in good repair, they do not have the time to disseminate their knowledge, and content themselves with instructing the men who work under their orders (Belidor, 1729, Preface).

Lefèbvre made a similar observation concerning the conduct of the sieges in the Netherlands in the 1740s (Lefèbvre, 1778, I, iii–iv).

Much of Vauban's *oeuvre* might have been lost with the fading memories of the old men and the fading ink of their portfolios if a number of writers had not taken the trouble to commit the tradition to print while it was still alive. De Quincy's *Maximes et Instructions sur l'art Militaire* (Paris, 1726) contained a useful resumé of the principles of siege warfare as they had been worked out in the reign of the last king. The beautifully illustrated *Science des Ingénieurs* of Belidor performed the same service for the practical business of fortress-building – the first of many editions was published in 1729, and the work was considered of enough enduring value to go through a last printing 101 years later. The corresponding viewpoint of the serving soldiers was represented by the personal recollections which informed the Chevalier de Guignard's *École de Mars* (2 vols., Paris 1725).

It was perhaps inevitable that the immediate heirs of Vauban in the engineering corps should appear in the nature of pygmies, scuttling around the feet of their dead master. This impression was reinforced by the character of the otherwise deserving Lieutenant-General Claude-François-Bidcal, Marquis d'Asfeld (1667–1743), who succeeded Le Peletier as *Directeur-Général* in 1715, and who remained in this post until his death in 1743. D'Asfeld was a cavalryman by origin (like Vauban himself), and by the end of the War of the Spanish Succession he had accumulated a considerable experience of command, siegework and administration. However, people were aware that the new chief engineer was descended from a line of prosperous textile merchants, and he was dismissed as a 'good-natured nobody' by the supercilious, who were amused by his quiet good humour, his modest ways, and his paternal solicitude for the corps. Indeed, in the reign of d'Asfeld the French engineers took on something of the character of a family-based guild, recruiting heavily from sons of engineers, who accounted for about 190 of the 300 or so admissions.

The works of fortification were concerned almost entirely with plugging the gaps left in the frontiers by the treaties of 1697 and 1713. Now that everything beyond the watershed of the south-western Alps belonged to the Piedmontese, the improvised works which Berwick had made on the heights around Briançon were replaced by fortifications in permanent style, so as to secure the valley of the upper Durance. The Batterie des Salettes rose immediately above Briançon, while the hills beyond the Durance were crowned with Fort Dauphin and the sprawling works of Les Têtes and Randouillet. The gorge was traversed by Pierre Bourcet's bold single-span arch, named the 'Pont d'Asfeld' in honour of the marquis.

On the north-eastern angle of the frontier the loss of Luxembourg in 1697 had put Vauban himself in a state of some agitation, but it was left to d'Asfeld to see to the necessary security of the upper Moselle. Out of all the proposals drawn up by his engineers, d'Asfeld favoured those put forward by the confident and energetic young Louis de Cormontaigne (1696–1752), who was made *ingénieur en chef* at Metz in 1733. Three extensive double crownworks were built according to his designs – two at Metz (Bellecroix and Moselle), and one at Thionville (Yutz).

Cormontaigne was made director of fortifications of the Three Bishoprics in 1745, which was suitable reward for the security he had helped to give to the frontier during the recent penetrations of the Pragmatic Army and the Austrians over the Rhine.

The second generation
A harsher, more demanding age opened for the engineering corps in 1743, when, immediately after the death of d'Asfeld, the engineers lost their self-sufficient life and were incorporated in the Comte d'Argenson's ministry of war. A set of regulations of 7 February 1744 tightened up the discipline of the personnel and began a long process of militarisation which culminated in the *Ordonnance* of 31 December 1776, which re-named the body of engineers the *Corps Royal du Génie*. The personnel was fixed at 329 officers, and for purposes of siegework the active engineers were divided into twenty-one permanent 'brigades', ready to be sent to wherever in the world they were needed.

Towards the end of his reign d'Argenson had actually overeached himself. This was on 8 December 1755, when he combined the engineers and gunners into a single corps. The arrangement looked tidy, to bureaucratic eyes, but it was unworkable in practice (see p. 115). On 5 May 1758 a new war minister, the Marshal de Belle-Isle, promptly re-divided the personnel into separate corps under his overall authority.

In this period the engineers found a new focus of corporate pride in the new *Ecole du Génie*, which was established at Mézières in 1748. This was one of the happier inspirations of d'Argenson, who was appalled at the losses of the corps in the sieges of 1744–8, when forty-eight engineers were killed or mortally wounded, and four or five more were reduced to nervous wrecks. Nearly all of the casualties were youngish folk, and d'Argenson attributed the carnage to the cosy atmosphere of d'Asfeld's rule, which had left the formation of the engineers to the local *ingénieurs en chef*.

The standards of the Mézières school were pitched very high from the start. Candidates for admission had first to gain a letter of examination, and master three thousand pages of scientific texts to fit themselves to attempt the examination itself

93 The Durance gorge at Briançon, with the Pont d'Asfeld. Briançon town to the right, Fort de Randouillet to the left

– a double hurdle which brought down five out of six of the aspirants. This ordeal was but the preparation for two years of intensive study and practical training at Mézières, under the supervision of a small but very highly qualified directing staff. The most celebrated of the instructors was Gaspard Monge, who lectured at the school from 1769 to 1784, and who invented 'descriptive geometry', which was a systematic method of representing three-dimensional objects on paper.

The intellectual energy of the corps as a whole was impressive. It was one of its members, Milet de Mureau, who in about 1749 had the distinction of being probably the first draughtsman to apply contours to represent the height of locations on land. Better-known to the outside world was Charles-Augustin Coulomb (1736–1806), who amused himself during an uneventful tour of duty at Martinique by investigating the effects of stress on beams, arches and revetments, and ended up by making the cen-

94 The Roc de Briançon, Briançon town

152 A Time of Doubt

tury's most important contribution to structural theory. The other researches of Coulomb extended to subjects as diverse as magnetism, metallurgy, hydraulics, the workings of windmills, and the circulation of sap in trees.

Against this record of achievement must be set the indictment drawn up in the next century by General Prévost de Vernois, who claimed that 'for the art of fortification the century of Louis XV was an age of decadence and error. In that period everything bore the imprint of bogus science, mediocrity and bad taste' (Vernois, 1861, I, 117).

There was substance in the charge, for too many engineers came to believe that 'scientific' methods could be applied to fortification in general with just the same validity as to the investigation of materials and mechanics. A rigid, formalist spirit settled on Mézières, where the successive commandants were faced with the problem of collecting all the strands of tradition together into an authorised syllabus. The teaching of fortification was concentrated on the building-up of the pupils' *gâches*, or portfolios, which contained reams of paper relating to an ideal fortress of nine fronts and one bridgehead. A high value was placed on geometrical proportion, but little regard was paid to tactical considerations or the demands of terrain.

The corps as an entity came under the influence of the dull, ambitious and inexhaustible Charles-René de Fourcroy de Ramecourt (1715–91). At the beginning of the Seven Years War his superior, General Pierre Filley, had given him a good character, but by 1758 he was forced to report that 'Monsieur de Fourcroy has a high-handed and harsh method of exercising command, and owns a marked talent for winning himself protectors' (Blois, 1865, I, 128). The irresistible Fourcroy became a frequent visitor to Versailles, and in 1760 he obtained permission to put together an authorised text for the instruction of young engineers. After his victory he spent the best part of the next two decades drumming up support among his colleagues for a project of creating an engineer supremo, who would have direct access to the Minister of War. Fourcroy had never in his life directed a siege or a large-scale construction, but it must have surprised few of his acquaintances when the king established the office of supreme engineer on 30 September 1776, and chose Fourcroy as its first incumbent.

For thirteen years Fourcroy's word determined the fate of every engineer, every suggested innovation, every projected fortification. Mercifully and miraculously, his energy finally flagged, and in 1789 he delivered up all his papers to the *Dépôt de Fortifications*. He died on 12 January 1791 – 'a man who fulfilled his duties because he loved them' (Augoyat, 1860–4, II, 644).

In his years of bureaucratic tyranny Fourcroy did much to shape the course of French military engineering until the second half of the nineteenth century. Being devoid of inspiration, he turned to the papers of one of his early patrons, the prolific Louis de Cormontaigne (see p. 150). From the great mass of Cormontaigne's correspondence and memoranda Fourcroy compiled an 'authorised' French trace which was probably never executed in its entirety on French soil, but succeeded in paralysing invention for generations to come. While retaining the general proportions of Vauban's works, Fourcroy greatly increased the projection of the ravelins into the country, and abolished the bastion tower in favour of an elaborate retrenchment in the gorge. He associated wonderful properties with the arrangement of the successive fronts on a 'straight-line trace', ignoring the fact that no object in the known universe can be enclosed by a straight line.

Less comprehensibly still, Fourcroy greatly diminished the capacity of the new works for active defence by cutting Vauban's estimate for the proper armament for a six-sided fortress (ninety guns) by twenty-two pieces. Fourcroy and Cormontaigne, indeed, seem to have had little faith in the power of defensive artillery. 'The simple reason is that the besieger batters the fortress with heavy guns, and he has more of them than we can possibly pit against him' (Cormontaigne, 1806–9, *Mémorial pour la Défense*, 192–3).

The Fourcroy-Cormontaigne theories were first circulated in *gâche* form, then openly published as Cormontaigne's *Oeuvres Posthumes* in three volumes between 1806 and 1809. These were the first official French printed manuals on fortress warfare and fortification. As was explained in one of the prefaces, 'the three volumes of this *Mémoire* will spare the engineer officers the labour of having to carry about with them those great masses of manuscript notebooks' (Cormontaigne, 1806–9, *Mémorial pour la Fortification*, vii).

However, it was Fourcroy's doctrine of *moments de fortification* that constituted his most striking departure from the principles of Vauban. In his memorial of 1669 on the conduct of sieges Vauban had expressly stated that it was impossible to predict the progress of a siege with any exactitude. He sometimes worked out time-tables of imaginary sieges for some of his fortresses, but only as a rough means of estimating the quantity of provisions which should be stored there. Cormontaigne took the matter an important step further, when he used the imaginary siege as an instrument to test the worth of fortification projects. Fourcroy in his turn was inspired to propound the *moment de fortification* – a yardstick of the absolute worth of a projected fortress, which was produced by dividing the building costs, estimated in units of 100,000 francs, into the anticipated number of days of resistance. In 1786 Fourcroy and a few friends defended their *moments* against all comers:

The employment of this touchstone elevates our art to the status of one of the positive sciences; it identifies and separates everything that is military, useful and properly tested from all those specious ideas, armchair speculations, imaginary properties and vain promises which emanate from well-meaning authors who deal with fortification without understanding it. (*Mémoires sur la Fortification Perpendiculaire*, 23)

As fortress construction was often the largest single item in an eighteenth-century military budget, the search for the *moment de fortification* was an entirely laudable one, which had much in common with the twentieth-century ambition to squeeze the maximum 'cost-effectiveness' out of expensive military projects. The *moment* nevertheless remained an entirely arbitrary figure, being compounded from two near-imponderables – the actual cost of construction, and the effect of moral forces on the resistance of strongholds.

Fourcroy claimed that he was the only authentic transmitter of Vauban's teaching, but what he gave posterity was his own version of Cormontaigne's misrepresentation of a great man whom neither of them knew.

The crisis of permanent fortification

The spirit of controversy was awakened rather than stilled by the leaden hand of Fourcroy. The bitter arguments among the engineers succeeded in dividing fortification into two contending schools – the official 'French' on the one hand, and the 'polygonal' or German on the other. More alarming still, military men began to question the value of any kind of permanent fortification, and they might well have brought about the wholesale dismantling of defensive systems if the wars of the French Revolution had not supervened from 1792, and shown that fortification was just as vital for the survival of modern states as it had been for the old kingdoms.

The external attack
Philippe Maigret's *Traité de la Sûreté et de la Conservation des Etats par le Moyen des Forteresses* (Paris, 1725) was widely accepted as a classic statement of the purposes of fortification. For Maigret the necessity of fortification was grounded in reason, experience and instinct, and he conducted his argument in calm and rather old-fashioned terms, with appeals to the authority of Aristotle, Plato and Vitruvius, and much talk of 'princes' and 'citadels'.

For a number of reasons the manner and content of Maigret's treatise proved unacceptable to more restless spirits. In part the thing was a simple response to the manifest power of the new siege attack. Eighteenth-century soldiers conceded that, in any normal siege, the attack invariably overwhelmed the defence. Struensee wrote half-jokingly:

The fortress commandant is unlikely to hold out until it is a question of repelling a storm. . . . At the present time the besieger does not hesitate to grant the garrison an evacuation with all the honours, or even, when it is possible, to allow the defenders to march out through the breach. This is regarded as a compliment – and nowadays people are not sparing with their compliments. (Quoted in Müller, 1892, 117)

This was a time when the boundaries of science had not yet been defined, and when mathematics and geometry were being pushed into areas of human activity whence they later retreated. It was the same with warfare. The siege attack was the one branch of the military art in which a 'scientific' method had been applied with evident success. As Marshal de Puységur put it, 'of all the component parts of warfare, the only ones which are established on known principles are those which relate to the attack and defence of fortresses, and the ways of building them' (Puységur, 1749, I, 76). Puységur saw this as a good reason to try to work out similar principles for the regulation of field warfare. Old Fritz himself likened the two lines of the order of battle to the parallels that were dug in sieges.

Developments in eighteenth-century artillery only served to increase the relative advantages of the attack. These comprised a host of minor improvements in the design and manufacture of cannon, gun carriages, gunpowder and harness which cumulatively enhanced the power and mobility of ordnance by about 50 per cent. Almost the sole invention of exclusive value to the defence was Gribeauval's high-cheeked fortress carriage, which enabled muzzles to be levelled *en barbette* over parapets, without the necessity of cutting embrasures.

Some particularly valuable researches were associated with the name of Bernard Forest de Belidor (1693–1761), a Catalan orphan who had been adopted by a French artillery officer, and who ended his days as Inspector of the King of France's artillery. While a professor at the La Fère artillery school, Belidor directed a series of experiments which gave him the material for the useful tables of charges and elevations which he published in *Le Bombardier François* in 1731. Lieutenant Jacobi drew up the official Prussian tables from similar experiments in 1749. With the gradual elimination of guesswork, gunnery began to assume the aspect of a science to match engineering.

Belidor then addressed himself to the question of propellant charges, and by 1740 he was able to proclaim that it was useless to load a cannon with a charge heavier than one-third of the weight of the shot, for greater loads merely threw more and more powder out of the muzzle unburnt. The regulation charge amounted to one-half the weight of the shot, and Belidor's many enemies in the artillery corps were infuriated by the suggestion that for all these years they had been firing away one-sixth of their powder to no purpose. Belidor had to leave the artillery school, but he was saved from a worse fate by the intervention of his protector Marshal Belle-Isle, who whisked him away to the army in Bohemia in 1741. In later years Belidor's reduced charges were adopted almost universally.

All of this was sad news for the defence, as the more passive party in fortress warfare.

No less dangerous was the weariness felt by many people in the face of the textbooks produced by men who wrote so drily and repetitiously, and came from such unmilitary backgrounds as the abbés Le Blond and Deidier. The Prince de Ligne exclaimed: 'The more I see and the more I read, the more I am convinced that the best fortress is an army, and the best rampart a rampart of men' (Ligne, 1795–1811, XXVIII, 14–15).

Then again, the field officers were now finding immense satisfaction in their own specialised crafts, and were often unimpressed by the performance of such fortresses as they encountered on campaign. The Marshal de Saxe, the conqueror of the Netherlands in the 1740s, felt entitled to say 'I am not much of a student, but I have never been overawed by the reputation of Vauban and Coehoorn. They fortified towns at immense expense without making them any stronger' (Saxe, 1756, 141). He rejected the fortification of towns as fundamentally unmilitary, and claimed that it would be much better to set the army to work on entrenching vital strategic points in the open country. After de Saxe's death, the success of the French *places du moment* in the Hessian campaigns of the Seven Years War (see p. 116) kept improvised works before men's eyes as a valid alternative to permanent fortification.

Debates on strategy and field tactics appeared all the more exciting, now that fortress warfare seemed to have been reduced to such a dull routine. Few military men in France seemed to appreciate what they owed to the huge capital legacy of Vauban, or to the sacrifice of their engineers, who were spilling their blood in offensive operations beyond the

95 The fantastic elaboration of one of Virgin's traces

borders of France. Some new and interesting strands of thought were evident in the writings of the Chevalier de Folard, and in particular his *Commentaires sur Polybe* (1719–30). Folard was much taken with the idea of war *à outrance*, in the style of Charles XII of Sweden, and he was convinced of the value of the attack with cold steel. In the next generation the Comte de Guibert explored the notion of the offensive on the tactical, strategic and moral planes, and he claimed that the guiding principle of campaigns must be to 'leave all the so-called barriers behind you, and carry the war into the interior of the enemy states, against their very capitals' (*Essai Général sur la Tactique*, London, 1772, 66).

Masonry fortification appeared to be particularly irrelevant during the lively tactical arguments which developed in the 1760s, 1770s and 1780s. The issues

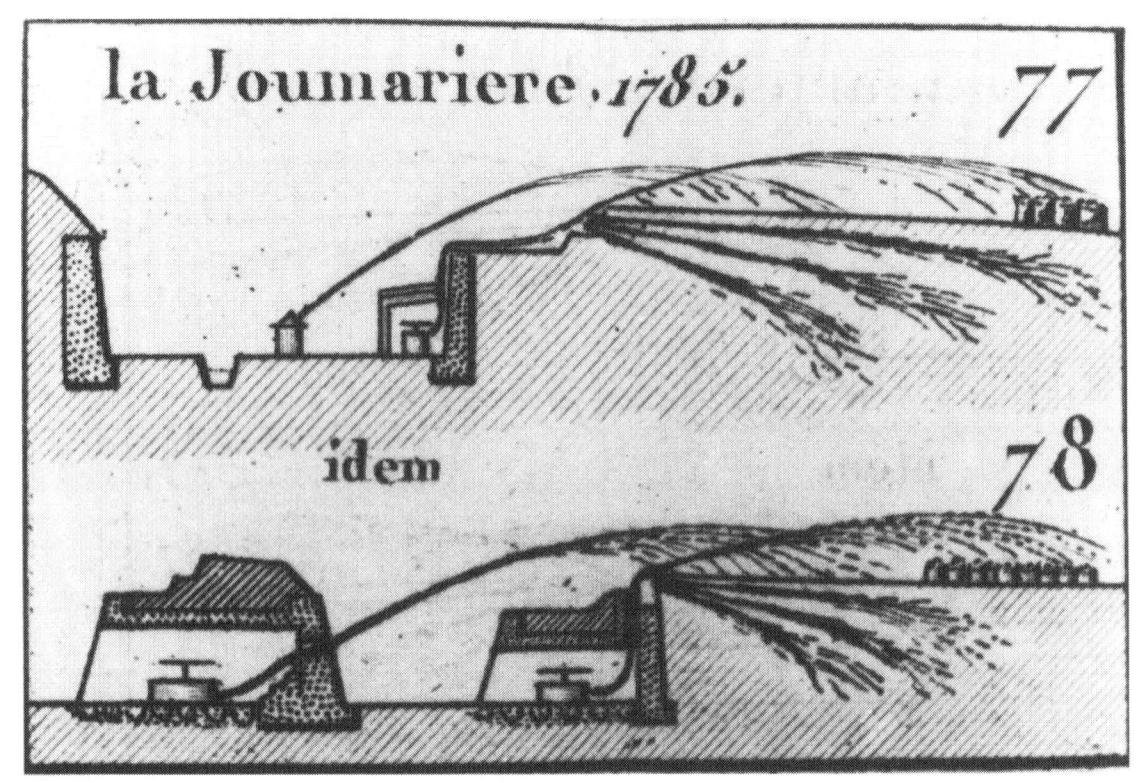

96 La Joumarière's squirt system 1785

of the moment seemed to be the contest between the 'Red' and 'Blue' schools of field gunnery, and the questions as to whether the infantry should close with the enemy in deep order or shallow, and with cold steel or fire. The Chevalier du Theil looked back with disdain to the days of Vauban and Coehoorn, when the principles of war were still in their infancy, and the science of gunnery was limited to the attack and defence of fortresses:

at the present time nobody can doubt that the fate of fortresses depends almost entirely on the outcome of battles, that fortresses are just an auxiliary element, that the system of war has entirely changed, and that what matters in warfare is to have well-found, mobile and manoeuvrable armies. From this it follows that artillery must participate in these fundamental changes, and that we must draw a distinction between field artillery and fortress artillery. (Du Theil, 1778, 2)

In the last decade of the *Ancien Régime* the scorn of the field tacticians was aroused by a revival of interest among polite society in the achievements and character of Vauban. In 1784 the fledgling engineer Lazare Carnot carried off the prize offered by the Academy of Dijon for an *Éloge de Vauban*. On 2 August the winning essay was read out to the assembled States of Burgundy, and the provincial governor-general, the Prince de Condé, bestowed the gold medal in person. Carnot thanked the future émigré chief with the undemocratic sentiment that he was 'heartened and proud to receive this palm from the hands of a member of the illustrious family of Condé, whose laurels are immortal!' Condé graciously replied that if he was ever called upon to command an army, he would be delighted 'to have the assistance of such a deservedly famous officer as you' (Carnot, 1861–4, I, 100–1).

Not to be outshone by its provincial rival, the French Academy offered a prize for a further panegyric of the long-dead Vauban. This was too much for military opinion. On 21 May 1786 the artillery officer Choderlos de Laclos (best known for his novel

Les Liaisons Dangereuses) addressed an open letter to the Academy, declaring that he could detect no sign of greatness in Vauban, a man who was devoid of originality, and who was responsible for spending four hundred million livres of national treasure on useless fortifications. Carnot and other engineers replied with some heat, and the War Minister, Ségur, tried to put an end to the dispute by forbidding military men to 'print any manuscript concerning the military art without having had the honour of submitting the paper to the minister and obtaining his approval' (Augoyat, 1860–4, II, 637). This order merely induced the polemicists to push out their pamphlets under the cover of anonymity.

The last prospect of containing the arguments disappeared with the setting-up of a highly suspect 'Council of War' within the War Ministry. The presiding genius was the distinguished field tactician de Guibert, who persuaded Fourcroy in 1788 to agree to the publication of a memorandum which bore the challenging title *Recueil de Quelques Mémoires sur la Trop Grande Quantité de Places qui Subsistent en France*. D'Arçon, Foissac-Latour and Carnot sprang to the defence of the threatened strongholds, and pointed out that the element of stability, as represented by the fortresses, was an essential complement to the natural volatility of French soldiers (C. Michaud d'Arçon, *Considérations sur l'Influence du Génie de Vauban dans la Balance des Forces de l'Etat*, no place of pub., 1786; *Considérations Militaires et Politiques sur la Réforme Projetée d'un Grand Nombre de nos Places de Guerre*, Metz, 1788; *Observations sur les Fragments de Mémoires Attribués au Maréchal de Vauban*, Landrecies, 1789; Foissac-Latour, *Examen Détaillé de l'Importante Question de l'Utilité des Places Fortes*, Amsterdam, 1789; Carnot, *Mémoire Présenté au Conseil de la Guerre au Sujet des Places Fortes*, no place of pub., 1789).

The internal debate
Ingenious writers of the middle and later eighteenth century put forward a large number of more or less insane alternatives to the regular bastion trace, ranging from the circular systems of Cugnot and some of the styles of Pirscher, to the great triangle of Cass. In 1757 a certain Robillard surpassed them all by describing a 'demolition' fortress of ditches, planks and earth, which was supposed to blow itself systematically to bits during the siege. La Joumarière came a close second in 1785, when he proposed batteries of hoses to deluge the siegeworks with water.

It was left to Marc-René, Marquis de Montalembert (1714–1800) to propose systems of an originality and merit capable of gripping the whole of military Europe. Montalembert qualified himself for his work by having taken part in fifteen campaigns and nine sieges in his forty-five years of service in a very wide variety of capacities. He possessed a wide knowledge of European fortification, and while he was serving as military envoy to the Swedes in the Seven Years War he had become acquainted with such un-French works as Walrave's fortifications at Stettin, and the casemated towers of the Swedish engineer Dahlberg. Perhaps also this was the time when he might have learnt of the remarkable Austrian fort of St Elisabeth on the lower Danube, which had a flanking work which corresponded very closely indeed to the form of Montalembert's caponnières.

Modestly but firmly, Montalembert argued that it was time to advance the boundaries of fortification – 'Descartes was a great man, and we still regard him as such, even though we have abandoned his principles for others which are patently better'. It was the same with Vauban and Coehoorn: 'We do not attack them as men, but we do attack their opinions on engineering – an art which has been kept in its infancy by the weight of their authority and of those who scrupulously profess their teachings' (Montalembert, 1776–96, V, 265–6). Montalembert now ventured to compare himself with Captain Cook, who overcame ignorant detractors, and voyaged into seas unknown.

The war minister, Choiseul, had shown a lively interest in Montalembert's notions, but he wrote to him in 1761 that it would be far too dangerous to allow them to appear in print – 'Just remember how annoying it was that Vauban's *Traité de l'Attaque des Places* which was originally confided in secret to a few senior engineers, came to be transmitted to the foreigners' (*ibid.*, I, vii). Years passed without further word from the ministry, and in 1774 Mon-

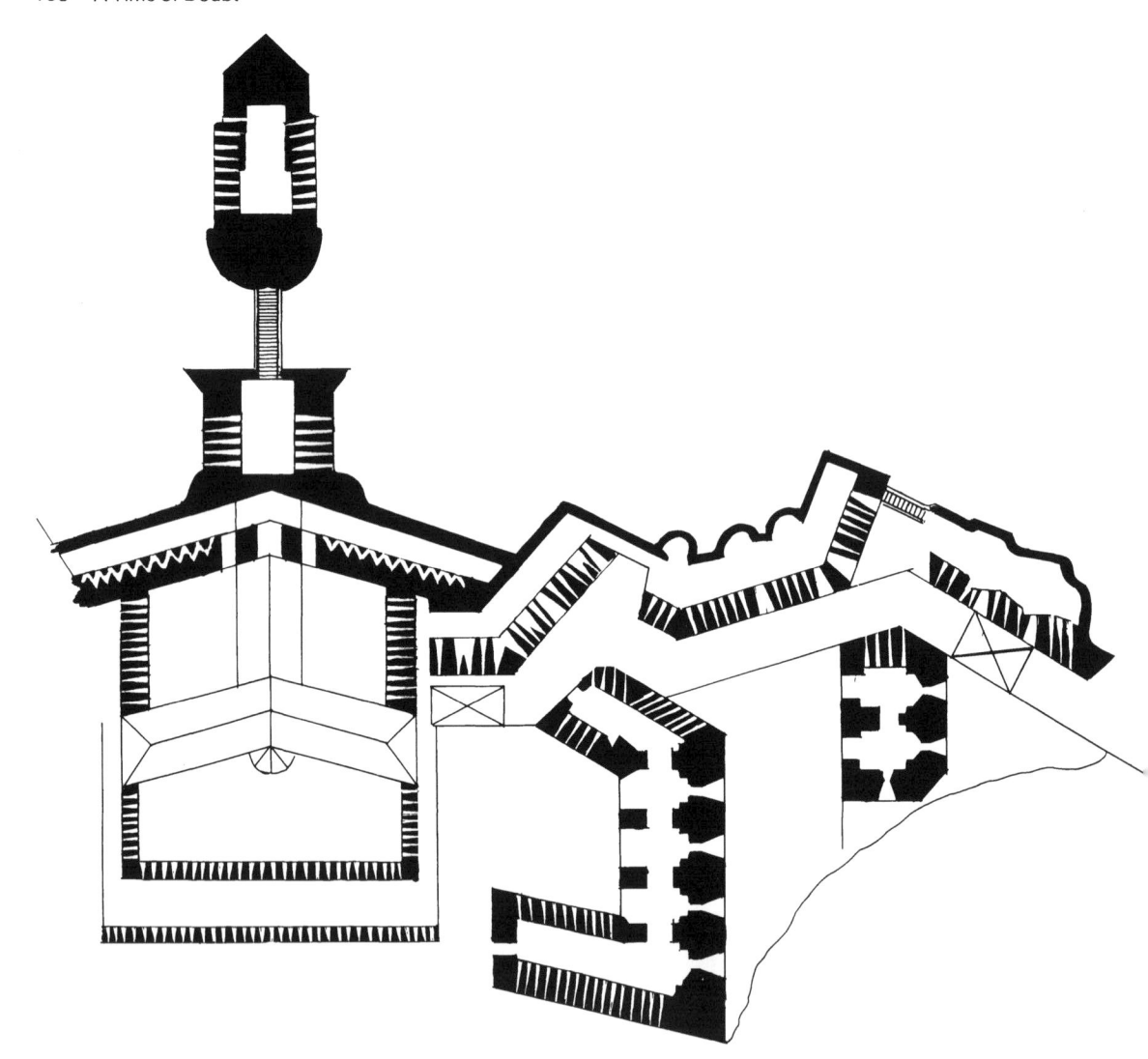

97 Fort St Elisabeth, showing the caponnière and part of the ground plan. This remarkable piece of architecture was completed in 1735, and almost immediately lost to the Turks. It stood on the southern, or Serbian, bank of the Danube, opposite the main fortress of Orsova on the isle of Ada-Kaleh. (Re-drawn from a MS plan in the British Library)

talembert had his project for fortifying Île de France (Mauritius) frustrated by the engineer Jean-Claude Le Michaud d'Arçon.

After this last affront there was no holding Montalembert, and in 1776 he brought out the first volume of the work which became known by the general title of *La Fortification Perpendiculaire*. The publication was completed in 1796, by when the cost of the eleven large volumes and the 165 engravings had drained away much of his fortune.

Amid much that was hackneyed and uninspired (not least the 'perpendicular' tenaille trace which gave its name to the work as a whole), Montalembert gave new force to three principles of far-reaching significance:

(i) 'Artillery is the weapon which takes fortresses – and by the same token artillery must defend them' (*ibid.*, V, 1). The first step towards gaining the necessary superiority of fire was to pack between three and four hundred guns into the fortress. Since

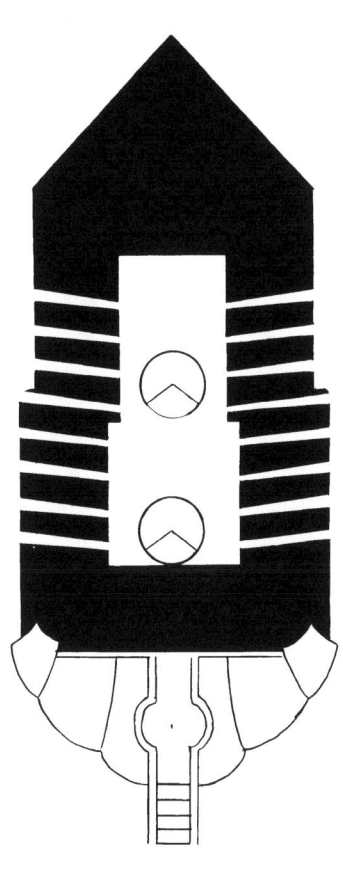

98 Details of the caponnière at Fort St Elisabeth

twelve or thirteen iron cannon could be produced for the cost of a single bronze piece, Montalembert reckoned that the expense need be no greater than for a conventional armament. This powerful artillery was to be housed in casemates, and not left exposed on the open rampart as in the usual 'solid' fortress.

For coastal defence the pieces were to be mounted in high triangular forts and soaring lighthouse towers. In dealing with ships, concealment was of less account than the ability to deliver a great weight of fire over a short period of time.

(ii) In the most influential of his traces, Montalembert proposed to supplant the heavily indented, all-purpose front of the bastion trace by a long straight curtain. This work saw to the long-range defence, and was provided to this end with two storeys of artillery casemates, which could also usefully serve as defensible barracks.

Projecting at right-angles from the centre of the curtain was a massive caponnière, possessing twenty-seven artillery casemates on each side, arranged in three storeys. As the business of the caponnière was purely to command the length of the ditch, the pointed head of the work was left blank, except for some loopholes for musketry. Montalembert claimed that the simple fronts of this 'polygonal' system could be more easily adapted to the ground than the bastion trace, of which every dimension and angle was closely interdependent.

(iii) The depth of the defence was to be increased by means of detached forts. Montalembert suggested that a girdle of such works would permit the defence to occupy any outlying heights, and hinder

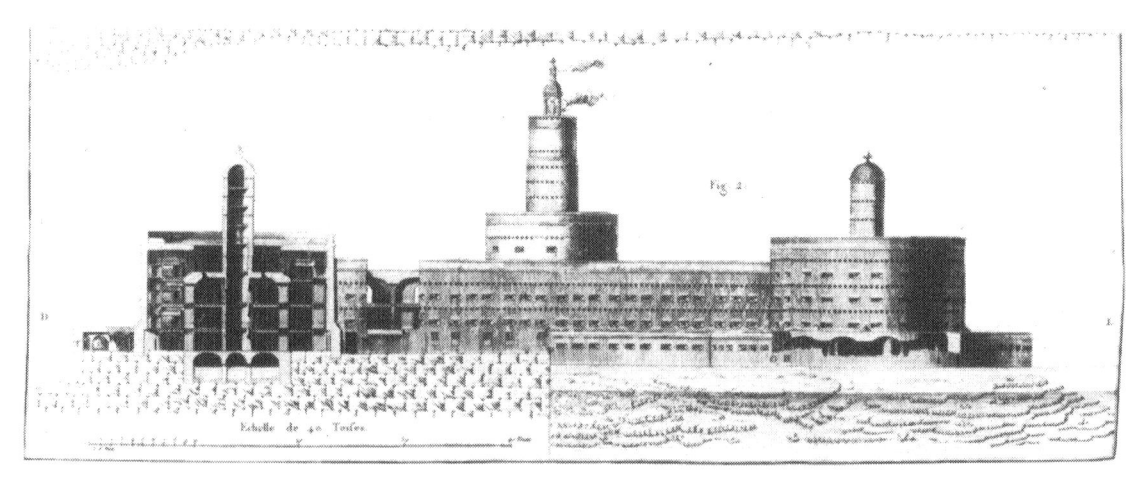

99 Montalembert's coastal tower (*Fortification Perpendiculaire*)

the besiegers from approaching the fortress proper. He allowed himself a fair latitude in the design of the forts, which could be circular, or three- or four-sided as the ground suggested. The simple, uncluttered polygonal trace showed to particular advantage in such small works.

The three principles amounted to a striving towards specialisation – to evolve works that were specifically designed to meet the respective requirements of long-range defence (the casemated curtain), short-range defence (the caponnière) and depth of defence (the detached fort). In contrast the bastion system was depicted as a general-purpose expedient, which performed none of the three functions particularly well.

Montalembert reinforced the effect of his writings by building a multi-storeyed wooden fort on the Île d'Aix. Since his enemies maintained that the accumulation of smoke would make the fort untenable, a commission of generals was assembled in October 1781 to witness an experiment at the new work. Sixty-seven pieces were fired at the highest possible rate for several hours, and at the end of the cannonade the commission unanimously declared that the smoke had caused no inconvenience, and that the structure of the fort was intact. According to the naval officers who were present, much less smoke seeped back through the gunports than was the case in warships.

Fourcroy was not the man to be moved from his opinions by proof, however incontrovertible, and he enlisted the aid of the long-retired Major Grenier and the young officer de Frescheville to compile the *Mémoires sur la Fortification Perpendiculaire* of 1786. They described their manifesto as a timely counter-blast against the pernicious opinions of Montalembert, which had been winning over so many converts, even among ministers of state, and which

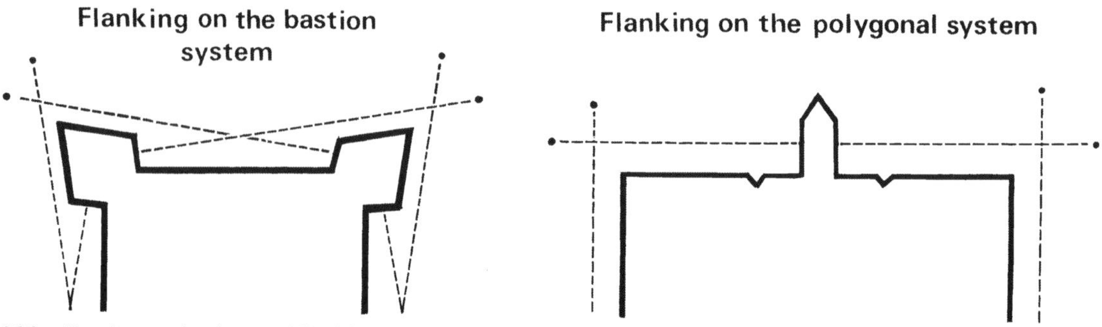

100 Bastion and polygonal flanking compared

now threatened the security of the realm itself. They predicted a smoky, splintery doom for Montalembert's casemates in the event of a siege (though, indeed casemates appear in the Fourcroy-Cormontaigne trace), and, in a notorious statement, they described any ambition to improve on the doctrines of Vauban as 'one of the distinctive characteristics of a man who is ignorant of the engineering art' (p. 38).

Somebody ought to write an extended study of the phenomenon of resistance to military change over the centuries. It is possible that he might discover that the opposition has less to do with the unacceptable *nature* of the proposals under consideration, as with their *source*. Montalembert was regarded as an alien intrusion, not a true son of the engineering corps, and so any suggestions emanating from him were dismissed as doubly objectionable.

Michaud d'Arçon, Montalembert's old enemy, added his voice in the same year of 1786 (*Considérations sur l'Influence du Génie de Vauban*), claiming that in theory it seemed a good idea to have every defender blasting off as much powder as he could, but adding that no governor in the real world could afford such an extravagant consumption of ammunition.

A blameless casualty in this first round of the controversy was the young engineer Lazare Carnot, who was violently attacked by Montalembert in the mistaken belief that he had contributed to the *Mémoires sur la Fortification Perpendiculaire*. Carnot made up the quarrel by writing to Montelembert on 22 August 1788 that he had no share in the work, and that on the contrary he and a wide circle in the engineering corps harboured the deepest admiration for Montalembert's endeavours – 'Now that your

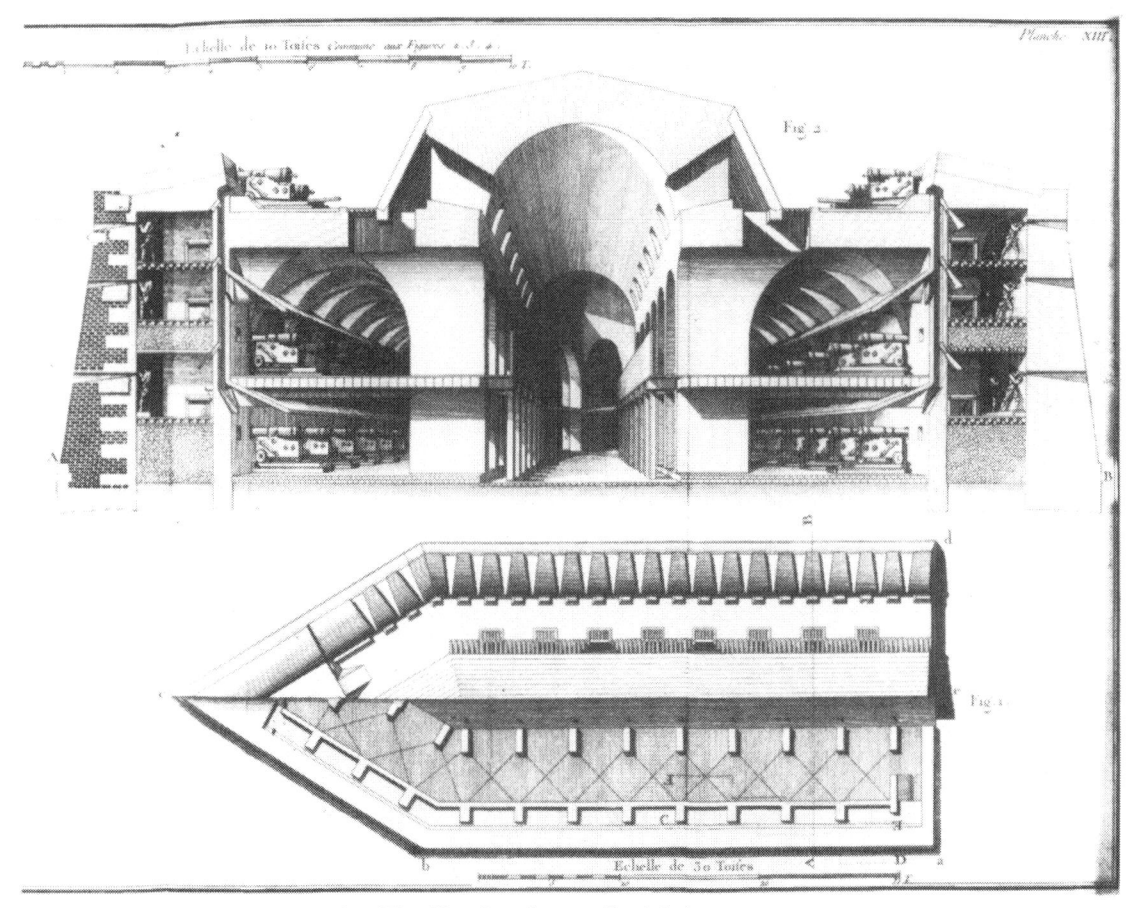

101 Montalembert's caponnière (*Fortification Perpendiculaire*)

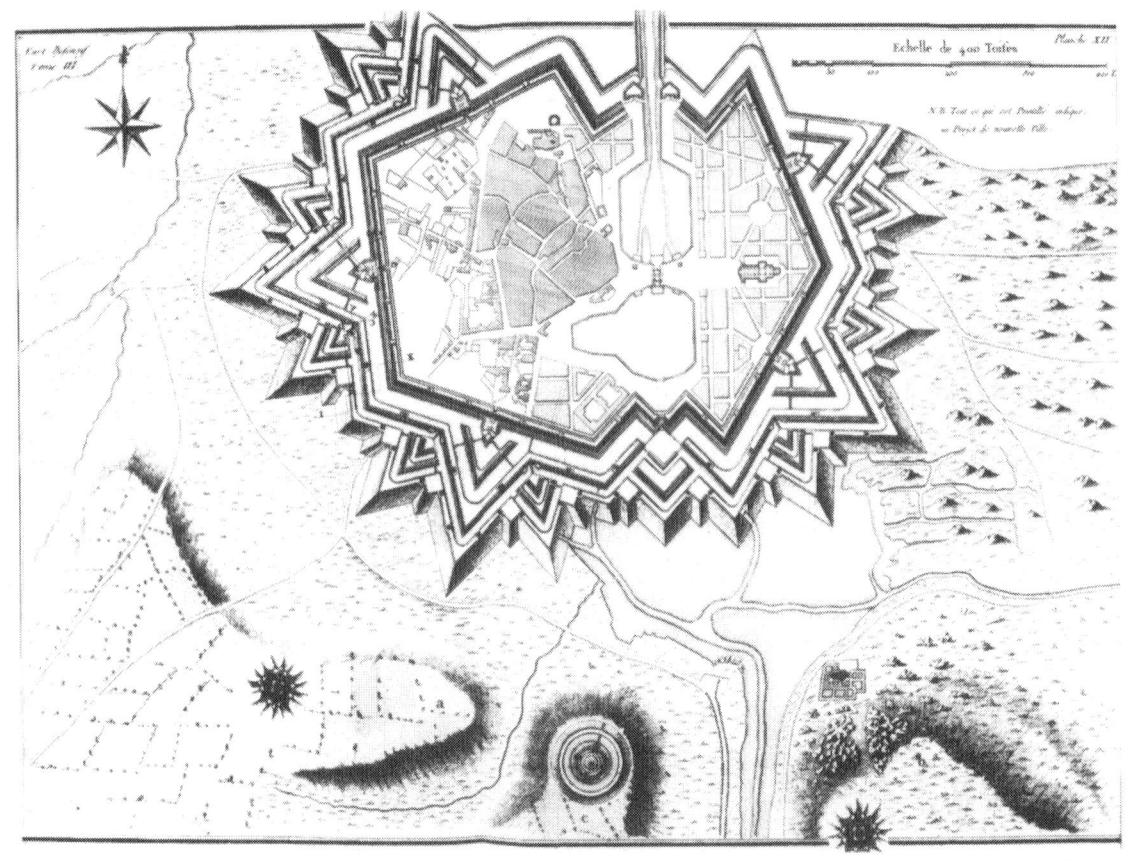

102 The polygonal manner, as illustrated by Montalembert in an imaginary scheme for the defence of Cherbourg. The long, straight fronts were to be very characteristic of German fortifications in the nineteenth century. To the south are three detached forts – two square and one circular (*Fortification Perpendiculaire*)

casemates are known and tested, engineering will take on a fresh aspect and become a new science' (Carnot, 1861–4, I, 147).

Carnot now strayed into the fire of the conservatives. He foolishly placed himself at their mercy in February 1789, when he deserted his garrison at Béthune and hastened to Dijon to settle accounts with a rich young infantry officer who had stolen his girl friend. He was hauled back to Béthune under guard before any blood was shed. He remained in prison until he was released as the person best qualified to guide his old acquaintance, Prince Henry of Prussia, on a tour of the northern fortresses. The people of Béthune illuminated their town to celebrate Carnot's liberation, and he felt sufficiently secure to send to the National Assembly a provocative *Réclamation contre le Régime Oppressif sous lequel est Gouverné le Corps du Génie*.

The original polemic between Montalembert and d'Arçon continued unabated. In 1790 Montalembert brought out a *Réponse au Colonel d'Arçon, Auteur des Batteries Flottantes*, a title which was designed to remind readers of d'Arçon's part in the catastrophic naval attack on Gibraltar in 1781 (see p. 164). The coming of the Revolution lowered the tone of the debate still further. D'Arçon now affected to style himself by the plebeian 'Darçon', and accused Montalembert of being a reactionary tyrant in his mental processes. He even resurrected an old story to the effect that Montalembert had gained permission to build his famous wooden fort on the Île d'Aix by getting his wife to disport herself enticingly on the stage of his private theatre in the presence of the bemused Maurepas, the minister of war.

The last hope that Montalembert's ideas might prevail in France disappeared when his friend Mirabeau died in 1791, before he could carry out his intention of proposing Montalembert to the National Assembly as chief of the engineering corps. Montalembert was too much the crusty old aristocrat to accommodate himself to the extreme Revolutionaries, but he retained the esteem of Carnot and his party, and he was left in peace to write and publish until he died at his Paris hôtel in 1800.

It gave Montalembert some consolation to know that his work was being enthusiastically received in Germany. As early as 1788 a Prussian engineer, Major Lindenau, wrote to him that he was translating *La Fortification Perpendiculaire* for the instruction of the officers under his charge, and that experiments had been made at royal command in the casemates at Schweidnitz which fully bore out the results of the demonstration on the Île d'Aix. Two years later Scharnhorst could sum up the controversy in the following terms:

All foreign experts in military and engineering affairs hail Montalembert's work as the most intelligent and distinguished achievement in fortification over the last hundred years. Things are quite different in France. The French engineering corps is a very considerable organisation which controls everything that has to do with the real and practical side of engineering in the kingdom. This corps was brought to its present high standing by a man who is justly famous [Vauban]. The prestige which was endowed on the corps by this great man has been maintained by mighty deeds in the attack and defence of fortresses... but it is extraordinary that such an important corps has failed to advance the state of its knowledge by so much as an inch. Its officers have not produced a single book on engineering, and its fortifications are still built according to the old forms and rules. (Jähns, 1889–91, 2, 802)

In the next century simplified forms of the polygonal system were employed all over northern Europe, and the Germans in particular accorded Montalembert a status little short of divine.

The triumph of engineering conservatism in France
By winning the confidence of the new Jacobin government, Michaud d'Arçon was able to settle every debated issue according to his own backward-looking lights. He celebrated his victory in his *Considérations Militaires et Politiques sur les Fortifications*, (Paris, l'an III), a work which was published on governmental order, and not, like his earlier pamphlets, printed furtively on some provincial or foreign press. According to d'Arçon, the fortress was a unique manifestation of permanence in the mutability of human affairs, and it had just proved its worth by enabling Revolutionary France to survive its defeats in the field at the beginning of the new war – 'the phantoms of terror dissipated under the ramparts of Lille and Valenciennes, just as clouds break up against high mountain tops' (p. 75).

As for the shape of fortifications, Montalembert was now officially discredited in France, and d'Arçon could afford to pose as an enlightened conservative, claiming that the details of Vauban's work 'are still capable of commanding our admiration, though they do not hinder us from striving after perfection' (p. 8). The ideal fortification remained the Vauban trace as it had been re-worked by Cormontaigne and Fourcroy.

Public affairs

The siege of Gibraltar 1779–83
Every now and again the attention of Europe was drawn to the fact that Britain owned a fortified presence in the Mediterranean. Minorca demanded a powerful squadron for its protection (as the British were reminded in 1756), but its safe anchorages and its fine harbour were tangible assets, and the island had a useful position between Barcelona and Toulon.

No such considerations applied to that geographical and strategic oddity, the Rock of Gibraltar, which had no real harbour at all, and did very little to seal the exit of the Mediterranean. Gibraltar had been taken in 1704, by the Anglo-Dutch squadron of Admiral Rooke, who made the attack almost as an afterthought. The place withstood a Spanish siege in 1726–7, and over the following decades the British made a few improvements to the old Moorish and Spanish fortifications. Work went ahead with a new sense of direction from 1770, which was when the chief engineer, William Green, submitted a detailed plan of defence. He urged the necessity of a strong and well-supplied garrison, of long-range artillery to keep hostile ships at a distance, and of additional fortifications designed in particular to strengthen the long western sea front. The most powerful of these new works was the King's Bastion, which rose about half-way along the sea line. With its heavily obtuse-angled salient, its straight retired flanks and its proportionately great width, the new work actually approximated less to Green's proposal than to the form of bastion proposed in the middle of the century by John Muller, who was an instructor at the Royal Academy of Artillery at Woolwich.

Having thus given the impetus to the new scheme of fortifications, Green also took on the responsibility of carrying them out on the ground. He was an accomplished theoretical engineer, and his knowledge of the practical side of things went back to the Netherlands campaigns and the siege of Quebec. His direction of the works at Gibraltar now proved to be meticulous in the extreme:

As a member of a corps, still in the throes of reorganisation and subjected to slights by the more autocratic branches of the armed forces, one can sympathise with, or at least understand his pedantry. The men he employed were engineering labourers hired by the hour, half soldiers, half civilians, and not particularly amenable to discipline. The engineer's job was no easy one in an age when gentlemen officers professed a knowledge of the art of fortification with which to dispute the recommendation of a professional. 'Such is the nature of an engineer's profession', wrote Green, 'that there's scarce a project can be proposed, but what there may be some objections raised.' (Hughes, 1981, 61)

Gibraltar became the object of mighty French and Spanish efforts during the War of American Independence. We must leave the detailed narrative of the operation to the veterans and historians who have chronicled the episode at length. Likewise, the strategic context has been authoritatively set out by Piers Mackesy (1964), who has shown how the winter relief expeditions mounted by the British left the Royal Navy dangerously weak in Channel and colonial waters, not least in 1781, when the fleet and convoy of de Grasse enjoyed a clear run to the West Indies. Here we merely touch on matters which struck contemporaries of being of the greatest technical interest.

After three and a half years of blockade the French and Spanish finally undertook the formal siege of Gibraltar in the late summer of 1781. The trenches, however, made little progress, and on 13 September the Duc de Crillon tried to hasten affairs by opening fire with 186 heavy guns, and sending in ten floating batteries which had been specially designed by Lieutenant-Colonel d'Arçon. The garrison took up the challenge with a murderous fire of its own, and by the morning of the 14th the siege guns had been largely silenced, and only four of d'Arçon's batteries were still afloat. The siege ended in prolonged and inconclusive bombardment with blockade.

Scharnhorst's comment on the siege was scarcely exaggerated:

If we except the largely mythical attack on Troy, there is no other operation of the kind quite so remarkable as the three-year siege of Gibraltar. The besiegers were prodigal in their employment of troops, invention and money, while the defenders distinguished themselves by their resource and endurance, and the skilful way they applied and exploited their rather limited means of resistance. (Scharnhorst, 1834, 28)

The warring parties carried the most varied experiences away from the siege. The British gunners devised ingenious 'depression carriages', which enabled them to fire steeply downwards from their rocky heights, while Captain John Mercer of the 39th Foot had the lucky inspiration of firing $5\frac{1}{2}$-inch mortar bombs from 24-pounder cannon, having cut the fuzes in such a way that the shells burst above the heads of the enemy working parties. The young gunner Henry Shrapnel saw what Mercer had done, and in later years he perfected the air-burst shells

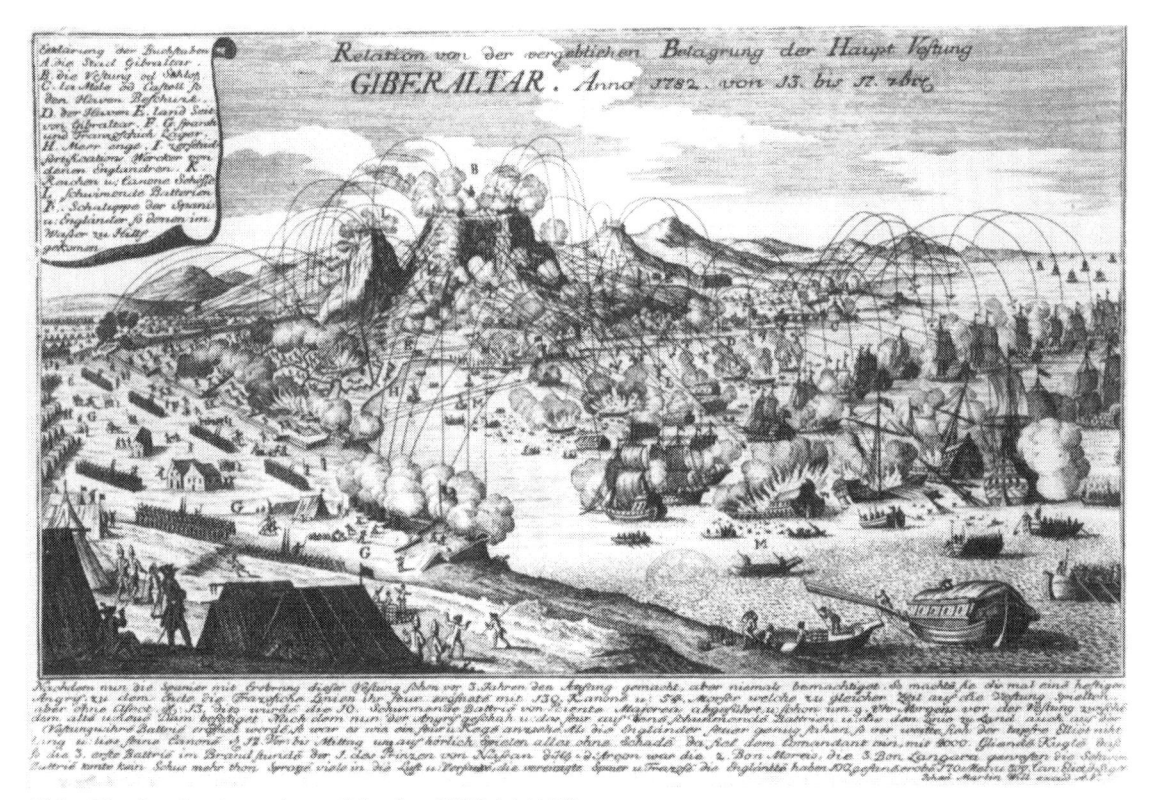

103 The floating batteries at Gibraltar 1781 (J. Will)

which largely replaced ricochet fire in the nineteenth century.

It may appear strange that the French, as assiduous bombardiers, had not invented 'shrapnel' themselves. They must have seen many occasions, like the one in their siegeworks at Namur in 1746, when by chance 'a mortar bomb, bursting a short distance from the ground, wreaked considerable execution among a party of thirty-odd men, of whom several were killed on the spot' (Virgin, 1781, 62). The Swedish engineer J. B. Virgin guessed that the backwardness of the French came from the fact that they persisted in applying the match to the bomb and the touch-hole of the mortar separately, which rendered the explosion of the bomb difficult to time with accuracy, instead of touching them both off with a 'single fire' like the British, who first cut the fuze, then left its ignition to the flame of the propelling charge, which licked around the bomb at the instant the mortar was fired.

The French were at least glad to have acquitted themselves somewhat better than the half-savage, chattering Spanish, who showed themselves thoroughly unfit for siege warfare:

What happens when they go to the trenches? They show plenty of bravado, but they arrive at the parallel in a mob, and proceed to create a great deal of noise, hawking and spitting, lighting up their pipes and exposing themselves carelessly, all of which draws on their working parties the fire of the enemy, who would otherwise have left them in peace. (Anon., 1783, 55)

Within the French army the technical experts were quick to discover very convincing vindications of their own viewpoints. Montalembert claimed that the success of the defence was due to 'the multitude of guns which were placed on the northern front, the only side on which that famous rock faced the Continent' (Montalembert, 1776–96, VI, 200).

One of the conservatives was just as certain that the siege showed the absurdity of Montalembert's principles:

If the English ... had by chance put their trust in men who were besotted with these fantasies, they would have neglected the cliffs in the interest of obtaining 'perpendicular defences' or some equally bogus properties. ... Instead of their barbette batteries, which are so simple, solid and easy to repair, they would have raised those multi-storeyed towers which become untenable as soon as they are hit. (Anon., 1785, 23)

Foissac-Latour was nearer the mark when he explained that the siege of Gibraltar proved that moral strength was one of the most important factors in fortress warfare. He attributed the success of the resistance to the character of old General Eliot, 'a very rare kind of person who combines the natural endurance of the Englishman with the skill of the French officer of artillery or engineers' (Foissac-Latour, 1789, 32).

Joseph II and the destruction of the Barrier 1781

One of the oddest episodes in international affairs in the 1780s concerned the peaceful demolition of the fortress system of the Austrian Netherlands. In 1781, soon after he became emperor in full sovereignty, the headstrong Joseph II made a tour of the Netherlands, that most remote and burdensome part of his dominions. On 25 June, once the inspection was complete, he called together the chiefs of the Brussels administration for an urgent conference. The greater number of the fortresses still laboured under Dutch military occupation, according to the terms of the old Barrier Treaty, and Joseph and his counsellors decided that the only way to get rid of their unwanted guests was to knock down the fortresses while the Dutch were still in them. Demolition gangs were accordingly set to work to slight every stronghold except the citadels of Antwerp, Namur and Luxembourg. This was an argument which managed to penetrate even Dutch ears, and on 18 April 1782 the Netherlands were at last free of the hated garrisons.

By dismantling one of Europe's outstanding defensive systems, Joseph was bound to diminish the role of permanent fortification in future wars. His action was, however, political rather than military in inspiration, for it was provoked by an international settlement that was at once intolerable and unenforceable.

The Prussian invasion of the United Provinces 1787

In September 1787 24,000 Prussian troops invaded the United Provinces in support of the Orangist party. The outcome was in no way calculated to enhance the prestige of permanent fortification. The Ijssel was still lower and more silted-up than at the beginning of the century, and the strongholds everywhere opened their gates to the Prussians. Gorinchem was the only one of the country fortresses to hold out long enough to undergo bombardment.

Amsterdam, as the last refuge of the pro-French 'patriots', defied the enemy from behind its inundations until an amphibious force crossed the Haarlem Lake and descended on the city from the rear. Amsterdam made its peace on 10 October, and William V of Orange was installed as hereditary Stadhouder under Prussian and British guarantee.

The coming of the Revolution in France

The balance between nobleman and commoner remained remarkably level among the French engineers for most of the period of the old regime. The policy of the corps was summed up in 1751 by the mathematician Charles-Etienne de Camus, who examined candidates for admission to the Mézières school:

There can be no doubt that when two people compete on otherwise fairly equal terms, the preference will be given to the nobleman, or to displaced officers who wish to give up the kind of work they did in their former regiments. ... But there is no intention whatsoever of excluding candidates who are not gentlemen, or who have not yet served in the army. (Augoyat, 1860–4, II, 445)

However, a number of changes became evident over the following decades. The passing of the cosy, inward-looking era of d'Asfeld was indicated by the decline in the intake of sons of engineers, from 47 per cent to 13 per cent between 1748 and 1777. Also the corps was not exempt from the influence of the aristocratic resentment which was building up against the rich bourgeois who had begun to buy their way into the field arms. The first fairly moderate control of the engineering intake dates from 1762. A more restrictive decree came into force in 1778, and finally in 1781 an exceptionally reactionary war minister demanded proof of four generations and four degrees of nobility from every prospective officer in every branch of the king's service. The intake of noble engineer recruits, which had long remained constant at just under one half of the whole, rose correspondingly to three-quarters in the period between 1778 and 1791.

The increasingly aristocratic tone of the engineers accounts only in part for the perhaps surprising fact that the Revolution commanded less than wholehearted support in such a hard-working and technically-minded corps. Fully one-third of the officers chose to follow the Royalist emigration, and two-fifths of these wandering heroes turn out to have been of bourgeois origin.

In 1789 the pamphleteer Foissac-Latour made a wonderfully mis-timed statement:

There is no state in the world more solidly fortified than France, and none where the princes have reigned with more gentleness, justice and benevolence. Call to mind the enthusiasm of the French for their kings, and tell me whether this pronounced and sustained national feeling could have arisen of its own accord, without being called forth by a régime which was founded on wise and moderate principles? (*Examen Détaillé*, 61)

Chief among these 'wise and moderate principles', in Foissac-Latour's opinion, was a belief in the value of permanent fortification.

With a few exceptions of this kind, we come across almost no trace of a correspondence between political and military views in the French army on the eve of the Revolution. Carnot was no less convinced than was Foissac-Latour of the necessity of strongholds, but he went on to become the incarnation of the Revolution Militant, and a patriot still more rabid than his fellow-Jacobin, Choderlos de Laclos, who deplored the spending of money on anything so useless as fortifications. Montalembert, the great revolutionary in fortress design, held that fortification *per se* was a necessity.

This explains why the coming of the Revolution, which shook so many institutions to the root, failed to break the continuity of the engineering corps with its past. D'Arçon and Carnot, however 'advanced' they were politically, found much to admire in the military achievements of the days of the old kings. The long-dead Vauban presented himself with new vividness to the generation of the Revolution as the guardian of the frontiers, and the embodiment of natural virtue as one who 'wished to check the frightful accumulation of prerogatives which condemns the most precious class of mankind to poverty and scorn' (Carnot's *Eloge de Vauban*, in Carnot, 1861–4, I, 112–13).

Six   The Subjugation of Ireland and Scotland

The Williamite campaigns in Ireland 1689–91

To all outward appearances the Cromwellian conquest of 1650–2 had spelt the end of militant Irish Catholic resistance to Protestant rule. In the 1680s Catholic Irishmen once more sprang to arms, but this time as loyal subjects of the most unlikely of masters – a Catholic king of Great Britain. The sovereign in question was James II, who was expelled from England by the Protestant supporters of Prince William of Orange.

In March 1689 James descended on Ireland with money and French officers. Almost all of Ireland proved to be loyal, and over the following months James devoted 12,000 troops to the object of reducing one of the last pockets of resistance – the ramparts of Londonderry on the western flank of the English and Scots plantation of Ulster.

Protestant Ulstermen are justifiably proud of the feat of their amateur garrison, which bid defiance to a royal army. At the same time the Jacobite historians are careful to point out that much of the Irish infantry was armed with nothing more than iron-tipped staves, and that the besiegers had only two heavy cannon at their disposal – and these had to be planted on the banks of the Foyle so as to cover the blockade boom.

The management of the siege too was grossly defective, because King James intervened sporadically and unhelpfully from his distant headquarters in Dublin. He granted rather too much authority to Lieutenant-General Richard Hamilton, who knew little about sieges, but certainly too little to the experienced Conrad von Rosen, who was born a Russian Balt, and who had served Louis of France in innumerable sieges over forty years. James allowed well over one thousand 'useless mouths' to leave the town in the early stages of the attack, and when Rosen threatened on 30 June to drive the Protestant countryfolk under the walls, if Derry failed to surrender at once, the king disowned the proclamation as something which emanated from a barbarous Muscovite. Here James displayed the same kind of mistaken humanity which held back Philip II from drowning the lands of his erring Dutch subjects in 1574.

A constant irritant during the operation was the difficulty which the foreign experts encountered in adapting themselves to Irish conditions and ways. Rosen complained that the Irish were slow of understanding and spoke an incomprehensible tongue. Conversely, James had every reason to expect that 'the French engineers, though very able men in their trade, may have been so used to having all things necessary provided for them and to want nothing that they are not so industrious, as other lesser-knowing men might be' (Anon., 1958, III, no. 13, 287).

After a purgatory of frustration the besiegers finally marched away on 1 August, having lost more than half of their number through action, sickness and desertion.

The coming of the year 1690 found James's Irish army battered and exhausted, and Ulster holding out as a bridgehead for invasion from Williamite England. King William III seized the opportunity, and during the spring he built up in Ulster one of the best-found armies ever to take the field in Ireland. The backbone of the expeditionary force was made up of a corps of 5,800 Danish troops under the command of the Duke of Württemberg. The duke brought with him as his principal technical adviser the much-travelled Julius Ernst von Tettau, who had learnt the trade of engineering under Turenne.

The army struck out along the same clockwise circuit which Cromwell had taken in 1650. William beat the Jacobites on the River Boyne on 1 July, which opened the way across the single natural barrier in his path, and the host went on to capture Waterford and Duncannon.

Meanwhile a detached corps under General Douglas had been sent directly across the chord of the arc of the circle against the middle Shannon at Athlone. There the ancient Colonel Richard Grace, a Royalist veteran of the English Civil War, gave him a splendid reception, drawing his pistol from his belt and firing it over the head of Douglas's envoy – 'These are my terms. These only will I give or receive, and when all my provisions are consumed I will eat my old boots!' Within a week all the Williamite powder was exhausted and several of their guns dismounted, which forced Douglas to break off the siege and join his royal master in front of Limerick, the Jacobite guardian-fortress of the lower Shannon.

The French major-general de Boisselot packed the 20,000 badly armed Jacobite infantry into Limerick, but the 3,800 horse roamed the open field under the command of Patrick Sarsfield, 'a man of amazing stature, utterly void of sense, very good-natured and very brave' (Berwick, 1779, I, 96). Sarsfield's troopers ranged the line of the Shannon, which prevented the besiegers from crossing to the Clare (western) side of the Shannon as Ireton had done in 1651, and, more important still, this marvellous idiot contrived to surprise and destroy the Williamite siege train at Ballyneety on the night of 11–12 August.

By the last week of August King William's siege of Limerick was in a sorry state. His trenches were flooded, his powder was low, and his light field cannon were able to effect only a narrow breach in the walls. On the 27th, therefore, William took what in other circumstances would have been an unjustifiable risk, and committed seven battalions and half the grenadiers of the army to an assault. The troops penetrated some way into the town, but were ultimately thrown out again in some disorder. The Danish contingent alone lost 441 men on this bloody day.

After this chapter of misfortunes William raised the siege on 30 August. He tried to persuade Europe that his misfortune at Limerick was due to the heavy rains, but the French royal historian attributes the outcome to the magnificent defence, which was 'regarded as one of the most brilliant ever staged in the reign of King Louis XIV. It bestowed great prestige upon de Boisselot and the troops who held this place' (Quincy, 1726, II, 340).

The Danes were shortly afterwards given an opportunity of exacting a measure of revenge from the southern Jacobites. In the late autumn the Duke of Württemberg led his corps away from William's army, and joined a force of ten regiments which was shipped from England under the command of John Churchill, Earl of Marlborough. The object of the enterprise was to capture the fortified ports of Cork and Kinsale, which, in Churchill's calculations, would help to isolate Ireland from France, and perhaps persuade a recently landed force of Frenchmen under de Lauzun to quit Ireland without a fight. By 15 October both Cork and Kinsale were in Williamite hands, and de Lauzun, having done nothing to promote the Jacobite cause, duly took ship with his men from Galway. This fag-end of the campaign had its corresponding absurdities on the Williamite side, for Tettau and Churchill could not agree on how to manage the sieges, and ended up by directing two completely separate attacks on each stronghold.

In marked contrast to their scrappy proceedings in 1690, the Williamites concentrated all their resources in the next year on the work of bringing down the strongholds of the Shannon.

In the first half of June 1691 the two corps of Ginkel and Württemberg met in front of Athlone, and on the 19th they assaulted and took the part of

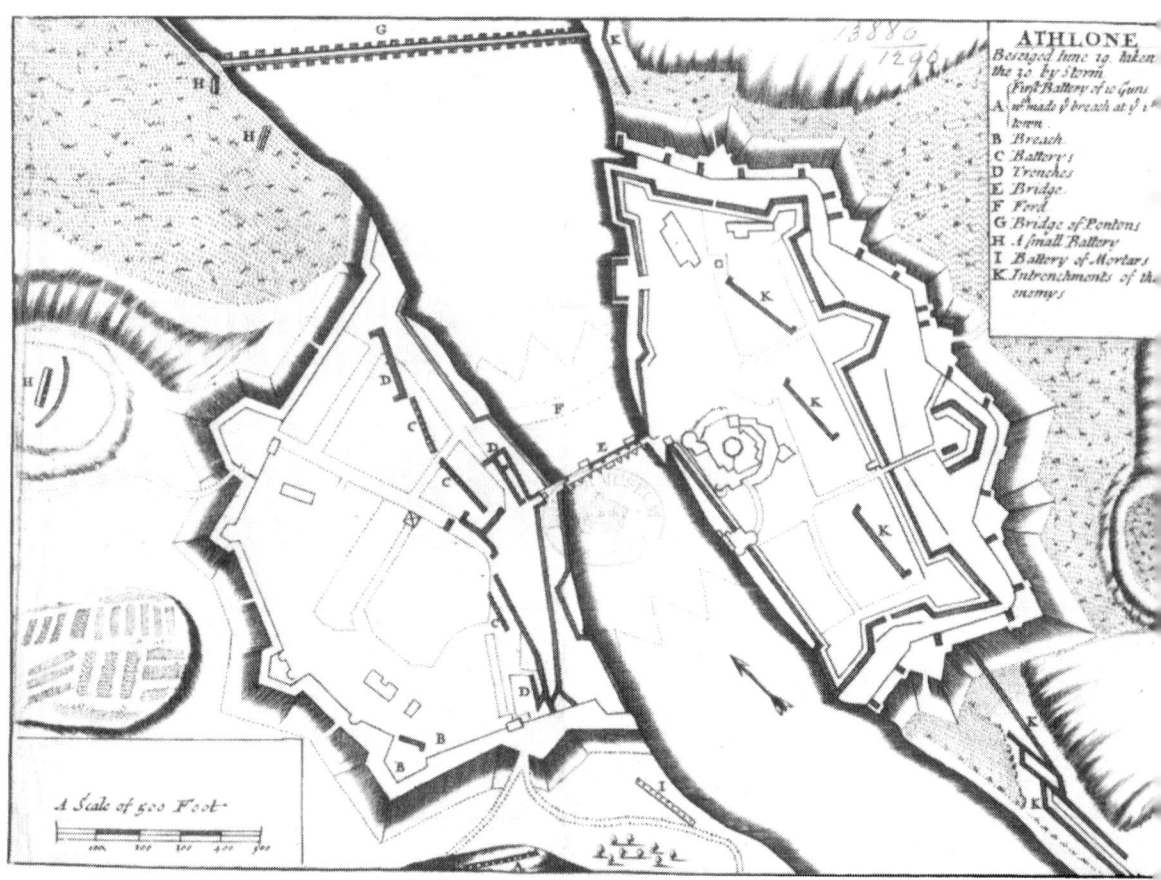

104 Siege of Athlone 1691

the town that lay on the left (east) bank of the Shannon. The Williamites then built a strong and high siege parapet along the river-front of the captured section, with platforms for six mortars and embrasures for fifty battering cannon, and over the next week they hurled 12,000 cannon shot, 600 bombs and several tons of pierrier stones into the defences on the far side of the river. This constituted the heaviest cannonade in Irish history. By the 30th the town was theirs for the taking – the riverside defences were down, the Shannon was at its lowest level in living memory, and the French lieutenant-general, Saint-Ruth, who commanded the Irish field army outside Athlone, refused to send in any reinforcements.

At three in the afternoon of 30 June, in the words of a Williamite soldier, 'on a sudden we bounced over our works into the river, and were a good way on before the enemy perceived us' (Parker, 1747, 32). Fighting for every yard of ground, the Irish were pushed through the town, over the rearward walls, and made their last stand in a line of redoubts outside. An English engineer reported:

As to the number killed, we cannot yet learn an exact account, though I think, there never was a more tragical spectacle in so short a time, and small a place. One could not set down his foot at the end of the bridge, or castle, but on dead bodies. Many lay half-buried under the rubbish, and more under faggots, and many not to be seen under the ruins, whereby the stink is insufferable. (Anon., 'A Diary', 1691, *The Irish Sword*, 1959, IV, no. 15, 92)

Saint-Ruth's inaction gave him only a temporary respite, for on 12 July the Williamites defeated and killed him in a battle at Aughrim. His broken army was divided in two parts. Some troops fell back westwards to Galway, where they shortly after capitulated on good terms, but the rest rallied for a stand at their last stronghold at Limerick.

Ginkel arrived before Limerick in late August, and undertook a siege on a truly continental scale. By 8 September forty battering cannon and eight mortars were in operation, and six days later the Danish Army Commissioner reported that the city looked like a heap of stones. There was no effective Jacobite force left in the open field, a circumstance which permitted the Williamites to bridge the Shannon above Limerick, and appear on the Clare side of the city on 22 September. Negotiations were set in train on the 23rd, and led to the famous capitulation which left the Jacobites with the choice of remaining in an Ireland under Protestant rule, or of taking service with the King of France. Almost to a man the troops who yielded at Limerick elected to take ship to the Continent – these 19,000 were the vanguard of the 'Wild Geese', the scores of thousands of Irish who were to seek their fortune in foreign armies over the course of the next century.

The English Secretary at War, George Clark, found it strange

that a numerous garrison, not pressed by any want, should give up a town which nobody was in a condition to take from them, at a time when those who lay before it had actually drawn off their cannon and were preparing to march away, and when that garrison did daily expect a squadron of ships to come to their relief, if they needed any. (Quoted in Simms, *The Irish Sword*, II, no. 5, 1955, 26)

It seems likely that the motives for the capitulation were rooted less in military necessity than in the desire of Sarsfield and his landless officers to search for fame and profit on the Continent.

What is at least certain is that the surrender of Limerick accelerated the work of social destruction which had been set in train by the fall of Kinsale and the Flight of the Earls nearly a century before. Deprived of their natural leaders, the Irish had to look elsewhere for champions of their liberties – Protestant aristocrats, atheistic Jacobins, Westminster politicians and last of all the poets and gunfighters of the twentieth century.

The Jacobite rebellions in Scotland

The '15

The legal basis for London's influence in Scotland was provided by the Union of the crowns of Scotland and England in 1603. Militarily, English rule was based on the control of the two tracts of land where the Scottish peninsula was most effectively constricted by salt firths or inland loughs or rivers – these were the Great Glen and the Central Lowlands.

The Great Glen slashed the Highlands transversely from north-east to south-west. At the southwestern exit the English had a garrison and listening-post at Fort William, which was in none too good a state when the agitations of the Scots Jacobites were first detected. The '15, however, proved to be a Lowland as well as a Highland rebellion and the deciding role in this campaign was played by the pro-Hanoverian forces which the Duke of Argyll gathered at Stirling in the marshy flats of the Central Lowlands. Based on this volcanic crag, the Hanoverian party effectively commanded the passage between the Highlands and the more 'civilised' areas of Scotland – eastwards stretched the unbridgeable Firth of Forth; to the west, the valley of the upper Forth snaked towards the Trossachs and the territory of the loyalist clan of Campbell, which could be relied upon to do its best to hold down discontented people like the Camerons.

Since the Jacobites did not have the means of taking Stirling by siege, the rebellion was effectively severed in two, and the Highland and Lowland Jacobites had to go to their separate dooms. The Duke of Argyll marched out of Stirling with 4,000 men, and on 13 November he defeated the Highland army of the Earl of Mar at Sheriffmuir. Meanwhile a force of about 1,500 Lowland and Northumberland gentry and their followers had made off into England along the same western path that the Scots had taken in 1648. The end came on the same 13 November, when the adventurers were bottled up on the line of the Ribble at Preston. They laid down their arms on the 14th, and Britain was saved for the benefits of thirty years of almost undisputed Hanoverian rule.

The '45

Following the defeat of the '15, the English were at great pains to open the Highlands to military penetration. From 1724 Field-Marshal Wade drove two carriage roads into the southern fringe of the Highlands at Crieff and Dunkeld, and he proceeded northwards, sometimes along a single passage and sometimes by way of widely separated passes, until he emerged into the Great Glen. He strengthened Fort William, and built Fort Augustus in the exact centre of the Glen to serve as the focal point for all the Highland garrisons. At the north-eastern exit rose Fort George (the first on the site), which was designed by the engineer captain John Romer and completed by him shortly before the outbreak of the '45 at a cost of £50,000. The system of regular forts was supplemented by defensible barracks at Bernara, Inversnaid, Kiliwhimen and Ruthven.

All the money and all the years of effort did little to stay the course of the new Jacobite rising which engulfed the Highlands in 1745. The English commander, Lieutenant-General Sir John Cope, had scarcely 2,000 mobile troops at his disposal, but under heavy political pressure from the government he marched north from Stirling to seek battle. The progress came to a halt at Dalwhinnie, for the promised Highland auxiliaries had failed to materialise, and the prospect of pushing over the Corrieyairack Pass to Fort Augustus was as uninviting as that of retreat to Stirling through the increasingly hostile countryside. To avoid being taken in a trap, Cope made for the east coast, and took ship at Aberdeen on 22 September.

Thus the forces of Prince Charles Edward were able to slip between the weakly held Great Glen forts, and wade the unguarded Forth above Stirling to descend on the Lowlands. The Hanoverian garrisons were about as well prepared to withstand the invasion as they were to meet the Second Coming. The small regular garrisons of Stirling, Edinburgh and Carlisle could place no reliance on the support of the militia or the townspeople, and they and the other slumbering strongpoints furnished Cope with 'gunners' who on the day of Prestonpans (21 September) were seen to charge cannon with powder but no shot, or to put the shot in first and the powder afterwards.

The citizens of Edinburgh went through a show of casting up earthworks under the direction of a professor of mathematics, but they offered no resistance once the Camerons had seized the city gates on the night of 16–17 September and opened the way for the entry of their lawful Prince. The 85-year-old Governor Guest on the Castle rock was content to leave the city in the hands of the Jacobites, as long as they allowed provisions to come through to the garrison.

Now the Jacobites had to settle on the best means of penetrating England:

His Royal Highness seemed determined to march straight to Berwick (i.e. down the east coast). This was represented by Lord George Murray as of very dangerous consequence, for it was a walled town with at least three hundred regular troops besides militia in it. Highlanders were not fit for making a siege, and the cannon they had could do no hurt to the walls, six of them being 4-pounders and the rest 3- and 2-pounders. General Wade was about Newcastle with an army stronger than that of His Royal Highness. He proposed going into England by Carlisle, which although walled and a castle, yet they would be unprepared. (Quoted in Tomasson, 1958, 68–70)

Thus the 4,500 Jacobites chose the same path of invasion along the western side of the Pennines which their fathers had followed in 1715, and which the Covenanters had travelled in 1648 – a compliment to the deterrent power of the fortress of Berwick.

Carlisle presented the Jacobites with the totally unaccustomed problems of conducting a siege. Their military commander Lord George Murray offended the Prince by declining to take charge of the operation, on the grounds that he 'understood nothing of sieges' (Quoted in *ibid.*, 74). This was unfortunate, for it alienated Charles Edward from the best natural soldier in his army. James, third Duke of Perth, took over in Murray's place, and racked his brains to recall the mathematics and fortification he had once studied in Paris. A more important qualification was his ability to keep the Highlanders at the uncongenial task of siege labour during the snowy nights. The townsmen were duly

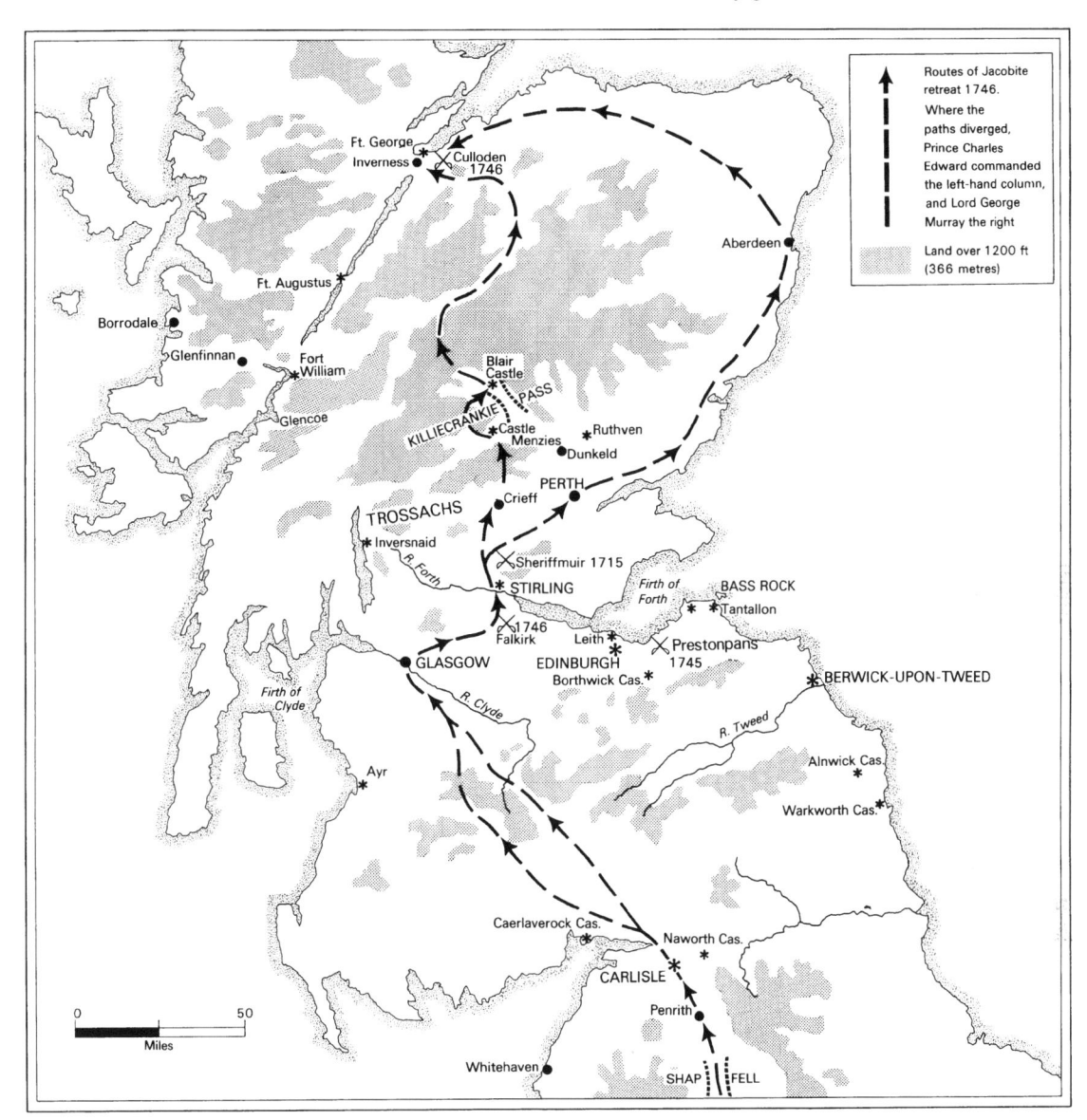

Scotland and the Borders

impressed by the imposing appearance of the batteries, and the governor was persuaded to yield on 14 November.

The Jacobites now laid the 'old bogey' of 1648 and 1715 by passing the Ribble unopposed, and marched on to the line of the Mersey, the southern border of the Lancashire strategic box. The rebels made a great show of repairing the Crossford bridge at Stretford, which put the Hanoverians in fear of a move by way of Altrincham and Knutsford to Wales or the Severn valley, but instead on 1 December the Jacobite force passed upstream at Cheadle and Stockport, and struck south-east through Macclesfield in the direction of London. For a time it seemed that the term of the Hanoverian dynasty was about to expire, and the Board of Ordnance recommended that London and the suburbs should be fortified with a ring of forts, 'such as were thrown up in the year 1642'.

The danger receded almost as unexpectedly as it

105 Fort George, Inverness. Designed by William Skinner in 1747 to secure the inner reaches of the Moray Firth after the '45. One of the very rare examples of eighteenth-century bastioned fortification on the British mainland

had materialised, for the rebels turned back to Scotland from the furthest point of their penetration at Derby. The invasion had been a gamble which was well worth the taking, but the Jacobites awakened as much curiosity – and as little real support – in England as did the scarecrow armies of Robert E. Lee in his offensives into the border states in the American Civil War.

The war of the rebellion now entered its second stage – namely the Jacobite attempt to convert Scotland into a strategic redoubt by reducing the Hanoverian strongpoints which the Prince had bypassed in his advance. The details are still somewhat obscure, for the historians are obsessed with marches and field actions, and pass on very rapidly from the about-turn at Derby to the combats at Falkirk and Culloden.

The year closed badly for the rebels, with the loss of Carlisle, the south-western door of Scotland. The Jacobites had left out of their calculations the ancient 'joker' in the English strategic pack, the ability to transport siege artillery swiftly and secretly by sea. The Duke of Cumberland moved against Carlisle overland, but his train of 12- and 18-pounders was disembarked at Whitehaven, thus avoiding the murderous climb over Shap Fell. Carlisle capitulated as soon as these guns opened fire on 30 December.

In the New Year of 1746, however, the threat of French invasion forced Cumberland to return to the south of England. This brief respite for the rebels coincided with the landing at Montrose of help from France in the form of a small siege train, together with one hundred troopers of Fitzjames Horse, fifty men from each of the six infantry regiments of the same Irish Brigade in the service of France, and the diminutive and volatile Mirabelle de Gordon, an engineer of Scots descent. Prince Charles Edward now had the means of prosecuting an important siege, and he made the sensible decision to attempt the reduction of Stirling Castle. With this strongpoint in his hands, he would have a good prospect of checking the English at the narrow constriction between the firths of Clyde and Forth.

Contrary to every expectation, the siege of Stirling Castle proved to be little better managed than the first Jacobite essay in fortress warfare at Carlisle. Mirabelle de Gordon turned out to be

a headstrong fellow that would have his own way and follow no man's advice. . . . He . . . had chosen such bad ground full of stones and very little earth, that the trenches could hardly be perfected anywhere, and his battery was so ill-made and so ill-placed that it could not resist. . . . The Highlanders would not undertake this work for fear of derogating from noble birth of which they were so proud, and the Lowlanders were too lazy to work in the trenches. There were thus only the [Irish] soldiers from France; and they worked even better than could have been expected. [Quoted in Thomasson, 1958, 160] . . . What a pity that these brave men should have been sacrificed to no purpose, by the ignorance and folly of Mirabelle. (Johnstone, 1821, 137)

An English relief column was defeated easily enough at Falkirk, on 17 January, but Stirling Castle was no nearer reduction when Cumberland approached with a powerful army at the end of the month. On 1 February the siege was raised amid considerable disorder.

For Prince Charles Edward there remained the hope of mastering the rearward strategic barrier of the Great Glen. In one of those rapid circling movements characteristic of the Scots Jacobites at their best, he reached Inverness well ahead of the Duke of Cumberland, and moved down the Glen, reducing the strongholds on his way. Fort George and Fort Augustus were wrested easily from their demoralised garrisons, but the Jacobite progress was stopped at Fort William, owing to the energetic defence which was conducted by the engineer Michael Scot. The siege was lifted on 3 April, and the Jacobites left behind their train of eight cannon and seven mortars.

The check at Fort William was all the more serious because Cumberland had meanwhile occupied Blair Castle and Castle Menzies, which helped him to close off the valleys of the southeastern Grampians. Cumberland therefore undertook his final advance against a force that was devoid of any *point d'appui*. The Jacobites met him in the open field at Culloden on 26 April and were beaten beyond hope of recall. Cumberland continued his march to the Great Glen, and made the half-ruined Fort Augustus his headquarters for the brutal suppression of the Highland culture. The subjugation of the British Isles was complete.

Seven The Battle for Sweden's Trans-Baltic Bridgeheads

The first bid, the war of 1674-9

During the middle decades of the seventeenth century the high tide of Swedish conquest had lapped around the shores of the Baltic, leaving them encrusted with a barnacle-like growth of fortresses which threatened to smother every other power which tried to breathe in the area. It was going to take the best part of a century to prise the garrisons loose, and in the process the Northern states displayed prodigies of effort and ingenuity which still remain almost unknown to students of military history in the West.

After a peaceful respite of fourteen years, Sweden came under a concerted counter-attack in the middle 1670s. To the west the Danes had a burning grievance to settle, for the Swedes had grabbed the provinces of Scania, Holland, and Blekinge (making up much of present-day southern Sweden), and they had thereby broken the territorial integrity of the Danish-Norwegian empire. In this new war the Danes were supported on the southern shores of the Baltic by some powerful allies, as we shall see. On the Scandinavian peninsula, however, the Danes were betrayed by their perpetual weakness in siege warfare. In 1676 they overran the open country of their lost provinces easily enough, but in this year and the next they were unable to evict the Swedes who held out in their rear in the Sound fortresses of Malmö and Göteborg. This failure helped to break the career of Denmark's foremost engineer and military reformer, Henrik Rüsensteen.

Meanwhile on the 'German' side of the Baltic the initiative was taken by the rising military state of Brandenburg, which defeated the Swedes at Fehrbellin on 8 June 1675, then set about throwing the enemy out of Swedish Pomerania. This ambition gave rise to a number of sieges of extraordinary vigour and crudity, which showed how far the techniques of Northern fortress warfare fell short of the economical and effective means which were being evolved by Vauban in France. The Great Elector Frederick William had just one technique at his disposal for this kind of operation – he simply trundled every available cannon and mortar into monster *Generalbatterien* and pelted the town with shot and shell. He reduced the fortress-port of Stettin in 1677 (at a second attempt), and Stralsund yielded in 1678 after almost every house in this wooden-built city had been destroyed by bombs and red-hot shot. The events at Stralsund were responsible for giving the word 'bombardment' its first currency in Germany, and for spreading among Northern lands as a whole the assumption that this usually wasteful technique was a valid alternative to a systematic siege attack.

Louis XIV found it intolerable that the Swedes no longer had a Baltic empire with which to divert the attention of the Elector of Brandenburg and the other German princes from the Rhine. The French diplomats accordingly showered the Northern powers with gold, threats and promises, and in 1679 they brought about peace settlements which bore

The Baltic lands

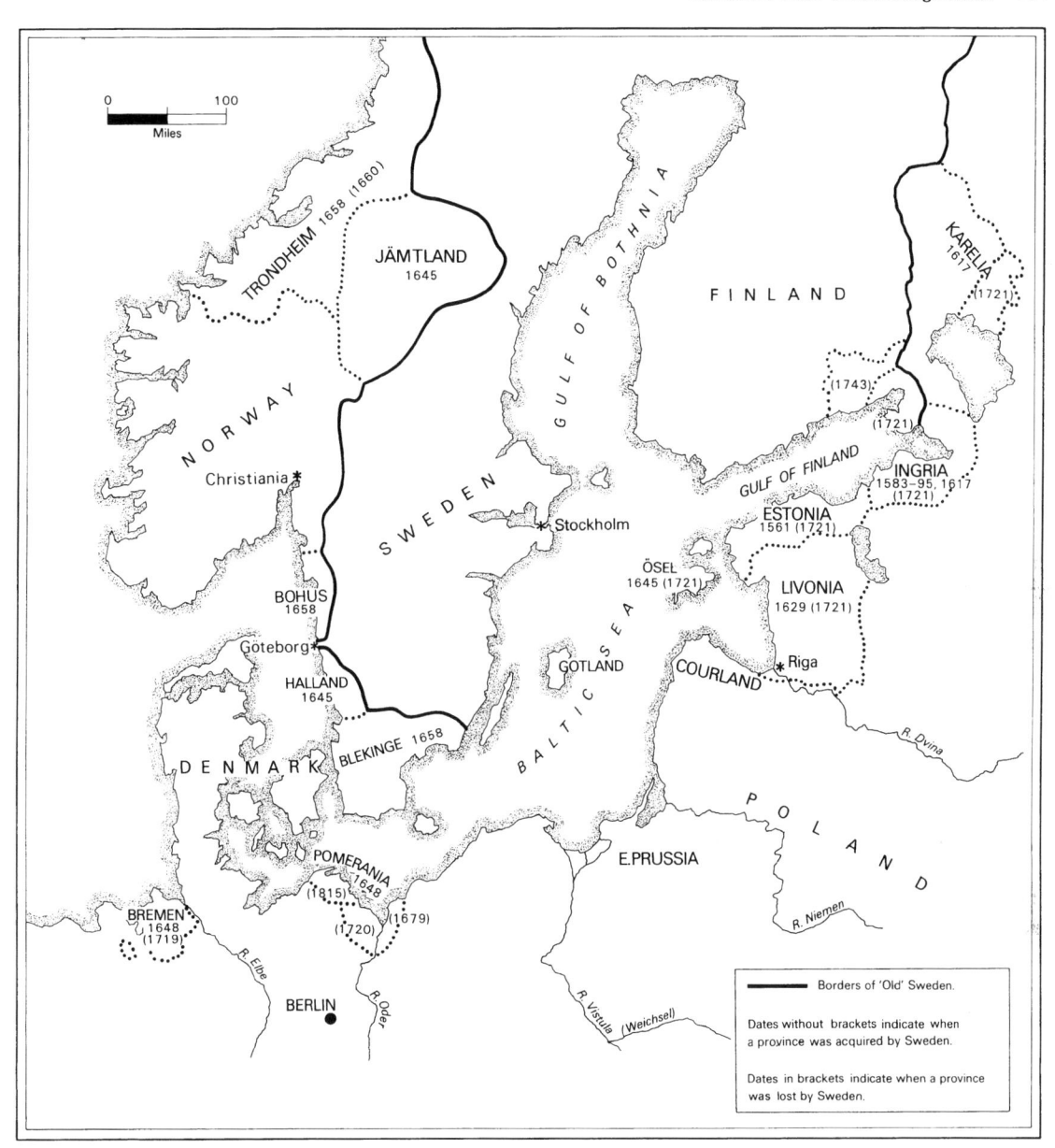

not the slightest relation to the way the war had gone. Brandenburg disgorged all Pomerania west of the Oder, while the Danes restored the lands of the Duke of Holstein-Gottorp, who was a client of Sweden.

This lucky escape helped to make up the mind of King Charles XI to undertake a radical re-shaping of the Swedish political and military organisation. The days were long past when, true to the principle of 'war must feed on war', the Swedes used to mount campaign upon campaign deep in central Europe with armies of German mercenaries. Likewise, Sweden could not always rely on such foreign assistance as was evident in the shape of the French interventions and subsidies, or the Dutch alliance of 1681. Charles accordingly imposed an absolutist but by no means unpopular regime on his own kingdom, unlocking the internal resources which enabled him to form an excellent army of Swedish soldier-farmers. The German provinces – so difficult and expensive to defend – were now prized chiefly for the fact that they continued to give Sweden a say in Western European affairs. Conversely, the eastern Baltic lands, and Livonia in particular, grew in relative value, for they clapped a muzzle on resurgent Muscovy, and helped to make up for the repeated failures of the Swedish harvest in the 1680s and 1690s. 'Quite suddenly the Baltic provinces assumed a new importance: they had become Sweden's granary, as necessary to her as Sicily was to Spain' (Roberts, 1979, 105). However, for reasons which have never been fully explained, the royal programme of fortress-building failed to take account of this fundamental shift in relationships.

Northern military engineering in the middle and later seventeenth century

Denmark
Danish fortress-building was prosecuted at a furious pace throughout these dangerous times, for the assorted disasters of the middle decades of the century had lodged the Swedes on the German flank of the Jutish peninsula, and left Copenhagen stranded as a frontier fortress facing eighty miles of Swedish-owned coastline beyond the Sound.

106 Gateway of Rüsensteen's *Kastell* at Copenhagen

The High Constable Anders Bille first sounded the alarm in 1646, calling for the establishment of a fortress in Jutland, and urging that Copenhagen 'should be as well and as completely secured and fortified as is humanly possible, for the whole welfare of the crown depends on this city' (Rockstroh, 1909–16, I, 174).

Frederiksodde (Fredericia), the fortress in Jutland, was completed just in time to fall into the hands of the Swedes in 1657. At Copenhagen the Inspector of Engineering Axel Urup made some additions and alterations between 1647 and 1656, but the perimeter as a whole was in a bad state of repair, and the city was lucky to survive the Swedish siege and blockade of 1658–9 (see Duffy, 1979, 186–8, 253).

The strengthening of Copenhagen, therefore, remained a matter of the first urgency, and in 1661 the Dutch engineer Henrik Rüsensteen contracted to build a citadel there 'in the course of three summers' (Rockstroh, in Bricka (1941) XX, no. 3, 19, 358), in other words by Martinmas Day 1664. He went about in some danger of his life, for the citizens were enraged by the brutal way he cleared the site, but by dint of using his own regiment as a labour force he was able to complete the pentagonal earthen *Kastell* within the agreed term. He was already designing a new city enceinte, which was a much more ambitious project. The construction began in 1667, and extended over four decades until the work was crowned by the completion of the East Gate in 1708.

Northwards along the coast the Kronborg fortress at Helsingør (Elsinore) not only retained its employment as collector of the lucrative Sound dues, but now assumed a considerable strategic importance, as the closest point to the newly hostile coastline of Scania, just two and a half miles across the Sound. In the 1570s Netherlandish masons had surrounded the handsome Renaissance castle with a bastioned enceinte, and several decades of work now began on an outer perimeter, which was completed in purest 'first Vauban' style in the 1730s.

In a wider context the Swedish push to the Sound and the Kattegat forced the Danes to take fresh measures for the independent defence of Norway, which was now deprived of overland communication with the rest of the Danish empire. For generations the office of southern outpost of Norway had been served by the castle of Bohus (Baahus), standing on a low hill above the division of the Nodre Älv and the Göta Älv a few miles to the north of Göteborg (Gothenburg) and the sea. However, this place was delivered to the Swedes in virtue of the Peace of Copenhagen in 1660, and it successfully resisted a determined siege by the Danish-Norwegian forces in 1678.

Now that the Swedes were so widely lodged on the westward-facing coastline, the defence of Norway recoiled one hundred miles to the north to the confines of Norway proper, where a number of rivers and lakes ran roughly parallel with the new borders. In 1659 and 1660 the Swedes laid siege no less than three times to the exposed and weakly fortified

107 Guardians of the Sound. Part of the seventeen-gun barbette battery at Kronborg Castle, Elsinore. This is one of the largest batteries of muzzle-loading cannon still in full working order. The carriages date from the nineteenth century, but the barrels were cast in 1638

180 Sweden's Trans-Baltic Bridgeheads

Halden, which commanded an important crossing of the Tistedal River. The successful resistance owed more to the obstinacy of the Norwegians than to the strength of the works, and after the war the able and popular Viceroy Ulrik Gyldenløve hastened to build a number of masonry fortifications on and around the Cretzensteen rock, which made this fortress, under the name of 'Fredriksten', one of the most formidable in the northern kingdom. The construction of the irregular pentagonal citadel was begun in 1661, to the designs of the Dutch engineer Quartermaster-General Willem Coucheron, and the whole complex, including the little forts or blockhouses to the east, was essentially complete by the end of the century.

In the strategic rear of Fredriksten, the channel and lakes of the Glomma River ran generally from north to south through vast forests to the fertile plain of Sarpsborg and Fredrikstad, and thus to the sea. This line too assumed a new importance for the defence of Norway after 1660. Up-river the fortress of Kongsvinger was planted on a height above a broad loop of the river – a site oddly reminiscent of the Tagus at Santarem – and it was fortified at the same time and in much the same style as Fredriksten. At the seaward end of the Glomma, Frederick III commissioned Colonel Coucheron to fortify the ailing little town of Fredrikstad on the left bank. The plans for the Dutch-style earthen enceinte were approved in 1663, and Fredrikstad ultimately became a most important military and naval establishment, serving as a base for Admiral Peder Wessel Tordenskiold's operations against the Bohuslän coast. Outside the fortress proper, the eerie outcrop of Gallows hill, 650 yards to the east, was ingeniously fortified with a perimeter of stone ramparts and countermines by General Johan Caspar von Cicignon. This 'Kongsten Fort' was connected to Fredrikstad town by a broad earthen caponnière.

As a final rearward defence for Norway, the Akershus citadel at Christiania (Oslo) was also strengthened under Gyldenløve's administration.

If we except the earthen ramparts of Fredrikstad town, the Norwegian fortresses were characteristically built with outer faces of natural blocks of granite, roughly dressed on the outside, with corners of cut stone and interiors of rubble and mortar. The

108 Kongsten Fort, Fredrikstad

Sweden's Trans-Baltic Bridgeheads 181

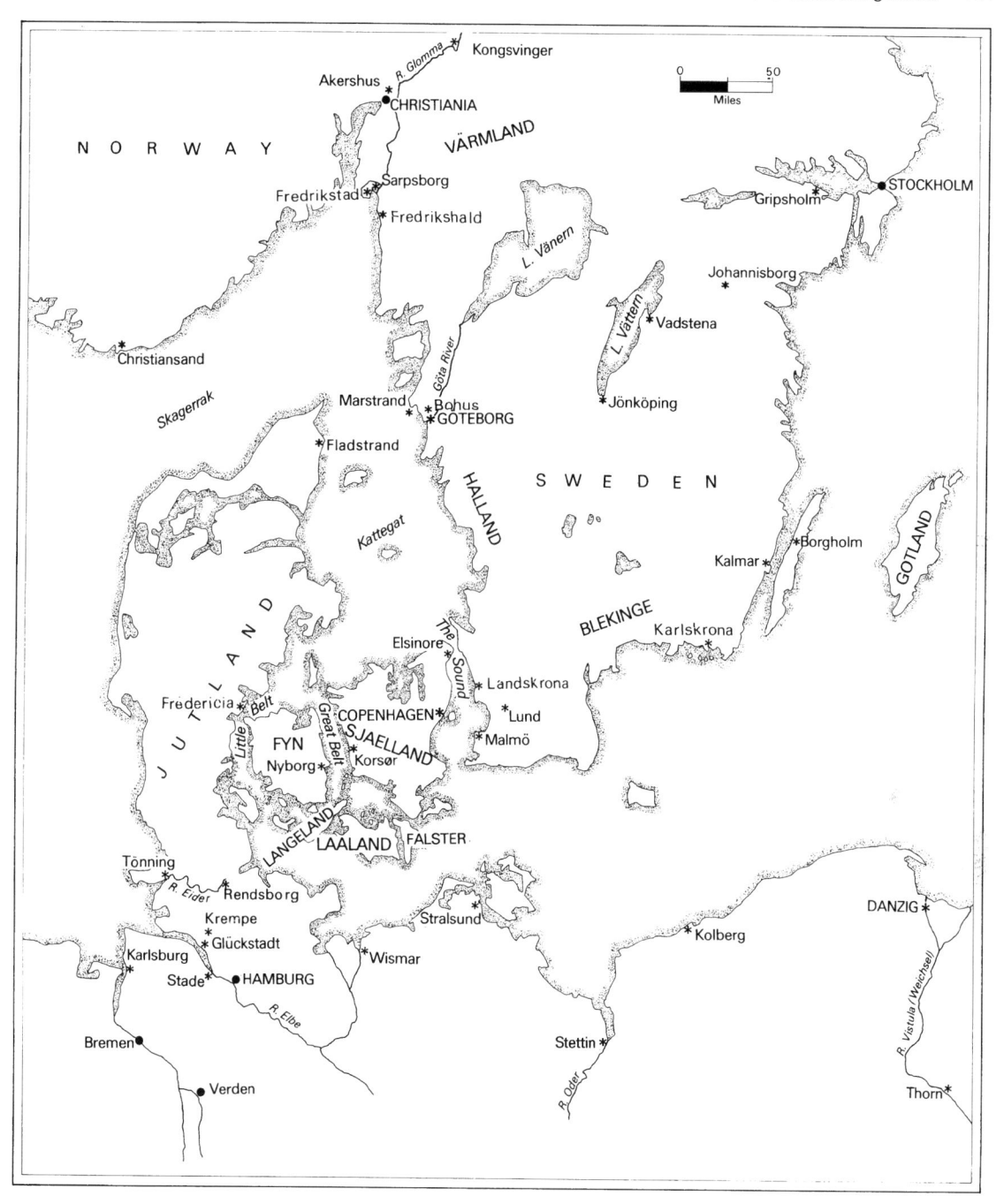

Denmark, with south Norway and south Sweden

foundations were excavated and levelled by dint of heating the living rock with huge fires, then cracking and crumbling the stone by pouring water or brine on top. The Norwegian National Regiments were called upon for the onerous labour of the building work proper, which went ahead in the short summer months, while the transport of stone (about 20,000 cubic metres for Fredriksten alone) was effected in winter by means of hired peasant sledges. The bastion trace was preferred, where the space was available, but the tenaille motif was adopted on the more cramped fronts of the works.

Far to the south, the exposed German flank of the Danish empire was at last given a measure of security when Rüsensteen built the seven-bastioned fortress of Rendsborg (Rendsburg) on the upper Eider between 1669 and 1671. Rendsborg occupied a well-chosen position at the centre of the base of the Jutish peninsula, and its size and strength made it the chief magazine and rallying-point of the Danish forces in Holstein and southern Jutland. Unfortunately, the pro-Swedish tendencies of the Duke of Gottorp made it difficult for the Danes to work out a rational scheme of defence for this part of the world. In 1689 the Danes unwisely returned the fortress of Tönning at the mouth of the Eider to the duke, who promptly rebuilt it with five bastions in the modern French style. In 1697 Sweden took over the command of the Gottorp troops, which further compromised the security of the Eider line.

In many lands of Europe the history of the development of military engineering is inextricably linked with that of growing royal absolutism. In seventeenth-century France and Sweden the royal despots kept the nobility under a tight rein, and ruled through a few native ministers and officers of great ability. In Denmark, however, as in Naples in the later eighteenth century, the monarch crushed the native nobility with full popular approval, and managed affairs with the help of a foreign-born nobility of his own creation.

Thus, when Frederick III (1648–70) established the absolute monarchy in Denmark, he was careful to import large numbers of officers of German or Dutch origin. Frederick was particularly pleased to win the services of our old acquaintance Henrik Rüsensteen, who had published a widely read book on fortification in 1654, and was a veteran of the Dutch, French, German and Venetian services. Rüsensteen came to Denmark in 1661, and was made head of the engineering arm as Quartermaster-General. He made his mark as a shrewd, energetic and ruthless rebuilder of towns and armies, and in the early 1670s he rose to the rank of lieutenant-general. In 1673 the king said that he had further promotion in view for him 'if he behaves well ... and if he takes his time about things and goes step by step' (*ibid.*, 360).

The arrogant Rüsensteen invariably spoke and wrote in German or his native Dutch, and he pushed into the background such Danish-born engineers as the widely travelled Axel Urup (1601–71) and the brothers Henning and Erik Qvitzow (1613–72 and 1616–78). He was described by one of the privy councillors as 'calculating and greedy' (*ibid.*, 359), and he eventually accumulated so many enemies that it was beyond the power of the king to save him. Rüsensteen was held responsible for the disasters of the campaign of 1677, and later in the same year he was required to meet a number of charges which were levelled against him by General von der Goltz and the *Generalkommissariat*. He put up a skilful defence, but he resigned from the service in December and shortly afterwards left Denmark for good.

The Danish monarchy being what it was, the place of Rüsensteen was taken by another foreign engineer, the Dutchman Jobst van Scholten (*c.* 1647–1721). Scholten was an altogether more trustworthy person than his prickly compatriot Rüsensteen, and in the Great Northern War he came to take the leading part in the management of the vast and elaborate Danish military machine. He was Inspector of Infantry in 1700, lieutenant-general in 1707, and full general and commander of the field army in 1710. He restored and reformed the army after the defeat at Helsingborg, introduced a new field artillery and built up a powerful siege train. He died in 1721 – an architect of the ruin of Charles XII of Sweden, and one of the last links with the great days of Dutch military engineering.

The Swedish Vauban – Erik Dahlberg (1625–1703)
Creative men rarely respond to the spirit of the times as completely isolated individuals, for there appears

109 The Dahlberg Monument, Karlskrona

to be a common background of circumstances and inheritance which encourages them to make simultaneous advances in the same fields of endeavour. Thus the date 1685 holds a special magic for musicians, as the year when Bach, Handel and Domenico Scarlatti were born. In the same way some of the greatest achievements in military engineering are linked with the names of three almost exact contemporaries, Coehoorn, Vauban and Dahlberg. Here the unifying feature was the power of late seventeenth-century despotism. Coehoorn opposed this despotism, as represented in the person of Louis of France, but the others were its devoted servants.

Dahlberg was a brisk, demanding man of a religious turn of mind, whose asperities were tempered with a sense of humanity and humour. 'The air about him was always fresh and breezy, like the wind about a pine tree on a high mountain' (Dahlberg, 1912, vii). He rebuilt over fifty fortresses, demolished scores of others, and argued cogently about national defence in general; he trained up a new generation of engineers, and he was well in advance of his time when he sought to create units of engineer troops. In all of this we could equally well have been talking about Vauban.

Erik Dahlberg was born on 10 October 1625 to a wealthy and old commoner family of the province of Västmanland. After his first schooling in Sweden and at Hamburg he was sent at the age of fifteen to serve in the administration of Swedish Pomerania. The Treasurer-General Gerhard Rehnsköld had occasion to beat him for a number of juvenile offences, but this hard master also discovered Dahlberg's bent for military engineering, and recommended him to the graces of Colonel Mardefeldt, the Inspector-General of the Swedish fortresses in Germany. 'Thus,' wrote Dahlberg, 'I entered for the first time into His Majesty's military service, and changed from being a clerk into a soldier' (*ibid.*, 37).

Dahlberg's active engineering career began in 1647, when he staked out the four-bastioned New Fort at the small Pomeranian town of Damgarten. In April 1648 he brought himself to the attention of Charles X Gustavus in the most spectacular possible fashion, when he blew up the fifteen-foot thick walls of an old tower at Demmin in the royal presence. The king was all the more taken with the demonstration because 'His Majesty needed some young people in his armies who were trained in fortification and other sciences' (*ibid.*, 39). Charles Gustavus appointed Dahlberg to the post of engineer with the army that was besieging Prague, but the war came to an end before he could take up the assignment.

Like many young Scandinavian engineers, Dahlberg managed to study and travel widely in foreign lands before returning to the narrower world of the Baltic. From 1650 to 1653 he was in Frankfurt-am-Main, engaged in the undemanding task of collecting and forwarding the monies that were due to Sweden by the peace settlement of 1648:

In the meantime I exercised myself in mathematics, geometry, perspective, fortification and other things with the distinguished engineer Georg Andreas Bökler; I practiced French with a learned priest, Maître Mohr by name; I also learned to play the mandolin ... and the flute. (*ibid.*, 48)

The same leisurely years gave Dahlberg the opportunity to acquire the social graces in the houses of prominent German families.

In 1654 Dahlberg set out on a pilgrimage to Jerusalem, in the company of a Portuguese merchant and the son of a French diplomat, but the trio was turned back just after crossing the Turkish border, on account of the state of tension then existing between the Porte and the Empire. In 1656, after guiding two sons of a Swedish nobleman around Italy, he tried to reach the Holy Land by sea. His vessel was forced to put back to Malta, because of the danger from Barbary pirates, and this time Dahlberg accepted the disappointment as God's will.

Back in Rome, Dahlberg received letters from Charles Gustavus inviting him to the war in Poland. Dahlberg took the summons as a *vocatio divina*, and on arriving with the army he was appointed Lieutenant-Quartermaster-General. His responsibilities were rather wider than the title implied, for he functioned as the chief engineer, and he was sent to negotiate in his fluent Latin with Sweden's ally, George Rakoczi of Transylvania. Now high in favour, Dahlberg accompanied the king on the Danish campaigns of 1657 and 1658, when he helped to plan the surprise of Frederiksodde and the crossing of the Belts over the ice.

Dahlberg was ennobled in the early 1660s, and he spent this decade in a peaceful but profitable fashion. He demonstrated his skill as a draughtsman in the illustrations to a *History of Charles X Gustavus*, and he compiled his review of great houses, *Suecia Antiqua et Hodierna*, which is considered one of the landmarks of Swedish art. In September 1668 he travelled to England, and was accorded three private audiences with King Charles II, who slapped him on the back and cried out: '*Vous seriez un homme pour moi!*' The king complained that his own engineers were either ignorant or villainous, but Dahlberg politely declined the invitation to enter the English service. At last Dahlberg was recalled to heavy responsibilities in Sweden when he was made Quartermaster-General in 1674.

The pace of reform and military building was quickening under the rule of Charles XI (1660–97), and in the space of six years from 1687 Dahlberg was made Master of the Ordnance, field-marshal and count. In 1697 the king appointed him governor of Livonia, because he wished to have in that province 'a man who is not excessively devoted to his own wellbeing, and who shows a faithful and disinterested attachment to us and our royal house' (*ibid.*, xvii). Riga, the chief fortress of Livonia, was saved for the Swedes by Dahlberg's vigilance at the outbreak of the Great Northern War in 1700. He was now a septuagenarian, and his health was broken by the same accumulation of years of travelling and labour which weighed upon his rheumaticky contemporary Vauban. He nevertheless accompanied the young King Charles XII on his campaign against the Saxons in 1702, and it was not until the next year that his many requests to retire were finally heard. Dahlberg died almost immediately after-

Dahlberg's Sweden

110 Vadstena Castle, Lake Vättern. A Renaissance pile featured in *Suecia Antiqua et Hodierna*. It was still in a state of defence in the seventeenth century, with cannon mounted on the drum towers, and on an outer perimeter (since demolished)

111 Kalmar Castle

112 The Eda Fort (from the plaque on the site)

113 The Eda Fort today. The entrance in the foreground is the one shown on the bottom of the model

114 The Aurora Bastion, Karlskrona. Part of the redoubt which closes up the eastern end of the dockyard wall

115 The Västerport, Kalmar town. Built by Wärnsköld in 1659, in close imitation of the Ancient Roman style

116 The central keep, Nya Älvsborg Fort, Göteborg. Cannon shot from Tordenskiold's attack of 1719 are still embedded in the surface

117 The Fars Hatt Tower, Bohus Castle. A four storeyed-work, built by Dahlberg to replace a small medieval tower badly damaged in the siege of 1678

118 The tower at Carlsten Fort, Marstrand. Built by Dahlberg after the recovery of Marstrand from the Danes in 1679. Marstrand was recaptured by the Danes in 1719, but restored by peaceful treaty. The grim tower is eighty feet in diameter, and stands nearly one hundred and twenty feet above the inner courtyard

119 Water gate, Kalmar town. With the monogram of Charles XI.

120 The Landskrona Bastion, Landskrona Citadel. Part of the earthen perimeter built by the Swedes in the 1660s and 1670s

121 The castle, Landskrona Citadel. The original fortress, built by the Danes 1549–59. After the construction of the outer perimeter, the castle served as an inner redoubt and for accommodation

wards on 16 January 1703, and was buried in a splendid Baroque tomb of his own design in the church at Turinge in Södermanland. On the window behind there is a representation of Jerusalem, the goal he never reached on earth.

Dahlberg's main achievement in fortress-building was to make secure the various provinces which had been snatched from the Danes, Norwegians, Germans, Poles and Muscovites in the earlier wars of the Swedish monarchy. In the bishoprics of Bremen and Verden, the most isolated of the Swedish holdings in Germany, the defence rested chiefly upon the Elbe fortress of Stade, and the new stronghold of Karlsburg (Bremerhaven) at the mouth of the Weser, which the French-born Colonel Mell built in 1672, 'giving much food for thought to not a few neighbouring powers' (Wimarson, 1897, I, 230). These and the smaller works were strengthened under Dahlberg's administration.

The main stepping-stone to Bremen and Verden was the Baltic port of Wismar, where Dahlberg began a lengthy programme of construction in 1681. Eastwards along the coast the lagoon fortress-port of Stralsund, the 'Mantua' of the North, was re-fortified after the Swedes got it back in 1680. Dahlberg's original schemes were overthrown in favour of those of the French engineer Roger, but after that gentleman retired in 1688 Dahlberg completed the massive crownworks according to his own lights.

On the great Scandinavian peninsula, the westward facing coastlands of Bohuslän, Halland and Scania were the objects of particular attention, for the king considered that Denmark was the most immediate and dangerous of Sweden's enemies. Dahlberg worked on Malmö, he attended to the citadel of Landskrona (after the Danish occupation of 1676–9), he extensively rebuilt the battered fortress of Bohus (after the terrible siege of 1678), and he did the same for Carlsten Fort (held by the Danes 1677–9), which stood watch over the lonely harbour of Marstrand.

However, the most important commission came in 1687, when Dahlberg received a generous grant for the works at Göteborg (Gothenburg), which was to become the largest fortress of Sweden, and the chief base for the defence of the western coast, entirely eclipsing the old fort of Älvsborg and the little inland fortress of Bohus. Göteborg town, lying on the left bank of the lower reaches of the Göta Älv, was encased in a perimeter of dark stone ramparts, which gave on to a wet ditch and the river. Dahlberg also secured two outlying heights which could not be taken into the fortress proper. The little Gullberg knoll to the east was surmounted by the compact Lejon tower, while a higher and wider hill to the south-west of the town became the site of Kronan fort, with its tall faceted central tower, and rings of outer fortifications. Finally Dahlberg pushed to completion the projects of Quartermaster-General Johan Wärnskold for the fort of Nya Älvsborg, which sprawled over a rocky island hard by the narrow shipping channel at the seaward entrance of the Göta Älv. Under cover of the new fortifications, Göteborg became a base for the shipmasters who turned to privateering with the end of normal trade in the Great Northern War. The young Danish admiral Tordenskiold therefore attacked Nya Älvsborg in 1717 and again in 1719, and on the night of 26–27 September of the latter year he was able

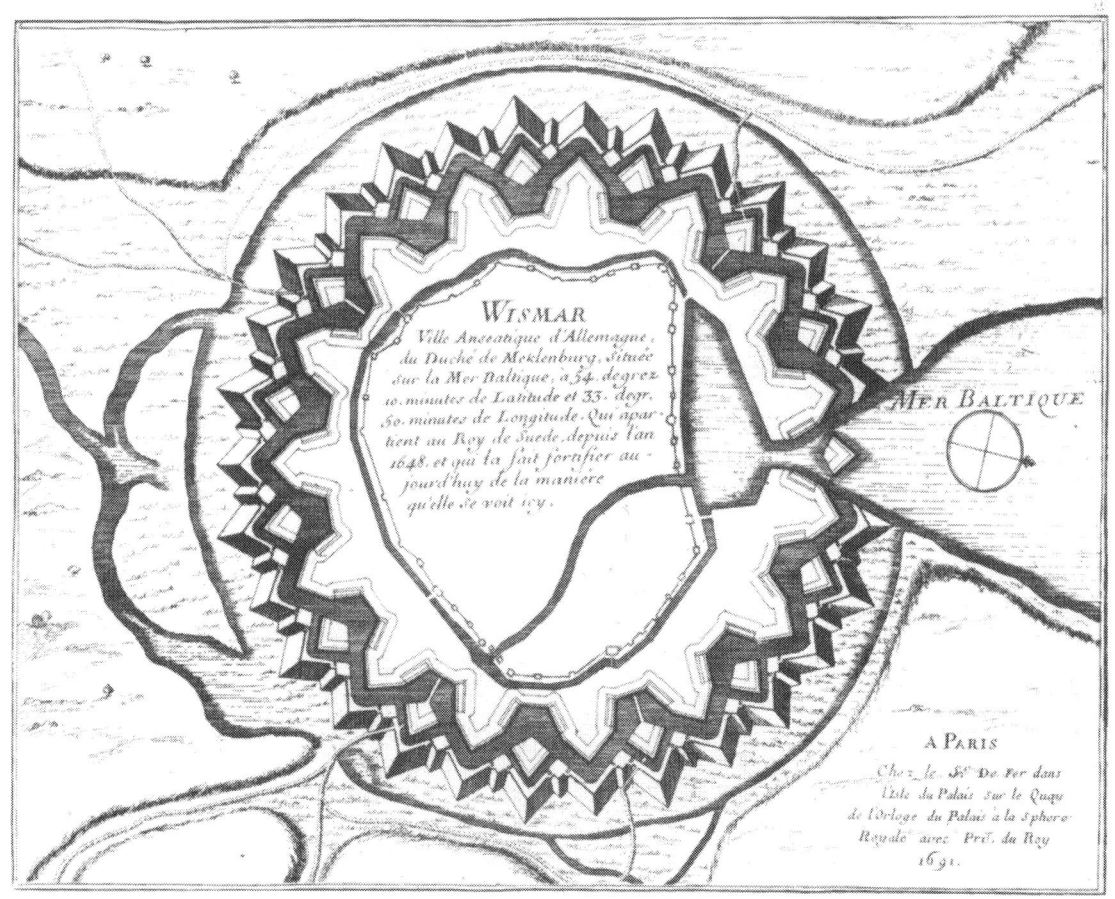

122 Wismar, the new fortifications by Dahlberg (De Fer, 1690–5)

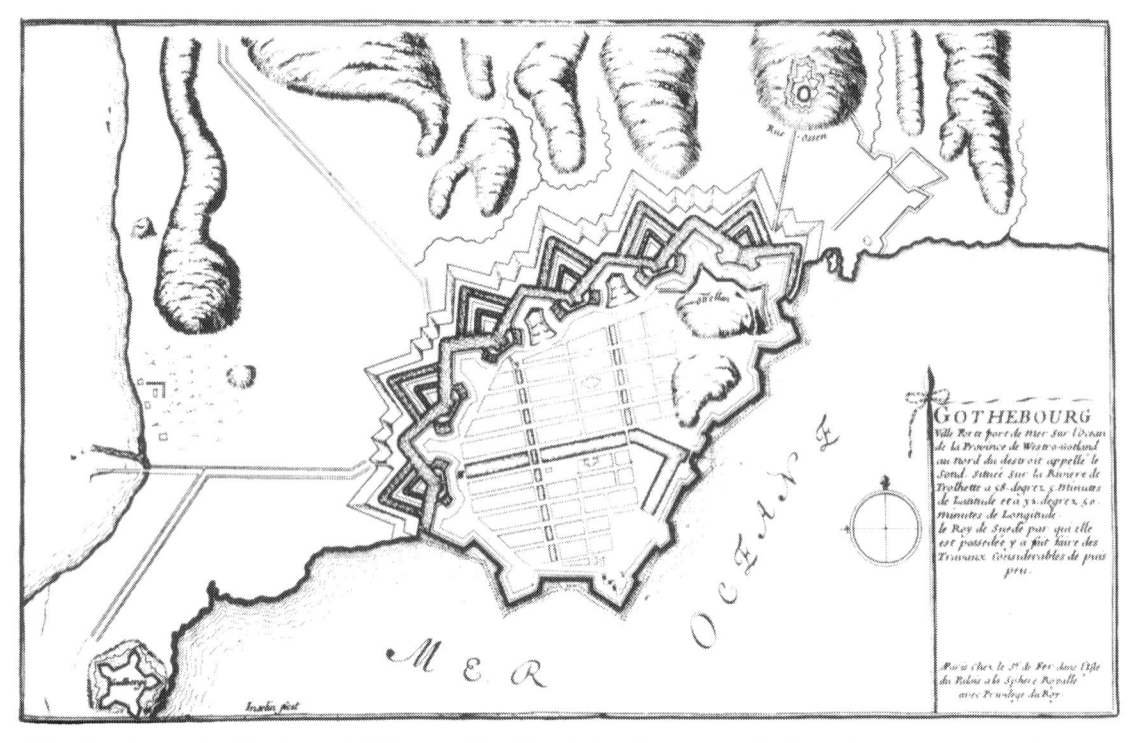

123 Dahlberg's fortifications at Göteborg. The Göta Lejon Fort on the Gullberg (now surrounded by railway yards) is at the bottom left. Kronan Fort is at the top right (De Fer, 1690–5)

to elude the vigilance of the garrison and push small boats upstream to devastate the Swedish shipping.

In comparison, the eastern, or Baltic coastline of Sweden had always been fairly lightly fortified. The defence of Stockholm rested as much upon the intricacies of the archipelago as on batteries and forts. Elsewhere the only fortifications of strength were to be found at Kalmar, where the harbour and therefore the short crossing to the island of Öland were secured by the thick outer rampart of the spectacular Castle, and by the new fortress town on Kvarnholmen, with defences laid out by Wärnsköld in the 1650s. Inside the walls of Kalmar, the streets followed the gridiron plan of the Renaissance urbanists, and the Cathedral of St Christopher (Nicodemus Tessin, 1660–82) gradually filled with the peculiarly ornate Swedish military funeral hatchments, embowered in carved and gilded wooden foliage, making the place a spiritual home of the Swedish army to rival the sailors' Admiralty Church at Karlskrona.

This last place was called into being by the experience of recent wars, which indicated that the naval establishments at Stockholm were too distant from the Danish and German theatres of war. In 1679 Dahlberg accordingly founded the new port of Karlskrona in the conquered southern province of Blekinge, to serve as Sweden's premier naval base in the Baltic. The site, on Trossö, was inaccessible by nature, and to secure the new facilities Dahlberg needed only to plant forts on outlying islands, and run a loopholed wall across the northern side of the dockyard. Provisioning was easier than in the inhospitable north, for Karlskrona backed on to fertile Blekinge, with its gentle, almost English landscapes. More important still, vessels could enter and leave Karlskrona throughout the year, for in these more southerly waters the formation of ice was rare and light.

In all of this the Swedes wished to convey the impression that their kingdom was not just a first-class military power, but one with a more southerly European orientation. If the canals of Göteborg hinted at the ambience of Amsterdam, then a stronger

Sweden's Trans-Baltic Bridgeheads 193

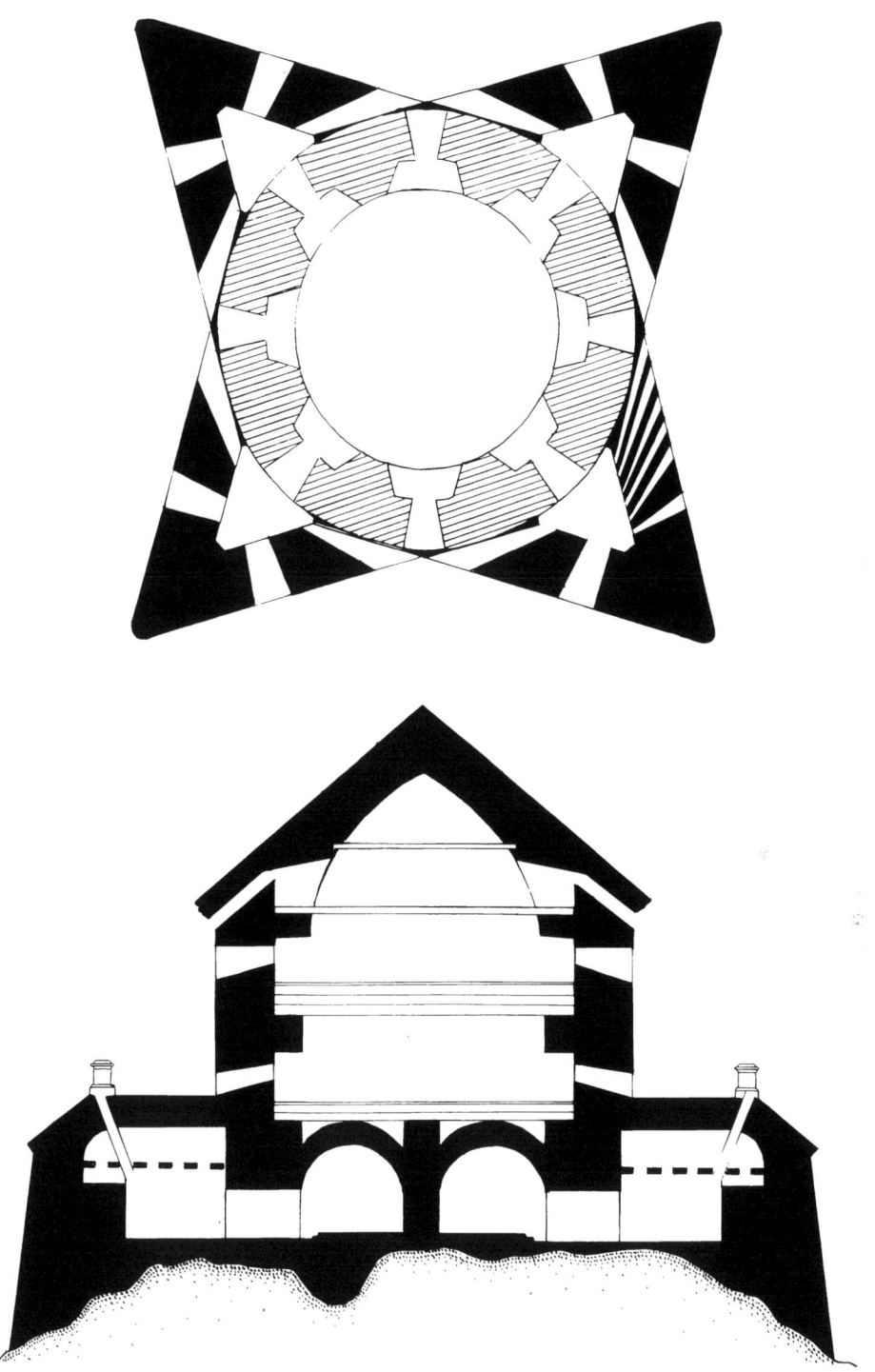

124 Trace and profile of the Göta Lejon Fort. Each of the four salients has embrasures for artillery, and (as shown for the salient at the bottom right-hand corner) loopholes for musketry. Grenades were rolled down the slanting embrasures on the third floor. (Re-drawn from a MS plan in the Swedish Military Archives)

125 Göta Lejon Fort

and more specific affinity with the Latin world was recalled by the piazzas and more-than-Jesuitical churches of Kalmar and Karlskrona.

On the inland borders of old Sweden, Gustav Gabrielsen Oxenstierna had laid out an entrenched camp in 1657 on a low rise between two lakes in Värmland, to secure the Eda Passage against raids from Kongsvinger in Norway, The earthen fort was strengthened and extended by Dahlberg in 1676, and it became an important link in the chain of northern frontier posts.

Further south, an artillery train was kept in constant readiness at the southern end of Lake Vättern at Jönköping. On the subject of this place the English diplomat Molesworth remarked that it was:

the sole inland fortress in Sweden, which [she] less needs such artificial strengths, as well for other reasons, as because nature in very many places has provided it with such passes, as a handful of men may defend against a great army. (Molesworth, 1738, 263)

In 1681 Dahlberg voyaged across the Baltic to the Gulf of Finland, and inspected the appallingly neglected fortresses in Karelia and Ingria. He recommended that Narva and Fort Nyen should be rebuilt, but he was never given the money to put his schemes into proper effect. The next year he went to Estonia and Livonia, where he effected repairs to Riga, Pernau and Dorpat. His plans for a much more ambitious rebuilding of Riga were approved in 1684.

About 3,600,000 riksdaler were spent by Dahlberg between 1689 and 1695, which were the years of his most intensive fortress-building. Each dollar had to be wrung from the miserly Charles XI, and his assemblies of ministers and generals who met for the *diskussion* and *ventiliring* of Dahlberg's projects. Fortunately, the labour costs were low, since the construction was carried out by gangs of soldiers, sometimes as many as 2,000 men at once, who worked for a small supplement to their usual pay. The grants were eked out still further by the contributions made by the nobility and townspeople of the trans-Baltic provinces to the building and upkeep of their fortresses.

Towards the end of his life Dahlberg became increasingly worried by a serious lack of proportion in the way these resources were being expended. Charles XI was obsessed with the danger from the old enemy Denmark, and he put his money into Göteborg, Karlskrona and Wismar, places which contributed to the defence of old Sweden, as 'the very heart of the monarchy' (Ericsson and Vennberg, 1925, 246). Dahlberg, however, could not shake off his concern as to the unfinished business in the Gulf of Finland, and maintained that the greatest threat to the kingdom lay in 'Tsar Peter's insatiable appetite' (Dahlberg, 1912, xviii). The old king had been deaf to his pleas, but on 22 February 1698 Dahlberg presented the new monarch, Charles XII, with twenty-seven folio sides of text and plans concerning the state of the empire's fortresses. Dahlberg insisted that the work on Narva 'must be tackled with the greatest seriousness, if Your Majesty wishes to guarantee Ingria for the future' (Ericsson and Vennberg, 1925, 247). He added that it was still more important to hold Fort Nyen at the mouth of the Neva River, otherwise the Russians would gain one of the best harbours on the Gulf and launch a fleet on the Baltic. These views were altogether too far-reaching to be accepted in Stockholm, and the Gulf fortresses remained in the same wretched state as before. Thus the Swedish field armies were to be largely deprived of secure *points d'appui*, where the provisions and stores could be heaped up in safety.

In the matter of fortress design, Dahlberg broke away from Sweden's slavish dependence on the Netherlandish style. There was certainly Dutch influence at Göteborg, just as there was French at Narva, but again and again we see evidence of Dahlberg's fondness for spaciously proportioned bastions and places of arms, ample casemates, and double ditches and curtains. The surest signs of Dahlberg's presence were, however, his idiosyn-

126 Kronan Fort. For plan see Duffy (1975) p. 155

cratic multi-storeyed casemated towers, which he employed variously as island batteries, hilltop forts and inner keeps. There were towers of this kind at Riga, Wismar (Havalfisken Fort), Malmö, Göteborg, the Carlsten Fort at Marstrand, Dalarö and Karlskrona (Drottningskär Fort). His successors preserved the tradition into the later eighteenth century, when it was plundered by the Frenchmen Montalembert and Carnot.

Dahlberg appreciated the value of having a corps of trained sappers at hand to carry out the orders of his engineer officers proper. A body of two hundred troops of this kind was set up at Stralsund in 1682, but Charles XI (like Louis XIV and Frederick the Great in similar circumstances) felt that this step signified that the engineers were getting above themselves, and in 1688 he converted the unit into an ordinary company of infantry. Dahlberg likewise strove in vain to disabuse Charles of another favourite notion of despots, namely that military engineers, like civil architects, ought to be bound to the monarch by individual contracts. To Dahlberg's regret the salaries still varied greatly among engineer officers of the same rank, and the payment often remained well in arrears.

In all other respects Charles XI gave powerful support to Dahlberg's schemes for the engineering corps. In 1683 the king combined the fortification establishments of Sweden, Ingria, Livonia and Pomerania into a single formation. The personnel grew steadily in number, and in 1696 the corps was given an authorised establishment of 376 officers, administrative officials and tradesmen. The business was regulated by Dahlberg's *Fortifikationsordning*, which was approved by the king on 3 July 1695, and remained in force with some modifications until the twentieth century. This code was a useful weapon to employ against recalcitrant people such as the German engineers in the trans-Baltic provinces, who had been slow to recognise Dahlberg's authority, and were addicted to the reprehensible habit of selling off copies of fortress designs to interested foreigners. Not surprisingly, Dahlberg recruited the corps as far as possible from reliable, native-born Swedes.

One of the most creditable of Dahlberg's achievements was to bequeath to Charles XII an army in which the knowledge of military engineering was wider-spread than in almost any other of the time. He had the excellent idea of placing 'information officers' with the other arms of the service. Among these experts were such luminaries as Hans Zader and Barthold Schmoll, who were the authors of the first Swedish text-books on fortification (respectively the *Manuale Fortificatorie*, and the *Architectura Militaris*). Further officers saw to the education of royal pages in fortification and mathematics. Charles XII's own tutor in these subjects was Carl Magnus Stuart, the future Quartermaster-General, who held his classes at a fixed hour every Wednesday and Saturday:

Charles was naturally inclined towards difficult sciences which demanded a great deal of penetration. He became adept at putting up a vast number of questions and objections, and it was not long before he cultivated a pronounced taste for these subjects. (Nordberg, 1748, I, 13)

However, the Swedish heavy artillery lacked the kind of continuous direction which the long career of Dahlberg had given to the engineering arm. The siege guns had probably been at their most mobile in the later stages of the Thirty Years War, after Gustavus Adolphus had reorganised the artillery on the duodecimal system, and Queen Christina had abolished the cumbersome 48-pounder.

After a period of stagnation, the artillery was restored to a high state of proficiency by Charles XI and a number of experts. In the 1680s the Master of the Ordnance Johan Siöbladh introduced a new and comprehensive range of siege and field artillery, which replaced the long and heavy guns which had made an appearance under Charles Gustavus, and the howitzer and the cohorn mortar were imported from Holland at the same time. Siöbladh also took the theoretical and practical training of the gunners in hand, and in 1690 he published a detailed code of artillery regulations.

Big guns assumed a secondary place in the design of Charles XII, who was fond of resolving military problems by a charge with cold steel in the open field. General Carl Cronstedt did wonders for the field artillery, but in comparison the siege gunners were sorely neglected.

Russia turns to the West

Engineering as yet had no institutional base in Russia, and until the end of the seventeenth century the Muscovites remained entirely dependent upon such foreigners as could be persuaded to visit their climes. During the early years of his relentless programme of self-education, Tsar Peter the Great (ruled 1682–1725) learnt what he could from two men of this kind – the Catholic Scot Patrick Gordon, and the Dutch officer Franz Timmermann. However, the costly attacks on the Turkish fortress of Azov (see p. 241) showed that his knowledge was still dangerously incomplete, and in 1697 and 1698 he took himself off to Western Europe. He travelled amongst other places to Riga, where he measured the fortifications with his own arms, to Coehoorn's fine new works a-building at Bergen-op-Zoom, and to the Royal Arsenal at Woolwich, where he tried his hand at casting a mortar bomb. Peter returned to Russia an arch-barbarian still, but one who had increased his knowledge of the most barbaric aspect of Western society – the systematic application of force.

The second bid, the Great Northern War 1700–21

1700, the busy year

At the beginning of the new century a hostile league moved against Sweden's trans-Baltic empire at three points – a poorly equipped army of Danes laid siege to Tönning, the main fortress of Sweden's friend, the Duke of Gottorp; King Augustus of Saxony-Poland sent a force against Riga in Livonia; lastly Tsar Peter invaded Ingria on the Gulf of Finland and began an attack on Narva.

The Swedish holdings were saved by the fact that, for a few months at least, the Dutch and British fleets were willing to help Charles XII to move his forces over the sea. In May a detached expedition of 18,000 Swedes, Lüneburgers and Dutch strode across Holstein and forced the Danes to raise the siege of Tönning. Charles and the main army, however, took to the water, and landed on Sjaelland between Helsingør (Elsinore) and Copenhagen on 25 July. Charles then marched on the Danish capital with 10,000 troops, but he was stopped short by nagging memories of the failure of Charles Gustavus before Copenhagen nearly half a century earlier, and by the news that the Danes and the Duke of Gottorp had signed a treaty of peace. Denmark had thereby withdrawn from the enemy alliance, but the warships and the fortified naval base at Copenhagen were intact, and in later years the constant threat of the waiting Danish troops and the 'fleet in being' forced Charles to keep 17,000 men locked up in Sweden.

It was some consolation that the watchful old Dahlberg was working out his own salvation at Riga. On the night of 11–12 February he foiled an attempt by the Saxons to surprise the fortress while the heads of the garrison troops were still throbbing from the effects of the Carnival. This was just a preliminary to a more serious attack, but Dahlberg assured the king that he would defend the city 'as long as the blood courses in my veins' (Dahlberg, 1912, xviii). The Saxons duly reappeared on 27 July, but after subjecting the place to blockade and bombardment they marched away on 9 September.

The Russians showed more determination, if not much more skill, when they opened their siege of Narva on 17 September. The saps were so badly managed that two of the 'attacks' had to be abandoned in the course of the operation, and the lines of circumvallation were dangerously overextended at four miles in length, as well as being dominated in the centre by higher ground outside.

All of this helped to preserve Livonia and Ingria until Charles hastened to the rescue across the Baltic. Landing at Pernau, he marched eastwards across the wastelands and on 20 November he assailed Tsar Peter's raw army in its lines in front of Narva. The Swedes executed the same plan of attack they were to attempt again at Poltava in 1709 – the cavalry moved out to either side to take the position by its flanks, while the infantry assembled by columns in the middle, and drove through the centre of the entrenchments with the bayonet. By the end of the day's fighting the 11,000 Swedes had killed or wounded about a quarter of the 34,000 Russians, driven the survivors from the field, and captured four guns.

1701–7, the indecisive years

The next phase of the war got off to a brisk start, when Charles forced the lower Dvina just below Riga in July 1701, and hustled an army of Saxons and Russians from Livonia and the Polish duchy of Kurland.

The ease of the victory, together with the chaotic state of Polish politics, persuaded Charles to embark on a crusade to evict Augustus of Saxony from the electoral throne of Poland. It is exceedingly strange that two greybeards, the engineer Erik Dahlberg and the chancellor Bengt Oxenstierna should have been alive to the long-term danger to Swedish interests from Russia, while the nineteen year-old King Charles chose to embroil Sweden once more in Poland, where he went on to capture and lose towns with the same frequency and lack of consequence as had his grandfather back in the 1650s.

The Swedes got possession of Warsaw and Cracow in central Poland in 1702, and in the following year Charles reduced Thorn by one of his rare formal sieges, which usefully opened up the Vistula route into the interior. Otherwise the rival armies groped their way around the incoherent mass of Poland like wrestlers in a bath of mud. Otto Haintz has remarked:

A state like Poland was not to be conquered by military means, but only by political ones. It is astonishing, but true that this undeveloped, spineless organism, which lacked everything that makes for national strength, was fundamentally impregnable. An aggressor could force Poland to obey his rule only after he had won over a considerable part of the noble class to his side. (Haintz, 1936–58, I, 216, 1st edn)

In 1706 Charles finally imposed a political solution of sorts, when he invaded the electorate of Saxony and forced Augustus to recognise the Swedish puppet Stanislaus as king of Poland. Charles stayed in Saxony for another year, taking care that the slippery Augustus lived up to his obligations, and making the diplomatic and military preparations for an offensive against Russia.

The king's campaigns up to date – the move against Denmark, and the long drawn-out war in Poland, belonged in their objectives and manner to the time of Charles X Gustavus. He had made no provision to stay the advance of the most potentially dangerous of Sweden's enemies, Tsar Peter, who was meanwhile crushing the resistance in Ingria, Estonia and Livonia. The commanders of these provinces were often left out of contact with the wandering king for months at a time, yet Charles bequeathed them no unified command, and on at least one occasion he strictly forbade the Defence Commission in Stockholm to send any help in men or money. As a manager of a multi-front war Charles was clearly inferior to Frederick the Great of Prussia, who fifty years later demonstrated what could be done by keeping small but adequately nourished forces on his strategic flanks, and intervening with the main striking-force when things were near collapse.

Only the culpable neglect of Charles XII can explain how the Russians, as beginners in the art of artillery siegework, were able to reduce the Swedish fortresses in the Gulf of Finland. On 11 October 1702 the Russians stormed and took the little fortress of Nöteborg, 'the key of Sweden' (Adlerfeld, 1740, I, 187), which stood sentinel for Karelia and Finland on the isthmus that separates Lake Ladoga from the Gulf of Finland. Peter refortified the site and gave the new fortress the name of '*Schlüsselburg*' ('Key Fortress-Town').

In 1703 the Russians moved down to the seaward end of the River Neva and captured the Nyen Fort on 4 May. This achievement was paltry in itself, but it severed the Swedish provinces in the Gulf of Finland in two, and gave Peter his first access to the Baltic. Dahlberg had warned the Swedish monarchy of this very eventuality some years before (see p. 195).

Over the following seasons the tsar built the city of St Petersburg on the south bank of the Neva, below the site of Nyen. This new capital lay within easy cannon shot of the ramparts of the Peter-Paul Fortress, which were springing up on Yanni-Saari (Hare Island) on the far side of the Neva, while the seaward access was guarded by the extensive island of Kronstadt, where Peter planted a fort and a naval base.

In the damaging year of 1704 Sweden lost the strongholds of Dorpat and Narva, and with them

Sweden's Trans-Baltic Bridgeheads

Gulf of Finland

the greater part of her provinces on the southern side of the Gulf. The Russians were not yet equal to besieging Revel, Pernau or Riga, which were the last major centres of resistance, but in the autumn of 1705 Peter brought this phase of the war to an entirely satisfactory end when he reduced the little towns of Nimlau and Bauske, and overran the open country of Kurland.

Over the last three years the Russian siege operations had accounted for about 8,000 Swedish troops, and given Peter a large park of captured guns with which to prosecute his further campaigns. He had shown an admirable sense of strategic purpose, though the tactical performance was abysmal even by the generally low standards of Baltic wars. At the siege of Dorpat his troops had opened their trenches at an excessive distance from the fortress, while at Narva they went to the other extreme and began digging perilously near. They never advanced their guns to the lip of the glacis, for this operation would have overtaxed their engineering knowledge, but preferred to bombard the civilian population and batter the walls at considerable range. The protracted business was usually brought to an end when the troops delivered an assault against the steep and narrow breaches.

For the Swedes, the loss of their eastern Baltic provinces was an avoidable, but comprehensive disaster, which did more than anything else to reduce their kingdom to a second-class power.

The Poltava campaign 1708–9
After making two limited offensives against the Russians in Poland, early in 1706 and in the winter of 1707–8, Charles XII committed all his disposable force to an all-out attack on the heartland of Russia in the summer of 1708. The relief to the wretched Baltic provinces, if any was intended, took the most indirect form – indeed 12,500 men and large quantities of precious supplies were taken from these lands and sent off under General Lewenhaupt to support the effort in Russia.

The one element of consistency in this great Eastern campaign is provided by the conduct of the Russians, who by frantic digging and breathless counterstrokes managed to turn Charles aside from the approaches to Moscow, sever his communications, and finally bottle him up in the Ukraine.

The Swedes were devoid of any support, except for the rebel Ukrainian and Zaporozhian Cossacks, and midwinter found Charles and his army stranded in an uncomfortably cramped area of the Ukraine about 450 miles south of Moscow. He won himself a little more room by taking Veprik on 7–8 January 1709 after a short but very violent siege which cost him one thousand of his best men. Eight thousand more troops were lost to him in the spring, for he had to send reinforcements to prop up his puppet regime in Poland against a renewed attack by the Russians and the faithless Saxons.

On 1–2 May 1709 Charles opened a languid formal siege of the isolated Russian garrison in Poltava. Nobody has yet provided a satisfactory explanation of what he was at. The Russians were reasonably strong, at 4,000, yet Poltava was just a Cossack-style stronghold, hastily fortified, which stood on a spur on the west bank of the Vorskla, a tributary of the Dnieper. The trenches, which proceeded with painful slowness, were directed from the south across low-lying ground against a suburb, instead of taking the level and easy ground to the west of the main fortress.

Perhaps the operation was being disrupted by the high casualty rate among the Swedish engineers, some of whom were killed or wounded every day:

By the end the king had to employ as engineers such officers of the infantry and cavalry as had studied fortification in their youth. The king directed them in person, and since he had a thorough knowledge of engineering he was in frequent conversation with them. (Nordberg, 1748, II, 307)

Perhaps Charles was just making time, while the talks for the intervention of the Crimean Tartars were still in train. Perhaps, as some contemporaries believed, he wished to lure Peter south to a decisive battle. If the last supposition was correct, the king was only too successful.

The Russians rapidly built up a force of 45,000 men around Poltava. Some were pushed into the place as reinforcements, while the rest assembled in a fortified camp to the north. Charles was wounded in the foot, in one of the many skirmishes, and he

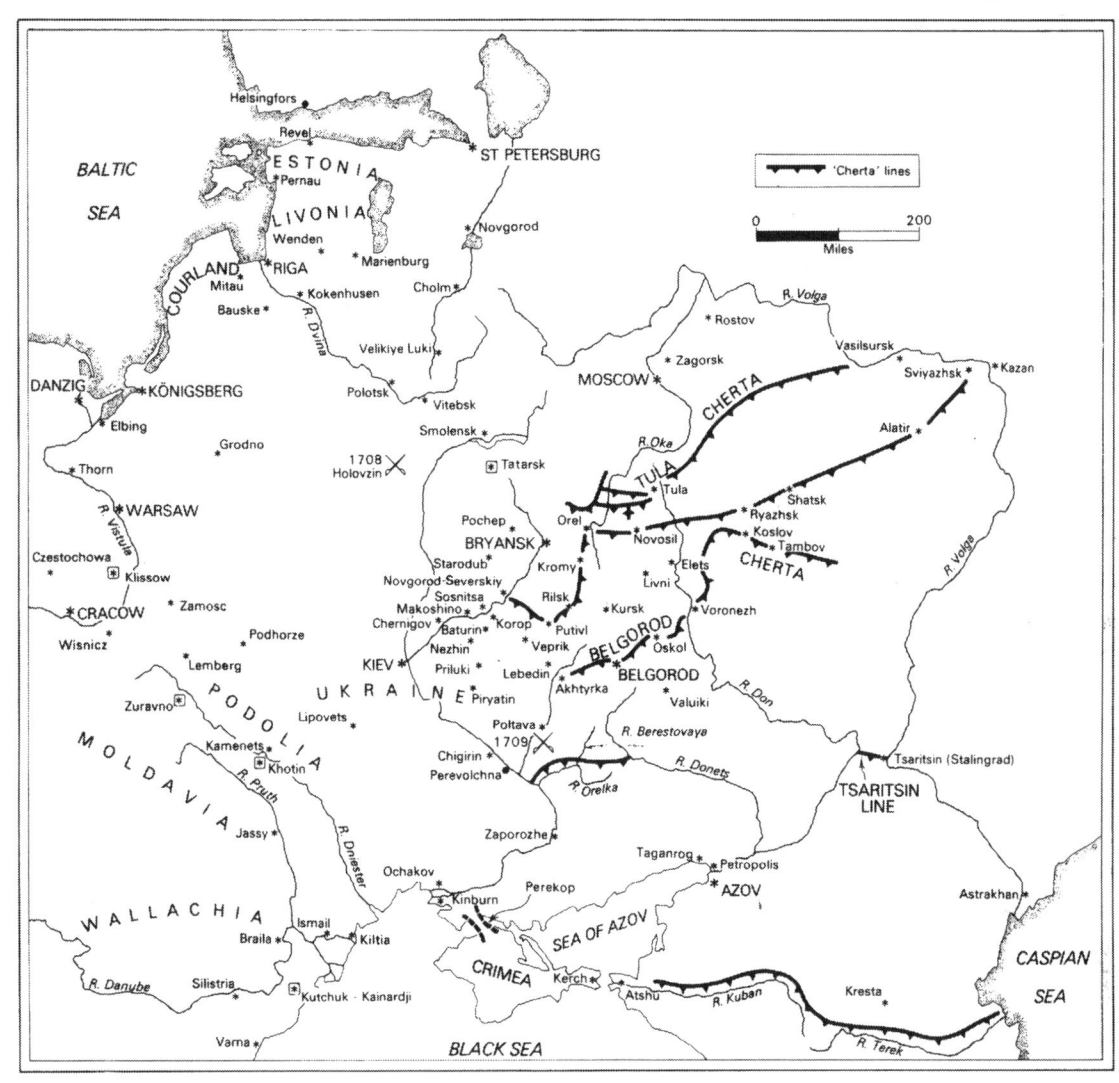

Poland and western Russia (reprinted from vol. I, 166)

had to relinquish the active command to General Lewenhaupt.

On 28 July Lewenhaupt and his 24 or 25,000 disposable troops launched a full assault on the position of the Russian army. The Swedish plan was similar to the one which had been carried out so successfully at Narva in 1700, but this time the attack was disrupted by a number of heavily garrisoned redoubts which projected from the centre of the Russian field works. The Russian army came out from its lines and broke the hopelessly outnumbered and out-gunned Swedes. Charles and a few companions fled to safety in Turkey, leaving Lewenhaupt in command of about 16,000 panic-stricken survivors, who surrendered on 1 August.

It is a frustrating exercise to try to reconcile King Charles's conduct in the Poltava campaign with any of the accepted principles of military engineering – he slaughtered his men in the wild assault at Veprik, he let them waste away in the inordinately prolonged siege of Poltava while the Russians were gathering their forces, and he left the remnants without any of the fortified refuges which a Gustavus, a Frederick or a Napoleon would certainly have provided if they had been in his place.

On their side the Russians knew little enough of

the niceties of the engineering art, but their purposeful digging had risen magnificently to the demands of the campaign. The host of improvised fortresses had placed the Swedes in a quandary:

they could either keep well clear of these strongpoints and renounce any idea of taking them (vital though it was to have them in their possession), or they could go ahead and capture them, as at Veprik... and incur frightful losses which were completely incommensurate with the military results of their 'victory'. (Tarle, 1958, 62–3)

The allied counter-attack 1709–15
The news of Poltava encouraged Russia, Saxony and Denmark to renew their old anti-Swedish alliance, and set about some ambitious military operations.

At the eastern end of the Baltic, Tsar Peter divided his forces in two, so as to overrun the opposite shores of the Gulf of Finland. Mitau, Riga, Revel and the other fortresses of Livonia and Kurland were reduced in the course of 1710. At the same time Russian detachments seized Vyborg and Kexholm, which effectively battered down the gates of Finland. After a long pause the Russians renewed the advance on Finland in 1713 and 1714. They neatly circumvented the difficult coast route by piling their troops into galleys, and they ended the operation as masters of Finland and of the Åland Islands, which placed them within striking distance of Stockholm. With the loss of Finland, the Swedes were now deprived of one of their main sources of recruits and supplies.

At the other end of the theatre the Danes were making a further bid to recover their lost provinces across the Sound. They put into operation the same plan they had used in 1676, and saw it fail for precisely the same reason – namely their inability to take fortresses. Early in 1710 the Swedish commander Magnus Stenbock manoeuvred the Danes out of the 'bread basket' of south Schonen, broke their investment of the Sound fortress of Malmö, defeated them in the field and shut them up in Helsingborg. He thereby secured Sweden from the threat of invasion for six years to come.

The one joint effort of the alliance concerned the reduction of the Swedish strategic bridgeheads on the German Baltic coast. Danes, Saxons, and later the Prussians all had a say in the proceedings, and they argued so bitterly among themselves that the Swedish commanders were able to keep up the fight until Charles staged his almost miraculous reappearance on the theatre in 1714. By then the Swedish holdings were confined to Stralsund and Wismar.

On 15 July 1715 Stralsund at last came under investment by the allied host. The Prussians made available their huge siege train of eighty 24-pounders and forty mortars. The Danes obligingly embarked these pieces at Stettin, and landed them at Greifswald in late September.

The new allied commander-in-chief, King Frederick William I of Prussia, at first laboured under the delusion that he could reduce Stralsund by a simple bombardment of the kind his grandfather had employed at the same place in 1678 (see p. 176). He was soon disabused of this notion by the Danish chief engineer van Scholten and his Saxon counterpart, the well-read General von Wackerbarth. These gentlemen pointed out that Stralsund now demanded a formal siege, for the Swedes had since thrown up some powerful bridgehead fortifications, guarding the causeways across the lagoons which embraced the city on three sides. 'According to the Comte de Croissy, the French ambassador, these works equalled or surpassed the lines which the French had thrown up in Brabant and Flanders' (Nordberg, 1748, III, 215). The garrison amounted to 12,000 men.

Scholten got his way, and he won over Frederick William to the idea that he must begin by imposing a tight investment. The king was a little out of his depth in the technical arguments, and he made a characteristic marginal note opposite a particularly complicated passage in one of Scholten's memoranda – 'I really don't understand this at all. But I rely on the Danes, who seem to know what it is all about' (Generalstab, 1899–1934, VII, 121). In accordance with Scholten's scheme, the Danes took up position to the north-west so as to assail the defences in front of the causeway of the Kniepertor. The Saxons and Prussians concentrated in the south-east and attacked in the direction of the Tribseertor and the Frankentor.

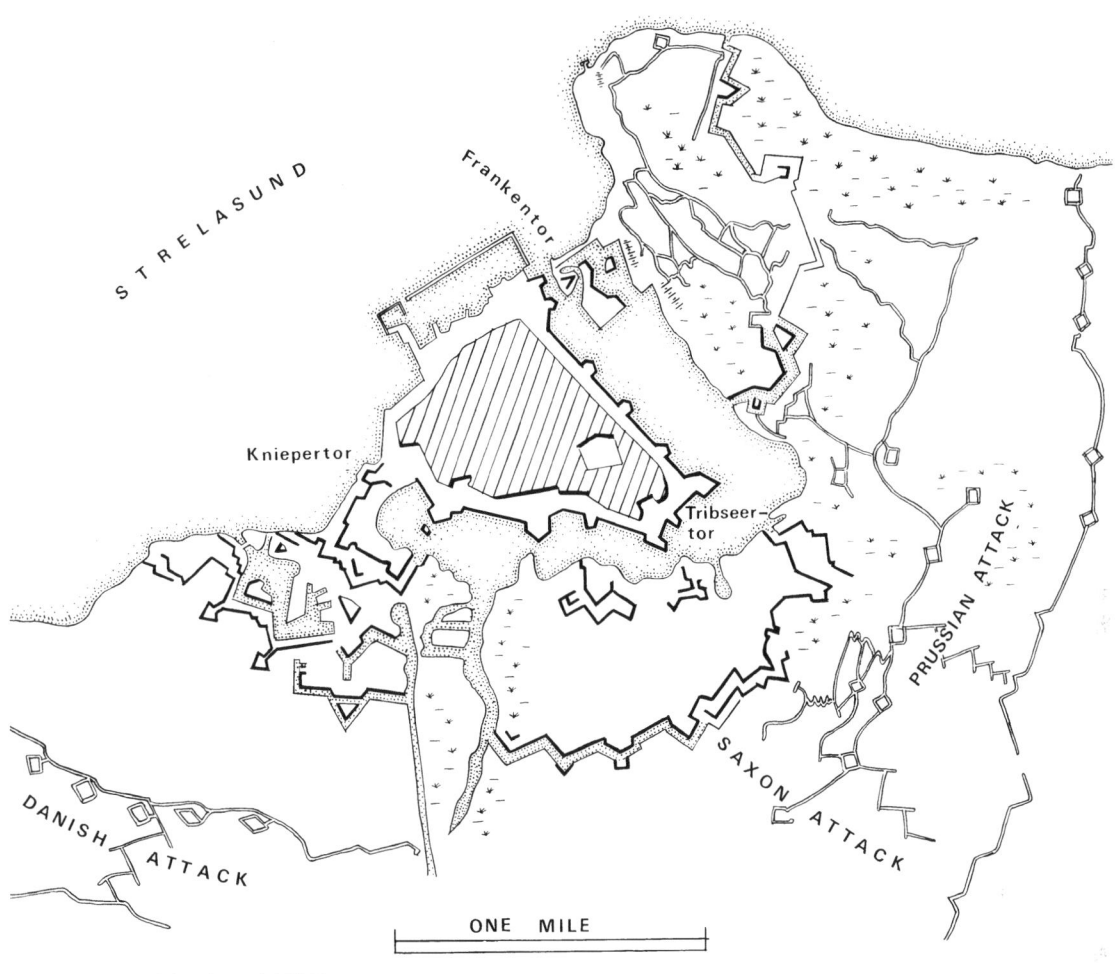

127 Siege of Stralsund 1715

Once the siege got under way the Danes discovered that their lack of heavy artillery told heavily against them in their duels with the enemy and their arguments with their allies. The whole episode was excessively hurtful to Danish feelings:

In 1711 and the following years we had involved ourselves in the great effort and cost of transporting the Danish siege artillery to and from Pomerania, without ever having the opportunity of using it. If we had had it with us in 1715, we could have operated to great effect, and been independent of the Prussians and Saxons, who very rapidly forgot how dependent they themselves had been on the Danish sea-power. (*ibid*., VII, 175–6)

The first parallel was opened on all sides on 19 October, but the Danes made very little further progress, whereas the Saxon and Prussian attack surged ahead with the support of its powerful artillery. All of Scholten's skill went for nothing.

On 29 November the chastened King Frederick IV of Denmark agreed to give up the attack from the west and throw all the weight of the Danes behind the effort of his allies. The covered way on the combined front of attack was taken by storm on 5 December, but the troops suffered terribly during the next days when they had to hack out the iron-hard earth under a scourging fire from the bastion flanks. On 17 December one thousand men rushed across the frozen ditch and took the hornwork in front of the Frankentor, thus placing the enceinte in immediate peril. The exploit cost the allies eight hundred dead and wounded. Five hundred further troops were lost on the 18th, as the price of fighting off a counter-attack which was led by King Charles in person. Charles had done everything that lay within his power to save Stralsund, and now that the fall was imminent he escaped by boat on 21 December. Two days later General Dücker yielded up the garrison as prisoners of war.

1716–21, the fatal years
By 1716 the Swedes had retreated from the Central European mainland (except for the foothold at Wismar, which was lost in April), and they were isolated by the waters of the Baltic on all sides except the frontier with Norway.

It was a little fortress on the southern Norwegian border that helped to determine the outcome of the Great Northern War, and possibly also Sweden's standing in the world – though that was probably already forfeit with the loss of the eastern Baltic provinces.

The place in question was the fortress-complex of Fredriksten (see p. 180), which sprawled over a series of rocky heights commanding the base of the Halden peninsula. The main fortress was a work of five bastions, surmounting a 650-foot high ridge. From here the ground fell away steeply towards Halden town and Tistedalen valley, but the terrain to the east was an awkward tangle of rocky crags and little valleys, which were commanded by a scattering of fortlets or blockhouses. A particularly dangerous knoll three hundred or so yards away was crowned by Fort Gyldenløve, a narrow work of dry stone and turf. The saddle between there and the main fortress was cunningly enfiladed from the south by two further forts – Stortårnet and more distant Overberget.

Charles knew that if he could take Fredriksten from the Danes, he would breach the barrier which had held up the Swedish advance northwards from Götenborg up the coast into Norway ever since the 1650s. Furthermore he would gain a strong bulwark for the Swedish county of Bohuslän, and win an outlet for his exports at the harbour of Halden,

128 Fredriksten, the main fortress

129 Fredriksten, with Stortårnet (left) and Overberget (right) forts. Seen from the main fortress

immediately below Fredriksten.

Charles carried out a first, badly-organised attack on Fredriksten in the summer of 1716. He lost five hundred men in a vain assault on the night of 3–4 July, and four days later a small Danish naval squadron captured his siege train as it was trying to make its way up the 'inner leads' from Göteborg. The last Swedish troops disappeared from the neighbourhood on 9 July, leaving Fredriksten in the hands of its garrison of just 1,300 men.

All of this time the allied high command had sought to assemble 22,600 Danes and 27,000 Russians in Sjaelland for the purpose of invading Sweden. Tsar Peter went to Copenhagen to this end, but he lost his nerve and on 24 September flatly declared that the Russians would have nothing to do with the scheme. He distrusted the weather, and he distrusted the faculties of the aged Scholten.

Throughout 1717 and for the best part of 1718 the warring parties shunned active operations and devoted all their efforts to building up their military establishments. Not everybody in Denmark-Norway appreciated the mighty services which had been rendered by Fredriksten, and in February 1717 the engineer Peter Nobel wrote a highly critical memorandum in which he expressed doubts as to whether 'the fortress serves any further use, since it can neither guard the town, which lies near its foot, nor dispute the passage. It is too small to receive a beaten army, and there is no room for large magazines' (*ibid.*, IX, 351).

Fortunately for the Danes, Jobst van Scholten used his influence in favour of a sensible plan of defence. He opposed the idea of disposing the troops in a cordon, but set in train a timely programme of work on the Norwegian fortresses, and insisted that

Fredriksten must be adequately garrisoned. The place was duly replenished with ammunition, and the defence entrusted to the experienced Lieutenant-Colonel Barthold Landsberg and a garrison of 1,800 troops, most of them veterans.

The Danes were in the dark as to where and when the Swedish blow might fall. Great was their astonishment when Charles came across the extreme southern border of Norway with 35,000 men at the end of November 1718, and laid formal siege to Fredriksten. This time he had assembled the siege artillery (eighteen pieces, including six 36-pounders and six 75-pounder mortars) close at hand in his new fortress of Sundsborg, and on 1 December he started to arrange his guns in three batteries against Fort Gyldenløve. This was the beginning of the most regular, the least typical and the last of the king's sieges. Major-General P. B. von Schwerin was in overall command of the operation, but the real authority lay with the French engineer Colonel Philippe Maigret, whose presence accounts for the purposeful nature of the attack.

Ground was broken on 5 December, and the trenches were directed against the southern flank of Fort Gyldenløve, so as to bring the Swedish troops within assaulting distance of the breach. On 8 December Charles led two hundred grenadiers out of the trenches and took the fort by storm. After this first success the Swedes prolonged the trench around the rear of the fort, thus forming a 140-yard long first parallel which confronted the main fortress of Fredriksten, rising on the far side of the saddle. The soil was shallow and stony, and every day the work of building up the trench parapet above ground required 3,000 fascines and about 500 gabions. Charles kept a close eye on the progress, and lodged himself in a cabin of planks a short distance from the trenches.

On the evening of 11 December the Swedes dug the first arm of a zigzag sap in a west-north-westerly direction from the first parallel. This alignment betrayed a professional touch, for the diggers were

130 Fort Gyldenløve, the southern face

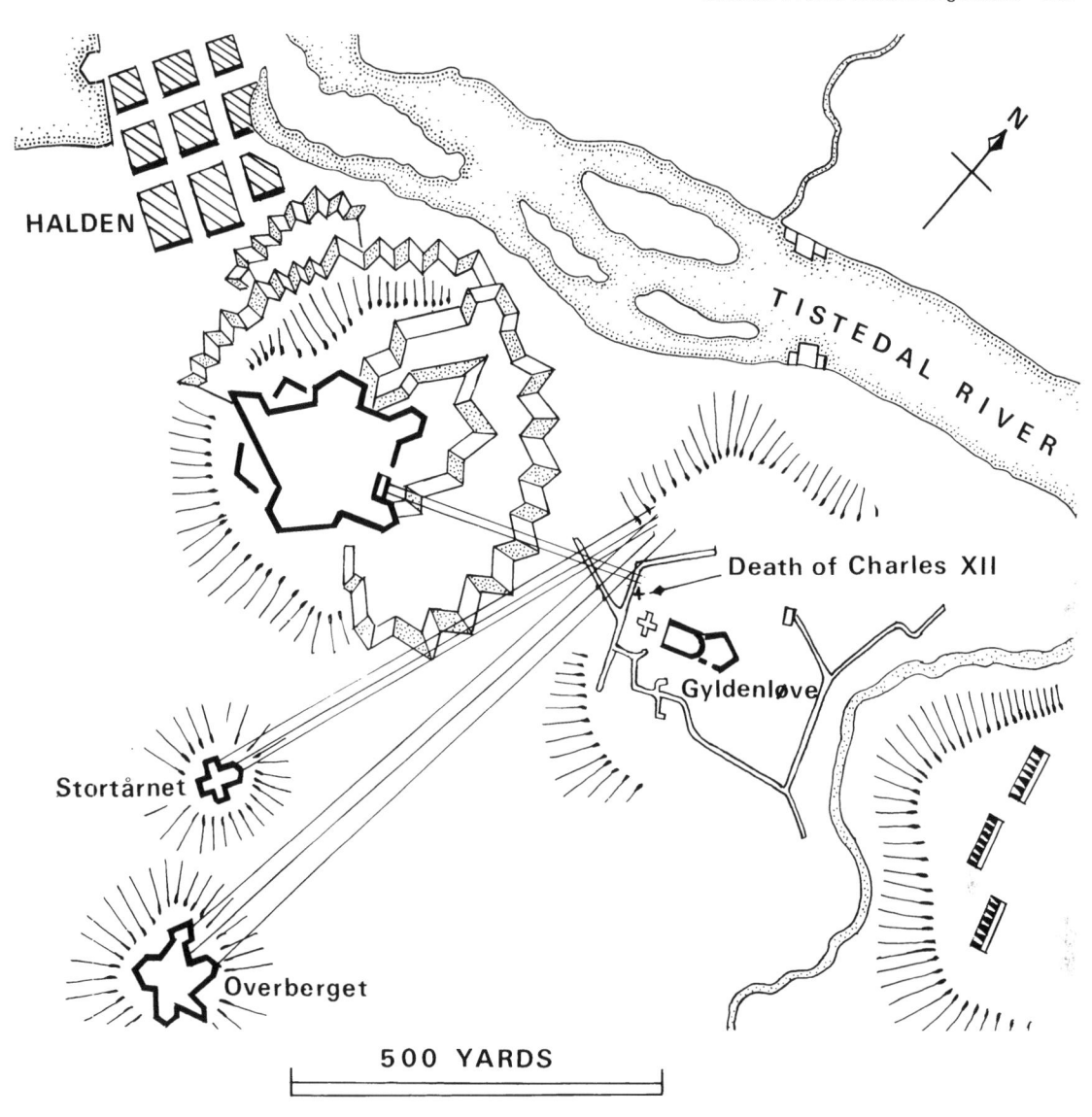

131 Siege of Fredriksten 1718

moving away from the enfilade fire from Stortårnet and Overberget forts to the south, and the imaginary prolongation of the sap reached across the waters of the Tistedal River safely away from the muzzles of the guns on the Prins Christian bastion of the main fortress.

As the moon rose, Charles stationed himself in the first parallel immediately behind the new sap:

He placed his two arms on the parapet and rested his head upon them (for this dangerous habit see also p. 100). He stayed in this attitude, as if he was asleep. The officers who were nearby at first assumed that he had dozed off, but when they saw him remain without motion for some time, which was against his usually active nature, they decided to approach him. You may imagine their consternation and terror when they found him stone dead. (Nordberg, 1748, III, 359)

A missile travelling at great velocity, probably an unaimed grape-shot, had pierced the king's head from left to right.

(The time was about half past nine in the evening. Every capable fortress commander was careful to keep up a fire at night against the known or suspected locations of enemy working parties, and Colonel Landsberg is known to have had plenty of ammunition in the magazines at Fredriksten. For good discussions of the 'assassination theory' and other suppositions see Haintz, 1936–58, III, 288–310; Hatton, 1968, 495–509, and Eriksen, 1979, 21–3. In their attempts to shed some light on the event, investigators have examined the poor, shattered head of Charles's mummified corpse no less than four times, and twice dug up the ground in the area of the parallel.)

The king's body rolled out of the stretcher as it was being carried back to his hut, and the appalling news spread rapidly through the army. It was unthinkable to continue the siege, and all the Swedish invading forces were recalled from Norway.

In July 1719 the allies moved in on Sweden from all sides. A Russian force devastated the eastern coast, while King Frederick IV invaded Bohuslän from Norway with 34,000 men, and the enterprising sailor Tordenskiold bluffed the island fortress of Marstrand into surrender.

The Swedes had to buy off their enemies one by one. According to the two treaties signed at Stockholm in 1719 and 1720 they demolished the works at Wismar, yielded Bremen and Verden to Hanover, and relinquished Stettin, south Pomerania, Usedom and Wollin to the Prussians. The old Swedish empire in Germany was now confined to a shrunken patch of Pomerania around Stralsund.

In 1720 the Danes agreed to evacuate their conquests on the Scandinavian mainland, but in return they forced Queen Ulrica of Sweden to pay a large indemnity, to admit liability to the Sound dues, and give up her support for Gottorp.

The Russians were not to be placated so easily. At the settlement of Nystadt in 1721 they won Livonia, Estonia, Ingria, the province of Kexholm and the fortress of Vyborg, in other words the 'corner' and the southern shore of the Gulf of Finland.

The eighteenth century

The contest for Finland 1741–3 and 1788–90
Eighteenth-century Sweden was slow to come to her senses after more than ten decades of staggering military effort. In particular it was difficult to resolve what was to be done to defend the national interests against Russia. In 1723 some good ideas were put forward by the Director of Fortifications, Major-General Axel Löwen, who had been a confidant of the late king. Löwen appreciated how the obsession with the southern flank of the empire had left Stockholm and the east coast vulnerable to the Russian galleys, which in the late war had ranged along the Finnish littoral and penetrated the Stockholm archipelago itself. He proposed to counter the danger by a strategy of active forward defence, based on Finland.

Starting from the supposition that the lakes and woods of the hinterland would channel the Russian advance along the coastal strip, Löwen suggested that the Swedes could check the first impetus if they took the trouble to build a new fortress at Degerby. The resistance of this place would win time for reinforcements from Sweden to reach the rearward base at Helsingfors (Helsinki), which should be built into a first-class naval and military establishment. It was patently impossible to form a fleet of ships of the line against Russia as well as Denmark, and Löwen instead advocated the construction of an 'Army Fleet' of light craft, specifically designed to match the Russian galleys in the Gulf of Finland, and assist the operations of the land forces.

Some of the Swedish politicians objected that military work on the scale proposed by Löwen would give undue offence to the Russians, who were to be placated at any price. Other people, more confident, said that it was no use fortifying the present borders when there was every hope of winning back the lost lands by an offensive war. The result was that the Swedish government made no provision for any defence at all.

The Swedish National Assembly, in an access of improvident belligerence, forced the government to declare war on Russia in 1741. The 'Hat' party of aristocratic politicians and ambitious young officers was in the ascendant, and their thirst for military adventure was whetted by expressions of admiration and encouragement from France.

The existing Swedish establishment in Finland amounted to 9,500 troops, and most of these were piled into the earth and fascine fortress of Willmanstrand. Without waiting for the Swedes to make up their minds what to do, the Russian field-marshal Peter Lacy brought an army of 26,000 men over the border, smashed into Willmanstrand on 23 August, and sent 4,500 prisoners back to Russia.

In 1742 Lacy once more contrived to take the Swedes unawares. He overran the vast earthworks at Frederikshamn without opposition, and in a brilliant stroke he got across the path of the Swedish army's retreat and shut it up at Helsingfors. The 17,000 Swedes capitulated on 24 August. Lacy finished off the campaign by reducing the whole of Finland, and in 1743 the threat of a Russian seaborne descent on their homeland forced the Swedes to come to terms. By the Peace of Åbo they ceded all southern Finland beyond the Kyumen, with the fortresses of Willmanstrand, Nyslott and Frederikshamn. The Swedish holdings on the Gulf of Finland had receded a further sixty miles.

Towards the end of the eighteenth century Swedish military ambitions flared up and finally burnt themselves out in the person of King Gustavus III, who restored the absolute monarchy. In 1788 he committed his forces to an offensive war against Russia. Two campaigning seasons passed without a clear advantage being gained by either party. In 1790, however, the Swedes strove for more positive action, and on 8 May their amphibious striking force appeared off Karlshamn in Russian Finland. The Russian commander Sislov had hardly any troops, but he arranged his galleys across the entrance to the bay, and beat off some determined landing attempts on the night of 16–17 May and on 18 May.

The Swedes decided to leave this hornets' nest alone, and see if they would fare any better at Vyborg at the head of the Gulf of Finland. The move was met by a concentration of the Russian fleet, and on 3 July the Swedes had to fight their way out of Vyborg Bay, barely escaping annihilation. The series of abortive sieges confirmed what the British already knew, that an amphibious attack on a fortress was one of the most difficult operations of war. The Swedes were aware that if they kept up the fight, they would soon be the subject of the undivided attention of the Russians, who were finishing off their war against the Turks. The Russians, on their side, were anxious to bring to an end a conflict that was being waged so close to St Petersburg. On 14 August, therefore, the Peace of Värälä confirmed the line of the existing border along the Kyumen.

The War of 1788–90 represented far more than a defensive victory for the Russians, for they had built their Baltic Fleet up to a strength of forty-six of the line by the end of the war, and inflicted losses which reduced the number of Swedish battleships to sixteen. The balance of power in the Baltic was swinging decisively against the Swedes, and in 1808, in a new war with Russia, they lost the whole of Finland in a matter of three months. This time the Russians were not prepared to let their conquest go.

Swedish eighteenth-century engineering
That lively and many-sided person Augustin Ehrensvärd (1710–72) is counted as one of the leading figures of the Swedish Enlightenment. It is a tribute to the diversity of his intellect that he also became known as Sweden's leading engineer and

132 Augustin Ehrensvärd

pundit on national defence.

Ehrensvärd was born in 1710 to a talented but not particularly well-off military family. His youthful readings in military technology were encouraged by his maternal uncle, the famous gunner Carl Cronstedt, who secured his admission to the artillery in 1726. Two years later Ehrensvärd was given leave to study at the University of Uppsala, where he cultivated such a taste for mathematics that for a time he entertained the ambition of becoming professor. This dream was shattered by the death of his father, a misfortune which compelled him to resume his military career. In the 1730s, however, he was given an extremely interesting commission to inspect and report on arms manufacture in foreign countries. He toured arsenals and fortresses in Denmark, Germany, Holland, France and England, and took the opportunity to learn the art of engraving and make the acquaintance of modern literature – the works of Alexander Pope became his favourite reading. He returned to Sweden in 1738 with an enhanced military and cultural reputation, and in the next year he was admitted to the newly-founded Academy of Sciences through the sponsorship of the great botanist Linnaeus. His education was completed by the experience of accompanying Frederick of Prussia on his arduous campaign of 1745.

Upon coming back to Sweden a second time Ehrensvärd embroiled himself deeply in public affairs. In 1746 he was counted among the young officers in the National Assembly who supported the demand of the Generalissimus and Crown Prince Adolphus Frederick for a more effective defence after the disasters of the last war with Russia. In his turn the royal patron managed to set aside the authority of the *Fortifikationskontor* and give Ehrensvärd direct powers to undertake a programme of fortress building in Finland.

Ehrensvärd's scheme for Finland was based upon the suggestions which had been put forward by Axel Löwen in 1723. Under the name of 'Lovisa', the eastern border fortress was built at Löwen's designated site on the skerries at Degerby. The construction of the main stronghold, at Helsingfors, was a taxing task, since the works were scattered across the entrance to the roadstead on seven granite islets. To offset the difficulties of the site Ehrensvärd had the help of French subsidies and the labour of up to 8,000 troops, and in 1747 he confidently predicted that he would finish this new fortress of 'Sveaborg' in four years.

The year of 1751 came and went with the works nowhere near completion, and in 1752 Adolphus Frederick, who was now king, visited the site in person to see what had gone wrong. Ehrensvärd admitted that there were still many obstacles ahead, but testified 'with a clear conscience that I have managed the building of the fortress with clean and unsullied hands' (Juva, in Hildebrand, 1946–9, XII, 426). The king went back to Stockholm, and announced that Ehrensvärd had let 'artistry run away with him, so that on occasion the works have been more costly and stronger than should have been required by the actual site' (*ibid.*, XII, 427).

Over the years Ehrensvärd was hauled before three commissions of enquiry, but survived with his reputation and strategy almost intact. He once declared:

we must inevitably contract some expenses, for it is a question of whether we are to live as freemen or vassals... If you are against making Sveaborg into a first-class fortress, it shows that you do not know what sea warfare in Finland is all about. (*ibid.*, XII, 431–2)

The aristocratic 'Hat' party came to power in 1769 and reinstated their old friend Ehrensvärd in direct control of the Finnish fortifications. The victory came too late, for Ehrensvärd was a badly-preserved 60-year-old, and was bent on retiring from public life. His wish was fulfilled in the following year. Already mortally ill, he was made a field-marshal on 14 September 1772. He died on 24 October. In the 1780s his body was re-interred in a tomb on Vargön Island at Sveaborg where, as the inscription reads, he lay 'surrounded by his own creations, the fortress of Sveaborg and the Army Fleet'. People say that he emerges from the vault on stormy nights and goes for a prowl around the ramparts.

Ehrensvärd borrowed his strategy from Löwen and his style of fortification mostly from Vauban, yet in one respect he stands out as the most modern engineer of his time. He alone among his contemporaries knew what it was to pilot immensely

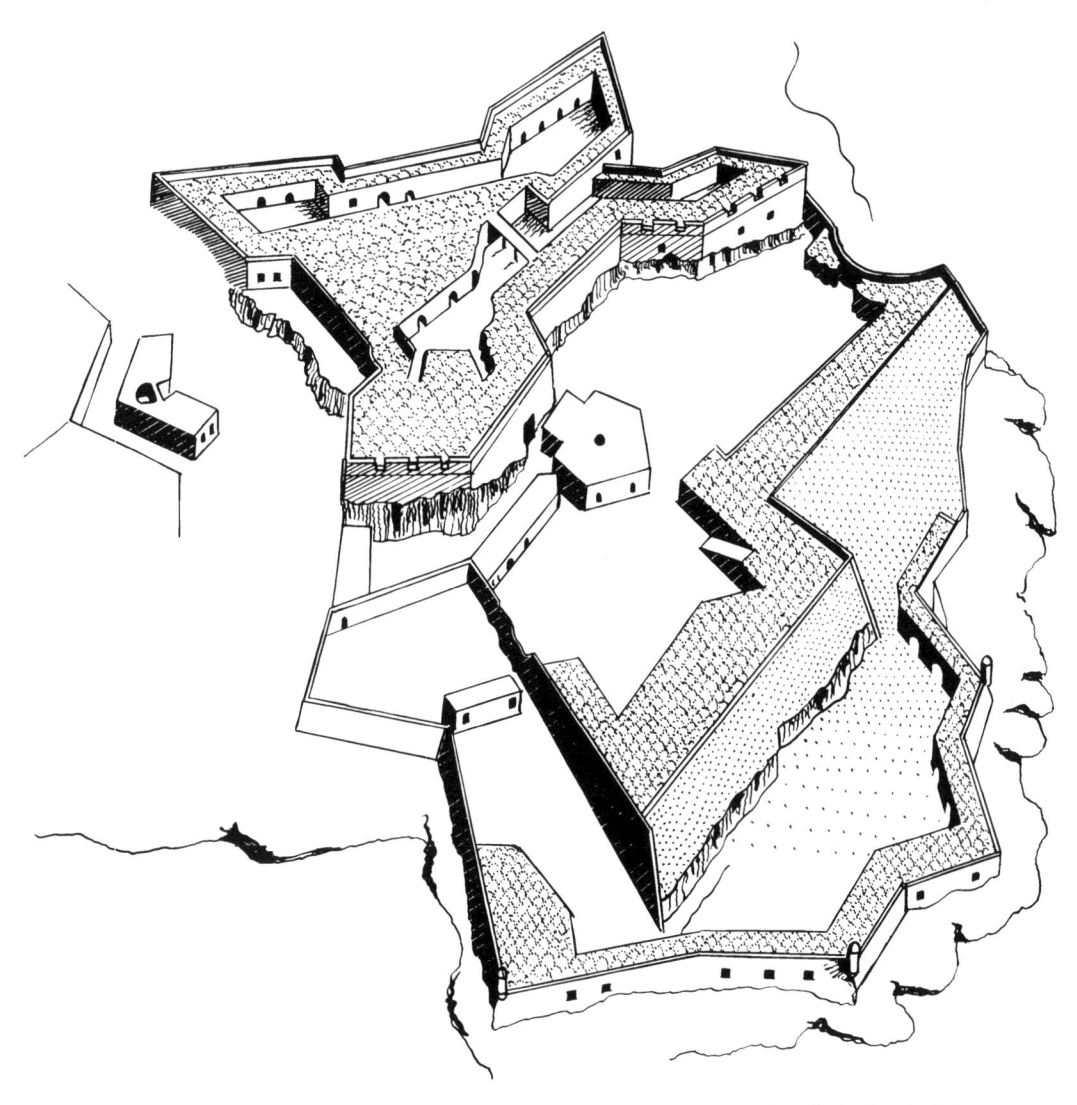

133 The Gustavsvärd Fort, Sveaborg. The first and the strongest of the fortified islands. It is liberally littered with blockhouses and caponnières

expensive and long drawn-out schemes of fortification and national defence through all the vicissitudes of domestic party politics. The experience was to become common in the next two centuries.

It was left to other engineers to continue the evolution of a truly 'Swedish' style of fortification. In 1755 Lieutenant-Quartermaster-General Carlberg proposed a system of round casemated towers, arranged in two storeys and an upper platform battery. In this he was clearly one of Dahlberg's spiritual heirs. The concept of the casemated tower was developed by one of Ehrensvärd's rivals, Quartermaster-General J. B. Virgin, who had watched the French reduce the Netherlands fortresses with disturbing ease in 1746 and 1747. In a work published in 1781 (*La Défense des Places, Mise en Equilibre avec les Attaques Savantes et Furieuses d'Aujourd'hui*, Stockholm) he proposed a number of traces which incorporated the motifs of an outer perimeter with bastion towers, and a tall inner keep. The keep was to contain an arcaded courtyard, from which well-hidden mortars were to lob their bombs

134 Virgin's mortar casemates

over the walls. He thereby hoped to give the fortress artillery

an incontestable and decisive advantage. . . . This superiority is to be derived from a fire which is to be delivered from the interior of the fortress, or the rearward side of the outworks, and not, as is usual, from the exterior fronts of the stronghold. (Virgin, 1781, iv–v)

The French polymath Montalembert was attached to the Swedish army in the Seven Years War, and he was undoubtedly influenced by the Dahlberg-Carlberg tradition when he proposed his system of high, heavily gunned coastal works of the 'Fort Sumter' type (see p. 159). In the early 1800s Montalembert's countryman Carnot carried the plagiarism still further, when he made Virgin's mortar casemates the foundation of an allegedly novel design of his own. These in turn became a component part of Prussian fortification later in the nineteenth century, at Königsberg and other places.

Altogether the record of Swedish military engineering is a highly impressive one. Its chief practitioners were men of the widest culture and interests, and long after they died their inspirations helped to shape fortress designs throughout the world.

The work of Tsar Peter and his successors
The fortresses. Peter the Great built or repaired his fortresses at great speed, according to the various demands of his many campaigns. The wonder is that the result was a reasonably balanced and tenable system of national defence.

In the north Peter was enterprising enough to snatch from Sweden the fortresses of Vyborg and Kexholm, which furnished him with a ready-made barrier against Finland. In these circumstances the rearward strongholds at Schlüsselburg and Narva lost some of their earlier importance, though the six-bastioned Peter-Paul Fortress at St Petersburg (built first in earth, then in brick from 1703) was still considered vital for the immediate defence of the capital.

Sweden's Trans-Baltic Bridgeheads 213

In 1703 Peter laid the foundation stone for the fortress and harbour of Kronstadt, on Kotlin Island a dozen miles out in the Gulf of Finland. This establishment served as a strategic outwork for the capital, and its deep waters offered a more suitable base for the new Baltic fleet than the Neva at St Petersburg. At the same time Kronstadt and St Petersburg shared a number of important disadvantages – they were remote from the open waters of the Baltic, they were ice bound for half of the year, and only a good easterly wind was capable of sweeping the vessels out of this extreme corner of the Gulf. Furthermore, the timbers of the ships soon rotted in the near-fresh water, and there was no good oak to be had anywhere in the neighbourhood. These considerations persuaded Peter to turn his attention to the Estonian port of Revel, and the nearby bay of Rogervik, where he began some very extravagant harbour works. Revel and Rogervik were well sited for offensive warfare, almost directly opposite Helsingfors, and the ice in their waters melted while the head of the Gulf of Finland was still ice-bound.

However, Kronstadt emerged as the ultimate victor. Empress Elizabeth and General Ludwig Louberas completed the fifty-vessel inland basin there in 1752, 'a work worthy of the ancient Romans' (Manstein, 1860, 408). Catherine was at first inclined to favour Revel and Rogervik, but she too finally gave the preference to Kronstadt, for she came to appreciate its importance for the defence of the capital. A new programme of works was undertaken from the end of 1781, and by 1783 it was so well advanced that the Admiralty was moved thither from St Petersburg.

At the beginning of the eighteenth century the vast border with the West possessed no strongpoints apart from the antiquated fortresses of Pskov and Smolensk. In 1707 Peter therefore built an earthen citadel at Velikii Luki, which did something to fill the gap between these two places, and he went on

135 Virgin-style mortar casemates at Fort Concepçion, Spain

to connect all three fortresses by a line of abatis and earthworks. The defensible border was prolonged to the south by the newly strengthened towns of Bryansk and Chernigov, and it ended at the very powerful new works at the city of Kiev, which gave the Russians a strategic bridgehead on the far side of the Dnieper, and formed the corner bastion of the western and southern borders. The strongpoints of the Kiev position were formed by the existing defences of the city proper, and the perimeter of the nearby Pecharsk Monastery. The work of extending the monastery into a major fortress began in 1706, and under the name of 'Novo-Pecharsk' this place was eventually linked by earthworks to the defences of the original city (Staro Kiev). Moscow still counted as a rearward garrison town, and the Kremlin owned an enceinte of earthen bastions in the emergency of 1708.

Most of Peter's fortresses on the western borders were so well sited – and so incomplete – that his successors were kept busy finishing what he had begun. They added the imposing Anna crownwork to Vyborg, and reclad the river fronts of the Peter-Paul Fortress with granite in the 1780s. The Russians, however, did not attempt to restore the weak and decaying works at Willmanstrand and Frederikshamn in the area of Finland which was ceded to them in 1743, preferring to defend the new border by throwing up field works at the likely crossing-points on the Kyumen.

We look in vain for any survival or emergence of a specifically Russian way of fortifying in the eighteenth century. What we have instead is a series of unrelated styles which were produced by whatever foreign architects happened to be at hand. The years 1706 and 1707, for example, saw work going ahead in Lambert and Trezzini's faceless Frenchified-Italian mode at the Peter-Paul Fortress, in German style at Kiev, and in Coehoorn's manner around the Kremlin and the Kitai-Gorod at Moscow. The ghost of Coehoorn continued to strive mightily against the French influence, and it inspired some works at Kronstadt in 1721 and Rogervik in 1723 which we may set against a very passable imitation of Vauban's 'second manner' at Kresta on the Persian border in 1722. Thereafter the patronage of Goulon and Münnich (see below) gave the school of Vauban the ascendancy, though there was a significant departure from convention in 1759, when a committee of engineer and gunner officers decided that the important new fortress of Dmitrya on the Don was to be built on a tenaille trace and incorporate artillery casemates. Montalembert was a champion of the tanaille system in his earlier years, and he could well have influenced (or been influenced by) the committee's decision when he acted as the French liaison officer with the Russian armies in 1759 and 1760.

The knowledge of the classic books on fortification was filtered through the cloudy medium of translations which rarely showed a complete mastery of Western technical terms. Between 1708 and 1711 there appeared the first Russian editions of works by some of the acknowledged foreign authorities on fortification and gunnery. Peter followed the translations and the process of production very closely, and he was so angered by the bad printing of the first edition of Rimpler (1708) that he had the work re-set and published again in the following year. Coehoorn (1710) was another of Peter's favourites. He had read the book when he was in Holland, and he particularly liked the clear explanations which accompanied the illustrations.

In 1724 Vasilii Ivanovich Suvorov bravely brought out a *True Method of Fortifying Towns, Published by the Famous Engineer Vauban*. His son was the famous Aleksandr Vasilevich, who became an authority on fortification in his own right. One of his associates testifies:

He knew Vauban almost by heart, and he once told me the reason why. 'My late father translated the work from French to Russian at the command of Emperor Peter the Great. Every day he used to read it over with me, and by comparing the Russian text with the original he was good enough to instruct me in this art, which is so necessary and useful for military men. (Fuchs, 1827, 23)

For a variety of reasons the Russian fortresses were very long a-building, and not particularly well made when they were complete. Reliable surveying instruments had to be brought all the way from Western Europe, for the Russian products were liable to give false readings. Then again the foreign-born

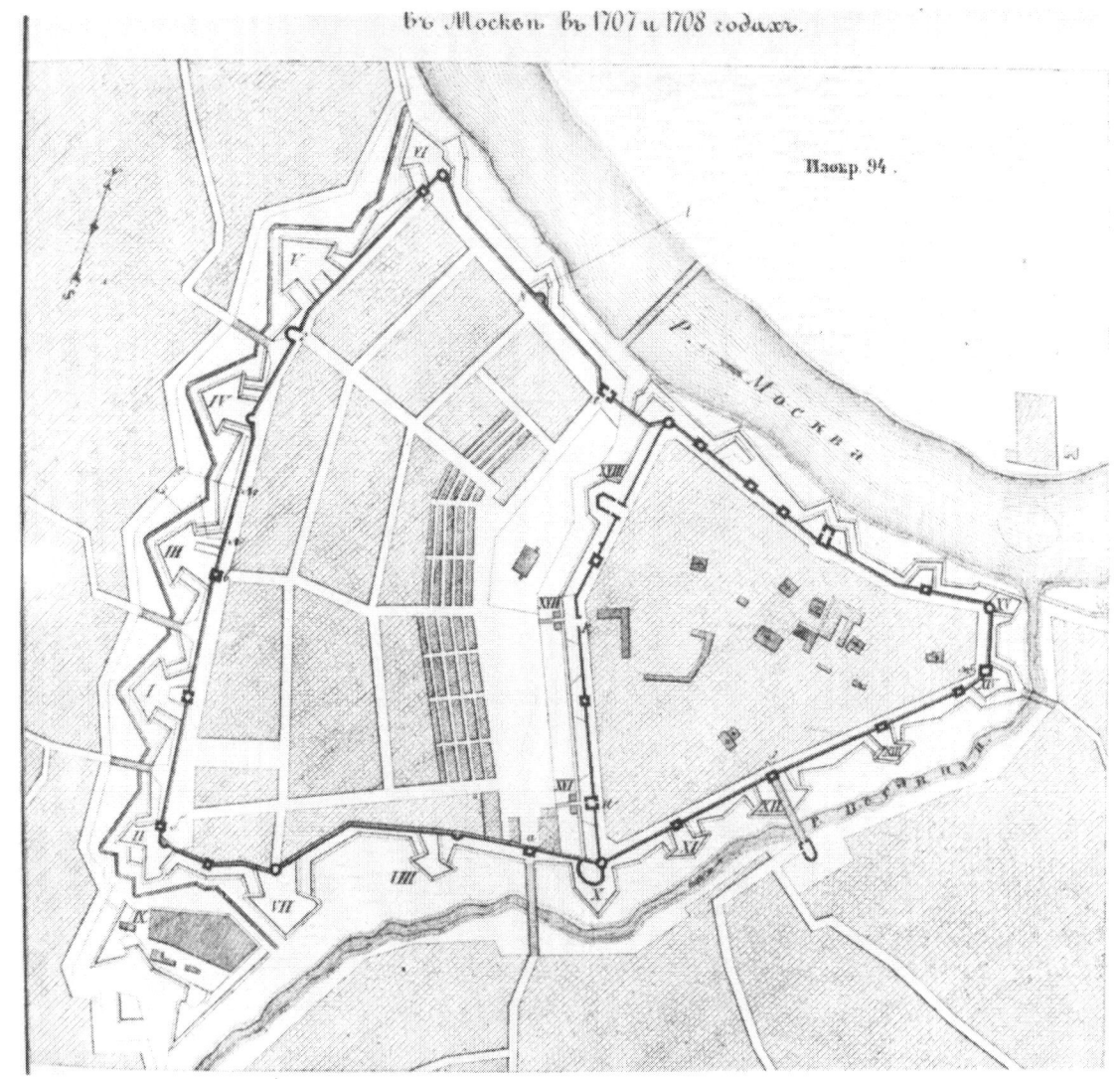

136 The bastioned fortifications at Moscow, built 1707–8. The Kremlin is on the right, and the Kitai Gorod on the left. Red Square extends in front of towers XVI, XVII and XVIII of the Kremlin. Nothing remains of the early eighteenth-century fortifications save a few bumps in the Alexander Gardens which stretch along the foot of the south-eastern wall of the Kremlin

engineers might draw up the finest plans in the world, but they did not find it easy to explain their intentions to their Russian assistants, or to travel to distant sites to supervise the work in person. In this respect Field-Marshal Münnich tried to blacken the reputation of one of his rivals by claiming

General Goulon used to reason that in Russia you should make a point of doing nothing but what you are expressly ordered to do. The junior engineers took him at his word, and remained immobile at St. Petersburg.... They also argued that it was enough to wait until war actually arrived before you set to work on the fortresses, and so these false and dangerous principles resulted in a state of general neglect. (to Empress Elizabeth, 28 August 1749, Vorontsov, 1870–95, II, 499)

The palace revolutions and the long and exhausting wars militated against any continuity of construction, on top of the natural difficulties proceeding from the great distances and the harsh climate. Also the building contractors lacked resources and experience, and when they fell down on a job the government was hard put to it to supply a labour force of its own. With reference to the coastal works. Bode observes:

The construction of the harbours, together with their defence by girdles of fortifications that were appropriate to their intended size, was a process that dragged out over many years or was sometimes never finished at all. It was fortunate that Russia's victories by land and sea spared her from having the resistance of her harbour fortresses put to the test. (Bode, 1979, 55)

In fact, Russia stood in no urgent need of fortresses in the later part of the eighteenth century, except for the defence of St Petersburg, or as way-stations and offensive bases. Many well thought-out schemes of defence were devised, like those for the western frontier by Friedrich Wilhelm Bauer in 1780 and Aleksei Tuchkov two years later, but all of the projects were overtaken by the headlong onrush of Russia's borders in this period. The Livonian fortress system, which had been one of the main objects of attention for Peter and Münnich, was now buried deep in the interior.

The engineers. The nascent Russian engineering corps was very slow indeed to show signs of independent life. We first discover the engineers as two 'commands' of officers, who were attached to the field artillery. Peter took them under the wings of the Chancellery of Artillery and Fortification, when it was set up in 1712, and in the same year he magnanimously endowed them with reproductive organs when an engineering school admitted pupils at Moscow. A second school was set up in 1719, in the more fashionable surroundings of St Petersburg, and it absorbed the Moscow school five years later. The teaching was largely in the hands of Germans, but Peter kept a lively interest in what was going on. He emphasised that the

instruction of engineers and miners is not just a question of paperwork, but of getting down to digging in the earth. We must begin with the construction of small models, then proceed to the execution of such common works as approaches, saps, galleries across wet and dry ditches, and mines. (Laskovskii, 1858–65, II, 195)

In December 1722 Peter created the post of Director-General of fortresses, and entrusted it to the Huguenot refugee Major-General de Goulon, who was a veteran of the French and Imperial services. This paved the way for the reorganisation of 1724, when the engineers won their partial independence from the artillery and were constituted into a regiment. By the end of Peter's reign, in 1725, the new corps stood under the direction of a lieutenant-general (the German Burchard Christoph Münnich) and two major-generals (Goulon and Louberas), and comprised no less than 243 engineers and assistants.

In 1727 the dictatorial Münnich won the title of *Ober-Direktor*, with extensive powers. In the following year he put the engineering personnel on a proper establishment, and in 1731 he published a corresponding establishment of fortresses, which were fixed at thirty-one in number, and divided into seven departments for administrative purposes. Russia's first code of regulations for the engineering service followed in 1737. Nothing came of Münnich's proposal for a gallery of fortress models, but he succeeded in having work begun on an atlas of fortifications, the *Sila Rossiiskoi Imperii*, a magnificent undertaking that was completed by Prince Repnin in 1746.

Münnich was disgraced in 1741, and his orphan engineers very soon lost their independence, with the same dire results as were to follow the union of the gunners and the engineers in France. Worse still, the native Russian nobility failed to show any enthusiasm for the trade of engineering. Already in 1731 the government was forced to take the humiliating step of inviting foreign officers to supply the deficiency, and two years later Frederick William I of Prussia sent out a large number of engineers to help with the war in Poland.

The 1740s was a period when fortifications were in every sense on the defensive. Münnich was influenced by some of the preoccupations of European engineers as a whole when he wrote from his exile to Empress Elizabeth in 1749, asking in vain to be readmitted to the service:

True engineers, Most August Sovereign, have always been difficult to find in every country. The French engineers are most expert at siegework, but it is pathetic to see how they have recently set about fortifying Metz, where they have piled up useless works and useless expense. Since the death of Coehoorn the Dutch have not produced a single engineer of any competence in either the offensive or defensive roles, and you have only to reflect on the great number of fortresses which the French have besieged and taken in a single war [the Austrian Succession in the Netherlands] to conclude that little is understood about the art of the defence at a time when we excel in the art of the attack. (Vorontsov, 1870–95, II, 499)

Münnich therefore offered himself as a supremely skilful engineer, and one who had been privy to the most secret plans of Peter the Great. Elizabeth was unimpressed.

The promise of a revival of Russian engineering came with the appointment of Petr Shuvalov as Master General of the Ordnance in 1756. This inventive and tireless person restored order to the management of engineering affairs, and in 1757 he commissioned *General-Anshef* Fermor to investigate all the fortresses, evaluating the state of their repair, and how far the original reasons for their construction measured up to present military needs. However, Shuvalov died before the end of the Seven Years War, and the advent of Catherine II and her favourites deprived Russian military engineering of any directing principle. The engineers remained what they had always been – isolated foreigners, lost in the vastness of Russia.

Even in Shuvalov's heyday the Russian methods of besieging fortresses corresponded much more closely to the ordinary tactics of the field army than they did to the systematic proceedings of the French engineers (see p. 118). Thus the field guns and unicorns were supposed to act as mightily as the specialised 24-pounders and mortars of the Western siege trains. Later in the century Suvorov placed the burden on the infantry instead, and employed techniques of assault which exploited to the full the endurance, devotion and what seemed (however wrongly) to be the limitless numbers of the Russian soldiers.

Eight The Last Crusade – the Repulse of Ottoman Turkey

Venice and the defence of the water avenue

The contest for Candia
The opening of our period finds Christendom's ancient enemy battering at the gates of Europe, for the Ottoman Empire had developed new force under the inspired leadership of the successive grand viziers Mehmet Köprülü (ruled 1656–61) and his son Ahmed (1661–76). Central Europe was endangered by a Turkish breakthrough along the Danube, while Turkish amphibious forces threatened to spill out over the Mediterranean as soon as they managed to force the Venetians from Candia, the chief stronghold of Crete, which was the cork in the bottle of the Aegean.

The Turks had laid Candia under intermittent blockade and attack for years, but in 1668 they came on with a new sense of purpose. This time they concentrated their efforts against the two sectors where the town wall met the sea. These were the Sabbionara Bastion in the far west, and the corresponding Sant'Andrea Bastion in the far east. The Turks thereby evaded much of the flanking fire which had plagued them in their siege of 1667, and their cunning engineers took good account of the nature of the ground – they built up lodgments on each of the rocky heights in front of Sant'Andrea, but were careful not to strike out fresh approaches until they obtained effective support from the artillery. In contrast, the sandy soil before Sabbionara inspired them to construct a maze of stone-revetted redoubts, which were connected by tunnels and low doors.

The new Turkish attacks placed the fortress in much greater jeopardy than before, and by the spring of 1669 the Sabbionara had become almost untenable, and the heap of ruins that marked the site of Sant'Andrea was being systematically blown into the air by the rival miners. On 13 May the Venetian governor, the able and conscientious Catterino Cornaro, was standing on one of the intact ravelins when

he saw a 500-pounder bomb about to fall nearby. He at once cried out and threw himself in the opposite direction in the hope of avoiding the missile. But the bomb exploded immediately it hit the ground, giving him no chance to escape. It ripped his belly away. (Solaye, 1670, 321)

The spirits of the defenders were somewhat revived by the coming of a powerful French contingent of twelve regiments, which were carried to Crete by Admiral de Beaufort and his fleet of eighty transports and warships. On 19 June the Turks saw the Duc de Navailles and other high-born French officers disembark with 'sixteen thousand Infidel pigs who intend us no good' (Hammer, 1834–5, III, 631).

We set out to view the town [recalls one of the Frenchmen], and at the very door of our lodging we came across two soldiers who had had their heads removed by a cannon shot in the middle of the street. It was pitiful to see the state of the town – the streets were littered with cannon shot, musket

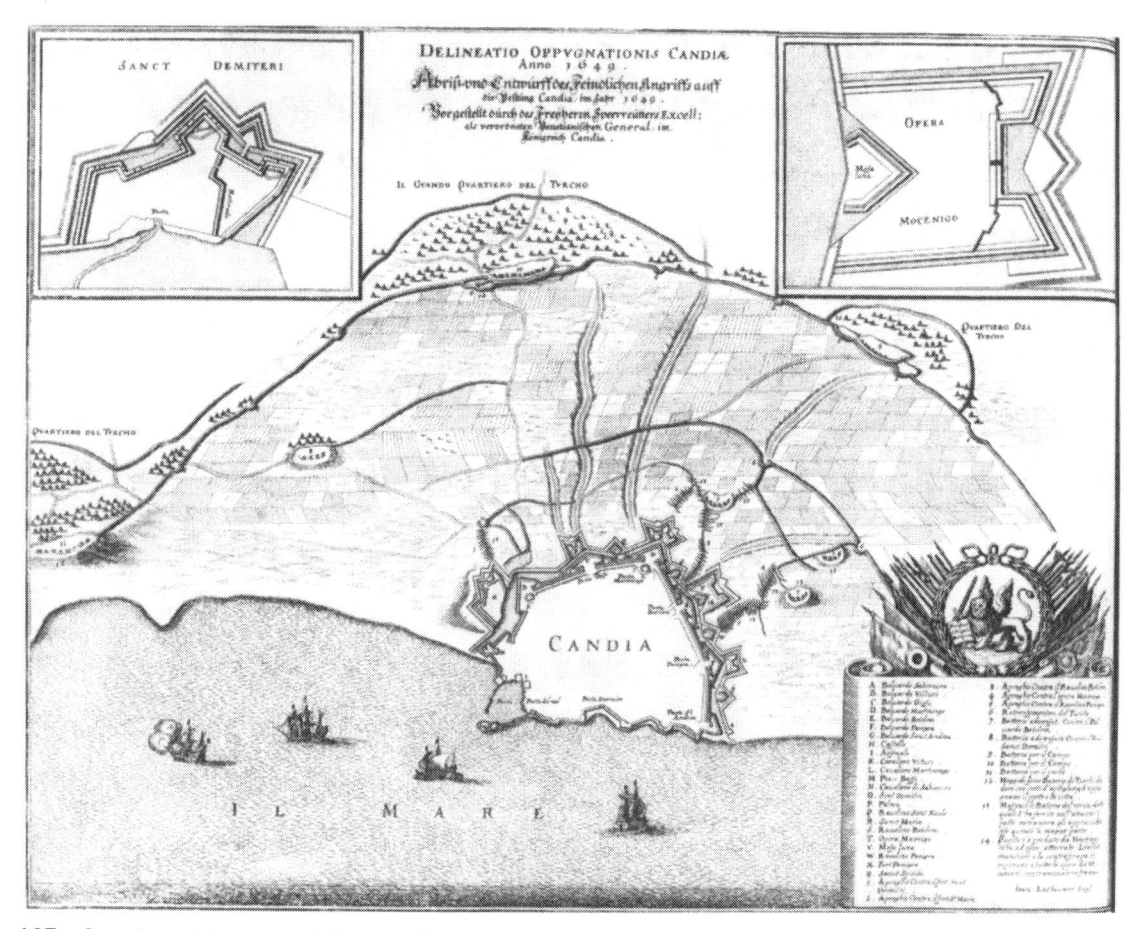

137 Opening of the siege of Candia 1649

balls, stones, and fragments of bombs and grenades; there was not a single church, not a single house which did not have its walls riddled and almost demolished by the cannon fire. (Reaux de la Richardière, 1671, 57–8)

The newcomers were consumed by a suicidal desire for glory. In a hare-brained sortie from the Sabbionara on 25 June they managed to fight their way as far as the Turkish batteries, but they were thrown into confusion when one of the magazines blew up. They lost four hundred men while they were running back to the fortress, and Admiral Beaufort disappeared without trace, though people said that the grand vizier paid a bounty for his head and sent the trophy back to Constantinople. The physical losses were covered by the arrival of more than one thousand Bavarian and Imperial troops on 29 June, but the morale of the defenders had suffered a mortal blow.

Hardly less catastrophic was the attempt of the Christian flotilla to bombard the Turkish camp on 24 July. The Papal and Maltese galleys shot so badly that most of the missiles fell into Candia. The French made rather better practice, but the 54-gun ship *La Thérèse* was hit by the Turks, caught fire, and blew up with her crew of four hundred men.

For a while the depleted French contingent soldiered on beside the Germans and Venetians. The enemy deluged the wilting defenders with arrows, grenades, cannon shot and pierrier stones, and they took care to fire their mortars at the times of day when the sun shone directly in the eyes of the Christians, who were then unable to see the

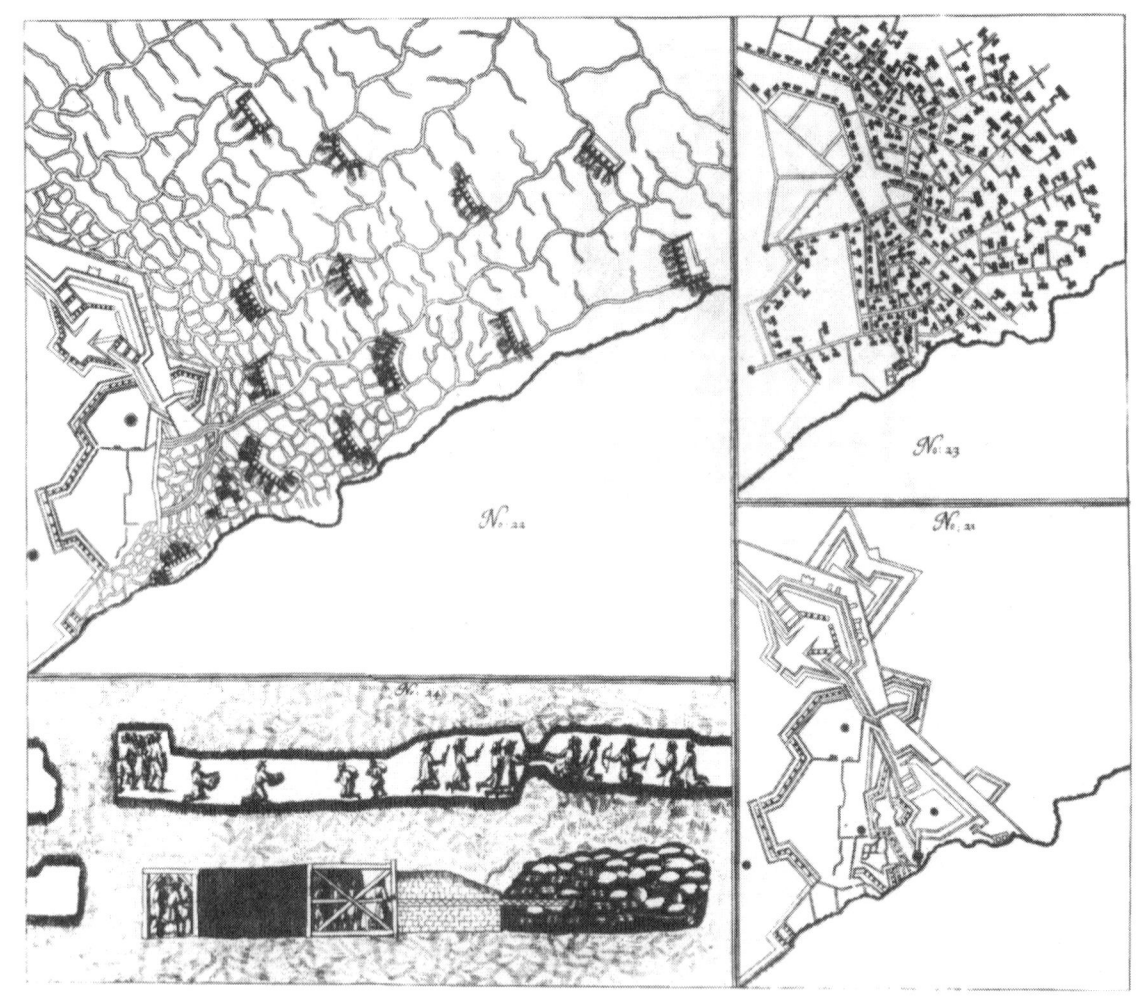

138 The Panigra and Sant'Andrea Bastions, Candia
no. 21 plan of the defences
no. 22 Turkish batteries and siegeworks
no. 23 plan of the Christian countermines
no. 24 underground combats; the Turks will shortly be annihilated by an enormous charge of gunpowder (Scheither, 1672)

bombs in flight. The Bavarian colonel Bürken exclaimed that he had served in many wars, but 'never in my life had I been in so many hot spots as at Candia' (Staudinger, 1901, I, 586). Not a day passed without one or more mines being exploded, and the rival works were so close that now and then a Turkish soldier would be propelled through the air and deposited, irate but intact, in the Christian trenches.

The reason why the Turks were shooting so well was that they used

bribes and force to take the gunners ... from the Dutch and English ships trading in the Mediterranean, and employed these men to serve in the cannon batteries and fire the mortars. (Scheither, 1672, 80)

On the Christian side Johann Bernard Scheither, an officer in the Brunswick-Lüneburg contingent, complained that

the available gunners were mostly Italians and Greeks – stupid and inexperienced oafs who never bothered where they aimed or hit. Sometimes they fired right into us, when we were defending the summit of the breach, and killed a great many of our troops.... When these clowns had fired one of the fatal shots they only burst out laughing. (*ibid.*, 79)

Ignoring the pleas of the Venetians, Navailles set sail on 20 August with the survivors of the French contingent which he had done so much to ruin. Only three hundred of his men remained behind. The deserted garrison numbered less than four thousand troops, and these were being depleted at a rate of a hundred a day in the defence of the retrenchments behind Sabbionara and Sant'Andrea.

Negotiations with the Turks began on 30 August 1669, and on 6 September the parties agreed on a capitulation and a general peace. The garrison was allowed a free evacuation with the honours of war, and the right to take away eighty pieces of artillery. The Venetians were to retain their small Cretan strongholds of Suda, Spinalonga and Carabusa, and also Clissa and the other Venetian conquests in Dalmatia, Bosnia and Albania. The Grand Vizier Ahmed Köprülü acted with the greatest honesty and courtesy, and the terms as a whole were so unexpectedly favourable that the Venetian Senate did not hesitate to ratify the treaty.

The defence of Candia was in every way worthy to be ranked with the epic siege of Ostend at the beginning of the century, both as a feat of arms, and an academy of fortress warfare for a new generation of engineers:

Though the war bore no other denomination than of the Venetian and the Turk, yet so great was the confluence of both parts of the world to this little isle, as if it had been chosen by unanimous consent for a stage to try the title to the Universal Empire. (Rycaut, 1679–80, 'Mahomet IV', 233)

So writes Mr Rycaut, the English consul in the Levant. Among European authors the Germans Rimpler and Scheither, who took part in the bitter fighting of 1669, and the Dutchman Coehoorn, who heard about the siege at second hand, were all struck by the powers of resistance of casemates, shelters and galleries, and they incorporated them in various ways in their 'systems' of fortification. At the same time it is more than possible that Vauban was encouraged to develop his stone-throwing mortars and his technique of siege parallels, from what the French survivors told him about the Turkish methods at the same place.

The mighty operation was just as rich in lessons for the Turks. According to the well-informed Marsigli, 'this siege brought about some changes in the ancient discipline of the Janissaries, and the training of troops in the ways of besieging fortresses' (Marsigli, 1732, pt 1, 133). The Turks now departed from the strict provisions of Suleiman's regulations, and began to use their provincial infantry in the trenches as well as the Janissaries. The reform of the artillery had to wait until late in the eighteenth century, but deserters from Candia taught European standards of mining and thereby increased the relative importance of the underground attack in Turkish siegework, with effects that were to be felt at Vienna in 1683.

The winning and loss of the Morea

By acceding to the Pope's Holy Alliance of 1684, Venice became a partner in what was virtually Europe's last crusade. Contingents of Germans, southern Slavs, and Maltese, Florentine and Papal troops therefore gave the Republic a striking-power quite out of proportion to her own forces, which were in a parlous state. The Irish-born officer Jacob Richards exclaimed that the Venetian vessels were 'more like floating brothels than warships' (29 September 1697, Stowe Mss 461, British Museum), while his brother John ascribed the loss of Candia to the ignorance of military service among the nobility, and to a Republican constitution that was quite unfitted for time of war, 'when every deliberation must go through so many hands, so that often, before they come to the execution, the occasion is past' (Diary 1699, Stowe Mss 462, British Museum).

Venice decided to apply her newly found strength to the work of conquering the Morea – the tongue-like southernmost projection of the Grecian peninsula, which separated the Aegean from the Adriatic, and thus from the access to Italy. In the course of 1685 and 1686 the colourful international force duly captured the little fortresses around the coasts –

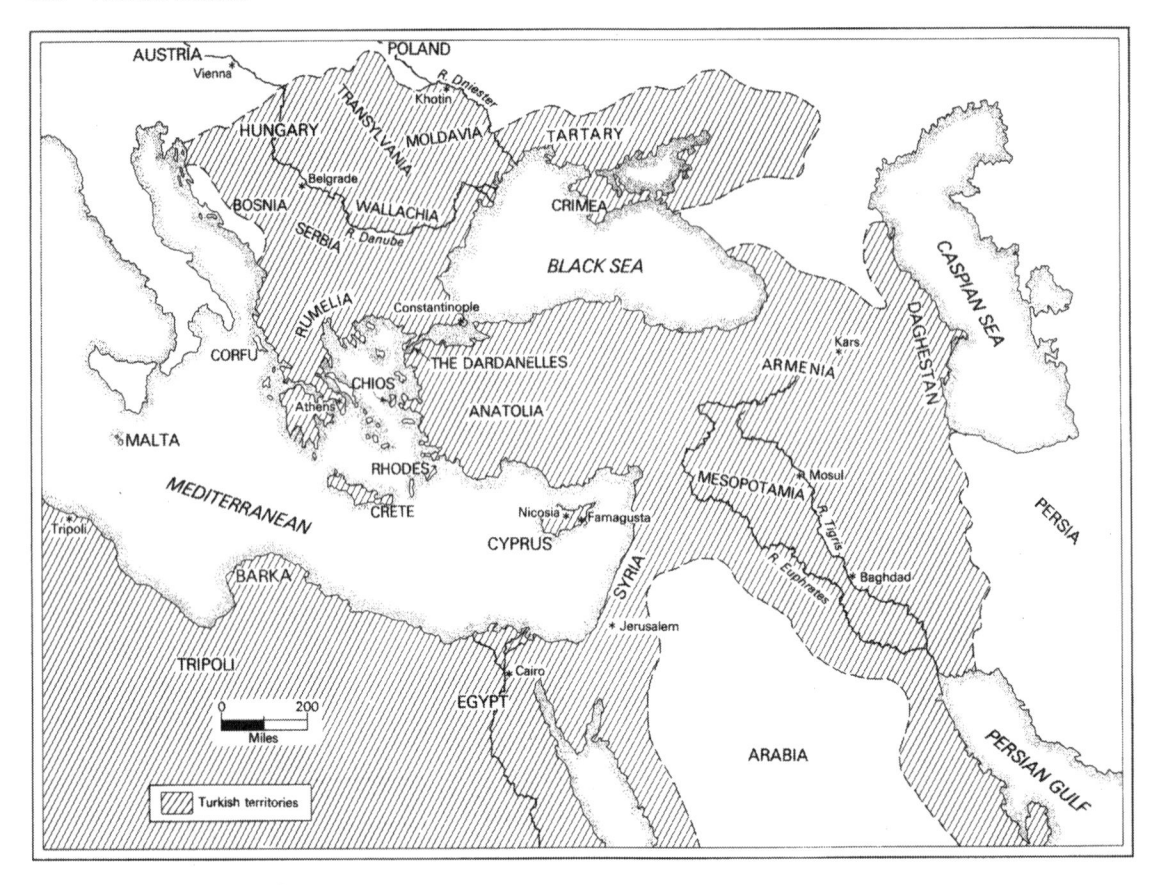

The Turkish empire 1683

Koron, Navarino, Modon, Argos, and Napoli di Romania (Nauplia).

These sieges were conducted in a peculiar style which was the product of the difficulties of the terrain and the incompetence of the engineers. The Venetians seldom had an exact idea of what fortifications they were going to encounter, beyond the usual Morean acropolis on its lofty crag. Also the rocky ground and the absence of brushwood made it almost impossible for the army to conduct an elaborate formal siege. The only course remaining was to bombard the Turks in their stony perches.

The Germans were loud in their accusations against the Venetian artillery commander, Count San Felice, who adjusted the range of the mortars by the elevation of the barrels, rather than the Germanic method of measuring out greater or lesser quantities of gunpowder for the charge. The shooting was certainly wild. At Navarino in 1686 only 2 per cent of the bombs actually hit the fortress – out of the other shells, some flew overhead and into the sea on the far side, some split on the rocks, and the rest landed in the besiegers' own trenches.

The apogee of the conquests was reached in 1687. The Christians secured their hold on the Morea, and in September more than ten thousand Italian and German troops were ferried over the Gulf of Aegina to Porto Leoni (Piraeus), the port of Athens. Porto Leoni and Athens were undefended, but six hundred determined Turks and twenty-eight guns were ensconced on the Acropolis rock just to the southwest of Athens town. The twelve hundred paces of the perimeter were enclosed by a high wall set with towers, and the steep hill slopes ruled out any possibility of attack except against the western side. Even here the Christians were confronted by the loopholed Odeum, two ledge batteries and the sixty foot-high wall itself. The Swedish field-marshal Königsmarck, commander of the land forces, found that 'even the most experienced general would be embarrassed to decide where he ought to attack' (Schwenke, 1854, 148).

On 22 September 1687 the Venetians began the siege by establishing a battery of four 500-pounder mortars on the Areopagus Hill to the west of the Acropolis. The notorious San Felice was in charge, and, as might have been expected, many of his bombs landed in Athens. The deafened and dusty townspeople addressed their complaints to Königsmarck, who obligingly moved two mortars to the eastern side of the Acropolis. These pieces scored several hits on the prominent Parthenon on the summit, but they caused no significant damage until a Lüneburg lieutenant adjusted the range on the evening of the 27th, and succeeded in blowing up a magazine. The explosion buried two hundred Turks, and gave that cold pagan monument a new and picturesque aspect.

On the next day a further bomb caused an extensive conflagration, and the last hopes of the garrison were dashed by the failure of a force of Turkish cavalry to break through the Christian positions. On the 29th the Turks capitulated for a free evacuation.

The rest was something of an anti-climax. Athens and the Acropolis were very soon abandoned as untenable, for the Turks still lurked off the coast of Thessaly on the large island of Euboea, where they held the useful fortress of Negroponte (Chalcis). From here they could pass at will to the mainland over a bridge. In 1687, when the capture of Negroponte might have been practicable, the Venetians had preferred the empty conquest of Athens. Afterwards the reduction of Negroponte proved to be beyond the power of the Christians. An expeditionary force made a landing in 1689, but it was almost immediately overtaken by the plague. Königsmarck himself died on 15 September, and the surviving Germans were ordered home to defend the empire against the French.

The Venetians were now reduced to their own resources, and the Morea was increasingly troubled by Turkish raids over the Isthmus of Corinth. This neck of land was not properly secured until 1696–7, when the Venetians adopted the plans of the Austrian gunner Steinau and their own major-general of artillery Jacob Richards, who suggested that watch-towers and redoubts should be built in the mountains north of the Isthmus to guard the passes from Megara and Thebes. Richards was even inspired to suggest that the Republic should bring a regiment of one thousand Irish troops into the service, and settle the men and their families in the Morea as the foundation of an Irish military colony (20 March 1698, Stowe Mss 460, British Museum). If the proposal had been carried out, it would certainly have produced the most bizarre of all the seventeenth-century military borders.

Meanwhile the Venetians had been making solid progress in the Adriatic provinces with the help of the local tribes, and by the late 1690s the Turks had been expelled from the Croatian coastlands and the area between the banks of the Unna and the northern plateau of Montenegro. The Venetians would probably have been well advised to confine their efforts to this part of the world from the first. An Englishman commented:

It lies just at their doors; it would make their dominion almost as weighty on this side of the gulf (the upper Adriatic) as on the other; and it would establish and secure their sovereignty over that sea, something better than their yearly marrying their Doge to it. Of all the places in the world it lies most convenient for them: one foot of ground in Dalmatia is worth two or three elsewhere. (Anon., 1689, 39)

By 1699 Turk and Venetian were equally spent. In the Peace of Carlowitz the Turks ceded the Morea to Venice, and renounced all Dalmatia except for a narrow corridor which led to the sea at the independent republic of Ragusa.

The Venetians did what they could to entrench themselves in their newly won Greek empire. Powerful bastions were built at Koron and Methone, and between 1711 and 1714 the French engineers La Salle and Levasseur designed and constructed a remarkable series of five detached forts on the summit of the Palamedi Mountain above Napoli di Romania. The Palamedi forts represented one of the last great achievements of Venetian fortress-

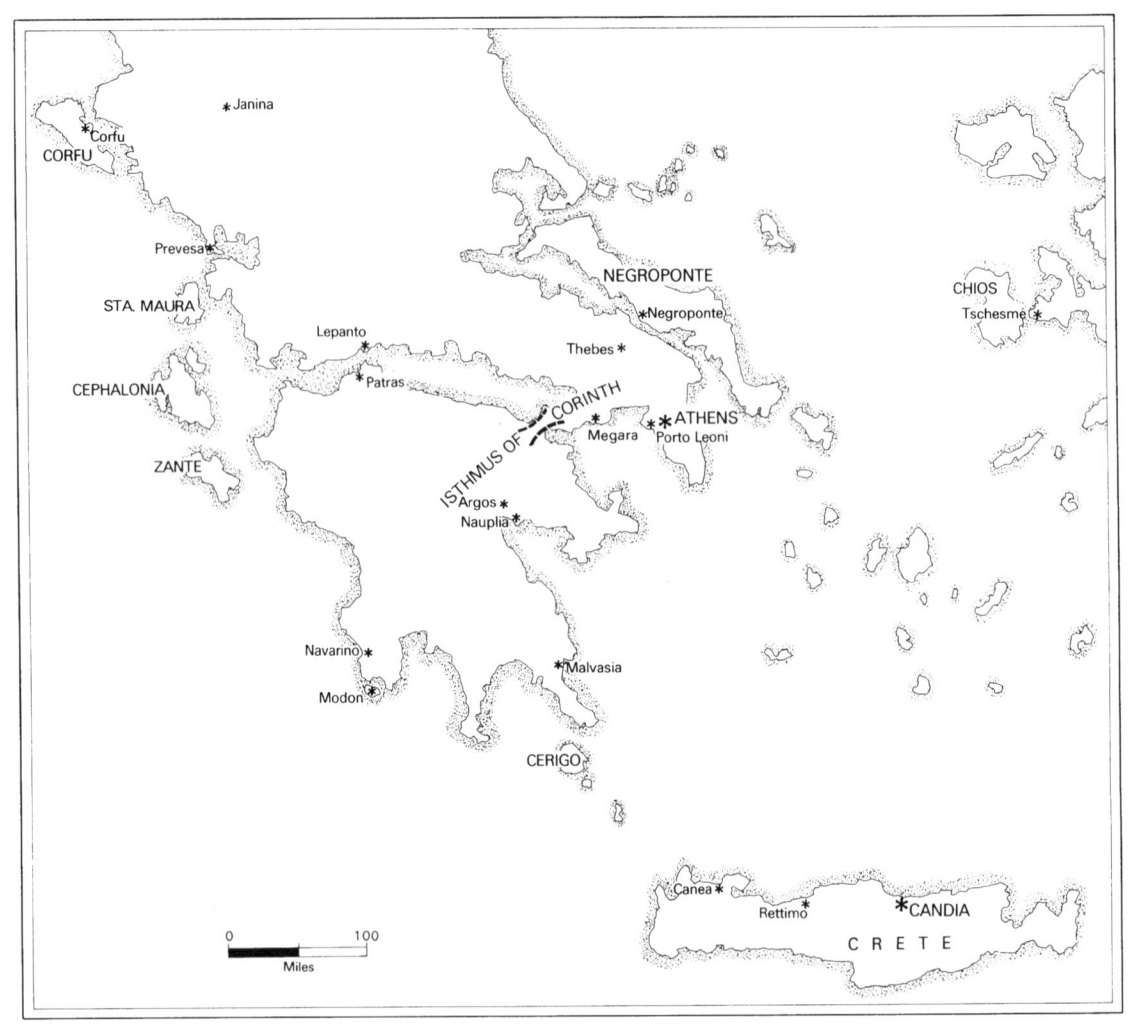

Southern Greece and Crete

building, but static defences like these were not enough to secure an empire which had expanded beyond all tenable limits. The Venetians had enjoyed adventitious foreign help in the 1680s, but the crusading spirit of the European princes was in temporary abeyance, and the Republic was thrown almost entirely upon the resource of its own decadent military institutions.

The Turks gathered enough confidence to re-open the war in 1714, and in the following year they overran the whole of the Morea in a single campaign. The proud Palamedi forts were abandoned after an eight-day defence. The collapse bears all the marks common to such notorious disintegrations of fortress systems as occurred in Holland in 1672 and Prussia in 1806 – we encounter decaying works, elderly commandants, a general relaxation of military standards after a decade or more of peace, and a feeling of alienation between the garrisons and the populations.

The defence of the Adriatic 1716–18
The loss of the Morea was a humiliating reverse. What was far more serious was the Turkish threat to Corfu, the northernmost of the Ionian Islands and the guardian of the mouth of the Adriatic. Prince

Eugene of Savoy, who was no alarmist, feared that the fall of Corfu would open the way to the invasion of Italy and a Turkish penetration of the Alps, and he persuaded his master the Emperor to renew the old Venetian alliance.

Fortunately, the Venetian Senate secured the services of the Saxon veteran Count Johann von der Schulenburg, one of those useful Germans who were wont to put in an appearance in the hour of need. In 1716 Schulenburg hastened to Corfu to build up the landward defences of the fortress of the same name, and

to this end I laid out six places of arms, and made bonnets of timber in front of some of the salient angles. I dug retrenchments and caponnières in the ditches and prepared mines and fougasses. Generally speaking I made every conceivable and practicable provision for the internal and external defence of the fortress. (Schulenburg, 1834, II, 77)

In 1717 the Turks ferried thirty thousand troops from the mainland and began the siege. The situation of the neighbouring hills greatly favoured the attack, but the progress of the operation suffered a grave setback on 19 August, when the Turks captured the Scarpone outwork but almost at once lost it again to an enterprising sortie. They were afraid of being stranded on Corfu, and shortly afterwards they raised the siege and returned to the mainland. The significance of the Corfu episode was not confined to the Adriatic, for their diversion of Turkish

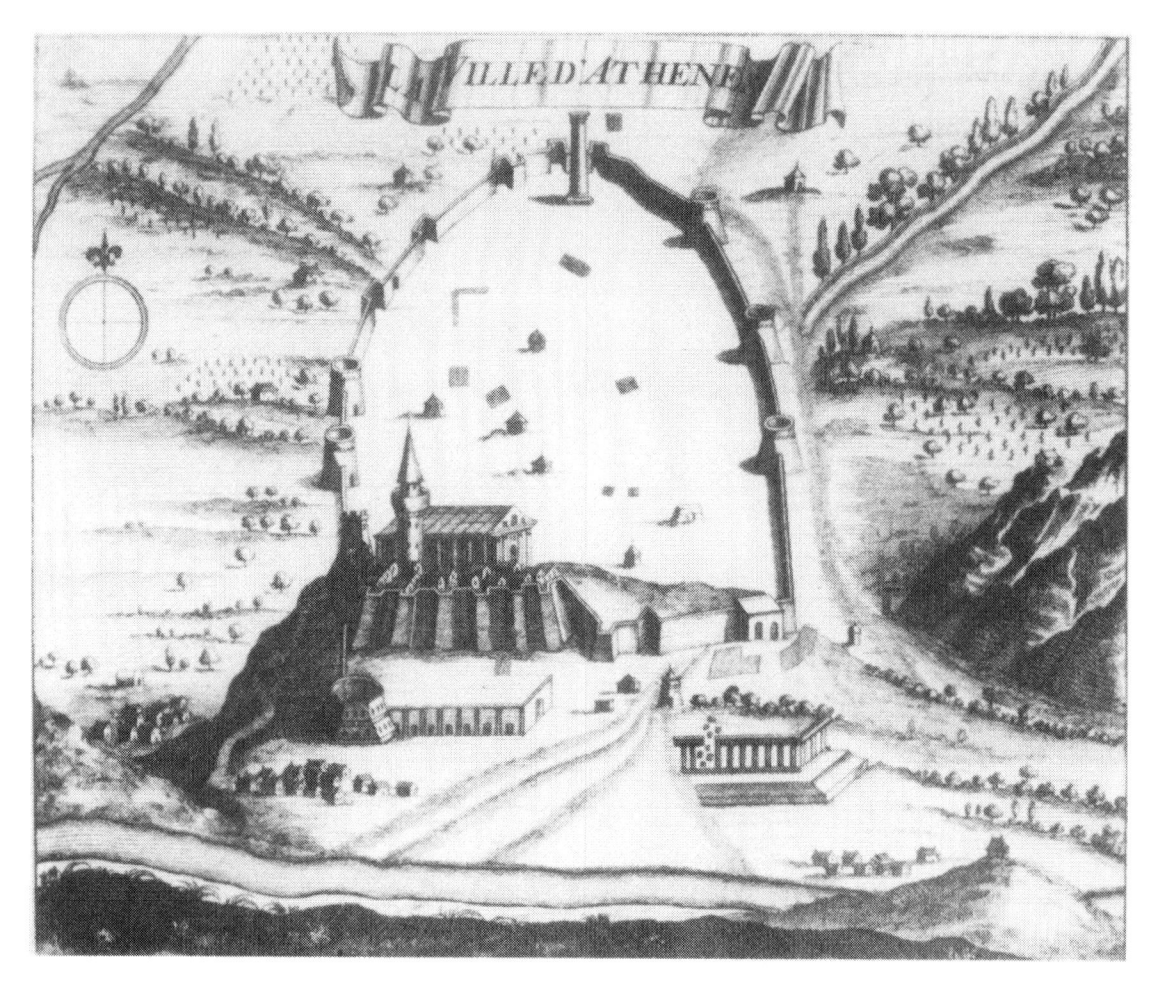

139 The Athens Acropolis as a Turkish fortress (Coronelli, 1687)

forces weakened their army on the Danube, and so contributed to their defeat at Peterwardein.

The initiative now lay with the Christians. Schulenburg wisely set himself against exotic expeditions in the old style, and persuaded the Venetians that they ought to reduce the Adriatic coastlands step by step. This was the best means to assure Corfu and the island of Santa Maura (Levkas) – 'the portals towards the Levant' (*ibid.*, II, 73). The Venetians got off to a good start by bombarding and capturing Preveza in 1717, but in the following year Captain-General Pisani committed the force to an attack on the very strong fortress of Dulcigno, which was an over-ambitious operation. The siege of Dulcigno was still in progress when an order came to cease hostilities.

The peace settlement of 1718 confirmed the Venetians in possession of Corfu and a good defensive border in Albania and Dalmatia. Having performed its last service to Christendom, the Republic settled into its final decades of gorgeous decline. The Venetians had to abandon all thought of joining the other powers in further adventures, for the cost of maintaining a defensive posture was as much as the treasury could bear. By the middle of the eighteenth century the trans-Adriatic provinces were bringing in an annual revenue of 210,000 ducats, but the upkeep of their fortifications and garrisons cost that amount and 45,000 more.

The Empire and the defence of the land avenue

Central Europe in danger 1663–83

In the early 1660s the Austrian monarchy proved to be slow to respond to the expansion of Turkish power through the pitiful remnants of Christian Hungary. The Austrian sympathisers in Transylvania were beaten down with scarcely a fight, and the only sense of urgency was displayed by the independently-minded Hungarian magnate Nikolaus Zriny, who began work on his new fortress of Serinvár (Zrinyburg) south of the Danube at the confluence of the Mur and the Drava (Drau), so as to counter the Turkish stronghold of Kanisza.

In 1663 Ahmed Köprülü surprised the Austrians by launching a sudden offensive along the north bank of the Danube. On 24 September the guardian fortress of Neuhäusel succumbed to a formal siege, and now at last the Austrian court was afflicted with

so dreadful apprehensions of the Ottoman fortune and fury, that they hastened the finishing of the works and fortifications of Vienna; cutting down all the woods and bocage thereabouts, which might benefit or shelter the enemy. (Rycaut, 1679–80, 'Mahomet IV', 143)

An army of twenty-three thousand Austrians and Hungarians began 1664 in fine style, when they burnt Suleiman's famous old bridge over the Drava at Esseg, thereby breaking the communication between the two principal Turkish fortresses on the Danube – Belgrade and Ofen. After this prosperous start the campaign was ruined by the wranglings between Zriny and the imperial commander Montecuccoli. The Christian army failed to take Kanisza. Worse still, the Turks riposted by reducing the gallant little fortress of Serinvár, and Zriny left the army in disgust. For a time Austria was again threatened by invasion, this time along the southern bank of the Danube. Montecuccoli fought the Turks at St Gotthard-on-the Raab on 1 August. However, the Turkish army was still formidable, and Montecuccoli's master, Emperor Leopold I, still regarded the Hungarian theatre as an annoying diversion from affairs in the West. Hence he shortly afterwards concluded peace at Vasvár. By the very disadvantageous terms Austria renounced Neuhäusel and Grosswardein, and promised never to rebuild Serinvár. The integrity of the Neutra line was broken, and the Austrians were forced to bolster up their weakened defences north of the Danube by building their new fortress of Leopoldstadt on the rearward line of the Waag.

Ahmed Köprülü was satisfied with the Vasvár provisions, as he had every reason to be, and he lived in peace with the Austrians until he died in 1676. He was succeeded as grand vizier by the fanatically anti-Austrian Kara Mustafa. The French were quick to sense the change of mood in Constantinople, and in 1677 their envoy gave the Turks the plans of Raab and Komorn. These valuable documents had been obtained through the good offices

Austro-Hungarian borderlands

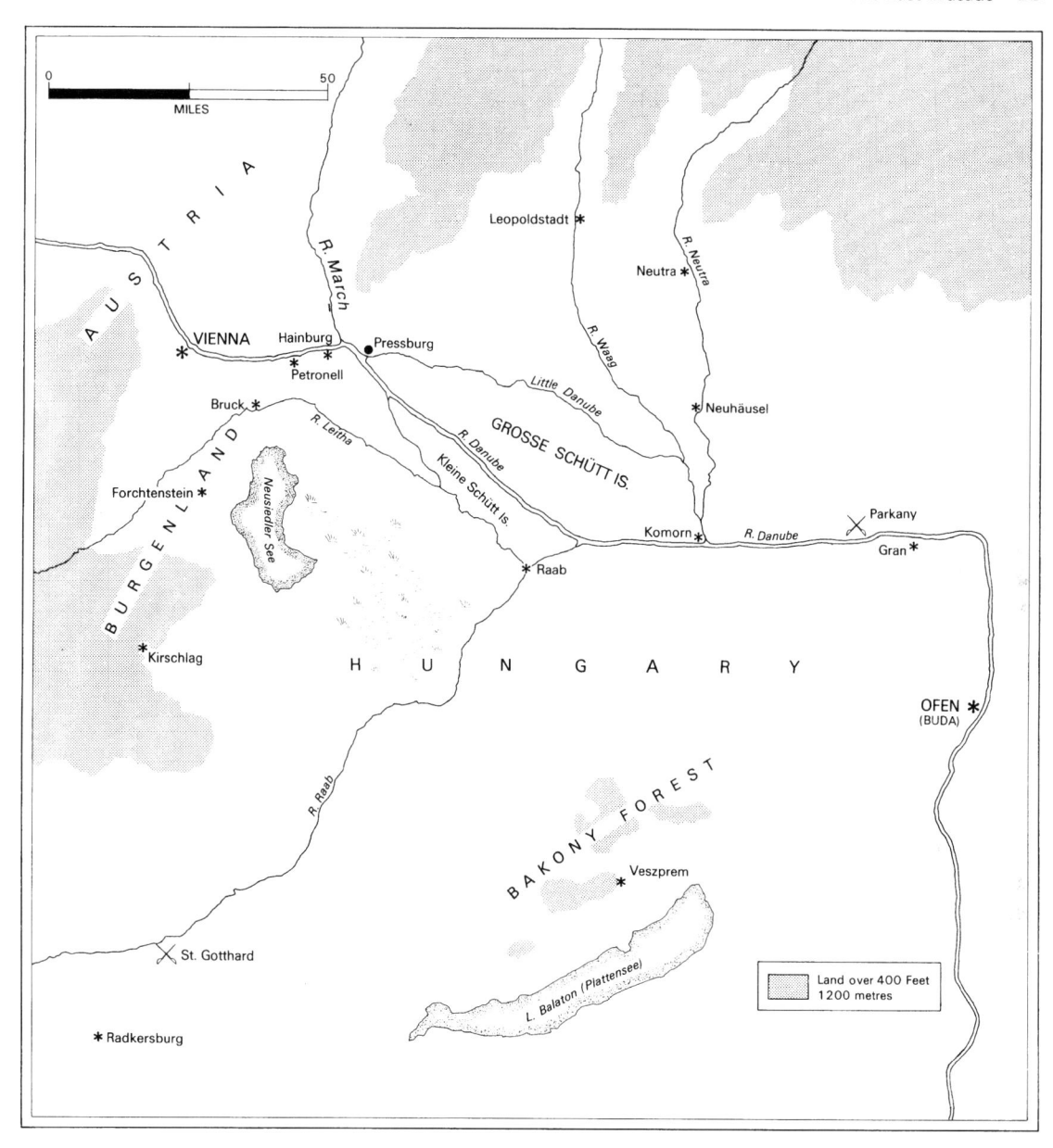

of a French Jesuit. The Turks looked on with a benevolent eye when the Hungarian magnate Imre Thököly entered into open rebellion against the Austrians in 1678, and gained the highlands of Upper Hungary. In 1682 the Ottoman-Hungarian friendship ripened into a full alliance, and the Turks made ready to renew the war with Austria.

In part the Turkish aim appears to have been the realistic one of stabilising their northern and northwestern frontiers by creating a vassal Hungarian buffer zone. However, Sultan Mehmed IV and some of his officers opposed the war (at least according to the chronicler Silahdar), and the initiative in fact derived from the Grand Vizier, whose character and ambitions are now recognised to have been crucial in determining the outcome of this new adventure. Kara Mustafa was greedy for power and money, and a man of cruelty even by the standards of his culture and time. He was by turns active and enterprising, and paralysed by the onset of indecision and superstitious fears. In his present undertaking he intended not, indeed, to overthrow the Christian West, but to return from campaign with such a prize as would reaffirm his power in Constantinople beyond all challenge.

The Austrians had for some time expected what was in store, and after carrying through a slight reduction in their forces after the Peace of Nijmegen in 1679, they actually raised new regiments in the years 1681 and 1682 – something that was highly unusual in peacetime. During the late war in the West, the sieges of Bonn, Trier and Philippsburg had already brought together some of the most important members of the team which was to shoulder the responsibility for defending the Danube against the Turks, namely Duke Charles of Lorraine (the future commander of the field army), Rüdiger von Starhemberg (commandant of Vienna in the great siege), and Margrave Hermann of Baden (President of the *Hofkriegsrath* from 1679). It was at the instigation of Baden that another of their old comrades, the much-travelled Georg Rimpler, was recruited in 1681 as chief engineer of the Empire and the Austrian Hereditary Lands at the enormous salary of two thousand florins per annum.

What made Rimpler so valuable was that he brought together a formidable book knowledge with a long experience of fortress warfare with the Swedish, Venetian, French and imperial armies. He had taken part in the last stage of the defence of Candia in 1669, and from this episode he derived a strategic doctrine of warfare against the Turks. This was committed to paper in Rimpler's *Befestigte Festung* of 1674. According to Rimpler, everything came down to a proper balance between fortifications and the mobile elements, and he maintained that the static defences must be 'arranged in such a way that they will be effectively co-ordinated with the forces on land and sea' (Kittler, 1951, 177). The numerical superiority of the Turks, and their aggressive manner of operations, indicated that the Christians should stand on the defensive in the initial phase of the war, then go over to the counter-attck after the invaders had been worn down.

Now Rimpler was able to apply his notions to the defence of the Danubian border. He made some urgent representations to the *Hofkriegsrath* on this head in June 1682, and he was finally rewarded by an Imperial resolution of 18 December, which sanctioned a detailed scheme.

North of the Danube the line of the Neutra had ceased to offer an adequate defence, now that the Turks held Neuhäusel as an enclave, and thereby interposed themselves between the fortress of Neutra and the Danube. It was all the more important for the Austrians to hold the fortresses of Leopoldstadt and Trentschin on the Waag, and maintain their ultimate defences along the March and at Pressburg.

At the centre of the Danubian defence rested the powerful Italian-style fortress of Komorn, situated on an island at the confluence of the Neutra and the two Danube arms which formed the huge marshy island of the Grosse Schütt.

More interesting to the strategists, however, were the plains, rivers, lakes and marshes south of the Danube. Here the rearward line was formed by the Leitha, which, together with Wiener Neustadt and other strongpoints, defended the way to the Alpine passes. In front of the Leitha, Rimpler expected that the conformation of the water obstacles would funnel the Turkish advance against the fortress of Raab, which stood little more than seventy miles from Vienna at the confluence of the River Raab and the

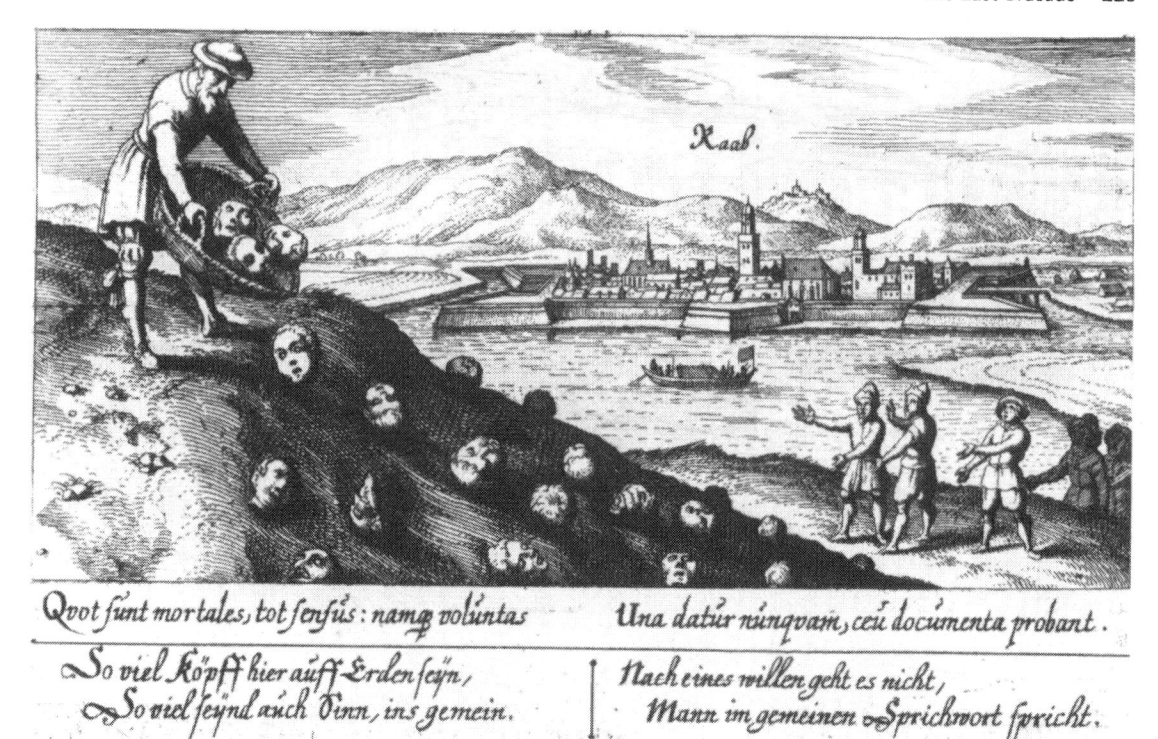

Quot sunt mortales, tot sensus: namque voluntas   Una datur nunquam, ceu documenta probant.

So viel Köpff hier auff Erden seyn,   Nach eines willen geht es nicht,
So viel seynd auch Sinn, ins gemein.   Mann im gemeinen Sprichwort spricht.

140 Raab, with reminders of the barbarities of the Turkish wars

southern arm of the Danube. This was where Rimpler intended to hold the Turks in the first, attritional stage of the coming war. Raab was given the first priority in labour and materials, and Rimpler received dictatorial powers to enable him to carry out the necessary work.

The Turks were very slow to make their appearance, which gave time for Rimpler to make his fortifications, and for the imperial diplomats to cement an alliance with King John III Sobieski of Poland. This respite was the consequence of the alternating haste and delay that were to characterise the Turkish conduct of the campaign of 1683. War against the Emperor had been declared on 2 January, months before the Ottomans were able to complete their march of hundreds of miles from their base areas. There was a long halt in Belgrade, and another while the Turks repaired the old bridge over the Drava at Esseg, but finally in the midsummer Kara Mustafa was ready to invade the Habsburg lands with 90,000 Turkish combatants and 20,000 Tartar auxiliaries. On 25 June, to the consternation of his subordinates, he announced that he was not interested in reducing the frontier strongholds, according to the accepted rules of Danubian warfare, and that he intended instead to push straight on to the 'golden apple' of Vienna.

Faced with somebody as unpredictable as Kara Mustafa, the Austrians were thrown into disarray. All told, Duke Charles of Lorraine had only about 33,000 troops at his disposal, and he lost valuable time by making a demonstration against the Turkish fortress of Neuhäusel. The Ottomans failed to respond, and the Austrians had to march south to confront the Turkish hosts which appeared to be intent on reducing Raab. On 1 July the Tartars swam the River Raab ten miles above the fortress, and Charles, who feared that the Turkish army was about to turn his right flank, promptly left Raab to its fate and fell back in the direction of Vienna. He was overhauled by a Turkish force at Petronell on 7 July, and received such a fright that he abandoned the Leitha line as well and gave the enemy a clear run to Vienna. However, he could have been mauled

Löwel Bastion **Burg Ravelin** **Burg Bastion**

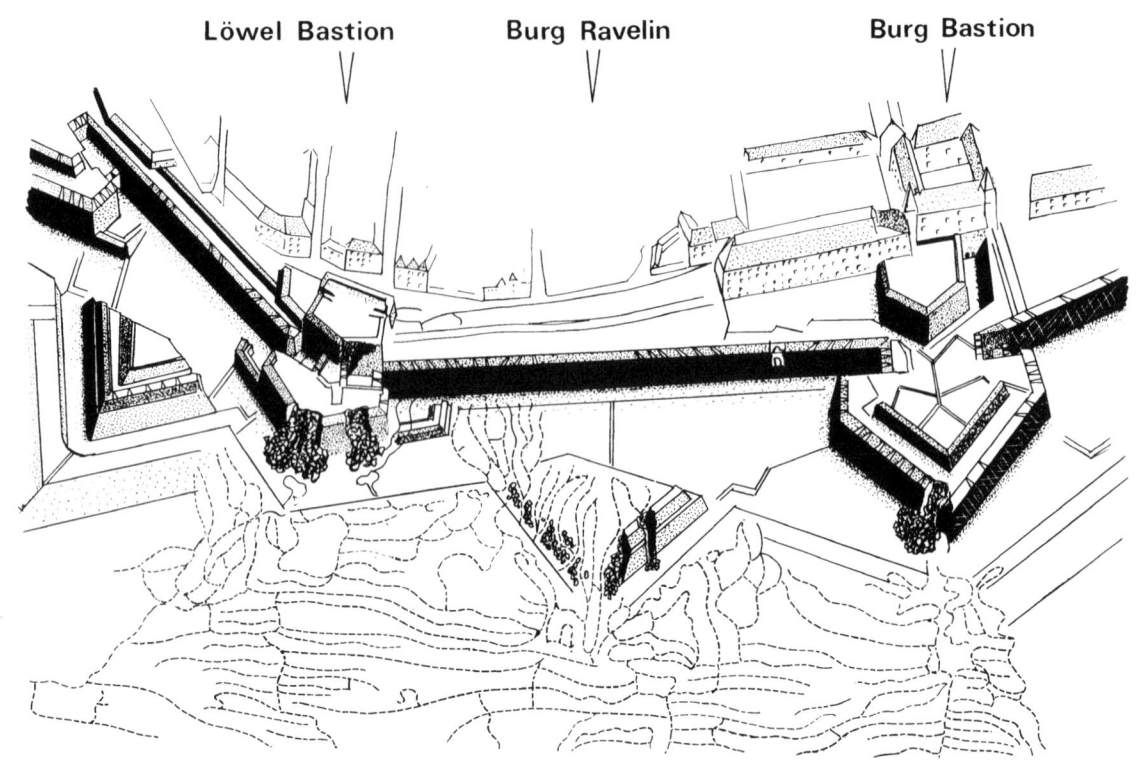

141 Siege of Vienna 1683

much more severely still, for Kara Mustafa held back the main Turkish army in front of Raab. The Grand Vizier had been gripped by a fit of doubt, and he had sent a messenger to Sultan Mehmed IV asking for his retrospective approval for the decision to move on Vienna. This third Turkish delay proved invaluable for the garrison of Vienna, which had been left to face the enemy unsupported. After the elapse of seven days Kara Mustafa left Raab blockaded by 12,000 troops (overturning the calculations of Rimpler, who had hoped to check the entire Ottoman army), and at last on 14 July 1683 the first of the 25,000 tents of the Turkish host appeared on the levels to the west of Vienna.

Every five generations or so Mars called the Viennese to account by planting a hostile army in front of the gates. The Turks had last descended on the place as long ago as 1529, and now in 1683 it was up to the engineer Georg Rimpler to review the defences of the city. He drew up the necessary plans between 15 January and 20 February, and his intention was to enable the sixteenth-century brick enceinte to put up a step-by-step resistance. Rimpler had proclaimed as a matter of principle: 'We must prepare the defences in good time, so as to be well dug in on all the important locations in advance. This is much better than having to meet the attack by constructing new lines of defence in the presence of the enemy' (Kittler, 1951, 217).

The experience of the siege of Candia indicated that the main threat would be posed by the Turkish miners, and Rimpler correctly anticipated that the presence of the Danube and the little river Wien would rule out approaches from the north and east. The resources of the defence were therefore concentrated on the south-west and southern sides of the city, along the fronts which were formed by the Mölker-, Löwel-, Burg- and Augustiner-Bastions and the intervening ravelins, especially the Burg-Ravelin. Embrasures were cut through the parapets of the existing works, to afford some protection to the artillery, and, where space allowed, strong retrenchments, with ditches and palisades, were built inside the bastions and ravelins. On the far side of the ditch the covered way was furnished with palisaded traverses and other strongpoints, in accordance with Rimpler's maxim: 'It is a demonstrable fact that a covered way, at small expense, may be so arranged as to cause the enemy more trouble than a strong fortress in the present conventional manner' (*Dreyfacher Tractat*, 1674, Kittler, 1951, 112).

In the actual ditch a lower outer rampart (faussebraye) was built close to the foot of the revetment, and a network of caponnières, or 'bonnets' in Rimpler's parlace, was run from the ravelins to the shoulder angles of the adjacent bastions. These caponnières were particularly close to Rimpler's heart. They were low-lying and apparently insignificant loopholed galleries, with sides built up of earth, wicker-work or other materials, and roofed over with planks and earth. They were difficult for the besieger to see and hit, while offering the defender almost complete protection from the elements and enemy fire.

Much remained beyond remedy. General Caplirs reported that there was

reason to fear the enemy miners, and especially at the Burg-Bastion, since it is devoid of vaulted galleries and countermines which might have enabled us to act against the enemy. Moreover we lack qualified miners, and in their place we have to employ men who do not have a full understanding of this trade – when they hear the enemy at work they run away, instead of advancing to meet them, such is their lack of experience and resolution. (Duncker, 1893, 269)

The adjoining Löwel-Bastion was particularly narrow and badly proportioned, and lacked the room for strong interior defences. Any breach here was therefore considered more than usually dangerous.

The garrison was under the overall command of Ernst Rüdiger von Starhemberg. Marshal Villars offers the sour comment: 'of all the qualities necessary for war, the only one which he is allowed to possess is courage, a trait which is rather more dangerous than useful to a general who is in sole command'. More narrowly he criticised Starhemberg for his policy of launching frequent sorties, instead of conserving the strength of the garrison. 'Foreign nations are more enthusiastic in their praises of Starhemberg than are the Germans, perhaps because they are envious of him or because they are better informed' (Villars, 1884–9, I, 438).

Closely associated with Starhemberg and indeed with the business of the defence as a whole was the ailing Bürgermeister Andreas von Liebenberg, who set an example to his fellow-citizens by transporting loads of earth on a barrow in the last days before the Turks arrived.

Christoph Börner, the artillery commander, was a self-made man of north German Protestant stock, like Rimpler himself. Börner's wanderings had begun from the day when, as an apprentice to a Berlin shoemaker, he had been ordered to buy a bottle of the well-known Bärnau beer. He walked all the way to Bärnau, instead of buying the beer locally, and he was so terrified when he discovered his mistake that he buried the bottle under a tree and fell into the hands of an Austrian recruiting party. He rose speedily in the Imperial artillery, that most democratic of arms, and after playing a distinguished part in the defence of Vienna he became a full general and Prince Eugene's right-hand man in gunnery matters. He was still troubled about the incident at Bärnau, and he could not rest until, as a very senior and respected commander, he returned to the spot and dug up the beer in its hermetically-sealed container.

For a city of the size of Vienna the garrison was a small one, of 10,000 regular troops. Starhemberg also commanded an urban militia of about eighteen hundred men, though these folk lacked the experience to be employed in the direct combat role in the early stages of the siege. Vienna was adequately, but not lavishly provisioned, and many of the 80,000 civilians enclosed within were refugees, who lacked shelter and food of their own. As some compensation Starhemberg owned the highly unusual advantage of a convincing superiority in artillery over his besiegers. Vienna was armed with no less than 312 cannon, of which forty-seven were 24-pounders or pieces of still heavier calibre.

The Turks, as a consequence of Kara Mustafa's

dash for Vienna, brought with them only five mortars and 112 cannon. They had no heavy pieces at all, and only seventeen of medium calibre (up to $22\frac{1}{2}$-pounders) (Mörz, 1983, 19). However, Kara Mustafa commanded a total of 90,000 men, of whom 15,000–20,000 were elite regulars. He was well provided with miners, and among his engineers he counted a certain 'Ahmed Bey', a renegade Capuchin monk who had a good knowledge of the enceinte from a visit he had made to Vienna in 1682, in the company of an Hungarian delegation.

From the beginning the Ottomans directed their attack with speed and skill, and already on 14 July they exploited a gross oversight on the part of the defenders, who had failed to demolish the nearest houses and gardens of the Suburbs:

And this is truly a sign of Allah's grace, for which we can never thank him enough [wrote the Ottoman Master of Ceremonies]. For if we had not enjoyed the facility of this Suburb, we would have had to open our trenches at a great distance, and spend several days in completing our first siegeworks. As things are, anybody who has to go to the saps can ride on horseback right up to the entry to the trenches. In short, the entire history of the Turkish Empire shows no precedent for what we have done here, namely, to lay out our trenches and siegeworks in a suburb, and amid palaces with all their gardens and pavilions. (Kara Mustafa, 1960, 31–2)

From the convenient base line offered by the Suburbs, the Janissaries drove forward three groups of trenches against the Löwel-Bastion, the Burg-Ravelin and the Burg-Bastion. The first batteries opened fire on the night of 22–23 July, and on the next day the Turks began the battle for the covered way when they exploded mines opposite the salients of the two bastions. The Christians responded by throwing in repeated sorties, and it was on the evening of 25 July, in the course of a successful counter-attack against a mine breach in the counterscarp of the Burg-Ravelin, that Rimpler's left arm was shattered. He was taken back to the city, where he died early on 3 August.

By that time the Turks had conquered a long stretch of the covered way, and they began to effect eight or nine 'descents' and 'passages' of the ditch. In this second stage of the siege, the battle for the ditch, the Turks worked forward by sap, mine and assault, while the Christians continued to launch their sorties, and maintained a deadly fire from Rimpler's low-lying caponnières. On the afternoon of 12 August the Turks exploded two mines at the salient of the Burg-Ravelin, and established their first lodgment in this triangle of earth and disintegrating brick. The defenders stood their ground on the ravelin until the Turks succeeded in burning one of the flanking caponnières, and virtually embraced the work with their saps. On the night of 2–3 September Starhemberg accordingly evacuated the ravelin and the surviving caponnières, having contested the ditch for a month. Now everything came down to the defence of the main enceinte.

The Turks burrowed ceaselessly through the stony earth, covering themselves as they went by roofings of planks, tree trunks and sandbags. All the time the Austrians pelted them with what seemed an endless supply of earthenware hand grenades, and every now and again a determined counter-attack sought to winkle the Turks out of the lodgments and reclaim the ground which had been lost.

The strain of the continuous battle was telling heavily on all the belligerents. The Turkish troops as a whole were disaffected from Kara Mustafa, on account of the miserly way he doled out their pay. The Tartar leaders were offended by the rude things he said to them, and their men wished to return to their native steppes with the booty they had garnered in the countryside. More serious still the Janissaries, the kernel of the Turkish forces, were disturbed by the elapse of the customary forty days maximum of Turkish siegework, and they feared the prospect of some deal between Kara Mustafa and the garrison, which might deprive them of the sack and plunder of Vienna.

On the Christian side the garrison was reduced to 4,000 effectives, and the artillerymen refused to stand by their guns unless they were awarded heavy cash payments. The citizens themselves appeared to lose interest in the survival of Vienna, and Starhemberg had to threaten them with death before they would set to work on what were literally the last ditch defences.

On 9 September the Turkish mines blew down the salient and one of the faces of the Löwel-Bastion. The Ottoman diarist testifies that the deed

gave rise to a struggle of great violence, and the Infidels were smitten so hard by the fire of our cannon and muskets, the impact of the bombs and stones and the blows of our swords that they lost more men than in any episode since the beginning of the siege. In this sector the whole ground was covered with the bodies of our dead enemies. Our brave protagonists of the True Faith managed to take twenty-one heads, and were duly rewarded by the grand vizier. (Kara Mustafa, 1960, 100)

The assault was beaten off (though you would hardly believe it from the description which has just been given) and the Turks reverted to formal siegework, pushing saps from either side of the Burg-Ravelin against the curtain behind.

It is doubtful whether Vienna could have survived these last critical days without signs that help was at hand. On the night of 7–8 September signal rockets soared from the Vienna Woods to the west, and on the following days the observers in the tower of St Stephen's Cathedral saw the cavalry of a Christian army of relief skirmishing in the plain around Vienna. By now the Austrian field forces had been joined by the 21,000 troops of King John III Sobieski of Poland, and by contingents from Saxony, Bavaria and other German states, which together amounted to a respectable army of nearly 68,000 men. Finally on 12 September the Christian force came storming down from the Vienna Woods 'like a herd of maddened swine' (Kara Mustafa, 1960, 108).

The Turkish army was already worn down by sixty days of combat before Vienna, and it was further weakened on the day of battle by Kara Mustafa's decision to leave 10–15,000 troops in the trenches. The Turks were heavily defeated, and they streamed away to the east, spurred on their way by a sortie from Vienna.

The defeat of the Turks at Vienna marked the beginning of the recession of the Ottoman tide from Central Europe. The Austrians and Germans grew in military strength, experience and prestige, and non-French Christendom began to assume a united front with the formation of the Holy Alliance with the Pope and Venice in 1684, and the accession of the Russians to the league in 1686. Emperor Leopold I was weary of the responsibility for guarding the Rhine against France, and for the first time he began to look to the East, attracted by the prospect of making conquests on the Danube at the expense of the Turks. Austrian strategy thereby acquired a literal 'orientation', a process which was to leave the Habsburgs off their guard against a new enemy which appeared at their back door in 1740, in the shape of Brandenburg-Prussia.

Was western civilisation saved by the resistance and relief of Vienna? Almost certainly not, because it was never seriously in danger. Kara Mustafa's ambitions probably did not extend further than humiliating the Austrians, consolidating his own standing at the Ottoman court, and establishing Vienna as a north-western outpost of the Turkish empire. The Turks were now at the very limit of their strategic tether, and they would probably have been incapable of exerting themselves to build the city into a major offensive base. This would have required the unseating of some fundamental Ottoman military institutions.

A Turkish Vienna would nevertheless have remained a source of chronic instability in Central Europe, and the perceived threat to the security of several Christian states was powerful enough to bind them together for the defence of common interests and values. A century later the Poles observed with an ironic bitterness that they were losing their freedom to the very folk that John Sobieski had come to save in 1683, but they had established beyond any doubt 'the fact that Poland was and is a part and parcel of the Western world. The king's personal attachment to and understanding of Christianity can probably also be considered an expression of this reality' (Barker, 1983, 5–6).

The Western reconquest of Hungary 1684–1718
The Christian counter-attack began in 1684 in an extremely inauspicious style, when forty-three thousand Austrians, Germans and Hungarians made an unsuccessful and badly managed 104-day siege of Ofen (Buda) on the Danube, the chief fortress of Turkish Hungary. Beyond the Danube

King John Sobieski of Poland encountered a similar check at the fortress of Kamenets.

A little reflection told the Imperial command that it was rather absurd to think of taking Ofen as long as the Turks still held the fortress of Neuhäusel, which was sited well up the Danube, and offered them a base for their raids into Austria and Moravia. This pocket of resistance was finally eliminated on 19 August 1685, when a corps under Field-Marshal Caprara stormed into the place and cut down the one thousand defenders *in der Furia*. The whole siege had lasted a month, and was creditable enough by the standards of the Eastern theatre, though it was pointed out that 'a French army would have had it in a week. They took Maastricht in fifteen days [see p. 12], which was twice as strong, had thrice as many men and was full as well provided' (Anon., 1689, 26).

In 1686 the Duke of Lorraine and Elector Max Emanuel of Bavaria brought an imperial army of seventy-four thousand men before Ofen. The besiegers made short work of the Lower Town, as had happened in 1684. A battery of six 24-pounders effected a breach so wide that 'three waggons could have been driven into it abreast' (Dolleczek, 1887, 264), and on 24 June Abdurrahman Pasha withdrew his garrison into the Upper Town on its high comb of rock.

On 22 July the main Turkish magazine exploded. The Duke of Berwick was an eye-witness, and records that 'the noise was terrible, all the windows three miles round were broken, and there were fragments of wall of an immense size, thrown on the other side of the Danube' (Berwick, 1779, I, 11). There were hopes that Ofen would capitulate there and then, but Abdurrahman rejected the summons 'in full trust in the assistance of Allah and his Prophet' (Zinkeisen, 1854–7, IV, 124).

The Turks beat off two determined assaults, on 27 July and 3 August, which seemed to indicate that Abdurrahman's prayers were being heard, and for much of the remainder of August the Christians had to slow down the progress of the siege, for they were compelled to detach forty thousand men to hold off

142 Explosion of the Turkish magazine at Ofen 1686. The event made a strong impression on the baroque imagination

143 Another view of the same

an army of relief. As was usual on such occasions, the Brandenburgers were bumptious and condescending:

I only wish that the Austrians would take prompt and military measures in their conduct of the siege [proclaimed Colonel Belling]. If they had done so, they would have had Ofen long ago. As things are ... they have committed so many blunders ... that I see no prospect of them ever taking a strong fortress like this. (Haake, 1910, 35)

The Duke of Lorraine re-sited his guns and finally cracked open the defences. He planted a battery of sixteen cannon on a nearby hill, which enabled the besiegers to direct their fire against the rear of a formidable retrenchment of earth-filled coffers. He placed another battery in an advanced position to the right of the original 'attack', and battered the inner wall at a point where it had no retrenchment. After these comprehensive preparations the besiegers launched a general assault on the night of 2–3 September and overpowered the two thousand surviving Turks. The body of the heroic Abdurrahman was retrieved from a pile of corpses, and was found to be covered with wounds.

In 1687 Lorraine managed to close with the elusive Turkish field army and defeat it at Mohács (Berg Harsan) on 12 August. This victory was the complement of the capture of Ofen, and it enabled the Imperialists to overrun the open country of Hungary as far as the Drava marshes. On 9 December Archduke Joseph of Austria could be crowned King of Hungary without any sense of incongruity.

In the following year the imperialists plucked up the courage to enter the Turkish preserve south of the Drava. The Turks had vanished from the open field, for their army had dissolved in mutiny, and Belgrade was taken by storm on 6 September. The year 1689 saw the new commander-in-chief, Margarve Ludwig of Baden, beat the Turks in three actions in Serbia, and take all the Danube fortresses from Widdin to Nikopolis. Within the Turkish empire the whiff of anarchy was in the air, with rebellion, mutiny, pestilence and crop failure threatening to bring orderly rule to an end. It seemed as if the work of Suleiman had been undone, and the Emperor and his advisers seriously debated whether the new Austrian border should extend as far as Constantinople, or merely up to Trajan's Wall.

In reality the Imperialists had already passed the line of equilibrium – the invisible border that was determined by the value of the leadership and the forces that were available to the fighting parties, and by their respective rates of 'strategic consumption'. The history of the next century was to show that it took unusually good leadership to enable the Austrians to hold the Danube quite so far downstream as Belgrade.

In 1690 the Austrian resources became perilously stretched through the necessity of putting two powerful armies into the field – one in the West against France, and the other in Transylvania to support the Habsburg party. The new grand vizier Mustafa Köprülü, another of the famous tribe, was therefore able to wipe out all the Austrian garrisons on the lower Danube in a matter of weeks. Belgrade fell to an assault on 8 October, and the integrity of the Danube defence line was therefore restored.

With the Austrians in possession of Ofen, and the Turks re-established at Belgrade, the strategic balance remained almost unaltered until the end of the war.

In 1692 the Austrians recaptured Grosswardein, which helped to strengthen the corridor to Transylvania, but they overreached themselves in 1693 when they made a new attack on Belgrade. The works had been reinforced in Western style by the Cretan renegade Cornaro, and the approach of an army of relief forced the Austrians to raise the siege in late August.

Otherwise the campaigns centred around the area of central Hungary north of Belgrade. At Peterwardein on the Danube the Austrians had a very useful camp from where they could observe Belgrade, while preserving the freedom to move laterally along the Drava in the south-west, or against the Theiss and the annoying Turkish fortress of Temesvár in the east. In 1697, therefore, the Sultan in person advanced with 100,000 men to crush the Austrian position. He was met and defeated at Zenta by the 35-year-old Prince Eugene of Savoy. Paradoxically, the Austrian lack of offensive force stood out more clearly than ever before, and Eugene warned in his victory report: 'I must

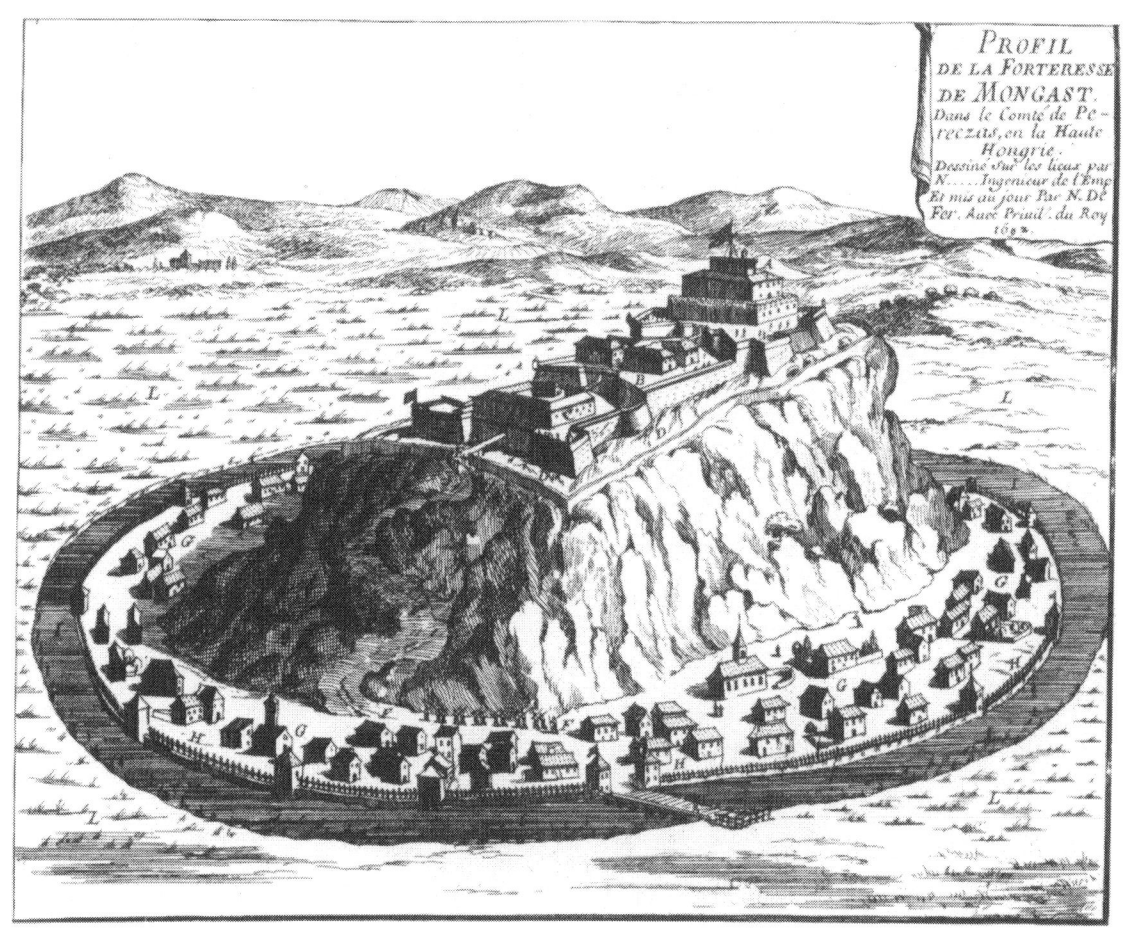

144 Munkacz, in the Carpathians. Typical of the smaller Austrian hill fortresses on the Hungarian theatre (De Fer, 1690–5)

humbly inform and assure Your Imperial Majesty that as long as the border fortresses are not put in a better state of defence, it will be impossible for us to move the army with freedom (Kriegsarchiv, 1876–91, II, Appx, 55).

Rather than continue to strive for hopeless goals, Austria and Turkey came to terms at the peace congress of Carlowitz in 1699. On the strategic flanks Austria retained Transylvania, and Croatia and Slavonia as far as the Unna; in the centre they kept Esseg and Peterwardein as the bulwarks of Ofen and an increasingly restless Hungary. The Turks, despite their losses, were still well-placed to meet the eventualities of a future war. The great base at Belgrade enabled them to operate with equal facility on the Sava and the middle Danube. On the eastern side of the great Danube bend the fortress of Temesvár guarded the remaining tract of Turkish Hungary, and positioned the Turks within fifty miles of the Austrian communications with Transylvania.

From 1703 until 1711 Hungary was swept by a great insurrection against the Austrians, and the Emperor was kept far too busy to think of expanding his borders any further to the east. He even found it necessary to furnish the suburbs of Vienna with a zigzag earthen rampart (the *Linienwälle*) as a safeguard against marauding Hungarian cavalry. When, at last, the Austrians were free to look ahead to the next confrontation with Turkey, Prince Eugene was appalled at the decay of the Hungarian fortresses, and the parlous state of their magazines. In despera-

238 The Last Crusade

tion the Austrians seized the private funds of two important Turkish officials, and devoted the money (400,000 florins in all) to restoring the eastern frontier. There was even enough cash to spare for an important new Transylvanian fortress called 'Karlsburg'. Work began in 1714, to the designs of Giovanni Morando Visconti, and the place was defensible by the end of 1716, though not completed for twenty-two years more.

Time was certainly at something of a premium, for in 1716 an army of 150,000 Turks descended on Hungary, in retaliation for the Emperor's new alliance with the Venetians (see p. 225). Eugene and his 64,000 men were shut up in the entrenched camp at Peterwardein, and they underwent two days of formal siege before sallying out on 5 August to beat the Turks in battle. Generals of an older generation would probably now have marched straight to Belgrade and catastrophe, but Eugene decided that he could most usefully devote the rest of the campaigning season to the capture of Temesvár – this would eliminate the last Turkish holding to the east of the great Danube bend, and protect the Austrian communications with Transylvania. The place surrendered on 13 October, after a costly and not particularly elegant siege.

Finally in 1717 Eugene brought the great age of the Imperial and Turkish wars to a fittingly spectacular end by going on to reduce Belgrade. In past decades both parties had invariably chosen to march along the right (west and south) bank of the Danube, whenever they were campaigning in the area between Ofen and Belgrade. They avoided the trouble of having to cross the Danube, but they were

145 The northern front at Karlsburg (Alba Iulia), Austria's principal fortress in Transylvania. The outer line of ravelins and envelope was a motif reproduced with some variations in the new works at Temesvár, which were a-building at the same time

forced to meet the Turks in their positions behind the transverse river line of the Drava. Eugene, on the other hand, preferred to make use of the wide operational base which he had secured when he conquered Temesvár and eastern Hungary in 1716. Forwarding his supplies and pontoons down the Dunavica and the Temes, he bridged the Danube below Belgrade at Pancsova, and on 19 June he appeared before the city itself. This wide, curling movement around the east of Belgrade is perhaps the closest eighteenth-century counterpart to the manoeuvre by which Napoleon contrived to isolate Mack at Ulm in 1805.

The core of the defence of Belgrade was formed by the fourteenth-century castle, which stood on a bluff rising 150 feet above the right (south) bank of the Danube. Along the foot of the plateau, on the river side, were crowded the houses of the Lower Town or Wasserstadt. Behind the castle, the landward slopes on the southern side were covered by the Varos suburb, whose bastioned works were built by renegade Christian architects in the 1690s, and formed a semi-circular perimeter extending from the Sava in the west to the Danube below Belgrade in the east.

Between 20 June and 9 July the Imperialists were hard at work building siege lines between the Sava and the Danube. The countervallation confronted the Varos suburb, and stretched for four and a half miles between the two rivers. The outer perimeter of Eugene's position was formed by a six-mile-long circumvallation.

Inside the siege lines foregathered a brilliant assembly of Europe's royal and noble houses, together with contingents of troops from most of the German states. Hundreds of thousands of fascines and gabions were fashioned by the united forces, and siege pieces to the number of two hundred were borne to Belgrade on the Danube, the Drava and the Theiss from the arsenals at Vienna, Ofen, Esseg, Szegedin and Peterwardein.

Active siege operations began on 23 July 1717, but the Imperial engineers had made little progress by the time the advance troops of the Grand Vizier's field army appeared on the 28th. The hills around Belgrade were soon covered with the red and green tents of the force of 150,000 Turks.

The next fortnight witnessed one of the last double sieges in history. On the night of 9-10 August the Austrians finally opened their first parallel against Belgrade. They kept up the bombardment at full intensity, and they were rewarded on the late afternoon of the 14th, when a lucky shot from a 10-pounder mortar bomb blew up the main Turkish magazine (see Duffy, 1975, 122-3). The minarets of the city mosques were swept away by the blast, and by the Turks' own estimate three thousand people lost their lives.

The surviving Turks harboured no thoughts of surrender. The truth was that Eugene was no better off than themselves. The Grand Vizier was thundering against the Christian camp with 130 cannon from the outside, and Eugene himself had to move his tent so as to gain some shelter from the shot. An officer with the Bavarian contingent writes that one day, while he was cowering on the lower banquette of the trench,

two soldiers were sitting side by side on the one above, with their backs against the parapet and their heads showing perhaps an inch and a half above it, when a ball tore away the earth just at this point and carried away the tops of their two skulls, which passed exactly over my head, covering my coat with the brains of these unfortunates. (Colonie, 1904, 435)

Altogether 90,000 troops were crammed into the increasingly dangerous and insanitary camp, and 'all this filth gave rise to much illness and engendered a great quantity of flies, which tortured man and beast alike' (Anon. account, Kriegsarchiv, 1876-91, XVII, 125).

By 15 August some of the Turkish saps had approached to within thirty paces of the circumvallation, which drove Eugene to take the same course he had followed when he had been surrounded by the Turks at Peterwardein the year before. On 16 August the Imperial army duly came out of its lines and routed the host of the Grand Vizier. Lieutenant-General George Browne was meanwhile left with 10,000 men to hold the siege trenches, but the defenders of Belgrade remained supine during the battle, and they were so taken aback by the defeat of the army of relief that they opened negotiations on the next day and capitulated on the 18th.

Thus the great age of the Baroque crusade came to an end amid clouds of sulphurous glory. By reducing Belgrade, the Austrians consolidated their hold on the Sava and the Hungarian Danube, and they helped to persuade the Turks to raise the siege of distant Corfu (see p. 225). The short and uneventful *Fieber-Campagne* of 1718 was closed by the Peace of Passarowitz, which recognised the Austrians in possession of Belgrade and the Sava fortresses.

The imperial achievement at Belgrade was therefore of high strategic and political significance. Its status as an engineering feat was, however, much lower – the ramparts had been surrendered intact, and Eugene had entered into possession of the fortress through the moral effects of his victory in the field, a kind of operation which suited German armies much better than did fortress warfare.

Turkey's northern neighbours, Poland and Russia 1672–1711

Even the extensive Hungarian theatre was tiny and compact, compared with the vast plains where the Ottoman empire gave on to Poland and Muscovy. Here too we notice a revival of Turkish confidence and offensive power. Poland and Russia, in contrast, were plagued by risings of Cossacks and discontented serfs, and Turkey seized the opportunity to claim the Polish Ukraine and begin hostilities in 1672.

In August of that year the Turks captured the key fortress of Kamenets. This gave them a firm base on the left bank of the Dniester, and opened up the whole of the south-west flank of the Polish Ukraine. John Sobieski campaigned gallantly against the Turks, first as Polish commander, then as king, but he was never able to redress the advantage which the enemy had gained.

In 1675 Sobieski was stretched to the utmost by the need to mount successive reliefs of the sorely-beset fortress of Lemberg, and in 1676 it was all he could do to hold the camp of Zuravno on the Dniester until hostilities petered out in general exhaustion. He had checked the further Turkish advance up the Dniester, but in the Treaty of Zuravno on 27 October he was forced to cede Podolia with Kamenets. It was to be much the same story in the war of the Holy Alliance, when the Poles laid vain siege to Kamenets in 1684 and again in 1687.

Russia's outpost in the western Ukraine was represented by the fortress of Chigirin, which stood among the marshes of the left bank of the Dnieper, half way between Kiev and the Zaporozhian Sech (the island fortress of the Dnieper Cossacks). Chigirin became the focus of Turkish ire in the Russo-Turkish War of 1677–81. An army of Turks and Tartars arrived before the place in the first year of the war, and cannonaded the castle with 36-pounder shot and 80-pounder bombs. 'Through the skill of their gunners, and the inexperience of the Russians in firing and concealing their own cannon, no less than seventeen of the best fortress pieces were knocked out in a few days' (Gordon, 1849–51, I, 438). Fortunately, the Scots engineer Patrick Gordon was at hand to help in the defence, and the Turks raised the siege on 28 August when a Russian army came to the relief. Chigirin withstood a further siege in 1678, again with Gordon's help, and a long drawn-out series of negotiations led to the Peace of Bakshai-Sarai in 1681, by which the Russians were confirmed in possession of Kiev and all its dependencies. The rest of the Ukraine west of the Dnieper was left as an independent buffer state.

The War of 1677–81 represented the first direct encounter of Russians and Turks since the siege of Astrakhan more than a century earlier. The Ottomans took a serious view of the development, and in the 1680s they did their best to fortify the main river entrances to the Black Sea. They strengthened the heavily fortified area of Azov still further, when they established the two Kalantshi castles a short distance up the Don. In the corresponding north-west corner of the sea they barred the mouth of the Dnieper by founding the fortress-towns of Kinburn and Ochakov, and planting the stronghold of Kasikermen a little way upstream.

The Turks had acted none too soon, for in 1689 the Russians sent an expedition against the Crimea, so inaugurating nearly two centuries of offensive warfare against the Black Sea coasts. The début was not particularly impressive, for the Russian army foundered from thirst amid the arid plains of the summer steppes without ever coming near the Lines of Perekop, which guarded the narrow isthmus lead-

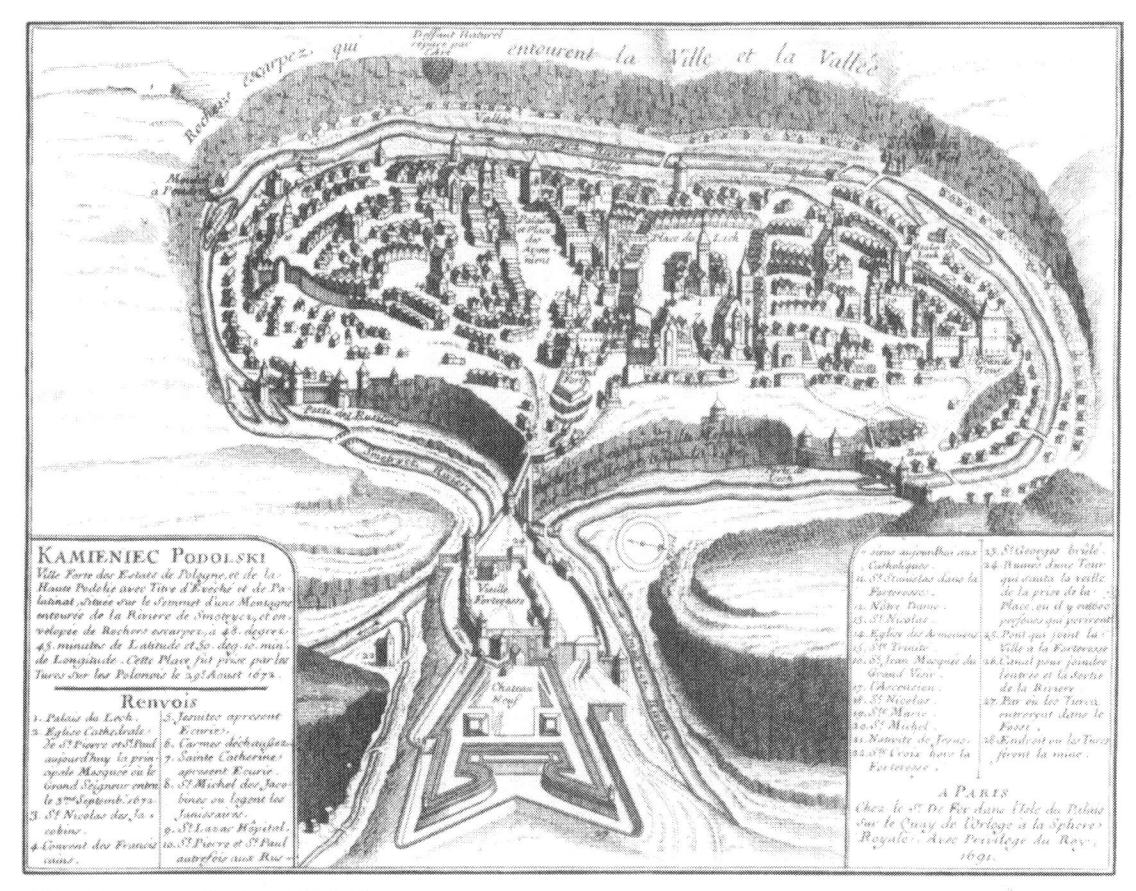

146 Kamenets (De Fer, 1690–5)

ing to the Crimea.

The young Tsar Peter I then turned his attention further to the east, and in 1695 he sought to break through to the Black Sea by way of the Don and the tutelary fortress of Azov. The campaign showed up the Russian defects of experience and temperament still more clearly than had the expedition against the Perekop. The various foreign engineers were scarcely on speaking terms, while the native Russians were disinclined to accept the guidance of any experts at all. Peter threw caution to the winds, and Gordon was unable to convince him that it was

most ill-advised to attempt to storm a fortress where the defenders are determined to hold out to the death, and especially when we have failed to effect breaches, whether by mine or cannon, when we have chosen to bring no scaling ladders to the siege, and when the trenches are such a long way from the ditch. (*ibid.*, II, 586)

The troops duly surged forward on 5 August, and were thrown back with a loss of more than 1,500 killed.

The siege was concluded by a feeble and belated attempt at a regular attack. The trenches wormed a short way forward, and on 15 September an inexperienced Russian miner touched off a fuze. The Turks saw the smoke issuing from the mouth of the tunnel, and temporarily abandoned their rampart. They might have spared themselves the trouble, for the gallery stopped short of the fortifications, and the explosion showered planks, beams and stones on the Russian trenches, causing over 150 casualties. The siege was raised at the beginning of October.

The Russians reappeared before Azov in 1696.

Peter took care to avoid the grosser of the mistakes that had been made in the earlier siege, and this time Gordon was supported by a number of competent German engineers and gunners. The fortress fell on 18 July, and Peter at once set about building Russia's first installations on the Sea of Azov. The new fort of Petropolis was planted beside the Don immediately opposite the conquered stronghold, and twenty thousand Ukrainian militiamen laboured on a fortified harbour at Taganrog, which was intended to accommodate the future Black Sea Fleet. The designs of the works were drawn by the foreigners who had helped to capture Azov.

In 1700 the Peace of Constantinople confirmed Peter as master of Azov. The Russians, however, had failed to break through to the Black Sea proper, for Azov and Taganrog merely gave the Russians access to the northern part of the almost landlocked Sea of Azov. The narrow entrance to the Black Sea was still guarded by the Turkish stronghold of Kerch, on the Crimean shore, and in 1697 the Turks strengthened their hold on the southern shore of the Sea of Azov as well, when they built the oblong castle of Atshu, at the mouth of the Kuban.

If the offensive value of Azov was limited, Peter now had the means to complete a strong and almost continuous border which ran from the Caspian Sea westwards along the lower Volga and the lower Don to Azov, then overland to the Dnieper and along that river by way of the new fortresses of Kamennyi Zaton (1704) and Samara (1688). The Zaporozhian Sech (see p. 240) was devastated after some of the Dnieper Cossacks made the miscalculation of allying themselves with Charles XII of Sweden, in his calamitous Ukrainian expedition of 1708–9.

Most of this achievement was cast away by Peter in 1711, when he executed a wide circuit roughly parallel with the south-western shore of the Black Sea and invaded Moldavia on the strength of promises of local support. The help did not materialise, and before Peter could extricate himself he was overhauled by the Grand Vizier on the River Pruth and forced to buy his freedom. By the provisions of the subsequent Peace of Pruth the Russians had to demolish and abandon Azov, Taganrog, Kamennyi Zaton and Samara.

The easy conquests made from Persia in the campaigns of 1722 and 1723 were no compensation for the loss of the defensible southern border – the Russians overran the whole of the western shore of the Caspian Sea, including the fortresses of Derbent and Baku, but twenty thousand troops were needed to retain the conquests, and Peter's heirs were only too glad to return to Persia the coastlands south of the Terek by treaties of 1732 and 1735.

The eighteenth century – Turkey on the defensive

The continuing struggle for Belgrade

The great achievement of Prince Eugene and his contemporaries had been to carry the strategic frontiers of Central Europe into the approaches to the Orient. This work was consolidated by a remarkable programme of fortress-building which extended over three generations. In the remote north-eastern outpost of Transylvania the Austrians built the small citadel of Klausenburg (1715–23) to support the main fortresses of Karlsburg (see p. 238). The vulnerable communications with Hungary were now safeguarded by the nine-bastioned fortress-town of Temesvár in the Banát (1732–56), and the works of General Harsch at Arad (1765–90). Along the Danube rose Fort St Elisabeth and the rebuilt fortifications at Belgrade (all too soon to be lost again to the Turks), and the vast and impregnable complex upstream at Peterwardein.

Meanwhile the Austrian advance had forced the Turks to reconsider the design of their Balkan fortresses. These had been built in the era of Ottoman expansion, when the principal requirement had been to offer a modicum of shelter and protection for the garrisons and military establishments. Now they had to answer the needs of frontier fortresses, and the Turks worked with energy and skill to replace the old walls of timber and earth with ramparts of masonry. At Nis, for example (completed 1727), the memoranda and plans extended to 230 sheets of paper in a large portfolio. On the marshy site at Widdin (completed 1723) the new works rested on no less than 673,845 piles.

Over the years the Christian crusading impulse died a natural death, and when the Austrian army

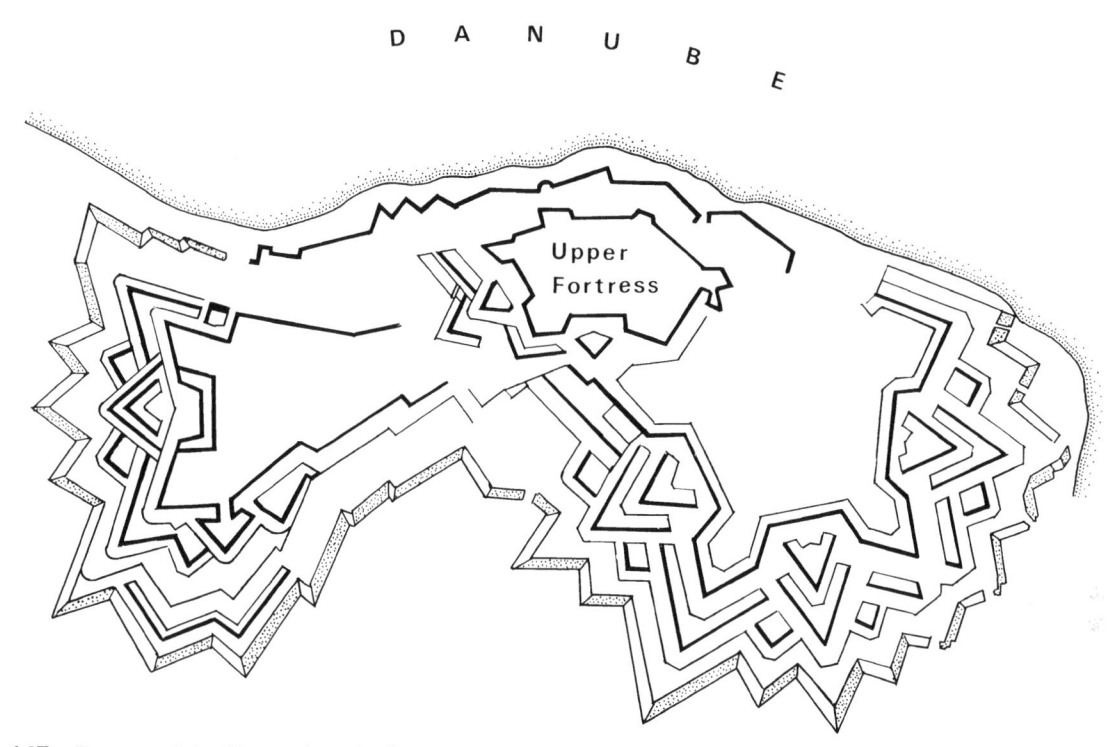

147 Peterwardein. Situated on the Danube, nearly fifty miles above Belgrade, Peterwardein became one of the most powerful fortresses of the Austrian monarchy. The first phase of construction lasted from 1692 to 1728, and concentrated on the Upper Fortress immediately above the river. An elaborate system of countermines was built between 1678 and 1776, and the hornwork and the extensive crownwork were mostly complete by 1780

once again went to war on the Danube it was no longer as the spearhead of the militant West, but as the instrument of narrower state interests. The Habsburgs were now concerned above all to stay the progress of Russian power into the Danubian theatre. Alliance with the infidel Ottomans was unthinkable, and so the only possible way of maintaining Austria's influence in that part of the world was to become an unwilling ally of the Russians, and join them in attacking an enemy with whom the Habsburgs had no particular quarrel.

Under these circumstances the aged Emperor Charles VI committed his ramshackle army to war against the Turks in 1737. The Ottomans quickly won back the initiative, and spent the next three years in the profitable business of reducing the little fortresses on the lower Danube. By the last week in July 1739 the Austrian army was cowering in an entrenched camp near Szalankemen, and the Turks, to their own surprise, were able to impose an unresisted blockade on the city of Belgrade. The place owned a new enceinte of eight large bastions, and was held by a powerful garrison of 13,700 men. However the morale of the Austrian authorities was shaky, and the diplomatic plenipotentiary, Field-Marshal Neipperg, was panicked into concluding a very disadvantageous treaty of peace, which delivered up Belgrade to the Turks.

This was doing the offensive capacities of the eighteenth-century Ottoman Empire altogether too much credit. A Prussian officer testified that

to be candid, engineers are not much use to the Turks. I have talked with some of the engineers who were in their army, when they besieged Belgrade in 1739, and they admit that the Turks pushed ahead the siegeworks in their age-old fashion, being unwilling to follow the advice of the engineers or any of the rules of the art. These officers are quite certain that the Turks would have been unable to take Belgrade, if it had not been delivered to them by the peace treaty. (Warnery, 1771, 94–5)

After this chastening experience, five decades passed before Austria could bring herself again to join with the Russians in another attack on Turkey. In 1788, the first year of the new war, the main Austrian army floundered about unhappily on the Sava and the Danube. To the south, however, Field-Marshal Gideon Ernst Loudon (see p. 125) made good progress on the Croatian borders, and reduced Dubitza and Novi by vigorous sieges. As always, the Turks excelled when they were on the defensive, and Loudon reported:

It is beyond all human powers of comprehension and description to grasp just how strongly these places are built, and just how obstinately the Turks defend them. As soon as one fortification is demolished, they merely dig themselves another one. It is easier to deal with any conventional fortress and with any other army than with the Turks when they are defending a stronghold. (To Joseph III, 22 September 1788, Kriegsarchiv, 1876–91, XVII, 227)

Inevitably Loudon was given the chief command in the next campaign, which had as its objective the recapture of Belgrade. He carried out his task in a way that made the operation one of the most striking sieges in history. The attack began in a curiously archaic style which was dictated by the discovery that much of Eugene's countervallation of 1717 was still standing. The governor, Osman Pasha, hung out the blood flag, the old symbol of defiance. Loudon now made a complete departure from accepted practice. He levelled the artillery of the entire army and Danube flotilla at Belgrade, and ordered the gunners to keep up the greatest possible rate of fire regardless of the expenditure of ammunition. The bombardment began at nine in the evening of 9 October 1789 and lasted until half past eight the next morning. After half an hour's rest the fire was taken up with the same ferocity as before and continued until two in the afternoon, when a new summons produced the reply from Osman Pasha: 'My lord, you name is terrible to our people; your fire cleaves the rocks in two; your cannon shot carry away my soldiers in the streets. I must yield to the pleas of my despairing garrison' (Dolleczek, 1887, 486). He delivered Belgrade forthwith.

The Turks were granted an evacuation, though without the honours of war, and Belgrade came once more to the Emperor. There was no sign of animosity between the garrison and the Austrians (who would rather have been fighting the Prussians anyway), and the Turkish traders stood smoking at their doors when the Christian troops came to see the city:

Every detail of the scene was calculated to refresh the eye and cheer the soul, when you saw the picturesque crowds thronging the banks of the Danube and the Sava. You noticed the Janissaries, beautifully decked up in a variety of rich and striking colours, intermingling with our grenadiers in their fur caps and our cuirassiers, as well as with their own spahis – beaten but not downcast, sporting magnificent weapons, and mounted on steeds which were as proud as they were. (Prince de Ligne, 18 October 1789, Ségur, 1824–6, III, 524)

The Russians managed things differently, as we shall see at Izmail.

However, the absence of atrocities in no way detracted from the magnitude of the Austrian achievement. In the seventeen hours of the bombardment 37,000 shot and shell had been fired from the main attack, and 150,000 from the peninsula formed by the confluence of the Sava and the Danube – an intensity of fire possibly unequalled until the Great War.

Loudon, who had put forward the most spectacular and convincing display of the technique of bombardment in the whole era of black powder, was awarded the diamond-encrusted Grand Cross of the Military Order of Maria Theresa. At the Peace of Sistova in August 1791 the Sultan renounced Belgrade, and delivered to Austria the fortress and region of Orsova at the Iron Gates on the Lower

Danube. Turkey no longer had any claim to be considered a Central European power.

The creation of Russian imperialism
Austria had met with such humiliating rebuffs on the Danube in the 1730s largely because she had been totally unprepared for the war. This did not apply with quite the same force to the Turks or the Russians.

Trouble had long been brewing on the Sultan's vague and disputed borders with Russia, and so the Turks gave a ready welcome to a new generation of Western adventurers who came to take the place of the useful Italian and Greek renegades of the seventeenth century. The grand vizirate of Ibrahim Pasha (1718–30) became known as the 'Tulip Period', when the Turkish elite displayed a lively curiosity about Western, and especially French artefacts and fashions. A printing press came into operation in the early 1720s, and it produced two useful maps for military purposes, as well as books on artillery and geography. A Janissary revolt in 1730 caused Ottoman society to turn once more in on itself, but the interest in Western military practice remained, and the Turks proved receptive to the teachings of one of the most valuable of their foreign guests, the French-born Claude-Alexandre de Bonneval.

Bonneval had distinguished himself with the Austrians at Peterwardein in 1716, but had then fallen out so badly with Prince Eugene that he was forced to leave the Imperial service. In 1731 he came to Constantinople, where he drew the attention of the Turks to the importance of attracting Western engineers by the prospect of 'distinctions and rewards' (Bonneval, 1738, III, 259). Bonneval proved his sincerity by renouncing Christianity and accepting the title of Pasha, and Sultan Mahmud (1730–54) willingly accepted his guidance in such matters as remodelling the artillery, rebuilding the old Bombardier Corps on French models, opening a school of mathematics, and translating various European technical treatises. The field operations were facilitated by the excellent maps which Bonneval drew of the Austrian and Russian theatres.

Russia too had been making preparations with foreign help. The Empress Anna harboured ambitions of revenging the Peace of the Pruth, and in 1732 she sent the Scots-born inspector-general of the army, James Keith, to organise and fill the magazines in the southern border fortresses. The forces as a whole were put in order by the energetic and ruthless military supremo Field-Marshal Münnich, who came from Oldenburg (see p. 216). He intended the sequence of campaigns to be a masterpiece of the military art, and at the same time he was 'careful to familiarise the army with the rules of siege warfare, for some time had passed since it had last attacked a fortress' ('Tagebuch', in Münnich, 1843, 136).

The Russians opened their new war in 1736. In the event they carried out their sieges in their accustomed muddled fashion, but they were rescued by the still greater carelessness of the Turks, who never learnt to safeguard their magazines properly. Azov capitulated to Peter Lacy in July 1736, after a Russian bomb blew up the main magazine. The same catastrophe visited the Dnieper fortress of Ochakov on 13 July 1737, whereupon the Russians overran the place and massacred the survivors.

Some of the details of the attack on Ochakov are only too indicative of the crudity and barbarity of Russian sieges, even when the Westerner was in nominal control. On the night of 12–13 July Münnich tried to storm the place in almost total ignorance of the defences. The Russians were checked at an outer ditch, and the Austrian colonel Berenklau reported that

the field-marshal, seeing that things were going badly, seized a colour and advanced to the very ditch. Not a man followed him, except the Prince of Württemberg and his suite.... Everybody was in disorder – you could see grenadiers hiding in the ditch in one place, and a group of officers in another.... The Red Indians do not throw in assaults with more confusion than did the Russians on this occasion. (Baiov, 1906, I, 144)

In the storm of the 13th, after the explosion of the magazine, 'the fire the russ and the Turks made during the attack is not to be conceived ... Field-Marshal Münnich's hat was shot through, as was also the folds on his coat ... there were so many Turks killed, that nothing but blood and dead bodies were to be seen in the streets' (C. Rondeau, SIRIO, LXXX, 1892, 133). Lieutenant Innes, a Scots volunteer with the Russians, was forced to kill a grenadier of the Guards, who was infuriated at being interrupted at his sport of tormenting a Turkish child with his bayonet.

Despite its bloody circumstances, the capture of Ochakov helped to open the path of advance down the western side of the Black Sea, and by the autumn of 1739 Münnich had brought an army across the Pruth and was beginning to revolve schemes of invading the heartland of European Turkey. All of this was brought to an end by the news that the Austrians had abandoned the war, which forced the Russians to come to terms as well in 1740. They abandoned all their conquests save Azov, and they retained the fortress only with the crippling restrictions of having to demolish the outworks and promise not to maintain a garrison. Altogether, Russia emerged from the war with little to show for the expenditure of more than 100,000 lives.

The winning of the equivalent of the favourable borders of 1700 had to wait upon the accidental, blundering but very profitable war which the Russians waged against the Turks between 1768 and 1774. The hostilities were provoked by some overenthusiastic officers, who pursued Polish rebels into Turkish territory, and in 1768 Russia was faced with the problem of how to conduct yet another major war on the south-western rivers. The Russians took the offensive not out of a spirit of adventure, but simply because they did not know how they could possibly defend the low-lying left bank of the Dniester.

In September 1769 Prince Golitsyn was lucky enough to worst the main Turkish army, and after this victory he found that there were only ten Ottoman troops who were willing to defend the important Dniester fortress of Khotin. Episodes such as these provoked Frederick the Great into calling the war a contest between 'the one-eyed and the blind'.

In 1770 a strong army under Prince Panin was directed against the fortress of Bendery, which commanded the lower Dniester. By the middle of September the Russians were ready to assault across the ditch, under the counterscarp of which one of their hired French technicians, Monsieur Chardon, had planted a globe of compression – the last word in military mining (see p. 127). At eleven on the night of the 15/16th the mine exploded 'with a frightful roar' (Strandmann, RS, XXXV, 1882, 312), and the consequent rubble enabled the Russians to reach the ditch on a battalion frontage. Lord Cathcart could not 'recollect of hearing of its having been anywhere used in service except at Schweidnitz, where it did not answer the intention of the engineer; here it had its full effect' (Public Record Office SP 91/86). On the inner side of the ditch the Russians climbed the walls at three places, to the accompaniment of a series of detonations from the Turkish magazines, which were being blown up by the Russian mortar bombs. The Russians were now masters of Bendery, and so 'this ancient and beautiful town, which had seen enemies before its ramparts on so many occasions, was now reduced in three days to a heap of ashes' (Strandmann, RS, XXXV, 1882, 314).

Count Rumyantsev meanwhile battled his way with another army to the lower Danube, and he reduced the guardian fortresses of Izmail, Kilia and Braila before the end of the season. The Turks managed to stay any further serious penetration until June 1774, when the Russians began to make dangerous progress on the south bank of the Danube. Constantinople lay scarcely two hundred miles away, and the Grand Vizier hastened out to parley at the Russian camp at Kutchuk-Kainardji. Terms were arranged after four hours of negotiation on 16 July, and 'never has an epoch-making peace been fixed up in so short a time' (Zinkeisen, 1854–7, V, 958).

The Russian Baltic fleet had meanwhile entered the Mediterranean and run through a variety of antics which had done singularly little to influence the course of the war. The Russians certainly got the enterprise off to a good start in 1770, when they destroyed the Turkish fleet at Chesmé (in the channel of Chios), and detached Admiral Elphinstone with the second division to force the Dardanelles. Confusion reigned at Constantinople, and the Turks delivered the entire seaward defence to the Frenchified Hungarian renegade François de Tott, who describes how he addressed himself for money to the Superintendant of the Coin, Ised Bey:

This Turk ... was desirous of possessing two canary birds which should both sing the same air. His servants had searched the city to procure them, but without success; and this minister was contriving how to gratify his fancy, when I arrived to consult by what means the capital might be preserved from the catastrophe with which it was threatened. (Tott, 1786, II, pt. 3, 32)

Little enough could be made ready before Elphinstone bore down on 26 July. He twice ran in close under Mehmed Köprülü's castle of Sedd el Bahr and tried to reach across the channel to get at the two warships and five galleys cowering under the Asiatic shore, but on both occasions he was forced back by the four- or five-knot current pouring from the Dardanelles. Tott frankly owns that the Turks were saved by the strength of the stream and the Russian ignorance of the weakness of the defences.

In August the discomfited Russians made a landing on the island of Lemnos, which would have been a useful base for a close blockade of the Dardanelles *à la Vénitienne*. Two breaches were battered in the citadel, but the Russians and rebel Greeks were thoroughly demoralised by the failure of their first assault, and they refused to come out of their trenches again, even when eighty British seamen from the Russian fleet and British merchantmen offered to lead the way with cutlasses and pistols. Early in October a Turkish landing made the Russians reembark in panic.

These latter-day Mocenigos and Morosinis cruised aimlessly around the Mediterranean for the next three years. Like Don John in 1572 and the British in 1915 they failed to appreciate that without a strong landing force there was little to be done against the Turks from the Mediterranean side.

It was Rumyantsev's advance over the Danube which, as we have seen, forced the Turks to make peace in 1774. The terms fell just short of giving the Russians a clear run to the Black Sea. At the eastern tip of the Crimea they certainly gained the fortress of Kerch, which commanded the straits of the same name and open the way from the Sea of Azov. The only Russian base on this inland sea was, however, Taganrog, which lacked the depth of water for a high seas fleet. To the west of the Crimea the Russians acquired most of the Bug-Dnieper estuary, with the fortress of Kinburn on its southern shore. After lengthy surveys, General Ivan Hannibal began work in 1778 on the new fortified base of Kherson, which was intended to take advantage of the new avenue. Kherson too failed to meet all the Russian requirements. Its water was shallow, like Taganrog, it was situated a little too far up the Dnieper estuary, and its access to the Black Sea was disputed by the Turkish fortress of Ochakov.

The desire to gain a site on which to build and base the new Black Sea fleet was therefore one of the motives which impelled the Russians to annex the whole of the Crimean peninsula in 1783. On 10 February 1784 a decree went forth: 'A great fortress, "Sevastopol", is to be built where Akhtiar now stands. This is where we shall bring an Admiralty, together with dockyards for first-rate ships, a harbour and a military settlement' (Bode, 1979, 33).

It is scarcely possible to exaggerate the importance of the bloodless conquest of the Crimea. By eliminating a Moslem strategic bridgehead, from where the Tartars had raided into southern Russia for centuries, the Russians could now at last enjoy the peaceful possession of the potentially rich agricultural lands already in their nominal possession. This circumstance, quite apart from the actual territorial gain, vastly increased the effective size of Catherine's realm.

In the context of the struggle against the Turks, the Russians acquired a base that was situated within three or four day's sailing of Constantinople. Already in 1787 French diplomats were astonished at the extent of the work that was going ahead at Sevastopol:

It seemed incomprehensible to us how in two years Prince Potemkin could have made establishments of this kind in a conquered territory eight hundred leagues from the capital. To have built a town, constructed a fleet, thrown up forts, and assembled such a quantity of inhabitants was truly a miracle of application. (Ségur, 1824–6, III, 182)

Scarcely less alarming to the Turks was the experience of the recent campaigns, which had shown that the Russians had the capacity to reach the Danube by the overland routes, and to launch expeditions on the south bank. In 1783 the French accordingly dispatched a commission of highly qualified officers to help their Turkish friends to shore up the crumbling northern flanks of their empire. The advisers included three engineers, namely Lieutenant-Colonel Marc-Antoine Chabaud de la Tour, Captain Joseph Monnier de Courtois, and the Major André de la Fitte de Clavé (Lafitte-Clavé) who became head of the representation in 1784. Lafitte-Clavé made extensive reconnaissances of the Black Sea and Asia Minor coasts, he tried to train up a dozen or more Turks as engineers, and he wrote a *Traité de Castramétation et de Fortification Passagère*, which was translated into Turkish and published in 1787. Unfortunately his experience of Turkish officials corresponded very closely to that of de Tott. These people could see no purpose in using measuring tapes or other surveying instruments, and on the Black Sea Lafitte-Clavé once encountered a pasha who insisted on planting his 'coastal' batteries well inland, out of sight of the shore. 'Everything depends on the will of Allah', explained the Turk. 'If it is his desire, our artillery will kill just as many enemy from here as anywhere else' (*ibid.*, II, 322).

Chabaud proposed to defend Constantinople by means of a line of detached bastions in front of the Byzantine wall, and Lafitte-Clavé himself made plans for new fortifications at Varna, Khotin, Sinope, but especially Izmail, as the most exposed and important of the fortresses of the lower Danube. Even the Turks could appreciate the utility of strengthening this place, for they knew 'how important it was for them to have a fortress on the Danube which would give them a defensible base, whether for carrying the war into Moldavia, or acting as a refuge for a beaten army (Richelieu, SIRIO, LIV, 1886, 153). Work therefore began on strengthening Izmail by means of a high and steeply-scarped rampart of very dense earth.

The Turks were unwise enough to take the initiative in opening hostilities against Russia in 1787. This gave the Russians the opportunity to clear up some unsettled business from the last war, by eliminating the fortress of Ochakov, which stood on the right bank of the Dnieper estuary opposite Kinburn.

Prince Potemkin's army of no less than 93,000 men arrived outside Ochakov in June 1788. An Austrian observer, the Prince de Ligne, judged that Ochakov could be brought down by assault, or a brisk formal siege of eight days. Potemkin, however, was unwilling to risk his reputation or his beloved troops, and the army settled down in a series of badly made earthworks. There was nothing to see but the sky, the sea, and a plain of tall grass that was crawling with snakes, lizards and poisonous tarantulas. The night brought little reprieve from the heat, and the pointless artillery duels illuminated the night for hours on end. A terrible mortality set in among the troops:

The epidemics proceeded from a number of circumstances – from the fact that the army was encamped in a square, from the loathsome stench that arose from the accumulated excrement despite the prevalence of strong winds, from the very unhealthy drinking water offered by the foul estuary . . . and from the drowned corpses you could see everywhere along the banks after the three naval battles staged on the firth. . . . In addition many horses and cattle had died from lack of fodder, and the inedible portions of their carcasses had either been deposited in the camp, or along the banks, which served to augment the noisome smell. (Tsebrikov, RS, LXXXIV, 1895, 170)

Cold north-west winds arrived in October, and it was

pitiful in the extreme to see how the frozen soldiers wandered about the camp collecting dung . . . as fuel to cook their *kasha*. Looking at their bivouacs, you shuddered with horror to think how they could endure the cold and frost, covered only by a cloak – and often a ragged one at that. (*ibid.*, 195)

After these inordinate delays the thing was ended by a bloody storm of Ochakov on 6 December. The Russians mastered the place at a cost of 2,800 casualties, and they killed more than 9,500 Turks on the spot.

As in the last war, the Russians followed up their success on the north shore of the Black Sea by exploiting down the western side towards Constantinople. Late in the campaigning season of 1790 the greencoats arrived outside Izmail to the number of 31,000. The French military mission had been ordered home from Turkey, at the start of the new war, and the fortifications of Izmail were defective in one important respect:

Lafitte-Clavé had proposed to plant the rampart with storm poles and palisades in the European style, but the Turkish engineer who replaced him, and who was merely . . . the head gardener of the seraglio, had no idea at all of fortifications. He found immense quantities of palisade stakes in store, and he could think of nothing better to do with them than set them up in the middle of the parapet, instead of planting them point-outwards on the exterior face, which would have made escalade almost impossible. (Richelieu, SIRIO, LIV, 1886, 153)

The siege, however, threatened to extend to Ochakov-like lengths, and the enterprise might well have been abandoned altogether if the aggressive Aleksandr Suvorov had not arrived on the scene on 2 December, and begun intensive preparations for an all-out assault. Fascines and scaling ladders were assembled in haste, and the troops were put through a number of realistic rehearsals – something that was unheard of in the military art of the time.

The assault was to be an affair of nine columns coming in from all sides at once on 11 December 1790. Three of these parties were actually to cross the Danube by boats and assault the riverine sector. Sharpshooters were to lead the way, and carry fascines. Then came labourers equipped with entrenching tools, and finally the main bodies of infantry with the scaling ladders. Every column was accompanied by a reserve, moving in square, and in addition each grouping of three columns had a larger reserve standing at the disposal of the appropriate general.

The height of the battle for Izmail lasted from half past five in the morning until eleven, by when the Russians had seized three of the fortress gates. Some of the most bitter fighting was waged for the possession of the Bendery Gate, where the assaulting column was made up of dismounted Cossacks. Adrian Denisov describes the first attack on the barricade:

I was stupefied by a cannon shot, which was thrown at me and hit me between the shoulders. Twice my clothing was pierced by spears, and I was hit several times over the head with a sponge-rammer. That first blow from the shot worked a very powerful effect on me. I crept away from the battery, and all the others abandoned it as well. Gathering my wits somewhat I tried to climb up again to the barricade, but all my efforts were of no avail – I got as far as the threshold, or breastwork, and summoned my men, but nobody came up to join me. (Denisov, RS, X, 1874, 42–3)

The reason was that his Cossacks were meanwhile being massacred by the Turks, who slashed at their lances with the sabre, leaving them holding useless stumps of wood. Here as elsewhere the contest turned in favour of the Russians when Suvorov committed his reserves.

The afternoon found the Russians inside the town, firing down the streets point blank with grape and musketry. Soon it was

impossible to imagine the horror and incongruity of the assorted sights. Most of the soldiers were laden with plunder and they were almost unrecognisable under their Turkish coats and clothing. Everywhere you could see half-naked survivors of the first butchery, who were running about in search of some refuge from the fury of the soldiers. . . . Horses galloped neighing around the ramparts, and the barks of the multitudes of dogs mingled with the shrieks of the dying and the shouts of the victors. (Richelieu, SIRIO, LIV, 1886, 184)

The Prince of Anhalt saw with horror that some of the infantry were up to their trick of throwing children into the air and impaling them on their bayonets. After the storm 26,000 Turkish bodies were thrown into the Danube, making the episode by far the most hideous in all of eighteenth-century fortress warfare. Indeed, the concept of 'Limited War' seems to have enjoyed little currency east of the Carpathians.

The Peace of Jassy in 1792 confirmed and extended the Russian mastery of the north shore of the Black Sea, and in 1794 the Russians began work on the great establishments of the future Odessa. The war had also been important for Russia because it ushered in the influential Suvorovian school of fortress warfare, with its incongruous blend of meticulous training and brutal assault. In a wider context, Russia's last three wars were typical of the record of her contest with Turkey. The sieges were crude in the extreme, and they were almost always terminated in a messy and spectacular fashion, amid colossal explosions and rivers of blood. On the Eastern theatre it seems that firepower and raw courage were always ready to take the place of the artistic siegework that was practised by Vauban and his followers.

Behind the spearheads of conquest, the Russians undertook a huge extension of their *cherta* (border) lines to protect the steppe settlements. The enterprise began on a modest enough scale in 1723, when they built the thirty-five mile-long Tsaritsyn (Stalingrad, Volgograd) Line, which joined the lower Volga and the lower Don into a continuous military border, reaching from Astrakhan to Azov. Cook describes the central sector as:

a ditch and rampart, reaching the whole length of sixty versts; the ditch is twenty yards broad, well formed, and proportionately deep. The rampart is very high, and the southern side, towards the Kalmyks . . . country, or the desert of Astrakhan, is planted with high and strong palisades made of fir trees, drove into the ground, and fastened together with cross-beams, so close, that a man cannot get through anywhere, except, I think, at two places, through which brooks of water run, and these are fortified as far as art hath hitherto been able. There are four strong forts built upon this line at equal distances, well stored with cannon, and betwixt the forts are many houses, where soldiers only live. Sentinel boxes are placed on top of the wall, the whole length, so near one another, that the soldiers on duty can almost speak together. (Cook, 1770, I, 287-8)

In 1731 Münnich and the Senate commissioned the major-generals Tarakanov and Debrini to build a westward extension: 'You are to make a line for the better protection of the Ukraine between the upper Donets and the rivers Berestovaya and Orelka, and you are to establish fortresses where you judge there exists a danger of enemy penetrations' (Laskovskii, 1858-65, III, 26). The line extended for 145 miles from the Donets westwards to the Dnieper, and it was studded with fifteen stout forts and a large number of intermediate redans and redoubts. Twenty-one thousand settlers came from the small gentry of the provinces of Kursk and Rilsk, and formed the Ukrainian Land Militia to defend the line. In the second half of the century it became necessary to plant a number of outposts, so as to cover the large population which had taken the risk of settling in front of the defended border. Westwards again, the area beyond the Dniester was settled and fortified after the peace with Turkey in 1740. However, none of the defences could keep out really determined Tartar raids, and as late as 1723 orders could still be issued for the strict upkeep of the Tula abatis, which was the rearmost and earliest of the *cherta* lines. Only the annexation of the Crimea in 1783 gave real security to the inhabitants of the black earth region.

By Western standards the various Ukrainian lines were of staggering extent, but they became mere garden fences in comparison with the defensive system erected against the wild peoples of the East. Taking the six hundred miles between the Black Sea and the Caspian as the first instalment, we discover lines creeping towards each other up the Kuban and Terek rivers until, in 1778, they were joined together by Aleksandr Suvorov. The eastward extension of the defences is found in the Ural Lines, which ran from the north shore of the Caspian up the Ural River to the southern passes of the Ural Hills. Orenburg was founded as a supporting fortress, and the arrival of the Russians in the area provoked the unappreciative Kirgiz tribesmen into a rebellion in 1735.

The Uisk Line was built between 1732 and 1743, and it provided a vital link between Russia's southern and eastern borders. Beginning on the upper reaches of the Ural River, it looped around the southern spurs of the Ural Hills and reached north-eastwards to the Tobol, a tributary of the Irtysh, along which Peter had established Omsk and other fortified towns. After 1743 a leap of more than a thousand miles carried a Siberian Line from the

Tobol due eastwards to the foothills of the Altay Mountains at Kuznetsk. South-west of Kuznetsk a matter of a mere 350 miles lay the stronghold of Ust-Kamenogorsk, the first of a cordon of widely scattered forts along the Chinese border. The central link in the chain was formed by Petropavlovsk (Ulan-Ude, fifty miles south of Lake Baikal), an important station for Chinese caravans, and the headquarters of the Yakutsk Regiment, which garrisoned the defences of the border with China. It is difficult to imagine the conditions of life in the Asian outposts:

The unfortunate officers are virtually buried in those frightful abodes in the Caucasus, Siberia and Orenburg. The places are often two hundred or more versts distant from any human habitation, and although they are dignified with the impressive name of 'fortress', they are made up of a single row of palisades and a gloomy surrounding ditch. You would have to possess a highly philosophical turn of mind not to endure such a fate without stupefaction. In the event, most of the commanders are speedily ruined by the misery, dejection and drunkenness that are the inevitable consequences of their boredom. (Langeron, RS, LXXXIII, 1895, 187)

At the north-eastern extremity of Asia, on the almost inconceivably remote Kamchatka Peninsula, the Russians held a series of small strongpoints (Verzhne-Kamchatsk, Bolsheretsk, Penzhinsk and Nizhne-Kamchatsk) which had been planted in the early 1700s. They were separated by fifteen hundred miles (little compared with the distance the Russians had already come) from North America, a land mass that was now being penetrated by the imperialist powers of the West.

Nadir Shah and the last great days of Persia
We have heard significantly little of Turkey's eastern neighbour, the ancient land of Persia, which was sunk in apparently irreversible decline. Afghanistan broke away in 1707, and further losses were sustained in the years after 1722, when the Sefavi dynasty finally collapsed. Peter the Great helped himself to the western shore of the Caspian (see p. 242), while the Turks captured Erivan, Tabriz and other important fortresses of the northern mountains.

A Persian national champion at last emerged in the unlikely form of the brigand Nadir Quli Khan, who gave a good account of himself in some sporadic outbursts of fighting with the Turks in 1730-1 and 1732. Other talents were revealed in Nadir when he persuaded the Russians to give up their Caspian conquests, a complaisance which is partly explained by the fact that they had lost some 130,000 men through sickness since they had entered into possession ten years before. Nadir now had 70,000 devoted warriors at his disposal, and he became effective ruler of Persia long before he took the title of Shah in 1736.

Nadir's later career of conquest shows that probably only the lack of heavy artillery and skilled engineers prevented him from being numbered with Marlborough, Eugene and Frederick as one of the outstanding commanders of the century. He was frugal, active and dominating, and possessed an extraordinary memory; he owned an excellent train of field guns; he handled cavalry in a way which looks back to Genghis Khan and forward to the Blitzkrieg of 1940. For all of this, he was nearly powerless when he came up against a stronghold which was held by a determined governor.

War with Turkey was renewed in 1733. One of Nadir's lieutenants was lucky enough to have the help of Russian engineers and gunners who contributed to the reduction of Ardebil, a stronghold which was situated on the mountain slopes leading down to the Caspian. Nadir himself led the main army to Baghdad in the spring, and ringed this great fortress with a countervallation of 2,700 towers, each standing within musket-shot of the other. In addition he barred the Tigris to relief by building strong forts on either bank nine miles above the city. All of the valiant spade-work was of no avail in the absence of siege artillery – the field guns could make little impression on the walls, and the Persians sat impotently before Baghdad until Topal Osman appeared on the scene with a relieving army and drove them away.

In 1734 General Levashev lent Nadir an engineer, four bombardiers and a quantity of siege artillery, but even this help was not enough to enable the Persians to crack open the Caucasian fortress of Genja. The Turkish strongholds might well have imposed a total stalemate if Nadir had not annihilated the Seraskier Abdullah Köprülü's army of eighty thousand men at Arpatshai on 10 June 1735. Scarcely one-tenth of the enemy escaped, and the fortresses of Erivan and Erzerum surrendered to Nadir after a token resistance. The Turks were soon expelled from the northern mountain region of Persia, and in 1736 they made peace on the basis of renouncing all their acquisitions except Baghdad.

Nadir could now devote 110,000 men to the work of recovering Afghanistan. The Persian progress in 1737 was, however, checked by the heroic resistance of Kandahar, and Nadir had to make a treaty of reconciliation in order to be able to enter the place at the end of the year. In 1738 Kabul and the remaining Afghan strongholds were taken by escalade, which was the one effective siege technique open to the Persians.

The capture of Kabul opened the way to Moghul India through the Khyber Pass, and on 14 February 1739 Nadir defeated the 160,000 men of the Great Moghul Mohammed Shah in a murderous battle on the plains of Karnal. As had already happened in the campaign of 1735, a Persian victory in the field brought down the fortresses without putting Nadir to the embarrassment of having to attempt a serious siege. The Moghuls ceded all their provinces up to the Indus, and yielded Delhi and its treasures.

Nadir deposited the booty from Delhi in his stronghold of Kalat-i-Naderi, perched amid the mountains of north Khuresan just before they descended to the steppe of Kara Kum. In the late nineteenth century Lord Curzon was to describe the position as 'one of the most extraordinary natural phenomena in the world and famous even in this land of mountain fastnesses and impregnable defiles for its inaccessibility and amazing natural strength' (Curzon, 1892, I, 113). Nadir had roamed these heights as a shepherd boy, and he chose and exploited the site for his refuge with great skill, whatever his limitations as a taker of fortresses. Kalat-i-Naderi was a kind of Asiatic Pirna, though on a grander scale than its Saxon counterpart, being a steep-sided plateau eighteen miles long and between six and ten wide. Circular towers guarded the few vulnerable points along the perimeter, and the main entrance, and the four-hundred-yard-long defile of Arghun on the southern side, was defended by a three-arched gateway bearing an inscription which describes the master as 'that king of kings, whose rank is as high as the firmament and whose throne is heaven itself, Nadir Shah, who, like his name, has no equal'.

The Turko-Persian war of 1743–6 proved yet again how little the proud Nadir could effect against a well-defended fortress system. In 1743 he advanced south-west from his base of Hamadan, but he was prevented from debouching from the mountains into the Tigris-Euphrates valley by the successful resistance of Mosul. In the next year he marched due west and met a corresponding check before Kars. On 3 August Nadir was at last able to defeat the main body of the Turks in open battle near Erivan, but by then the chaotic internal state of Persia ruled out any possibility of exploitation.

Nadir was assassinated in 1747, and Persia entered upon a new period of anarchy and impotence. The Turks gained some immediate benefit, but in the long term the eclipse of Persian power served to bring them face to face with the Russians in Caucasia. It was part of the same process by which the erosion of the buffer states of Byzantium, Rhodes, Poland, Transylvania, Hungary and Tartary drew the Turks into direct confrontation with the Christian powers of the West. By the end of the eighteenth century it was increasingly doubtful whether the Ottoman empire would be able to withstand the ordeal.

Nine   The Collision of the Colonial Empires

In the eighteenth century, the rivalries of Dutch, Portuguese and Spanish took second place to the world-wide clashes between British and French interests, as represented by trading companies, colonists and expeditionary forces. On occasion a large tract of territory was immediately at stake, as in North America; at other times the wars focused upon the struggle for possession of chains of West Indian islands, or for bases for commercial and political expansion, as in India.

The *relative* strength of fortification was all-important in contests like these. You might enjoy an enormous advantage, if you owned a couple of even remotely tenable forts, but your supremacy was liable to vanish at once if your enemy managed to bring some reasonably heavy artillery along with him. Thus the outcome of colonial campaigns was often decided by the advent of a well-found expedition on the theatre of war, and this in turn hung largely upon the command of the sea.

India

The British 'John Company' made a singularly bashful début on the fringes of the vast expanses of India. It planted its first permanent factory at Surat (1612), which remained almost the only sign of the presence of the British in the subcontinent until they founded Madras (1640), seven hundred miles away on the Coromandel (south-eastern) Coast. A report on the state of the fort at Madras in 1653 characteristically reads:

We have yet one curtain of our fort to seaward, the most part thereof is laid with loose bricks which a man may push down with his hand; which although we are loath to expend any of the Company's money in the building, yet we must be forced to do it less to save a penny we lose a pound. (Sandes, 1933–5, I, 7)

However, one great advantage of Madras lay in the fact that it was tucked out of the way of the Moghuls, and in the eighteenth century the place was to become the chief citadel of British power in India.

Bombay, on the western coast, came to the British in 1661 as part of the dowry of Catherine of Braganza. Its sole defence was a fortified house, surrounded by 'a delicate garden, voiced to be the pleasantest in India, intended for wanton dalliance, love's artillery, rather than to make resistance against an invading foe' (*ibid.*, I, 14). A new fort was begun there in 1669, and eighteen years later Bombay replaced Surat as the headquarters on the western coast.

By this time the directors of the East India Company were firmly convinced of the necessity of providing their establishments with much stronger fortifications than before. Not only did such works provide the English with a measure of security against the turmoils of the subcontinent, but they attracted Indian merchants to the protection of their walls, which provided further sources of revenue, and enabled the company to challenge traditional patterns of authority in India.

A number of smaller posts were destined to be of the greatest strategic importance in the struggle with France in the eighteenth century. In 1690 the company bought from the Marathas the site of the future Fort St David, on the Coromandel Coast an impudent fifteen miles south of the new and rapidly-growing French settlement of Pondicherry. Likewise, at the head of the Bay of Bengal the French factory at Chandernagore was matched by Fort William (Calcutta), which the British planted in a malarial swamp sixteen miles further down the Hooghly. The company could now draw on its ample experience of the power of attraction of its protected settlements, and Calcutta began to expand very rapidly indeed. Carical and Masulipatam were almost the only French establishments which were free of the immediate and unwelcome presence of the English.

These British forts were designed in a very casual way. The company's engineers were not put upon a military footing until 1759, and in earlier times the engineering work was left to officers seconded from the army and navy, or, failing that, to adventurers who hailed from all over Europe.

Towards the middle of the eighteenth century, the French began to reassert their position. The revival was linked with the names of Admiral de la Bourdonnais, and the governor and commandant-general Dupleix. Pondicherry and Chandernagore flourished, and the island of Mauritius (Île de France) was made into a useful though cramped naval base on the route between France and India.

The French were therefore well placed to take the initiative in the War of the Austrian Succession. In 1746 de la Bourdonnais captured Madras without meeting any great display of opposition from its merchant governor. The French sailor agreed to hand the place back in return for a large ransom and a personal bribe of £4,375, But Dupleix had strict views on this sort of thing and at once repudiated the deal. The best retaliation the British could make was a slapdash and unsuccessful attack on Pondicherry in 1747. The one good result of these misfortunes was to give some useful siege experience to the Company's best soldier, Clive, who escaped from Madras in the guise of a native, and served as a volunteer in the attack on Pondicherry.

The British rapidly made up the lost ground. Madras was returned to them in 1749, according to the terms of peace, and in the early 1750s they waged some successful campaigns against the native friends of the French in the hinterland of the Coromandel Coast. The tension was also rising in Bengal, where the nawab Siraj-ud-Daula captured Fort William in 1756 – the loss of a European fortress to a native prince was a rarity, but in this case Fort William was doomed because it mounted so few cannon, and because the governor and the Sepoy troops ran away.

Clive speedily built up the Company's forces, and in association with Admiral Watson he recovered Fort William on 2 January 1757. News of the outbreak of the Seven Years War reached Clive shortly afterwards, whereupon he and Watson pressed up the Hooghly and captured Chandernagore after a short but vigorous defence. The downfall of this post, the capital of French Bengal, provoked Siraj-ud-Daula into opening fresh hostilities. He was defeated at Plassey on 26 June, and the British replaced his sway over Bengal at first by sponsoring native authority, which did not work very well, and finally by direct Company administration.

In 1757, therefore, the British factory-fort at Calcutta ceased to be a mere excrescence on the coastlands of India, and became a base for wide territorial rule. In 1758 Clive began work on a great New Fort William, which was intended to serve as a fortified compound where all the forces, riches and white population of British Bengal could be concentrated in safety. The extremely elaborate works were built to the design of the gifted but dishonest engineer John Brohier, and they were ultimately completed in 1781 at a cost of two million pounds.

The French took up the challenge by sending out to India one of their most experienced soldiers, Thomas Arthur, Comte de Lally, whose personal knowledge of fortress warfare extended back to the sieges of Gerona and Barcelona in the War of the Spanish Succession. Neither the French nor the British yet considered that they were engaged in a contest for the direct rule of the subcontinent, and Lally was simply commissioned to wreck the British establishments on the Coromandel Coast.

When Lally arrived at Pondicherry his ship was

The Collision of the Colonial Empires

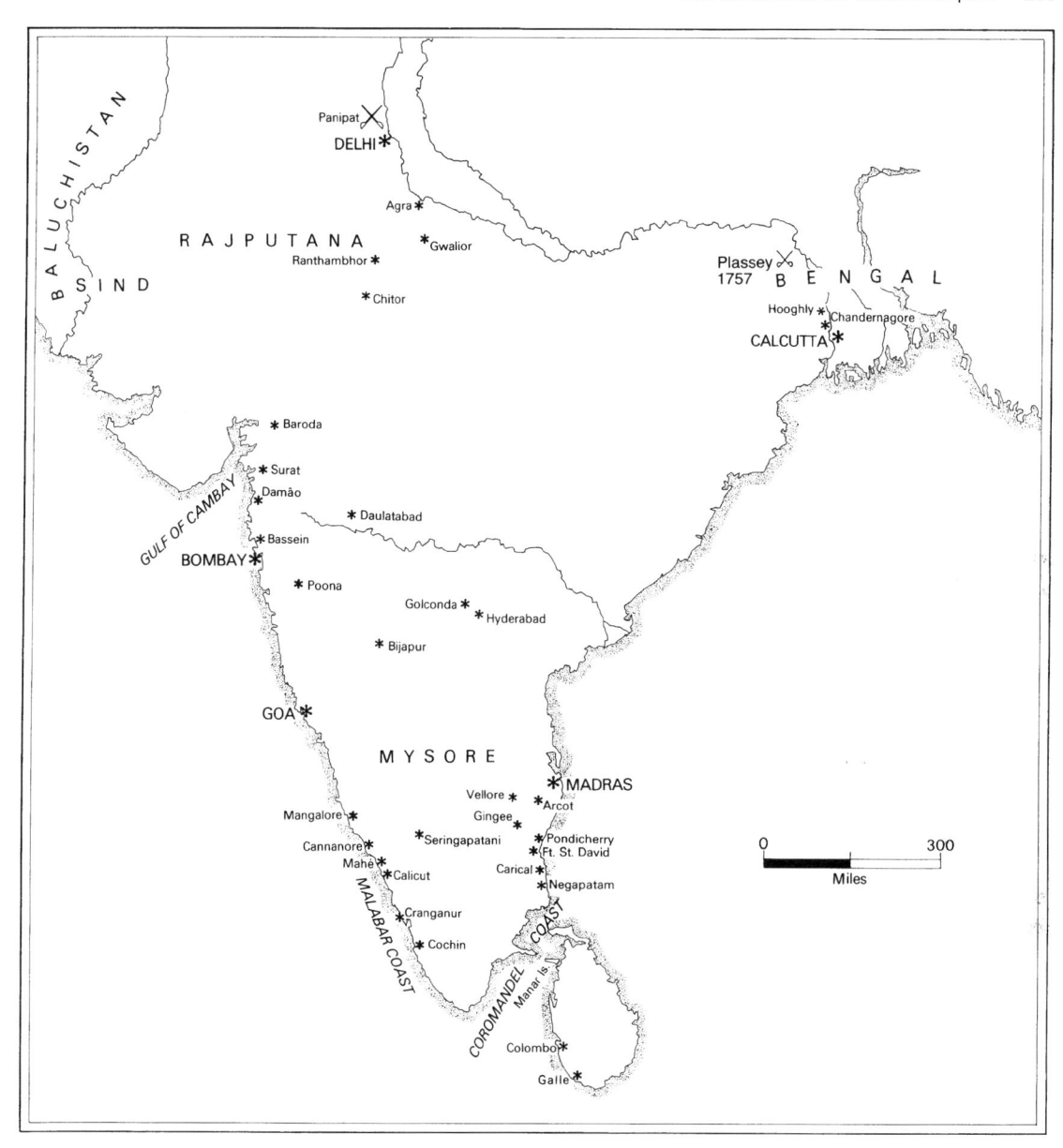

India

greeted by an accidental salute from shotted cannon – a blunder which offered a fitting introduction to affairs in French India. Lally had brought with him only his own regiment of Irish infantry and fifty gunners, but the authorities at Pondicherry had no tools, ammunition or worth-while troops waiting for him. The local officials did not even know the extent of the enemy defences and forces.

Lally decided to besiege nearby Fort St David, a move which was regarded as sensational. As the Comte d'Estaing noted in his diary, 'it was quite novel, in this part of the world, to undertake the formal attack of a strong fortress' (Lally-Tolendal, 1779, I, 60). Lally arrived before the place in May 1758, and proceeded to scandalise local opinion still further when he struck at the caste system, which did not permit a Sepoy infantryman to demean himself by digging so much as an inch of ground for a battery. Lally's son writes:

My father sought to overcome these prejudices by one of those dramatic gestures which make such an impact on crowds. Wishing to show the people that there is no such thing as servile labour in warfare, he journeyed to the trenches in all the regalia of his office and surrounded by his staff, and before the astonished eyes of the Indians he proceeded to assist the solders in wielding pick-axe and shovel, carting away the spoil, carrying burdens and dragging up the ammunition. (*ibid.*, I, 57–8)

In the event the Sepoys proved more ready to follow his example than did the old India hands among the French. Fort St David capitulated on 2 June, after the morale of the garrison collapsed.

Lally now turned against Madras, a fortress which was now considerably stronger than when de la Bourdonnais had taken it in 1746. Lally overruled his engineer d'Urre by directing the attack against the north front of the place, and, with rather less justification, when he opened fire on 2 January 1759 with only three hundred rounds of artillery ammunition at hand. The disgruntled d'Urre conducted the attack in a half-hearted way, and aligned the embrasures of the batteries so badly that it was physically impossible for many of the guns to hit their target. Every cannon that the French unmasked was immediately answered by three from the fortress. A British squadron of relief arrived on the scene, and on 17 February Lally was forced to raise the siege.

Over the next two years the British drove Lally back to the immediate neighbourhood of Pondicherry. The man chiefly responsible was Colonel Eyre Coote, who was a vigorous and systematic soldier in his thirties, and belied a name which brings to mind some ancient, moulting eagle. By the start of 1761 the French at Pondicherry were closely hemmed in. The garrison was starving, and the works were in a poor state to meet a formal siege:

The ditch was filled by the subsidence of the counterscarp; two-thirds of the covered way had been traced out but not completed; the dry-stone wall was four feet wide at the summit, of which two feet had been taken to form a little chemin de ronde; the bastions were so weak that the garrison did not dare to fire so much as an 8-pounder cannon, for fear of bringing them down – such was the condition of the capital of the French establishments in India. (*ibid.*, I, 57–8)

Lally was forced to conclude an unconditional surrender on 16 January 1761. Coote was full of admiration for what Lally had contrived to do, in the face of every difficulty, but French public opinion demanded a sacrifice, and after the war this gallant soldier was put on trial and executed.

The British returned Pondicherry to the French, in virtue of the peace of 1763, but they could console themselves with the thought that they had already inflicted irreversible damage on the enemy interests in India. The British took Pondicherry again after a month's siege in 1778, in the American War of Independence, and this time they took care to raze the fortifications before they handed the place back. For the rest of the war the French remained in India only as auxiliaries and advisers with the disaffected princes of central and southern India. The Marathas achieved some victories over the British in 1779, which brought Hyderabad and Mysore into the contest against 'John Company' in the following year. The British were more than once near to being thrown out of India altogether, but thanks to the generalship of Coote and some canny diplomacy they were able to wreck the hostile native coalition before an expedition from France reached India in 1783. In the next year the Peace of Mangalore resored the boundaries to the lines they had followed before the war. The British, however, had braved the fury of the strongest and best-advised of the local princes, and thereby established the company as a first-class Indian power.

The effects were to be seen in British military architecture. By now the forts at Bombay, Madras and Calcutta were incapable by themselves of containing the vast military establishments, or of guarding the increasingly wide areas under the Company's control. In the 1780s and 1790s more and more of the functions of the forts were taken over by the military suburbs called 'cantonments' or 'lines'. At Calcutta, for example, the authorities abandoned the principle of the closed city, and began to plant the troops around the periphery of the sprawling urban area in the cantonments at Dum Dum, Ballyganj and Barrackpore. The pressure of population at the centre of the city was now somewhat relieved, and the company cleared the area outside Fort William to form the spacious and breezy Maidan esplanade.

The development of British amphibious striking power

In the middle years of the eighteenth century, by dint of painfully-acquired experience, the British gradually learnt the arts of launching well-equipped expeditions across the seas, and dealing effectively with whatever forces or fortifications they encountered on the far side.

The start could scarcely have been less promising. There were certainly many tempting targets at hand, particularly in the Spanish colonial empire. 'No other territory', wrote Montalembert, 'is so vulnerable along its whole extent. The Spaniards, with their extraordinary indolence ... are inclined to regard their flimsy ramparts as insurmountable obstacles, and they believe that the defenceless sectors of their coastline are sufficiently protected by the adverse climate' (Montalembert, 1776-96, III, 96).

In 1741 the British staged an attack on the Spanish-American fortress of Cartagena, but the enterprise became a costly and humiliating debacle. The naval and land officers were at loggerheads, and Admiral Vernon or one of his party railed against the army's technical services:

And for the engineers, bombardiers and gunners, worse never bore the name or could be picked out of all Europe. Amongst the ten engineers there was but one who ever saw a siege, and that was the simple siege of Gibraltar [1727], and he was killed in Bocca Chica, in the midst of his own defenceless works, so that the rest may justly have been said to be left without a head. As for the bombardiers and gunners, the colonel commanding the train was in his grand climacteric, and consequently very unfit to be sent on this expedition. (Porter, 1889-1958, I, 153-4)

All of this reflected on the parlous state of the British military technologists. The Corps of Royal Engineers had been set up as an independent entity in 1716, with an establishment of twenty-eight officers, but the Chief Engineer was free to designate any officers as 'engineers' without formal examination, and the authorities made no provision for a systematic technical education until they founded the artillery and engineering academy at Woolwich in 1741.

The British now proceeded to launch a series of expeditions against strongpoints on the French coast which proved to be less bloody but hardly more glorious than the affair at Cartagena. The enterprises against Lorient in September 1746, Rochefort in September 1757 and Saint-Malo in June 1758 failed for identical reasons – the routes between the landing places and the objectives were too long or too difficult, and the commanders were so ignorant of the state of the fortifications that they were unwilling to test their luck. The one tangible military result from all this effort was to force the French to divert 134 battalions and fifty-four squadrons of regular troops to the defence of their coasts in the Seven Years War.

These defeats helped the British to grasp certain truths concerning amphibious operations. Thomas More Molyneux was provoked by the failure of 'the mighty parade of our Rochefort armament'

(Molyneux, 1759, I, 212) into undertaking a very detailed historical analysis of the nature of combined expeditions (*Conjunct Operations*, 1759), ranging from the landings of Julius Caesar to the disasters of the earlier part of the Seven Years War:

Our conjunct armaments go out freighted with good wishes, blessings, and huzzas; these they soon disburthen, and have too often come home loaded with reproaches, sorrow, and disappointments. We call ourselves the Neptune of the Sea, without knowing how, in many parties, to sway the trident. (*ibid.*, I, 2)

Molyneux identified consistent sources of failure in the discord between military and naval commanders, the neglect of providing material necessities, the ignorance of the locality, the lack of suitable boats and orderly arrangements for the landings and re-embarkations, but especially in the 'hardening' of enemy coasts through effective fortifications, which from the beginning of the seventeenth century became

more frequent, as well as more perfect. . . . Wherefore we may reasonably suppose, more art was required in making descents upon a coast fortified, than upon one open and defenceless. Nothing proves this plainer, than our conjunct expeditions from this period of time which gives us near on 160 years, not meeting with that success as they did before in the same length of time . . . we have not changed with the times, as we ought to do. We have not kept pace in our manner of attack, with the improved method of defence. (*ibid.*, II, 2, 29)

Among the practical military men the young Lieutenant-Colonel James Wolfe had been a witness of the events at Rochefort, and on his return he pointed out something which many people had been inclined to forget, that risk and uncertainty must be accepted as part of warfare, and that 'pushing on smartly is the road to success' (to Major Rickson, 5 November 1757, Wolfe, 1909, 399). Then again, the higher officers of the army and navy began to find out that it was more satisfactory to help one another out than to revel in the other's misfortune. The engineers too were in better heart, for they now enjoyed equivalent military rank, and they were more experienced and better educated than in earlier times.

In home waters the capture of the Breton island of Belleisle in 1761 was the first indication that the British were becoming more adept in amphibious warfare. Admiral Keppel had been disturbed by the composition of the first wave of the land forces to be sent out – 'It is impossible to tell you what a set of wretches I have for engineers, and none of them more worthless than the great Captain Walker' (Whitworth, 1958, 359). Fortunately, his lamentations were heard in Whitehall, and a new transport of infantry, miners and engineers came to join Keppel under the command of Colonel Desaguliers, who was the most scientifically minded gunner of the army. The British now proceeded to reduce the citadel of Palais by formal siege.

As we have seen, a comparable fund of experience had been gathered in India. At Madras Colonel William Draper was inspired to propose an expedition against Manila, the entrepôt of Spanish trade in the Far East. He scratched together a force of about two thousand regulars, Sepoys, and French and German deserters from Lally's army, 'such a banditti [as] never assembled since the time of Spartacus' (Thornton, 1957, 46). Admiral Cornish put the expedition safely ashore on 25 September 1762, and on 6 October Draper wrested Manila from the astounded Spaniards after a short but vigorous siege.

The change in the British style of operations was also evident in the West Indies, where the powerful expeditions had an excellent base in Barbados, a point from where they could run before the easterly trade winds to any of the French islands of the Lesser Antilles.

In January 1759 a devastating naval bombardment by Commodore Moore compelled the French to evacuate the town and citadel of Basseterre, which was the capital of the privateering and sugar-growing island of Guadeloupe. Colonel Barrington completed the task of occupying the island by the beginning of May.

Three years later sixteen thousand British and American troops descended on Martinique under the direction of General Monckton and Admiral Rodney. They first of all set about the technically

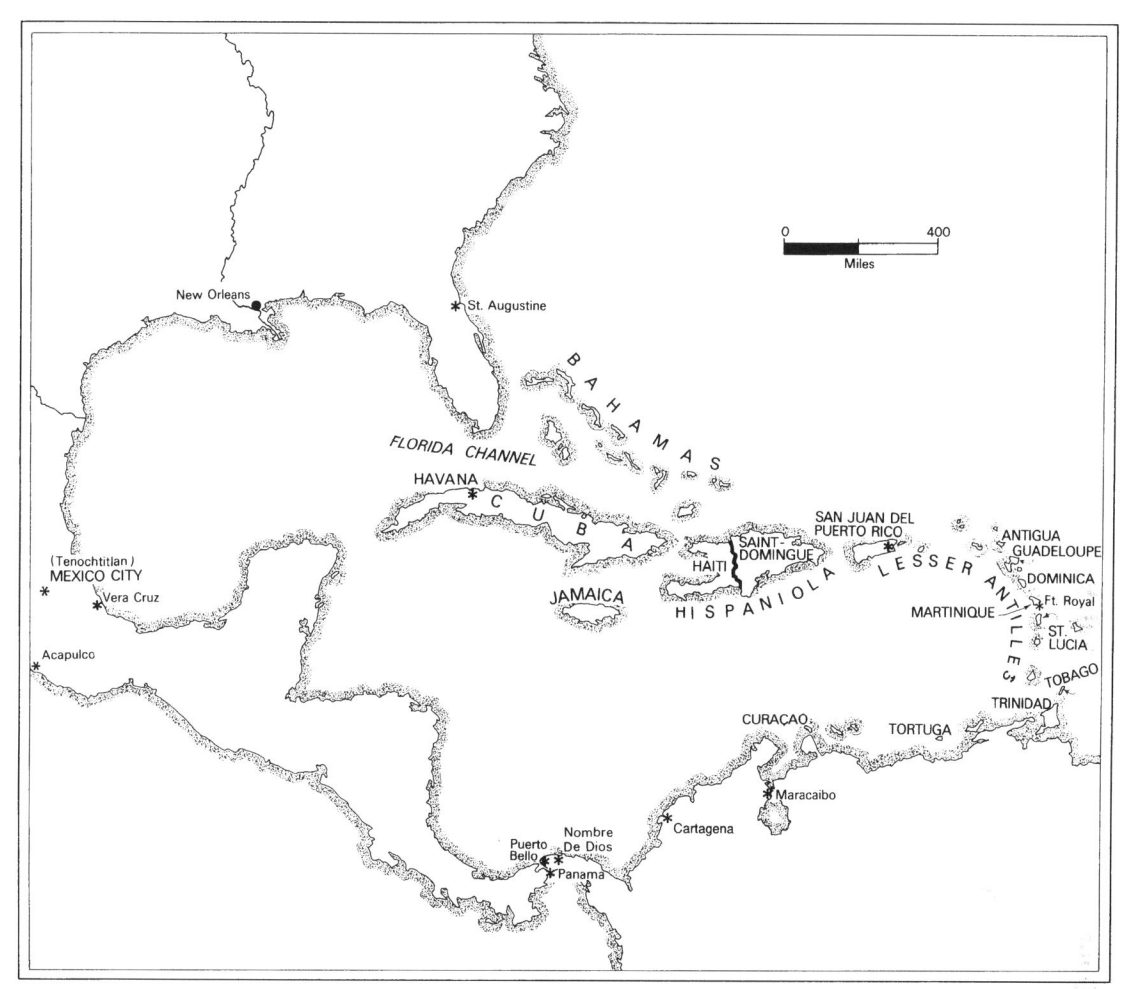

West Indies and Central America

difficult task of reducing the fortified hills, or 'deodands', behind Fort Royal. A thousand seamen came ashore to help, and they very soon succeeded in changing the ideas of many land officers as to what ground was practicable for siege artillery:

A hundred or two of them with ropes and pullies will do more than all your dray-horses in London. Let but their tackle hold, and they will draw you a cannon or a mortar on its carriage up to any height, though the weight be never so great. (Quoted in Corbett, 1907, II, 222–3)

By taking the hills the besiegers effectively cut off Fort Royal from the hinterland, and the defenders capitulated on 3 February 1762 rather than undergo an attack.

Later in 1762 the hitherto inviolate Spanish fortress of Havana on Cuba was reduced by the British, which was the most convincing proof possible of the power of their peculiar style of siege warfare. Charles III of Spain had inadvisedly ranged himself with the French when the Seven Years War was almost at an end, and the British, who had enjoyed naval superiority since their victory at Quiberon, decided to retaliate by attacking Spain's premier military establishment in the New World.

First of all a skilfully managed concentration of forces from England and Martinique brought together twelve thousand men for the landing north of the city on 7 June 1762. The expedition was accompanied by no less than fifteen engineers under the command of Lieutenant-Colonel Patrick Mackellar, who had distinguished himself at Quebec.

General Eliot was sent inland with a detached force to cut off communications between Havana and the country, while the principal army under the Earl of Albemarle closed in to make a formal siege of Fort Moro, which commanded the two-hundred-yard-wide channel leading from the sea to the harbour. Fort Moro was advantageously situated on the north side of the channel at the seaward end of the Cabaña ridge, and its strong if rather old works were protected by a landward ditch that was quarried out of the rock to a depth of between forty-four and sixty-four feet.

The Royal Navy rendered unstinting help under the direction of Vice-Admiral Sir George Pockock, which was of the first importance in forwarding the operation. On 1 July three ships of the line made an apparently disastrous attack on the Moro. Casualties were heavy on the warships, but the naval bombardment provided a useful distraction, which enabled the British land batteries to gain a superiority of fire. Several of the batteries were manned and armed from the fleet, and a land officer testified that:

our sea folks began a new kind of fire unknown to us, or, at all events, unpractised by artillery people. The greatest fire from one piece is reckoned by them from eighty to ninety times in twenty-four hours, but our people went on the sea system, firing extremely quick and with the best direction ever seen, and in sixteen hours fired their guns 149 times. (Quoted in Corbett, 1907, II, 274–5. These were iron naval cannon. Such a rate of fire could never have been maintained by the conventional bronze iron ordnance.)

The Navy also helped by sending ashore such commodities as provisions, water, cables, old sails to be cut up as sand bags, and bales of cotton for use as gabions.

The Spanish gunners, however, continued to shoot back with coolness and determination, and the progress of the artillery attack was delayed by an accidental fire which destroyed the main battery of eight cannon and two mortars on 3 July. The British also experienced great difficulty in building up their siege approaches across the bare rock in front of the Moro, and the expedition as a whole was suffering heavily from disease.

At last the siegeworks came to an end at the edge of the giddy drop to the floor of the ditch. Everything now depended on the miners, who bravely made their way to a bastion across a narrow comb of rock which served as a batardeau, closing off the ditch from the sea. During the siesta on 30 July the British exploded two mines, one behind the counterscarp and the other beneath the opposite bastion. The charges produced a ramp across the ditch and a steep but practicable breach, and the waiting assault parties fought their way into possession of the fort.

The loss of the Moro broke the back of Havana's resistance. Many invaluable Spanish grenadiers and seamen had been killed in the last minutes of the defence, and the imbalance of forces was accentuated when the first of three thousand American troops, who landed on 28 July, were made available for the siege. Also the British were now free to establish their artillery on the Cabaña ridge, which had been unaccountably left unfortified by the Spanish, and from where the besiegers could dominate the city and its mouldering enceinte on the far side of the channel. On 10 August the British opened fire from the Cabaña with their mortars and five batteries of cannon, and almost at once Havana's parapets crumbled away.

Both sides were eager to put an end to hostilities. The British were tormented by the sun, and five thousand of their men were already dead of disease. For his part Don Luis de Velasco, the brave defender of Havana, knew that his ammunition was so short that further resistance was numbered in hours. A capitulation with the honours of war was arranged on 12 August.

The capture of Havana eliminated about one-quarter of the Spanish navy, namely nine floating ships of the line, two more on the stocks and a further three sunk as blockships in the harbour. No less than 1,882,116 Spanish dollars were confiscated in cash, and 'when all the carnage is reckoned, the fact remains that probably no conquest, as once so rich, so decisive, and of so high a strategic value, was ever made against a civilised force at so small a cost' (Corbett, 1907, II, 282).

In a wider context the advent of such a powerful expedition to the New World compelled both the British and the Spanish to revise their colonial strategies. The fevers contracted at Havana continued to plague the victors when they were shipped on to New York, and so the enfeebled British military establishment was incapable of putting a rapid end to the dangerous rebellion of the Indian chief Pontiac, which broke out in 1763. The London government accordingly decided that the colonists ought to take a fair share of the burden of maintaining armed forces in America – a policy that was to lead directly to the fatal breach of the 1770s. 'The British took Havana and gained the Floridas, but at the cost of an army, and perhaps unknowingly set the stage for the loss of an empire' (Syrett, 1970, xxxv).

The Spaniards had to face up to the overthrow of a strategy which had stood them in good stead for almost two centuries, ever since Pedro Menéndez de Avilés had established his system of armed convoys and key fortified bases (see Duffy, 1979, 224). The British returned Havana to Spain after the war, but they had demonstrated their capacity to master the guardian of the Florida Channel, and the mainland of New Spain (Mexico) itself could no longer be considered invulnerable.

As regards conventional defences, the Spaniards strengthened Havana, Campeche, and Acapulco (on the Pacific coast). However, something more comprehensive was needed to safeguard New Spain, now that absolute trust could no longer be reposed in the defensive power of its winter storms, its summer fevers, its open coast, its roadless interior, or the low, sand-blown ramparts of the filthy, stinking, disease-ridden fortress-port of Vera Cruz, which was called the 'throat of New Spain', even if the name of another passage might have seemed more apt. The sole position of any strength was the island fastness of San Juan de Ulloa, standing off Vera Cruz. The Spanish therefore strove to found a local establishment of New Spanish regular infantry and cavalry, which would provide defence of a more active and independent kind. It was hoped at the same time to strengthen the links with the homeland by means of a regeneration of trade, and through the work of specially assigned Spanish officers, who would imbue the local forces with patriotism and the military spirit. In the event the native society proved almost completely unresponsive, and even the Spanish regiments were ruined by the corruption, negligence and hostility which reigned in New Spain.

As technical exercises, the operations against Havana and Belleisle were all the more creditable, since they had been undertaken against unusually skilful and tenacious defenders. Indeed it was only in the last stages of the Peninsular War that the British were to prove so competent in siegework as in the early 1760s. What was lacking was the element of continuity, which in turn was largely the product of the short-sighted pragmatism of the British.

In 1772, for instance, the naval lieutenant J. P. Ardesoif made a creditable attempt to interest his comrades in land operations when he published his *Introduction to Marine Fortification and Gunnery*. He told the naval officers that 'if they would consider their own consequences in a country that chiefly depends upon them, and their marines, they would blush that an officer should be sent from another corps to command and direct them in the simple operation of firing a bomb' (Ardesoif, 1772, xi. The mortars on the bomb-ketches were operated by bombardiers from the Royal Artillery). The pity is that Ardesoif could have done so much better. He gave stale enumerations of Le Blond's artillery tables, and of the real or fancied traces of Vauban and Coehoorn, when he could have helped young officers to appreciate all the things which had been shown in the Seven Years War to make for the success of a combined attack on a fortress – a sound knowledge of the fortifications and their surroundings, the moral impact resulting from the appearance of a heavily armed expedition over the horizon, the existence of a skilled and cheerful labour force in the seamen of the fleet, and the availability of immense quantities of heavy guns which no 'land' army could ever have transported to a siege.

Molyneux had alluded to some of these issues in passing, but his analysis was stronger in its negative criticisms than in its positive recommendations. Instead of exploring what was to be done with the forces and equipment available, he advocated the formation of special amphibious 'ranger' regiments of infantry and artillery, and in all seriousness suggested that maritime fortresses could be taken by escalade by means of ladders set up in boats – which would have made for a merry massacre.

North America

The Indian frontiers of New Spain

The *provincias internas* of Mexico were inhabited by a cowed, depleted Indian stock which was incapable of putting up effective opposition to Spanish rule. To the north, however, the Spanish penetration of the North American subcontinent was discouraged by a malevolent combination of unwelcoming terrain, limited resources and savages of a much more lively kind.

On the eastern flank, in Florida, the Spanish maintained the fort of San Marcos at St Augustine together with a chain of missionary stations. They had little inducement to expand these footholds, since the barren coastal dunes and the inland swamps produced neither precious metals nor bountiful crops, and the British had established their colony of Carolina to the north in the 1670s. Westwards the Mississippi zone was infested by the French. By the 1730s these daring folk were thickly planted in Biloxi, Mobile, New Orleans and their other settlements in southern Louisiana, and they had founded trading posts as far up the Mississippi as modern Minnesota.

When the Spanish began to advance north from Mexico, the initiative proceeded from the government, and the progress was fitful. The first slow push of settlers and missionaries into Arizona and Texas met with an abrupt check in the Pueblo Indian revolt of 1680, which caused the Spanish and the loyal Indians to abandon the outlying communities and congregate at El Paso on the Rio Grande.

French traders arrived on the Rio Grande in 1700s, which at last forced the Spanish authorities to summon up the energy to consolidate eastern Texas as a barrier against Louisiana. In 1716 alone they planted six missions and two *presidios* (garrisons) on the Sabine River. Two years later they founded San Antonio as a way station between these distant posts and the Rio Grande. This advance brought the Spanish into unpleasantly close contact with the violent ways of the Plains Indians, who had acquired firearms and stray horses from the Europeans, but showed no desire whatsoever to settle down as good Christians. Indeed, it would be difficult to think of more effective deterrents to curiosity than the barriers formed by the persons of the Apaches, who hunted from the Gila in the west to the Pecos in the east, and the no less intractable Comanches, who roamed to the rear and east of the Apaches in the area between the upper Pecos and the Gulf of Mexico.

The borders remained in this state until a number of motives bestirred the Spaniards into undertaking an extensive reorganisation in the 1770s. They had acquired Louisiana from the French in 1763, which removed one of the sources of anxiety, but a dangerous power vacuum was now felt along the missionary border, for the government had expelled the Jesuits from the Spanish dominions. Nor could the Viceroy afford to forget that the Russians were showing signs of interest in the Pacific coastlands.

The plans for the new frontier were based on information which had been gathered in the 1760s by the Marqués de Rubí, Nicolas de Lafera and José de Gálvez. The first fruit of this bureaucratic activity was a comprehensive *Reglamento e Instruccion para los Presidios* (1772), which realigned and regulated the borders on principles that remained in force until 1848, long after the Mexicans had claimed their independence. The detailed pattern of the frontier forts was likewise determined between 1776 and 1783 by the commandant-general, Field-Marshal Don Teodoro de Croix, who organised the line in two main sections, namely from Altar near the Gulf of California to Guajoquilla on the Rio Grande, and then down that river to San Juan Bautísta.

Two salients projected from this continuous frontier. The province of New Mexico stretched for about three hundred miles on either side of the upper Rio Grande, and terminated in the Sangre de Cristo Mountains near the *presidio* of Santa Fé. Meanwhile along the Pacific coast the missionaries were winning converts among the Indians of California ('Hot Furnace'). The northernmost *presidio* in that part of the world was established at San

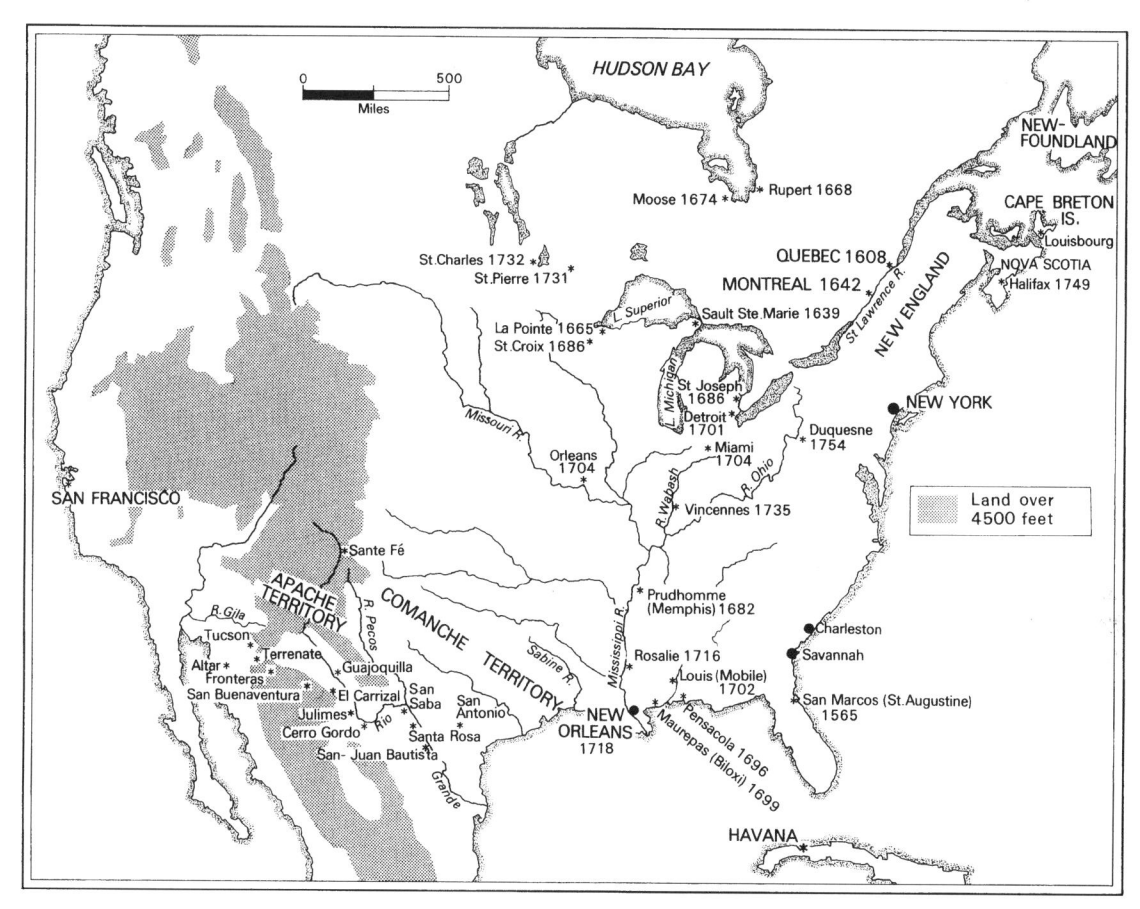

North America in the colonial period

Francisco on 27 June 1776.

The true Spanish power by no means corresponded with the immense tract of land which appears on the map to have been taken in by the line of *presidios*. The typical fort was little more than a rectangular enclosure of sun-dried brick, reinforced here and there by a small tower of round or square trace. The paltry armament consisted of small, crudely made cannon, often of Mexican manufacture. The interior of the fort was indistinguishable from that of many small Latin American towns, with shops to provide for the needs of soldiers and their families, and courtyards for the evening promenade and the occasional influx of refugees and their livestock.

The garrisons were unable to guarantee so much as an inch of ground outside their walls. In 1783, when New Spain's military force stood at the unprecedentedly 'high' number of 4,686 regulars, the Indians could still sweep down with impunity on the surrounding corrals and make off with the horses. In the open plains the Indians encountered little difficulty in evading or trapping the patrols of Spanish cavalrymen, encumbered as they were with their trains of remounts, their lances, their leather shields and their stifling leather coats. However, Teodoro de Croix did not hesitate to ascribe the parlous condition of the frontier above all to the failings of the garrison officers: 'They openly embrace all the abominable excesses of drunkenness, luxury, gambling and greed' (Thomas, 1941, 42).

Important contributory causes were the refusal of the settlers to help in the work of defence, and the dwindling of support from Spain towards the end of the eighteenth century. Thus the future of North America came to lie in other hands than the Spanish.

The new France and the new England – patterns of settlement

Champlain, the founder of French Canada, established Quebec in 1608, and planted Montreal upriver as a rampart against the western Indians. The St Lawrence valley between these two places remained the heartland of French Canada, and the dour colonists from northern and western France settled themselves in narrow strip-like holdings which ran inland from the river banks. Well to the west a faster moving vanguard of traders, missionaries, troops and fur-trappers built stockaded forts on the narrows of the Great Lakes and the portages of the rivers. The speed of the advance had much in common with the Russian penetration of Siberia, which likewise made use of waterways, and it is no exaggeration to say that the French spanned the Great Plains before the British broke in force across the tangled Appalachians.

In these western regions, however, the French were primarily interested in claiming the souls of the Indians for Christianity, and gaining their furs by trade – activities which relied on keeping the human and physical environment intact. A Francophile Iroquois Indian tried to make the point to his fellow tribesmen in 1754:

Brethren, are you ignorant of the difference
between our Father [the French] and the English?
Go and see the forts our father has erected, and you
will see that the land beneath their walls is still
hunting ground, having fixed himself in those
places we frequent, only to supply our wants;
whilst the English, on the contrary, no sooner get
possession of a country than the game is forced to
leave it; the trees fall down before them, the earth
becomes bare. (Eccles, 1969, 158)

Even counting in the St Lawrence settlements, the people of French Canada amounted to seventy thousand or less at the time of the Seven Years War, which put them at a numerical disadvantage of something like twenty to one compared with the British Americans to the south. Until almost the very end, however, the Canadians maintained a clear superiority in mobility and military prowess over the British – seemingly incredible assets which they owed to a greater centralisation of control (despite notorious corruption in high places), their skill at managing the canoe and the musket, the facility of water transport, and their generally good relations with the Indians.

In contrast, the open but far more thickly-settled British colonies of the eastern seaboard grew at the slow pace of self-sufficient agricultural communities. They were boxed in to the north by the nations of the Iroquois confederation and their French associates, and to the west by the Appalachians. There was little sign of common purpose among the British colonies. Indeed, out of all the expeditions mounted by the British in the earlier wars the only ones which bore lasting fruits were the enterprises which wrested New Amsterdam (New York) from the Dutch in 1664, and gained Port Royal (Annapolis Royal) and the mastery of Acadia in 1710. Louis XIV had to renounce Acadia (a lightly settled coastal province) and the great island of Newfoundland at the Peace of Utrecht in 1713.

The French appreciated that they would have to take fresh measures to safeguard the seaward approaches to the St Lawrence. Already in 1706 an anonymous memorandum had urged the government to set up a fortified colony on Île Royale (Cape Breton Island), which formed the southern shore of the entrance to the Gulf of St Lawrence:

The proposed establishment will concentrate all the
fisheries in the hands of the French and deny them
to the English altogether; it will defend the colonies
of Canada, Newfoundland and Acadia against all
the enterprises of the English . . . and ruin their
colony at Boston by excluding them from this great
tract of land; it will give refuge to our crippled
vessels . . . it will promote Canadian trade and
facilitate the export of its grain and other produce;
it will furnish the royal arsenals with masts, yards,
timbers and planks. (McLennan, 1957, 30–1)

The Conseil Royal decided in favour of the thing in 1715. The first small band of settlers came ashore in the following year, and the chief engineer of Canada, Jean-François du Verger de Verville began a series of lengthy reconnaissances. In 1721 work

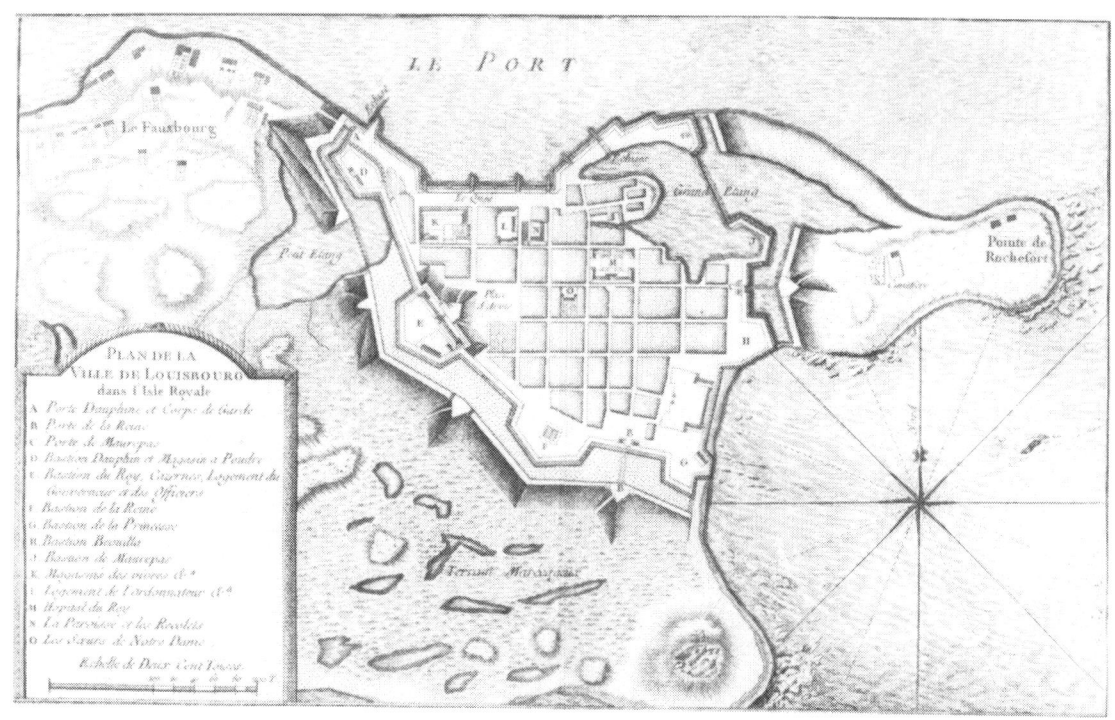

148 Louisbourg (Bellin, 1764)

finally began on the new fortress of Louisbourg. The chosen site was on the east coast of the island at Havre à l'Anglais, a roadstead capable of sheltering an entire French fleet, which might then bottle up any British ships that sailed into the St Lawrence. Verville planted the town on a peninsula, and closed off the neck by a perimeter of two full bastions, three curtains, and two half bastions – one on each of the seaward flanks. A highly original feature of the design was the way the full bastion to the right, looking from the town (Bastion du Roi) was formed into a miniature citadel with gorge wall, barracks, governor's lodging and chapel. The one factor which the French left out of their calculations was the absence of anything which could be termed a 'building season'. The fog and rain prevented the mortar from drying out during the summer, and the imprisoned water froze every winter, with devastating results to the masonry. Verville disliked the Canadian climate intensely, and the Canadians still more, and he spent every winter in the comfort of France. Thus Louisbourg absorbed immense sums of money, without ever being in good repair, and Louis XV complained that he almost expected to see the ramparts of this costly 'Dunkirk of America' rising above the horizon of France.

In a very rare display of joint effort the British North Americans managed to get this establishment into their possession in 1745. The canny and popular merchant William Pepperell gathered 4,000 troops from the New England colonies (which was a considerable achievement in its own right) and sailed to Cape Breton Island in the company of Commodore Warren and 1,000 marines. The many seamen and backwoodsmen proved to be an immense help in building the siege batteries, though somebody complained that the force was 'in great want of good gunners that have a disposition to be sober in the daytime' (*ibid.*, 152). There were no engineers with the expedition at all (until two officers arrived from Annapolis on 5 June), and the French were perplexed by the very irregularity and unpredictability of the conduct of the siege. Louisbourg fell on 17 June after six weeks of attack.

The new governor, Commodore Charles Knowles, had no very high opinion of any kind of fortress as a prize: 'Neither the coast of Acadia nor any of the harbours in Newfoundland (except St Johns and Placentia) are fortified, and these but triflingly, and yet we always be masters of the cod fisheries for that year whether there be a Louisbourg or not' (*ibid.*, 175). Indeed, the British government was not disinclined to listen to the instances of the French, who at the peace conference at Aix in 1748 were determined to regain Louisbourg at almost any price. The Comte de Maurepas, the minister of marine, viewed the place as the guardian of both New France and the Grand Banks fisheries, which latter were of great economic importance and a nursery of seamen. Out of these considerations the French sacrificed Madras in far-off India and the brilliant conquests of de Saxe in the Netherlands.

The British accordingly gave up Louisbourg. They partially made up for the loss in 1749 when they built four forts and a barricade at Halifax on the adjacent peninsula of Nova Scotia (Acadia). Within three years Halifax had a population of four thousand, and the potential to become one of the most important avenues of entry for British power to North America.

The North American crisis of the 1750s
In the middle of the eighteenth century the regular forces of France and Britain were for the first time drawn into direct confrontation in North America.

The reasons for the conflict are still a matter of debate. According to one interpretation (Higonnet, 1968) the encounter was by no means an inevitable collision of empires, but something that was engineered by local interests. On the British side, the governor of Virginia, Robert Dinwiddie, was a large shareholder in the Ohio Company, and had private commercial reasons for persuading London that the fate of Virginia and British North America hung on the domination of the inherently unimportant Ohio valley. His French counterpart Duquesne, governor-general of New France, had associations with a company of fur traders, and it was at least partly in their interest that he began the provocative French fort-building in the Ohio valley in 1753. Duquesne was skilful in representing his actions to Versailles in high-flown terms, and his style was adopted by his successor, the Canadian-born Pierre de Rigaud, Marquis de Vaudreuil (governor-general from 1755). Concerning the *pays d'en haut*, the Ohio and Illinois country, he once wrote to his masters: 'We must . . . hold on there at any cost. As things are at the moment, the salvation of the colony and Louisiana depend on this region' (Michalon, 1978, 71–2).

Montcalm was correct to treat rhetoric of this kind with some suspicion. There remained, however, an element in French policy which genuinely held to an ambitious and imaginative policy of containing British North America. This dimension is associated above all with the name of the Comte de la Galissonière, who was governor-general of New France from 1748 to 1750.

In a famous dispatch Galissonière ranged far in time and space. He foresaw a happy future for Canada, as a prosperous and viable settlement, but he maintained that in the meantime the French presence on the northern flank of the British colonies could act as a most useful military diversion, drawing British forces across the Atlantic from Europe. Exploiting the accident of geography which held the British at the Appalachians, he planned to prevent their emergence on the far side by establishing chains of posts which reached out from the St Lawrence and the Great Lakes by way of the Ohio and its tributaries to the Mississippi, and thence to southern Louisiana, where the French were already settled in some numbers.

Both low commercial calculation and grand strategic design therefore contributed to what seemed in hindsight to be a cunningly thought-out scheme to block British expansion northwards in the direction of Canada, and westwards across the Appalachians.

The northern avenue was formed of a chain of rivers and lakes which presented the most direct path between the British colonies and Canada. This led by way of the Hudson River, lakes George and Champlain, and the Richelieu River to the St Lawrence. Along route the French already owned Fort Saint-Frédéric (Crown Point), which had been planted on the western shore of Lake Champlain in 1731. Saint-Frédéric appeared inadequate to meet

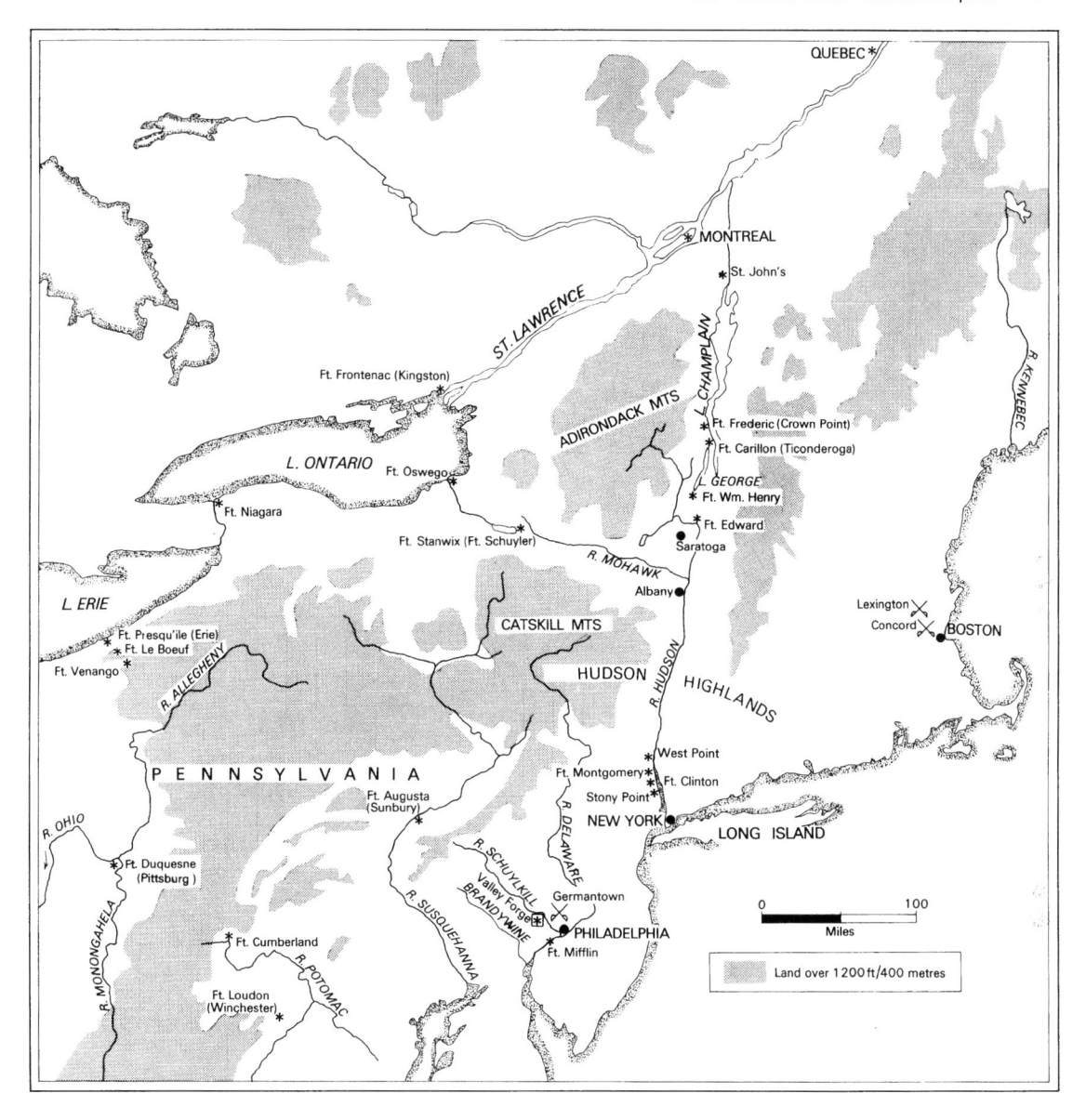

The theatres of war on the St Lawrence, Hudson and Ohio

the more strenuous demands of the 1750s, for it was disadvantageously sited under outlying heights, and it could do nothing to prevent the British getting onto Lake Champlain in the first place. On 20 September 1755 Vaudreuil accordingly instructed an engineer to prospect for a site for a new fort at the southern end of the lake at Carillon Point, so called after the tinkling sound made by the waterfall where Lake George flows into Lake Champlain:

As this Point is the head of the navigation of Lake Champlain, M. de Vaudreuil feared with reason that, the enemy gaining possession of it, it would be very difficult for us to dislodge him, and that being solidly established there we would be exposed to see him appear in the midst of our settlements at the moment we least expected, it being possible for him to make during winter all necessary preparations to operate in the spring. (Lotbinière to Versailles, 31 October 1756, Anon., 1931, 92)

The engineer in question was a Canadian, Michel Chartier, Sieur de Lotbinière, who was born in Quebec in 1723, and who had recently studied engineering in France at the expense of the colony. Lotbinière selected the site for the new 'Fort Carillon' (Ticonderoga) on a ridge of rock, and by prodigies of effort constructed what he claimed to be 'the best thought-out work executed in this country' (Anon., 1931, 96). The first ramparts were formed of a ten-foot thick bank, retained by revetments of massive oak logs, which were in turn braced against the rampart by timber cross-pieces running through the earth. The iron and glass for the fort had to be carried all the way from Montreal, but Lotbinière and his soldier-craftsmen made the necessary bricks from a bank of excellent clay nearby, and in 1757 they began to replace some of the timber revetments with blocks of the local limestone.

Meanwhile to the west the successive governor-generals were busy establishing a series of posts in echelon from Lake Erie to the upper Ohio region, so completing their strategic bridge between the regimes of the St Lawrence and the Mississippi. The Marquis de Duquesne took the first step in 1753, sending an expedition of two thousand colonial troops and two hundred Indians to the southern shores of Lake Erie, where they built Fort Presqu'Île (Erie) as an advanced base. The next bound was commemorated by the planting of Fort Le Boeuf, fifteen miles inland up French Creek. The Virginian Major George Washington reconnoitred the place in December, and reported that:

the bastions are made of piles driven into the ground, and about twelve feet above the sharp at [the] top, with port-holes cut for cannon and loopholes for the small-arms to fire through; there are eight 6-pounder pieces mounted, two in each bastion, and one piece of 4 pound before the gate; in the bastions are a guard-house, chapel, doctor's lodging, and the commander's private store, around which are laid platforms for the cannon and men to stand on; there are several barracks within the fort, for the soldiers' dwelling, covered, some with bark, and some with boards, made chiefly of logs. There are also several other houses, such as stables, smith's shop, etc. (Hunter, 1960, 88)

With a few modifications, this description could have been extended to almost any of the forts which the French and British built in North America.

The Virginia Assembly awoke tardily to the danger at its back door, and in February 1754 it voted £10,000 to build a four-bastioned fort on the upper Ohio. Work began in April, but the construction party had to retreat in the face of a new lunge by the French, who impudently took over the site and in little more than one month completed the defences of 'Fort Duquesne' nearby, which was the strongest, the most advanced and by far the largest of the French forts in the *pays d'en haut*. The French had just three hundred troops at Duquesne, and another hundred each at Presqu'Île and Le Boeuf, but their presence was enough to incline the Indians of the Ohio to the side of the French, and assist in the liaison with Fort Chartres and the other posts of the Illinois. These developments were a sad disappointment to the Lees, the Washingtons and the other magnates of the new Ohio Company, who had already parcelled out the Indians' land in their imagination.

Galissonière never intended to confine his Canadians to their fortifications, declaring 'You preserve nothing by sitting still. If you don't attack on your own account, you will come under attack your-

The Collision of the Colonial Empires 269

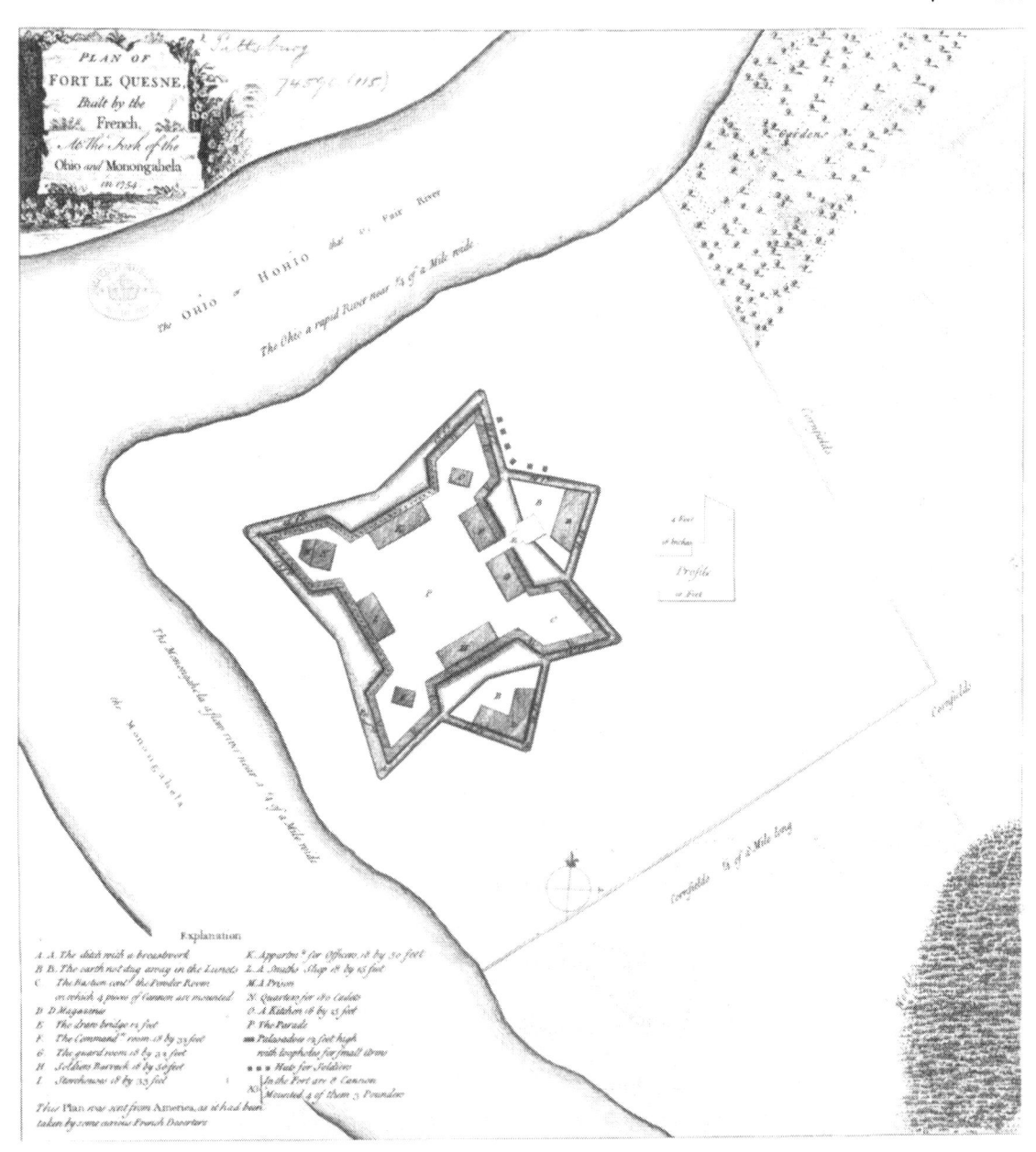

149 Fort Duquesne (Payne, 1755)

self, and the cost of the defensive will exceed that of the offensive' (Michalon, 1978, 79). This suggestion too was taken up with enthusiasm by Vaudreuil, who dispatched his Indians and Canadians on forays that were designed to paralyse and terrorise the British colonies, and hold the enemy as far distant as possible from the St Lawrence.

The expeditions of Washington and his small colonial band in 1754, and of General Braddock with his 2,200 well-found troops in the next year were both of them swallowed up by the forest, the French and the Red Men. The borders were now open to the depredations of the French and their Indians, and the alarmed British colonists and military men threw up a multitude of official and 'private' forts along the whole length of the Allegheny Mountains. Even Pennsylvania was prepared to forget its Quaker principles, and take up musket, axe and spade. Morris, the colony's governor, acquired a taste for fortress-building, and he sent out detailed instructions as to the dimensions and proportions of the works that were to be built. Washington's own experiment in this kind of thing at Fort Necessity in 1754 had led to a minor disaster, and on touring the chain of Virginia forts two years later he sourly reported that the garrisons were 'weak from want of men, but more so from indolence and irregularity' (Freeman, 1949-52, II, 222).

A more 'military' policy prevailed once the first panic had subsided. The defensive system of Pennsylvania came to be centred on the Susquehanna at Fort Augusta (Sunbury), a stronghold which had sides 204 feet long and exceeded in scale even the hated Fort Duquesne. To the south, Governor Dinwiddie of Virginia at last fell in with Washington's arguments and abandoned all his forts except Waggener and Loudon (Winchester) in the Shenandoah Valley, and the vital Fort Cumberland which guarded the gap which was carved by the Cumberland in the Allegheny Mountains.

The arrival of Major-General Braddock and his two regiments of infantry in 1755 was the first indication that the London government had taken the momentous decision to answer the French challenge by committing regular troops from Europe to the North American theatre. Every reasonable effort was to be made to safeguard the trade with the increasingly prosperous American colonies. The French responded in kind, as we shall see, but the British gradually exerted their naval superiority, which was of vital importance for shipping reinforcements across the Atlantic, and by 1760 they had about twenty regiments on the theatre, or a total of about sixty thousand troops if we include the colonials. Vaudreuil and Montcalm had at the most fifteen thousand French and Canadian troops at their disposal.

The advent of the European regulars effected a radical change in the relationships on the scene of conflict in America, and it still poses some interesting problems in the interpretation of the last French and Indian campaigns. Three thousand *Troupes de Terre* (French regulars) appeared in New France under the command of the ill-fated Dieskau in 1755, and a further three thousand disembarked in 1756 with a new chief, Maréchal de Camp Louis-Joseph Marquis de Montcalm. A proud and hot-tempered son of the *Midi*, Montcalm was determined to mend the ways of the Canadians, and before long he announced:

The foundation of warfare in this colony has completely changed. Hitherto the Canadians believed they were waging war, when all they did was go on raids which resembled nothing so much as hunting-parties. Now we have operations which are carried through a proper sequence. Now the savages are relegated to auxiliaries, whereas they used to play the leading part. There is therefore a need for fresh views, fresh principles. (Hitsman, 1968, 10)

Montcalm's entire military experience had been in European warfare, where he had survived sixteen or so sieges, as well as the murderous assault on the Colle dell'Assietta on 17 July 1747. He was an enemy not just of the offensive-defensive strategy of the Indian and Canadian raids, but of the concern with the forts of the *pays d'en haut*, which he ascribed to the ambitions of the fur traders. Instead he desired to incorporate the Canadians with the French regulars (which was to have disastrous results at Quebec in 1759), and to concentrate every effort on the defence of a central core: 'It is the trunk of the tree which is being attacked. Everything which has to do with the branches is a matter of supreme indifference' (Michalon, 1978, 81).

Likewise, the qualified French engineers like Desandrouins were scornful of the kind of log forts which were being built by the axemen of the militia under the direction of the officers *de Marine* (Canadian regulars):

Most of the forts show no sign of common sense. It used to be said that Vauban was formed as an engineer by the sight of the first fortifications he ever saw, however distant they were from perfection. But it is difficult to imagine even a Vauban deriving any benefit from the kind of works in this country. (Berenger, 1979, 81)

The French engineers failed to appreciate that in the circumstances of the theatre fortifications like these could be veritable backwoods Namurs or Turins, when the enemy possessed only light field guns, or indeed no artillery at all.

However, it is difficult to subscribe completely to the views of some North American historians who maintain that the European regulars were hopelessly adrift in the seas of Canadian greenery, and fault people like Jeffrey Amherst for their 'plodding thoroughness' (Eccles, 1969, 177). On the contrary, the story of the campaigns shows that it was worth setting about your marches, sieges and other operations in a systematic fashion. Indeed, as Hitsman has indicated, the disaster which befell Braddock in 1755 was due in part to the neglect of the regulation rules for marching in close country.

Vaudreuil, as governor-general, still had overall control of the war effort of New France, and in the summer of 1756 he directed Montcalm against the shabby fort of Oswego (Chouaguen), which stood on the southern shore of Lake Ontario. This place had been planted as long ago as 1724 by Governor William Burnet of New York, and it still offered an impudent challenge to the French mastery of the *pays d'en haut*. 'I cannot accord to see the operation against Chouaguen fail', wrote Vaudreuil, 'for on the success of this enterprise depends the security of the colony' (Michalon, 1978, 78).

Montcalm subjected Fort Oswego to a formal siege, and the sizeable garrison surrendered on 14 August 1756, after their commander had been decapitated by a cannon shot. The Ohio Indians once more inclined to the side of the French. However, Montcalm wrote almost apologetically to Versailles:

This is perhaps the first time that a force of three thousand men, which was inferior in artillery, has dared to besiege sixteen hundred troops who could have called on the rapid help of two thousand more, and opposed our disembarkation through their preponderance of vessels on Lake Ontario. Our success surpassed all expectations. My conduct in this affair, and the dispositions I made, are so contrary to the accepted rules that the risks I took in the operation would have been dismissed as excessive in Europe. (Michalon, 1978, 130)

The British were as inattentive and as slow to respond as they had been in 1754. All their available forces save three battalions of regulars and some militia were drawn down to the town of New York in 1757 in preparation for an expedition against Louisbourg, which did not take place. Montcalm promptly concentrated five thousand troops and a body of Indians against the recently-built Fort William Henry, at the south end of Lake George, and he captured the place on 9 August by the same technique of vigorous but formal siege which had cracked open Oswego. The haul of booty included twenty-six thousand pounds of gunpowder, and rations for six thousand men for six weeks, but instead of dispatching an expedition against Albany (as Vaudreuil wished), Montcalm retired tamely to Carillon.

The campaigning of 1758 reaffirmed what had already been proved by Montcalm, that meticulously-planned advances and formal siege attacks were as effective in backwoods warfare as in the plains of Flanders.

Major-General Abercromby had the task of redressing the humiliations of 1757 by taking the direct route to the St Lawrence by way of lakes George and Champlain. He assembled about six thousand regulars and nine thousand colonial troops for the enterprise, which was all well and good, but on approaching Carillon he was misled by a sketchy reconnaissance on the part of his engineer, Lieutenant-Colonel Matthew Clark, into leaving his artillery in the rear and launching an improvised assault on Montcalm's position on 8 July. The 3,500 or so French were waiting for him behind a log breastwork and an abatis which made the forest look as if it had been laid low by a hurricane. Montcalm was doubly disinclined to base his defence too narrowly on Carillon itself. The fort had been condemned by his experts on account of its small perimeter, its badly-sited embrasures and its narrow platforms. Also Montcalm and his engineer Desandrouins were veterans of the Assietta battle, and the experience had convinced them of the effectiveness of field defences.

The British lost nearly two thousand men in five attacks, and the survivors fled rather than face the ordeal of a sixth attack. A captured officer declared: 'Why, this was a second day of Assietta!' (Pell, 1953, 193).

On the tactical level the affair may be taken as a vindication of Montcalm's cautious proceedings, and the validity of the European experience of warfare. Vaudreuil, however, was angry that the victory was not followed up by offensive action, and the French government drew the dangerous conclusion that Canada could be left to defend itself, without the need of further help.

Meanwhile Lieutenant-Colonel Bradstreet and his force of 2,600 men, mostly colonial troops, were making ready to deliver what was to prove one of the most decisive of the blows against the western flanks of New France. He began by marching up the Hudson, like Abercromby, but he then 'turned left' just beyond Albany and took the back corridor of the Mohawk around the flank of the Adirondack Mountains, finally emerging on the shore of Lake Ontario. The expedition crossed the water on light craft, and on 27 August Bradstreet captured Fort Frontenac (Kingston), where the lake narrows into the St Lawrence for the surge through the Thousand Islands. Bradstreet did not intend to hold the site, which was exposed to counter-attack from Montreal downstream, but he destroyed the provisions he found there and the flotilla of nine boats, and consequently deprived the French of the means of supplying Duquesne and all the other posts beyond the southern shore of the lake.

Brigadier John Forbes and Colonel Henry Bouquet had the credit of taking the stranded forts. Deliberately avoiding the route which Braddock had taken from Virginia three years before, they struck out from the more northerly colony of Pennsylvania, and took care to establish their depots at intervals of about forty miles, according to the principles which Forbes had read in Turpin de Crissé's *Essai sur la Guerre*. From their last depot at Loyalhanna Creek a forced march with 2,500 men brought them on 25 November 1758 to Duquesne, which was found to have been burnt and abandoned by the French. Forbes was mortally ill, but he survived long enough to set up a stockade in the ruins and re-name the site 'Fort Pitt' (Pittsburg).

The French positions in the west and south collapsed altogether in 1759. Five thousand men under Brigadier John Prideaux came by way of Oswego and Lake Ontario to Fort Niagara, and subjected the place to a formal siege. Prideaux was killed by the premature bursting of a shell, but the energetic Sir William Johnson took over the command and forced Niagara to capitulate on 24 June. Canada was thereby isolated from the southern lakes and the Ohio country.

Meanwhile on the Hudson the new commander-in-chief Major-General Amherst was gathering 11,500 men and enough artillery to undertake regular sieges of forts Carillon and Saint-Frédéric. The French divined his intention, and rather than await the impact they fell back to the northern end of Lake Champlain.

The poor showing of the French was partly due to the fact that the British were simultaneously prising open the eastern, or seaward flank of New France by one of their new and formidable amphibious expeditions. The prime minister, Pitt, was prodigal in the resources he was willing to expend to recapture Louisbourg, at the entrance to the St Lawrence. The place could perhaps have been left to one side, considering the evident British mastery of the seas. The Chevalier de Lévis had already written: 'All the forces of this country [Canada] are unable to do anything for the security of the lower St Lawrence. It is up to our naval forces to hold this gateway open, and, if they are unable to do so, we are in for a bad time' (Masson, 1978, 4). Louisbourg, however, still owned a high political value, as was proved by the

150 Fort Chambly, Richelieu River, Canada. One of the earliest stone forts in Canada, it was built in a backwoods version of the bastion tower style in 1709, to guard the access to Montreal from the south-east. Seized by the British in 1760. (The model in the Fort Chambly Museum.)

price the French had been willing to pay to get it back in 1748.

In the late spring of 1758 Admiral Boscawen shipped 11,400 British troops across the Atlantic to Halifax, where they were assembled with 2,500 colonial troops under the overall command of Amherst. The expedition owned ten engineers, fifty-one siege guns, and so much ammunition that two-thirds remained unconsumed at the end of the year's operations.

Amherst's force landed on Capte Breton Island on 8 June 1758, and proceeded to open two trench attacks against the one-and-a-half mile-long fortified enclosure of Louisbourg. Brigadier Wolfe seemed to be everywhere, and the saying went about that 'wherever he goes he carries with him a mortar in one pocket and a 24-pounder in the other' (McLennan, 1957, 269). However, the digging proceeded slowly under the direction of the old and infirm Colonel J. F. Bastide, and Wolfe had some hard things to say about this side of affairs:

The parapets in general are too thin, and the banquettes everywhere too narrow. The trench of the parallel should be wide, and the parapets more sloping. Our next operations were exceedingly slow and injudicious, owing partly to the difficulty of landing our stores and artillery, and partly to the ignorance and inexperience of the engineers. It is impossible to conceive how poorly the engineering business was carried on here. The place could not possibly have held out ten days had it been attacked with more common sense. (Porter, 1889–1958, I, 185)

Fortunately for the British, Colonel Bastide was rendered *hors de combat* by a wound and Major Mackellar took over the command of the engineers. A new battery was planted on the left (northern) attack, which enfiladed the west front of Louisbourg from end to end, and on 25 July the British opened a breaching fire, causing large sections of the rotten revetment to fall into the ditch at every hit. On the 26th the French surrendered as prisoners of war.

There was every prospect of a still mightier operation in 1759. The pressure of events was already forcing the French to consolidate in the St Lawrence valley between Montreal and Quebec, and the new foreign minister, Choiseul, gave final sanction to Montcalm's defensive strategy, for he wished to limit French commitments to Canada and the war in Germany, and concentrate resources on an intended invasion of the mainland of Britain. Montcalm was promoted to lieutenant-general and given wide powers, and Vaudreuil was told that he must 'never lose sight of the main objective, which must be to retain and establish yourself in a sufficient part of the colony, so as to have a good chance of recovering the whole at the peace' (Masson, 1978, 8).

Vaudreuil and the other French-Canadians recalled episodes like the wreck of Admiral Walker's troops transports in 1711, and assumed that the British could never get a squadron intact up the St Lawrence. Montcalm, however, had lived in fear of just such an eventuality, and as it turned out, Major-General Wolfe gathered troops at Louisbourg from Nova Scotia, New York and Guadeloupe, and came up river with the aid of a renegade French pilot. It was now too late for the French to put Quebec in a respectable state of defence, and, in the absence of ditch, ravelins and counterscarp, Montcalm put his trust in an entrenched camp which was prepared on the bluffs of the north bank of the St Lawrence below the city.

Pointe Lévis, immediately opposite Quebec on the south bank, was left unguarded, which permitted the British to open a destructive bombardment, but Montcalm's strategic position remained inviolate until the enemy managed to get their ships upstream past Quebec. Finally on the night of 12–13 September 1759 Wolfe made a landing on the north bank at the Anse du Foulon, less than two miles above Quebec – a move which threatened Montcalm's communications with Montreal. On the 13th Montcalm came out of Quebec to fight, which was probably inevitable. However, nobody has provided a convincing explanation for the haste which induced him to give battle with just 4,500 troops, when a short delay would have given him three thousand more. The French were defeated and Montcalm mortally wounded, and in the evening Vaudreuil abandoned Quebec to its fate. Now acting under the orders of Brigadier Townshend, the British chief engineer Mackellar broke ground for a siege attack on 16 September. On the next day the depleted garrison capitulated under the threat of assault.

The French were left with a constricted, but intact central position in the area between Quebec, upper Lake Champlain and Lake Ontario. At the heart of the region lay the fortified city of Montreal. In the freezing spring of 1760 the French field commander, the Chevalier de Lévis, actually came out and subjected Quebec to attack. The operation failed, but it had better title to the name of 'siege' than the more famous British undertaking of 1759.

This stroke of enterprise did little to disconcert the British commander-in-chief Amherst, who went ahead with his plans for a three-fold offensive against Montreal. The main force of eleven thousand troops under Amherst's own command embarked on Lake Ontario and came at Montreal from the west. Amherst took and repaired Fort Lévis, at the exit of the lake, and on 31 August he made the perilous descent of the St Lawrence rapids with the loss of sixty boats. The train of artillery followed close behind, despite the obvious risks, which shows how much importance Amherst attached to having his guns with him. The two smaller expeditions arrived by way of Lake Champlain and the lower St Lawrence according to plan, and by the second week in September Montreal was bottled up by a force of seventeen thousand men. On 8 September Vaudreuil signed away Montreal, his garrison and the whole of French Canada.

Amherst's victorious progress in 1760, like every other North American campaign of the Seven Years War, proved that a commander was right to go to a good deal of trouble to make sure that he had enough artillery to deal with any fortifications he found in his path. It is part of the inherent injustice of things that the same laudable preoccupation caused General Burgoyne to be trapped in the American backwoods in 1777, and so went far to cost the British their possession of their old colonies in the south. We find this grossly unfair.

The American Revolution 1775–83

Whether we are talking about the second half of the twentieth century, or the events of two hundred years before, we notice that every generation seems to be taken by surprise by some age-old truths, namely that there is something very momentous about the commitment of regular combat troops to a theatre of conflict, and that (having by definition rejected less drastic forms of influence) the government responsible is faced with responsibilities and consequences which surpass anything that it envisaged at the time it made its first decisions. So it was with the great projection of British military force on to the North American theatre in the Seven Years War.

On the northern flank the imposition of British rule in Canada was accomplished with perhaps unexpected ease, for the Quebec Act of 1774 accomplished a working alliance with the society of New France, or at least its respectable elements. To the west, however, the British had assumed the management of the huge tracts of Indian land beyond the Appalachians, which had to be guarded and garrisoned, and preserved against the pressures of immigration and land speculation which were driving the Americans over the mountain barrier. Indeed, it began to appear to the Americans that the British and their Canadians had inherited the mantle of Galissonière. The London government now began to ask the Americans for a financial commitment to match the British military commitment – a demand that many of the colonists chose to regard as an attack on a *de facto* independence that was already theirs. During this period of tension the larger forts proved to be one of the most potent safeguards of the settlements. For reasons already noted, their far-reaching influence ran counter to the interests both of the conservative British administration and of the wretched Indians. William Smith observed in 1766:

Our forts keep the Indian towns at a great distance from us. Fort Pitt has effectively driven them beyond the Ohio, and made them remove their settlements at least sixty miles further westward. Were it not for these forts, they would settle close on our borders, and in time of war infest us every day in such numbers as would overpower the thin inhabitants scattered on our extensive frontier. (Smith, 1868, 139)

The fight for the strategic footholds 1775–6
Boston. In the spring of 1775 the disaffected folk in the North American colonies rose in revolt. The nine thousand royal troops were unable to hold the countryside of New England against the swarming native militia, and they were compelled to fall back to the small peninsula of Boston, where they dug themselves in. The rebel forces converged on the place and cast up a semi-circular line of investment.

The leisurely blockade of Boston gave the rebel commanders a welcome opportunity to accustom themselves and their troops to fire, much as the French had done during the investment of Philippsburg in 1734 (see p. 100). George Washington, the leading light in the rebel command, had acquitted himself passably well in the old war against the French, but he had spent the last sixteen years as a country gentleman at Mount Vernon. Experience even of this extent was rare, and most of the rebel officers were chosen on account of their political influence, or because they possessed some rags and tatters of warlike knowledge. Like Marquese Spinola of old, more than one amateur of the military art was suddenly called upon to put his bookish hobby into practical effect.

The effort was not as extraordinary as we might have expected, for in spite of the advances in the specialised trade of engineering in recent generations, men still regarded this art as a component of that corpus of knowledge that was accessible to gentry of an enquiring turn of mind:

fortification plans were ... familiar to both amateur and professional students of the military sciences. Indeed, the extent to which they had permeated a wider culture is reflected by their appearance in both the art and literature of the seventeenth and eighteenth centuries. A knowledge of fortification enhanced the education of a gentleman as well as that of a professional soldier. English travellers on the Grand Tour, for example, viewed the fortifications to the north of Venice as part of the 'standard package'. (Harley, 1978, 6)

In North America the interested public was *au fait* with all the common terms of fortification, and the draftsmanship of a formally untrained engineer like Jeduthan Baldwin would not have shamed some of the British professionals. This was perhaps the last generation in which such a thing was possible.

The rebel chief of artillery, Henry Knox, was a characteristic product of the age. As a fat young Boston bookseller he made a speciality of stocking military literature, and he rarely missed an opportunity to discuss his wares with the British officers who happened to pass by. At the beginning of the revolt he was asked by the lawyer John Adams for the names of some good authorities on fortification, and he obliged by tripping off the roll-call of Clairac, Muller and Pleydell on field engineering, and Vauban, Coehoorn, Blondel, Pagan and Belidor on permanent works.

Now, in the blockade of Boston, Henry Knox attracted attention when he worked with Colonel Joseph Waters on two fortifications at Roxbury, immediately opposite the neck of the British-held peninsula. Another amateur engineer, Colonel Richard Gridley of Massachusetts, laid out a redoubt forty yards square and six feet high on the top of Breed's Hill, on the Charleston peninsula just across the harbour from Boston. The British came across the water in force on 17 June, but it cost them more than one thousand casualties to storm the redoubt and the adjacent defences in the mis-named action of 'Bunker Hill'.

After this encounter the British regarded the enemy fortifications with more respect, and talked about works 'well finished and extremely well planned by engineers supposed to be French and Swedes' (Lieutenant William Feilding, Balderston and Syrett, 1975, 33). The blockade was prolonged through the winter into 1776, and the ground was still hard frozen when Washington planted a powerful force on the Dorchester Heights on the night of 4–5 March. Before the British could respond, the rebels had ensconced themselves firmly behind breastworks of fascines and bales of hay. This move more than made up for the loss of the Charleston peninsula, for the Dorchester Heights projected into the main roadstead of Boston harbour, and any hostile guns that were established there would soon made this stretch of water untenable for the British shipping. General Howe accordingly embarked all the British forces and set sail for Halifax on 17 March, leaving behind sixty-nine usable cannon.

Washington took the opportunity to view the abandoned British fortifications, and reported that Boston was 'amazingly strong ... almost impregnable, every avenue fortified' (Freeman, 1949–52, IV, 55). The rebels' own performance was much better than might have been anticipated from beginners, and Samuel Adams wrote:

When I visited headquarters at Cambridge, I had never heard of the valour of Prescott at Bunker Hill nor the ingenuity of Knox and Waters in planning the celebrated works at Roxbury. We were told here [in Philadelphia] that there were none in our camp who understood the business of an engineer or anything more than the manual exercise of the gun. (Callahan, 1958, 34)

The north and Canada. Boston was no great loss for the British, for it was separated from all the more promising theatres of war by the colonies of New England, with their stony ground, and flinty, rebellious hearts. It would have been far more serious if the Crown had lost Canada, which was its northern base of operations. Before the conflict, Colonel Guy Carleton was possibly the only British officer to draw attention to the continuing importance of the line of rivers and lakes which extended from the St Lawrence near Montreal, by way of the Richelieu, lakes Champlain and George, and the Hudson to New York. In 1767, as deputy governor of the province of Quebec, he urged the importance of restoring Fort Ticonderoga (Carillon) and the other strongpoints along this classic route of invasion, so as to facilitate the movement of a corps of ten or fifteen thousand troops between the St Lawrence and the American colonies:

This communication so established, will give security to the King's magazines, till then precarious, and doubtful who may avail themselves of them; will separate the northern from the southern colonies, will afford an easy and advantageous opportunity of transporting his forces into any part of the continent, and may prevent the greatest of all inconveniences, delay and loss of time in the beginning of a war. (Hitsman, 1968, 23)

Nothing effective was done, and rebel raiding parties grasped at their chance at the outset of the new hostilities. On 10 May 1775 the gangs of the giant outlaw chief Ethan Allen and the Connecticut apothecary Benedict Arnold seized delapidated Ticonderoga on Lake Champlain. Crown Point (Saint-Frédéric) succumbed two days later, and in the late autumn the rebel brigadier Montgomery descended the Richelieu, and reduced little Fort Chambly and the much larger St John's. Valuable ordnance and supplies thereby fell into the hands of the rebels, and in the winter Henry Knox had fifty-nine of the captured guns dragged on sledges to the lines before Boston. Thus the armament of the rebels was growing as fast as their experience.

Canada meanwhile lay almost without defence. Continuing down the Richelieu to the St Lawrence, Montgomery took Montreal without opposition on 13 November. He then proceeded to the neighbourhood of Quebec, where he joined Benedict Arnold and the six hundred survivors of a force of backwoodsmen who had made a harrowing march across Maine. Sir Guy Carleton, now governor-general of Canada, held Quebec with a force of about eleven hundred men, which was enough to compel Montgomery to make a formal siege in the depth of winter. The ingenious rebels filled their gabions with snow, then poured water over the top to freeze, but these solid, glittering breastworks flew to pieces under the impact of the British 32- and 42-pounder shot.

During a driving blizzard on the night of 30-31 December Montgomery threw eight hundred men at Quebec in a desperate assault. The Americans were beaten back with a loss of nearly five hundred. Montgomery was killed and Arnold wounded, but the survivors and the as yet uncommitted forces managed to keep up a ragged blockade until reinforcements arrived in April 1776, bringing the rebel numbers up to two thousand. On 6 May a British sortie broke the entire force beyond recall, and the rebels made for the Richelieu in disorder. The German veteran Riedesel fought alongside the British, but he was not at all impressed with what he had seen:

I have toured the entire fortress of Quebec. In Germany we would have subjected a place like this to a few hours' battering fire from between four and eight cannon, and opened a breach wide enough for half a battalion to enter at one time. (Eelking, 1856, III, 177)

It was not easy for a land-bound European to appreciate that the future of empires could depend upon the outcome of 'unprofessional' little actions like these. Carleton had succeeded in holding Canada as a dominion of the Crown, and, what was more immediately important, as one of the bases for the counter-offensive that was going to break over the rebels' heads.

New York. No plan for recovering the rebel colonies could leave out of account the opportunities offered by our famous avenue extending from the St Lawrence valley to New York. The Hudson was by far the most important of the component waterways, for it cut through the heart of the enemy land and offered a good navigation for the final 170 miles from Albany to New York. Henry Clinton, Arnold and the French engineer Duportail were among the people who also made the important observation that the rebel states on either side of the Hudson were not agriculturally self-sufficient colonies, for the easterners were as dependent upon western grain as the westerners were upon eastern cattle.

Altogether there was a good deal to be said for the British fixing themselves at New York, which would give them a base at the southern end of the strategic route which corresponded to Canada at the northern entrance. The rebels lived in fear of this eventuality, and by April 1776 eight thousand men were hard at work fortifying the inner recesses of New York harbour on the plans of Major-General Charles Lee, who was well versed in the techniques of regular warfare from his service with the British army. Manhattan Island was defended by batteries along the eastern and western shores, and by the powerful four-bastioned Fort Washington which stood near the northern tip hard by Harlem, 'a sweet little village with one church' (Freeman, 1949-52, IV, 184). Across the East River the heights of Brooklyn were secured against an enemy advancing over Long Island by means of a three-mile-long row of redoubts and forts which extended across the short neck of the Brooklyn peninsula between Wallabout Bay in the north-east and the deep inlet leading to Gowanus Bay in the south-west. But John

Adams could not conceal all his misgivings: 'The practice we have hitherto been in, of ditching round about our enemies, will not always do. We must learn to use other weapons than the pick and spade. Our armies must be disciplined and learn to fight' (*ibid.*, IV, 142).

On 22 August 1776 General Howe landed the first of his thirty-two thousand troops from Halifax on Long Island. On the following days the British convincingly outfought and out manoeuvred the rebels in the open field, and on 28–29 August they sat down before the Brooklyn Lines in preparation for a formal siege: 'No doubt the slaughter at Bunker Hill in the previous year was a major factor in Howe's calculations' (Cohn, 1962, unpaginated). Washington withdrew his men at once to Manhattan Island, rather than subject his men to a new test. This obliging conduct spared the British an ordeal of their own, as was appreciated by Howe's chief engineer Captain John Montresor, who explained that:

the lines on Long Island were so very strong that the morning they were evacuated it was with great difficulty that he and a corporal's patrol of six men could get into them to view them. The works could not be taken by assault or storm; they called for regular approaches. It would be a forlorn hope to commit naked men to storm redoubts without fascines, scaling ladders, etc. (Porter, 1889–1958, I, 204)

New York town lay just across the East River:

It was now a question, whether to defend the city, or evacuate it, and occupy the strong grounds above. Every exertion had been made to render the works both numerous and strong; and immense labour and expense had been bestowed on them; and it was now determined that the city should be obstinately defended (Heath, 1901, 50).

By well-aimed amphibious hooks Howe nevertheless manoeuvred Washington from New York town in mid-September, and again from the Harlem Heights on 12 October. Fort Washington was now isolated, and on 16 November the British stormed into the work and captured the garrison of three thousand men. George Washington gave up the struggle for the lower Hudson, and retired across the Delaware into Pennsylvania. His communications with New England described an awkward dog-leg which crossed the lower middle Hudson at Stony Point, thirty miles upstream of the British positions.

The British offensives of 1777
Howe in Pennsylvania. Howe had ended the campaign of 1776 in brilliant fashion by his capture of New York, and in the following year he put sixteen thousand of his men on ships and sought to bring the rebellion to an end by executing the biggest of all his amphibious turning movements. On 25 August 1777 the British landed at the head of Chesapeake Bay, an operation which placed them in the rear of the rebel defensive lines on the Delaware and the Schuylkill, and within sixty miles of the seat of the rebel administration at Philadelphia, the second city of the colonies. Howe broke through an improvised position along the Brandywine on 11 September, and after this accomplished performance he entered Philadelphia on the 26th.

The triumphant Howe placed the main body of his men in an open camp at Germantown, six miles north of Philadelphia, and detached three thousand troops to clear the rebel forts on the lower Delaware and open a shorter sea route to New York. Washington sensed an opportunity, and assaulted the Germantown camp on 3–4 October. Offensive operations of this kind were, however, still beyond the capacity of the rebel army, and the attack disintegrated under the malign influences of fog, an over-elaborate plan of converging columns, and the resistance put up by 120 British troops holding the stone-built mansion of the Chew family. The younger officers among the rebels had been in favour of leaving the 'Chew House' to one side, 'but the sages of the army, at the head of whom was General Knox, repelled at once the idea of leaving a fortified enemy in the rear' (Callahan, 1958, 123).

The British dug themselves in around Philadelphia in a system of redoubts, which helped to plunge Knox into another of his scholarly cogitations. He advised against any renewed assault, since he could not bring himself to believe

that we are on a par in military knowledge and skill

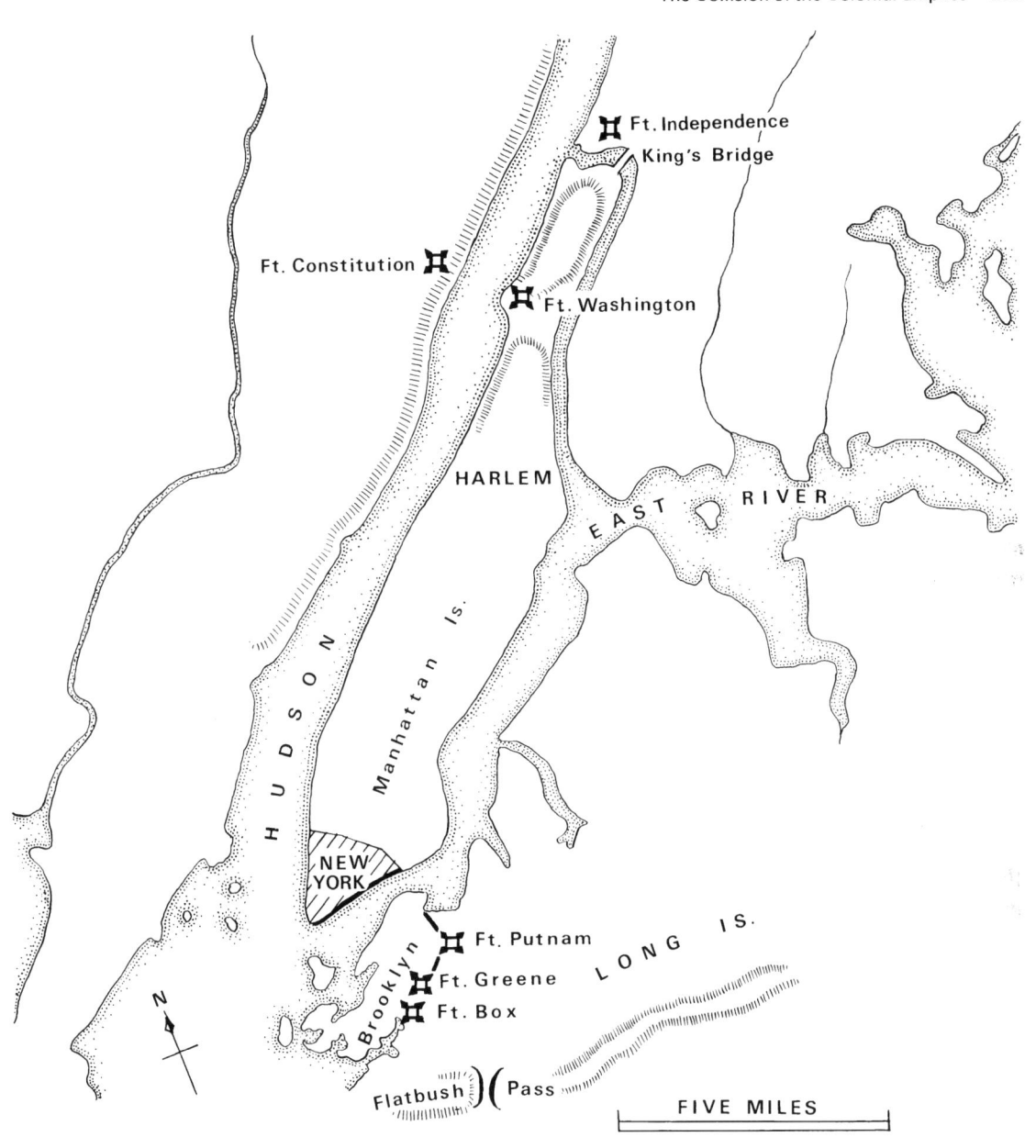

151 The Long Island and Manhattan fortifications

with our enemies ... Marshal Saxe says redoubts are the strongest and most excellent kind of field fortification, and infinitely preferable to extended lines – because each redoubt requires a separate attack, each one of which succeeding does not facilitate the reduction of the others. ...
Charles XII with the best troops in the world was totally ruined in the attack of some redoubts at Poltava, although he succeeded in taking three of them. (Ford, 1897, 194–)

Since there was no dislodging the British from Philadelphia, Washington withdrew twenty-four miles up the Schuylkill to the bleak winter camp of Valley Forge.

Washington's forces eventually emerged from winter quarters as something which began to resemble an army, as the term would have been understood in European military circles. On the engineering side the credit was indirectly due to the work of Benjamin Franklin, who as minister to France had been instructed 'to secure skilled engineers, not exceeding four' (Palmer, 1969, 133). The head of the French mission was Lieutenant-Colonel Louis Duportail, who came to the colonies in the company of his subordinates de la Radière and de Gouvion. Duportail was made a brigadier-general in the rebel service on 17 November 1777, though only after he had been forced to compete for billets with private soldiers, and show that he was not one of the international riff-raff who were flocking across the Atlantic under the guise of 'engineers'.

Duportail made a good job of building the earthworks around Valley Forge, and on 18 January 1778 he made so bold as to urge the rebels to set up a proper corps of military engineers. In his memorandum he also laid great stress on the importance of engineering work in general: 'If fortification is necessary in any armies, it is peculiarly so in those, which like ours, from a deficiency in the practice of manoeuvres cannot oppose any to those of the enemy' (Kite, 1933, 47).

Such enthusiastic diggers as the Americans hardly needed a reminder of this kind, and indeed the only doctrinaire opposition to fortifications *per se* appears to have been uttered by Major-General Nathaniel Greene, who was of the opinion that:

All fortifications in America, except for the security of particular objects, considering the nature of the country are rather prejudicial than useful: the country is taught to expect security, and always lose their confidence upon any unfortunate event. The enemy getting possession of the works, they serve them for strongholds to keep in awe all the circumjacent country. ... The security of the country must depend upon our superiority in the field. (Ford, 1897, 11)

Congress fell in with Duportail's plans, and on 27 May 1778 it authorised the setting-up of an Engineer Department of three companies, each with an establishment of four officers, eight NCOs and sixty privates or sappers.

Duportail was made Commandant on 11 May 1779, though little further seems to have been done about constituting the corps until Washington sent out a call for one man from every regiment in July 1780. Joseph Martin signed up as an NCO on 1 January the next year, and he declares:

This corps of Miners was reckoned to be an honourable one; it consisted of three companies. All the officers were required to be acquainted with the sciences, and it was desirable to have as intelligent young men as could be procured to compose it, although some of us fell considerably short of perfection. (Martin, 1962, 196)

The United States engineering corps was to be disbanded after independence was won, but it was reborn following a hiatus of eleven years and in the next century its officers went on to win an esteem which can be compared only with the status of the engineers in Duportail's native France.

The quiet, professional competence of Duportail was complemented in another field by the efforts of the bellowing Prussian charlatan, 'General' Steuben, who trained and drilled the rebel infantry until it could begin to think of meeting the British in open combat. At the same time Henry Knox, as chief of artillery, was assembling a powerful if varied train of ordnance.

The British adventure in Pennsylvania came to an end when the London government ordered the army to withdraw to New York. Washington's troops followed on a roughly parallel course, and the two forces resumed their positions of two years before on the Hudson.

Burgoyne's march 1777. The long diversion of British force into Pennsylvania becomes all the less justifiable, when we consider it alongside the advance which General Burgoyne undertook in 1777 from Canada to the upper Hudson. The disastrous outcome showed that Burgoyne would have benefited from all the help he could have been given from the direction of New York.

Burgoyne's operation began prosperously enough, with the effortless reduction of Fort Ticonderoga at the head of Lake Champlain. The veteran gunner Major-General William Phillips reconnoitred the heavily wooded Mount Defiance to the south-west of the fortress, and came back repeating the adage: 'Where a goat can go, a man can go: and where a man can go he can drag a gun'. The engineers cut a path to the top of the hill and hauled up artillery after them on 3 and 4 July, whereupon the Americans abandoned Ticonderoga without a fight.

Things began to go wrong when the seven thousand British undertook a difficult overland march to the headwaters of the Hudson. The progress was impeded by the train of fifty-two cannon which Burgoyne brought along with him to deal with any improvised rebel fortifications, and the enemy began to cluster about the column in unexpectedly great numbers. On 19 September the advance was checked at some redoubts which the Polish engineer Colonel Thaddeus Kosciuszko had built at Bemis Heights. Burgoyne was unable to break through, despite all his artillery, and on 17 October he surrendered at Saratoga.

The main British force under Howe was inextricably committed in Pennsylvania, as we have seen, though General Henry Clinton and the garrison of New York made a creditable attempt to support Burgoyne from the south. Clinton left his artillery behind (in defiance of all the rules of war), and on 6 October he surprised forts Montgomery and Clinton, in the Hudson Highlands forty-eight miles above New York. The effort was too late to affect the issue on the upper Hudson, and Clinton later had to abandon the forts on receiving orders from Howe to send reinforcements to Pennsylvania.

The Hudson in later years

Long after the lucky reprieve of 1777, the narrow neck of Washington's communications across the middle Hudson remained the most vulnerable point of rebel America. Defensive arrangements for this part of the world were in amazing disorder. The 'official' French engineer, Colonel de la Radière, appreciated that the best place to block the Hudson against any advance upstream from New York was at Fort Clinton, which could be converted into a compact and readily defensible fortress in the European style. This did not accord with the mental processes of the rough ex-farmer Israel Putnam, who was determined on a site further upstream where the Hudson described a tight bend through the granite hills at West Point. Putnam complained to Washington of the difficulties he encountered with the Frenchman:

I have directed the engineer to lay out the fort immediately but he seems disgusted that everything does not go as he thinks proper, even if contrary to the judgment of every other person. In short he is an excellent paper engineer and I think it would be well for us if Congress would have found business for him with them, our works would have been as well constructed and much more forward than they are now. (Kite, 1933, 85)

De la Radière found it impossible to continue, and work went ahead on the West Point site under the direction of Kosciuszko, who, as Washington explained, was 'better adapted to the genius and temper of the people' (*ibid.*, 95). The result was a sprawling arrangement of sixteen detached riverside batteries and hill forts 'which rise like an amphitheatre and consequently defend each other' (Closen, 1958, 60). The chief strongpoints were Fort Arnold (later renamed Clinton), which stood on the edge of the riverside cliff on the west bank, and Fort Putnam which crowned one of the rugged heights above. Drystone walling was used extensively for the foundations, the inner walls and some of the scarps of the various works, though as a matter of principle the parapets were invariably constructed of timber and/or earth, so as to obviate the danger of stone splinters. The ultimate purpose of the defensive complex was to guard the great chain, which ran from Fort Arnold to Constitution Island on the left bank.

Some Americans nowadays appear to regard the design of the West Point 'fortress' as an indication of a superior wisdom (Palmer, 1969, 166), but it was fortunate for their compatriots in the War of Independence that the place never came under siege. There was a dangerous plateau of level ground on the west bank (where the Cadets of the present Military Academy live and drill), the works were perilously scattered, and the parapets of some of the strongpoints were surprisingly low. On the last feature, the Comte de Clermont-Crèvecoeur explains: 'These fortifications were built to fulfil the same function as our high coastal gun carriages. The American [gun] carriages are all very low. They therefore had to invent some method of adapting them to their purpose at a time when they could not build others' (Rice and Brown, 1972, I, 41).

Still, the site was strong by nature, and it looked very impressive. Surgeon James Thacher once climbed Sugarloaf Hill, and

> looking down as from a cloud, we beheld the Hudson, resembling a vast canal cut through the mountains of stupendous magnitude; a few boats playing on its surface were scarcely visible. But to the pen of the poet and the pencil of the painter, be consigned the task of describing the wonders of nature there exhibited in the form of huge mountains, rocky cliffs, and venerable forests, in one confused mass. From this summit, too, we have a most interesting view of the fortress and garrison of West Point. Fort Putnam, on its most elevated part, the several redoubts beneath, and the barracks on the plain below, with numerous soldiers in active motion, all defended by the most formidable machinery of war, combine to form a picturesque scenery of peculiar interest. (*ibid.*, 166)

Closer examination would have shown the construction proceeding slowly. No sense of urgency was imparted to the proceedings even in the midsummer of 1779, when the rebels lost forts Stony Point and Verplanck, just thirteen miles downriver.

In 1780 West Point was very lucky indeed to survive the plot of its governor, Benedict Arnold, to deliver the fortress to Henry Clinton. By a mischance their go-between, Major André, was captured by the rebels on 25 September, and Arnold saw fit to disappear from West Point half an hour before the as-yet unsuspecting Washington was due to arrive on a tour of inspection.

The Hudson retained its importance until the very end. Hostilities did not cease with the fall of Yorktown, and the year 1782 found the American Republic in an enfeebled and divided condition, and the British still ensconced with their powerful garrison at New York. In this crisis Washington drew an army together in hutted camps on the middle Hudson, and maintained a force there until the British finally withdrew.

The British and Loyalist offensives in the South 1779–80

The Loyalist element in the American population was nowhere totally negligible, and in the South these faithful 'Tories' were so numerous that they were waiting only for British forces to arrive as the signal to rise against their rebel 'liberators'. The first British venture in the South had taken the form of an expedition from Boston, which was repulsed from the entrance of Charleston Harbour in June 1776. A much more significant project materialised at the end of 1778 and the beginning of 1779, when 3,500 troops from New York seized Savannah against weak opposition, and Brigadier Augustine Prevost moved into Georgia from the isolated British base of St Augustine (ceded by Spain in 1763). The loyalists of Georgia rose *en masse* to greet the British troops.

The Loyalists of Georgia stood in little danger from the local malcontents, but in the autumn of 1779 more than three thousand French troops came from the French West Indies at the invitation of the Continental (i.e. rebel) command in the South. The expedition appeared at the mouth of the Savannah River, the Atlantic gateway to Georgia, whereupon 'Old Bullet-Head' Prevost threw himself into a frenzy of activity, casting up a chain of interconnected redoubts around the landward end of Savannah town, which stood on a sandy bluff amid

The Southern States in the War of Independence

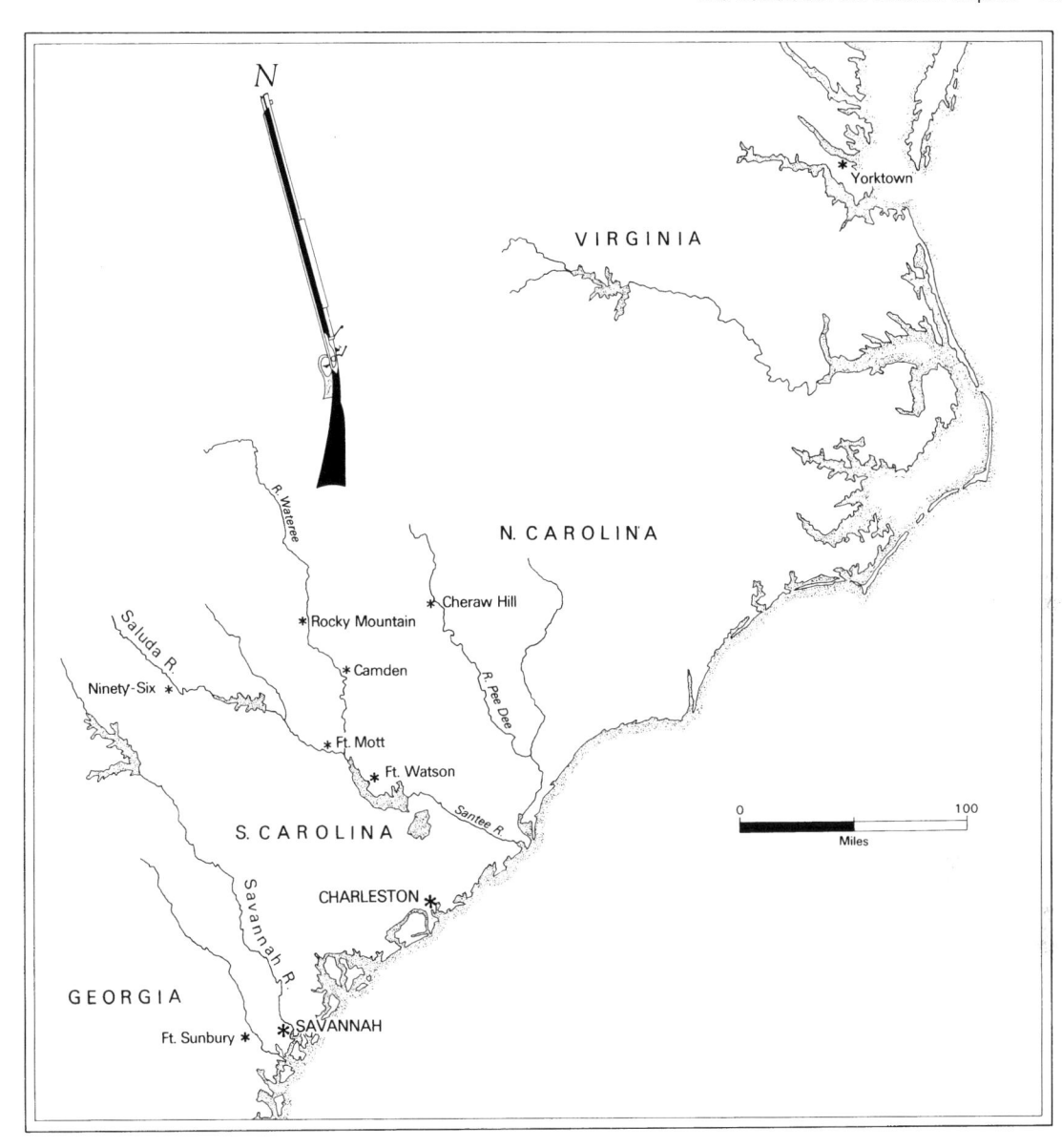

rice fields and savannah on the right bank of the river. The fortifications were easy to build and repair, since they were made of sand revetted with planks and fascines, and there was ample slave labour to be had from the plantations. Four redoubts were ready by the time the French and rebels arrived outside on 16 September, and this number was increased to thirteen in the course of the siege. It is not very often that you come across a fortress that was stronger at the end of an attack than at the beginning.

This was the first time the Southern rebels had seen siege operations in the European manner, and they were very taken with the mortar battery which the French set up behind the trenches. D'Estaing, the French commander, commented that 'in American eyes, the mortars represent the ark of the covenant and the sure way of making the walls of Jericho fall. I hoped so, but I doubted it' (Lawrence, 1951, 62).

The French artillery duly opened up on 3–4 October:

At midnight, on Monday, the bombardment begins. It ceases at two o'clock, by order of M. de Noailles, because the mis-directed bombs fell in great numbers in the trench he commanded. This bad firing was occasioned by the mistake of a ship's steward who had sent to the cannoneers a keg of rum instead of a keg of beer. (Quoted in Jones, 1874, 25)

The aim was re-adjusted, but the bombardment produced little effect on the sandy works. The hurricane season was now approaching, and the French decided to settle the issue one way or another by throwing in an assault on the early morning of 9 October. Even before the storm the French were chilled by the *lugubre harmonie* of bagpipes emanating from Savannah, and when they attacked the British lines they were met by gales of grape, nails and scrap iron. The supporting rebel troops fared little better, and they huddled in the ditches of the fortifications until d'Estaing gave the order for a general retreat:

Seldom has the sun of a warm October morning looked down upon a scene so mournful and appalling. The smoke of the muskets and cannon hung broodingly over the place, gathering denseness and darkness from every discharge; and the roar of the artillery, the rattling of small arms, the calling bugle, the sounded retreat, the stirring drum, and the cries of the wounded blended startlingly together. (Quoted in Hough, 1866, 42)

After this bloody repulse the siege was raised on 18 October, and the French sailed away two days later. There could have been no greater encouragement to the Tories and the loyal Cherokee Indians, while in New York a delighted Henry Clinton acclaimed the defence of Savannah as 'the greatest event that has happened the whole war' (Clinton, 1954, 149). The victory nevertheless exercised a pernicious influence on the shape of operations. The British were prompted to commit more and more forces to the South, a peripheral theatre of war, and thereby neglected the Hudson Highlands, where they still had a chance of attaining decisive results. New York offered the British a firm base, which nobody could take from them, whereas their decision to fight in the South presupposed that the Royal Navy would have an unchallenged command in American seas.

In accordance with the developing new strategy, Clinton came from New York early in 1780 with a force of over 8,500 men to wrest South Carolina from the rebels. The British landed thirty miles south of Charleston on 11 February, after a storm-tossed passage in which most of their heavy cannon were lost with the ordnance ship *Russia Merchant*. Under the pressure of public opinion the rebel general Lincoln gave up any idea of escaping into the interior, and shut himself up in Charleston with some five thousand troops, who dug themselves in along a line of redoubts which stretched between the Ashley and Cooper rivers across the peninsula to the north of the town.

The British laid Charleston under formal siege. Clinton explains that:

The attack had been planned with so much judgment by the commanding engineer Captain Moncrieff (who had already given the most honourable proofs of his skill in the late successful defence of Savannah), that I had not the smallest

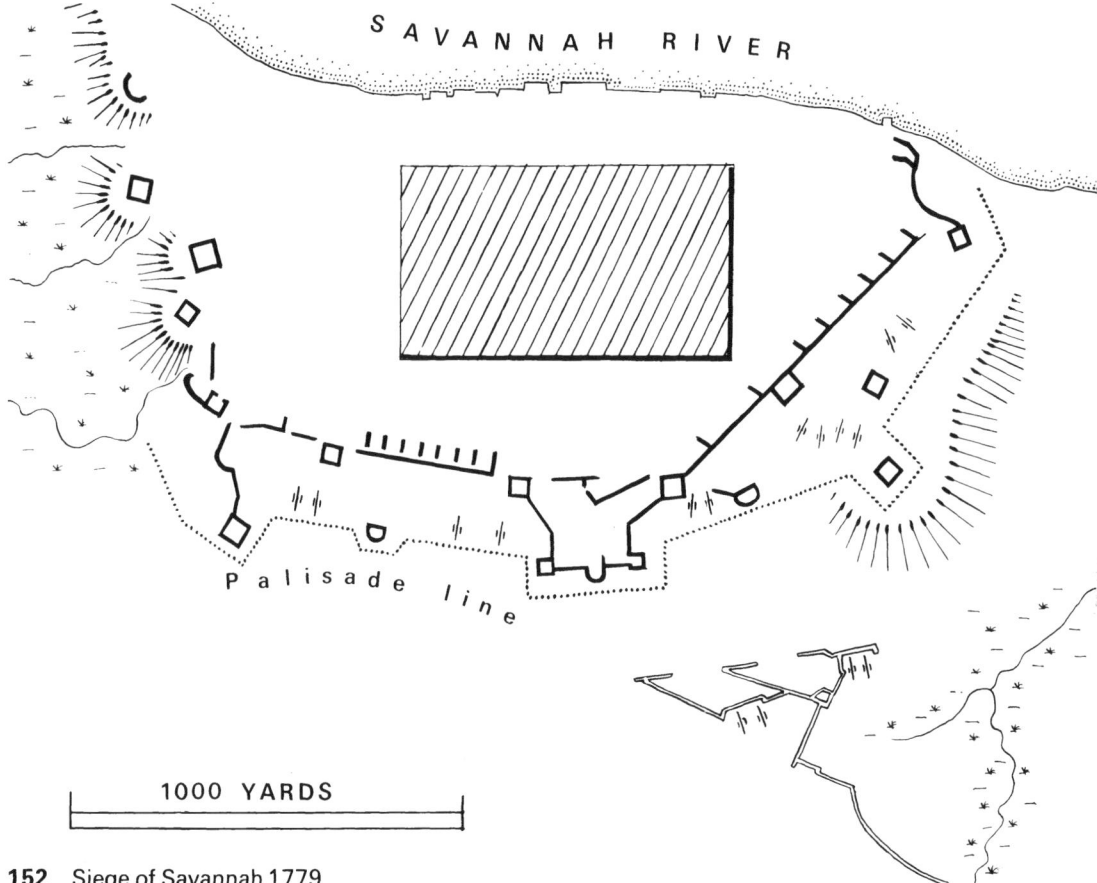

152 Siege of Savannah 1779

doubt of my becoming master of the town without much loss. This consideration alone would have been a sufficient incitement for me to prefer the mode of regular approaches to any other, less certain though more expeditious, which might have sacrificed a greater number of lives on both sides. Other important motives also influenced me on this occasion, among which *to secure the capture of all the rebel corps in Charleston* had been from the first a very principal object with me, as I saw the reduction of the rest of the province in great measure depended upon it. (Clinton, 1954, 95)

In the second week of March the saps came within musket-shot of the defences, and the artillery duels began to cause great destruction in the town. Lincoln once more gave way to civilian outcry, and surrendered his men as prisoners of war on 9 May. Duportail was numbered among the captives, but the British unwisely exchanged this valuable prize for one of their own officers in November.

A Hessian captain gave a continental European perspective on how the British had performed at Charleston. He admired the courage of his friend James Moncrieff, but found that his proceedings were slow and confused: 'I assert . . . that this man could hardly serve as an errand-boy for an engineer during a siege in a European war, although he has served as a subengineer during the sieges of Louisbourg, Havana, St Augustine and several more in the Seven Years War, where he may have learned this method of war from his superiors' (Ewald, 1979, 236).

The British and Tory hold on the South now rested on a comprehensive system of strongpoints. The fortified posts of Savannah, Beaufort, Charleston and Georgetown provided a base along the coast. Between one hundred and one hundred and fifty miles inland a corresponding chain of garrisons guarded the upper reaches of the main rivers of the region: Augusta on the Savannah River acted as a way-station between Savannah and the fort of Ninety-Six, on the Saluda; the Wateree, another tributary of the Santee, was commanded by the outpost of Rocky Mountain and the important depot and rallying-point of Camden; below the junction of the Wateree and the Santee the post of Fort Watson guarded the hinterland of Charleston and Georgetown; Cheraw Hill, on the Great Pee Dee River, formed one of the bastions against North Carolina.

Clinton departed for New York in June 1780, leaving the command in the South in the hands of General Charles Cornwallis, who beat the rebels on the few occasions he could catch them in the course of the fast-moving and complex operations that followed. Cornwallis reached the conclusion that he could never finish with the southern rebels until he had run them to ground in Virginia, which was their principal base of operations. In April 1781 he accordingly committed himself to a campaign in the Old Dominion, a decision which was to doom the green-coated Loyalists of the South and the British rule in the American colonies.

The loss of the American colonies 1781–2
The south. Now that Cornwallis had left for Virginia, all the energy of the young Lord Rawdon could do little to postpone the ruin of the Tory cause in South Carolina and Georgia. Rawdon commanded eight thousand troops, more than half of them Loyalists, but most of the force had to be devoted to holding the vital strongpoints, which left only about two thousand men for operations in the field. On his side the rebel commander Greene possessed a core of fifteen hundred Continental regulars, and a fluctuating but rapidly growing number of militia and guerrillas.

The rebels reduced the loyal posts in a series of bizarre little sieges, and by the middle of 1781 the stockaded village and fort of Ninety-Six remained the only stronghold of consequence in the back country. Lieutenant-Colonel John Cruger and his garrison of 550 Tories resisted attack by trench, firearrow, siege tower and assault. The rebel colonels Kosciuszko and Henry Lee had run through their fund of engineering techniques to no purpose, and on 20 June their commander Greene raised the siege when he heard that Lord Rawdon was nearly upon them. Rawdon destroyed the isolated post, and carried the brave garrison back to safety in Charleston.

This gratifying episode could not affect the general issue of the war in the south. The Loyalists in the coastlands came under increasing pressure, and by the end of hostilities the Tories had abandoned all their holdings except Savannah.

Meanwhile the rebels and their allies were eroding the distant flanks of the British positions in the subcontinent. The rebel George Clark had been pursuing a semi-private war with the British forces which were based on Detroit, and on 25 February 1779 he captured the small post of Vincennes on the Wabash for the second time. The reduction of this place contributed significantly to the worsting of the British and their Indian allies in the Middle West in the following years.

The Spanish had a direct interest in the outcome of the war, as new masters of Louisiana and past owners of Florida, and they made a notably energetic showing in some of these peripheral campaigns. With the help of the infamous Clark they successfully defended St Louis on the Mississippi against the British in May 1780. In the south they went over to the offensive, and expeditions from Louisiana reduced Mobile in March 1780, and nearby Pensacola in May the next year. Fort George in West Florida was taken on 9 May 1782, and the Spanish recovered Florida as a whole in the peace settlement of 1783.

Yorktown 1781. We left Cornwallis at the time when he had entered Virginia with the British forces from the South. The rebels continued to evade him most annoyingly, and there arrived orders from Clinton, as overall commander, to send three thousand troops by sea to New York, which stood in some danger of coming under attack. Cornwallis accordingly moved to the mouth of Chesapeake Bay. The fears for New York proved to be exaggerated, as we shall see, and so Cornwallis dug himself in with his entire force of eight thousand men at Yorktown, on the north side of the Williamsburg peninsula.

Since July 1780 Washington had had at his disposal a force of five thousand French troops which had landed at Newport, Rhode Island, under the command of the Comte de Rochambeau. This gave Washington a total of about 10,500 men, and all the expertise he required to conduct a regular siege, but the numbers still fell short of the force required to drive Clinton's army from its positions on Manhattan and Staten Islands. The prospect of this very considerable operation gave pause for thought to Henry Knox, Washington's military-scientific 'guru', and to Duportail, when he returned from British detention. Meanwhile the new corps of American sappers and miners was set to work making fascines and gabions – the classic instruments of European-style siegework. Joseph Martin helpfully explains the use of the latter device: 'Three of four rows of them are set down together, the trench is then dug behind and the dirt thrown into them, which, when full, together with the trench, forms a complete breastwork. The word is pronounced *gab-beens*' (Martin, 1962, 218. This rendering is on a par with the *ou is dair?* and the other sayings that were being painstakingly taught to the French at about the same time.)

Could the Franco-American force be used more profitably elsewhere? The opportunity came when the British lost the total command of the American waters, an advantage upon which all their strategic combinations had been based. The Channel Fleet had been drawn into operations for the relief of Gibraltar, with the consequence that Admiral de Grasse was able to set sail from Brest to the West Indies in 1781. He picked up 3,500 troops at Haiti, and fell in with Washington's scheme for a combined attack on Cornwallis at Yorktown. Washington asked the Board of War for the maximum material support for the enterprise, since 'we must look forward to a very serious operation' (Kennett, 1977, 143).

The French fleet appeared at the mouth of Chesapeake Bay at the end of August, while Washington and Rochambeau marched their armies overland from the Hudson. Much of the rebel artillery was sent by sea from Newport, at the risk of falling into the clutches of Admiral Grave's fleet from New York, but the activity of de Grasse and the coming of stormy weather forced the British ships away from the Virginia capes in early September. On 28 September 1781 Cornwallis was invested at Yorktown by an army of eighteen thousand rebels and French.

The British had been entrenching themselves amid the scattered woods and sandy fields since the beginning of September, which was two or three weeks short of the time that Cornwallis needed to build adequate fieldworks without destroying his army in the sultry heat. The broad York River covered the rear of the position, and a good line for the frontal defences ran across the half-mile-wide Pigeon Quarter, a plateau which rose between the muddy and impassable Yorktown and Wormeley Creeks. Cornwallis built four redoubts to close the access, but he abandoned them on 30 September in order to concentrate on an inner perimeter of interconnecting redoubts and batteries around Yorktown. Cornwallis thereby hoped to conserve his force until he received help by sea from New York, but the immediate effect was to allow the enemy to march through the gap, and permit them to open their attacks against the eastern sector of the fortifications.

The Americans took the prospect of their first major formal siege very seriously indeed. They were given the place of honour on the right of the line, as principals in the quarrel with the British, and Rochambeau later testified:

I must render the Americans the justice to say, that they conducted themselves with that zeal, courage, and emulation, with which they were never backward, in the important part of the attack entrusted to them, and the more so as they were totally ignorant of the operations of a siege. (Rochambeau, 1838, 69)

On 6 October the Americans issued a fifty-two-article set of *Regulations for the Service of a Siege*, and on the same day Washington disarmingly confessed that

our works go slow, the heavy artillery hard to get up; not one piece of cannon yet fired at them; indeed, I discover very plainly that we are young soldiers in a siege; however, we are determined to

153 Siege of Yorktown 1781

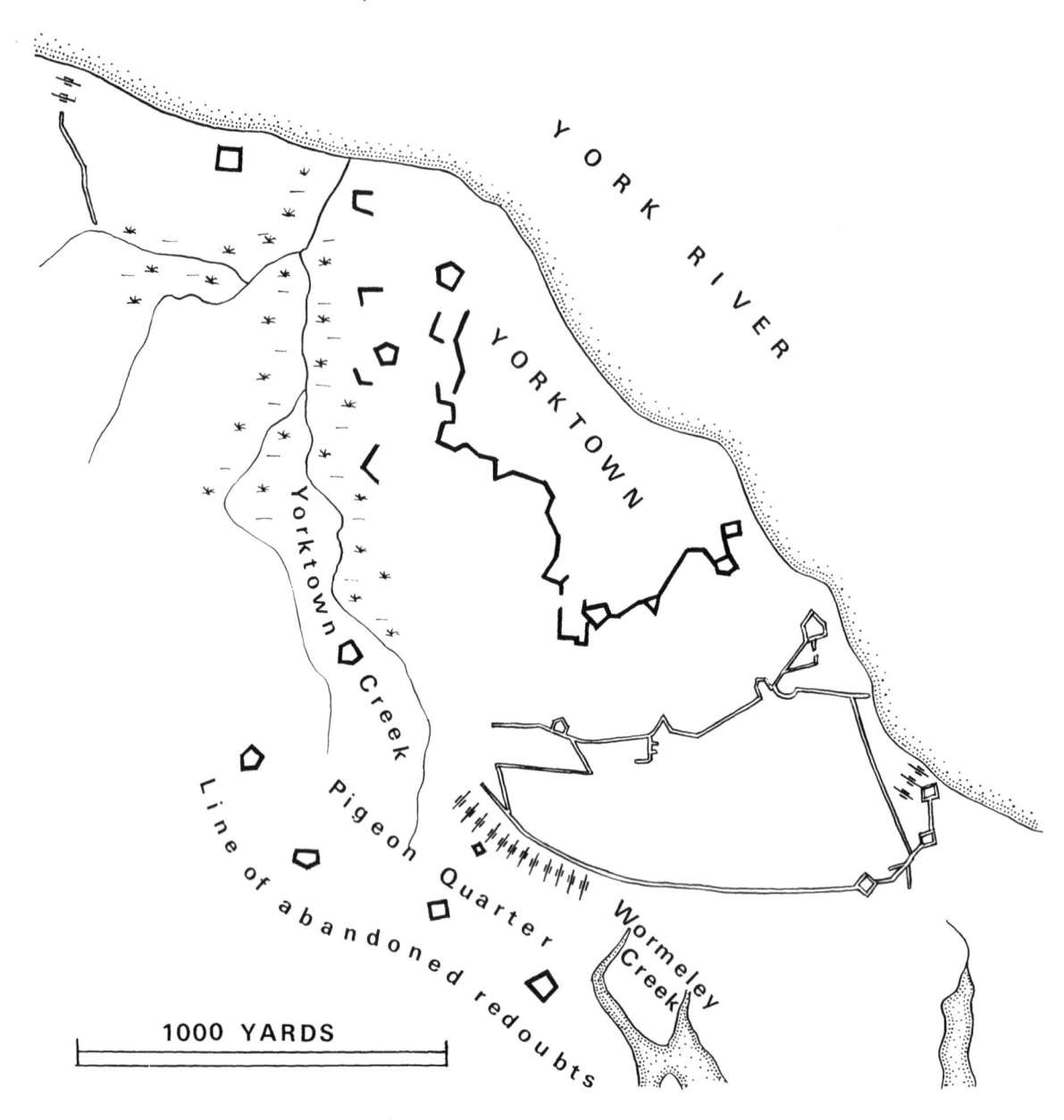

benefit ourselves by experience; one virtue we possess, that is perseverance. (Callahan, 1958, 183)

The opening of trenches was preceded by a period of careful reconnaissances. Ebenezer Denny noted:

Generals and engineers in viewing and surveying the ground, are always fired on and sometimes pursued. Escorts and covering parties stationed at convenient distances under cover of wood, rising ground etc., afford support. This business reminds me of a play among the boys, called 'prison-base'. (Denny, 1859, 41)

Washington selected the line for the first parallel in person, and on 5–6 October the American miners and sappers prepared the site: 'It was a very dark and rainy night. However, we repaired to the place and began by following the engineers and laying laths of pine wood end-to-end upon the line marked out by the officers for the trenches' (Martin, 1962, 231). On the night of 6–7 October the ground was broken along the indicated line, which ran at a distance of between six and eight hundred paces from the defences. This potentially dangerous operation was accomplished without any interruption, and before long the first parallel formed 'a large ditch, broad enough for carriages to travel in, about four feet in depth, and covered with a rampart of gabions, or cylindrical baskets, fixed upon the ground, by means of projecting stakes, filled and covered over with loose dirt, and forming a height of about seven feet on the side towards the town' (Robin, 1783, 57). It is uncertain just how earnestly the French regarded this siege by European technical standards (see the contradictory evidence uncovered by Kennett, 1977, 142, and Harley, 1978, 15), though they were evidently displeased that Washington had paid the British the compliment of breaking ground at such a long range.

At three in the afternoon of 9 October the Continental and French flags were run up above the siegeworks, whereupon six batteries were unmasked and opened fire. In the instant before the general conflagration the first shot was distinctly heard clattering from house to house within the town, and as the bombardment augmented a French chaplain could see the cannon balls striking or rebounding from the redoubts of the enemy, and driving through the air the planks and timber which formed the embrasures for the great guns. I followed with my eye, in its downward path, the slow and destructive bomb, sometimes burying itself in the roofs of houses, sometimes when it burst, raising clouds of dust from the ruins of the buildings, at other times blowing the unfortunate wretches, that happened to be within reach, more than twenty feet high in the air, and letting them fall at a considerable distance most pitiably torn. (*ibid.*, 58)

The heavily-outgunned British artillery made what reply it could, and every time one of their mortars fired a fierce and patriotic bulldog left the defences and made a one-dog sortie across no-man's land. Surgeon Thacher says that

the bomb shells from the besiegers and the besieged are incessantly crossing each other's path in the sky. They are clearly visible in the form of a black ball in the day, but in the night they appear like fiery meteors with blazing tails, most beautifully brilliant, ascending majestically from the mortar to a certain altitude, and gradually descending to the spot where they are destined to execute their work of destruction . . . the whole peninsula trembles under the incessant thunder of our infernal machines. (Callahan, 1958, 187)

By the evening of 10 October the outlines of the British parapets were visibly ragged, and on the night of 11–12 the allies set about digging their second parallel at less than three hundred yards from the fortifications. Only seven men were killed in the process. Washington was struck with admiration at the proficiency of the French engineers and gunners, and he wrote to Congress: 'The experience of many of these gentlemen in the business before us, is of the utmost advantage in the present operation' (Freeman, 1949–52, V, 395).

On the night of 14–15 October the allies stormed two redoubts lying towards the York River, and gained sufficient obtuse angles to permit the French gunners to open up ricochet batteries in front of the second parallel. The British breastworks, platforms, guns and gun carriages were pounded into a heap of rubbish. Inside Yorktown 'one could not take three steps without running into some great holes made by bombs, some splinters, some balls, some half-covered trenches, with scattered white or negro arms or legs, and some bits of uniforms' (Closen's later inspection, Closen, 1958, 155).

The British made a sortie on the night of 15–16 and managed to spike two of the French guns. This was the last show of spirit on the part of the defenders. The allied fire reached an intolerable intensity on the 17th, and the shot and bombs were fast carrying away the storm-poles on the British works when Cornwallis asked for a truce. He knew that his soldiers were as patient and firm as always:

A successful defence, however, in our situation was perhaps impossible. For the place could only be reckoned an entrenched camp, subject in most places to enfilade, and the ground in general so disadvantageous that nothing but the necessity of fortifying it as a post to protect the navy could have induced any person to erect works on it (Clinton, 1954, Appx., 586).

That night, the last of the British presence in the Old Dominion, the three armies settled down to rest under a silent celestial bombardment:

A solemn stillness prevailed. The night was remarkably clear, and the sky decorated with ten thousand stars. Numberless meteors gleaming through the atmosphere afforded a pleasing resemblance to the bombs which had exhibited a noble firework on the night before, but happily divested of all their horror. (Tucker, in Scheer and Rankin, 1959, 567)

On the 19th Cornwallis surrendered his forces, and the British marched out of Yorktown to captivity. One of the airs the British musicians played on this occasion was particularly well chosen. The Americans have ever since been persuaded that they had listened to *The World Turned Upside Down*, though to British ears the tune also recalled the expectation of *When the King Enjoys His Own Again*.

In London Lord North received the news of the fall of Yorktown 'as he would have taken a ball in his breast'. Britain lost the will to continue the war, and a new administration concluded preliminary terms of peace with the new American nation on 20 November 1782.

The French, as allies of the rebels, could congratulate themselves on having helped to let loose a spirit of discord and discontent in the world. Montalembert prophetically warned the French and Spanish that they too ought to expect 'a general revolt' in their colonies, inspired 'by the example of the Americans, whose brilliant success will certainly give rise to imitators' (Montalembert, 1776–96, III, 134).

Ten Conclusions

After taking a very circuitous route, I must return to seek an answer to the question posed at the beginning of this work, namely, why it was, despite the efforts of Vauban, Coehoorn and all the rest, that fortress warfare by the time of the coming of the Revolution was of less account than it had been when Louis XIV first claimed despotic power.

This is not to discount the significance of later episodes like the young French Republic's defence of its fortress barriers, the celebrated sieges of the Peninsular War, or the allied attack on Sevastopol. Specialists will be tempted to recall Radetzky's use of the Austrian Quadrilateral of fortresses in northern Italy, or the defensive work of General Séré de Rivières on the eastern borders of France, which encouraged the Germans to think of coming at Paris by way of Belgium.

What does seem worthy of serious attention is the fact that by 1789 the time was long past when the business of sieges had been the central, formative experience of warfare – the school of soldiers and captains – and when the military art had been understood to consist largely of operations relating directly and indirectly to the attack or defence of strongholds. Plainly the explanations must lie in processes that were at work in the period of the *ancien régime*.

Two conjectures spring immediately to mind. The first concerns the perfection which Vauban brought to the art of the attack through his parallels and saps, and his specialised batteries of siege artillery which knocked over men and guns in calculated progression, until they could be brought close enough to knock holes in the walls. However, the siege of a major fortress remained a very considerable operation of war, and it still brought with it an element of risk for the attacker, as witness the French débâcle at Turin in 1706. Even a small place, resolutely defended like Cuneo in 1744, might ruin an invading army. Therefore the increasing power of the attack cannot by itself account for the decline of fortification.

I used to be much impressed by what I had read about the unwieldiness of eighteenth-century armies, and what I described in a primitive draft as 'the geography of unregulated rivers and roadless hills' which, I thought, must have added so much to the stopping-power of fortresses. I shared the general assumption that the opening up of natural barriers and the improvement of roads in the nineteenth century must consequently have detracted from the efficacy of the fortress defensive. This explanation too now seems inadequate. Much remains to be discovered concerning the nature of eighteenth-century warfare, but having travelled some distance in the tracks of Frederick the Great and his enemies, I must say that I am impressed, almost disconcerted by the very high level of mobility of the monarchial armies. The invention of the sheet-copper pontoon enabled these old warriors to take a river barrier in their stride, as Frederick rightly claimed; they pushed and hacked their way through vast, gloomy forests; they and their guns passed over the merest hillside tracks;

they were halted by nothing short of genuine mountains, of the kind which have their peaks capped with snow for most of the year. In other words, before the advent of the railway and the internal combustion engine, the physical improvements in mobility were ones of degree rather than kind. Moreover, such advantages as the nineteenth century enjoyed were partly counteracted by specially-designed small barrier forts (*forts d'arrêt*, *Sperrforts*), which were sited on choke points of communication, in the hope of holding up invaders as effectively as Fort Bard delayed the irruption of the French into north Italy in 1800.

Having thus exploded the equivalent of a globe of compression under my preconceptions, I had to search elsewhere for the causes of the changes that had undoubtedly taken place.

The events of the Netherlandish campaigns of the 1790s, immediately following our period, showed what important consequences flowed from the decision which Emperor Joseph II had taken in 1781, to dismantle the majority of the fortresses of the Austrian Netherlands. Once they were forced on the defensive by the French Republic, the allies were thus deprived of refuge, and the possession of the land hung largely on the outcome of field battles, such as the one which turned to the allied disadvantage at Fleurus in 1794. Inasmuch as the Netherlands had for centuries past been the theatre of the most intensive fortress conflicts in Europe, the removal of so many strongholds from the strategic map served to detract from the prominence of fortification in warfare as a whole.

It is a more lengthy business to explore the effect on the standing of fortification that was wrought by the changes in the character of the field armies in the seventeenth and eighteenth centuries. In the old wars of Parma, Wallenstein and the like, fortresses had provided an element of stability at a time when armies were ill-regulated, semi-mercenary affairs, which were known to dissolve in mutiny even when the enemy were still far distant. Fortresses were also predominant because, according to a rough rule of thumb, we find that the smaller the forces engaged on a theatre of war, the more importance attaches to the available strongpoints.

The advent of permanent, standing armies in the second half of the seventeenth century began to effect a striking transformation in the relationships between field forces and static defences. Now the regulated state army offered the military world a new fixed point of reference, as enduring as the ramparts of the engineers. Moreover, the bureaucratic structures of absolutism enabled sovereigns to put on foot larger numbers of well-equipped soldiers than had been possible before. In 1672 Louvois increased the size of the French army from 30,000 to 120,000 men to fight the Dutch war, and in 1688 some 360,000 troops at the outset of the new struggle that was to last, with one interval, until 1714. It is strange that the same impulses which made possible the oeuvre of Vauban also rendered engineering of less relative consequence in the long term in the art of war.

The eighteenth century manufactured further numbers by the machinery of conscription, whether the strictly limited form adopted in states like Russia or Prussia in the earlier decades, or the less selective practice for which Republican France set the example in the 1790s. No less important than crude numbers was the facility of employing them effectively on campaign. Already in the *ancien régime* we encounter the first strivings towards a grouping of the scores of individual regiments into the handy intermediate formations which became the divisions and corps of the early nineteenth century. By that time the 'career open to talents', and its less democratic equivalent in monarchical lands, had engendered theatre commanders of a quality which old Frederick would have been surprised and delighted to see in his old generals. Any defects in the paperwork of these great men was made good by the new race of staff officers, especially trained in the sciences of articulating and supplying the component parts of the mass armies.

Now it was far more difficult to hold the aggressor in a border zone. Offensives were likely to break across the frontier along several sectors at once, presenting the defender with the horrid vision of seeing his strongholds masked, and the invaders waging a war *à outrance* in the heart of his country. Numbers and depth could, however, also serve the purposes of the defensive.

Long before the trench warfare in Virginia in

154 Modern French engineer troops clearing vegetation at Blaye. An expression of the current world-wide interest in the restoring of artillery fortifications

1865, or the deadlock of 1914–18, armies had on rare but significant occasions taken to a form of linear, positional warfare which confronted the challenge which the fortresses alone had been unable to meet. This posture was adopted by the French in their lines in the last campaigns in the War of the Spanish Succession, and it was taken up again by the Austrians when they held the Prussians on the upper Elbe in 1778. The thing was made feasible by a high ratio of force to usable frontage, and by the importance which the warring parties attached to the ground in question – in other words it did not hang exclusively on advances in weapons technology.

The corresponding element of defensive depth was clearly manifest in the Napoleonic period, when mass armies were raised to confront mass armies, and when a protracted resistance could be offered with the active assistance of the populace, which Clausewitz rightly counted as one of the most useful resources of the defensive.

All of this detracted from the value of the static and highly specialised kind of strength represented by the fortress: the stronghold was replaced, rather than overcome, and it surrendered not so much to invaders as to its powerful new allies in the business of the defensive. The useful device of the corps of observation, as developed by de Saxe in the 1740s, had already offered the attacking commander the facility to concentrate his attention almost exclusively on events in the open field. Now, in the nineteenth century, the co-ordinator of a defensive viewed his fortresses as one weapon available to him among many.

Paradoxically, the phenomenon of engineering professionalism contributed to the process of withdrawing strongholds from their commanding position in warfare. The fact is all the more striking because, in one perspective, this institutionalised military expertise was the ultimate expression of continuity and political stability.

Extraordinary things were possible to such a machine as was inspired by a Louis XIV, administered by a Louvois, and directed by a Vauban. Other states were impressed by the outward manifestations, without necessarily appreciating all that lay behind them. Hence the relative impotence of the divided German empire concerning siegework. Hence also the struggles of Coehoorn, Rüsensteen and Verboom, who earned the character of bloody-minded Dutchmen, but who had to battle with an environment that was much less sympathetic than anything known to Vauban. Where Vauban had absolute power at his beck and call, Coehoorn had to work through impassioned argument.

Even in France, however, much remained to be won and held by the effort of the engineers, for this was a time when European engineering corps were still in the process of acquiring independence and cohesion, and some field commanders like de la Feuillade, Villars, de las Torres and Frederick the Great were still sometimes tempted to stray across the new lines of demarcation and wrest the management of sieges from their engineers. On their side, the engineers of France, Holland, Denmark, Sweden, and Spain sought with remarkable unanimity to acquire the things that would endow them with professional status:

(a) the right to direct sieges
(b) control of the candidates for entry to the corps
(c) equal status with the field arms, and recognised hierarchies of rank and reward
(d) an engineering 'depot' of records, plans and fortress models
(e) a body of trained sapper troops, proficient in the procedures of siegework.

If we accept the notion of systematic fortress-building and siege attacks as the product of a highly developed organism, tenderly nurtured in certain states of Europe, then there is a certain interest in following the attempts to plant this exotic bloom in foreign climes. It is the incongruity of the import and the alien surroundings which helps to account for the frustrations which Rosen experienced with his Irish, the Duke of Perth with his Highlanders, Münnich and Shuvalov with their Russians, Lally-Tollendal with the French in India, Lafitte and his associates with the 'idiotic' Turks, Montcalm with the Canadians, and de la Radière with individuals like Israel Putnam.

There were certain compensations. The advent of a well-found regular force, with trained engineers and a proper siege train, was likely to work to decisive effect in a low-technology environment, as in Ireland in 1690-1, and Havana in 1762. When resources on this scale were lacking, any honest attempt to put into practice conventional engineering and gunnery was nearly always amply rewarded.

Occasionally the local conditions proved to be unexpectedly congenial. For Vauban and Dahlberg, the creation of sapper troops remained an unattainable vision. In the later eighteenth century, however, French technicians were fortunate enough to light upon foreigners who were willing to appreciate the advantages of what they were proposing. Thus Gribeauval became the spiritual father of the Austrian sappers who contributed to the epic defence of Schweidnitz in 1762. Less than twenty years later Duportail accomplished the same with the Americans. They were already skilled defensive engineers, but they saw that to share in regular siegework would be the culmination of their process of military education.

Despite this record of achievement, the change in the character of military engineering, which we sum up as 'professionalism', did not in every respect work to the integration of the engineering art in warfare. It is remarkable how the men who excelled in exploring new ideas in fortification and siegework, or setting up bureaucratic structures, were succeeded by specialists who, for the most part, lacked the impressive breadth of vision of their spiritual fathers. Whereas Vauban, Dahlberg, Rimpler, Coehoorn and even d'Asfeld were drawn by instinct to military engineering from the field arms, the new engineering corps, once established, attracted a significant minority of fuss-pots and the kind of people who regard a profession primarily as a field for the exercise of their ambitions.

By the time of the end of old monarchical Europe, the new race of pedants and careerists had devised a 'science' of engineering which seemed to outsiders at the same time unapproachable and unchallenging. The émigré engineer Bousmard looked back from his viewpoint near the end of the eighteenth century and concluded that the field commanders were

> persuaded that the science of Vauban and the engineers he had trained was beyond their reach. They always had engineers with them when they wished to carry out an attack, and this was another reason why they did not think it was worth their while to learn engineering. The astounding progress of the art of engineering tended in some degree to act to its disadvantage – it seemed arcane and unattainable to people who had not made it their speciality, and so all the officers gave it up. (1797–9, I, 18)

The new engineers were interested above all in the geometrical interrelationships of the component parts of fortification, and they forgot, to some extent, the essential military properties. No longer did an accomplished field commander have the confidence, like Montecuccoli of old, to pronounce that a good ditch ought to be about as wide as a big tree is tall. Altogether, the emergence of engineering professionalism must be counted as one of the most powerful of those agents which worked to remove the conduct of the fortress defence and attack from the purview of the commander-in-chief, and thus to relegate those skills to a secondary place in warfare.

Glossary

(Reprinted from Duffy, 1975)

ABATIS   A defence made of felled trees.
APPROACHES   Trenches dug towards a fortress to enable the besieger to approach under cover from fire.
ASSAULT   A storm made against a fortification.
ATTACK   1 An operation (usually by formal siege) aiming at the reduction of a fortress.
   2 A body of trench approaches, directed against one of the fronts of a fortress.
AUGET   A square-sectioned wooden channel which protects a length of fuze in a mine.
BANQUETTE   An infantry fire-step, built behind the parapet of a rampart, a covered way or a trench.
BARBETTE   A cannon is positioned *en barbette* when the carriage is high enough (or the parapet low enough) to permit the barrel to point over the top of the parapet without the necessity of cutting an embrasure.
BASTION   A four-sided work which projects from the main rampart, and consists of two faces and two flanks.
BATARDEAU   A dam which retains water in a ditch.
BATTER   The slope given to the outer face of a revetment.
BATTERY   1 An emplacement for cannon or mortars.
   2 A group of cannon or mortars.
BERM   A space left between the edge of a ditch (or trench) and the foot of the slope of the rampart (or parapet).
BODY OF THE PLACE   *see* ENCEINTE
BOMB   1 A shell fired from a mortar or howitzer.
   2 A mortar boat.
BOMBARDMENT   A generalised cannonade of a fortress town.
BONNET   A triangular work placed in front of the salient angle of a ravelin.
BOYAU   A communication trench.
BRANCH   1 A small mine gallery.
   2 A long straight stretch of a work of fortification.
BREACH   An opening made in a rampart or wall by artillery-fire or mining.
BREASTWORK   *see* EPAULEMENT
BRICOLE   A cannon fires *en bricole* when the ball strikes a revetment on a horizontal plane which departs markedly from the perpendicular.
CALTROP   An obstruction consisting of a small iron tetrahedron with pointed ends.

CAMOUFLET   A mine charge which is intended to take all its effect against enemy mineworkings underground.
CANNELURE CUTTING   A technique for breaching a wall by cannon fire.
CAPITAL   An imaginary centre-line, running through the salient angle, which divides a work into two equal parts.
CAPITULATION   An agreement to give up a fortress on terms.
CAPONNIERE   1 A covered communication, usually in the form of a trench with raised sides, running from the enceinte to a detached work.
2 A powerful casemated work, projecting perpendicularly across a ditch for the purpose of delivering flanking fire.
CARCASS   An incendiary shell.
CASEMATE   A covered chamber, usually of masonry. A defensive casemate is one which is pierced with loopholes or embrasures for musketry or artillery. *See also* HAXO CASEMATE.
CAVALIER   A raised interior battery, usually in the centre of a bastion.
CHAMBER (FOURNEAU)   A space made in a mine for the housing of an explosive charge.
CHEMIN DES RONDES   A sentry walk running round the top of the masonry of a revetment.
CHEVAL DE FRISE   An obstruction made of a squared beam to which are attached wooden stakes.
CIRCUMVALLATION   A line of siege works which faces the open country so as to hold off the army of relief.
CITADEL   A compact, independent and very strong work of four or five sides. It is usually sited next to a town enceinte.
CORDON   A continuous, rounded coping stone which surmounts the revetment of a masonry rampart.
COUNTER-APPROACH   A trench dug from the fortress against the siegeworks.
COUNTERFORT   An interior buttress.
COUNTERGUARD   A detached bastion, standing in front of a bastion of the enceinte.
COUNTERSCARP   The slope or retaining wall on the outer side of the ditch.
COUNTERVALLATION   A line of earthworks made at the beginning of the siege and facing the fortress under attack.
COVERED WAY   An infantry position, running along the rim of the counterscarp.
CREMAILLERE   A work *en crémaillère* is in saw-toothed form.
CREST   The innermost edge of a glacis or parapet.
CROCHET   A miniature parallel in the approach trenches.
CROWNWORK   A kind of hornwork, composed of two long branches on either side and two small bastioned fronts at the head.
CURTAIN   A stretch of rampart running between two bastions.
CUVETTE (or CUNETTE)   A narrow ditch sunk in the floor of the main ditch.
DEBLAI   Material excavated in the digging of the ditch.
DEFILEMENT   The science of aligning the summits of fortifications in a vertical plane, so as to evade gunfire from a height outside the fortress.
DEMI-LUNE   *see* HALF-MOON *and* RAVELIN
DESCENT OF THE DITCH   The process of advancing siegeworks from the crest of the glacis to the floor of the ditch.
DISCRETION   A garrison surrenders at discretion when it delivers itself to the mercy of the besieger without terms.
DOUBLE CROWNWORK   A kind of crownwork with three bastioned fronts at the head.
ECHAUGUETTE   *see* GUERITE
ÉCLUSE DE CHASSE   An entry sluice.
ÉCLUSE DE FUITE   An exit sluice.
ÉCOUTE   A small mine gallery.
EMBRASURE   An opening made through a parapet or wall, to enable a cannon to fire through the thickness.

ENCEINTE (BODY OF THE PLACE)   The main, continuous perimeter of a fortress.
ENFILADE   Fire coming from the flank in such a way that the effect is felt along the length of a fortification or a body of troops.
ENVELOPE (COUVREFACE GENERALE)   A continuous outer enceinte.
ÉPAULEMENT (BREASTWORK)   A parapet which protects troops or guns against enfilade fire.
ESCALADE   The climbing of a work by means of ladders.
ESPLANADE   The open space left between a citadel and the buildings of a town.
EXPENSE MAGAZINE   A small magazine placed close to a battery.
EXTERIOR SIDE OF FORTIFICATION   An imaginary line drawn from the salient of one bastion to the salient of the next.
FACES   Outer sides of a work which converge to form a salient angle.
FASCINE   A bundle of branches used in sieges.
FAUSSE-BRAYE   A low outer rampart, usually built of earth.
FLANK   The side of a work, more particularly the part of a bastion which connects one of the faces with the curtain.
FLECHE   An arrow-shaped outwork, usually of light construction.
FORT D'ARRET (SPERRFORT)   An isolated fort guarding a pass or passage.
FOUGASSE   A small mine placed a short distance below ground to take effect against troops.
FRAISES   *see* STORM-POLES
GABION   A basket of woven brushwood which is filled with earth and used extensively in siege-work and as a supplement to fortifications.
GABION FARCI   *see* SAP ROLLER
GALLERY   The largest kind of mine tunnel.
GARDE-FOU   A free-standing tablette, running along the outer rim of the chemin des rondes.
GLACIS   The open slope descending from the crest of the covered way to the open country.
GORGE   The side or neck of a bastion or detached work which faces towards the centre of the fortress.
GUERITE   A sentry box which is sited on the ramparts.
HALF-MOON (DEMI-LUNE)   A ravelin.
HAXO CASEMATE   A vaulted defensive casemate, sited on the terreplein.
HORNWORK   An outwork composed of two branches at the sides and a small bastioned front at the head. *See also* CROWNWORK
INSULT   The taking of a fortress by surprise or storm, without recourse to formal siege.
LINE OF DEFENCE   An imaginary line, extending from the salient of a bastion along a face and thence to the curtain or flank of an adjacent bastion.
LUNETTE   1 A detached triangular work standing on or beyond the glacis.
   2 A small work sited to the side of a ravelin.
MANTLET   A wheeled timber screen, employed to protect the head of a sap.
MERLON   The solid portion of a parapet between two embrasures.
ORILLON   A projecting shoulder of the bastion, which partially screens a retired flank from fire.
PALANKA   A small fortification made of logs or palisades, more particularly on the Turkish theatre of war.
PALISADE   A fence of close-set, pointed wooden stakes.
PARADOS   *see* PARAPET
PARALLEL   A wide and deep siege trench, describing an arc roughly equidistant along all its length from the covered way of the fortress.
PARAPET   A stout wall or bank of earth, placed along the forward edge of fortifications or siege-works, and giving protection to the troops behind. A rearward parapet is called a 'parados'.
PAS DE SOURIS   A narrow flight of steps, set in the counterscarp revetment.
PETARD   A bell-like device, used for blowing in a gate.
PLACE OF ARMS   An enlargement of the covered way, at the re-entrant or salient angles, where

troops are assembled for sorties or for the obstinate defence of the covered way.
PROFILE   A cross-section of fortification.
RAMEAU   A medium-sized mine tunnel.
RAMPART   A thick wall of earth, masonry, or both, which forms the main defence of the fortress.
RAVELIN   A triangular detached work, placed in front of a curtain and usually between two bastions. NB in French the ravelin is termed the *demi-lune*.
REDAN   A V-shaped work, open to the rear.
REDOUBT   1 A detached work, enclosed on all sides.
2 A small, powerful work, usually in the form of a redan, which is placed inside a bastion or a re-entrant place of arms.
RE-ENTRANT   An angle facing inwards from the field.
REMBLAI   The material (usually from the excavation of the ditch), which is piled up to form the body of the rampart.
RETIRED FLANK   A recessed portion of a bastion flank.
RETRENCHMENT   An interior defence.
REVETMENT   A retaining wall. In works in demi-revetment, the masonry covers only the lower part of the rampart.
RICOCHET FIRE   The firing of cannon shot or howitzer shells at high trajectory and low charges, so that the missile drops over the parapet of a work and bounces along its length.
SALIENT   An angle pointing outwards towards the field.
SALLY-PORT   A small gate, usually set in a curtain, which permits troops to leave on a sortie.
SAP   A narrow siege trench which is established by the planting of gabions or sandbags. In a flying sap, a row of gabions is planted simultaneously, and not (as is usual) in succession.
SAP ROLLER (French GABION FARCI)   A stout gabion which is rolled horizontally in front of the head of a sap.
SAUCISSON   A fuze made of a powder-filled hose of canvas or leather.
SCARP   The outer slope of a rampart.
SHOULDER ANGLE   The angle of a bastion which is formed by the meeting of a face and a flank.
SPERRFORT   *see* FORT D'ARRET
STORM-POLES (French FRAISES)   A palisade planted in the scarp of a work, and projecting horizontally or slightly downwards.
TABLETTE   A low wall crowning the cordon of a rampart.
TAIL   The entrance to the siege trenches.
TALUS   1 The rearward slope of a rampart.
2 Any earthen slope.
TAMBOUR   A small palisaded perimeter.
TENAILLE   A low work stationed in the ditch in front of a curtain.
TENAILLE FORTIFICATION   A fortification on a zigzag trace.
TENAILLON   A small work standing to one side of a ravelin.
TERREPLEIN   The wide upper part of a rampart (or covered way), stretching from the banquette to the edge of the talus (or counterscarp).
TRACE   Ground plan.
TRAVERSE   A bank or wall, usually set at right-angles to the main alignment of the work, which protects the defenders from enfilade.
WALL-PIECE (French MOUSQUET A CHEVALET)   A very long and heavy musket used in sieges.
ZIGZAGS   Approach trenches.
ZONE OF SERVITUDE   An area beyond the glacis on which civil building is restricted or forbidden.

Bibliography

NB: The titles of contemporary manuals which are mentioned in the text are not generally repeated in the Bibliography, unless they are used as a source of quotations. Many of the authorities cited in the Bibliography of *Siege Warfare. The Fortress in the Early Modern World 1494–1660* (1979) are also relevant to the later period.

Abrahamovich, Z. (1983), *Islamische Quellen zur Geschichte des Türkenjahres 1683*, paper delivered to the Conference of the International Commission of Military History, Vienna, 1983.

Adelung, F. V. (1846), *Kritish-Literärische Übsersicht der Reisenden in Russland*, 2 vols, St Petersburg.

Adlerfeld, G. (1740), *The Military History of Charles XII*, 2 vols, London.

Allmayer-Beck, J. C. and Kaindl, F. (eds) (1983), *Bedrohung und Befreiung Wiens 1683*, Vienna.

Allmayer-Beck, J. C. (1983), 'Bedrohung und Befreiung Wiens 1683. Eine weltgeschichtliche Einführung', in Allmayer-Beck and Kaindl (1983).

Alquié, F. S. (1670), *Les Mémoires du voiage de Mr. le Marquis de Ville au Levant, ou histoire curieuse du siège de Candie*, 3 pts, Amsterdam.

Amoretti, G. (1965), 'Le Gallerie di contromina delle "Mezzaluna della Porto del Soccorso" della citadella di Torino', in *Armi Antiche*, Turin.

Amoretti, G. (1978), 'Il sistema di centromine dell'Antica Torino', in *Commission Internationale d'Histoire Militaire*, no. 39, Rome.

Anburey, T. (1789, reprinted 1969), *Travels through the Interior Parts of America*, 2 vols, London (reprinted New York).

Anderson, R. C. (1910), *Naval Wars in the Baltic*. London.

Anderson, R. C. (1952), *Naval Wars in the Levant*, Princeton.

André, L. (1906), *Michel le Tellier et l'organisation de l'armée monarchique*, Paris.

Andrews, K. (1953), 'Castles of the Morea', in *Gennadeison Monographs*, IV, Princeton.

Anon. (1688), *A Journal of the Venetian Campaigns, A.D. 1687*, London.

Anon. (1689), *Observations upon the Warre of Hungary*, London.

Anon. (1702), *A Journal of the Several Sieges of Keiserswaert, Landau and Venlo*, London.

Anon. (1707), *A Journal of the Siege of San Matheo*, London.

Anon. (1709), *History of the Campaign in Flanders in the Year 1708*, London.

Anon. (1745), *The Theatre of the Present War in the Netherlands and upon the Rhine*, London.

Anon. (1747), *An Authentic and Accurate Journal of the Siege of Bergen-op-Zoom*, London.

Anon. (1772), *An Authentic Narrative of the Russian Expedition against the Turks by Sea and Land*, London.

Anon. (1773), *Histoire de la guerre entre la Russie et la Turquie*, St Petersburg.

Anon. (1783), *Histoire du Siège de Gibraltar*, Cadiz.

Anon. (1785), *Conseil d'état privé sur l'événement de Gibraltar en 1782*, Paris.

Anon. (1785), *Conseil d'état privé sur l'événement de terzügen aus dem Leben Friedrichs des Zweiten*, 4 vols, Berlin.

Anon. (1886), 'Der Antheil der Kurfürstlich Sächsischen Truppen an der Erstürmung von Prag 25/26 November 1741', in *Kriegsgeschichtliche Einzelschriften*, VII, Berlin.

Anon. (1887), 'Die Hessen vor Belgrad und auf Sicilien 1717 bis 1721. Aus dem Nachlasse eines Kurhessischen Offiziers', in *Beiheft zum Militär-Wochenblatt*, Berlin.

Anon. (1931), *Bulletin of Fort Ticonderoga Museum*, Ticonderoga.

Anon. (1958), 'James II and the Siege of Derry', in *The Irish Sword*, III, no. 13, Dublin.

Anon. (1959), 'A Diary' (1691), *The Irish Sword*, IV, no. 15, Dublin.

Archenholtz, J. W. (edn of 1911), *Geschichte des Siebenjährigen Krieges in Deutschland*, 2 vols, Leipzig.

Archer, C. I. (1977), *The Army in Bourbon Mexico*, Albuquerque.

D'Arçon, C. Le Michaud (1786), *Considérations sur l'influence du génie de Vauban dans la balance des forces de l'état*, no place of publication.

D'Arçon, C. Le Michaud (1788), *Considérations militaires et politiques sur la reforme projetée d'un grand nombre de nos places de guerre*, Metz.

D'Arçon, C. Le Michaud (1789), *Observations sur les fragments de mémoires attribués au Maréchal de Vauban*, Landrecies.

D'Arçon, C. Le Michaud (l'An III), *Considérations militaires et politiques sur la fortification*, Paris.

Ardesoif, J. P. (1772), *Introduction to Marine Fortification and Gunnery*, Gosport.

Arneth, A. (1863-79), *Geschichte Maria Theresias*, 10 vols, Vienna.

Augoyat, M. (1839), *Notice historique sur le Lieutenant-Général Lapara des Fieux*, Paris. Lapara was one of the most gifted engineers of Vauban's generation.

Augoyat, M. (1860-4), *Aperçu historique sur les fortifications, les ingénieurs et le Corps du Génie de France*, 2nd edn, 3 vols, Paris. Very important.

Baiov, A. (1906), *Russkaya Armiya v Tsarstvovanie Imperatritsy Anny Ioannovnyi*, 2 vols, St Petersburg.

Balderston, M. and Syrett, D. (1975), *The Lost War. Letters from British Officers during the American Revolution*, New York.

Balesi, C. J. (1978), 'French Mississippi under the British Régime 1765-1777', in *Proceedings of the International Military History Colloquy*, Ottawa.

Barker, T. M. (1967), *Double Eagle and Crescent. Vienna's Second Turkish Siege and its Historical Background*, Albany.

Barker, T. M. (1983), *The Year of the Turk, 1683. A Turning-Point in European History?* Paper delivered to the Conference of the International Commission of Military History, Vienna 1983.

Beatson, R. (1804), *Naval and Military Memoirs of Great Britain*, London.

Beaurain and Grimoard (1782), *Histoire des quatre dernières campagnes du Maréchal de Turenne*, Paris.

Behr, J. H. (1690), *Der aufs Neue-verschanzte Turenne*, Frankfurt.

Belidor, B. F. (1729), *La science des ingénieurs*, Paris.

Benedikt, H. (1959), *Der Pascha-Graf Alexander von Bonneval 1675-1747*, Graz and Cologne.

Bengtsson, F. H. (1960), *The Life of Charles XII*, London.

Berenger, J. (1979), 'Rélations des Troupes Reglées, Troupes de Terre et Troupes de Marine, avec les Canadiens' in *Revue Historique des Armées*, no. 1, Vincennes.

Bertin, P. (1978), 'Les forces en présence pendant la conquête de 1674' (i.e. of Franche Comté), in *Revue historique des armées*, no. 2, Vincennes.

Memoirs of the Duke of Berwick (1779), 2 vols, London.

Beskrovnyi, L. G. (1958), *Russkaya armiya i flot v XVIII veke*, Moscow.

Bienemann, F. (1902), *Die Katastrophe der Stadt Dorpat während des Nordischen Krieges*, Revel.

Bigge (1899), 'Der Kampf um Candia in den Jahren 1667-1668', in *Kriegsgeschichtliche Einzelschriften*, XXVI, Berlin.

Bird, H. (1968), *Attack on Quebec. The American Invasion of Canada 1775-1776*, New York.

Blanchard, A. (1970), 'Les ci-devant Ingénieurs du Roi', in *Revue internationale d'histoire militaire*, XXX, Paris.

Blanchard, A. (1979), *Les Ingénieurs du 'Roy' de Louis XIV à Louis XV*, Montpellier.

Blanchard, A. (1981), *Dictionnaire des ingénieurs militaires 1691-1791*, Montpellier.

Bleyl, W. (1939), *Silberberg. Die Passfestung Schlesiens*, Breslau.

Bleyl, W. (1981), *Der Donjon. Eine Bautechnische Typologie des Verteidigungsfähigen Wohnturmes*, Cologne. Traces an enduring Northern tradition of defensible towers.

Bliver, B. (1956), *Battle for Manhattan*, New York.

Blois, E. (1865), *De la fortification en présence de l'artillerie nouvelle*, 2 vols, Paris. Blois was one of the few French advocates of the technique of bombardment.

Blondel, F. (1684), *La Nouvelle Manière de fortifier les places*, The Hague.

Blondel, F. (1685), *L'Art de jeter les bombes*, The Hague. The first 'scientific' treatment of the subject.

Bode, A. (1979), *Die Flottenpolitik Katharinas II und die Konflikte mit Schweden und der Türkei (1678-1792)*, Wiesbaden.

Bonin, Lieutenant (1877), *Geschichte des Ingenieurkorps und der Pioniere in Preussen*, vol 1, Berlin.

Mémoires du Comte de Bonneval (1738), 3 vols, The Hague.

Bonneville (1762), *Esprit des lois de la tactique et de différents institutions militaires, ou notes de Mr. le Maréchal de Saxe*, The Hague; especially on the sieges in Holland in 1747.

Borus, J. (1983), *Moderne Militärtechnik und alte Kriegswaffen in den Türkenkriegen 1663–1698*, paper delivered to the Conference of the International Commission of Military History, Vienna, 1983.

Bothen, A. (1980), *Nya Älvsborg*, Göteborg.

Bousmard, H. J.-B. (1797–9), *Essai Général de Fortification et d'Attaque et Défense des Places*, 2 vols, Berlin.

Braubach, M. (1963–4), *Prinz Eugen von Savoyen*, 2 vols, Munich.

Brinckerhoff, S. B. and Faulk, O. B. (1965), *Lancers for the King. A Study of the Frontier System of Northern New Spain*, Phoenix.

Brisac, C. C. (1981), *La Musée des Plans-Reliefs: Hôtel National des Invalides*, Paris.

Broucek, P. (1983), 'Der Feldzug 1683 und der Entsatz Wiens', in Allmayer-Beck and Kaindl (1983).

Brun-Lavaine and Elie Brun (1838), *Les Sept Sièges de Lille*, Paris and Lille.

Callahan, N. (1958), *Henry Knox. George Washington's General*, New York.

Cambridge, R. O. (1762), *An Account of the War in India between the English and French on the Coast of Coromandel*, London.

Canadian Automobile Association (1978), *Heritage of Canada*, Montreal. Contains excellent short histories and descriptions of forts in Canada.

Memoirs of Capt. George Carleton (1808), Edinburgh.

Carnot, L. H. (1789), *Mémoire présenté au conseil de la guerre au sujet des places fortes*, no place of publication.

Mémoires sur Carnot. Par son fils (1861–4), 2 vols, Paris.

Carter, A. C. (1976), 'The Dutch Barrier Fortresses in the Eighteenth Century, as Shown in the Ferraris Map', in *La Cartographie au XVIII siècle et l'oeuvre du Comte de Ferraris (1726–1814)*, Brussels.

Mémoires et correspondance du Maréchal de Catinat (1819), 3 vols, Paris.

Çeliker, F. (1983), *Zweite Türkenbelagerung Wiens und Ursachen der Misserfolge*, paper delivered to the Conference of the International Commission of Military History, Vienna, 1983.

Chandler, D. G. (1976), *The Art of War in the Age of Marlborough*, London.

Chidsey, D. B. (1962), *Victory at Yorktown*, New York.

Chotard, K. (1890), *Louis XIV, Louvois, Vauban et les fortifications du nord de la France*, Paris.

Churchill, W. S. (1947), *Marlborough, His Life and Times*, 2 vols, London.

The American Revolution. Sir Henry Clinton's Narrative of his Campaigns, 1775–82 (ed. W. B. Willcox) (1954), New Haven and London.

The Revolutionary Journal of Baron Ludwig von Closen 1780–83 (ed. E. M. Acomb) (1958), Chapel Hill.

Coehoorn, G. T. (ed. 1860), *Het leven van Menno Baron van Coehoorn*, Leeuwarden. By the great Coehoorn's nephew.

Coehoorn, M. (1685), *Nieuwe vestingbouw op een natte of lage horisont*, Leeuwarden. Our quotations are from the French ed. of 1741, *Nouvelle Fortification*, The Hague.

Coehoorn, Stitching van (1956 and still in progress), annual *Jaarboek*, and *Atlas van historische vestingswerken in Nederland*, The Hague.

Coehoorn, Stitching van (1982), *Vesting vier eeuwen Vestingbuow in Nederland*, The Hague.

Cohn, M. (1962), 'The Fortifications of New York during the Revolutionary War 1776–82', New York (duplicated typescript).

Colin, J. (1901–6), *Les Campagnes du Maréchal de Saxe*, 3 vols, Paris.

Colonie, M. de la (1904), *The Chronicles of an Old Campaigner*, London.

Cook, J. (1770), *Voyages and Travels through the Russian Empire*, 2 vols, Edinburgh.

Corbett, J. S. (1907), *England in the Seven Years War*, London.

Cormontaigne, L. (ed. C. R. Fourcroy) (1806–9), *Oeuvres posthumes de Cormontaigne*, comprising I, *Mémorial pour la fortification permanente et passagère*; II, *Mémorial pour l'attaque des places*; III, *Mémorial pour la défense des places*, Paris.

Cornet, H. (1867), *Siège de Prague 1742*, Paris.

Corvisier, A. (1983), *Louvois*, Paris, Emphasises the place of Vauban as member of a bureaucratic team.

Cousine, A. (1976), 'La Campagne de 1674–1675 du Maréchal de Turenne', in *Revue historique des armées*, no. 1, Vincennes.

Criste, O. (1904), *Kriege unter Kaiser Josef II*, Vienna.

Curzon, Lord (1892), *Persia and the Persian Question*, 2 vols, London.

Cyrus, A. (1947), *Vaxholms fästnung*, Vaxholm.

Erik Dahlbergs Dagbok (1625–1699) (ed. H. Lundström) (1912), Stockholm.

Delmas, J. (ed.) (1978), *Conflits des sociétés au Canada Français pendant la Guerre de Sept Ans et leur influence sur les opérations*, Vincennes.

Denisov, A. K. (1874), 'Zapiski', in *Russkaya Starina*, X, St Petersburg.

Military Journal of Major Ebenezer Denny (1859 reprinted 1971), Philadelphia (New York).

R. Deputazione Sovra gli Studi di Storia Patria (1907–10), *Le Campagne di guerra in Piemonte (1703–1708) e l'assedio di Torino (1706)*, 10 vols, Turin.

Diepenbach, W. (1928), *Die Stadtbefestigung von Mainz*, Mainz.

Dirrheimer, G. and Fritz, F. (1967), 'Einhörner und Schuwalowische Haubitzen', in *Schriften des Heeresgeschichtlichen Museums in Wien*, III, Graz.

D.M.V.L.N. (1756), *Histoire de la dernière guerre de Bohême*, Amsterdam.

Dolleczek, A. (1887), *Geschichte der Österreichischen Artillerie*, Vienna.

Dollot, R. (1902), *Les Origines de la neutralité de la Belgique et le système de la barrière (1609–1830)*, Paris.

Amiable Renegade. The Memoirs of Capt. Peter Drake (1960), Stanford.

Duffy, C. (1964), *The Wild Goose and the Eagle. A Life of Marshal von Browne 1705–1757*, London.

Duffy, C. (1974), *The Army of Frederick the Great*, Newton Abbot.

Duffy, C. (1975), *Fire and Stone. The Science of Fortress Warfare 1660–1860*, Newton Abbot.

Duffy, C. (1977), *The Army of Maria Theresa*, Newton Abbot.

Duffy, C. (1979), *Siege Warfare. The Fortress in the Early Modern World 1494–1660*, London.

Duffy, C. (1981), *Russia's Military Way to the West. Origins and Nature of Russian Military Power 1700–1800*, London.

Duke, W. (1952), *The Rash Adventurer*, London. On the '45.

Duncker, Major v. (1893), 'Drei Berichte aus dem belagerten Wien', in *Mittheilungen des K.u.K. Kriegs-Archivs*, N.F.VII, Vienna.

Dupuget (1771), *Essai sur l'usage de l'artillerie*, Amsterdam.

Dupuy, R. and Dupuy, T. (1963), *The Compact History of the Revolutionary War*, New York.

Duro, C. F. (1900–1), *Armada Española*, vols VI and VII, Madrid.

Duvernoy, Lt.-Col. (1901), 'Die Anschauungen Friedrichs des Grossen vom Festungskriege vor Ausbruch des Siebenjährigen Krieges', in *Beihefte zum Militär-Wochenblatt*, Berlin.

Duvigneau, K. (1830), *Exercise sur les fortifications*, 2 vols, Paris. Written for the instruction of the Mézières engineering school in 1768.

Eccles, W. J. (1969), *The Canadian Frontier 1534–1760*, New York.

Eccles, W. J. (1972), *France in America*, New York.

Eelking, M. (1856), *Leben und Wirken des Herzoglich Braunschweig'schen General-Lieutenants Friedrich Adolf Riedesel*, 3 vols, Leipzig.

Eimer, G. (1961), *Die Stadtplanung im Schwedischen Ostseereich*, Stockholm.

'A Diary of the Siege of Athlone . . . by an Engineer of the Army' (1691 reprinted 1959), in *The Irish Sword*, IV, no. 15, Dublin.

Ericsson, E. and Vennberg, E. (1925), *Erik Dahlberg*, Uppsala and Stockholm. An important study.

Eriksen, R. R. (1979), *Fredriksten Festnings Historia. Carl XII's Død*, Halden.

Ewald, J. (1979), *Diary of the American War. A Hessian Journal*, New Haven.

Fabritsius, I. G., 'Glavnoe Inzhenernoe Upravlenie, Istoricheskii Ocherk' in D. A. Skalon (1902–c. 1911), *Stoletie Voennago Ministerstva 1800–1902*, VII, pt. 1, St Petersburg.

Foissac-Latour (1789), *Examen détaillé de l'importante question de l'utilité des places fortes*, Amsterdam.

Ford, W. C. (1897), *Defences of Philadelphia in 1777*, Brooklyn.

Foster, W. (1906), *The English Factories in India*, Oxford.

Francis, D. (1975), *The First Peninsular War: 1702–1713*, London.

Fraser, J. (1742), *History of Nadir Shah*, London.

Oeuvres de Frédéric le Grand (1846–7), 30 vols, esp. I–VII (historical) and XXVIII–XXX (military), Berlin.

Politische Correspondenz Friedrichs des Grossen (1879–1939), 46 vols, Berlin; the supplementary vol, 1920, consists of *Die Politischen Testamente Friedrichs des Grossen*.

'Friedrichs des Grossen Practische Instruction im Festungskriege im Jahre 1752', in *Archiv für die Officiere der Königlich-Preussischen Artillerie- und-Ingenieur-Corps* (1836), 2nd series, III, Berlin.

Fredrikstad and District Travel Association (1978), *Fredrikstad. The Fortified Town. Kongsten Fort. Norway*, Fredrikstad.

Freeden, M. (1952), *Festung Marienberg*, Würzburg. Especially on the conditions of German fortress-building.

Freeman, D. S. (1949–52), *George Washington*, 5 vols, New York.

Fregault, G. (1969), *Canada. The War of Conquest*, Toronto.

French, A. (1928), *The Taking of Ticonderoga in 1775. The British Story*, Harvard.

Fuchs, E. (1827), *Anekdoty knyazya Italiiskago, Grafa Suvorova rymnikskago*, St Petersburg.

Geikie, R. and Montgomery, I. (1930), *The Dutch Barrier 1705–1719*, Cambridge.

Gembruch, W. (1972), 'Zur Kritik an der Heeresreform und Wehrpolitik von Le Tellier und Louvois in der Spätzeit der Heerschaft Ludwigs XIV', in *Militärgeschichtliche Mitteilungen*, Freiburg.

Generalstab, *Bidrag til den store Nordiske krigs historia, utgivne av generalstaben* (1899–1934), 10 vols, Copenhagen. The Swedish General Staff's counterpart, *Karl XII pa Slagfåltet* (1918–19), is criticised by modern Swedish historians for glorifying Charles XII, while underestimating the work of Charles XI.

Gibson, C. (1966), *Spain in North America*, New York.

Gipson, L. H. (1936–70), *The British Empire before the American Revolution*, 15 vols, New York.

Tagebuch des General Patrick Gordon (1849–51), 2 vols, Moscow and St Petersburg.

Göyünç, N. (1983), *Osmanische Festungen auf dem Balkan im 18. Jahrhundert*, paper delivered to the Conference of the International Commission of Military History, Vienna 1983.

Grosser Generalstab (1890–1914), *Die Kriege Friedrichs des Grossen*, comprising *Der Erste Schlesische Krieg, Der Zweite Schlesische Krieg*, and *Der Siebenjährige Krieg*, 19 vols, Berlin.

Guasco, Lt.-Gen. P. (1846), *Rélation de la défense de Schweidnitz*, Paris. By the command of Schweidnitz in the famous defence of 1762.

Guilbert, J. A. (1772), *Essai général de tactique*, London.

Guignard, Chevalier de (1725), *L'Ecole de Mars*, 2 vols, Paris.

Guthorn, P. J. (1966), *American Maps and Map Makers of the Revolution*, Monmouth Beach.

Guthorn, P. J. (1972), *British Maps of the American Revolution*, Monmouth Beach.

Guttin, J. (1957), *Vauban et le Corps des Ingénieurs Militaires*, Paris.

H++++ (1774), *Ausführliche Erzählung, nebst Grundrissen der Belagerung der Festung Schweidnitz ... 1762*, Hanover.

Haake, P. (1910), *Generalfeldmarschall Hans Adam von Schöning*, Berlin.

Haintz, O. (1936–58), *König Karl von Schweden*, 3 vols, Berlin.

Hammer, J. (1834–5), *Geschichte des Osmanischen Reiches*, 2nd edn, vols II and III, Pest.

Hamont, T. (1887), *Lally-Tollendal*, Paris.

Handen, R. D. 'The End of an Era. Louis XIV and Victor Amadeus', in Hatton (1976).

Hanway, J. (1753), *An Historical Account of the British Trade over the Caspian Sea ... With the Particular History of the Great Usurper Nadir Kouli*, 4 vols, London.

Harley, J. B., Petchenik, B. B. and Towner, L. W. (1978), *Mapping the Revolutionary War*, Chicago.

Hart, F. R. (1931), *The Siege of Havana 1762*, Boston.

Hatton, R. (1968), *Charles XII of Sweden*, London.

Hatton, R. (ed.) (1976), *Louis XIV and Europe*, London.

Hatton, R., 'Louis XIV and his Fellow Monarchs', in Hatton (1976), London.

Hayes-McCoy, G. A. (1969), *Irish Battles*, London.

Memoirs of Major-General William Heath (1901 reprinted 1968), New York.

Held (1847), *Geschichte der drei Belagerungen Colbergs im Siebenjährigen Kriege*, Berlin.

Henning, (1965), *Das Barocke Wien*, 3 vols, Vienna.

Heuser, E. (1913), *Die Belagerungen von Landau 1702–13*, Landau.

Higham, R. (1978), 'Military Frontiersmanship – an Hypothesis from the Point of View of the Encroacher', in *Proceedings of the International Military History Colloquy*, Ottawa.

Higonnet, P. L.-R. (1968), 'The Origins of the Seven Years War', in *Journal of Modern History*, London.

Hildebrandt, C. (1829–35), *Anekdoten und Charakterzüge aus dem Leben Friedrichs des Grossen*, 6 vols, Halberstadt and Leipzig.

Hitsman, J. M. (1968), *Safeguarding Canada*, Toronto.

Hogg, F. O. (1963), *English Artillery 1326–1716*, Woolwich.

Holbrook, S. H. (ed.) (1965, etc.), *American Forts*, series, Englewood Cliffs, N.J.

Horneck, W. (1738), *Remarks on the Modern Fortification*, London.

Hough, F. B. (ed.) (1867 reprinted 1975), *The Siege of Charleston*, Spartanburg.

Hozier, H. M. (1876), *The Invasions of England*, 2 vols, London.

Huber, R., Rieth, R., Pflüger, H., Truttmann, P. and Hughes, J. Quentin (1979), *Festungen: Die Wehrbau nach Einführung der Feuerwaffen*, Munich.

Hughes, J. Quentin (1969), *Fortress Architecture and Military History in Malta*, London.

Hughes, J. Quentin (1974), *Military Architecture*, London.

Hughes, J. Quentin (1981), *Britain in the Mediterranean and the Defence of her Naval Stations*, Liverpool.

Hummelberger, W. (1983), 'Totale Verteidigung Wiens', in Allmayer-Beck and Kaindl (1983).

Hummelberger, W. and Peball, K. (1974), *Die Befestigungen Wiens*, Vienna and Hamburg.

Hunter, W. A. (1960), *Forts on the Pennsylvania Border 1753–1758*, Harrisburg.

Intelligence Branch of the Quartermaster-General's Dept.

(1884), *British Minor Expeditions 1746 to 1814*, London.

Jähns, M. (1889–91), *Geschichte der Kriegswissenschaften vornehmlich in Deutschland*, 3 parts, Munich and Leipzig.

Jakobsson, T. (1943), *Artilleriet under Karl XII:s Tiden*, Stockholm.

Jarvis, R. C. (1971), *Collected Papers on the Jacobite Risings*, vol. I, Manchester.

'Captain James Jefferye's Letters from the Swedish Army 1707–1709' (1954), ed. R. Hatton, in *Historiska Handlingar*, XXXV, Stockholm.

Johnston, H. P. (1900), *The Storming of Stony Point*, New York.

Johnstone, Chevalier (1821), *Memoirs of the Rebellion in 1745 and 1746*, London.

Jones, C. J. (ed.) (1874 reprinted 1968), *The Siege of Savannah in 1779*, Albury (New York).

Juva, E. W. (1946–9), 'Augustin Ehrensvärd', in B. Hildebrand, *Svenskt Biografiskt Lexikon*, XII, Stockholm.

Kalkreuth, Field-Marshal (1840), 'Kalkreuth zu seinem Leben und zu seiner Zeit', in *Minerva*, vol. IV for 1840, Jena.

Kamen, H. (1969), *The War of Succession in Spain*, London.

A Fragment of a Memoir of Field-Marshal James Keith (1843), Edinburgh. Especially on Gibraltar 1727.

Kennett, L. (1977), *The French Forces in America, 1780–1783*, Westport.

Keppel, S. (1982), *Three Brothers at Havana*, Salisbury.

Aus der Zeit Maria Theresias. Tagebuch des Fürsten Johann Josef Khevenhüller-Metsch (1907–72), 8 vols, Vienna.

Kinsky, Count (1790), *Ueber Türkenkrieg*, Wiener Neustadt.

Kite, E. S. (1933), *Brigadier-General Duportail*, Baltimore.

Kittler, G. A. (1951), 'Georg Rimpler. Kaiserlicher Obristleutnant und Oberingenieur im Türkenkriege 1683', in *Zeitschrift für Geschichte des Oberrheins*, XCIC,

Kohl, E. (1972), *Die Geschichte der Festung Glatz*, Würzburg.

Korobkov, N. M. (1940), *Semiletnyaya Voina*, Moscow.

Kotasek, E. (1956), *Feldmarschall Graf Lacy*, Horn.

Kreutel, R. F. (trans. and ed.) (1960), *Kara Mustafa vor Wien*, Graz.

Kriegsarchiv (1876–91), *Feldzüge des Prinzen Eugen von Savoyen*, 20 vols, Vienna.

Kriegsarchiv (1896–1914), *Oesterreichischer Erbfolge-Krieg*, 9 vols, Vienna.

Krockow, Lieut. (1884), 'Erinnerung an die letzte Campagne Friedrichs des Grossen', in *Jahrbücher für die Deutsche Armee und Marine*, LIII, Berlin.

Lacrocq, N. (1981), *Atlas des Places Fortes de France (1774–1788)*, Vincennes.

Mémoire Produit au Conseil d'Etat du Roi, par Trophime-Gérard, Comte de Lally-Tollendal (1779), 2 vols, Rouen.

Memorias Militares de La Mina (1898), 2 vols, Madrid.

Langeron, A. (1895), 'Russkaya Armiya v God Smerti Ekateriny II', in *Russkaya Starina*, St. Petersburg.

Lantzeff, G. V. and Pierce, R. A. (1973), *Eastwards to Empire*, London.

Laskovskii, F. (1858–65), *Materiali dlya istorii inzhenernogo iskusstva v Rossii*, 3 vols, St Petersburg.

Lautzas, P. (1973), *Die Festung Mainz im Zeitalter des Ancien Regime, der Französischen Revolution und des Empire (1736–1814)*, Wiesbaden. Important and wide-ranging.

Lawrence, A. A. (1951), *Storm over Savannah. The Story of Count d'Estaing and the Siege of the Town in 1779*, Athens, Georgia.

Le Blond (2nd ed. 1762), *Eléments de la guerre des sièges*, comprising I, *L'Artillerie raisonnée*; II, *L'Attaque des places*; III, *La Défense des places*, Paris.

Lecomte, C. A. (1904), *Les ingénieurs militaires en France pendant le règne de Louis XIV*, Paris.

Oeuvres complètes de M. Lefèbvre (1778), 2 vols, Maastricht.

Lenman, B. (1980), *The Jacobite Risings in Britain 1689–1746*, London. Especially on inter-clan relationships.

Leonard, E. G. (1958), *L'Armée et ses problèmes au XVIII siècle*, Paris.

Levy, A. (1980), 'Military Reform and Political Development in the Ottoman Empire in the 18th Century', in *War and Society in East Central Europe during the 18th Century*, Brooklyn College Studies on Society in Change, XI, Brooklyn.

Ligne, C. J. (1795–1811), *Mélanges militaires, littéraires et sentimentaires*, 34 vols, Dresden.

Lisk, J. (1967), *The Struggle for Supremacy in the Baltic 1600–1725*, London.

Livet, G. 'Louis XIV and the Germanies', in Hatton (1976).

Lockhart, L. (1938), *Nadir Shah*, London.

Lockhart, L. (1958), *The Fall of the Safavi Dynasty and the Afghan Occupation of Persia*, Cambridge.

Loeber, R. (1977–9), 'Biographical Dictionary of Engineers in Ireland, 1600–1730', in *The Irish Sword*, XIII, nos. 50–3, Dublin.

Löfberg, T. (1975), *Bohus Fästning*, Kungälv.

Longworth, P. (1965), *The Art of Victory. The Life and Achievements of Generalissimo Suvorov*, London.

Longworth, P. (1969), *The Cossacks*, London.
Lonnröth, E. (1975), 'Sweden's Coastal Defence', in *Actes du 2e Colloque Internationale d'Histoire Militaire* (in Stockholm, 1974), Brussels.
Lorenzen, V. (1953), *Axel Urup*, Copenhagen.
Oeuvres de Louis XIV (1806), 6 vols, Paris.
Campagne de Hollande en MDCLXXII, sous les ordres de Mr. le Duc de Luxembourg (1759), The Hague. A collection of documents.
McGuffie, T. H. (1965), *The Siege of Gibraltar 1779-1783*, London.
McKay, D. (1977), *Prince Eugene of Savoy*, London.
Mackesy, P. (1964), *The War for America 1775-1783*, London.
Mackey, H. D. (1973), *The Gallant Men of the Delaware Forts 1777*, Philadelphia.
McLennan, J. S. (1957), *Louisbourg from its Foundation to its Fall 1713-1758*, Sydney (Nova Scotia).
McLynn, F. J. (1981), *France and the Jacobite Rising of 1745*, Edinburgh.
McLynn, F. J. (1983), *The Jacobite Army in England 1745. The Final Campaign*, Edinburgh. Excellent.
Macrory, P. (1980), *The Siege of Derry*, London.
Mémoires du Marquis de Maffei (1741), 2 vols, Venice.
Maigret, P. (1725), *Traité de la sûreté et de la conservation des états par le moyen des forteresses*, Paris. English trans. (1747), *A Treatise on the Safety and Maintenance of States by Means of Fortresses*, London.
Mallet, A. M. (1673), *Travaux de Mars*, 3 vols, Paris. Especially on Portuguese fortresses.
Manstein, C. H. (1860), *Mémoires historiques, politiques et militaires sur la Russie*, 3 vols, Paris.
Marguerite, S. (1838), *Journal historique du siège de la ville et de la citadelle de Turin en 1706*, Turin. By the chief gunner of the garrison; most detailed and vivid.
The Letters and Dispatches of John Churchill, First Duke of Marlborough (ed. G. Murray) (1845), 5 vols, London.
The Marlborough-Godolphin Correspondence (ed. Snyder, H. L.) (1975), 3 vols, Oxford.
Marsigli, Conde di (1732), *Stato militare dell'imperio Ottomanno (L'État militaire de l'empire Ottoman)*, The Hague and Amsterdam.
Martin, J. P. (1962), *Private Yankee Doodle*, Boston.
Maslovskii, D. F. (1888-93), *Der Siebenjährige Krieg nach Russischer Darstellung*, 3 vols, Berlin.
Masson, P. (1978), 'La Marine Française et la Perte du Canada', in *Proceedings of the International Military History Colloquy*, Ottawa.
Mauvillon, J. (1794), *Geschichte Ferdinands Herzogs von Braunschweig-Lüneburg*, 2 vols, Leipzig.

Mengin, G. (1832), *Rélation du siège de Turin en 1706*, Paris.
Michalon, R. 'Vaudreuil et Montcalm', in Delmas (1978). Important.
Milliet Dechales, C. F. (1677), *L'art de fortifier, de défendre et d'attaquer les places*, Paris.
Milligan, C. D. (1948-50), *The Walls of Derry*, 2 pts, Londonderry.
Milligan, C. D. (1951), *History of the Siege of Londonderry*, Belfast 1951. The viewpoint of a fervent Orangeman.
Millner, J. (1733), *A Compendious Journal*, London.
Ministère d'Education (1981), *Vauban et ses Successeurs en Franche Comté. Trois Siècles d'Architecture Militaire*, Besançon.
Mirabeau, H. G. and Mauvillon, J. (1788), *Système militaire de la Prusse*, London.
Molesworth, Lord (1738), *An Account of Sweden as it was in the Year 1688*, London.
Molesworth, Lord (1738), *An Account of Denmark as it was in the Year 1692*, London.
Molyneux, T. M. (1759), *Conjunct Operations. Or Expeditions that have been carried on jointly by the Fleet and Army*, London.
Correspondance de Mons. le Marquis de Montalembert ... pendant les Campagnes de 1757 ... 61 (1777), 3 vols, London.
Montalembert, M. R. (1776-96), *La fortification perpendiculaire*, 11 vols, Paris.
Montecuccoli, R. (1735), *Mémoires*, Strasbourg.
Moore, J. (1780), *A View of Society and Manners in France, Switzerland, and Germany*, 2 vols, London.
Mörz, K. (1983), 'Befestigung und Armierung Wiens', in Allmayer-Beck and Kaindl (1983).
Muller, J. (1746), *A Treatise containing the Elementary part of Fortification*, London.
Müller, H. (1892), *Geschichte des Festungskrieges*, Berlin.
'Tagebuch des Generalfeldmarschalls Grafen von Münnich' (1843), in Hermann, E., *Beiträge zur Geschichte des Russischen Reiches*, Leipzig.
Munthe, C. O. (1906), *Frederikshalds og Frederikssten Historia indtil 1720*, Kristiania.
Munthe, L. (1902-52), continued by Ericsson, E., Grabe, G. and Enger, P. H. *Kungl. Fortifikationens Historia*, 6 pts, Stockholm. The later parts were published as appendices to the *Tidskrift i Fortifikation* – 4 (ii) in 1932-42, and 5 (i) in 1951-2.
Nikula, O. (1948), *Sveaborg*, Helsingfors.
Nilsson, S. (1968), *European Architecture in India 1750-1850*, London.
Noailles, Marshal (1850), *Mémoires politiques et militaires*,

in *Nouvelle collection des mémoires*, 3rd series X, Paris.

Nordberg, J. A. (1748), *Histoire de Charles XII*, 3 vols, The Hague.

'Letters of Samuel Noyes' (1959), in *Journal of the Society for Army Historical Research*, London. Especially on the siege of Huy 1703.

Ochwadt, K. (1977–83), *Wilhelm Graf zu Schaumburg-Lippe. Schriften und Briefe*, 3 vols, Frankfurt.

O'Meara, W. (1965), *Guns at the Forks. The Story of Fort Duquesne and Fort Pitt*, Englewood Cliffs, N.J.

Orrery, Earl of (1677), *A Treatise on the Art of War*, London.

Osman (1962), 'Der Gefangene der Giauren'. *Die Abenteurlichen Schicksale des Dolmetschers 'Osman Aǧa aus Temeschwar*, trans. and ed. R. F. Kreutel and O. Spies, Graz.

Palmer, D. R. (1969), *The River and the Rock. The History of Fortress West Point, 1775–1783*, New York.

Pankov, D. V. (ed.) (1952), *Iz Istorii Russkogo Voenno-Inzhenernogo Iskusstva*, Moscow. Copy available in Library of Congress, Washington DC.

Pajol, Comte (1888–91), *Les Guerres sous Louis XV*, 7 vols, Paris.

Pares, R. (1936), *War and Trade in the West Indies 1739–1763*, Oxford.

Parker, R. (1747), *Memoirs of the Most Remarkable Military Transactions*, London.

Parnell, A. (1905), *The War of the Succession in Spain*, London.

Peckham, H. H. (1958), *The War for Independence. A Military History*, Chicago.

Pell, R. T. (1950), 'The Cradle of Carillon. Assietta', in *The Bulletin of the Fort Ticonderoga Museum*, VIII, no. 6, Ticonderoga.

Pell, R. T. (1953), 'The Strategy of Montcalm', in *The Bulletin of Fort Ticonderoga Museum*, IX, no. 3, Ticonderoga.

Pell, R. T. (1966), *Fort Ticonderoga. A Short History*, New York.

Penny, F. (1900), *Fort St George, Madras*, London.

Peters, Capt. (1902), 'Die Österreichischen Befestigungen an der Oberen Elbe', in *Mittheilungen des K.u.K. Kriegs-Archivs*, V, Vienna.

Petersohn, J. (1958), 'Stralsund als Schwedische Festung', in *Baltische Studien*, NF XLIV, Hamburg.

Petrie, C. (1953), *The Marshal Duke of Berwick*, London.

Pezzl (1789), *Skizze von Wien*, Vienna.

Pfau, T. P. (1790), *Geschichte des Preussischen Feldzuges in der Provinz Holland*, Berlin.

Pfister, P. (1845), *Der Krieg von Morea in den Jahren 1687 und 1688*, Kassel.

Pirscher (1771), *Méthode nouvelle et facile pour fortifier les places*, Berlin.

Porter, W. and others (1889–1958), *History of the Corps of Royal Engineers*, 3 vols, London and Chatham.

Powell, P. W. (1952), *Soldiers, Indians and Silver*, Berkeley.

Preuss, J. D. (1832–4), *Urkundenbuch zu der Geschichte Friedrichs des Grossen*, 5 vols, Berlin.

Centre Pro Civitate (1965), *Plans en relief de villes Belges levés par des ingénieurs militaires français XVIIe–XIXe siècles*, Brussels.

Puységur, Marshal (1749), *L'Art de la guerre*, 2 vols, Paris.

Quincy, Marquis de (1726), *Histoire militaire du règne de Louis le Grand, Roy de France*, 8 vols, Paris. vol. VIII is an exposition of contemporary techniques called 'Maximes et Instructions sur l'art militaire'.

Des Reaux de la Richardière (1671), *Le Voyage de Candie, Fait par l'armée de France en l'année 1669*, Paris.

Redlich, O. (1921), *Österreichs Grossmachtbildung in der Zeit Kaiser Leopolds I*, vol. VI of *Geschichte Österreichs*, Gotha.

Reid, D. M. (1945), *The Story of Fort George*, Madras.

Reinhardt, M. (1950), *Le Grand Carnot*, 2 vols, Paris.

Retzow, F. A. (1803), *Nouveaux mémoires historiques sur la Guerre de Sept Ans*, 2 vols, Paris.

Rice, H. C. and Brown, A. S. (1972), *The American Campaign of Rochambeau's Army 1780, 1781, 1782, 1783*, 2 vols, Princeton.

Richards, Jacob and John, letters and diaries, British Library, Stowe Mss 447, 448, 451, 459–62, 466.

Richelieu, A. E. Duc de (1886), documents and letters, in *Sbornik imperatorskago istoricheskago obshchestva*, LIV, St Petersburg.

Richmond, H. (1941), *Amphibious Warfare in British History*, Exeter.

Roberts, M. (1979), *The Swedish Imperial Experience*, Cambridge.

Roberts, R. R. (1980), *New York's Forts in the Revolution*, Cranbury.

Archibald Robertson, Lt.-Gen. Royal Engineers. His Diaries and Sketches in North America 1762–1780 (ed. H. M. Lydenberg) (1930), New York.

Robin, Abbé (1783 reprinted 1969), *New Travels through North America*, Philadelphia (New York).

Memoirs of the Marshal Comte de Rochambeau (1838 reprinted 1971), Paris (New York).

Rochas d'Aiglun, A. (1867), *D'Arçon. Ingénieur militaire. Sa vie et ses écrits*, Paris.

Rockstroh, K. C. (1899), *Et Dansk Korps' historie 1701–1709*, Copenhagen. On a Danish contingent in the War of the Spanish Succession.

Rockstroh, K. C. (1909–16), *Udviklingen af den nationale haer i Danmark i det 17 og 18 aarhundrede*, 2 vols, Copenhagen.

Rockstroh, K. C. (1940–3), engineering biographies in C. F. Bricka, *Dansk biografisk leksikon*: 'Erik Qvitzow' and 'Henning Qvitzow' in XIX, no. 1; 'Henrik Rüsensteen' in XX, no. 3; 'Axel Urup' in XXIV, no. 4.

Romaňák, A. (1980), 'Zur Geschichte des Festungsbaus in Böhmen am Beispiel der Festung Theresienstadt', in *Militärgeschichte*, no. 6, Potsdam.

Rondeau, C. (1892), reports in *Sbornik imperatorskago Russkago istoricheskago obshchestva*, LXXX, St Petersburg.

Rousset, C. (1864–79), *Histoire de Louvois et de son administration politique et militaire*, 4 vols, Paris.

Russell, J. (1965), *Gibraltar Besieged 1779–1783*, London.

Rycaut, P. (1679–80), *History of the Turkish Empire from the Year 1623 to the Year 1677*, London.

Mémoires de Saint-Hilaire (1903–4), 6 vols, Paris.

Saluces, A. (1817–18), *Histoire militaire du Piémont*, 5 vols, Turin.

Sander, L. (1881), 'Eindrücke aus der Geschichte des Preussischen Ingenieur Corps', in *Jahrbücher für die Deutsche Armee und Marine*, XXXVIII, Berlin.

Sandes, E. W. (1933–5), *The Military Engineer in India*, 2 vols, Chatham.

San Felipe, Marques (1957), *Comentarios de la guerra de España*, 2 vols, Madrid.

Santa Cruz, A.N.O.V., Marques de (1735–40), *Reflexiones militares*, 12 vols, The Hague.

Sautai, M. (1899), *Le Siège de la ville et de la citadelle de Lille en 1708*, Paris.

Savory, R. (1966), *His Britannic Majesty's Army in Germany during the Seven Years War*, Oxford.

Les Rêveries ou mémoires sur l'art de la guerre de Maurice, Comte de Saxe (1756), The Hague.

Scharnhorst, G. J. (1834), *Geschichte der Belagerung von Gibraltar*, Hanover.

Scheer, G. F. and Rankin, H. F. (1959), *Rebels and Redcoats*, New York.

Scheither, J. (1672), *Novissima praxis militaris*, Brunswick. By a veteran of the siege of Candia.

Leben und Denkwürdigkeiten Johann Mathias Reichsgrafen von der Schulenburg (1834), 2 parts, Leipzig.

Schütz, M. (undated), *Rundgang durch die Heutige Festungsruine Rothenberg*, Hersbruck.

Schwenke, A. (1854), *Geschichte der Hannoverschen Truppen in Griechenland 1685–1689*, Hanover.

Ségur, Comte de (1824–6), *Mémoires ou souvenirs et anecdotes*, 3 vols, Paris.

Shaw, S. J. (1976), *History of the Ottoman Empire and Modern Turkey*, I, Cambridge.

Shy, J. (1978), 'Armed Force in Colonial North America: New Spain, New France, and Angloamerica', in *Proceedings of the International Military History Colloquy*, Ottawa.

Silva, Marquis de (1778), *Considérations sur la guerre de 1769 entre les Russes et les Turcs*, Turin.

Silva, Marquis de (1778), *Pensées sur la tactique, et la stratégique*, Turin.

Simcox, G., 'Louis XIV and the Outbreak of the Nine Years War', in Hatton (1976).

Simms, J. G. (1955), 'The Surrender of Limerick', in *The Irish Sword*, II, no. 5, Dublin.

Simms, J. G. (1964), 'The Siege of Derry', in *The Irish Sword*, VI, no. 25, Dublin.

Simms, J. G. (1969), *Jacobite Ireland*, London.

Skrine, F. H. (1906), *Fontenoy and Great Britain's Share in the war of the Austrian Succession*, Edinburgh and London.

Smelser, M. (1955), *The Campaign for the Sugar Islands, 1759*, Chapel Hill.

Smith, W. (1761), *An Authentic Journal of the Expedition to Belleisle, and of the Siege of the Citadel of Palais*, Dublin.

Smith, W. (1868, 1st ed. 1766), *An Historical Account of the Expedition against the Ohio Indians, in the Year MDCCLXIV*, Cincinnati.

Solaye, L. de la (1670), *Mémoires ou rélation militaire ... de la défense de la ville de Candie depuis l'année 1645*, Paris.

Sonnino, P., 'Louis XIV and the Dutch War', in Hatton (1976).

Speck, W. A. (1982), *The Duke of Cumberland and the Suppression of the '45*, Oxford.

Spielman, J. P. (1977), *Leopold I of Austria*, London.

Stacey, C. P. (1959), *Quebec 1759. The Siege and the Battle*, Toronto.

Staudinger, K. (1901–9), *Geschichte des Bayrischen Heeres*, 3 vols, Munich.

Stefanović-Vilkovsky, T. (1908), *Belgrad unter der Regierung Kaiser Karls VI (1717–1739)*, Vienna.

Stille, C. L. (1763), *Les Campagnes du Roi de Prusse en 1742 et 1745*, Amsterdam.

Stoye, J. (1964), *The Siege of Vienna*, London.

Strandmann, G. (1882), 'Zapiski', in *Russkaya Starina*, XXV, St Petersburg.

Sturm, L. C. (1710), *Le Véritable Vauban se montrant au lieu du faux Vauban*, The Hague.

Sturm, L. C. (1736), *Architectura militaris hypothetico-eclectica*, Nuremberg.

Sturminger, W. (1955), 'Bibliographie und Ikonographie

der Türkenbelagerungen Wiens 1529 und 1683', in *Veröffentlichungen der Kommission für neuere Geschichte Österreichs*, XLI, Graz.
Sumner, B. H. (1949), *Peter the Great and the Ottoman Empire*, Oxford.
Sutton, J. L. (1980), *The King's Honor and the King's Cardinal. The War of the Polish Succession*, Lexington (Kentucky).
Syrett, D. (ed.) (1970), *The Siege and Capture of Havana 1762*, Navy Records Society, London.
Tarle, E. V. (1958), *Severnaya Voina*, Moscow.
Taveira, A. P. (1906), *Summario historico sobre a defeza de Portugal*, part 1, Lisbon.
Taylor, F. (1921), *The Wars of Marlborough*, Oxford.
Taylor, W. (1976), The Military Roads in Scotland, Newton Abbot. For details on military posts and the Wade road system.
Tengberg, N. (1857–60), *Bidrag til historien om Sveriges krig med Ryssland åren 1741–1743*, 2 vols, Lund.
Ten Raa, F. and others (1911, etc.), *Het staatsche leger 1568–1795* (still in progress), The Hague and Breda.
Terry, C. S. (1903), *The Rising of 1745*, London.
Theil, Chevalier du (1778), *De l'usage de l'artillerie nouvelle*, Metz.
Thomas, A. B. (1941), *Teodoro de Croix and the Northern Frontier of New Spain 1776–1783*, Norman.
Thornton, A. P. (1957), 'The British in Manila 1762–1764', in *History Today*, London.
Tielke, J. G. (1788), *An Account of some of the most Remarkable Transactions of the War between the Prussians, Austrians, and Russians*, vol. II, London.
Tomasson, K. (1958), *The Jacobite General* (i.e. Lord George Murray), Edinburgh.
Memoirs of Baron de Tott (1786), 2 vols, London.
Trevelyan, G. M. (1931), 'Peterborough and Barcelona, 1705. Narrative and Diary of Col. John Richards', in *Cambridge Historical Journal*, III, no. 3, Cambridge.
Truttmann, P. (1976), *Fortification, architecture et urbanisme aux XVII et XVIII siècles*, Thionville.
Tsebrikov, R. M. (1895), 'Vokrug Ochakova v 1788 god', in *Russkaya Starina*, LXXXXIV, St Petersburg.
Tuetey, L. (1908), *Les Officiers sous l'ancien régime*, Paris.
Tychsen, V. E. (1893), *Fortifikations etaterne og Ingenieurkorpset 1684–1893*, Copenhagen.

Vauban's writings

Rochas d'Aiglun, A. (1910), *Vauban, sa famille et ses écrits. Ses oisivetés et sa correspondance*, 2 vols, Paris.
Abregé des services du Maréchal de Vauban (ed. M. Augoyat) (1839), Paris.
Mémoires inédites du Maréchal de Vauban sur Landau, Luxembourg et divers sujets (ed. M. Augoyat) (1841), Paris.
Mémoires militaires de Vauban et des ingénieurs Hué de Caligny (ed. M. Favé) (1847–54), 2 vols, Paris.
Le Directeur-Général des Fortifications (1676 or 1677), printed as appx. to Goulon's *Mémoires pour l'attaque et la défense d'une place* (1730), The Hague.
Mémoire pour servir d'instruction dans la conduite des sièges et dans la défense des places (1667–72) (1740), Leyden, trans. and ed. G. A. Rothrock as *A Manual of Siegecraft and Fortification* (1968), Ann Arbor.
Traité des sièges et de l'attaque des places (1704) (ed. M. Augoyat) (1829), Paris.
Traité de la défense des places (1706) (ed. de Valazé) (1829), Paris. Also contains Deshoulière's *Discours sur la défense des places* (1675).

Works on Vauban

Blomfield, R. (1938), *Sébastien le Prestre de Vauban 1633–1707* (1938), London.
Guerlac, H. (1944), 'Vauban. The Impact of Science on War', in *Makers of Modern Strategy*, ed. E. M. Earle, Princeton.
Halevy, D. (1923), *Vauban*, Paris.
Lazard, F. (1934), *Vauban 1633–1707*, Paris. The fullest biography.
Lloyd, E. M. (1887), *Vauban, Montalembert, Carnot. Engineer Studies*, London.
Michel, G. (1879), *Histoire de Vauban*, Paris.
Parrent, M. and Verroust, J. (1971), *Vauban*, Paris.
Rebelliau, A. (1962), *Vauban*, Paris.
Ricolfi, H. (1935), *Vauban et le génie militaire dans les Alpes Maritimes*, Nice.
Sauliol, R. (1924), *Le Maréchal de Vauban*, Paris.
Sautai, M. (1911), *L'Oeuvre de Vauban à Lille*, Paris.
Toudouze, G. C. (1954), *Monsieur de Vauban*, Paris.

Vault, ed. Pelet (1835–62), *Mémoires militaires relatifs à la Succession d'Espagne sous Louis XIV* (1835–62), 11 vols, Paris. A prime documentary and cartographical source.
'Prospero Jorge Marqués de Verboom', anon. article in *Enciclopedia Universal Illustrada* (1929), LXVII, Bilbao.
Prevost de Vernois (1861), *De la fortification depuis Vauban*, 2 vols, Paris.
Mémoires du Duc de Villars (1884–9), 3 vols, Paris.
Virgin, J. B. (1781), *La défense des places, mise en équilibre avec les attaques savantes et furieuses d'aujourd'hui*,

Stockholm.
Vischer, M. (1938), *Münnich. Ingenieur, Feldherr, Hochverräter*, Frankfurt.
Arkhiv Knyazya Vorontsova (1870–95), 40 vols, Moscow.
Walker, P. K. (1981), *Engineers of Independence. A Documentary History of the Army Engineers in the American Revolution, 1775–1783*, Washington.
Warnery, C. E. (1771), *Rémarques sur le militaire des Turcs et des Russes*, Breslau.
Warnery, C. E. (1788), *Campagnes de Frédéric II*, Amsterdam.
Watson, I. B. (1980), 'Fortifications and the Idea of Force in Early East India Company Relations with India', in *Past and Present*, LXXX, Oxford.
Wendt, H. (1936), *Der Italienische Kriegsschauplatz in Europäischen Konflikten: seine Bedeutung für die Kriegführung an Frankreichs Nordostgrenzen*, Berlin.
Whitworth, R. (1958), *Field-Marshal Lord Ligonier*, Oxford.
Wieringen, J. S. (1980/81), 'De "Fransche Methode" en Ingénieur Paul Storf de Belleville', in Stichting Menno van Coehoorn *Jaarboek*, The Hague.
Wieringen, J. S. 'De overgang van het Oudnederlandse naar het Nieuwnederlandse Stelsel 1648–1704', in Stichting Menno van Coehoorn *Jaarboek* (1982).

Wilkinson, S. (1927), *The Defence of Piedmont 1742–48*, Oxford.
Willax, F. and Schütz, M. (1975), *Die Belagerung der Festung Rothenberg 1744*, Hersbruck.
Wimarson, N. (1897), *Sveriges krig i Tyskland 1675–1679*, Lund.
Witt, P. (1887), *Une invasion Prussienne en Hollande en 1787*, Paris.
Wolfe, J. B. (1968), *Louis XIV*, London.
The Life and Letters of James Wolfe (ed. R. Willson) (1909), London.
Wraxall, N. W. (1806), *Memoirs of the Courts of Berlin, Dresden, Warsaw and Vienna*, 3rd edn, 2 vols, London.
Wylly, H. C. (1922), *A Life of Lt.-Gen. Sir Eyre Coote, K.B.*, Oxford.
Zastrow, H. (1854), *Geschichte der Beständigen Befestigung*, 3rd edn., Leipzig.
Zeller, G. (1928), *L'Organisation défensive des frontières du nord et de l'est au XVIIe siècle*, Paris.
Zimmermann, Ritter v. (1788), *Ueber Friedrich den Grossen* (1788), Leipzig.
Zimmermann, Ritter v. (1790), *Fragmente über Friedrich den Grossen*, 3 vols, Leipzig.
Zinkeisen, J. W. (1854–7), *Geschichte des Osmanischen Reiches in Europa*, vols II–IV, Gotha.

General Index

(Dates in brackets denote year of siege)

Aachen, G., 17
Åbo (Peace of, 1743), 209
Acapulco, 261
Aire, 44, 87; (1676), 12; (1710), 41
Aix-la-Chapelle (Peace of, 1668), 8
d'Ajot, Brigadier-General, 131, 133
Akershus, 180–2
Alès, 87
Alessandria, 103; (1746), 104
Alghero (1717), 99
Alicante (1709), 60, 61
Almeida (1762), 148
Alsace, 19, 20, 32, 45, 47
Altar, 262
Älvsborg, 191
Anhalt-Dessau, Prince Leopold of ('The Old Dessauer'), 134, 138
Anklam, 118
Annecy, 32
Antibes, 87; (1746–7), 104
Antwerp, 35
Aragonese (1717), 99
d'Arçon, J. C. Le Michaud, 157, 158, 161–4
Ardebil (1733), 251
Ardesoif, J. P., 261
Ardres, 106
Argos, 222
Armentières, 12
Arnhem (1672), 9
Arnold, B., 277, 282
Arras, 42, 87
d'Asfeld, C.-F.-B., 61, 150, 166, 294
Assietta, Colle dell' (action of 1747), 104, 105, 270, 272
d'Astier, Lozières, 49–50, 56
Ath, 8, 12, 31; (1667), 7; (1697), 30–1, 80; (1706), 37
Athens (1687), 222–3
Athlone (1691), 169–70

Atshu, 242
Augusta (on Savannah River), 286
Augusta, Fort (Pennsylvania), 270
Augustus, Fort, 172; (1746), 175
Avesnes, 87
Azov, 240, 246; (1695), 241; (1696), 241–2; (1736), 345

Badajoz, 148; (1705), 58
Baden, Margrave Ludwig of, 45, 85, 236
Baghdad (1733), 251
Baku, 242
Balbi, Colonel, 123, 125, 135, 138
Baldwin, J., 275–6
Barcelona: (1697), 33; (1705), 60; (1706), 60; (1714), 62
'Barrier, The' (in southern Netherlands), 35, 106, 114, 166
Bastide, J. F., 273
Bayonne, 90
Beaufort, 285
Behr, J. H., 13–14
Belfort, 20, 83, 85, 87, 91, 96
Belgrade, 226; (1688), 236; (1690), 236; (1717), 238–40; (1739), 243–4; (1789), 244
Belidor, B.-F., 127, 149, 154
Belleisle (1761), 258
Belleville, P. S., 13, 70
Bendery (1770), 246
Bergen-op-Zoom, 12, 34, 64, 71, 197; (1747), 107–10, 138
Bergues, 87
Berlin, 23
Berwick, 172
Berwick, Duke of, 57, 58, 62, 98, 99, 100, 150, 234
Besançon, 83, 84, 87
Béthune, 87, 94; (1710), 41
Black Sea, 240, 242
Blaye, 90, 95, 96
Bohemia, 132, 134
Bohus (Baahus), 188, 191; (1678), 179

Bohn, P., 119
Bökler, G. A., 184
Bombay, 253
Bonn, 20; (1673), 25; (1689), 28, 63; (1703), 37, 65
Bonneval, C. A. ('Pasha'), 245
Borgsdorf, E. F., 16
Börner, C., 231
Boston, Mass. (1775–6), 275–6
Bouchain, 12, 42, 44, 87; (1676), 12; (1711), 42–3
Boufflers, Marshal, 33, 35, 36, 38
Bouquet, H., 272
Bousmard, H., 295
Brabant, Lines of, 35, 37, 85
Braila (1770), 246
Breda, 12, 13
Breisach, 19, 32, 44, 45, 47, 87
Breslau, 113, 119, 142, 145; (1757), 122
Brest, 90
Briançon, 48, 57, 150, 151
Brieg, 142; (1741), 113
Broglie, Marshal, 116–17
Brouage, 89
Bruges (1706), 37
Brünn, 112; (1741), 113
Brunswick, Prince Ferdinand of, 116, 117
Brussels (1706), 37
Bryansk, 214
Burgoyne, J., 281
Burgundy, 90

Cagliari (1717), 99
Calais, 74, 106
Calcutta, 257
Camaret, Tour de, 90
Cambrai, 12, 42, 43, 44, 87; (1677), 12
Cambray, Chevalier de, 149
Cambrin, Lines of, 41
Camden, 286
Campeche, 261
Canche, river, 42
Candia (1649–69), 13, 14, 67, 218–21, 230

General Index

Carabusa, 221
Carcassonne, 87
Carillon (Ticonderoga), Fort, 268, 272; (1758), 271–2
Carlberg, General, 211
Carleton, G., 276, 277
Carlisle (1745), 172–3, 174
Carlowitz (Peace of, 1699), 223, 237
Carnot, L., 111, 156–7, 167, 196, 212
Cartagena (Spain) (1706), 60
Cartagena (Spanish America) (1741), 257
Casale, 26, 32, 33, 87; (1694–5), 32
Cassini, J., 99
Cermeño, J. Martin, 98
Chambly, Fort, 273; (1775), 277
Champlain, Lake, 268
Chandernagore, 254
Charleroi, 8, 12, 31, 38, 44; (1667), 7; (1677), 12; (1693), 29
Charles XI, King of Sweden, 178, 195, 196
Charles XII, King of Sweden, 195, 196, 198, 200–2, 204–8, 279
Charles Emmanuel II, Duke of Savoy, 49
Charleston, 286; (1776), 282; (1780), 284–5
Charleville, 87
Château-Porcien, 90
Château-Queyras, 72
Cheraw Hill, 286
Chernigov, 214
Chigirin (1677, 1678), 240
Chouaguen (Oswego), Fort (1756), 271
Cicignon, J. C., 180
Ciudad Rodrigo (1706), 58
Clare, Lines of, 35
Claris, A., 16, 17
Clerville, Chevalier de, 8, 71, 75
Clinton, Fort, 281
Clissa, 221
Coblenz, 20
Coehoorn, M. van
—career and character, 12, 28, 29, 30, 34, 36, 37, 63–6
—and engineer corps, 65–6
—fortification, principles of, 66–71
—fortress construction at: Bergen-op-Zoom, 34, 64, 71; Breda, 64; Coevorden, 64, 71; Grave, 64; Groningen, 64, 71; Namur, 63, 71; Nijmegen, 71; Zutphen, 64; Zwolle, 64
—siegecraft, 28, 30, 51, 64–5, 96
—strategy, 36
—writings, 64, 66–71, 219
Coevorden, 34, 64
Colbert, J.-B., 6, 75
Colmars, 76, 77, 87
Cologne, 20
Conçepcion, Fort, 213
Condé (fortress), 12, 41, 87
Condé, Louis, Prince de, 6
Copenhagen, 178–9, 197

Coquille, P., 18
Corbie, 90
Corfu (1717), 225
Cormontaigne, L., 150, 150–3
Cornwallis, C., 286–7, 290
Coucheron, W., 180
Coulomb, C.-A., 151–2
Courtois, J. M., 248
Courtrai, 8, 12, 31; (1683), 27
Crete, 218, 221
Crimea, 240, 242, 247
Croix, T. de, 262, 263
Cronstedt, C., 196, 210
Crown Point (Saint-Frédéric), Fort, 266–8; (1775), 277
Cumberland, Fort, 270
Cuneo (Coni) (1744), 103, 104, 291

Dahlberg, E.
—career and character, 182–4, 190–1, 194–6
—and engineer corps, 183, 196
—fortification, principles of, 195–6
—fortress construction at: Bohus, 188; Damgarten, 184; Eda Fort, 194; Göteborg, 191; Jönköping, 194, 226, 228; Kalmar, 192; Karlsburg, 190; Karlskrona, 192, 196; Landskrona, 191; Malmö, 190; Marstrand, 188, 191, 196; Narva, 195; Riga, 194, 196; Stade, 190; Stralsund, 190; Wismar, 190, 196
—strategy, 190, 192, 194–5, 198
Damvillers, 90
Danzig (1734), 100
Daun, W., 52–3, 55
Dechales, C. F. Milliet, 49
Delhi, 252
Dembach, P., 18
Demmin, 118
Denain, 42
Denia (1708), 60
Derbent, 242
Deshoulières (engineer), 41
Dilich, W., 13
Dillenburg, 117
Dinant, 87; (1675), 12
Dinwiddie, R., 266, 270
Dmitrya, 214
Dögen, M., 13, 23, 24
Dorpat, 194; (1704), 198, 200
Douai, 8, 41, 87; (1667), 7; (1710), 41; (1712), 44
Dresden, 14; (1760), 125
Driesch, J. B., 16, 17
Dubitza (1788), 280, 287
Dunkirk, 44, 85, 87, 106
Duquesne, Governor-General, 266, 268
Duquesne (Pitt), Fort, 268, 269, 272
Dürer, A., 15

Eda Fort, 186, 194

Edinburgh (1745–6), 172
El Paso, 262
Elvas, 146–7, 148
Entrevaux, 87
Erie, Lake, 268
Erivan, 251; (1735), 252
Erzerum (1735), 252
L'Espinasse, C. du Puy de, 30, 64
Esseg, 226, 229, 237
Eugene, Prince of Savoy, 25, 38, 39, 40, 43, 44, 47, 55, 57, 101, 231, 236–9
Exilles, 48, 105; (1708), 57

Fenestrelle (1708), 57
Ferdinand Maria, Elector of Bavaria, 24
Feuillade, Duc de la, 49, 50–2
Filley, P., 45
Finland, 202, 208–10
Foissac-Latour (writer), 156, 167
Folard, Chevalier de, 155, 157
Forchheim, 17, 21, 22
Fourcroy de Ramecourt, C.-R., 152–3, 160
Franche-Comté, 7, 8, 12, 20
Frankenthal, 20; (1688), 31
Frankfurt-am-Main, 116, 117
Frederick II ('The Great'), King of Prussia
—and engineer corps, 114, 122, 123, 127, 128, 134–7, 144–5
—fortification, principles of, 119–20, 139–42
—fortress construction at: Breslau, 142–4; Brieg, 142, 144; Glatz, 142, 143; Glogau, 142, 144; Graudenz, 144–5; Kosel, 144; Neisse, 142, 143–4; Schweidnitz, 120, 142, 144; Silberberg, 144
—siegecraft, 120, 122, 125, 137–8
—strategy, 142–5, 147, 198
Frederick III, King of Denmark, 180, 182
Frederick William, Elector of Brandenburg ('The Great Elector'), 23
Frederick William I, King of Prussia, 134
Frederikshamn, 214; (1742), 209
Frederiksodde (Fredericia), 184; (1657), 178
Fredrikstad, 180
Fredriksten (Halden), 180, 204–5; (1718), 206–8
Freiburg, 20, 26, 32, 44, 87; (1677), 25; (1703), 45; (1713), 47; (1744), 106
Freudenstadt, 20
Frontenac, Fort (1758), 272
Fuenterrabia (1719), 99
Furnes, 12, 44, 87, 106; (1744), 106

Gaeta (1708), 57
Galissonière, Governor-General, 266, 268–70

Genja (1734), 252
Genoa, 104; (1684), 27; (1746-8), 104
George, Fort (Scotland), 172, 174; (1746), 175
George, Fort (West Florida) (1782), 286
Georgia (N. America), 282, 286
Gerona, 98; (1694), 33; (1711), 60
Ghent, 39; (1678), 12
Gibraltar (1704), 60, 163-4; (1727), 100, 164; (1779-83), 164-5
Giessen, 117
Givet, 29
Glatz, 131, 139, 142, 143, 144; (1741), 113; (1760), 119
Glogau, 119, 139, 142, 147
Gontzenbach, P., 144
Gordon, Mirabelle de, 174-5
Gordon, P., 197, 240
Gorinchem (1787), 166
Gork, G., 14
Göteborg (Gothenburg), 176, 187, 191-2, 193-4, 195
Göttingen, 117
Goulon, Major-General, 214, 215, 216
Graudenz, 144-5
Grave, 12, 13, 70; (1674), 12
Gravelines, 87, 106
Greene, N., 280, 286
Gribeauval, J.-B., 119, 128, 130, 154, 292
Gridley, J., 276
Groningen, 34
Grosswardein, 226; (1692), 236
Guadeloupe (1759), 258
Guasco, P., 126, 128
Guibert, J.-A., 155, 157
Guignard, Chevalier de, 149
Gustavus III, King of Sweden, 209

Haguenau (1675), 25
Halden, see Fredriksten
Halifax (Nova Scotia), 266, 276, 278
Hamburg, 90
Hameln, 117
Hamilton, R., 168
Hannibal, I., 247
Harsch, General, 105-6, 131, 242
Havana (1762), 259-61, 294
Heidemann, C., 24
d'Heintz, Count, 136
Helsingborg, 202
Helsingfors (Helsinki), 210; (1742), 209
Helsingør (Elsinore; Kronborg Fortress), 179
s'Hertogenbosch, 12
Hesse-Darmstadt, Prince George of, 60
Howe, W., 276
Hudson, river, 266, 272, 276, 277, 281-2, 284
Huningue, 20, 47, 90
Huy, 35; (1675), 12; (1693), 29; (1703), 37; (1705), 37

Inverness (Fort George), 4
Izmail, 248; (1770), 246; (1790), 249

Jassy (Peace of, 1792), 249
John III Sobieski, King of Poland, 229, 233, 234, 240
Johnson, W., 272
Jönköping, 194
Joseph II, Emperor of Austria, 166, 292
Josephstadt, 132-4

Kaiserswörth: (1689), 28; (1702), 36, 64, 65
Kalat-i-Naderi, 252
Kalmar, 185, 187, 189, 192, 194
Kamchatka Peninsula, 251
Kamenets, 241; (1672, 1684, 1687), 240
Kamennyi Zaton, 242
Kampen, 12
Kandahar (1737), 252
Kanisza (1664), 226
Kara Mustafa, 226, 228, 229-33
Karlsburg (Bremerhaven), 190
Karlsburg (Transylvania), 238, 242
Karlshamn (1790), 209
Karlskrona, 187, 192, 194, 195
Kasikermen, 240
Kassel: (1759), 116; (1760), 116; (1761), 117; (1762), 117
Kehl, 17, 19, 20, 32, 44, 47, 134; (1678), 25; (1703), 45; (1733), 100
Keith, J., 245
Kerch, 242, 247
Kexholm, 208, 212; (1710), 202
Kherson, 247
Khotin, 248; (1769), 246
Kiev, 214
Kilia (1770), 246
Kinburn, 240, 247
Kinzig, river, 20
Klausenburg, 242
Knocke, 87, 106; (1744), 106
Knox, H., 276, 277, 278-9, 280, 287
Kolberg, 23, 144, 147; (1761), 119, 125-6
Komorn, 226, 228
Kongsvinger, 180
Königgrätz, 130, 131
Königsberg, 23
Köprülü, Ahmed, 218, 221, 226
Köprülü, Mehmet, 218, 247
Köprülü, Mustafa, 236
Koron, 222, 223
Kosciuszko, T., 281, 286
Kosel, 139, 142, 144
Kresta, 214
Kronach, 18
Kronborg Fortress, see Helsingør
Kronstadt, 198, 213, 214
Küstrin, 119; (1758), 118
Kutchuk-Kainardji (Peace of, 1774), 246

La Capelle, 90
Laclos, Choderlos de, 156-7
Lacy, F., 130, 131
Lacy, P., 209, 245
La Fère, 90
Lafitte-Clavé, A., 248
la Mina, Marqués de, 98-9
Landau, 20, 83, 87; (1702), 45; (1703), 45; (1704), 46-7; (1713), 47
Landrecies, 87; (1712), 44
Landsberg, Colonel, 13, 16, 38
Landskrona, 189, 190, 191
Lapara des Fieux, L., 32, 33, 45, 60, 75
Le Castelet, 90
Lefèbvre, S. D., 127, 128, 135, 149
Lemberg (1675), 240
Lemnos (1770), 247
Leopold I, Emperor, 27, 226
Leopoldstadt, 228
Le Peletier de Souzy, M., 75, 78
Le Quesnoy, 42, 87; (1712), 43-4, 45
Lerida, 61; (1707), 60
Le Tellier, M., 2
Leutrum, General, 104
Liebenberg, A., 231
Liège (1702), 37, 64
Lille, 7, 8, 12, 38, 44, 81, 82, 87; (1677), 7-8; (1708), 38-9
Limburg (1675), 12
Limerick (1690), 169; (1691), 171
Lindenau, Major, 163
Lippstadt, 23, 117
Londonderry (1689), 168
Longwy, 6, 87
Lorient (1746), 257
Lorraine, 7, 87
Lorraine, Duke Charles of, 228, 229, 234, 236
Lotbinière, Sieur de, 268
Loubéras, L., 213
Loudon, G. E., 125, 244
Loudon, Fort, 270
Louis XIV, King of France, 2, 6-9, 10, 12, 20, 26, 27, 29, 32, 33, 36, 41
Louis du Rhin, Fort, 20
Louisbourg, 266, 271, 272; (1745), 264; (1758), 273
Louvois, M. L. Le T., Marquis de, 2, 6, 27, 29, 72, 73, 75, 78
Lovisa, 210
Löwen, A., 208, 210
Löwendahl, Marshal, 107
Lüttich, Captain, 134
Luxembourg, 20, 31, 44, 150; (1667), 7; (1684), 27, 28, 79

Maastricht, 9, 12; (1673), 6, 10, 63, 78; (1676), 12; (1748), 110
Mackellar, P., 260, 273
Macquire von Inniskillen, J. S., 125
Madras, 253; (1746), 254; (1759), 256
Madrid, 58, 60

General Index

Magdeburg, 23, 134, 142, 147
Maigret, P., 153
Maintenon aqueduct, 73
Mainz, 20; (1689), 17
Malines (1706), 37
Malmö, 176, 190, 202
Manila (1762), 258
Mannheim, 19, 20, 71; (1688), 31
Mantua, 47–8, 101
Marburg, 117
Marchiennes (1712), 44
Marguerite, Solar de la, 52
Mariembourg, 87
Marienberg Citadel (Würzburg), 17, 18, 19
Marlborough, John Churchill, Earl, later Duke of, 36–43, 46–7
Marstrand, 188, 191; (1719), 208
Martinique (1762), 258–9
Maubeuge, 12, 30, 42, 87, 106
Max Emanuel, Elector of Bavaria, 45, 234
Maximilian I, Elector of Bavaria, 24
Medrano, S., 98
Meesters, W., 27
Memmingen (1703), 45
Menin, 12, 87, 106; (1706), 37; (1744), 106
Mercer, J., 164
Messina (1718), 99
Methone, 223
Metz, 87, 150
Meuse, river, 11, 12, 29, 35, 36, 37, 38, 41
Mézières, engineering school, 150–2
Micca, P., 55
Minden, 116
Minorca (1756), 148, 163
Mitau (1710), 202
Mobile (1780), 286
Modon, 222
Molyneux, T. M., 257, 261–2
Moncrieff, J., 284, 285
Monge, G., 151
Mons, 38; (1691), 28–9; (1709), 41
Montalembert, M.-R., xiv, 157–63, 165–6, 196, 212, 214
Montcalm, Marquis de, 270–2, 274
Mont-Dauphin, 87
Montecuccoli, R., 25, 226, 295
Mont-Genèvre Pass, 48, 49, 57
Montgomery, Fort, 281
Mont-Louis, 5, 80, 90, 92, 93
Montmédy, 4, 5, 87, 90; (1657), 90
Montmélian, 32, 48; (1691), 32
Montreal, 264; (1760), 274; (1775), 277
Montresor, J., 278
Montreuil, 88
Mont-Royal, 90
Morea, the, 221–4
Mortagne, Fort de, 87
Moscow, 214, 215
Moselle, river, 20, 47

Mosul (1743), 252
Muiden, 9
Muller, J., 164
Munkacz, 237
Münnich, B. C., 100, 214, 215, 216–17, 245, 250, 294
Münster, 117; (1760), 116
Mureau, Milet de, 151

Naarden, 8, 9, 12, 66–70
Nadir Quli Khan, 251–2
Namur, 12, 38, 44; (1692), 29, 63; (1695), 45, 63; (1746), 107
Napoli di Romania, 222, 223–4; (1715), 224
Narbonne, 87
Narva, 194, 195, 212; (1700), 197, 201; (1704), 198, 200
Navarino (1686), 222
Necessity, Fort, 270
Negroponte, 223
Neisse, 123, 136, 139, 142, 145; (1741), 113; (1758), 144
Ne Plus Ultra, Lines of, 36, 43
Neubauer, C., 13, 14
Neuburg (1703), 45
Neuf-Brisach, 20, 79, 84, 86
Neuhäusel, 228; (1664), 226; (1685), 234
Neuingen, 47
Neumann, B., 18, 19
New Spain (Mexico), 261, 262–3
New York, 281, 287; (1776), 277–8
Niagara, Fort (1759), 272
Nice, 32, 48; (1691), 32
Nieupoort, H., 28
Nijmegen (1672), 9
Nijmegen (Peace of, 1678), 12
Nikopolis (1689), 236
Nîmes, 87
Ninety-Six, Fort (1781), 286
Nis, 242
Nobel, P., 205
Nöteborg (Schlüsselburg) (1702), 198
Novara, 101, 103
Novi (1788), 244
Nuremberg, 18, 19
Nyen, Fort, 194, 195; (1703), 198
Nyslott, 209
Nystadt (Peace of, 1721), 208

Ochakov, 240, 247; (1737), 245–6; (1788), 248
Oder, river, 112, 119, 142, 144
Ohio valley, 266
Olmütz, 112, 119, 131; (1758), 123–5
Omsk, 250
Ontario, Lake, 271
Orange, Prince William of (later King William III of England), 11, 12, 13, 26, 64
Orsova, 244
Ostend (1706), 37

Oswego (Chouaguen), Fort (1756), 271
Oudenarde, 8, 12; (1667), 7; (1674), 12; (1706), 37
Oudewater, 9

Pabliczek, Captain, 128
Papacino, A., 103
Passarowitz (Peace of, 1718), 240
Peenemünde, 118
Pellegrini, General, 132
Pensacola (1781), 286
Pepperrell, W., 265
Perekop, Lines of, 240
Pernau, 194, 197
Perpignan, 87
Persia, 242
Perth, Duke of, 172, 294
Pescara (1708), 57
Peter I ('The Great'), Tsar of Russia, 195, 212–14, 241–2
Peterborough, Earl of, 60
Peterwardein, 236, 237, 238, 242, 243
Petropavlovsk, 251
Petropolis, 242
Philadelphia (1777), 278
Philip V, King of Spain, 98–100
Philippeville, 87, 106
Philippsburg, 17, 19, 20, 26, 32, 44, 46, 87, 134; (1688), 31; (1734), 100–1
Philips, W., 281
Pillau, 23
Pinerolo, 27, 32, 33, 48
Pinto, Colonel, 136
Pitt (Duquesne), Fort, 275
Poltava (1709), 200–1
Pondicherry: (1747), 254; (1761), 256; (1778), 256
Pont Saint-Esprit, 87
Prague, 112; (1741), 105; (1742), 105; (1744), 114; (1757), 120, 125
Presqu'Île (Erie), Fort, 268
Preveza (1717), 226
Prevost, A., 282–4
Pskov, 213
Putnam, I., 281
Puységur, Marshal, 154

Quebec, 264; (1759), 274; (1775–6), 277
Querlonde du Hamel, L., 133
Qvitzow, E., 182

Raab, 226, 228–9, 230
Radière, L. de S. de la, 280, 281
Rain (1704), 22
Regler, Colonel, 136, 143, 144
Reichelsheim, F. C. Reichel von, 17
Rendsborg (Rendsburg), 182
Revel, 213; (1710), 202
Rhine, river, 9, 19, 20, 26, 31–2, 36, 37, 44, 47, 87, 100
Richards, Jacob, 221, 223
Richards, John, 58, 61, 221

General Index

Riga, 194, 196; (1654), 14; (1700), 184, 197; (1710), 202
Rijnberk (1707), 37
Rijswijk (Peace of, 1697), 31, 44, 83
Rimpler, G., 14–15, 214, 221, 228, 229–32
Robin, B., 107
Rochepine, P. F. Bechade de, 131
Rocky Mountain (post), 286
Rocroi, 87
Roermond (1702), 37
Rogervik, 213, 214
Römer, C., 23
Romer, J., 172
Rosas (1693), 33
Rosen, C., 168, 294
Rosenberg Fortress (Kronach), 18, 21
Rothenberg Fortress (Schnaittach), 18–19
Roveda, I., 103
Rüsensteen, H., 176, 178, 182, 294

St Augustine (Fort of San Marcos), 262, 282
St David, Fort (India), 254; (1758), 256
St Elisabeth, Fort, xiv, 157–9, 242
Saint-Frédéric (Crown Point), Fort, 266–8, 272; (1775), 277
Saint-Hyppolite-du-Fort, 87
St John's, Fort (1775), 277
St Lawrence, river, 264, 265, 268, 270, 272, 274
St Louis (1780), 286
Saint-Malo (1758), 257
Saint-Martin de Rhé, 88
Saint-Omer, 12, 87, 106; (1677), 12
St Petersburg, 198, 212, 213, 217
Saint-Venant, 44; (1710), 41
Samara, 242
Sambre, river, 8, 9, 29, 30, 41, 42
San Antonio, 262
San Francisco, 262–3
San Juan Bautísta, 262
San Juan de Ulloa, 261
San Matheo (1705), 61
San Sebastian (1719), 99
Santa Cruz, Marqués de, 98–9
Santa Fé, 262
Sardinia, 99
Sattler, J. H., 13
Savannah, 286; (1779), 282–4
Saverne (1675), 25
Saxe, Marshal de, 107, 154
Scharnhorst, G., 163, 164
Schaumburg-Lippe, Count W. of, 116, 148
Scheither, J. B., 13, 14, 220, 221
Scheldt, river, 8, 12, 35, 38, 39, 42, 43
Schenkenschans (1672), 9
Schlüsselburg (Nöteborg), 212
Schmoll, B., 196
Scholten, J., 182, 202, 205

Schönborn, J. P. von, Elector, 16
Schönborn, L. F. von, Elector, 17, 21
Schulenburg, J., 225–6
Schweidnitz, 120, 139–42; (1757), 120, 142; (1758), 122–3; (1761), 125, 144; (1762), 119, 126–30, 294
Sech, Zaporozhian, 240, 242
Sedan, 87
Sedd el Bahr, 247
Sehrs, Colonel, 142
Seignelay, Marquis de, 75
Serinvár (Zrunyburg) (1664), 226
Sevastopol, 247
Shrapnel, H., 164–5
Shuvalov, P., 118, 217
Siberian Lines, 250–1
Silberberg, 136, 139, 144
Sinope, 248
Siöbladh, J., 196
Sisteron, 77
Skinner, W., 174
Sommières, 87
Spandau, 23, 24
Spinalonga, 221
Stade, 190
Starhemberg, G., 60, 62
Starhemberg, R., 14, 228, 231, 232
Stenay, 90
Stettin, 119, 134, 142, 147, 157; (1677), 176
Stirling, 171, 172; (1746), 174–5
Stollhofen Lines, 45
Stony Point, Fort, 278; (1779), 282
Stralsund, 118; (1678), 176; (1715), 202
Strasbourg, 19, 20, 26, 87, 100
Stuart, C. M., 196
Sturm, L. C., 13, 15, 16, 149
Suda, 221
Sundsborg, 206
Surat, 253
Susa: (1690), 32; (1704), 49
Suvorov, A. V., 214, 217, 249, 250
Suvorov, V. I., 214
Sveaborg, 210–11

Tabriz, 251
Taganrog, 242, 247
Temesvár, 237, 242; (1716), 238
Tettau, J. E., 30, 169
Theil, Chevalier du, 156
Theresienstadt, 131–2, 134
Thionville, 87, 150
Ticonderoga (Carillon), Fort, 268, 271–2, 276; (1775), 277; (1777), 281
Timmermann, F., 197
Tönning, 182; (1700), 197
Tordenskiold, P. W., 180
Tortona, 101, 103
Tortosa (1708), 60
Tott, F., 246–7
Toulon (1707), 56–7
Tour, M. A. Chabaud de la, 248

Tournai, 8, 12, 38, 44, 82, 87; (1709), 41; (1745), 107
Transylvania, 226, 236
Trentschin, 228
Tsaritsyn Line, 250
Turin, 49; (1706), 45, 50–6, 291
Turenne, H. de La Tour d'Auvergne, Vicomte de (Marshal of France), 6, 26

Uisk Line, 250
Ulm: (1703), 45; (1704), 46
Ural Lines, 250
Urup, S., 182
Ust-Kamenogorsk, 251
Utrecht (Peace of, 1713), 44, 106

Vadstena, 185
Valencia (town), 60
Valenciennes, 12, 41, 42, 87; (1677), 12
Valley Forge, 280
Värälä (Peace of, 1790), 209
Varna, 248
Vauban, S. Le Prestre de
—career and character, 6, 7, 8, 10, 27, 29, 33, 45, 50–1, 54, 71–3, 75, 78, 83, 90, 94, 96–7
—and engineer corps, 75, 78
—fortification, principles of, 81–4, 86
—fortress construction at: Arras, 82; Bayonne, 90; Belfort, 83; Besançon, 83, 84; Breisach, 73; Briançon, 87; Brouage, 89; Colmars, 76, 77, 87; Entrevaux, 76, 87; Landau, 20, 83; Lille, 7, 8, 81, 82; Luxembourg, 20; Mont-Dauphin, 87; Mont-Louis, 90; Montmédy, 90; Sisteron, 77; Strasbourg, 23, 73; Tournai, 82; Villefranche du Conflent, 82; Ypres, 81
—reputation and influence, 60, 110, 124, 137, 138, 149, 152, 153, 154, 157, 163, 214, 276, 294–5
—siegecraft, 10, 27, 29, 30, 78–80, 221
—writings, 81, 214
Vauban, du Puy, 38, 72
Vaudreuil, Marquis de, Governor-General of Canada, 266, 268, 270, 272, 274
Velikii Luki, 213
Vendôme, Marshal, 33, 36, 38, 48, 49
Venlo (1702), 65
Veprik (1709), 200–2
Vera Cruz, 261
Verboom, J. P., 99, 100, 294
Vercelli, 49
Verdun, 87
Verplanck, Fort (1779), 282
Verrua (1705), 49, 50
Verville, J. F. du Verger de, 264
Victor Amadeus, Duke of Savoy, later King of Sardinia, 32, 48, 64, 101
Vienna, 226, 229, 237; (1683), xiv, 230–3

Villars, Marshal, 35, 41, 43–5, 47, 101
Villefránche (Villafranca), 87; (1691), 32
Villefranche du Conflent, 82, 83
Villeroi, Marshal, 35, 37
Villingen, 20
Vincennes (N. America) (1779), 286
Virgin, J. B., 155, 165, 211–12
Vistula, river, 119, 144, 198
Vitozzi, A., 49
Vyborg, 208, 212, 214; (1710), 202; (1790), 209

Wackerbarth, General, 202
Waggener, Fort, 270
Walrave, G. C., 114, 134–5, 144
Wärnsköld, J., 187, 191
Washington, G., 268, 270, 275, 276, 278, 280, 281, 282, 287, 289
Waters, J., 276
Watson, Fort, 286
Welsch, Colonel, 134
Werdmüller, Colonel, 13, 16
Wesel, 116, 144; (1760), 117
West Point, 281–2
Widdin, 242; (1689), 236
William, Fort (Calcutta) (1756), 254
William, Fort (Scotland), 171
William Henry, Fort (1757), 271
Willmanstrand, 209, 214
Wismar, 190, 191, 195, 196, 202; (1716), 204
Woerden, 9

Wolfe, J., 258, 273, 274
Wrede, Major, 143
Wülzburg Fortress, 18
Würzburg, 16, 17, 18, 19

Yorktown (1781), 286–90
Ypres, 12, 38, 44, 81, 87, 106; (1678), 12; (1744), 106–7

Zader, H., 13, 196
Zastrow, H., 13, 196
Zeger, J., 27
Ziegenhain, 117
Zittau (1757), 120
Zriny, N., 226
Zutphen (1672), 9

Subject Index

Engineers
Engineering professionalism, xiii–xiv, 78, 110, 135, 137, 150–2, 164, 196, 216, 258, 294–5
Engineers in service of
- American Revolution, 275–6, 278–80, 281–2, 287–9
- Austria, 17, 24–5, 37, 38–41, 105–6, 113, 119, 131, 133, 228, 237
- Bavaria, 23–4, 45
- Britain, 107, 110, 164, 168, 172, 174, 184, 254, 257, 261, 271–2, 273, 285
- Denmark-Norway, 180, 182
- Dutch Republic, 12–13, 63, 15–16
- France, 49–50, 55–6, 75, 78, 98, 110, 115, 149–53, 163, 166–7, 168, 265, 268, 271, 280
- Germany as whole, 13–18, 22–4, 116–17
- Palatinate, 20, 31–2, 45
- Persia, 251
- Piedmont-Sardinia, 49, 103
- Portugal, 57, 148
- Prussia, 22–3, 114, 122–3, 127–8, 134–7, 144–5
- Russia, 23, 118, 197, 214–17, 240, 242, 246
- Spain, 98–9
- Sweden, 13, 117, 184, 196, 200, 209–12
- Turkey, 232, 236, 243, 245, 246–7, 248, 249
- Venice, 223, 225

Fortification, parts of
Barracks, 74
Bastions, 1, 2, 3, 14, 164
Bastion towers, 83–6
Caponnières, xiv, 111, 134, 139, 142, 158–61, 231
Casemates, mortar, 111
Constructional details, 2, 6, 18, 68–9, 132, 136, 149, 151–2, 180, 194–5, 268
Countermines, permanent, 41, 52, 75, 138–9
Covered ways, 1–3, 5, 231
Ditches, 1, 2, 3, 68, 69, 134, 139, 142
Entrenched camps, 57, 84–5
Forts, 120, 127, 130, 139–42, 159–60, 292
Gateways, 6, 73
Glacis, 2
Hornworks, 81
Lines of earthworks, 35–6, 250–1, 293
Lunettes, 30, 45, 47, 123
Magazines, powder, 74
Ramparts, main, 1, 2, 4, 14, 111, 140, 142
Ravelins, 1, 3–5
Towers, 195–6, 211, 212

General topics
Civil communities, 9, 53, 72, 74, 137, 179, 231, 232, 253, 263
Garrisons, 8–9, 72, 74, 137, 263, 270
Logistics, 11, 22, 29, 39, 49, 62, 112, 116, 117, 132
Symbolism, 6, 18–19, 21–2, 73–4, 143, 187, 192–3
Town planning, 74, 79

Siegecraft
Austrian and Allied in War of Spanish Succession, 36–41, 42, 51
Austrian in Seven Years War, 119
Austrian against Turks, 236, 241–2
British, 257–62, 265
Dutch, 27–8, 64–5
French, 10–11, 14–15, 29, 30–1, 33, 60, 65, 78–81, 107–10, 115, 256
German as whole, 22–3, 25, 116
Prussian, 122–5, 127–8, 137–8, 202
Russian under Peter the Great, 197, 200
Russian in Seven Years War, 118, 217
Russian against Turks, 245, 249–50
Swedish under Charles XII, 200
Swedish in Seven Years War, 117–18
Turkish, 218, 221–3, 230–3, 243

Strategic geography, State defence
America, North, 264, 266–72, 274, 276, 277, 284, 285–6
Ansbach, 18
Austria, 24–5, 105
Austria, against Turks, 223–4, 226, 228–9, 233, 236–8, 242–3
Austrian Netherlands (*see also* Spanish Netherlands), 106, 114, 166, 292
Austrian North Italy, 101, 103, 104
Bavaria, 18–19, 23–4, 46
Denmark-Norway, 176, 177, 179–82, 197, 202
Dutch Republic, 8–9, 12–13, 28, 34–5, 166
France, 1–2, 6, 8, 10–12, 20, 25–6, 31–2, 35, 37, 39, 41–5, 48, 56–7, 85, 87, 90, 94, 97, 106, 150
Germany as whole, 13–14, 16–20, 22–4, 116–17
India, 253–4
Palatinate, 20, 31–2, 45
Persia, 242, 251–2
Piedmont-Sardinia, 32–3, 47–50, 103
Poland, 198, 240
Portugal, 57–8, 148
Prussia, 22–3, 142–7
Russia, 195, 212–14, 216, 240, 242, 247–8, 250–1
Spain, 33
Spanish America, 257, 261, 262–4
Spanish Netherlands, 8, 29, 35, 37
Sweden, 178, 184, 190–2, 194–5, 198–200, 202, 204, 208–10
Turkey, 218, 233, 236, 237, 240, 242, 244–5, 247–8, 252
Venice, 218, 221, 223–6
Württemberg, 20
Würzburg, 17–18

Weapons and techniques, defensive
Artillery, 3, 4, 81, 128, 139, 152, 154, 158, 164–5

Subject Index

Countermining, 41, 107–8, 127–30, 220
Inundations, 138, 143
Musketry, 3
Sorties, 81, 128, 139, 231

Weapons and techniques, offensive
Artillery in general, 1, 22, 29–31, 33, 51, 79, 124, 165, 196
Bombardment, 79, 118, 120, 125, 176, 202
Circumvallation, lines of, 100, 197
Coups de main, 125
Howitzers, 27–8, 65, 138, 196
Mining, 54, 80, 127–30, 231, 246
Mortars, 27, 79–80, 222–3, 239

Mortars, cohorn, 65, 196
Mortars, pierrier, 80
Observation, armies of, 107, 138, 293
Trench attack, 10, 11, 27, 37–9, 78–9, 110, 206–7, 287, 289

Printed in Great Britain
by Amazon